THE XML & SGML
COOKBOOK

The Charles F. Goldfarb Series on Open Information Management

"Open Information Management" (OIM) means managing information so that it is open to processing by any program, not just the program that created it. That extends even to application programs not conceived of at the time the information was created.

OIM is based on the principle of data independence: data should be stored in computers in non-proprietary, genuinely standardized representations. And that applies even when the data is the content of a document. Its representation should distinguish the innate information from the proprietary codes of document processing programs and the artifacts of particular presentation styles.

Business data bases – which rigorously separate the real data from the input forms and output reports – achieved data independence decades ago. But documents, unlike business data, have historically been created in the context of a particular output presentation style. So for document data, independence was largely unachievable until recently.

That is doubly unfortunate. It is unfortunate because documents are a far more significant repository of humanity's information. And documents can contain significantly richer information structures than data bases.

It is also unfortunate because the need for OIM of documents is greater now than ever. The demands of "repurposing" require that information be deliverable in multiple formats (paper-based, online, multimedia, hypermedia). And information must now be delivered through multiple channels (traditional bookstores and libraries, online services, the Internet).

Fortunately, in the past ten years a technology has emerged that extends to documents the data base's capacity for data independence. And it does so without the data base's restrictions on structural freedom. That technology is the "Standard Generalized Markup Language" (SGML), an official International Standard (ISO 8879) that has been adopted by the world's largest producers of documents.

With SGML, organizations in government, aerospace, airlines, automotive, electronics, computers, and publishing (to name a few) have freed their documents from hostage relationships to processing software. SGML coexists with other data standards needed for OIM and acts as the framework that relates objects in the other formats to one another and to SGML documents.

As the enabling standard for OIM of documents, SGML necessarily plays a leading role in this series. We provide tutorials on SGML and other key standards and the techniques for applying them. Our books are not addressed solely to technical readers: we cover topics like the business justification for OIM and the business aspects of commerce in electronic information. We share the practical experience of organizations and individuals who have applied the techniques of OIM in environments ranging from immense industrial publishing projects to self-publishing on the World Wide Web.

Our authors are expert practitioners in their subject matter, not writers hired to cover a "hot" topic. They bring insight and understanding that can only come from real-world experience. Moreover, they practice what they preach about standardization. Their books share a common standards-based vocabulary. In this way, knowledge gained from one book in the series is directly applicable when reading another, or the standards themselves. This is just one of the ways in which we strive for the utmost technical accuracy and consistency with the OIM standards.

And we also strive for a sense of excitement and fun. After all, the challenge of OIM – preserving information from the ravages of technology while exploiting its benefits – is one of the great intellectual adventures of our age. I'm sure you'll find this series to be a knowledgable and reliable guide on that adventure.

About the Series Editor

Dr. Charles F. Goldfarb is the inventor of SGML and HyTime, and technical leader of the committees that developed them into their present form as International Standards. He is an information management consultant based in Saratoga, CA.

About the Series Logo

The rebus is an ancient literary tradition, dating from 16th century Picardy, and is especially appropriate to a series involving fine distinctions between things and the words that describe them. For the logo, Andrew Goldfarb, who also designed the series' "Intelligent Icons", incorporated a rebus of the series name within a stylized SGML comment declaration.

The Charles F. Goldfarb Series on Open Information Management

As XML is a subset of SGML, the Series List is categorized to show the degree to which a title applies to XML. "XML Titles" are those that discuss XML explicitly and may also cover full SGML. "SGML Titles" do not mention XML *per se*, but the principles covered may apply to XML.

XML Titles

Goldfarb, Pepper, and Ensign	*SGML Buyer's Guide™: Choosing the Right XML and SGML Products and Services*
Megginson	*Structuring XML Documents*
Jelliffe	*The XML and SGML Cookbook: Recipes for Structured Information*
Leventhal, Lewis, and Fuchs (Coming Soon)	*Designing XML Internet Applications*
Goldfarb and Prescod (Coming Soon)	*The XML Handbook™*

SGML Titles

Turner, Douglass, and Turner	*ReadMe.1st: SGML for Writers and Editors*
Donovan	*Industrial–Strength SGML: An Introduction to Enterprise Publishing*
Ensign	*$GML: The Billion Dollar Secret*
Rubinsky and Maloney	*SGML on the Web: Small Steps Beyond HTML*
McGrath	*ParseMe.1st: SGML for Software Developers*
DuCharme	*SGML CD*

Rick Jelliffe

THE
XML & SGML
COOKBOOK

Recipes for Structured Information

Prentice Hall PTR
Upper Saddle River, New Jersey 07458
http://www.phptr.com

Library of Congress Cataloging-in-Publication Data

Jelliffe, Rick.
    The XML and SGML cookbook: recipes for structured information/
    Rick Jelliffe.
        p.cm.--(Charles F. Goldfarb series on open information
    management)
        Includes bibliographical references and index.
        ISBN 0-13-614223-0
        1. XML (Document markup language) 2. SGML (Document markup
    language) I. Title. II. Series.
    QA76.73.X56J45 1998
    005.7'2--dc21   98-4504
                                                     CIP

Editorial/production supervision: *Nicholas Radhuber*
Cover design director: *Jerry Votta*
Cover design: *Anthony Gemmellaro*
Acquisitions editor: *Mark L. Taub*
Marketing manager: *Dan Rush*
Editorial assistant: *Mary Treacy*
Manufacturing manager: *Alexis R. Heydt*

© 1998 by Rick Jelliffe
Published by Prentice Hall PTR
Prentice-Hall, Inc.
A Simon & Schuster Company
Upper Saddle River, NJ 07458

Prentice Hall books are widely used by corporations and government agencies for training, marketing, and resale. The publisher offers discounts on this book when ordered in bulk quantities.

For more information, contact:
Phone: 800-382-3419   Fax: 201-236-7141
E-mail: corpsales@prenhall.com.
or write:
Corporate Sales Department
Prentice Hall PTR
One Lake Street
Upper Saddle River, NJ 07458

Printed in the United States of America
10 9 8 7 6 5 4 3 2

ISBN: 0-13-614223-0

Prentice-Hall International (UK) Limited, *London*
Prentice-Hall of Australia Pty. Limited, *Sydney*
Prentice-Hall Canada Inc., *Toronto*
Prentice-Hall Hispanoamericana, S.A., *Mexico*
Prentice-Hall of India Private Limited, *New Delhi*
Prentice-Hall of Japan, Inc., *Tokyo*
Simon & Schuster Asia Pte. Ltd., *Singapore*
Editora Prentice-Hall do Brasil, Ltda., *Rio de Janeiro*

Notices

Portions of Chapter 23 are derived from reference material provided on the X11R6 distribution, which is copyright 1994 X Consortium. This material has been used under the terms of its copyright, which grants free use:

TEI material has been used under the terms of its copyright, which grants free use. (The TEI special character public entity sets are also the basis for recent ISO special character sets, which are available under the ISO copyright conventions.)

Opinions expressed in this book are those of the Author and are not necessarily those of the Publisher or Series Editor.

The Author of this book has included a diskette or CD-ROM of related materials as a convenience to the reader. The Series Editor did not participate in the preparation, testing, or review of the materials and is not responsible for their content.

To my sweet parents, for their love and care.

Acknowledgments

For technical material and discussions, to my former colleagues at Allette Systems especially Nick Carr; to my former colleagues at Uniscope Inc especially Robin Masson; to my fellow members of ISO JTC1/WG4 especially Jim Mason, to my fellow members of the CJK DOKP especially Yushi Komachi; to my fellow members of the W3C XML SIG especially Jon Bosak; to the guinea pigs who suffered through early versions of the first chapters in my DTD course; and to all my various email correspondents.

For particular ideas and quotes, to Tim Bray, Martin Bryan, Len Bollard, Marcus Carr, Nick Carr, Dan Connolly, Charles Goldfarb, Elliot Kimber, Robin Masson, Yasushi Nakahara, Steve Newcombe, Gavin Nicol, Yasuhiro Okui, Peter Pacers, Dave Peterson, Lynne Price and Don Stollee. Thanks to Amy Shiu for translations from Chinese. Thanks to Christopher Keener of Kamo Inc and Hiroshi Tokui for introductions in Japan. Special thanks to Greg Palmer of Active Systems, Ottowa, and Athula Ginige of the School of Electrical Engineering, University of Technology, Sydney, who graciously contributed articles, originally intended to be appendixes, analyzing experiences from real SGML projects: these articles could not be included because of space restrictions only.

For reading and editorial advice, to Marcus Carr, Andrew O'Connor, Scott Tia and the patient Charles Goldfarb. For design advice, to Nicholas Radhuber. For the cartoons, to Andrew Goldfarb.

For access to software, Roger Schutz of T.I.M.L.U.X. for EditTime, Lani Hajagos of Adobe for FrameMaker+SGML, Tony Mudie of OmniMark, and Dallas Powell of Corel for WordPerfect.

For support emotional and financial during the writing of this book, which was unduly prolonged due to poor-health and the need to track XML, my parents Robin and Jill, my brother Peter, Hideki John Reekie, Kuni Hashimoto, Danny Odang, Somkiat Trakarnkitti, Stephen Tawaru, Sadahiko Ohata and Fumiaki Yamada, and my other friends who have put up with so much.

Special thanks to M. Chabot of ISO, Michael Gunnerson, Keld Simonson and David Bruce-Steer for their assistance in navigating ISO copyright issues.

Contents

Part 1: Systems of Documents

Part 2: Document Patterns

Part 3 : Characters & Glyphs

Appendixes

Foreword

Every chef has his special recipes. Not to mention an array of sauces, stocks, and seasonings that can add flavor to any dish.

Rick Jelliffe is no exception. He is a master chef *par excellence*, although his cuisine is structured information—the data and documents that support the workings of enterprises and that underpin electronic commerce and the World Wide Web. For a decade he's been helping clients throughout the world master structure and gain control over their information processing.

Rick's secret ingredients are SGML—the International Standard for structured information—and XML—the subset of SGML designed for the World Wide Web. In fact Rick works with me on the committees that develop these standards.

Over the years Rick has collected an amazing collection of recipes and he shares them with you in this book. All the basics are included, of course, but also hard-to-find expertise in subjects like East Asian languages and internationalization.

And Rick is a raconteur as well as a gourmet. The book is spiced with fascinating historical and cultural background that adds to understanding and retention of concepts.

So read *The XML and SGML Cookbook* and join Rick for a feast of structured information techniques. Or, as he might say to you in his native Australian:

"Come on in and we'll throw another structure on the barbie!"

Charles F. Goldfarb
Saratoga,
California February 20, 1998

Preface

As I complete this book today, I have two exciting new publications fresh from the Net, still warm from the laser printer: the final texts of XML 1.0 (the World Wide Web Consortium's subset of SGML, the *Extensible Markup Language*) and Web SGML (the corrections and enhancements to the SGML standard, ISO 8879, for WWW uses such as XML).

These two publications together revolutionize electronic publishing; they make SGML's traditional advantages for large-scale corporate publishing available at the desktop. Most importantly, they give you, the owner of data and the creator of data systems, control of your documents: SGML and its Web-optimized subset XML represent the triumph of the Open Systems movement. Not only can we have open systems for network protocols and languages, but also for the data which animate them.

This book is a practical guide for this brave new world—ideas and declarations for SGML and XML element type sets and entity sets that implement the important and useful document structures. I have tried to put in many resources which may be hard to track down otherwise. And I have paid particular attention to trying to bring out the deeper model in XML, one which will not be familiar to readers coming from HTML or proprietary markup languages: processing instructions and notations in particular.

This is not a tutorial on syntax: there are many excellent books available, including the previous books in this series. In particular I have avoided reference to SGML declarations and to the more rarely implemented, optional features of SGML. I have included a particularly detailed treatment of one area for which there has until now been little detailed treatment: characters, glyphs and internationalization.

Order, Structures, Patterns & Forms

This book is about order, structures, patterns and forms. In this book,

- *order* means the underlying, abstract (and sometimes ineffable) relationships and natures of things,

- *structure* means how some order is captured in some concrete markup,

- *pattern* means a kind of template or recipe used for creating structures (i.e., "pattern" in the dressmaking sense, not the text-processing sense), and

- *form* means a particular conformance between one structure and another (i.e., "form" in the concrete-laying sense, not the metaphysical sense).

Like any good cookbook, as well as showing *how* to make a structure, *The XML & SGML Cookbook* also tries to explain *why*, to explore the alternatives, and give the various pros and cons.

The freedom of a highly generalized technology like SGML can cause unease for new document-system designers. Being able to move in any direction is not much comfort if you cannot afford to go in the wrong direction! Fortunately, during the ten years of SGML's existence as an International Standard, convergent approaches and solutions to many common document patterns have emerged. This book attempts to catalog and discuss the best, the most instructive and the most useful of them.

Document Systems

A consideration of system constraints and factors outside the scope of the document type declaration is so often the thing that makes a project successful. Because of this, this book is aimed at the *document–system designer* rather than just the "DTD writer." Information is never managed in a vacuum; documents exist as part of a document system. Sometimes the system is closed, sometimes open-ended. If the information is valuable enough to warrant management, your whole document system should usefully be considered when creating a great DTD.

In any case, this book also will be of use to those who generate XML documents, and who might not ever even create formal declarations for elements types using SGML as their notation. If you are one of these people, I urge you to learn and attempt to use SGML content models in your informal documentation at least: SGML provides a very convenient and well-thought-out notation, suitable for many kinds of structures, and there are graphical visualization tools available to help.

So even though order can be discovered in all kinds of places in documents, many times the structures are loose, have exceptions or are incomplete. Consequently, the patterns for element type sets in this book are presented as prototypes and exemplars that you can take and reshape to your particular needs, rather than as templates which you must obediently cut and paste.

The document-system designer needs to be aware of the limits of DTD elegance. A pattern that the designer may perceive as the archetype for authors may in fact merely be a stereotype of their needs. A pattern can only be used successfully to reveal some actual order, never to impose a spurious order.

Document-system designers tend to have neat and schematic minds that reject disorder, sometimes at the price of wanting to see order where there is none: a mirage from some previous document. So this book, as well as giving patterns, also gives some principles for selecting patterns. The need for elegance must be moderated by the need for success. I hope that readers coming to this book expecting neat cookie-cutter solutions will be empowered and enabled; you will understand the issues and tradeoffs most appropriate for your individual needs.

Terminology

XML is bringing a rich influx of people from different disciplines and technologies into the SGML world, and so there is quite a variety and duplication of terminology. In order to keep sentences under control, I have used some common simplified terms which emphasize the SGML keywords used.

This Book	ISO-ese
ANY element	element having a declared content type of ANY
CDATA attribute	attribute having a declared value of CDATA
CDATA element	element having a declared content type of CDATA
CDATA entity	CDATA entity
CDATA marked section	CDATA marked section
container element	element having subelements
EMPTY element	empty element
ID attribute	attribute having a declared value of ID
IDREF attribute	attribute having declared value of IDREF
NDATA entity	NDATA entity
NMTOKEN attribute	attribute having declared value of NMTOKEN
RCDATA element	element having a declared content type of RCDATA
SDATA entity	SDATA entity
SUBDOC entity	subdocument entity

In this book, *an attribute ID* means *an attribute with the name ID*; *an ID attribute* means *an attribute having the declared value ID*; but *the attribute ID* means *that attribute with the name ID in the example snippet*. It is good usage that *an attribute ID* should be *an ID attribute* and that *an attribute IDREF* should be *an IDREF attribute*.

I intend to maintain a Web page giving any errata for this book, at the Prentice Hall PTR Web site `www.phptr.com`.

Rick Jelliffe
Sydney, Australia
1998-2-12

Index of Patterns, Structures & Forms

Colophon

Set in 10.5 pt Bitstream Aldine, Prestige and Futura by the author, using Pyrus TypeTool to partially redraw the fonts and to create various new symbols.

This book was produced from SGML documents, using DOCBOOK and customized HTML DTDs. Edited in custom version of TimeLux EditTime and several other editors. Drafts created with Adobe Framemaker+SGML and Softquad Panorama. Typeset in Corel WordPerfect 8. Text processing used OmniMark, and GNU `sort` and sed.

Cats and fishy tessellations by Andrew Goldfarb.

Part 1
Systems
of
Documents

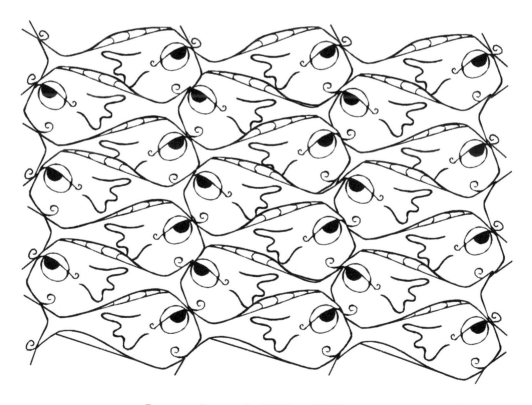

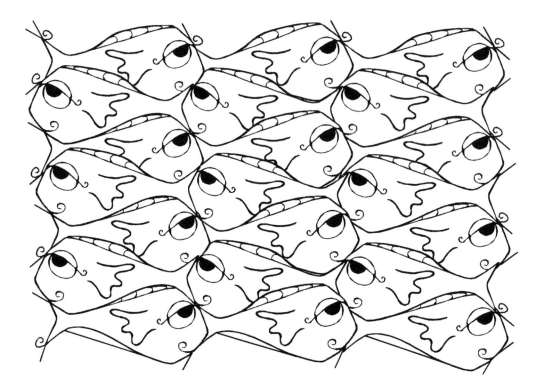

The SGML Cookbook

Documents & Publications

Chapter 1

This chapter

…shows how documents can be analyzed in many different ways, and that some of these ways are more valuable than others.

The *document* is the central organizing mechanism of SGML. A document is a thing that *documents* or *notates* information: it is a container, gaudy or plain, with something interesting inside.

ISO Definition

4.96 document: A collection of information that is processed as a unit. A document is classified as being of a particular document type.

4.102 document type: A class of documents having similar characteristics; for example, journal, article, technical manual, or memo.

(ISO 8879:1986 glossary)

Documents are the raw material used to create *publications*, which are renditions that can be perceived by human beings. Publications are not random assemblages of words in various typefaces; they have structures. Between publications and documents of different types we can see common structures: chapters, numbered lists, bibliographic information.

SGML allows us to separate out a document's structure, storage and rendition, perhaps even farming out each of them into separate documents. This in turn allows us to group documents together into *document types*, based on their common structures rather than, for example, which word processor happened to produce them or how they look.

This book collects many useful patterns, recipes for these structures to help you create your own [*SGML*] and [*XML*] [1] markup languages.

---

1. This book generally focuses on SGML features that are widely used in mainstream SGML applications or that are available in XML. But please note that XML 1.0 does not support NAME and NAMES attributes; use NMTOKEN instead. Also, many markup declarations in this book have comments inside the declarations: XML 1.0 does not support this, so XML users should strip out the comments.

Explicit and Implicit Document Type

Like documents, applications have built-in structures. Every application that deals with collections of information accepts and implements some document type: a word processor program implements structures that its designers think will be good for publications of the type found in offices, for example.

For every document type there is some kind of document type definition.[1] Whether it is implicit and hard-coded into C++ code of the application or explicit in the design documentation, there is a notional *Document Type Definition*. It says: *"my documents contain paragraphs and headings and tables, and tables have rows and rows have cells"* or *"cells can span horizontally, but not float vertically."* Even for XML documents (which use a simple selection of readily-implementable SGML features, perhaps with no explicit markup declarations) the users of the document will have some idea of where it is sensible to put elements.

The *implicit DTD* of an application can often be gleaned by looking through its plain-text dump format: Microsoft's Rich Text Format (RTF) for example. Of course, implicit DTDs usually are not rigorously documented for the general public; some vendors prize their ability to gratuitously change a plain-text format to suit the whims of their perceived markets and may use plain-text format incompatibility to encourage across-the-board upgrades of applications. There is no reason why the implicit DTD of an off-the-shelf application created by strangers should (or should not) match what you need.

One of the major skills of the document-system designer is to know when to adopt a structure that is convenient for applications (reverse-engineering an application's implicit DTD) and when to use a structure that transcends any particular application.

---

1. Even though it may only be equivalent to `<!ELEMENT X ANY>`.

Love, Bloat and Prudence

The sad history of applications, especially in the personal computer market, seems to be that vendors add feature after feature until they (i.e., the applications) are bloated. Then vendors add GUI customization tools to let you make unloved features go away. Then they provide scripting languages and add-ons to let you play with the data more. Finally they realize the whole thing has been made too complicated to inflate further and add embedded links to other specialist applications, which themselves get the same bloat. [1]

A famous book by [*Wirth*] is *"Algorithms + Data Structures = Programs."* Programmers love elegant algorithms and they aim to use data structures that are easy for programs to manipulate. This lack of a data-centered view encroaches into software analysis and system design: the fundamental high-level design decision to formally model text-data provides an immediate high-level modularization of the system design. It may not make complex systems less complex, but it certainly can make small and medium-sized systems tractable.

We need tools to let us actually model our text-data directly, and then to map whatever parts of the data are interesting to the implicit DTD of the application. This is where SGML steps in: it makes the owner of the text-data the controller of its form.

It is not a matter of saying *"application DTDs – BOO!...information DTDs – HURRAH!"* One criterion of a good SGML DTD is that it allows you maximal use of whatever facilities the application vendors provide.

A document does not need to be marked up so that every high-level structure is exposed. Sometimes, for the more difficult and labor-intensive parts of the document, it is convenient to reverse-engineer a presentational-structure *element type set* from the implicit DTD of the application. This is particularly the case for tables and equations: the most readily portable element structures use generic yet fairly presentational element type sets.

---

1. In the mid 1990s this trend seemed very apparent in Web browsers and the proprietary Active X and OpenDoc APIs.

ISO Definition

4.112 element type set: a set of element, attribute definition list, and notation declarations that are used together.

(ISO 8879:1986 glossary)

Sometimes the implicit DTD is particularly ill-defined or difficult to determine. In such a case, you may find it prudent to not store your data in SGML at all, but to keep it in its native form in an external NDATA entity (for example, as an XML *resource*). [1]

People may think that if you advocate SGML, you believe everything should be marked up in SGML. SGML was developed by pragmatic people for practical reasons, and is most used in high-pressure production environments. SGML's constructs for marking up where things that are not SGML go (NDATA entities) and for adding processing instructions (PIs) at appropriate points are not concessions that the structured text methodology is somehow flawed. Rather it indicates that SGML is designed to give users of documents *control* over the kinds of information present in markup, even the arbitrary and unstructured events for which PIs are often used. [2]

---

1. This is still how most graphics and line drawings are incorporated into most SGML documents. It is also often how tables are done, in some markets: the ubiquitous Western [*CALS*] table model does not model well what East Asians do in their tables, for instance (e.g., the diagonally split corner header cells in so-called "3D" tables), and also for what is needed for more free-form document structures like charts.

2. The other strange misconception people have about SGML is that it is only useful for character text: as the [*SGML*] definition of document given earlier makes clear, the SGML idea of a document is not a thing that holds character text, but rather a collection of information that is processed as a unit, which might not include any character-text information at all. See *About Non-Text* below.

A Six-View Model of Publications

Markup is conventionally classified into two different categories: *logical markup* (models) and *presentational markup* (views). Logical markup is how an electronic publication looks and acts in cyberspace; presentational markup is how it looks and acts on your screen. People like to deem one good and the other bad—the theory seems to be that your markup should be rich enough to derive any view you need from it. This two-fold classification is convenient for introducing the ideas of generalized markup, yet it is over-simple for sophisticated document-system designers like us![1]

Logical Markup

Presentational Markup

I would like instead to propose a deeper model, showing six views of what can be marked up in publications. These six views can all be present simultaneously, and might not have the same boundaries or connections. Of course, usually one type of structure will piggyback on a higher structure—it is when they do not that complications arise and a skillful DTD designer is needed. And I want to avoid the idea that any type of markup should be deemed universally bad.

To explain the six views, we will use two running examples. One, flagged with ∿, is based on tracking what structures we can see as we gaze at a page. The other, flagged with 🖳, uses dialog boxes from some imaginary GUI-based publication system to show what controls are relevant for each view.

---

1. Separating presentation concerns from logical structure is not only an output-time issue but also an input-time and processing-time issue. However, SGML's advantage over binary formats is that even the most complex SGML documents are still editable in common text editors.

Viewing Page Layout

ꙮ First stare at it like those 3D image books – with the image out of focus. All you can see is the *layout*: various blocks of fuzzy text arranged in columns. If the page has been poorly typeset you may also see a river running through text from top to bottom.

🖥 This is the kind of thing that a WYSIWYG DTP application would have under the control of a *"page layout"* dialog box

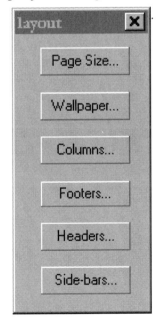

Viewing Page Objects

～ Now, if you focus your eyes a little better you can see that the columns are formed by *page objects* flowed into the columns: the objects include word segments in lines, symbols, logos and pictures.

⌨ This is the kind of thing that a WYSIWYG DTP application would have under the control of a *"paragraph format"* dialog box.

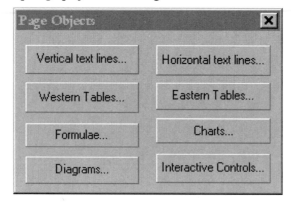

Viewing Glyphs

ꝏ Focusing further, we can see that the logos are composed of *glyphs*: a character in particular size and typeface from a particular font vendor, for example.

ISO Definition

glyph: a recognizable abstract graphical symbol which is independent of any specific design.

(ISO/IEC 9541-1:1991)

⌨ This is the kind of thing that a WYSIWYG DTP application would have under control of a *"font"* menu.

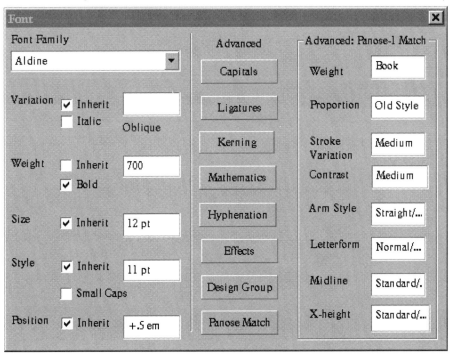

Viewing Characters

⤳ Now the brain kicks in. When we see a glyph, we recognize it as a particular instance of a universal: the glyph "f" is a Latin small letter f *character*.

🖳 This is the kind of thing that a WYSIWYG DTP application would have under the control of a "*Key Caps*" dialog box and the keyboard.

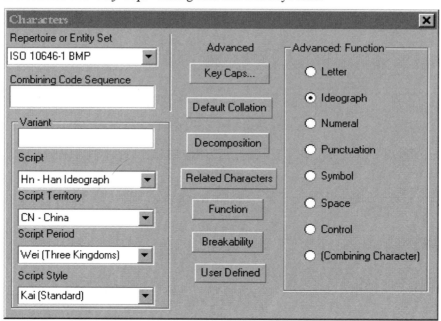

Viewing Editorial Structure

↳ Our poor relentless brains still can't stop their job! The characters spell words, which are arranged in some grammatical and editorial-structures: words, phrases, sentences, paragraphs, sections. These are called *editorial–structures*.

🖵 Editorial-structure encompasses the kinds of thing that a WYSIWYG DTP application might have under a *"Collapsible Outline"* dialog box from the *"View"* menu, and a *"Make Link"* or *"Make Anchor"* dialog box from a *"Hypertext"* menu. The lower-layer structures, phrases and sentences, are generally avoided by DTP applications, though the detection of words is required for line breaking.

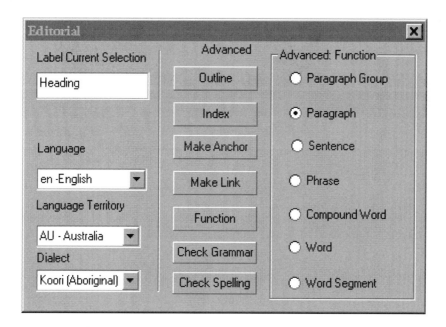

Viewing Topic Structure

〜 And language expresses thought: semantics and *topic–structures*. This is the domain of logic, rhetoric and meaning. The topic-structures include what is often called *information–content*.

⌨ This is the kind of thing that a WYSIWYG DTP application usually is utterly incapable of representing, except by embedding external database objects

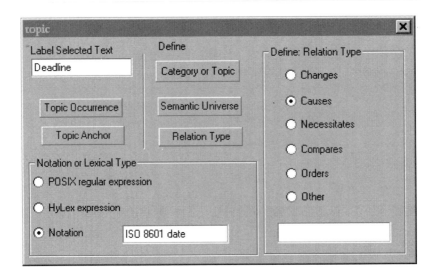

The Flow of Dependence

Text media involves all these things: topic-structures, editorial-structures, characters, glyphs, page objects, and layout. And SGML document type declarations can be written that describe each of them. However only some of them will be important for any given publication; the big issue for DTD writers is to find what is important, then to make that accessible and convenient.

Figure 1: Simple Forwards Dependence

We can see that, in most cases, and for most publications, the presentation (view) is dependent on the logical structure (model). There is a simple forwards flow of information and control from the higher (more mental) to the lower (sensed) structures.

- The topic-structure of some piece of a document will largely determine what layout structure it uses (e.g., an *index* has one layout, a *section* has another),

- the editorial-structure with the topic-structure determines the page-object view it uses (e.g., a paragraph will be rendered as a text block), and

- the character with the editorial-structure and the topic-structure will largely determine the glyph to be used (e.g., the character "f" will almost always get a glyph that is some kind of an f).

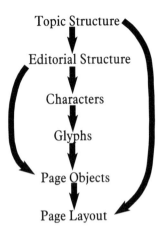

Topic Structure

Editorial Structure

Characters

Glyphs

Page Objects

Page Layout

Figure 2: More Realistic Forwards Dependence

When analyzing a publication to find its structures, we follow this dependency flow. Before you make an element type, first think if there is a higher-level way to represent it. By marking data up in the highest-level way possible, you maximize the chance of useful side-effects, where you can mine some unexpected value out of your text at some later stage.

When a structure belonging to one view has the same extent and fits neatly inside a structure of another view, only one element type needs to be used to mark them both up: this is called *piggybacking*. Typically, the highest view is used for the *element type name*; [1] rather than tagging a string as `italic` (which relates to the glyphs used), we tag it as a `keyword` (which relates to the editorial view).

We may even take the topic-structure view and tag it as a `computer-term`. Usually, lower-level structure is caused by the higher; the string is a computer term, **therefore** it is a keyword, **therefore** it is bold. Marking it up according to the highest-level view allows you to disconnect this: to say *"give me all computer terms"* for example, or *"keywords are now to be rendered in bold"*.

Most typesetting can be performed using just this kind of logical markup; a typesetting system can figure out most other details—the glyphs to be used, the hyphenation, and the line and page breaking—without needing any explicit markup. Indeed, it is one of the major benefits of generalized markup that so little needs to be marked up explicitly.

---

1. In this book I will often use the term *element type name* in preference to the older, less clear term *generic identifier* (GI).

I do not need to defend generalized, logical markup: it has been used successfully for many of the Western world's large publications for the last decade or more ① SGML met with initial resistance or disbelief outside the West: the typesetting issues of many non-Latin-based languages present interesting challenges. However, I have not seen any reason why generalized markup will not be appropriate for the same kinds of documents it is used for in the West. SGML is particularly language-, locale-, character-set- and script-neutral. ②

If all structures belonging to each view exhibited a simple dependence and could be piggybacked onto a single element hierarchy, life would be simple. Indeed, when structures can fit in this way, SGML document systems are very straightforward.

ISO Definition

4.113 element structure: The organization of a document into hierarchies of elements, ...

(ISO 8879:1986 glossary, extract)

Some kinds of publications do not fit into this category. Some kinds of technical publications get loose-leaf single page updates to replace existing pages, for example. To do this without upsetting the page-breaking on subsequent pages, there needs to be some kind of feedback mechanism to insert into the original SGML text the pages breaks from the typesetting system.

Because such a mechanism is complex, sometimes you must make other rules affecting the design of the document so that production is manageable. For example, you might make a rule that paragraphs cannot break over a page: this ensures that the page structure (layout) is synchronous with paragraph structure (editorial structure). You can then piggyback a layout attribute to force page-breaks on editorial-structure element types.

---

1. Refer to [*Ensign*] *SGML: the Billion Dollar Secret* for more on this.

2. Those who think that typesetting rules cannot be codified and therefore computerized should consider the opinion of [*Jan Tschibold*], who designed Penguins, that good typesetting is *"the opposite of an adventure"* and *"eminently logical."* But, of course, even the most sophisticated typesetting expert system may require tactful intervention on occasion.

The exceptions that break the simple one-way dependence come from the nature of the medium, ergonomics or æsthetics: paper pages have a particular length, only so many glyphs of a size can fit on a line, chapters should not end with a small amount of text on an odd page.

Such constraints should be expected: usually an appropriate page design can reduce the amount of hand-tuning (by adding processing instructions, or tweaking the rendering application at runoff-time) needed to a minimum. For example, the use of *floatable* illustrations and tables rather than anchored ones when the illustrations or tables are larger than a paragraph, is an appropriate design decision for automated layout, as well as for humans. ①

We can now say which kinds of documents are not straightforward for generalized markup: any documents in which this dependence flow is reversed:—

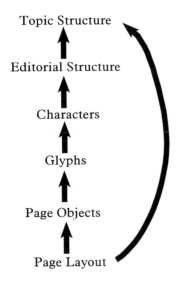

- ☒ Where page design determines the types and numbers of page objects allowed in the document;

- ☒ where the page design or type of page object determines the glyph style, regardless of the character, editorial-structure or topic-structure;

- ☒ where the typeface used determines which characters can be used.

Figure 3: Reversed Flow of Dependence

This reversal of dependence is particularly true with more graphical information, with small page and column sizes compared to the size of the page objects (i.e., where there is a packing problem), and in nations whose typesetting systems do not yet have adequate heuristics to place page objects in a culturally-pleasing fashion.

---

1. A floatable page element is one that is marked-up in-line in a position that will be satisfactory for non-paginated presentations, but can float in paginated presentations.

Fads, Trends, Polemics

In the early days of text processing the first three of our six views (the presentational structures: layout, page objects and glyphs) were the province of the compositor and typesetter (following the designer) while the latter three (the logical structures: topic-structures, editorial-structures, characters) were the province of copy editors (following the author and editor).

With the advent of computing, the boundaries have shifted in most countries, so that there is no longer the same two-part division between editorial and production.

In the initial round of computerization, characters from the editorial system were marked up with codes to select glyphs, break lines and perform layout. Very early on, line-breaking and hyphenation became automated.

As early technology progressed, it became obvious that, especially for large and complex documents, it was more expedient to mark the documents up according to the editorial-structure view into paragraphs, headings, and so on. Marking up according to the editorial-structure of the text and then using a *style–sheet* to get formatted output is called *generic coding*. It has the advantage that highly consistent and flexible documents can be created—documents that can be reformatted quickly.

Marking up documents by even higher-level criteria, by tagging them according to their topic, creates documents that are akin to text databases—the tags identify fields.

WYSIWYG suddenly threw out of fashion text-processing systems based on batch processing, generic coding and publishing from databases. Users like *direct manipulation* systems, where they can see the direct fruits of their labor; WYSIWYG desktop publishing software clouded the issue, by allowing direct manipulation of presentational markup only, ignoring the needs of logical markup. Yet gradually all those things have crept back; word processor applications have scripting languages, style-sheets and embedded links to database software.

They have crept back because, despite the desires of the designers of personal publishing software, logical markup (named characters, generic coding and topic-structure markup) is useful. Often using logical markup can be only the only practical way to get a result.

The SGML industry, in its need to get this last point across, also may be accused of too-extreme a position: that you must *never* have presentational markup and should *only* markup according to logical structure.

Eschewing such polemics, we can ask instead *"What is a reasonable approach?"*—

- In some documents and parts of documents, the value of the information is in the logical structures of the data: logical markup should be used; in other documents and parts of documents, the value of the information is in the presentational structures: presentational markup should be used. SGML lets you do both. ⚐

- Where presentational structure can be derived automatically from the logical structure by a program, you should favor logical markup—it is more flexible and manageable.

- Presentational structures and logical structures are not always co-extensive. And it is not always possible to derive the former from the latter. Sometimes you need to intersperse presentational markup in with the logical markup. If you need to do this, first check whether processing instructions are not the better choice.

- Unless your documents are targeted for a single system and will be short-lived, use generic rather than specific markup.

Principle

Model the Real Information

SGML was originally adopted by producers for large, corporate, technical and legal publications. These kinds of publications are partic. ularly suited for logical markup. Yet just because you can strip out the presentational structures from a document so that only its logical structures remain, it does not mean that you must, or that you have to want to. Presentational markup, even in the form of generic hints about typeface or page-objects, is a poor master but a good servant:

---

1. An extreme example of where layout aspects are utterly intrinsic to the text is the *calligram*, a text picture with a shape that reflects the topic, for example, a cruciform devotional poem. Refer to [*Gaur*].

The SGML Cookbook

just because an element type has presentational attribute, it does not mean you have to obey it to the letter when publishing the document.

······This is one of the great differences between SGML and other markup systems: in SGML you can treat presentational attributes as an indication of how the source document looked, not as how it *must* look in the future. It can be worthwhile, in legacy text, to not strip out presentational information, but to store it in attributes of a convenient element; these can help subsequent rendering of the text, and may also contain hints about structures you have missed or did not realize you needed. It is especially true when you are processing legacy documents through a series of interim DTDs, and exploring what information will be provided by the final DTD: don't exclude legacy markup early.

Conflicts of Interest:

HTML and SMDL

The big issue is appropriateness and value. HTML has a simple generic document type declaration, though polluted with presentational element types in its early days. As HTML developed in the mid 1990s, it was being pulled in at least four directions:

> 1. text authors require a broader, better range of generic element types: tables, etc.;
>
> 2. advertising and public relations folks place a lot of emphasis on glyphs, lines and layout: much or most of the value of their publications is not in logical content at all but in being eye-catching;
>
> 3. people who need to search or study the data need better element types so that specific fields can be represented, linked, queried and traversed;
>
> 4. software vendors want to allow browsers to take over more GUI functionality, to allow new kinds of navigation and for more flexible and integrated systems.

In all four cases , the value of the document is in a different place. Rather than extend HTML in all four ways with no guarantee that the result will be particularly useful to anyone, SGML lets you write your own document type declaration – modeling whatever is important – so that you can later transform the documents into whatever is the best available form. For even a small number of documents it is easier to change a transformation program or a style-sheet than to edit all the documents by hand.

The Standard Music Description Language ([*SMDL*], ISO/IEC 10743) is an SGML application for describing music and performances. It was one of the test cases for the development of [*HyTime* '97], the ISO Hypertext and Time-scheduling language. SMDL says that musical works can be represented in terms of four basic domains which mirror the four directions that HTML is being pulled in:

♪ the *logical domain* is the basic content of the music: what the music is after removing the accidents of any particular performances, analyses or visual notation;

♪ the *visual domain* is how the music is printable in some edition;

♪ the *analytical domain* is how the music can be annotated with classification information and used in other texts;

♪ the *gestural domain* refers to dynamic aspects of the music's performance: in a sense it records the user's (i. e., the performer) choices during a specific session with the data (i.e., the music).

SMDL can get away with attempting to model all four domains whereas HTML cannot, because HyTime is a much more powerful linking and scheduling system.

What about Non-Text?

People sometimes have confused the fact that SGML is a simple text-based language, and not some machine-readable-only binary, with the completely wrong notion that SGML can only be used to model and represent text. SGML can be used to model and notate systems for encoding thought and order other than sequential text on paper pages. —

Metadata

The most important type of non-text information is *metadata*, which means *data about the data*. This includes bibliographic information, resource descriptions, graphic bounding boxes, copyright notices, revision histories, the create-size or bounding box of graphics, and other classifications given as annotations to some entity, object or resource. In general, metadata is implemented by header blocks of fielded data[1] and by attributes of elements. Perhaps SGML's greatest strength for many users is the ease with which metadata can be added to – and located from – anywhere, in a disciplined way that is convenient for applications.

Hypertext documents

These are often arranged into nodes, which are analogous to pages. However, unlike pages, nodes are not limited to a particular size, and indeed may overlap with other nodes, and they may not have an author-defined sequence. *Hypertext* documents may have intelligent links, where the history, language, system or skill of the user determines in part the target node.

Charts and graphs, database records

These are just renderings of numeric data. The data and format information for the chart can be represented in SGML. Indeed, all sorts of database records can be stored and transmitted as SGML—the entry-level subset of SGML called [*XML*] (the eXtensible Markup Language) has been particularly designed for this purpose.

Electronic circuits

Most circuit board design is done by entering a *netmap* of the components and connections (logical markup) and then letting the program lay the board out (presentation). The netmap can be easily defined as an SGML document type; the layout could also be, but with much more complication. Western ([*Pinnacles*] Group) and Japanese (E-CALS) microchip companies are providing chip data

---

1. See chapter 10, *Databases*.

sheet information in SGML form, with the chip package connections and electrical specs modeled in SGML.

CDROM fantasy games

Games are often highly customizable, and to be successful, some game manufacturers need to make their software readily portable between PC operating systems and Macintosh. This can be done by separating the structure of the game from the implementation of navigation and rendering. The structure of a fantasy game, rooms, paths, objects, interactivity, messages etc. can be represented with SGML. The rendering engines are usually highly optimized for each specific operating system and hardware.

Music, conducting and performance

These can also be notated in SGML. In fact, there is an ISO standard for this: [*SMDL*] the Standard Music Description Language. ①

Speech

There is not enough information in plain text for computers to speak pleasingly in most languages. Extra information about tone, stress, pronunciation, pacing and quality of voice can be added by markup. The [*JSML*] Java Speech Markup Language DTD is an example of SGML being used for this purpose

Graphical User Interfaces (GUIs)

The resource files for GUIs can be represented in SGML: the HTML element type INPUT is an example of this use.

Computer function arguments

When an application programming interface (API) is becoming complicated, with many options, or where the API invoked is to send some message to a remote computer or external process, or where each function call is highly reliant on another and it is safer to be kept as atomic operations, it may be practical to send a string containing SGML markup. The receiving routine parses the text and itself makes the appropriate calls.

Literate programs

Programming languages do not, typically, allow convenient integration of source code, diagrams and comments with any typographical sophistication. The literate programming movement says that program fragments can be usefully embedded inside non-program markup. That way the program becomes a unified document. The extra information kept in markup could just be extra metadata relating to

---

1. ISO/IEC 10743:1996. SMDL was developed by Drs Steven R. Newcomb and Charles F. Goldfarb, both of whom have had musical careers outside their well-known work on HyTime and SGML.

how to use and find the source code, for example version information and compiler dependencies. [*DSSSL*] defines an SGML DTD to be used for these kinds of purposes.

It is possible to go all the way and make up a whole programming language using SGML: the IETM (U.S. military Interactive Electronic Training Manual project) [*MID*] (Metafile for Interactive Documents) DTD is one example. While this may be cumbersome and require some effort it can also allow the advantage of being able to program at a higher level than usual, by being able to make up a language highly geared to the needs of the particular project. One of the most famous proprietary SGML parsers is, in fact, written in SGML in just this fashion: it even has element types for function preconditions.

Documents *versus* APIs

What distinguishes the SGML family of markup languages?—

- [*SGML*] (Standard Generalized Markup Language),

- [*Web SGML*], the 1997 adaption of SGML to allow simpler parsers for use on the World Wide Web,

- [*HTML*] (HyperText Markup Language), and

- [*XML*] (Extensible Markup Language), a subset of Web SGML.

They put at center stage the *document*: the thing that ties information together and labels its parts.

They do not—

- attempt to distill the most computationally pure and elegant method of storing data (like the relational database), or

- try to encompass all possible format needs (like high-end text-processing systems).

Instead, SGML's focus is narrow, or rather, highly targeted: to provide a format that can be storage-neutral and application-neutral, yet which allows documents to be rigorously marked-up. So that the marked-up structure of the document encodes some interesting part of the order in the document. ①

SGML's approach is attractive and works② . The rigorous markup of data and the separate specification of the processing to be run on the marked-up document have proved to be a more successful way to divide and conquer information-rich problems: text, hypertext, multimedia, multiple media. In the West, a great proportion of technical and reference material is now produced in this way; in some industries, SGML is ubiquitous.

A paper by [*Brown and Duguid*] in the worth-reading book *Bringing Design into Software* [*Winograd*] names SGML among other technologies as one in which the old distinction between program and content has become blurred.

On first glance, this is a rather *startling assertion*, given that SGML was invented to implement generalized markup and to free documents from thralldom to procedural markup. But generalized markup allows unconfused use of SGML documents by programs, even for non-textual data: allowing a disconnection between a document and its use, it paradoxically provides a clean level of abstraction which allows far tighter coupling of the document and the program using the document. ③

---

1. In 1997, SGML's power was extended by the SGML Extended Facilities (given in Annex A of [*HyTime* '97], ISO/IEC 10744:1997): this book includes some of the most useful of these facilities, though HyTime's sophisticated hypertext and time scheduling technology itself is not treated.

2. Robust and rude applications like the World Wide Web prove it. However the WWW's evolution has at times been a demonstration that programmers habitually try do do things using program languages rather than markup languages. Programmers are trained to expect APIs or algorithms to be the best approach to implementing information systems—many compound document systems and hypertext systems have foundered on this bias.

3. The paper [*Crampton Smith, Tabor*] in the same collection agrees with Marshall McLuhan that the *"medium is the message."* This may seem to run contrary to the principles of generalized markup, in which information exists disembodied and independent of any medium.

However, the thrust of their argument is, in effect, against the notion of an abstract, universal, context-independent presentation DTD. They are saying that because the user fuses the medium with the information, the medium must be conformed in some way to the message and the user to achieve maximal understanding of the in-

The SGML Cookbook

Summary of Chapter 1

This chapter discussed documents and views.

The simplistic *logical* structure versus *presentation* structure was abandoned in favor of the senocular model of topic-structures, editorial-structures, characters, glyphs, page objects, and layout.

The chapter emphasized that there may be many kinds of structures present in your document. Figuring out which are important or needed is the DTD writer's task.

"We understand material things by abstracting ideas of them from their images, and then use such knowledge to attain knowledge of immaterial things," St Thomas [*Aquinas*], *Summa Theologica,* [Ia] q. 85.

---

formation. SGML attributes and processing instructions can provide rich hints and instructions for the new generation of conformable user interfaces the paper calls for.

In any case, a document marked-up in SGML itself is not medium-independent: SGML prescribes and perhaps *is* a medium – markup using characters in plain text.

The SGML Cookbook

The Nature of
Markup

Chapter 2

This chapter

…explains the kinds of markup you can use in SGML documents.

M arkup is the information used by an SGML parser to construe the document as a tree of entities (starting from the document entity) and a tree of elements (rooted at the document type element). Entities and elements can be decorated with attributes which may themselves name other entities and attributes. This allows structures more complicated than trees to be represented.

⚠ ······ In SGML elements can span entities: you can have a start–tag in one entity, and its corresponding end–tag in another. However, try not to do this: when the entity structure hangs off the element structure, your elements become like *micro–documents* which can both stand alone by themselves or be reused as components of other documents. (NOTE: XML 1.0 does not allow elements to span entities.)

ISO Definition

4.183 **markup:** Text that is added to the data of a document in order to convey information about it.

4.120 **entity:** A collection of characters that can be referenced as a unit.①

4.110 **element:** A component of the hierarchical structure defined by a document type definition; it is identified in a document instance by descriptive markup, usually a start-tag and end-tag.

(ISO 8879:1986 glossary)

SGML is different from most markup systems: an SGML tag doesn't prescribe *do X here*, it describes *this is an X*; in the jargon this is *descriptive markup* rather than *procedural markup*. It is entirely up to the application to decide, based on the tags, what to do. When the same data must be used by many different processes, procedural markup becomes an untenable approach.

___

1. An entity is a system-independent interface to data storage, and can be contrasted with the hypertext **resource**, which is *"an addressable unit of information or service which is participating in a link. Examples include files, images, documents, programs, and query results. Concretely, anything which happens to be reachable by the use of a locator in some linking element."* [XLL] Not all the entities of a document are resources, since they may be included by entity references and form part of the document itself; similarly, not all resources are entities, in that some may not be declared using the SGML entity mechanism.

ISO Definition

4.183 **descriptive markup:** Markup that describes the structure and other attributes of a document in a non-system-specific manner, independently of any processing that may be performed on it. In particular, SGML descriptive markup uses tags to express the element structure.

(ISO 8879:1986 glossary)

The first question you should ask when thinking about how to mark a particular structure up best is: *Is this a structure in entities, in elements, or in processing instructions?* Where, what or how. It is a fundamental question that is sometimes unasked

Entities are most often used for structures involving characters and glyphs. Elements are most often used for structures involving topic–structure and editorial–structure. Processing instructions are most often used for structures involving page–objects and layout.

ISO Definition

4.234 **processing instruction:** Markup consisting of system-specific data that controls how a document is to be processed.

(ISO 8879:1986 glossary)

Element and processing instruction structures are, one would hope, preserved between SGML systems during the life of a document. However, entity structure, in particular text entity structure, rarely is maintained: the act of importing by some editors and document management systems often merges text entities into a single, fat document.

ISO Definition

4.126 entity structure: The organization of a document into one or more separate entities.

(ISO 8879:1986 glossary)

This *de facto* constraint – that you cannot guarantee the entity structure of the document downstream – is sometimes a freedom: you can restructure the document to suit your data storage system, and the capabilities of your entity manager.

For example, if you receive a dictionary in a single 10 Meg SGML file, the first thing you might decide to do is to process it out into a hub document which invokes each dictionary entry or section, marked up as external entities. Apart from any other consideration, this allows you fast access to tweak poor markup. If you want to force an entity structure that will be maintained downstream, you should use subdocuments, or links to external documents. Or only use tools that respect the entity structure.

What is Good Markup?

A workable answer to this question will allow you to cull your DTD of poor structures and their declarations quickly. We can eke out a response with a simple positive and negative test:

- The negative is the bottom line: good markup won't prevent you or your computers from understanding and manipulating your document. This is the big reason why presentational markup is inappropriate for documents where the value is in the logical structure: you lose access to the things you most need to manipulate.

- Now the positive: good markup presents the valuable information in the most direct and simple way.

The SGML Cookbook

So what is good markup for humans? What is good for computers? Some document type declarations are made for humans; some are made for computers; most are intended for both. The DTD writer can structure a document type declaration to be suitable for either.

Good markup for humans will

- ✓ have short and simple identifiers for common element types and attributes, and descriptive ones for less common,

- ✓ follow the house- or industry-jargon the users are familiar with,

- ✓ allow easy formatting, perhaps even have format hints, and not gratuitously depart from a useful presentational order, so that formatted drafts can be readily generated,

- ✓ allow the use of features such as omitted tag and short references only in ways which do not obscure the effect of what is being done,

- ✓ not use obscure markup tricks and hacks,[1]

- ✓ not gratuitously confuse users: if your users all know HTML, they should not be given a DTD where <h1> identifies something other than a heading,

- ✓ have a high locality of data, so the reader does not have to search too much,

- ✓ minimize the chances of introducing errors or incompatibilities for authors of the document.

Principle

Identifiers should be simple and clear.

---

1. A well-known example: HTML Cascading Stylesheets ([*CSS*]) are supposed to be embedded in comment delimiters <!-- and -->. An SGML or XML parser or a CSS-supporting HTML browser will know the declared content type is CDATA and allow the rest, while an old-style browser will treat the characters as comment delimiters and strip out the style-sheet.

Good markup for computers and networks will

✓ be compact,

✓ be complete,

✓ label, name, address, or position all the information that will be needed for searching, sorting, interaction and presentation,

✓ avoid forward references, since most large SGML documents are processed as using data streams rather than in-memory methods,

✓ have a granularity of entity that matches the application,

✓ use *fielded names* for identifiers of objects that are part of a fixed series. [1]

Principle

Garbage Markup, Garbage Documents.

The threshold of goodness is determined by the technological and skills context of the computers and users. A DTD intended only ever to be edited using a custom computer program may be impossible to fathom or use with a simple text editor. If it is a good DTD used well, the document instance will have all the information needed, rigorously tagged, and the tagging will be no more complex than needed.

ISO Definition

4.160 **instance (of a document type):** The data and markup for a hierarchy of elements that conforms to a document type definition.

(ISO 8879:1986 glossary)

---

1. See Chapter 5 *The Document in Use*.

Generic and Specific Tagging

There is another axis apart from the six views of markup discussed in chapter 1: the axis that goes from generic to specific tagging. Here are examples of generic and specific versions for each of the six levels. —

Type of Markup	Generic	Specific
Layout	`<page design="dlr">`	`<page columns="1" in-gutter="72" type="recto">`
Object	`<text-block type="para-design">`	`<text-block font="times-roman" first-indent="1 em">`
Glyph	`<!ENTITY bullet "&#149;" -- US MS Windows -->`	`<!ENTITY bullet SDATA "[GLYPH: round filled black bullet, helvetica 12 point, best followed by em space]">`
Character	`<!ENTITY bullet SDATA "[bullet]">`	`<!ENTITY bullet PUBLIC "-//My Company::My Section//ENTITY in-house bullet for top level bullet point lists//EN">`
Publication-Structure	`<paragraph>`	`<stanza>`
Topic-Structure	`<keyword>`	`<killer-bug>`

You can have the generic value as the element type identifier (GI) and the specific value as the declared value of an attribute, of course: `<keyword type="killer-bug">`. Or *vice versa*: `<killerbug class="keyword">` or `Class` and `Type` are the common attribute names used to decorate elements with specific or generic element type names. If a finer granularity is required, attributes with names using biological terms such as `species` and `genus`, or computing terms like `superclass` or `subtype` can be appropriate.

It would be nice if Class always denoted a higher-level abstraction, and Type always denoted a particularization.[1] In [*HTML*] the class attribute names the general styles to be used to render that element. Because of this, it is probably unwise to declare an attribute class with any different intent.

Attribute names like Class, Species, Genus and Type are themselves very generic. More specific attribute names may be useful: <bug danger="none"> rather than <bug type="nodanger">. Another possibility is to use more verbal attribute names like is-a and has-a, is-part-of and has-part, like-a and has-copy.

Parent and child are fairly clear terms to be used in attribute names. For example, parent-type may be preferable to supertype—though both are so generic that they convey little meaning.

······When an attribute name or element type name is vague or broad, the danger is that it does not capture enough information to be useful. For example, an attribute declaration like

```
<!ATTRIBUTE text
        presentation CDATA #IMPLIED >
```

does provide a clear place for presentational data to go, but it does not give any indication of what values are allowed. When it comes time to make use of an attribute like this, the future user must, in the absence of some Markup Policy Document or Data Type Dictionary,[2] inspect all the document instances and try to find the format and allowed values. So, if you know your future users will not have the skills or technology to do this, you should use more specific attributes. Changing the name of the attribute to be more specific is not the point: the attribute named and its value must be in a useable form.

---

1. Unfortunately, because class and type have meanings in programming, and because type also has a meaning in typesetting in English, some well-known public document type declarations use one term when the other is appropriate. The horse has bolted. The richness of the English language, in overloading words with multiple meanings, sometimes results in a good specific names causing confusion because of ancillary meanings—class is one such word.

2. See *Declarations are not Enough* on page 1-104.

The development of generic coding and generalized markup in the 1960s and 1970s was based on the flexibility and longevity gained by keeping markup as generic as possible. Rather than hard-coding the rendering and layout into the document, a separate style-sheet can be maintained to allow greater consistency of markup and rapid, global style changes.

It is possible to have specific markup of presentation using SGML. However, there are many excellent presentation-oriented software packages with direct manipulation user interfaces (for example, desktop publishing packages) that do this: SGML has not flourished as an interchange format for documents of this type.

There can still be advantages in using SGML even in this unfriendly territory: the [*Rainbow*] DTD is a format-oriented DTD for use when converting presentation-oriented word processing documents into SGML. For example, the Rainbow DTD lets you have RTF-in-SGML (most word processors support export to Microsoft's rather erratic export format RTF); once the document is in SGML, high powered off-the-shelf SGML-processing tools can be used to finish the conversion.

Using SGML can open new ways of working with documents that take advantage of the human and computer resources available. For example:

- You can create some kind of keyword list by visual inspection of a document, which can be attached at the head of the document or chapters, one element per keyword.

- These keywords can be added to any glossary or keyword terms already marked up in the document.

- A computer program can then extract, sort and make unique all the keywords and output them as an SGML document.

- If needed, the author or editor can then prune this list, add attributes and other keywords missed.

- Finally, the list can be used as input data for a text–processing program to further mark up the original document.

The document now is richly indexed and cross–referenced. You did not need to explicitly mark up each document and a domain expert did not have to supervise the whole process.①

Which is Better: Generic Markup or Specific Markup?

Specific, presentational markup has proved itself to be a poor performer for long-life documents, for the reasons already given. However, it is interesting to note that there are some niche markets, in particular the market for read-only distribution of electronic facsimile versions of printed documents, where specific, procedural, presentational markup is strong: Adobe's Portable Document Format [*PDF*] is the leading example of this.

I do not know if industry experience particularly favors generic markup or specific markup for editorial-structure markup or topic-structure markup. —

> • The skill of the person (or program) doing the markup is one limiting factor. An author will be in a position to know specific details about an element's topic, but a technical editor may not. And a WP operator who is not a domain expert probably can only mark up editorial-structure elements, not topic-structure elements.

> • The other limiting factor is how specialized the processing software can be. This, in turn, will be determined by the value of the information, the size of the publication or document series, and so on. ②

---

1. This is a commonly-used method:—I have used it successfully on encyclopedias, dictionaries and thesauruses. With these very large works it is impractical to mark the document up by hand:—maintaining links by hand for a large and evolving document makes consistency difficult. Humans are bad at this repetitive work; computers produce consistent results. In any case, there may be no suitable tools for doing these kinds of simple, yet powerful, automated transformations in a given proprietary format.

2. [*Nihimura and Imago*] propose an approach using two related DTDs, one using specific GIs and the other using generic GIs. A holding attribute in each DTD is used to contain the appropriate GI from the other DTD, to allow transformation between the two forms.

To give an example, let us have an SGML paragraph:

```
<para>He was bitten by a Blue-Ringed Octopus.</para>
```

A WP operator who is not a domain expert can only be expected to detect the grammatical and editorial structures in the text. In this case, that the Blue-Ringed Octopus is a name:

```
<para>He was bitten by a <name>Blue-Ringed Octopus</name>.</para>
```

A technical editor (who can read and understand the meaning of the text yet, may not be a domain expert) can be expected to detect generic topical characteristics of the data. In this case, that the Blue-Ringed Octopus is an animal:

```
<para>He was bitten by a <animal>Blue-Ringed Octopus</animal>. </para>
```

The author however, is a domain expert who can be expected to put in specific markup by topic. In this case that the dreaded Blue-Ringed Octopus is a lethal but pretty animal:

```
<para> He was bitten by a <marine-animal habitat="coastal"
look="pretty"  poison="deadly"  dread="appropriate">Blue-Ringed
Octopus</marine-animal>. </para>
```

☼····· When you are writing a DTD you need to have a model of the expertise of those performing the markup. If the markup expertise required for the intended use of the document is greater than that available, the project cannot succeed.

Underlying Forms

Time and time again documents contain structures that have common underlying forms. Lists and cross-references are examples of these forms.

But beware! The craft terms used by editors and writers for the structures may be different from the element type identifiers (GIs) given by the DTD designer. And these GI may be different from the terms used to name the underlying forms. A "table of contents" is called a *table* in industry parlance, and may have an element type identifier (GI) like TOC, but its underlying form is typically more like a fancy list than a table.

ISO Definition

4.145 **generic identifier:** A name that identifies the element type of an element.

4.114 **element type:** A class of elements having similar characteristics; for example, paragraph, chapter, abstract, footnote, or bibliography.

(ISO 8879:1986 glossary)

The table is one of the most powerful and obstinate forms. A table is like a cut-up and embedded page. Like a page it has its own layout: columns. These columns contain objects – cells in rows – and the cells contain various text blocks and other objects: paragraphs, graphics, lists and even nested tables.

In order to talk about structures and to make document type declarations to model them, we occasionally have to make fairly unsatisfactory demarcations: informed demarcations but sometimes arbitrary. The list and the table are really just two structures from a continuous range of forms: where one begins and another ends is a matter for conjecture. A sophisticated table *markup language*[1] and a sophisticated list markup-language can each represent many of the same structures, though with different markup.

---

1. By markup language I really mean an element type set, which would be a fragment of the document type declaration.

Some vendors and users of batch-processing typesetting software took a long time to become aware of the disadvantages of specific presentational markup. Since then some WYSIWYG vendors and users have taken a similarly long period to learn the same thing. So it is hardly surprising that tables are still usually marked up according to their specific presentation, even when a more generic approach or even language-structure or topic-structure markup might be more appropriate. [1]

In SGML you can annotate element types with attributes that specify some other underlying pattern found in the elements. Such attributes are called *architectural forms*. You mark your document up using generic identifiers that are appropriate for that document type, but then nominate the elements as also conforming to some other pattern: the difference between a normal attribute and an architectural form is that an architectural form refers to a structure you have modeled in some other DTD: this DTD is often called the *meta–DTD*. For example, you could mark up a table of contents with generic identifiers to name the elements in each row as—

```
<sect>
  <sect-no>...</sect-no>
  <title>...</title>
  <page-no>...</page-no>
</sect>
```

Then you could use architectural forms (probably with #FIXED attributes in the document type declaration) to give—

```
<sect form="row">
  <sect-no form="cell">...</sect-no>
  <title form="cell">...</title>
  <page-no form="cell">...</page-no>
</sect>
```

---

1. The subject of tables is dealt with in chapter 11.

ISO Definition

5.1 Architectural forms: Architectural forms are rules for creating and processing elements (just as document architectures are rules for creating and processing documents). Architectural forms are specified primarily by attribute definitions...

(ISO/IEC 10744:1992 HyTime, extract)

The structures that architectural forms represent are often dependent on or derived from some particular medium: so, for example, a table is an architectural form that has a dependency on visual media. For the medium of the relational database, the data must conform to the underlying form of records and fields. Patterning data as a visual table may not be very useful if the output medium is a voice synthesizer—though perhaps the left-to-right visual arrangement could be imitated by panning or changing the voice!

Applications are judged on how well they support these underlying forms directly. *"This program supports 3D tables!"* we say with enthusiasm, and fork out our money. An SGML document which is an instance of an SGML DTD that directly mirrors these forms will be trivial to translate into input for that application: a <cell> becomes a {cell or whatever.

Things become more complicated when a document with a given DTD must be translated into very different structures; the simple architectural form approach will not work, and a transformation program of some kind must be used – or human intervention. Similarly, when the document must be translated into several different structures for different uses, each application or function may use a different implicit DTD.

SGML does not always make complexity simple, but it can make it manageable and doable.

Embedding Other Kinds of Data

You can notate most things in SGML, but it may not be desirable or practical to do so. SGML lets you embed any kind of object into a document using data entities and data content notations. In fact, for some types of document, it can be practical just to have a *hub document* in SGML which invokes pre-formatted, non-SGML chapters.

Data content notation is *SGML*'s mechanism for identifying the representation format of some data. It is particularly useful for labeling data held in external non-SGML files or database fields, or that must be generated on-the-fly.

ISO Definition

4.75.1 **data entity:** An entity that was declared to be data and therefore is not parsed when referenced.

4.75 **data content notation:** An application-specific interpretation of an element's data content, or of a data entity, that usually extends or differs from the normal meaning of the document character set.

4.213 **notation identifier:** An external identifier that identifies a data content notation in a notation declaration. It can be a public identifier if the notation is public, and, if not, a description or other information sufficient to invoke a program to interpret the notation.

(ISO 8879:1986 glossary)

On PCs and Macintosh systems, this information is usually determinable from the file extension or from a built-in signature; however, these are sometimes not enough to describe the format in enough detail to be useful. Sometimes formats get revised incompatibly several times, yet retain the same extension. The UNIX family of operating systems is weak in this regard: there are usually no application restrictions to promote using particular file extension and the signature mechanism (/etc/magic) is not mandatory.

You should usually define and use data content notations,[1] although you get away without them if—

☒ all your documents are only used in-house, and you hard-code the format information into your SGML system; or

☒ all your documents and data are created, maintained and archived on computers with applications that store files with adequate and compatible file extensions (e.g., DOS, Windows, OS/2, NT); or

☒ all your documents and data are created, maintained and archived on computers with applications that store files with adequate and compatible signature information (e.g., Macintosh resource fork); or

☒ some other system is in place in your system to determine the format of resources reliably (e.g., [*MIME*] Multimedia Internet Mail Extensions); or

☒ there are incompatible versions of the notation that are not adequately self-documenting (e.g., files with the extension .CGM).

Elements, attributes, and SDATA entity references for special characters are familiar to everyone who has marked up documents using HTML. But SGML has much more: the entity mechanism is very rich, and with data content notations and data attributes allows all kinds of sophisticated and creative ways to compose documents from parts of many kinds. (Note: XML 1.0 does not support data attributes.)

A recent buzzword for marketing has been *document–centric*, rather than *application–centric*. This has been used to deride monolithic applications in favor of documents made from parts, with each part controlled by a lean and mean *applet*. Scratch the surface, and you find that the programming API is still king, not the data. SGML offers an alternative way that can be far more flexible and stand the rigors of time and the changing winds of commercial fortune: rich, useful markup.

---

1. We say *notation* rather than *format* to avoid confusion with formatting (i.e., presentation or rendition).

The SGML Cookbook

The Worst DTD in the World?

DTDs like the following do exist: I have seen them with my own eyes! It is a waste of SGML, and very difficult for humans to use.

```
<!-- The worst DTD in the World! -->
<!ELEMENT element (element | #PCDATA)* >
<!ATTLIST element
 attribute1 CDATA #IMPLIED
 attribute2 CDATA #IMPLIED
 attribute3 CDATA #IMPLIED >
```

If the aim is to make a generic DTD, a better approach would be to make element types with common attributes with a widespread use. ①

However, even though the DTD above is so inadequate – and violates the SGML standard – a valid use for insanely generic GIs and attribute names does exist!

The SGML declarations are designed to allow tightly-specified content models, where the details about element containment are known in advance. In [*SGML '86*], the only intermediate step available between the constraints of a content model and the freedom of the ANY declared content type is the SUBDOC feature. SUBDOC allows embedded micro-documents with their own DTDs and name-spaces. It is an attractive yet fairly unexplored optional feature of SGML.

But SUBDOC misses the main requirement of some document systems to be able to arbitrarily decorate and rename elements on the fly. The most flexible way to do this is to use *architectural forms*: you can have as drab and uninteresting element type identifiers and attribute names as you like, and use attributes with some selected names which map the element to some other architecture. The other architecture can be specified formally with a *meta–DTD*.

So even this worst DTD in the world can have some use if you really do not want to commit yourself to saying anything descriptive with your element names or to constrain your document structure. Of course, the SGML content models are only one way of constraining your document structure: you are always perfectly free to impose your own declarations and modeling system on top of SGML. ②

---

1. See chapter 6 *Common Attributes* for sets of common attributes that you can simply cut-and-paste into your declarations for a good head start.

2. See page 1-104, for a further consideration of Additional Requirements.

The cost of developing your own schema representation system is the loss of standardness and therefore portability—SGML is designed to provide the most basic content-modeling and usually you will find it more convenient to maximize your use of SGML's capabilities rather than reinventing the wheel, and losing standardness. Before deciding to make your own schema system, check through books (such as this one) to see how SGML document system designers have approached the problem in the past. Certainly for archiving and static publications, SGML is the fruit of almost twenty years of use and development; the newer online media offer some different challenges, but it is important not to forget that the solutions to the problems of scale and complexity will generally be valuable for any transmission or presentation medium.

⚠ ⋯⋯ You may also be forced to use such highly generic element types if your applications are particularly inflexible. SGML systems that require the pre-compilation of DTDs before instances can be processed can have a fairly high setup cost compared to the cost or ease of altering the SGML systems scripts to handle a new, different attribute value.

Summary of Chapter 2

This chapter discussed structures and markup in general, "specific" tagging *versus* "generic" tagging, architectural forms and data content notations.

All things are lawful unto me, but all things are not expedient. (KJV)

St. Paul, I Corinthians 6, 12

Software Engineering
Chapter 3

This chapter

…gives methods you can use to analyze documents and develop DTDs.

What method should you use to design your DTD? There are several methodologies or approaches from both the SGML and software engineering literature:[1]

- DTD assembly from reusable components or architectures;

- waterfalls and spirals;

- exploratory DTDs and prototyping; and

- viewpoint or scenario analysis

The essence of software engineering is not to apply some magical methodology uncritically, but to understand the problem well and thereby be able to justify that your solution is appropriate. A methodology is useful because it assures us that some kind of disciplined thought has been applied and has been documented. Choosing the correct approach to use for any production environment can be as important as applying it well – the military saying is *"time spent in reconnaissance is seldom wasted."*

Software engineering does not mean a dry, bookish or imposed solution. Using the appropriate methodology can be the way to make sure that the people to be affected by the DTD are onside, and that their skills have been tapped.

---

1. Refer to [*Sommerville*] p 6 et seq. for more on this. Many methodologies for analyzing structure will be usable for SGML: in particular, as SGML and XML become the markup languages of choice for database schema, database schema methodologies will become more appropriate to apply to SGML.

DTDs and Patterns

Reusable Components

The most direct use of the patterns in this book is as *recipes*: if you need tables, you can copy an element type set for tables. If I have done my job right, this will be a satisfactory method both for casual DTDs and for extending existing DTDs. If you apply experience and judgment, and weigh up the factors given in the discussions, it should even be a satisfactory method for larger, new DTDs.

If you decide to use this approach, you first have to determine which patterns you will need element type sets for. Along with your declarations you will have to include details about the semantics of the element types (and so on) you are declaring, to make a useful *Document Type Definition* (often called schemas or *schemata*) from the various components.

But before you plunge into making your own DTD, I suggest you check if your industry has an applicable standard DTD. After a generation of development, these can be very useful, and may be a good DTD to tailor at least. Also, there may be off-the-shelf tools developed for industry DTDs which make the use of these DTDs compelling for cost or time reasons. The [*CALS*] table model is widely used for this very reason; and if you need some simple text with simple formatting, HTML cannot be ignored.

On the contrary side, the DTD may be biased towards some party in the industry; it may model the information that a supplier wants to give, yet not be practical for users. So even if an industry DTD does exist, it still needs to prove itself in your workflow.

A variation on these approaches is used in both the [*DOCBOOK*] DTD for technical and computer-related publications, and the Text Encoding Initiative ([*TEI*]) DTDs for preexisting literary, scholarly and reference works. Both provide standard DTDs which seem at first to be crazily large. You subtract the parts you don't need to derive a DTD of appropriate complexity. ①

---

1. See chapter 6 *Common Attributes* for a list of attribute definitions for all occasions. You may find it useful to start with all these attribute definitions at the start of your development and pare them down as you become more familiar with your documents and with how SGML and XML operate. Though some may call this approach *quick and dirty* or *brute force and ignorance*—I prefer "DTD assembly from *reusable components*."

Architectures

The previous method, *DTD assembly from reusable components*, lacks flexibility. What if you want to use your own names for GIs? What if you need additional element types or attributes? What if you want to change the order of element types within a container?

A better method is to use *architectural forms*. The great advantage of the architectural approach is that it can build the notion of *constraints* into the DTD development process—

- First, express all the constraints on the element type sets imposed by your systems and your house style. Where possible, express even these constraints as element type sets: such sets are often called *meta–DTDs*. For example, your pre-existing software investment may force the constraint on you that all tables must follow the [*CALS*] table model, and that all hypertext links should be [*XLL*] links.

- Next, model your DTD using some conventional document analysis approach. Concentrate on capturing the structure of the document rather than external constraints.

- Finally, reconcile your DTD with the meta-DTDs. At best, this involves merely adding fixed attribute definitions to the DTD that point to the element in the meta-DTD. [1] You will probably find it easiest if you massage your DTD so that its content models are compatible with the meta-DTDs, as much as possible.

Architectures are a great way to have your cake and eat it to: once you have decided to use architectures, then you are freer to use the local jargon for generic identifiers and other names. However, you may have to include in your document system model an extra processing stage if your software cannot process documents according to architectural forms (which largely comes down to being able to key your processing to attributes as well as *element type identifiers*, also known as GIs).

---

1. It may be that you will also need to remap attribute names and attribute values as part of this. And what you have modeled as an attribute value for an EMPTY element may be modeled in the meta-DTD as #PCDATA. The [*HyTime '97*] standard has an annex, *Architectural Form Definition Requirements* (AFDR) that gives conventions for reconciling these differences using a standard vocabulary of keywords and attribute names.

The SGML Cookbook

There is great connection between *patterns* as used in this book, and *architectures*. An architecture is really a concrete implementation of a pattern, and in many sentences the two terms can be used interchangeably without violence to the meaning of sentences. ① A good document system developer will have a mental library of patterns, and also be aware of the most common architectures that are floating around: in particular the architectures of [*HyTime '97*], [*XLL*] links and [*ICADD*].

⚠ ······ The HyTime AFDR system is powerful enough to allow you to retrofit architectural forms onto pre-existing DTDs: the architecture does not have to come first. You may be able to move your documents to a new architecture without any explicit markup of the instances – just by adding the appropriate fixed attribute definitions to the DTD.

Information Units

[*Maler and el Andoloussi*] introduce the useful idea of an *information unit*. An information unit is an element type set that can be understood or exist standing alone. Material that is often typeset in displays – with a different indent or typeface – are good candidates for treatment as an information unit. Material that is structured like a database would be an information unit also.

An information unit can be modeled in SGML with an element type set. Many of the patterns in this book are prefabricated information units.

If your analysis determines that your information fits neatly grouped into discrete information units, you may find it useful to implement your SGML system using a *micro–document* architecture: using a series of smaller individual documents eases many maintenance problems, such as ID management. It also promotes a document-construction-by-linking style rather than a document-construction-by-pasting style. This is more flexible and manageable. ②

---

1. Some people find the term "architecture" a little confusing: if you are one of these, then try mentally substituting the term "pattern" or "schema."

2. A good example of information units in use are the Information Modules of the Swedish CALS DTD *Fösverats Materielverk (FMV) Grund–DTD* (a base DTD) developed by [*Bergström and Karlsson*] and available over the Internet.

Cohesion and Coupling

In the software engineering terminology of [*Constantine and Yourdan*], who developed the ideas of *cohesion and coupling*, an information unit has elements that are highly cohesive, and which can be decoupled from the rest of the document.

Constantine and Yourdan identify seven levels of cohesion which may useful to pin down the kinds of information that should be grouped together into information units. Their original list was developed for software components; I have taken some liberties with it to make it applicable for us. —

Coincidental cohesion

Some texts get grouped together because it has no where better to go – metadata at the start of an HTML document, for example. This is the weakest kind of cohesion, and not a particularly good reason to group element type declarations into an information unit.

Logical association

Components that do the same kind of thing can be bundled together. For example, rather than having all footnotes in-line, they may usefully be bundled together in a footnotes section. And the footnotes section and endnotes section may usefully be bundled together in a notes section. In [*Maler and el Andoloussi*]'s methodology, these high-level groupings perhaps are top-level hierarchy element types rather than information units. (*Pools*, treated below, often have this kind of cohesion only.)

Temporal cohesion

Some material needs to be accessed at the same time as some other material. A warning paragraph in a technical manual is an example of this: there needs to be some mechanism in markup to tie the warning to the procedure it warns about. When typeset, this warning material must be typeset on the same page as the procedure.

Procedural cohesion

Instructions and procedures make little sense if taken singly. There needs to be some mechanism in markup to tie procedures together – tagging them as a list for example.

Communicational cohesion

When all the components relate to the same external thing, they should be tied together. Attributes often have this kind of cohesion with their element types too.

Sequential cohesion

When sequence is important, the individual components need to be contained in some markup to signify this – tagging them as a numbered list, for example.

Functional cohesion

When material makes no sense if some component is removed, the parts need to be tied together to prevent escapes. The most straightforward example of this is the paragraph: each word is needed for the sentences. Consequently, the words exhibit extreme cohesion and should be connected by markup. This is the strongest kind of cohesion.

The information unit can be contrasted with the *pool*, which the documentation of the semiconductor industry's [*Pinnacles*] DTD (PCIS) promotes. A pool is a grouping together of all the kinds of element types that might appear at roughly the same level. For example, sections, chapters and appendixes might all be put in one pool, and all the kinds of elements found in running text (e.g., inside paragraphs) might be in another pool.

While the element types in an information unit can be expected to occur together, there is no expectation that element types in a pool will occur together: a pool is really a way of simplifying the element type declaration structure. Pools are often naturally modeled with parameter entities.

For example, you may decide that all *running text* will have the same content model. Even though your document analysis may show that headings never have footnotes, you would rather not have different content models for each type of heading, paragraph, and so on. Your DTD is simpler and more flexible because you have not added an arbitrary restriction.

ISO Definition

4.55 **(content) model:** Parameter of an element declaration that specifies the model group and exceptions that define the allowed content of the element.

(ISO 8879:1986 glossary)

The best way to divide the labor of marking documents up is to allocate work by pool structures rather than information units. For example, rather than giving one person responsibility for all chapters, one person responsibility for all backmatter, and one person responsibility for all frontmatter, to take a perhaps extreme view of *information unit*, it is better to give one person responsibility for sections, headings and paragraphs, the second person responsibility for tables and lists, and the third person responsibility for in–line elements. This allows each person to develop good expertise, without taxing them overly with a multitude of dissimilar elements. Another good division for our three people would be to give one responsibility for editorial–structure markup, the second for topic–structure markup, and the third for characters and presentational markup.

You can see pools in DTDs: when you see an element type declaration with a parameter entity reference on the left-hand side, that is a pool structure:

```
<!-- generic pool structure (on left-hand side) -->
<!ELEMENT ( %all; )            ( something ) >
```

Several element types with the same content models (the right-hand side), also indicates a pool structure.

```
<!-- generic pool structure (on right-hand side) -->
<!ELEMENT something            ( %sundry; ) >
```

Waterfalls and Spirals

Most of the approaches found in the SGML literature are broadly similar in rationale and approach, and are completely analogous to the *waterfall and spiral* approaches in software engineering literature.

- The most complete methodology is the highly structured bottom-up methodology of [*Maler and el Andoloussi*]. It is appropriate for large and new SGML projects and emphasizes human factors and the need for development processes to be documented.

- [*Alschuler*] gives a six-stage method which combines [*Maler and el Andoloussi*]'s with a simpler four-stage method attributed to LePeyre. Alschuler has a pleasing emphasis that the intended use of the documents will determine what information is important and therefore what should be marked up, and that bottom-up design may not work best in all situations.

- [*Colby, Jackson, et al*] have a broadly similar top-down approach to the others, as part of a four-part model:

  - define the goals;

  - analyze the publications;

  - model the document by marking up real samples from the publication set; then

  - validate that document type declaration and instances conform to standard SGML.

- A less prescriptive description of the tasks in document analysis can be found in [*Travis and Waldt*]. This is a spiral model, emphasizing the need for iteration. Their description mentions many useful and specific technical issues and has a good awareness of the kinds of processes involved in using SGML.

- [*Colby, Jackson, et al*] also have a tantalizing few pages on applying object-oriented methodologies to SGML development. Their most interesting point is that because a DTD fulfills important steps in both Booch's (spiral) and Rumbaugh's methodologies (waterfall), SGML document systems are well-fitted to object-oriented implementation. [1]

Prove your analysis! No matter what method is used to construct a DTD, it is worthwhile to prove the DTD by marking up a representative document. It is amazing the number of DTDs that are launched at the trusting world which have never even been tried on a representative document.

The document preferably should be chosen by someone who was not on the DTD team, and it should not have been used as part of the document analysis. The aim of the test is to prove the analysis process rather than the DTD: if the DTD has a few minor elements missing or incomplete, that is to be expected. But if there are

---

1. [*Bray*] mentions that modeling each element type by a Java class is a convenient design technique for writing DTD-specific parsers.

whole information units missing, or if important common elements are missed, it suggests a flaw in the analysis process.

If you are getting your DTD written by external contractors, add to the deliverables that they must provide a marked-up example of a complete document, to be chosen by you. This is a deliverable, prior to any (perhaps more scientific) acceptance testing at your end: if even they cannot make their DTD work, you should not accept delivery. ①

Diagrams

The various books use different diagraming techniques. Diagrams are essential for novices to understand SGML structures.

> • [*Van Herwijnen*] gives the syntax for structure diagrams. These "railway" charts are a variation on the Pascal syntax charts, and really just present an element type's content model in different form. Several different flavors of structure diagrams exist, with different conventions for showing attribute definitions and inclusions, for example.

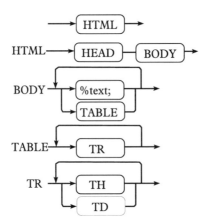

---

1. See *Growth of DTDs* in chapter 5, page 1-119, for some typical faults in DTDs, as revealed by change logs.

The SGML Cookbook

- [*Maler and el Andoloussi*] use syntax tree diagrams. These give a hierarchical view of the DTD. [*Colby, Jackson, et al*] also suggest syntax tree diagrams, and use Microstar's Near & Far DTD diagraming software.

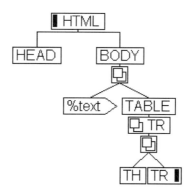

- Many content models are diagramed using indented lists. A very appealing and simple diagraming version is used in the [*Pinnacles*] Group's PCIS DTD documentation. The PCIS DTD uses a restricted version of content models,[1] so the PCIS documentation can use very simple bullet lists, with a bullet for each level of indentation, with some list items finishing with the words "and/or" to indicate specialized sequencing.

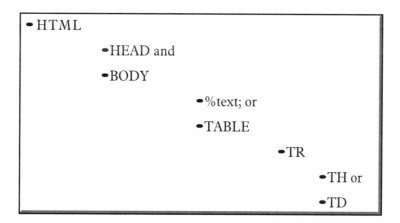

---

1. See *Your own Simplified SGML* in chapter 4 at page 1-91.

• Box diagrams, which show element types as boxes containing other boxes, are very intuitive and useful, but not very powerful. I find repetition and optionality difficult to see in them, especially for content models with many choices. Box diagrams are often best used to diagram element types that have element content, particularly those element types above the paragraph-level.

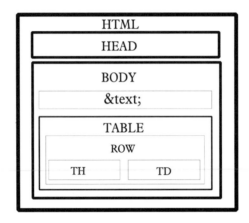

Maler and el Andoloussi's Methodology

The modeling methodology from the book *Developing SGML DTDs* by [*Maler and el Andoloussi*] typifies, but is more systematic than, the modeling approaches elsewhere in the SGML literature.

The SGML Cookbook

The methodology is basically a bottom-up approach, yet with a top-down stage (5.) and a middle-out stage (6.). I would paraphrase it like this:

1. List (embracingly) the possible components;

2. Categorize (thoroughly) them;

3. Review (critically) other DTDs for similar documents;

4. Cull (explicitly) useless components;

5. Model (hierarchically) the top element types – the containers such as volume, section, part, chapter, list;

6. Model (methodically) the information units;

7. Model (kindly) the bottom element types – what general text contains;

8. Stick it (generously) all together;

9. Model (happily) references and links;

20. Validate (systematically) that the DTD seems complete.

DTDs made according to Maler and el Andoloussi's methodology may tend to have three pools: a top-level pool, a phrase-level and references pool, a pool with the paragraphs and information units. The [*Pinnacles*] PCIS DTD, developed using a proprietary methodology, has five pools.

[*Alschuler*]'s version emphasizes finally testing your analysis by applying it to a section or sample document. The more extensive the testing, the better. Maler and el Andoloussi also suggest sending the DTD out for review.

[*Travis and Waldt*] have the important variation that there should be some notion of iteration built into these steps. I cannot agree enough.

Exploration and Prototypes

Exploratory design is appropriate if you need a once-only conversion of large amounts of poorly-structured legacy text from all sorts of ✎ formats to SGML. It is only by actually manipulating the document and trying and evolving various DTDs that any interesting order within the document can be detected economically.

The owners of existing documents often do not have a realistic idea of the state of their text. A fair degree of latitude to tailor DTDs must be allowed even when some structured DTD design methodology was used to build the original DTD. Making a simple *pretty good DTD* lets you examine your documents further, to zero in on a more suitable DTD. You may decide to use a stricter, better DTD for new documents, using the result of your explanation as a prototype. But you need to keep in mind the difference between a DTD that describes what some pre-existing documents contain and a DTD written to allow optimal future use by computers. ①

In a legacy conversion run there will often be a few documents with a completely aberrant order. The temptation is to loosen and enlarge the document type declaration to fit all documents. A better approach is to create a special document type declaration for the worst offenders: one cannot fit a square peg into a round hole. Where there is a particularly gratuitous exception to an otherwise common structure, it may be warranted to get the offending parts of the document re-written, rekeyed, deleted or even just incorporated into the document in some fixed non-SGML form. This simplifies the number of special cases of DTDs you will require, which makes for easier programming.

⚠······ The key issue is sample size. Unfortunately the only way to detect all the structures in most sets of legacy documents is by exploratory DTD design for over 80% of them. In fact, there is often no reason to expect that the last 20% of documents won't have some novel order not found in the first 80%, if they have been created by different people at different times. The less that style–sheets were used in the legacy documents, the more chaotic their markup will be: highly chaotic documents may be better scanned in with OCR or re–keyed rather than processed using text processing.

---

1. Many times when I hear people criticize DTDs, it is the lazy re-use for new documents of a DTD designed for legacy text that is being criticized. The issue is not so much element structures as it is the vision or decisions of the technical management.

The SGML Cookbook

🔅 ······ For legacy conversions, it is important to have someone with expertise in tailoring document type declarations on-tap on a continuing basis, someone who has the expertise and authority to make minor changes to the DTDs to keep the day-to-day work progressing. At the very least, have vanilla element types in which unaccounted-for structures can be parked, and dealt with later. This is true of document type declarations created by the other approaches.

Prototyping

How can you do exploratory DTD design if you do not have domain expertise coming out of your ears? You can use the patterns in this book and your judgement to make a *hopeful monster* DTD, perhaps just for only part of your document set: there should be enough discussion of the various options available for a reasonable prototype DTD. Actually using a DTD is the best way to get experience. You should only expect your DTD to fully stabilize after a year, when you should hold a major review!

You may even decide to go the route of institutionalizing change, and decide on *periodic prototypes*, for example deciding that you will have a scheduled DTD revision every three months. To accompany these visions, you may also revise your goals and strategy. As the DTD is deployed, a workflow for using it develops; the problems and needs of the workflow provide an additional source of information about the nature and needs of your documents.

This will have a particular impact on the way in which your SGML applications and documentation are written: with an emphasis on reconfigurability and modularization. And DTDs will have more features to allow transformations of text: ubiquitous use of ID attributes, architectural forms, information units and information pools. SGML is often touted as a medium for archiving information, but it can also be used a tool for accelerating response to changing needs.

Expecting there to be a second version of the DTD is probably prudent even when expertise is available. Almost all major DTDs, even when designed by expensive consultants, are redesigned within three years. User requirements, expectations, experience and demands all grow.

New and unforeseen uses come up, requiring documents to be decorated with new element types and attributes. Undreamt of technologies suddenly become commonplace, devaluing proprietary SGML element type sets. For example, a proprietary syntax for external hyperlinks implemented in 1994 may have had to be replaced by URLs in 1996. The future-proofing flexibility of SGML, to allow such incremental upgrades and partial changes to systems, should not be under-estimated.

Exploratory DTD Design

Exploratory design methods tend to be rather specific to their problem domain. Here are steps[1] to derive DTDs for legacy, non-SGML documents.

- Audit the documents: glance at the document set to get a broad yet realistic view of all the parts.

- Fence in the requirements: figure out the inputs and outputs required for the application.

- Hunt for interaction between documents: very often similar informat-ion will be found in different places – sometimes one is clearly better, sometimes it is useful to make a composite. Useful information can be sometimes found in unexpected places: I know a case where the only reliable source for data needed for *frontmatter* was found to be the accounting system!

- Make a *good–enough–for–80*% document type declaration from a repre-sentative sample: with skillful and lucky selection of the initial samples, this 80% document type declaration will act as a base for all the instances of that type of document with only minor changes.

- Start marking up using the 80% document type declaration: when a document comes which really doesn't fit very well, loosen or expand the content model, make a new document type declaration derived from the base, or make a subset DTD. You want to avoid the temptation to make a single document type declaration that fits all cases by allowing any ele-ment type anywhere. Such document type declarations may make pro-cessing difficult; one size need not fit all.

---

1. Thanks to Nick Carr, Allette Systems (`www.allette.com.au`), private com-munication.

If you are using Exploratory DTD Design in an environment where there are many documents in progress, or many people involved in marking up or processing the documents, you have the additional consideration of how to promulgate changes.

If the change is

☑ a tightening of a content model,

☑ the addition of required elements, or

☑ the removal of an element type,

you will have to go over old documents and mark up the changes. However, because markup is already present, you have a head start – you can often write a program or editor macros to do much of what you need.

⚠ ⋯⋯ You may find it is good practice to start off with a very loose content model,[1] except for absolutely essential elements. After markup has finished check through the instances and find if any elements are almost always found in a particular position: the exceptions may be mistakes in the data itself that should be corrected, rather than mistakes in your structural analysis.

Then go through the DTD and find out which optional element types or attributes are so useful they really should be mandatory: this may be as basic as checking whether element types for figures have required ID attributes, or only impliable. The exploratory process can be a two–way street, both exposing a document's valuable information and pinpointing deficiencies in quality.

---

1. See *DTD Style Checklist* in chapter 4 at page 1–74 for an explanation of loose and tight content models.

The Human Side

Viewpoint Analysis

One criticism I have of the approaches above is that they tend to assume that the information exists as a document only in a single document type declaration, or a single document type declaration with some variants to allow for weird data. For sophisticated sites with access to decent programmable tools, it may be worthwhile to use an approach taken from viewpoint analysis in the Software Engineering world.

Viewpoint analysis presumes there is a division of labor into tasks[1] and that it is most efficient to have a semi-customized document type declaration for each stage and to automatically transform the document between them. Because there is a division of labor, there is also a *workflow*.

> 1. In this approach, the first thing to do is to identify all the stakeholders: the parties who use the document – writers, editors, copy editors, typesetter, proofreader, revisor, indexer/hyperlinker, book reader, CD-ROM reader, and so on, and to determine the workflow. Computers have needs too. The viewpoint analysis rejects the idea that there is a single, generic user of the document, or even that there must be a single DTD for a document: a document goes through a lifecycle of birth, feeding, growth, use and transformation.

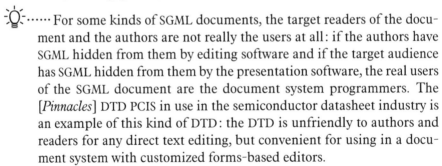 For some kinds of SGML documents, the target readers of the document and the authors are not really the users at all: if the authors have SGML hidden from them by editing software and if the target audience has SGML hidden from them by the presentation software, the real users of the SGML document are the document system programmers. The [*Pinnacles*] DTD PCIS in use in the semiconductor datasheet industry is an example of this kind of DTD: the DTD is unfriendly to authors and readers for any direct text editing, but convenient for using in a document system with customized forms-based editors.

---

1. Not a novel idea, even before Adam [*Smith*]'s pin factory, yet one which managers of markup operations often forget.

The SGML Cookbook

2. The next step is to make, in consultation, the perfect DTD for each of these groups of users. The questions asked are:

- *What information will this user need, use, name, point at, affect or provide in the document?*

- *What technology is appropriate for this user: what information will this technology need, use, name, point at, affect or provide?*

- *How will this user interact with the document as presented: what information will the user need, use, name, point at, affect or provide for this interaction?*

Make element type sets to implement your answer to these questions, and combine them into a DTD. Note that again, we are interested in the document system, not just the document.

3. Finally, attempt to reconcile neighboring DTDs. Reconciliation involves specifying, for use by a programmer, the transformations and additional element types needed to transform a document from one DTD to the next. If there are few transformations or additions involved, the DTD and its neighbor may be merged into one. In the nature of things, the initial writer's DTD may be fairly sparse, and subsequent stages may have richer DTDs as element types and attributes appropriate to the various tasks are added.

One particularly useful way of reconciling DTDs is to use architectural forms. Each of the stakeholder DTDs is treated as a meta-DTD, and the equivalent stakeholder names are put into fixed attribute definitions in the actual DTD. Whether you use architectural forms like that or pro-grammed transformations depends on the concrete technical constraints of your site: in particular how architectural-form-aware your users' applications are. Architectural forms can be thought of as a method of avoiding the need for custom software for simple transformations of data: general purpose software can be used instead – the specification for transforming the document is shunted from being a task of programming to being a task of DTD specification.

The difficulty with a straightforward transformation occurs whenever there must be cycles in the workflow. If there are localized cycles in the workflow between adjacent stages, the two DTDs may have to be coalesced to some extent; an author's DTD may need to have to have an editor's feedback annotation element type as an inclusion, for example.

Where there is large cycling of documents in the workflow, a different implementation should be considered: storing the document in a database as many micro-documents or fragments, and combining them as needed into documents with the appropriate DTD as discovered by viewpoint analysis.

Viewpoint analysis is not simply saying ""There is a storage DTD and some usage DTDs." Depending on the workflow, there may be several or no storage DTDs as such, especially if the information cycles around a workflow rather than being booked in and out of a repository. ①

Scenario Analysis

The previous methods tend to assume that there is one DTD, or there are many different DTDs. What about where there are several document types, but they share common information units or information pools?

Scenario Analysis is useful for creating the top-level design, especially where the site will be in transition, or where a DTD solution must be useful for a wide variety of levels of implementation of SGML.

- Interview or model a range of users, and find out what their plans for implementing SGML are. Some may only want to implement SGML wrappers for PDF files, to allow more consistent interfaces with scanned and legacy documents, but with searching and indexing of keywords possible.

Others may require full SGML. Still others may need full SGML for export only, and store and work with proprietary structured-document systems.

---

1. A similar emphasis on the workflow as the organizing principle of DTD development is apparent in the general description by [Kennedy] of the proprietary "Organic Information Management" methodology of the Sagebrush Group. Apart from an identification of the SGML *stakeholders* (viewpoints), this methodology also apparently deals with project structure (workflow), and risk analysis.

- Find out which information units are needed for each user-group's scenario.

The result of the scenario analysis is a series of diagrams, with a box representing the document or micro-document under consideration. There is at least one box per scenario. Within each box is a series of sub-boxes, representing different selection from the top-level major information units or non-SGML entities or DTDs, for example:

- metadata and administrative text,

- navigation information,

- frozen format text (e.g., PDF),

- non-SGML source text, or

- SGML source text.

Each diagram has a different selection of these sub-boxes, depending on the scenario.

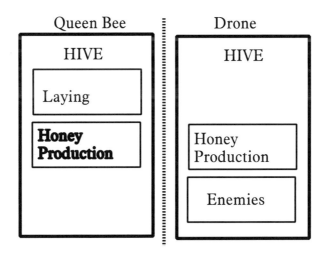

Between each sub-box there can be arrowed lines to indicate when one sub-box is automatically generated from another, and – using a different type of line – when one sub-box has links pointing to another. External links or sources and sinks of information can be represented as external sub-boxes.

Scenario analysis is useful to maximize the common use of element type sets between slightly different sites or workflows.

Scenario analysis can also be useful if you discover that peer departments think they use the same document structures, but in fact use very different structures. It can help you concentrate on factoring out into subdocuments the structures that vary between the different departments.

For example, analysis of the needs for certain military technical manuals disclosed that, though the structure of the body matter was fairly compatible between services, each had irreconcilable frontmatter and metadata needs. A technique like Scenario Analysis provides a way to model and document this.

User Interfaces are Documents

Generally, document analysis is made based on paper documents. The DTD for a book may have metadata element types to give information needed for navigation – for example, an element type for the short-form running header that some books use when the normal title of a chapter is too large.

An online document may need metadata element types and attributes connected to the needs of that medium also. For example, a hypertext version of legislation documents may display the exact reference to be used for wherever the cursor is positioned. The numbering conventions may be too eccentric to be automatically derived from the element context, especially if the text contains annotations or has been reordered for explanatory purposes.

When doing document analysis of *legacy material*, it is increasingly important not to merely analyze old paper documents, but also to look at legacy hypertext and browser applications, to get a sense of the information that is useful to the document.

Users not only just read publications, they also interact with them. This is true even for a cool medium like print: childrens' books in particular.

When you are designing a document system, you must have some idea of the nature of your users' interaction. Having a working model of your anticipated users' anticipated interaction with various forms of the rendered document does not mean you need to build in any specific form: use the model to figure out what information would be needed to perform the interaction, then use generalized markup concepts to actually model it with element type sets. This way your markup can be used a building blocks for future systems, perhaps involving presentations and interactions you have not dreamt of.

Including interaction information is not a reason to let procedural markup in the back door. For example, if your browser application lets you turn on and off various sections of text, depending on the expertise of the user, do not mark this up with tags like—

```
<if menu.view.show_difficult="yes">...</if>
```

Rather, mark the document up as—

```
<expert>...</expert>
```

This allows your browser system to change without making your markup misleading.

Computer programs are rarely conveniently specified in SGML. But most interactive development environments (IDE) allow the replacement of the built-in editor with one of your choice, so using SGML is far from impossible.

It is generally regarded as good programming practice to separate constants out of program code, in a similar fashion to the way SGML entity declarations must be kept together in the prolog. SGML may definitely be useful wherever you need to specify complicated data structures in a representation-independent fashion, using a program to automatically generate the target source code as required.

ISO Definition

4.236 prolog: The portion of an SGML document or SGML subdocument entity that contains document type and link type declarations.

(ISO 8879:1986 glossary)

Involvement

Participants regularly attribute the success or failure of projects not to methodologies as ways to be systematic, but to methodologies as ways to rope in and involve the people who have expertise or who will have to use the resulting DTDs. [1]

Even if the initial DTD was developed with less involvement than desirable, for many projects the involvement can be built in later by making sure there is a good response and feedback system in place, as an expectable part of maintenance. Even a DTD from the dreaded Lone Ranger SGML consultant, who rides in, delivers a DTD, and rides into the sunset again, can be made useful by this method.

No methodology can enumerate and weigh all the issues and structures present in a large document in one fell swoop. The utilization of the skill and expertise of the stakeholders and of an experienced document system designer will augment and nurture the development of a successful DTD.

Useful Skills

Being able to make a nesting DTD from the flat visual evidence of a paper sample is a fundamental skill. A few years ago, this skill was often all that was needed to write a DTD:

- you recursively box in visual page components, identifying at each stage whether the text is variant or invariant between documents of that type (logical invariance), and between different possible uses or renderings of that text (presentational invariance).

---

1. This is particularly alarming for the writer of a book of predefined patterns! There is the distinct possibility that if you make up a whizz-bang DTD, yet do not adequately tap the expertise and needs of the stakeholders, your DTD may fail. See *Top 10 Reasons Why DTDs Fail* in chapter 5, page 1-123, for some other reasons.

Now, however, some other skills are just as important:

- the skill to track down an industry standard DTD;[1]

- the skill to cut and paste a useful element type set from a cookbook like this one, or from some convenient DTD, or to augment HTML with higher-level container element types and whatever particular extra attributes and element types are needed;

- the skill to be aware of any industry consensus and experience about the kinds of things that work and don't work: however, be aware that many such judgments may be pragmatic calls based on a particular state of technology; and

- the skill to look for the topic-structure: the common method of deducing a DTD from the visual clues sometimes misses important relationships in the text: things that look visually separate on the page sometimes do belong together.

The bottom-up visual approach can make you focus on the wrong level of information: the entries in a geographical atlas may be better modeled as a DTD that looks like a database schema, despite looking like complicated free text.

DTDs are often written by programmers rather than domain experts. It is good to get a domain expert involved; however the patterns in this book can be of use when the expert is not available, or as a last resort, or even just to check that some important consideration has not been missed.

---

1. Robin [*Cover*]'s SGML site, hosted at the Summer Institute of Lingustics at `www.sil.org/sgml`, is the first place to start looking.

Summary of Chapter 3

This chapter discussed document system design as an application of software engineering.

The most common approach to document system design uses a waterfall or spiral model. Most of the literature uses some variation on this. The concepts of the information unit and the pool are important, and are clarified by the software engineering concept of cohesion and coupling.

Other approaches to the particular task of DTD design are:

- direct assembly from reusable components and architectures;

- exploratory DTD design and prototyping; and possibly

- viewpoint and scenario analysis.

My object all sublime...
To let the punishment fit the crime.
W.S. Gilbert, The Mikado.

Implementation Choices

Chapter 4

This chapter

...gives a range of options available to you when you implement SGML and generalized markup.

Before you start making a DTD, there are some practical issues you should double-check:

☑ Do you even need to use SGML? SGML has been created with some specific big problems in mind. If you are not clear why SGML is useful to you, you may be trying to use it to solve a problem it won't.

☑ Can you do anything to prepare the way for easier SGML adoption in the future?

☑ SGML seems bigger and more complicated than you need: is there some simpler version? What are the options available for SGML?

☑ What other information is needed apart from the SGML markup declarations?

DTD Style Checklist

We have already seen that DTDs can have various element types that deal with markup of topic-structure, editorial-structure, characters, glyphs, page objects, and layout. But many different DTDs can model the same source text. Choosing the appropriate element structure sometimes comes down to judgments of taste and experience; perhaps in their cocooned form: *house style*.

DTDs can be categorized in many ways: each of these ways is appropriate for some DTDs. You can use this list as a checklist for preliminary specification of the DTD, to help you select appropriate versions of the element type sets given in part 2.

Linear versus nested
A nested element structure is where container elements in turn hold other container elements. A linear element structure is where any containment must be inferred just from the position of the elements, or from clues in their element type identifiers (GIs). The early [*HTML*] DTDs were highly linear, for example. The HTML definition list is like this:

```
<!-- A linear definition list -->
<!ELEMENT dl      ( dt? , dd? )* >
```

```
■ dl
[₁]
□ dt   □ dd
```

A nested DTD gives greater value to explicitly marking up *belongs to* structures, and need not be as intentionally loose as HTML is. For example:

```
<!-- A nested definition list -->
<!ELEMENT dl      ( dl-item )* >
<!ELEMENT dl-item ( dt, dd ) >
```

```
dl-item
dt   dd
```

It is easy to convert a nested structure into a linear one, but it can be more difficult to convert a linear structure into a nested one: this explains why some text formatting programs with linear formats are difficult to convert *to* SGML, but easy to convert to *from* SGML. SGML omitted-tag minimization is an attempt to have the nested cake and eat it, linearly, too—it can let you leave out explicit tags for required elements in particular.

Programmers consistently prefer nested element structures, text-entry people consistently prefer linear DTDs, since linear DTDs tend only to have elements for things that appear on the page. This is because a programmer's tasks often involve manipulating whole structures, while text entry jobs often involve manipulating just one element after the next. Jobs where there is considerable need to have easy text input, yet where the document must be useful for programs, can have two DTDs: a linear DTD which can be transformed to and from a nested DTD. These in-house transformations have more knowledge of the DTD and the nature of the document than the SGML omitted-tag minimization rules.

Tight versus loose

A loose content model is where elements are allowed anywhere in any sequence. A tight content model is where elements are constrained by position and number.

```
<!-- A loose content model -->
<!ELEMENT name
        ( title | family | given | nickname | #PCDATA )* >
```

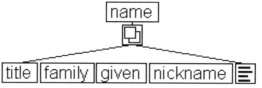

In this element type, a name could be marked up to contain several family names all mixed in with other elements in any order. This is an invitation to wrong markup, but may be needed for some strange names.

```
<!-- A tight content model -->
<!ELEMENT name
        ( title, family, given, nickname ) >
```

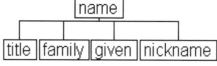

Too-loose markup is often of little use. Even for documents that are only destined for simple formatting it adds no value compared to proprietary markup. However, legacy text often does not fit in tight content models.

Looseness and linearity make a very poor combination. You can see in the dl definition list examples above that the linear version actually has quite a strong tightness, despite the optionality delimiter ?: the use of the sequence delimiter , gives that. One approach is to have a loose DTD for conversion work, and then transform documents to a tighter DTD.

Building blocks versus paragons

Element types can be regarded as building blocks, to be shaped as required, or as paragons, which must be kept intact. A paragon DTD has a policy note *"do not touch."* A building-block DTD, even though it may recommend a particular tight element set, allows a certain latitude in use. A building-block DTD often will be highly parameterized, so that any content model can be overridden in the prolog of the doctype declaration. If your text was not written to a DTD, there may be little point attempting to make it fit into a paragon DTD, unless that DTD is so loose as to be useless.

However, before loosening up content models or parameterizing them, check to see if your unruly text secretly is conforming to several alternative content models. For example, when you analyze the entries in a dictionary that has been under preparation for many years, you may find no single consistent structure; but check to see if there are actually a couple of alternative structures, each being used consistently.

You may be able to get a paragon DTD, with a great degree of tightness, by *kicking the looseness upstairs.* —

```
<!-- A loose dictionary entry -->
<!ELEMENT dict-entry
        ( key,  (short | num | phonetic | text | entry )* ) >
```

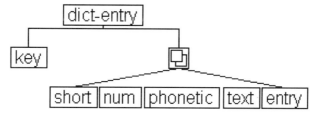

This structure can be modeled more tightly:—

```
<!-- Two tighter dictionary entry types -->
<!ELEMENT old-dict-entry   ( key,  num?,  phonetic,  text ) >
<!ELEMENT new-dict-entry   ( key,  short,  num?,  phonetic?, text ) >
```

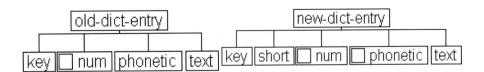

Of course, if you require a customizable building block DTD because of a relatively small number of naughty entries, you should consider the alternative route of making the problem disappear by re-marking up, and possibly rewriting, the naughty entries. A DTD problem suggests a document problem: knock the rough edges off the documents, and you get a simpler and more implementable DTD.

Generic versus specific

Specific markup[1] is needed for smarter searches and custom indexes, where the elements are to be treated as database fields, or where it is the *species* and never the *genus* that is the valuable information. For example, if you are interested in marking up pets that are corgi dogs or English Blue cats, but the other cats and dogs are of no interest, you will have the following specific element types:—

```
<!-- Two specific element types -->
<!ELEMENT corgi    ( %text; ) >
<!ELEMENT eblue    ( %text; ) >
```

---

1. See chapter 2, page 1-35, for a description of generic and specific markup.

And you would not have any of the more generic elements:—

```
<!-- Three less specific element types -->
<!ELEMENT pet     ( %text; ) >
<!ELEMENT dog     ( %text; ) >
<!ELEMENT cat     ( %text; ) >
```

Topic-structures versus editorial-structures

Text that is only marked up according to its editorial-structure[1] is not very valuable for uses like automatically constructing indexes or topic maps, resolving cross-references or for smart searches: the less topic-structure in your markup, the more appropriate it is to use *brute-force full-text searches*. However, you need someone with domain expertise to mark up topic-structures: this expertise might only be as trivial as deciding whether a name is a family name or a given name, but the expertise is still needed.

Database versus literature model

A database element type set keeps everything in nice fields, reminiscent of records and fields in databases. These records may be in-line, or they may be collected at the head of the document or the head of the major element such as a chapter. When a field value is needed in running text, element references can be used: an EMPTY element is placed in-line in position in the running text, with an IDREF attribute specified. This IDREF attribute references the field element with the desired content.

A literature model will keep the text in-line in running text, but mark it up in a container element with attributes to identify the fields.

The literature model is easier to read as plain text, and with off-the-shelf browsers. The database model requires customized software. However, the database approach is more appropriate when the database records need to be gathered together, managed and used as an information unit. Using a technique like *element references* (also known as *reflections*) allows the dynamic customization of references more easily: you might make a typesetting rule that the first reference to a database record on any hypertext page will expand to a full name, and subsequent references to only contracted names.

---

1. See chapter 1, page 1-8, for a description of topic-structure and editorial-structure.

Attribute versus element type

Often it is clear when a thing should be represented with an attribute and when to use an element type. Sometimes it is not. The usual rule[1] invokes some idea of belonging: a thing should be an element if it *is* the subject of the element type identifier (the GI); it should be an attribute if it merely is *owned* or *had* or *inherited* by the subject of the element type identifier.

For example, the number at a paragraph in a law is part of the data, not just an attribute of the paragraph. However, an automatically generated paragraph number, in some text in which all cross references are resolved automatically and in which there is no need to maintain numbers, is merely an attribute.

When there are information units containing large sequences of EMPTY elements with all their information in attributes, it may be useful to promote some attributes up to data content.

In-place floating elements versus at-end

Floating elements are sometimes declared in-line and sometimes at the end of the major section. Footnotes are an example. Following the rule that you should not use something before it has been declared, it would be best to put footnotes at the head of the current major section. However, this is too strange for many document users, who are comforted by page-isms.

If you enter floating elements after they may be used, you may have an extra processing step before some applications can use them. So in-place elements are perhaps slightly more flexible.

Startup versus mature DTD

A startup DTD may be used to prove the concept of SGML to management. It may err on the side of simplicity. Once the documents are simply marked up, and the concept proved, the DTD can be progressively enriched, and the documents marked up accordingly, to tap additional value in the data.

Terminal or intermediate DTD

A terminal DTD is aimed at humans, an intermediate DTD is aimed at computers and their text processing programmers. Terminal DTDs tend to be fixed and modification involves large programming changes to the SGML applications that use the DTD, especially GUI-based editors and typesetting systems that will require

---

1. See *Thumbs Rule, OK!* in this chapter, page 1-96, for some more rules of thumb for figuring out whether to use an attribute or an element type.

　　　　　　　　The SGML Cookbook

rules to be rewritten and recompiled. Intermediate DTDs are hidden from users, and tend to be more readily tweakable as the programmer requires.

Authoring, repository, or export

Each of these DTDs will reflect the nature of the technology used to manipulate them, as well as the skills and concerns of their users. An authoring DTD may be fairly loose. A repository DTD will have IDs on every element. An export DTD may be very tight.

Internal markup versus external markup

Some documents might be available read-only, or not be SGML documents at all. Rather than marking them up further, and altering an existing DTD, it may be more efficient and simple to have an external document and DTD, with markup elements that point to identifiers and locations and strings in the original document. [*HyTime '97*] provides standard mechanisms for this. ①

Active versus passive

A passive DTD just allows you to give relationships between elements. An active DTD goes further and prescribes some functional attributes of elements and links. Unless these functional attributes are highly generic, an active DTD is application-specific.

Personal versus impersonal payoff

[*Rubinsky*] suggests that traditional large SGML DTDs have been made for applications where the benefits of that complexity and indirectness end up in the laps of someone downstream. DTDs where the end-user is also the creator (such as HTML) are better to be smaller, pay more attention to formatting and immediate effects.

Self-labeling or external-labeling

SGML and HyTime provide a rich set of language constructs to let you point to external entities (and other objects), and label them by their notation or type, and give particular details using data attributes. This is called external-labeling. HTML and XML, on the other hand, rely far more on a self-labeling style, where each object carries around enough information about itself to be useful. A self-labeling style document will be rich in metadata in headers yet probably relatively poor in elaborate entity declarations.

Marketplace versus hierarchy

A conventional mistake when analysing documents is to assume that hierarchical structure is the ideal. To get to any information, all we need to do it just to drill

---

1. As does [*XLL*], see chapter 6 *Common Attributes*.

down through the layers of labelled containers until we finally reach the information we seek. Everything is neatly in its place:

```
<!-- A simple hierarchy -->
<alive>
    <edible>
        <thing>banana</thing>
        <thing>orange</thing>
    </edible>
</alive>
```

This approach to modeling information fails when the classifications important for one bit of information is not important for another. A human may be considered edible in some cultures and on some airflights yet for most of us such a classification serves little use.

```
<!-- A pointless hierarchy -->
<alive>
    <edible>
        <thing>banana</thing>
        <thing>human</thing>
    </edible>
</alive>
```

Indeed, some classifications important for one object may be entirely impossible to make for another:

```
<!-- A "not applicable" distinction -->
<alive>
    <edible>
        <thing>banana</thing>
    </edible>
    <inedible>
        <thing>sea-slime</thing>
    </inedible>
    <other>
        <thing>power cable number 3</thing>
    </other>
</alive>
```

The alternative form for modeling information that is not hierarchical is the *marketplace*: data is bundled as separate objects with enough signs on display to allow the viewer to determine whether the object is of interest, using the viewer's own criteria. [1]

```
<!-- A marketplace pattern; a list of objects -->
<objects>
 <object type="alive, edible,   splitable" >banana                 </object>
 <object type="alive, edible,   juice-able">orange                 </object>
 <object type="alive, inedible, scrofulous">sea-slime              </object>
 <object type="alive, electric, fraying"   >power cable number #3 </object>
 <object type="alive, electric, fictitious">Frankenstein's monster</object>
</objects>
```

This distinction between hierarchies and marketplaces is analogous to that found in object-oriented analysis: class/inheritance systems versus agent systems.

---

1. The distinction of markets versus hierarchies is discussed in [*Malone, Yates and Benjamin*].

Do You Need Full SGML?

SGML allows all sorts of strategies: which one you choose and implement in your DTD depends on where the value lies in your text and on how much your text's structure matches the implicit document type of applications and proprietary text formats. —

- ☑ Is it fairly regular?

- ☑ Is it big or numerous or complicated?

- ☑ Must it last a long time?

- ☑ Does it need to be rigorously defined?

- ☑ Does it come from multiple sources?

- ☑ Must it go to multiple destinations?

- ☑ Is the editing and production process spread over multiple sites all with different platforms?

- ☑ Do you need to search it like a database yet print it like free text?

- ☑ Are your current systems not quite smart enough to accomplish all you need?

- ☑ Is some of your publishing system satisfactory yet another part of it is fatally limited?

- ☑ Do your documents need more intelligence? For example, hypertext links, database queries, embedded documents, dynamic content generation, invisible text, extractable fields.

Any of these things indicate full SGML might be useful. If you are lucky, you may find XML is enough for your needs: SGML was developed for large and long-term document publishing; the 1997 Web SGML corrections to the SGML standard adapted it to be also suitable for efficient, small and short-term document-systems on the World Wide Web, in particular to support XML documents.

SGML is often used to improve the productivity of old, stable systems. Completely replacing one obsolete, monolithic system with another system that will, in due time, itself become obsolete, along with its data format, will not make sense to astute managers. Augmenting with SGML the parts of your production system that are working smoothly allows you to stage partial upgrades rather than monumental upheavals.

So if you have simple, small, temporary, free-form, single-source, single-destination, presentation-oriented documents, and you are happy with the current proprietary tools on offer, and are not tooled up for SGML, then full SGML is not the appropriate technology for you. Or, at least, a custom DTD is probably not what you need—an off-the-shelf DTD with XML will probably serve you better, or SGML used transparently with some WYSIWYG editor.

Almost SGML

You do not need to plunge directly into full SGML. Here are five preparatory or introductory choices available to you:

- ◉ non-standard generalized markup,

- ○ HTML markup,

- ○ XML markup,

- ○ simplified SGML, or

- ○ SGML with user extensions.

Non-Standard Generalized Markup

The days when vendors would pass off completely non-SGML tools as SGML seem to have passed. SGML is not "pointy brackets": it is the full set of rules and selectable features of ISO 8879, the [SGML] standard. But non-standard generalized markup is not always a bad thing: adopting generalized markup practices even in non-SGML, proprietary tools can be more than half the battle.

There are things you can do now to make the path to SGML easier when it is time. These will help both in creating your DTD, converting your legacy text, and moving your staff to the structured markup way of thinking.—

- Standardize your editorial structure:

  - high-level structures like document names, filenames, and the names of parts;

  - medium-level structures like the house style for section and list numbering, indentations and bullets;

  - low-level structure like whether tables are entered using tabs or hard spaces or using the proprietary table system provided by the document processing application.

- Use style sheets for all headings and emphasis, rather than hard coding the text with font settings and rulers. ① Many word processors allow you to disable various menu items. You should consider disabling the menus relating to hard-coding.

- The style sheet styles should be named and used to reflect the role or nature of the text they are marking up—this is called generic coding. A side benefit of marking up text this way is that you can make last minute global style changes merely by redefining the style.

- Emphasize to the operators, authors and editors that the most important thing for documents is no longer just the look of the page, but that the look is achieved by having the document marked up according to generalized, logical structures. Have a quality control process to sample and check that staff aren't faking the markup using the wrong styles.

⚠ ······ The use of inappropriate styles may be a sign that the predefined styles you have do not reflect what is actually cropping up in your documents. Welcome this: it will make the DTD analysis easier, and help train you to understand your documents better.

---

1. I have seen a document where there were 200 ways in which simple paragraphs had been keyed in—this makes it difficult to convert into other forms when needed.

The SGML Cookbook

• If you are not using a direct manipulation text system (WYSIWYG) but batch processing with some database or typesetting system, start to adopt SGML-isms in your text. I don't mean simple visual things like using < for the open delimiter of a start-tag: rather, try to generate text which is consistent and well structured and which uses generic coding.

• If you are maintaining a home-grown text processing language, then moving towards SGML might also involve such things as not having attributes (or whatever your equivalent is) in end-tags, and knowing exactly when white space is significant or not in your markup language. And if you are in luck, you could find that your text is already SGML![1]

HTML

[*HTML*] is a simple SGML DTD used on the World Wide Web, which combines

• a small element type set, using element type names similar to those in the General Document example DTD of Annex E of the [*SGML*] standard but with more linear and loose content models,

• an extended addressing mechanism, Universal Resource Locators [*URL*], and

• a way to send queries, Common Gateway Interface [*CGI*].

HTML browsers generally have such a robust error handling strategy that many HTML users have little inkling of the actual structure of the DTD. That strategy, and the resultant frequent non-conformance of HTML documents to standard SGML, means that many are not even aware that HTML is an application of SGML at all.[2]

---

1. SGML optionally allows you to change delimiters and to omit many tags or parts of tags. XML has foregone these conveniences to gain simplicity.

2. Cooperation on HTML by vendors and others has improved under the leadership of the World Wide Web Consortium, [*W3C*].

There has been an ISO effort to make an ISO standard HTML. By using [*ISO HTML*], users can have a clear idea of what element types are portable across different browsers. ISO HTML is not a rival HTML; it is fully compatible and based on the best, most common and most useful features commonly agreed on by industry representatives, but made safe for organization use. ISO HTML also forces headings to only appear at the start of divisions; this brings to HTML the advantages of nested-structure navigation and fragment exchange.

HTML is appropriate where you need simple, generic, rich text. Many documents are well modeled as linked *microdocuments*, where some micro-documents are fielded tables (topic–structure), such as found in a relational database, and some micro–documents are simple text (editorial–structure). HTML can be useful as both the base DTD for the simple text microdocuments and as the base DTD for the contents of the database fields.

This is a very attractive option, since there are so many books and applications now about using HTML. Database–style micro–documents are often better not stored as HTML, but kept in databases, as entities which can be searched and sorted using the database management facilities provided, and only converted to HTML (or XML or full SGML) at use–time.

For implementors rolling your own HTML-based system, you might find the lexical analyzer developed by the World Wide Web Consortium useful. It implements a simple HTML, which is probably most useful for implementing proof of concept prototypes.

Most HTML applications and tools are designed to keep going regardless of errors. For example, the following text has overlapping tags.—

```
<!-- Text with overlapping tags -->
<p><b>hello<i> </b>world</i></p>
```

Many WWW browsers will parse the above to give the following *effective markup*:

```
<-- Non-standard effect of the overlapping tags -->
<p><b>hello<i> </i></b><i>world</i></p>
```

The correct SGML could be any of the following, depending on which tag minimization regime had been declared:

```
<!-- Effect of different SGML normalization regimes  -->
<!-- 1. b="- -" i="o o" -->
 <p><b>hello<i> </i></b>world<i></i></p>
<!-- 2. b="o -"  i="- -" -->
 <p><b>hello<i> <b></b>world</i></b></p>
<!-- 3. b="o o"  i="- -" -->
 <p><b>hello</b><i> <b></b>world</i></b></p>
```

This may be because many early HTML developers saw tags as things that switch on and off a visual effect at certain points, rather than as things that delimit a range of text as part of a hierarchical (tree) structure. They were interested in *tags* not *elements*. If you avoid using tools that allow you to generate bad SGML, you will make future translations of text more useful.

XML

The next approach is to use SGML, but only a very simple subset.

The World Wide Web Consortium [*W3C*] has sponsored the development of recommendations for such a language, called [*XML*], the Extensible Markup Language. Involved in its development were many of the heavyweights of the SGML and WWW industries.

ISO 8879:1986, the SGML Standard, is reviewed regularly to allow industry experience and evolving needs to be incorporated. The ISO working group involved, [*JTC1/WG4*], has bound itself to not change SGML in any way which would make any existing document no-longer conforming SGML.

XML is interesting in that it shows that SGML can be improved, not by adding features for extra power, but by making simpler parsers possible. [1] At the same time XML was developed, the ISO standard for SGML was also adapted to support the needs of small, lightweight and entry-level SGML systems such as XML better. (These adaptations are known as Web SGML and may not be available on every SGML system.)

---

1. However, it is a testament to the foresight of the original designers of SGML, and is confidence boosting, that SGML can be used for very large projects without having to add non-standard kinds of markup. This can be compared to the limitations of a fixed element type set approach, like HTML, in which few large-scale or rich problems can be dealt with.

The aim of XML is to allow simple and small parsers, perhaps even with off-the-shelf tools, suitable for building into small applications, for example as the input language for a table renderer, for efficient use over the World Wide Web. For implementors rolling their own minimal SGML system, a public domain XML parser is the best bet.

XML can be thought of as any SGML after it has been parsed, but then re-emitted as SGML. This type of SGML is sometimes called the *fully normalized element structure information set* (ESIS), or *fully-tagged SGML*. The key is to remove all of SGML's typist-oriented shortcuts, and almost pathological configurability, which complicate SGML parsing so much. SGML is particularly rich in *syntactic sugar* —language features added to make use easier, but which do not, at their core, provide any greater modeling capability.

With these kinds of restrictions, it is possible to make SGML documents which, provided they have been type-validated against a document type declaration when they were generated, do not need a document type declaration to parse—the delimiters alone give enough information. ①

ISO Definition

K.2.2.2 **type-valid SGML document** A SGML document in which, for each document instance, there is an explicitly associated document type declaration to whose DTD that instance conforms.

K.2.2.3 **fully-tagged SGML document** A SGML document, all of whose document instances are fully-tagged. There need not be a document type declaration associated with any of the instances.

K.2.2.1 **conforming SGML document** ...A conforming SGML document must be either a type-valid SGML document, a fully-tagged SGML document, or both. ...

(ISO 8879:1986 Annex K *Web SGML Adaptations*)

---

1. Web SGML also allows an implied document type name:

```
<!-- Simplest document type declaration -->
        <!DOCTYPE #IMPLIED SYSTEM>
```

Your Own Simplified SGML

SGML is a highly configurable language. If you find SGML is too big for you, and XML does not quite meet your needs, you can define your own simplified version: selecting which optional and base-level features you need, and specifying markup policies (additional requirements) to restrict usages that you do not want. ① The XML language is a well-thought-out example of a limited SGML.

A good example of a simplified SGML is the *monastic rule*, which is useful wherever document fragments must be created, joined and potentially parsed separately. ②

Document fragments which follow element boundaries (the SGML terminology for this is an *integrally-stored document instance*) can be reliably stored and incorporated into other documents without any nasty surprises if your DTD does not use

- ☒ exceptions (inclusions or exclusions),

- ☒ short references,

- ☒ #CURRENT attributes, and

- ☒ the instance has had all marked sections resolved. ②

---

1. Note that some additional requirements (such as those marked with ② later) are maybe constraints not allowed by the SGML standard: conforming parsers cannot enforce them, which impacts their portability.

2. The term *monastic DTD* is attributed to Wayne Wohler of IBM and Elliot Kimber of ISOGEN in [*Pinnacles*]. The rules have been further developed in [*SGML Open*]'s Technical Resolution **TR9601:1996** "Fragment Interchange" [*DeRose, Grosso*]. See *Fragment Interchange* in chapter 16 *Embedded Notations*.

ISO Definition

K.2.3.1 integrally-stored document instance   A document instance in which every element and marked-section ends in the entity in which it began.

(ISO 8879:1986 Annex K Web SGML Adaptations)

Another simplification that is fairly useful is to restrict mixed-content content models. Whenever a mixed content model includes optional sequences, especially with choices between PDCATA and sub-elements, it is very easy for users to introduce spurious REs (record ends) data into the content model, which may cause unexpected validation errors.

```
<!-- A mixed content model which may cause nasty surprises -->
<!-- Note: XML 1.0 does not allow this kind of content model -->
<!ENTITY    % sub.elements  " ( a | b | c )* " >
<!ELEMENT   example         ( #PCDATA | %sub.elements; ) >
```

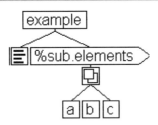

The Pinnacles DTD PCIS is the most well-known DTD that restricts this kind of mixed content. The only type of mixed content model allowed is like the following:

```
<!-- A mixed content model with only "or" connectors -->
<!-- Note: XML 1.0 allows this kind of content model -->
<!ENTITY    % sub.elements  " a | b | c ">
<!ELEMENT   example         ( #PCDATA | %sub.elements; )* >
```

The SGML Cookbook

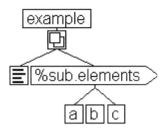

Other simplifications which can be worthwhile considering—

    ☒ Trimming from a public entity set for special characters all the entity declarations you do not want to support. This is the approach taken in the HTML public entity sets, which select the most commonly available characters from the ISO public entity sets.

    ☒ Restricting processing instructions in the body of the instance. ⑦

    ☒ Altering other standard delimiters. In particular, when your DTD includes CDATA elements and the data to be marked up contains many characters which would be parsed as delimiters, it can be easier to alter the standard delimiters rather than to mark up the document instance. For example, altering the Entity Reference Open delimiter (ERO) from & to && may save many keystrokes if your data has many & characters.

    ☒ Relaxing the naming rules to allow almost any character which non-English users might want to be in a name to occur in SGML identifiers.

    ☒ Restricting further the allowed declared values of attributes, perhaps to just CDATA, and banning the #FIXED keyword.

    ☒ Requiring that IDs must be declared before they can be used in IDREF attributes. [*HyTime* '97] has a standard mechanism to declare that this requirement is in force.

-☼-····· If you do use home-grown tools for SGML, HTML or XML, you should seriously consider using a third–party SGML parser to type–validate your documents.① Programmers are often over–confident in this regard. It is prudent to remember that conforming SGML is not what your program produces, but is what ISO 8879 says. A third–party SGML type–validator is an essential item for quality control.

⚠ ····· If you have the luxury of a fixed DTD, you are using some simplified SGML such as XML, and you are creating your own custom parser, then a whole new world of error–recovery and robustness possibilities are open to you. This can make the rest of the production process easier: you can generate and manipulate less than type–valid SGML documents, but get acceptable results at the end. You will be reaping the rewards of generalized markup, not of standardization *per se*: many projects fail because of this;—your text is non–standard and must be re-marked up to some extent if ever you need to use third–party tools.

The SGML approach of requiring (or at least, promoting) type-valid documents is because, for any large document set, it is better to catch errors at their source rather than at their destination.② However, note that SGML type-validation is only a technology to enable the rigorous markup of documents: if the documents are not well marked-up, they will be useless even if they happen to be type-valid SGML. Your quality assurance process must attend to the quality of the markup, not just the results of type-validating a document through an SGML parser.

SGML with User Extensions

You can invent your own markup system that you run in concert with or instead of standard SGML markup. For example, you may decide to use the C prepro-cessor (cpp) to incorporate #include statements to construct entities. Or you may define your own type of non-SGML tags to allow multiple concurrent trees

---

1. [*OmniMark*] Corporation's OmniMark program and James Clark's public domain [*SP*] parser are both useful for this role.

2. This is the catch cry of everyone I know who has successfully completed large SGML projects.

within your text to be directly marked up. Or you may define some context-setting instruction to allow a parser to process fragments of SGML documents, rather than having to start from their beginning.

These types of markup are generally bad if they duplicate what SGML can do already.

- For example, SGML already has a simple mechanism for marked sections and external entities: it is probably unnecessary to use cpp.

- Similarly, multiple concurrent trees can be marked-up in SGML using empty tags (e.g., <start.tree2.level3/> and <end.tree2.level3/>), though this must be checked by something other than the parser. Or you could use HyTime linking and addressing.

- If you need to be able to process fragments, then the use of a *monastic DTD* can make the whole process possible without requiring special constructs.

SGML is meant as an open standard. It aims to free you from being tied into slackly-defined markup methods which prevent generalized markup. However, SGML is not a superstition: there may be good practical reasons to sometimes refrain from using SGML markup. It is quite proper to embed application-specific markup in your data: the notation mechanism has been provided for this. For example, you might have an eight-bit SGML parser, and encode all characters in data with codes greater than 255 inside special non-SGML delimiters (e.g., <p>Mr [[345]] from Okinawa.</p>). The SGML parser does not recognize this as markup, the application must.

The kind of user-defined extension to SGML which really should be avoided is markup that will confuse an SGML parser: markup which requires a custom parser. Text which uses this must be clearly marked "non-SGML" or "SGML-like" and be stored in NDATA entities. If there is a genuine need for syntax additions, the ISO JTC1/WG4 can be approached to discuss them.

When a new technology is being developed, there is a proliferation of different ideas and implementations. When it is standardized, the main value of a technology should be conformability. There were three or more main versions of C before standardization. Now, the standardization of ISO C means in turn that other technologies, such as ISO C++, can be defined in terms of it. And the standardization of ISO C++ means that other higher level technologies, like the Standard Template Library, can be built on top of it, in turn. Standardization is not the stultification of a technology; it can be the foundation for greater things.

It is important to stress that HTML, XML, simplified SGML and user-extended SGML still are all conforming SGML. None of them need define markup that conflicts with what the ISO 8879, the [*SGML*] standard, allows.

Thumbs Rule, OK!

When should something be an attribute, an element, a processing instruction or an entity? And which sequence should elements and attributes go in? There are various rules of thumb to help you decide. Not every rule will give the same answer.

Language Analogy

☑ A simple way is to think about which part of speech corresponds to what you are trying to model—

Is it like a general or collective noun, or gerund?
☑ Use an element type.

Is it like an adjective?
☑ Use an attribute.

Is it like verb or a command?
☑ Use a processing instruction.

Is it like an adverb?
☑ Use a pseudo-SGML attribute in the processing instruction. ①

---

1. Pseudo-SGML markup refers to markup used inside processing instructions, element data, and CDATA attribute values that uses SGML "pointy bracket" conventions. It looks SGML-ish but is actually a user extension or defined by some other standard. See chapter 16 *Embedded Notations* for more.

Is it a specific noun, for something inside the document?

☑ Use an ID or IDREF attribute.

Is it a specific noun, perhaps the name or location of something outside the document?

☑ Use an entity.

Is it like an adjectival phrase for the name (e.g., the "island" in "the island Australia", or the "CGM-program" in "the CGM-program X.CGM")?

☑ Use a notation.

Is it like an adjective for a thing that is an entity (e.g., *the green island Australia* or *the 2cm by 3cm CGM-program X.CGM*) or a *version 1.0* CGM figure?

☑ Use a data attribute. (Data attributes are not available in XML 1.0.)

```
<!-- Declare a notation for image/jpeg -->

<!-- It could have the URL of the handler in system identifier -->
<!NOTATION JPEG SYSTEM >

<!-- Example of declaration for attributes -->
<!ATTLIST #NOTATION JPEG
    version CDATA #IMPLIED
    x       CDATA #IMPLIED
    y       CDATA #IMPLIED >

<!-- Example of an entity declaration with data attributes -->
<!ENTITY thing SYSTEM "X.CGM" NDATA JPEG
              [ x="2 cm" y="3 cm" version="1.0"]>


<!-- Example of an element type with data attributes
    (Web SGML only) -->
<!ATTLIST small-figure
      type DATA JPEG
              [ x="2 cm" y="3 cm" version="1.0" ] #IMPLIED >
```

While we have the example of sizes in data attributes, we can clarify the difference between attributes and data attributes. Let us say that say that an entity that is a graphic has `size` data attributes giving the size of the bounding box of the file, independent of scaling. An element `<figure>` has an attribute of type ENTITY to nominate the graphic to be used, and `size` attributes giving the size required for the graphic. The application has to divide the element `size` attributes by the entities `size` data attributes, and scale the graphic by that amount.

Object Relationships

Various relationships between objects[1] suggest DTD policies. —

X has-a Y
☑ Use

- a container element if only one X has Y, or

- IDREF element reference if multiple Xs have Y;

X uses Y
☑ Use

- an IDREF element reference if only X uses Y, or

- an entity reference if multiple Xs use Y.

X is-a Y
☑ Use

- a GI for the primary type,

- an architectural form for aliasing the object to another type, and

- IDREF element reference for arbitrary extended class, pointing to some object (e.g., refer to [*TEI*] glossaries).

---

1. Refer to [*Colby, Jackson, et al*] for a brief discussion of applying Rumbaugh's object-oriented methodologies to DTD analysis. However, the statements that one can ignore everything except the logical structure of the document when processing a document seem is perhaps an ideal, only reached after the kinds of steps expounded in *The Tweak*, in chapter 5 at page 1-118.

Occurrence

A key factor in determining what information can go into a DTD when analyzing documents, is to figure out what text and structures are unique to each particular document instance, and which text and structures are invariant.

We can use occurrences as a cue to what kind of markup to use—

- ◉ for structures repeated in most documents: **element types**;

- ○ for text which is the same in all documents: **fixed attribute values**;

- ○ for text that reappears regularly: **internal text entity**;

- ○ for structures which are unique to a document: **generic element type with attributes**;

- ○ for text that is unique to a document instance: **data**;

- ○ for structures which are unique to a particular presentation or medium: **architectural forms**;

- ○ for text which is unique to a particular presentation or medium: **links or external documents**.

After enumerating, group the least common element types into a more generic element type, with attributes to distinguish them, and the most common as default.

Sequence

It is difficult to back-propagate attributes with stream-based text tools. Although these tools cannot look ahead, they are very common; they are often appropriate because the large sizes of many SGML documents makes "in-memory" processing impractical. The problem is particularly true for attributes that are like metadata, and which will be needed by SGML applications to make decisions about how to use the SGML text.

-̣Ọ̈-······ You should attach attributes to elements before or where you anticipate they will be needed, not after.

So

```
<!-- An attribute given after it may be required -->
<sect><heading section-id="S234">Blah...
```

is not preferable to

```
<!-- An attribute given where or before it may be required -->
<sect id=S1234><heading>Blah...
```

unless there is a strong requirement to be able to minimize the <sect> element.

Similarly, put the metadata-ish elements first, since programs are more likely to need this information when processing non-metadata-ish elements. So

```
<!-- Metadata given after it may be required -->
<section><heading>Blah</heading><number>3</number>...
```

is less preferable to

```
<!--Metadata given where or before it may be required -->
<section><number>3</number><heading>Blah</heading>...
```

Summary of Chapter 4

This chapter discussed some questions that should be asked before designing or implementing an SGML document system. The first is, of course, whether SGML is really an appropriate solution—and if so, whether only in some simplified kind like HTML or XML, or with some of the optional, user-friendly features.

This art, like so many other famous inventions, owed its birth or at least improvement and perfection, to an effect of chance, but was established upon solid reasons and hath flourished in this island ever since with great luster. All agree that it first appeared upon the decay and discouragement of bagpipes, ...

Jonathan Swift, Mechanical Operation of the Spirit.

The Document in Use

Chapter 5

This chapter

...looks at how SGML documents are processed and used. This will help you understand the reasons why some element types are preferable to others, and why more mature DTDs tend towards particular structures.

Declarations are Not Enough!

Document type declarations and element type sets are not enough to deal with every problem of a document. To complete a document architecture, the document type definition requires statements of policy about how the document is marked up, and what the meaning of the markup is.

ISO Definition

4.97 document architecture: Rules for the formulation of text processing applications.

4.105 document (type) definition: Rules, determined by an application, that apply SGML to the markup of documents of a particular type. NOTE — Part of a document type definition can be specified by an SGML document type declaration. Other parts, such as the semantics of elements and attributes, or any application conventions, cannot be expressed formally in SGML. Comments can be used, however, to express them informally.

(ISO 8879:1986 glossary)

Lay users of SGML often find large document type declarations difficult to follow. Element types and their intended usage are often documented in an *element type dictionary* (or *Data Dictionary*). The element type dictionary will have entries in some convenient format for each type, often accompanied by diagrams of the content models. Railway diagrams are a diagraming technique that has proved successful – railway diagrams are like augmented Pascal syntax diagrams.

Markup policy (*additional requirements*)[1] documents can be just as important. They state what the markup policy is for all the issues that SGML does not address—

• integrity checks like "*the number of cell elements in a table must match the number given in some attribute*,"

---

1. If you are using a Web SGML system, put the public identifier for your additional requirements document in the SEEALSO parameter of the SGML declaration.

　　　　　　　　The SGML Cookbook

- restrictions to SGML to govern the use of certain types of markup in certain places, like "*processing instructions must start with a notation name*," and

- conventions about naming, like *ID attributes should start with the type identifier (GI) of the element*" or "*element type names should start with the entity name of the entity in which they were declared.*"

Of course, small, personal or transitory projects will probably not need such documentation. If you have significant additional application requirements, you should make sure your SGML document notes them, or has a reference to a document that does.

Principle

Do talk to strangers.

These references could be just in a comment, but you might also like to provide a *notation declaration* with a public identifier or a URL system identifier for the additional application requirements. Your aim may be to make sure that every instance carries enough information about its type with it to be useful during its life. For a closed and short-term system, there may be no need to send any information about document type; for a variable and open-ended system, then the more type information the better. Future users of the documents will thank you if they have every thing they need.

Additional requirements could also be used by customized computer applications to switch in extra syntax-checking conventions. —

⊠ Are new lines significant?[1] Some SGML applications completely ignore all returns in text: record starts and record end characters having no impact on the final document. If records are significant, what as? Word separators or paragraph separators?

⊠ Are spaces allowed inside a particular element or should they be moved outside?

⊠ Is there a spacing discipline within particular element types?

---

1. SGML calls each line in the SGML text a *record*, to avoid confusion with the lines in formatted output.

☒ What is the syntax of CDATA attribute values? The [*HyTime* '97] lexical language *HyLex* is useful for this.

☒ How are empty elements to be treated? For example, what is done with empty paragraphs like the following?

```
<p></p>
```

☒ How are missing or excess columns or cells in tables handled?

One of the most useful techniques for keeping element identifiers (IDs) under control is to have a naming convention by which you can know to what type of element an identifier reference (IDREF) refers. For example, the identifiers for all cross–references may start with X, all footnotes may start with F, all tables may start with T, etc. This allows a very simple kind of validation to be made, so that an identifier used in an IDREF that appears to be a table reference does indeed correspond to the ID of some table. And it allows boilerplate text to be generated based on the type of the reference, for example, "*See table 5*" or "*See figure 4.*"

This convention is an example of a *fielded name*: the identifier is good for humans, yet it also incorporates some information that a computer can use. The fielded name is an important pattern and crops up in many guises—

• The SPREAD entities, for example, have a fixed prefix to introduce a code number, which indexes into the [*ISO 10646*] character set: an intelligent SGML entity manager can use the information in the name to locate the entity efficiently.

• Element type identifiers (GIs) can be disambiguated by using *meaning-namespace* prefixes. For example:—

```
                    <p>My
<lipstick:color> violent blue </lipstick:color>
             is different from your
    <idiom:color topic= "movie"> violent blue
               </idiom:color>.</p>
```

The SGML Cookbook

The strings "::" or ":" are most commonly used as hierarchical namespace delimiters – [*ISO 9070*] recommends using "::" but ":" may result in some small filesize saving. ① You can document the namespace prefix further in your DTD with a notation declaration, a comment, or some processing instruction of your own construction: make sure you point out in your documentation what the function of the notation is! The use of namespace prefixes is an extension away from [*SGML '86*]; it is perfectly legitimate to use SGML in this way, but make sure that your approach is adequately documented.

• The affixing of a checksum number to a locator, to ensure that the text received is the same as the text requested. This is, of course, only suitable for systems where the checksum can be calculated and distributed as part of the identifier.

Another example borrows a construct from a draft of WIDL, the Web Interface Description Language [*WIDL*] under discussion at W3C. If your ID names were like `table[3].tr[2].td[6]` (assuming HTML-like tables), then they could be used to navigate through the GROVE (the complex tree of information that an SGML parser nominally produces): the ID acts as much as a locator as a name. Note: If you want to do this, you must add [and] to the list of characters possible for use in SGML names by creating a special SGML declaration for the purpose.

---

1. A simple experiment by Gavin Nicol suggests that the advantage may not hold for Internet transmissions, which are often compressed at various bottlenecks.

Processing SGML

SGML documents are hierarchical data notated in text and sourced from entities. You get three stabs at processing documents:

✓ as arrangements of entities;

✓ as the data structured into hierarchical elements; and

✓ as plain text.

If you want to make the best use of SGML you need good tools for all three.

SGML Tools

Validator

This is the most useful and important tool for using SGML. It lets you have confidence that your text is regular enough to be useful in the next stage of its existence, helps you pin down errors, or at least gives you an idea how bad your text is.

⚠······ Unless all your text is generated by computer, and you have confidence in the generating software, somewhere in your workflow you should include a validation stage. If you hand your SGML documents on to others, you should include a validation stage as part of your Quality Assurance procedures. If you receive SGML documents, you should include a validation stage at the outset, to prevent you wasting your time trying to process invalid documents. If you are writing contracts for document delivery, you should write validation into the contract, so that the parties involved have a clear delineation of responsibility for document quality.

Normalizer

Not all SGML systems are the same; they may have different parser conventions or features. A normalizer takes the document and generates an equivalent document with omitted tags filled in and other forms of minimization removed. It is very useful to have the source code of your normalizer available—you can tailor the normalization to your particular requirements.

A limited-SGML normalizer transforms your SGML document into a limited-SGML document. Not only are all kinds of minimization removed, but also delimiters may be changed to allow easier DTD-less parsing. [1]

Structure editor

A structure editor lets you move around text by the information in the document type declaration or according to the markup. A key criterion of any SGML editor is often whether the performance is adequate when editing long (more than 1 meg) and densely marked-up files.

SGML filters

An SGML filter is a program that takes the structures in the document and the data and produces some output in SGML or some other notation based on it. A good SGML filter program will allow you to treat attributes with as much interest as you do GIs: sometimes you may be more interested in the attribute values than GIs. For example, when you are processing the document according to an external architecture and have attributes acting as architectural forms.

SGML delivery vehicle

A program that processes SGML and renders it for the end-user.

Text Tools

General-purpose text tools are not only useful for processing text entities, but also for processing the system files associated with manipulating the storage objects in which the entities live: .BAT files, shell scripts and program text.

For larger systems, the systems issues involved in storing, naming and managing storage can be as complex as those involved with the element structure. This is why SGML has such a strongly developed notion of entity and notation: to allow a document to carry with it as much information about these external systems issues as will be needed.

Perhaps the strongest confirmation of the importance of being able to represent the external is the success of the World Wide Web. HTML originally was a very simple DTD, but the development of URLs has allowed the development of an enormous web of information.

---

1. See *XML* in chapter 4 at page 1-89 for more details.

One great advantage of the text processing tool is that it does not try to expand entities, and you do not need to make special efforts to do so.

Text editor
SGML can be edited by any text editor. Ideally it should
     ✓ handle very large files,

     ✓ handle very long lines,

     ✓ handle numbers of files,

     ✓ preserve white space,

     ✓ allow macro-recording of editing moves, preferably with an optional confirmation mode,

     ✓ have sophisticated search and replace, including wildcards,

     ✓ allow display of non-ASCII characters, and is 8 bit (or 16 bit) clean,

     ✓ allow you to re-output cut text, for example, to transform **aaa** to

```
find "aaa" output "<text>aaa</text>"
```

or (sed or vi)

```
1,$s/aaa/<test>&<\/text>/
```

☼ ······ In this way you can convert lists of keywords into programs, shell scripts or batch files that can mark up data automatically.

Stream editor
Stream editing by batch files was made famous by UNIX, but the tools from UNIX are now available on many platforms. `Sed`, `awk` and `perl` are the most common. `Emacs` and some commercial text editors also often have a stream mode, which is useful because it lets you process large numbers of files in batches using familiar editing commands. There are public domain SGML toolkits available for `perl` and `python` languages, and freely distributable, stripped-down versions of several SGML processing applications.

Stream selection

The UNIX command line utility `grep` is a strange beast: it looks at the input one line at a time, and if the line has a match of a pattern, it prints out the line (or suppresses it). This has two great uses: first to track down strings in a whole lot of files quickly from the command line. Secondly, you can use it to extract fields from marked-up files quickly.

This second use requires you to have generated your text with extra conventions. Particularly useful is the convention that all titles must be marked up on a single line.—

```
<sec><title>A TITLE</title>...
```

You can now generate a table of contents simply[1] by giving the command such as:

```
grep -i "<title" filenames | wc
```

Sort

The key to sorting is that you want to sort lists of keys that reference entities, and not the contents of the entities themselves.[2] The sort utilities provided with some popular operating systems are insufficient for handling large files. I can recommend the FreeSoft Foundation's [GNU] `sort` and UNIX `sort`.

Unique and duplicate

A unique-izing sort is very useful (GNU `sort -u`) to make a list of keys. The well-known utility `uniq` does this just for successive lines.

The companion utility to this would be one that finds duplicated lines. None exists though, that I know of, so you have to roll your own using what ever tools are at hand.

---

1. This technique also requires that no start-tags have been omitted from markup.

2. The issue of sort keys is discussed in *Collation* in chapter 18 *About Characters and Glyphs* on page 3-16.

Cutters and concatenators

A program that can cut up documents into separate entities based on some criteria is most useful. Many common text-processing utilities can do this, for example, `split` and `cat`, but it is best to use structure-utilizing tools that can create entities divided up following element structures. Dividing up a document into small, neat entities that follow an element boundary makes each entity easier to include in other contexts.

Cross platform converters

Every operating system uses different linefeed and carriage return conventions. Some software acts strangely on files with the wrong conventions. The standard UNIX commands `dos2unix` and `unix2dos` are useful. Microsoft has some useful tools for converting between character sets, including [*Unicode*].

Comparison

It is useful to have a tool to compare two text files, and print out any differences. The common UNIX tool for this is called `diff`. When large documents are slightly updated, it can be useful to only send the changes, as caught by `diff`. A tool called `patch` applies these changes to a document. In the PC world, the shareware program ARC also allows this kind of patching.

Storage Management Tools

What should you store your entities in?—

- ◉ A file system?

- ○ A database?

- ○ A source code control system?

File systems and source code control systems are, of course, only particular kinds of databases highly optimized for particular uses.

The file system rather than a database may be more than enough for your needs in many situations. —

⊠ If you are using a file system which allows long filenames and naming conventions flexible enough for you to use a filename as a key, and

☒ you only need to access the entities by a single key, and

☒ you organize it so that you only keep numbers of files *per* directory to a manageable level,[1] and

☒ you can usually keep entities not much smaller than the minimum block size of the file systems. [2]

The more powerful the GUI tools you have, the less useful the *command line tools* are, however command line tools are still the basis of much text processing. Batch files and command–line invocation systems are the skeletons on which large document–processing systems hang; time spent by programmers familiarizing themselves with their command–line tools is time well spent: the UNIX shells, REXX, AppleScript, COMMMAND.COM, ECMAScript (JavaScript), SQL and the macro languages used in word processors.

You should have good tools that can help you track down strings and files easily – a database browser, the UNIX shell tools, REXX command language, or a visual aid like the XTree product on PCs.

Source code control systems can be good choices for storing SGML entities, especially if the entities will have a long life and pass through many successive edits. Of course, an SGML document is not source code in the sense that a file containing a C program is source code, but both are parseable character-based representations of information.

---

1. Some file systems experience performance problems when the number of files is greater than 100 to 250.

2. I discovered to my alarm when setting up a large website that fifty thousand 200 byte files will take up a `tar` archive file of about 10 meg, but take up 100 meg on a LINUX system with 2K file blocks, and at least 400 meg on DOS FAT, actually much more on large disks! One well-known object-relational SGML database advises that SGML files may expand by **ten times** when placed in the database.

Hybrid Tools

In practice, it is useful to have SGML tools that also can do some rudimentary processing of the SGML as plain text, and to have text applications that have some awareness of the structures or markup of the document.

Many people who edit SGML files choose to use their favorite powerful text editor (Emacs, Multiedit) because the powerful macro languages of these editors let them build in structural navigation and markup highlighting while maintaining the simplicity and speed of direct text editing.

And, even when you have good SGML tools, there is no reason why all markup in an SGML document in progress should be SGML markup. For example, you might decide that some unique string, for example, $$QQQ$$ should be a place-holder for some name, and then run a script

```
sed "s/\$\$QQQ\$\$/my name/" infile > outfile
```

to convert the SGML boilerplate to a usable SGML document. Especially if you have no good normalizing tools and are unwilling to alter the document type declaration (to declare an extra element type or SDATA entity).

You should use whatever markup is easy for your tools to process. ① Gaining expertise with professional-quality and powerful tools helps you understand the constraints on DTD designs that exist at your current state of technology.

See *XML* in chapter 4, page 1-89 *et seq*, for some recommendations on the parts of SGML you should avoid if you want to use simple sub-SGML tools.

Groovy Steps with SGML

Working with SGML, rather than being an end- user, can involve taking the text through various steps.

The Scrub

The first step is purely textual: it is to make text that is regular and consistent enough to be useful. Many of these scrubbing steps should be automated. The aim of *scrubbing* is to produce a valid SGML document which is free from trouble—

• Some processing systems generate empty paragraphs, and sometimes users generate empty elements just so that an over-tight content model can be satisfied: these must be removed and the DTD rectified.

• Many times spacing around elements is wrong: when you see some text with a bold word abutting hard against a word in plain text (e.g., `helloworld`) `you know that the markup looked like this:`

```
<p><bold>hello</bold>world.</p>
```

You may be able to devise a post-process to ensure that all bold tags must be followed by a single space, for example. If you do this, document it also in the DTD or the markup policy (additional requirements) document. A similar problem occurs sometimes with [*SGML*] '86 when the original markup looked like this:

```
<p><bold>hello ⏎
</bold>world.</p>
```

because the SGML record handling rules will probably cause the Record End character ⏎ to be stripped out.

 ⋯⋯⋯ The same problem can occur when using the well-known method of keeping all Record End characters inside markup, for example just before the tag close delimiter in a start-tag or end-tag. This has the advantage that no complex rules need to be learned, or smart programs written to handle records. However, it does again make the SGML plain text look as if it has a newline, which can be confusing. —

```
<p><bold>hello</bold⏎
>world.</p>
```

• Sometimes a document may be delivered with a CDATA or NUTOKEN attribute when an ID attribute would be more appropriate. It can be worthwhile to convert all these to real IDs. This can catch duplicate errors in the process. The next step is to validate IDs and IDREFs across documents, where this occurs. The HTML equivalent is to check that every href URL corresponds to one only URL and name attribute.

• It is possible that the same data could be marked up in a few alternative ways, especially with presentational markup. For example,

```
<b>hello <i>world</i></b>
```

and

```
<b>hello </b><i><b>world</b></i>
```

or models which allow lists inside paragraphs and outside, and which have *continuation paragraphs*. This is particularly true of text in the first stages of conversion from unstructured legacy formats, for example through the [*Rainbow*] DTD. 1

• Especially with automated translation, strange sequences of entities may exist: an entity for ellipses might be a thin-space entity, three periods, and another thinspace;

Replace combined special character entities with their combining forms, or vice versa, depending on what the collating and rendering requirements of your document system are. For example, to convert ä to a combined with an entity reference for the umlaut, taken from the SPREAD entities, using UNIX `sed`:

```
s/\&auml;/a\&U0308;/
```

You should keep some kind of record of the scrubbing steps you have to take, to provide feedback for the people doing the mark-up, and for reviewing the DTDs in the future. Usually, our memories are not reliable enough: by reviewing a well-kept log-file, we can pinpoint problems objectively.

The Massage

The purpose of the massage is to convert good documents from one valid SGML form into another, perhaps with a different SGML declaration, perhaps with a different entity structure—

◉ normalize;

---

1. I once worked on a project where visually identical paragraphs, originally marked up by many different human operators using a well-known high-end desktop publishing application with little support for structure, had been marked up in two hundred different ways—very difficult to convert.

O normalize, but output as XML or some other limited SGML;

O normalize with some additions; or

O loosen document type declaration or add element types for bad markup or unresolved issues.

The Tweak

Now your text has been scrubbed to the 99.99% correct level, you have massaged the recalcitrant text so that it will not ruin the party, and you come to use your SGML text in an application. Sometimes it still does not work!

Even after the text has been scrubbed, and the markup massaged, every application must have certain work done:

☑ registering the document type and SGML declaration;

☑ setting up the public entity mappings;

☑ setting up the appropriate SDATA entity mappings. (NOTE: [*XML*] 1.0 does not have SDATA entities.)

This is OK, but what happens very often is that each application requires or works best with slight variations in the SGML text.

• SGML declarations for documents are often varieties of the *house SGML declaration* from whomever last had the document, rather than reflecting the document itself – often quantities may be too high; some features may be YES but not used; a character set may be declared in an unusual way. All these things are minor housekeeping, and tedious, but are commonly needed.

• In instances, newlines may not be able to be made significant to the application: in <pre> sections. They have to be replaced by SDATA entity references or EMPTY elements like <br>. And sometimes the entity set used is not available and it is easiest to re-map the document to a familiar entity set: for example to the ISO standard — from &em-dash;.

- Sometimes names will exceed the maximum name-length, requiring the SGML declaration, the element type declarations or the instance to be changed.

- Sometimes the error correction on one application is better than in another – especially on large documents, minor errors in minimization can become a great problem.

Growth of DTDs

There are many DTDs now that have had five to ten years of use and evolution. The change logs of these DTDs reveal the deficiencies and infelicities of the original design, the increased sophistication of the users, the changing patterns of usage of the document, and the results of reviews of markup problems from the existing DTD.

In lieu of a complete study of these logs, here are some changes that recur. —

- Revising too-simple content models. In particular, early designs often do not allow multiple paragraphs in list items, or metadata elements on information units, or optional headings in container elements, or option number setting for list items (not all lists should be auto-numbered). For example,

```
<!ELEMENT list-item ( %text; ) >
```

often gravitates towards

```
<!ELEMENT list-item ( num?, head?, p+ ) >
```

Many lists end up with a form similar to chapters and sections.

Another common over-simple content model comes from not allowing emphasis elements in paragraphs.

• Allowing unnecessarily exclusions of links, note references, or cross-references inside links, note references, cross-references, footnotes, equations, quotations and facsimile material. (Note: [XML] 1.0 does not have inclusions or exclusions.) Often such exclusions are a concession to the limitations of particular target applications – a paper formatter may not allow a footnote to have a footnote, for example. The better way is to allow them, but to convert the SGML into some intermediate form suitable for your target application.

Altering the DTD to suit a particular formatter or to prevent a particular markup practice is, of course, entirely legitimate and practical, as long as the downside is recognized: what you remove today you may have to build in tomorrow. To continue the example, hypertext browsers usually have no trouble with footnotes inside footnotes: in fact, the World Wide Web style of hypertext tends to reduce everything to nothing but notes that refer to other notes.

• Tightening up identifiers declared in CDATA attribute values so that the attribute can be redefined to be an ID attribute. Commonly, most element types end up with ID attribute definitions.

• Requiring end-tags on medium-level container elements, especially where there is a possibility that the element type can contain itself somewhere: for example, lists within lists.

• Loosening the content models of container elements that mark names, addresses and references, in order to get more position independence. Usually the inefficiency of marking up and repositioning such text into a standard order by hand is eventually realized: as long as the fields are marked up rigorously, a computer program can be used to sequence the fields, perhaps even on demand at rendering-time.

• Standardizing on the element type set that can appear inside text, and coalescing information units that are very similar. This may result in possibly inappropriate structures if used without attention to guidelines in a markup policy (application requirements) document, yet the human and maintenance benefits of a simpler DTD may outweigh this problem.

A common change is to make the text in paragraphs in table cells just as rich as text in ordinary paragraphs. Rather than a special content model for table entries, the usual paragraph content model is used.

• Changing content models so that low-level container elements favor "+" rather than "*" and so that higher-level container elements favor "*" and "?" more than "+". The tightening of the low-level container-element content models is because very often this is fielded data which must have certain information present. The loosening of the higher-level container-element content models is because many DTDs are created for use with large documents: sometimes small documents require an excessive, tedious and confusing number of dummy higher-level elements to be valid. For example, do not require an Appendix section if it will be empty for some documents, especially if the document is being newly created.

• Changing table models to use [*CALS*] tables instead of a proprietary table structure. ①

• Abandoning in-house conventions and adopting HTML or HyTime conventions, where it does not affect the data modeling.

• Obsoleting *hopeful monsters*. A hopeful monster element set, to borrow a term from evolution literature, is one added because it might be useful. If it does not prove itself, it is removed, or declared obsolete. These are often elements relating to user interaction or presentation, or some anticipated markup need. HTML's MENU and DIR element types are examples.

---

1. The [*SGML Open*] Table Exchange Model subset of this is the best version of CALS table for most uses.

It is useful for the DTD maintainers to keep a planning version of the DTD, in which they can note anticipated element type sets: this can help them keep the working DTD as simple as possible, and allow you to make sure any custom software that gets developed will be flexible enough to cope if the extra element type sets do get adopted.

- Adding a whole new type of markup to the document. In particular, many older DTDs do not have much markup for hypertext links. The widespread use of ID attributes means that most SGML documents are already rich with easy-to-use anchors (destinations).

Many times, owners of text are not aware of the kinds of topic-structure information that is present in their documents. For example, in a mechanical manual, there may be value in explicitly marking up parts with a `part` tag, to allow easy searching and the construction of indexes to the occurrence, and hypertext links from the part to a data sheet. It could also serve as a consistency check: when a part design or model is updated, or a warning issued on the part, the text relating to all the references to the part can be checked for veracity. Often, references to mechanical parts and other objects with standard-form names can be marked up automatically.

- Augmenting appendix elements to allow richer content. All sorts of material can be added to an appendix: interactive forms, graphics, complex tables, indexes. Appendixes often should allow the same content as a section, but also almost everything else under the sun.

Top 10 Reasons Why DTDs Fail

⚠ ······ Sometimes DTDs fail, and with them a whole project. Sometimes DTDs just fail to thrive, not bringing the expected benefits.—

Too loose or too tight
◆ Probably the major problem is content-model looseness. The result is documents that a computer cannot do much with. For example, I have heard of a DTD in which the heading levels were not tied to the division structure:

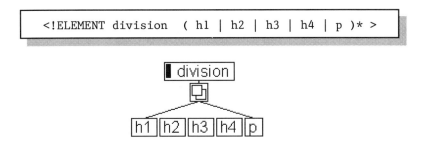

```
<!ELEMENT division  ( hl | h2 | h3 | h4 | p )* >
```

You could have a division with an h1 heading nested inside a division under an h4 heading! However, to pose as Goldilocks for a while, a corresponding problem is over-rigidity, where the DTD is so tightly constrained that there is no way to squeeze the document into it.

Fitness for purpose
◆ Most high-end publishing involves very specific problems. There is no reason to expect the use of general purpose DTD, or a DTD from another industry sector, to work. DTDs fail if they ignore the immovable constraints of the workflow: human factors, technical limitations and the availability of resources.

Inappropriate adoption
◆ The early [ATA100] DTD allowed little topic-structure markup but, because it was an "air industry standard," some airline companies' management tried to impose it even when a topic-structure DTD was appropriate.

Not enough accompanying smarts
◆ SGML makes your valuable information accessible to your computer. Making your computer do something useful with it is usually a job which involves programming. Quality programming should involve professional programming tools, robust programming environments, and skilled, trained and bright programmers. Any SGML house needs to have at least one *guru/nerd/whizz–kid* who can solve

tricky problems as they arise. ⚀ If no accompanying smarts are available, the DTD must avoid anything tricky.

Sometimes even the best guesses will get it wrong

◆ All DTDs involve tradeoffs. It is no secret to anyone in the software industry that many projects do not succeed. Using a structured methodology is a good way of making sure that the failure was not due to mere negligence or incompetence, and for allowing a *post mortem* of the DTD design.

Cheating

◆ Anyone who uses a database understands that data should be put into the correct fields, and that the fields should have a specific and useful meaning. But this knowledge mysteriously goes AWOL sometimes when people use SGML. SGML is well placed to be specified as an interchange format in contracts, for when document workflows are split between several companies.

So the first step of document acceptance upon receiving documents from a supplier should be to validate the document against the agreed DTD: beware that sometimes document suppliers will loosen the DTD, making required elements optional and altering the sequence in which elements must appear, to make their text validate correctly. Make sure to validate the text against your own copy of the DTD, not the one that happened to come with the text: at the very least it can tell you the real state of the documents you have to deal with. Even if the document is valid, it does not mean the document is properly marked up: some kind of sampling and inspection should be carried out.

Tag abuse

◆ When documents are consistently marked up incorrectly, there is a problem in the DTD, in the workflow, or in quality assurance. If the DTD does not contain element types for something that is in the document, operators will mark up the document using the nearest best thing. When the human operators are overloaded, and trying to mark up too many element types at the same time, they will also tend to confuse and misuse element types. Without some kind of quality assurance mechanism, these cannot be caught. The age of the proofreader is not over.

---

1. SGML text processing sometimes involves manipulating hundreds of megabytes of text, sourced from thousands of entities. The lengthiest script I have generated for manipulating SGML was seven meg: some jobs require this kind of work.

Sabotage

◆ The move to SGML-based systems can be threatening, especially as it can involve changes in workflows and the devaluing of existing, hard-won skills. Those who use the DTD or who can benefit quickly from its use can often be won over by being in the loop at some stage—in creation or maintenance. The document system should be designed to try to win over a slightly hostile user. DTDs can fail if they confuse their readers, especially by being too big, and by not using expected terminology.

Quirks and foibles

◆ Sometimes DTDs fail because there was too much attention to the application's quirks and foibles, especially when homegrown tools are used. For example, I know a firm who never used attributes in their document type declarations—handling attributes with their tools required some programming while elements could be handled by just filling out table-forms. They could not make use of any of the capability of SGML to guarantee unique identifiers; they could only validate that kind of thing at the final application, not at text-entry time.

Unavailable expertise

◆ If the project involves conversion of legacy text, you need SGML expertise on tap for day-to-day contingencies, especially in the initial deployment.

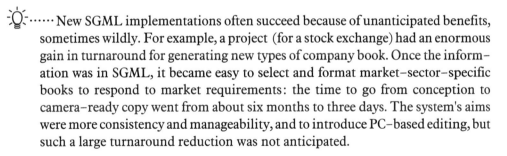 New SGML implementations often succeed because of unanticipated benefits, sometimes wildly. For example, a project (for a stock exchange) had an enormous gain in turnaround for generating new types of company book. Once the information was in SGML, it became easy to select and format market–sector–specific books to respond to market requirements: the time to go from conception to camera–ready copy went from about six months to three days. The system's aims were more consistency and manageability, and to introduce PC–based editing, but such a large turnaround reduction was not anticipated.

SGML implementations that are in trouble can often be turned around when the right mix of expertise, attitude and technology are applied. If your DTD and the prototype project have failed, and you are not sure why, take it to some consultants with a proven track record in the area. Indeed, there are even companies that specialize in salvaging stalled or botched SGML implementations.

Summary of Chapter 5

The SGML markup declarations alone do not specify everything that is needed for a complete document type definition.

If you are serious about processing SGML, you need good tools and good skills in them for storage management (database or file system), text management (editors), and structure (SGML-aware text languages). And you need a good validator to make sure that any document has all three in correct order.

The tools and skills you can apply to a document system directly determine how adventurous your DTD can be: an unadventurous DTD which sticks closely to the needs of your presentation system will probably be unproductive – the value of your information is left unmineable.

ALONSO
This is as strange a maze as e'er men trod,
And there is in this business more than nature
Was ever conduct of. Some oracle
Must rectify our knowledge.
PROSPERO Sir, my liege,
Do not infest your mind with beating on
The strangeness of this business.

William Shakespeare, The Tempest, Act 5, Scene 1.

Design

Principles

The first question you should ask is: *Is this a structure in entities, in elements, or in processing instructions?* Similarly, when you want to give an attribute to something you should ask *Does this attribute belong to an entity, an element or a process?*

Then consider the following principles—

Model the Real Information
Presentation is a good servant, but a poor master.

Expose your Valuables
If it is not marked up, maybe your computer cannot find it.

Ignore Constraints at your Peril
"My surprise in SGML after all these years is the insistence by some that authors should be not be constrained by even the simplest disciplines of programmers."[1]

---

1. Len Bullard, of Oxford University and TEI, (who rejoices in the appellation the gadfly of SGML), *private correspondence.*

Present Information in the most Direct and Simple Way
Use all the tools available in the SGML toolbox for their intended purpose.

Don't Reinvent the Wheel
If there is a standard or common DTD or architectural form or convention, try it first.

Identifiers should be simple and clear
If humans can read your SGML, it can make debugging easier.

One size should not fit all, or you cannot fit a square peg in a round hole
Do not try to stretch a DTD to fit text it cannot describe.

The more something is repeated, the more it should be a flyweight.
Put repeated and important text in an entity declaration or use element references (*reflection*). The term flyweight comes from the Pattern movement in object-oriented programming languages: refer [*Gamma*].

The more complex the document, the more strong typing is useful.

Things should be declared before they are used
SGML can be parsed in a stream, and for very large documents this is sometimes the most efficient way to process the documents.

Do talk to strangers
Documents going outside need more documentation than documents that stay in-house.

Garbage Markup, Garbage Documents

Simplicity for Big Things; Directness for Small Things

Every thing (that is a thing and not merely a part) should be able to have a label
If it is individually important label it with a name (e.g., an ID attribute). If it is generally important label it with a type label (e.g., a NOTATION attribute).

Part 2

Document
Patterns

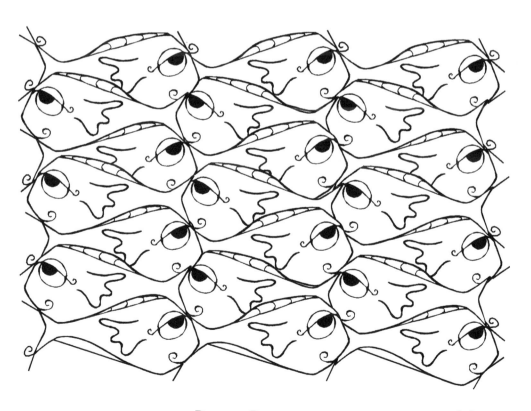

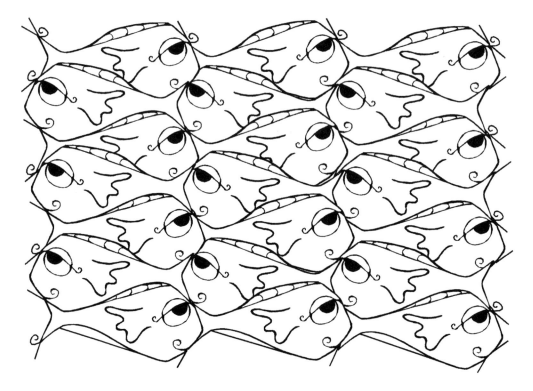

The XML *&* SGML Cookbook

Common Attributes
Chapter 6

This chapter

…will help you to quickly add the most common attributes.

et us start by cheating! A lot of the most common attributes of elements are really no-brainers. If you want to get a DTD up and going fast, just add all these attribute definitions to all the attribute definitions. ①

```
<!ATTLIST xxxx
    %common_SGML_attributes;
    %common_HTML_attributes;
    %common_XLL_attributes;
    %common_TEI_attributes;
>
```

As you then use and develop your DTD, you can cut out the definitions you do not need or which do not make sense, and add more specific ones. Chapter 3, page 1-47, gives several more formal methodologies for developing DTDs that are more appropriate for serious DTDs. Some valuable, but more complicated, attributes can be found on page 2-8 below, *SGML Extended Facilities*.

---

1. If you need reminding, the% is the opening delimiter of a reference to a "parameter entity". In a document instance, you use **&xxx;** to refer to a general entity; in markup you use **%xxx;** to refer to a special kind of entity that can be used to group and simplify parameters. The namespace for parameter entities is separate from general entities, so "**&xxx;**" is not the same text as "**%xxx;**".

SGML

Vanilla [*SGML*], with its companion standard [*HyTime*] Annex A SGML Extended Facilities, provide us with a good place to start locating common attributes.

Here are common generic attributes using SGML names:

```
<!ENTITY % common_SGML_attributes
'id       ID       #IMPLIED -- short, unique name for this element type --
 etfullnm CDATA    #IMPLIED -- full, unique name for this element type —
                            -- Use #FIXED --
 refid    IDREF    #IMPLIED -- points to another element --
 refids   IDREFS   #IMPLIED -- points to lists of other elements --
 entity   ENTITY   #IMPLIED -- points to an entity --
 notation NMTOKEN  #IMPLIED -- names a notation --
'>
```

For standard attributes smu, gn and gd for measurements of time and space, see *Data Content Notations* in chapter 14, page 2-83.

HTML & XML

[*ISO HTML*] has some standard generic attributes for internationalization and to help formatting:

```
<!ENTITY % common_HTML_attributes
' lang  NMTOKEN   #IMPLIED     -- RFC 1766 language code --
                               -- If you are using XML, then XML:lang -
_
  dir   (ltr|rtl) #IMPLIED     -- text direction --
  alt   CDATA     #IMPLIED     -- alternative text --
  class NMTOKENS  #IMPLIED     -- list of GIs from source, for style --
  align ( left | center | centre | right | justify )
                  #IMPLIED     -- alignment --
```

```
'>
```

The `class` attribute can be used when converting legacy text into your DTD; you can use it to list the GI and context GIs of the original DTD. For example,

```
<p class='paragraph table row entry paragraph'>...</p>
```

might indicate that this p element was originally part of a table nested inside a paragraph. The HTML attribute `class` should not be confused with the attribute `type` (as used in [*TEI*] documents, for example), which is used to provide finer detail on the meaning of the element type name(GI).

XLL

The Extensible Linking Language [*XLL*] has generic attributes you can use for linking elements:[1]

```
<!ENTITY % common_XLL_attributes
' href      CDATA       #IMPLIED -- URL or XML link       --
  title     CDATA       #IMPLIED -- nickname of link      --
  role      CDATA       #IMPLIED -- role of link          --
  behavior  CDATA       #IMPLIED -- for application        --
  show      (new|replace|embed) "replace"
  actuate   (user|auto)         "user"
_ xml:attribute CDATA  #IMPLIED -- Remap "href" to use some other name -
'>
```

You can flag to your application that the attributes are the XLL attributes (i.e., that you are using the XLL element type set as an architectural form) by using a fixed CDATA attribute `XML-LINK` that takes one of several values, typically `SIMPLE`. I.e.,

---

1. XLL was still in draft stage at this writing.

```
xml-link CDATA #FIXED 'SIMPLE'
```

The XML attributes are treated later in this part, in *Interactive Systems*, chapter 12, page 2-69.

TEI

The [*TEI*]-based TEIlite DTD has some good generic attributes:

```
<!ENTITY  % common_TEI_attributes
' ana     IDREFS #IMPLIED  -- points to aliases (also known as) --
  corresp IDREFS #IMPLIED  -- points to corresponding element --
  next    IDREF  #IMPLIED  -- points to next in series --
  prev    IDREF  #IMPLIED  -- points to previous in series --
  n       CDATA  #IMPLIED  -- sequence number --
  rend    CDATA  #IMPLIED  -- presentation information --
  type    CDATA  #IMPLIED  -- subtype of the element type -- '>
```

You can flag to your application that the attributes are the TEI attributes (i.e., that you are using the TEI element as your architectural form) by using a fixed CDATA attribute **TEIform** that takes the value of an GI defined in a TEI-compliant DTD, like TEIlite. I.e.,

```
TEIform CDATA #FIXED 'XXX' -- the corresponding TEI element --
```

Other attributes defined in TEI that you can use include—

```
<!ENTITY % less_common_TEI_attributes
' default   (YES | NO) "NO"
  scheme    IDREF      #IMPLIED
  function  CDATA      #IMPLIED  -- role in context --
  value     CDATA      #REQUIRED -- computer-friendly value  --
```

```
subtype    CDATA      #IMPLIED  -- subtype of the type attribute --' >
```

······Note that TEIlite also has some attributes which you may have to look at more closely: the TEIlite attribute `lang` is `idrefs` and not CDATA, for example, and the TEIlite attribute `notation` is CDATA.

SGML Extended Facilities

SGML's attribute mechanism is very straight-forward, but has a couple of limitations. The SGML Extended Facilities annex to ISO/IEC 10744:1997,[1] 2nd Ed. [HyTime '97] provides some interesting patterns to increase the power of SGML. These are called the General Architecture facilities and aim to fill in some gaps of ISO 8879.[2]

Default Value Lists

The first extended facility deals with attribute defaulting: how can you specify in your document instance default values for attributes?

The SGML Extended Facilities answer is called the *default value list*—

```
<!ELEMENT dvlist (#PCDATA) -- attribute specifications -->
<!ATTLIST dvlist
id      ID       #REQUIRED -- everything needs ids! --
preatts NMTOKENS #IMPLIED  -- preempt these attributes --
defatts NMTOKENS #IMPLIED  -- default these attributes --
dvgi    CDATA    #IMPLIED  -- list: GIs of elements with the
                              attributes-->
```

---

1. For full details, refer to the HyTime standard.

2. Lexical typing, another thing provided by the SGML Extended Facilities annex, is dealt with in chapter 16, *Embedded Notations,* on page 2-109.

For example, the instance—

```
<dvlist id='atts1' dvgi='#ALL hr' defatts='size'>size='4pt'</dvlist>
```

sets the default value used for any unspecified `size` attributes on any `hr` elements to '4pt'. The following instance overrides (preempts) any specified values too:

```
<dvlist id='atts1' dvgi='#ALL hr' preatts='size'>size='4pt'</dvlist>
```

so that all `hr` elements have a `size` attribute with the value `'4pt'`.①

Data Attributes for Elements

The second facility we will look at allows data attributes for elements (DAFE, [*HyTime*] A.5.3). Note: [*XML*] 1.0 does not support data attributes.

When an entity is declared, you can also specify a notation for it: this documents the format of the entity and lets an application select the appropriate handler for that entity. Each notation can have an appropriate list of attributes definitions for it. Entities declared with that notation can have these *data attributes* specified. With data attributes, you do not have to embed references to external resources in elements if you also need attributes. And you can separate attributes that belong to the resource itself (for example, the size of the bounding box of an image) from attributes that belong to the particular invocation of the resource (for example, how the image should be scaled in a particular place). In use, these data attributes look like this:

```
<!NOTATION   gif        SYSTEM>
<!ATTLIST    #NOTATION gif
```

---

1. The SGML Extended Facilities also define attributes `subdvl`, `subdvl` and `selfdvl` that allow individual elements to invoke default value lists by `idref`.

```
    size    number #REQUIRED >
<!ENTITY x SYSTEM 'x.gif' NDATA gif [ size='3' ]>
```

One shortcoming in ISO 8879:1986 is that element types can also have notation attributes (using NAME or NMTOKEN attributes), but SGML does not provide any way to allow data attributes on elements. [1]

The simplest form is merely to add a CDATA attribute NotNames with the value '#DEFAULT'. (The 'not' in NotNames is short for 'notation'.) For example:

```
<!NOTATION regex          SYSTEM   -- POSIX regular expression -->
<!ATTLIST  #NOTATION      regex    -- (Not available in XML 1.0 ) --
   case    (case|icase)  case    -- case sensitivity -->
<!ATTLIST string
   type     NAME          regex
   NotNames CDATA         '#DEFAULT'
   case     (case|icase)  case >
```

informs the application that the case attribute on the string element type is to be interpreted as if it were the data attribute case. The element string is now clearly marked-up as containing a case-insensitive regular expression:

---

1. Web SGML allows you to specify the type of attribute values using a similar mechanism: data attributes in attribute definitions. The attribute must have the type DATA. (Lexical Typing is dealt with in more detail in chapter 16, *Embedded Notations*, on page 2-115.) For example, in the following defines a type for a simple date attribute.

```
<!ATTLIST some-element
        date    DATA    regex
                        [ case="icase" model="[0-9]+-[0-9]+-[0-9]+"]
#IMPLIED >
```

```
<string>(abc)+</string>
```

Limiting the Target Element Types of IDREFs

The third facility we will look at lets you specify that a particular IDREF (or IDREFs) attribute should correspond to IDs of certain element types only. A predefined attribute `ireftype` is used.

Here is a simple example of IDREF type-limiting. This example specifies that the target of the current element type's IDREF attribute should correspond to an ID of an element with the GI figure.

```
<!ATTLIST   figure-pointer
     refid    IDREF  #REQUIRED
     ireftype CDATA  'figure'>
```

Common Data Attributes

The General Architecture specifies some common data attributes. Just as with the common attributes given above, these are suitable for cutting and pasting directly into attribute definition list (ATTLIST) declarations for any notations you are using. You can prune them later. If you are cautious and do not wish to over-burden your users, you may decide to just paste them into comments and uncomment them when and if needed.

```
<!ENTITY % common-SGML-data-attributes
'  included ENTITIES #IMPLIED -- entities included in this one --
   altreps  ENTITIES #IMPLIED -- alternative representations --
   supdcn   NMTOKEN  #IMPLIED -- notation on which this one is based --
'>
```

`included` is a list of entities that the entity itself includes. This allows your SGML document to list all the non-SGML files or text locations that indirectly are called into the document. For example, an entity with a notation that identifies the entity as a C program might nominate all the files included by the C preprocessor:

```
<!NOTATION C          PUBLIC 'ISO/IEC 9899:1990//NOTATION
                             Programming languages - C//EN'>
<!NOTATION java       PUBLIC '-//SUN//NOTATION
                             Programming languages - Java//EN'>
<!NOTATION Cminusminus PUBLIC '-//Simple Simon//NOTATION
                             Programming languages - C--//EN'>
<!ATTLIST #NOTATION ( C | java | Cminusminus )
    %common-SGML-data-attributes >
<!ENTITY stdio  SYSTEM 'stdio.h' NDATA C>
<!ENTITY hello  SYSTEM 'hello.c' NDATA C
    [ included='stdio' ]>
```

And the entity declaration for a Java version of the program can specify that the C version is an alternative representation. The system could use this alternative, if needed:

```
<!ENTITY j.hello   SYSTEM hello.jav NDATA java
    [ altreps='hello' ]>
```

Finally, the data attribute **supdcn** allows you to specify the *notation derivation source*. (Object-oriented programmers may think of this as the supertype of the notation.) For example, let us say we now have a language called C--, which is derived somehow from the C language; presumably it is a subset. We can then document all this with the following declaration:

```
<!ENTITY s.hello   SYSTEM 'hello.simp' NDATA C--
    [ supdcn='C' ]>
```

`supdcn` is therefore to non-SGML data what the Web SGML Additional Requirements parameter (SEEALSO) is to SGML text.

The Unspecified Attribute

Given a declaration like the following:

```
<!ATTLIST x
   y  CDATA #IMPLIED>
```

you need to set a policy about the difference in meaning between the following two elements:

```
<x y=''>
<x>
```

The former usually means "an empty string" or "no value," while the later usually means "system-determined". System-determined will often also mean either "no-value" or "inherited" – it is usually fairly clear from context which is appropriate. Whenever you have an IMPLIED attribute that is not one of those choices you should document it. And the very best way is to provide an explicit default value for attributes: that way everything is clear.

If your document is fully normalized – so that every attribute is explicitly marked-up in the start-tag – you should define some unique value to indicate that the attribute was originally not specified. For example:

```
<x y='**UNSPECIFIED**'>
```

Skim Milk Masquerades as Cream

It is a good convention that if your attribute has the same name as a built-in SGML type, do not use it for something else. Almost every important DTD ends up with plenty of ID attributes. So, rather than using—

```
id CDATA #REQUIRED   -- unique name for this element --
```

use—

```
id ID     #REQUIRED -- unique name for this element --
```

It is a good idea to design your system so that every important element type can have an ID attribute. Force your document generators to make more easily cross-referenceable documents by declaring the ID attributes on all the head elements of all information units (see chapter 3, page 1-51) to be #REQUIRED. Similarly, force your document to be more indexable by forcing all elements for keywords, names and addresses to have required id attributes. And when processing document sets which have a frequent but not universal markup error, you can key the remedy to the elements' IDs.

Architectural Forms

I mentioned the subject of architectural forms early (see chapter 2, *Underlying Forms*, in *The Nature of Markup*, page 1-40) because it is an important technique. The basic technique is for you to define a separate DTD (the meta-DTD) that all your applications will use. For example, you might define ISO HTML to be the meta DTD you are using. Now you can go ahead and make up your custom DTDs, which can be as specific as you like: the trick is that you include in the declarations in your custom DTD some attribute definitions to map your elements in the instance to the element forms in the meta-DTD.

For example,

```
<!ELEMENT dog                        ( breed, characteristics)>
<!ELEMENT ( breed | characteristics ) ( %text; )>
```

```
<!ATTLIST dog
        HTMLform CDATA "DL">
<!ATTLIST breed
        HTMLform CDATA "DT">
<!ATTLIST characteristics
        HTMLform CDATA "DD">
```

marks up the document to note that the **dog** element has the same structure as the HTML definition list: **dog** is a more specialized form of the same structure. An ordinary SGML processor will accept instances of **dog** at face value and perform the normal application processing. However, an SGML system with an "architecture parser" can read it as HTML directly. The saving is that you can make many different document types but use the same software to process the various instances.

The SGML Extended Facilities in ISO/IEC 10744 Annex A. 3 Architectural Form Definition Requirements (AFDR) puts together well-thought-out requirements for architectural forms. It lets you map attribute names and notation names as well as generic identifiers.

If you decide to use architectural forms, this can be an additional constraint on your DTD. You may decide to limit yourself strictly to structures that directly correspond to structures in the meta-DTD, to make architectural parsing trivial. You may decide that all your tabular data will only use the simple structure of HTML tables, for example.

If you go down this simple path, then it is worthwhile studying the AFDR. Among other things, it provides a means of suppressing the association of an element form: not every element type of your document may be interesting for each architectural DTD.

Your architecture may decide to allow pseudo-markup in some architectural attribute values: this is the route that [*ICADD*] has taken. (See chapter 16, page 2-109 for more examples of pseudo-SGML markup.) To continue our example we might also allow an attribute called **HTMLprefix** which can contain things like run-in headings.

```
<!ELEMENT dog                               ( breed, characteristics)>
<!ELEMENT ( breed | characteristics )  ( %text; );
<!ATTLIST dog
        HTMLform    CDATA "DL">
```

```
<!ATTLIST breed
        HTMLform    CDATA "DT"
        HTMLprefix CDATA "<I>Breed:<I>">
<!ATTLIST characteristics
        HTMLform    CDATA "DD"
        HTMLprefix CDATA "<I>Nature:</I>" >
```

······ How far you go with pseudo-markup in designing your own architectural forms depends largely on how custom your system needs to be.

• The simplest is simply to have a one-to-one correspondence between your meta-DTD and your document DTD's structures. The AFDR provides "control attributes" for managing the relationship, including a suppression function.

• If that is not enough, utilize additional Architectural Form Definition Requirements facilities, including attribute forms and notation forms. Use of a standard maximizes the likelihood that off-the-shelf SGML and HyTime systems will be able to process your documents.

The DTDs you should investigate for use as meta-DTDs are: [HTML], [Docbook], [TEIlite], and the various [CALS] and ISO DTDs.

The Document Shell

Chapter 7

This chapter

…helps you understand that the high-level structure of documents is a pattern that recurs for information units.

D ocuments are naturally made up of three parts:

- the data belonging to the subject;

- annotations to the subject; and

- various resources needed to use and manage the document: this is customarily called **metadata**.

```
<!-- Top level form of a natural document  -->
<!ELEMENT   natural      ( metadata, data, annotations)>
```

The metadata and annotations of the document can be

- bundled as elements with the data , so the document is **self–describing**, as above,

- given as part of the **reference**, for example using SGML notations and data attributes to augment an entity declaration, or

- external to SGML as part of the **application**'s function, for example using file extensions to encode metadata.

Just as attributes allow simpler content models and more generic identification of an element's type (hence the name *generic identifier*), so metadata elements simplify the element type set for the body element types. The usefulness of separating metadata from data can be seen, in the Java Database Connect [JDBC] `java.sql.DatabaseMetaData` and `java.sql.ResultSetMetaData` interfaces, for example. Not only is it useful to be able to mark up attributes of individual elements within a document, it is also useful to be able to mark up attributes relating to the document as a whole.

HTML

HTML began as a very small DTD, and it still is, especially in subsets such as ISO HTML which are designed to avoid the gilded gogo-cage of unmanageable proprietary extensions.

HTML was created for small, freely-structured pages, and simple reports: small documents linked together as a hypertext web. But we can see that even a modest, but serious, DTD like HTML has evolved quite a few elements to cope with the administration and document control issues: **metadata**. And annotations are taken as so important to HTML that they have been promoted to equal rank with the body: every document can use any other document as an annotation.

The following is a fragment of a rather strict HTML 3-2 -conforming DTD:

```
<!-- Top element types for a kind of HTML 3-2 -->
<!ELEMENT      html       ( head?, body)>
<!ELEMENT      head
       ( title, isindex?, meta*, base?, link*, style*, script*)>
<!ELEMENT      body       ( %body-content; )*>
```

HTML documents can be cleanly partitioned into two parts: a head and a body. The body contains the data that will be directly presented to the browser of the document in the main document windows; the head is where everything else goes.

Information Units

The body of a document may be further divided into other information units. ①
HTML frames are an example of this.

```
<!-- Top element types for a kind of HTML 3-2 with frames -->
<!ELEMENT      html      ( head?, ( body | frameset), plaintext)>
<!ELEMENT      head
        ( title, isindex?, meta*, base?, link*, style*, script*)>
<!ELEMENT      body      ( %body-content; )*>
<!ELEMENT      frameset  ( %body-content; )*>
<!ELEMENT      frame     EMPTY>
<!ATTLIST      frame
          src             CDATA #IMPLIED >
<!ELEMENT      plaintext ( %literal; )>
```

Information units are themselves natural documents, which will in turn be structured with a head for metadata, a body, and annotations. In the case of HTML
framesets, which allow you to switch between information units using GUI tabs,
the information units are each complete external HTML documents. This
extreme simplicity of HTML implements – but perhaps hides the fact from view
somewhat – that information units should have the features of full documents.
Conversely, the presence of a content model which boils down to (head,
body, tail?) or (metadata, data, annotations?) or (front
matter, text, backmatter?) is a good indicator that the element should
be considered an information unit.

In general, each type of specific medium or each DTD that the text passes
through on its journey to the end-user can be considered a natural document.
Each may require its own specific head, annotations and metadata structures.

For example, a DTD for a book will consist of a core of element type declarations
for the chapters that make up the body of the book, and declarations for the
element types in the head: in particular, frontmatter such as the table of contents,
the data for the title page of the book and the publishing details. If the text of
this book document is itself sent over an electronic medium, it will need another
head containing data about the electronic form of the text: encodings and locations and conversion histories. In the case of the WWW, some of this information
will be sent in the MIME headers.

---

1. See chapter 3 *Software Engineering*, page 1-51.

```
<!--  Top level form of documents with subdocument  -->
<!ELEMENT document-container (metadata, contained-document, annotat-
ions)>
<!ELEMENT contained-document (metadata, data, annotations)>
```

The News Industry Text Format DTD, which is used for newswiring stories to newspapers, is a highly augmented version of HTML, and has the following upper-level structure:

```
<!-- Top element types for a kind of NITF -->
<!ELEMENT      nitf      ( head, body)>
<!ELEMENT      head
      ( (%head.html;), ( %head.docdata;), (head.links)?)>
<!ELEMENT      body
      (( %body.head;)?, ( %body.content;)*, ( %body.end;) )>
```

Apart from the usual HTML-inspired head element types, the element type head also has elements for containing or pointing to headers of older format data allowing a measure of backwards inter-convertibility. This is what the parameter entity head.docdata provides.

Inside the body, we can see a further division into a head (the parameter entity body.head) and body (the parameter entities body.content and body.end.) This head contains element types for headline, copyright, notes, bylines and a dateline. These are a kind of metadata about the story in the body of the body

The [TEIlite] DTD has a very clear example of these: the division elements body, div, div0 .. div7 all have versions of this three part structure—

```
<!ELEMENT div6 (
      (argument | byline | docAuthor | docDate |
            epigraph | head | opener | salute | signed)*,
      ((div7
            | divGen)+
            | ( bibl | biblFull | l | lg | p | sp | cit
                  | q | label | list | listBibl | note | stage)+,
      (div7 | divGen)* ),
      (byline | closer | epigraph | salute | signed | trailer)*
) >
```

This kind of nested structure, where information units in a document are themselves natural documents, can be represented either:

• **directly**, by a hierarchy of elements, for example NITF or TEIlite;

• **loosely**, by making each thing and its subthings into separate SGML documents, and linking them with in-line locators, for example HTML URLs

• **tightly**, by using the SGML SUBDOC feature, which provides the modularity of the HTML web approach but, because it is built on declaring entities, lets you exactly specify notations and data attributes for the subdocuments;

• **indirectly**, by putting the metadata for each information unit into a separate SGML document. This is the preferred method when, for example, a document has to travel through many stages, and each stage includes a completion checklist as part of the metadata that will not be of interest to a subsequent stage.

The Advantages of a Simple Head

SGML documents are often used for multiple purposes, often in larger organizations and for larger projects. Consequently, the metadata and other head information required or provided for in SGML DTDs can be quite large: in some cases the element type sets for the head can be as large as for the body. XML metadata, designed for the smaller kinds of documents pushed and pulled over the World Wide Web, will probably not be so complex. ①

 ······ Head information is usually difficult to understand by just reading the generic identifiers of the element types. A new user of the DTD will often try to make a small instance to familiarize themselves with the DTD. In a similar way to how computer languages and GUI programming interfaces are judged by how many lines it takes to print out "hello world", new users usually will be frustrated

---

1. Though each medium has unique metadata requirements. World Wide Web documents may have metadata to establish ratings for parental control, for example. Refer to [*PICS*] for more.

and antagonistic if they must wade through a dozen or so obtuse required administrative elements before they get near to entering the body matter of the document.

Fixes for this problem include—

☑ making a special "training-wheels" version of the DTD with a simplified head section;

☑ requiring an explicit head section and a body section, so that the user is not confused about the status or the intended function of the elements; organize the DTD declarations to make it clear which declarations belong to the head and which to the body;

☑ in the head section, making only the title a required element;

☑ apart from the title, removing all the metadata into a separate, external subdocument with its own DTD – if you have confidence that your entity management system (or your human procedures) will not lose parts.

Note that metadata removed to a separate external document or entity is also an information unit, and may need its own metadata and annotations sections.

Paragraphs

Chapter 8

This chapter

...helps you understand paragraphs: the most fundamental editorial-structure.

Paragraphs group together sentences that have a running theme, and separate sentences where there is some change in theme.

In our six-view model of structures, generic paragraphs are editorial-structure element types. They relate to how information is signaled and written, rather than describing the contents. They are usually the structure above embedded-list and sentence structures.

As well as the generic simple paragraph, there are an unlimited number of specific paragraph element types: quotes, notes, warnings. However, the same issues of structure apply.

Paragraphs versus Text Blocks

Given that the paragraph is such a basic unit, you might expect representation of paragraphs to be simple. And generally it is. The big complication is that people have different conceptions of *"paragraph"* from the one I gave above. The confusion, at least in terminology, is most easily seen with paragraphs containing lists, which paragraphs often do.

When a paragraph is split into two by a contained list, many people insist that the sandwiching **text blocks** are both paragraphs. They see the paragraph as a layout-structure element type, not a editorial-structure element type.

Those who want to represent the editorial-structure will use an element type declaration which allows embedded lists, like the following:

```
<!-- Language-structure conception of paragraph -->
<!ELEMENT      %general;      (p)* >
<!ELEMENT      p             ( %text; | %list; )* >
```

Those who want to represent the layout-structure will use an element type declaration in which lists cannot be embedded, like the following:

```
<!-- Layout-structure conception of paragraph -->
<!ELEMENT      %general;      ( para | %list; )* >
<!ELEMENT      para          ( %text; )* >
```

The problem with this second approach is that there is then not enough information to indicate when the editorial-structure paragraph begins or ends, or for proper indentation. In such a case, element type declarations for **paragraph continuations** (i.e., a second kind of text block, often with different presentation
characteristics) have to be created:

```
<!-- Linear form of simple paragraph with paragraph continuation -->
<!ELEMENT      %general;                (para, ( %list; , para-cont? )? )*
>
<!ELEMENT      ( para-cont | para )   ( %text; )*>
```

To me, paragraph continuations element types are a poor pattern. However that
is not to say that they do not mark up the underlying structure of interest in a
way that is not useful. A better element type set for marking up the same kinds
of patterns is the following:

```
<!-- Nested form of simple paragraph -->
<!ELEMENT      %general;         ( p )* >
<!ELEMENT      p                ( block | %list; )* >
<!ELEMENT      block            ( %text; )* >
```

This model has the advantage of clearly delimiting the end of each paragraph.
You can simply attach any attributes which belong to the whole paragraph to the
parent "p" element type. In the linear form previous (i.e., the one using paragraph continuations), such attributes must be attached to the "para" element,
which complicates processing requirements. If the information given in the attribute is needed during processing or using a "para-cont", the processing
language must be able to navigate back to the last found element "para" at the
same level to look – looking at the parent is simpler to specify and program.

This issue is also found in lists: when a list item contains multiple paragraphs,
some document analysts will make an element type declaration for **list-item
continuations**. In fact, we can use the same examples, but just rename the generic
identifiers:

```
<!-- Linear form of simple list -->
<!ELEMENT      list              ( li, ( list, li-cont? )? )* >
<!ELEMENT      ( li-cont | li )  ( %text; )* >
```

The underlying design issues are whether editorial-structure or layout-structure should have primacy, and whether the element type set should be linear or hier-archical.

```
<!-- Nested form of simple list -->
<!ELEMENT    list            ( li )* >
<!ELEMENT    li              ( p | list )* >
<!ELEMENT    p               ( %text; )* >
```

Avid readers of DTDs will see that this HTML uses the nested form of the simple list, and the editorial-structure conception of a paragraph, which reflects good practice.

Element type declarations for paragraph and list continuations are often indicat-ions that the DTD was written with the pragmatic idiosyncrasies of particular software in mind: in particular, software that cannot tell if an element (e.g., the element "block" above) is first in its parent. If your custom software forces you to use element type declarations for continuations you may find it easier to simply add the parent-context lookup routines to your software rather than fore-go the advantages of hierarchical markup.

One of the themes of this book is that the consideration of such pragmatic issues is vital to the success of any project. It is not only proud, but imprudent to criticize strange-looking element type sets if you cannot ask the document archi-tect why they chose a design.

In our particular case, even though there are many reasons to prefer the nested form of paragraph, reasonably simple processing software can convert between the nested and the linear forms without much difficulty: the same information is present implicitly in both. So which to prefer should not be the cause of great agonizing or dogmatism: these can be reserved for cases where different forms are not inter-convertable.

Paragraphs versus Paragraph Groups

We can safely predict that since the term paragraph is also sometimes used to mean something less than the editorial-structure paragraph, someone somewhere will also be using it to mean something greater than a editorial-structure paragraph.

A notable case is found in the very successful 5629A DTD used for military CALS projects in Australia. The Australian military editorial rule is that every paragraph must have a number. This is a commonly-made rule for reference material with life-critical or legal importance.

However, for many readers, long paragraphs are difficult to follow and sometimes are better if broken up, even when there is not an absolute break in topic. To give numbers to such paragraphs that are really artifacts of ergonomic concerns rather than topical coherence is misleading—the paragraphs have a strong cohesion and should be grouped together. These conflicting needs can reconciled by a sleight of hand in naming, using an element type set like the following:

```
<!-- Simple paragraph group -->
<!ELEMENT    para0       ( para+ ) >
<!ELEMENT    para        ( %text; )* >
```

This is quite unusual, but is very flexible. In particular it allows quibbles over the definition of a paragraph to be sidestepped: people must say "*a para0 paragraph*" or "*a para paragraph*" in order to distinguish what they mean. More importantly, it allows much more complicated types of paragraph groups to be constructed. We will take up this topic[1] again in *Paragraph Groups* below.

---

1. Thanks to Peter Pacers of Allette Systems for his detailed discussions of the issues of paragraph grouping dealt with in the 5629A DTDs.

Paragraph Contents

Very often, the content model of the element type declaration for a paragraph will be a few parameter entity references to running text, graphics, the major types of semi-graphical text, and various specialized nested paragraphs, notably the block quotation and the poetic stanza.

```
<!ELEMENT ( p | bq )  ( %in-line-text; | %graphics; | %tables; |
                        %lists; | %equations; | %nested-paragraphs; )*
>
```

When you are first browsing a new DTD, the content model in the element type declaration for paragraphs can be a good place to start – you can usually quickly see whether there are any exotic element types, for example, *reflections*.

Paragraphs Nested Inside Paragraphs

It is rare that the content model of the element type declaration for a DTD's general paragraph will directly allow other immediately nested general paragraphs: this would reduce the usefulness of omit-tag minimization and make processing more difficult. Often a nested paragraph inside a paragraph is better modeled as an unmarked list item.

However, there are several types of **display paragraphs** which can nest directly. To prevent confusion with general paragraphs these are often given unique generic identifiers rather than, for example, an attribute indicating type—

- The **block quote** is the most common. It is often set in italic and indented. The most common generic identifiers are BLOCKQUOTE or BQ. The most common generic identifier for in-line quotations is Q.

- The **stanza** in poetry. Stanzas usually contain lines or couplets, which may be elements or just implicitly represented using a line-break element like BR.

- Computer **source code**. A ruler and tab system (see chapter 22, page 3-101) is the most simple way to typeset this kind of code. Computer source code is very commonly typeset with a mono-space font which tames the various evils that make tabs so inappropriate and clumsy with proportional-width fonts. Many programming systems include pretty printers that can indent computer source code automatically. It may well be worthwhile integrating these into the typesetting process instead of explicitly marking up the source code.

• **Footnotes, endnotes, marginalia,** or popup notes: these are often entered in-line as paragraphs inside paragraphs, but are not rendered as such. Actually, these type of notes get rendered in almost any position in different typographical traditions, including the tops of pages.

• The Japanese **in–line paragraph,** the *warichu*, is the most direct form of a nested paragraph. It is a note that is typeset in parentheses in-line, but at half the type size in doubled lines. There is no native Western equivalent of this.

• The **bullet point** is a type of paragraph preceded by a typographical device, typically a bullet •, to call out the character of the paragraph. In the West, bullet points are usually handled as bullet lists, since bullet points are rarely found alone. Other typographical marks tend to be used for paragraphs that are single points: for example, the warning icon and the tip icon in this book. In certain traditions and designs, in-line bullet points of various kinds are common – topical reference works often use condensed, in-line icons rather than full explanatory text. For example, a document instance like this:

```
<place>
<name>Coffs Harbour</name>
<p class=climate>Subtropical, but not too steamy.
The area is protected by mountains from
frost, and is kept cool by sea breezes. </p>
<p class=fruit>The banana industry is waning, due to imports
of genetically altered, cosmetically more attractive,
but blander fruit. <p></place>
```

may be rendered as:

Coffs Harbour: Subtropical, but not too steamy. The area is protected by mountains from frost, and is kept cool by sea breezes. ☞The banana industry is waning, due to imports of genetically altered, cosmetically more attractive, but blander fruit.

In this example, the element type `place` is typeset as one text block, despite being marked up as several different paragraphs.

Subparagraphs

A general principle is that *"Everything that is generically important should have a type label."* The generic identifier (i.e., the name of the element type) is often used as the fundamental type label, but you can also use SGML attributes for any kind of subtyping, inheritance-specification, schema-association and multiple type-specification that you require.

Some kinds of documents allow or require subparagraphs. These are not paragraphs nested inside other paragraphs, but rather material that is perhaps too brief to warrant a formal subsection (with the heading that subsections usually have) and not digressionary enough to be diverted into a footnote. A subheading might interrupt the flow of the text, and some readers might incorrectly infer from the presence of a subsection that the main treatment of a topic had finished. [1]

A simple element type set for subparagraphs is:

```
<!-- Simple subparagraph -->
<!ELEMENT section
            ( heading, ( para0, ( para1, ( para2, para3* )* )* )* ) >
<!ELEMENT ( para0 | para1 | para2 | para3 )
            ( %text; | %list; )* >
```

This model is good for simple content models, but becomes somewhat unwieldy when other types of display text are added which belong to the subparagraphs, and which may need to be formatted to reveal this.

---

1. Let me immediately contradict myself by pointing out that the 5629A DTD even has element types for titles and subtitles in the content model for subparagraph groups. So, what people may call a paragraph may vary from a simple container to an elaborate element type set resembling a list or a subsection. In English at least, the word "paragraph" is almost as plastic as the words "table" and "list". The prudent document system designer will find out what the trade usage of these terms is for the particular users of the DTD, and include these discoveries in the DTD documentation.

```
<!-- Unwieldy subparagraphs -->
&!lt;!ENTITY % para0-stuff
        '(para0, ( %list; | %table; | %graphic; | %equation; )* )'>
&!lt;!ENTITY % para1-stuff
        '(para1, ( %list; | %table; | %graphic; | %equation; )* )'>
&!lt;!ENTITY % para2-stuff
        '(para2, ( %list; | %table; | %graphic; | %equation; )* )'>
&!lt;!ENTITY % para3-stuff
        '(para3, ( %list; | %table; | %graphic; | %equation; )* )'>
<!ELEMENT section
        ( heading, ( %para0-stuff;, ( %para1-stuff;,
                        ( %para2-stuff;, %para3-stuff;* )* )* )* ) >
<!ELEMENT ( para0 | para1 | para2 | para3 )
        ( %text; | %list; )* >
```

The difficulty with this content model is that processing software must determine the most recent element para*n* to figure out how to indent lists, graphics, etc.

A better approach is to house subparagraphs in elements that look like heading-less sections:

```
<!-- Rich subparagraphs -->
<!ELEMENT section
    ( heading, para0,
            ( %list; | %table; | %graphic; | %equation; | para0 )* )
>
<!ELEMENT para0
    ( p, ( p | %list; | %table; | %graphic; | %equation; | para1 )* ) >
<!ELEMENT para1
    ( p, ( p | %list; | %table; | %graphic; | %equation; | para2 )* ) >
<!ELEMENT para2
    ( p, ( p | %list; | %table; | %graphic; | %equation; | para3 )* ) >
<!ELEMENT para3
    ( p, ( p | %list; | %table; | %graphic; | %equation; )* ) >
<!ELEMENT p
    ( %text; | %list; )* >
```

⚠ ······ Subparagraphs are often used when house style only allows a certain fixed depth of subsections but the material requires more. When subparagraphs are used in conjunction with markup to simulate headings, there is clearly some conflict between the house–style and the needs of the document. It may be prudent to include an extra level of subsections and subparagraphs than house–style allows, merely to provide a place to park out–of–spec text. The Markup Policy Document should note this.

💡 ······ As a matter of convention, it is a good idea if the generic identifier **p** is only used for paragraph types with simple content models like that of HTML. If your paragraph's content model is structured more tightly than HTML's paragraph content-model, and has required or optional elements allowed at certain points only, or includes another element that actually contains the text, it will be less confusing for new HTML-grounded users of the DTD if some variant of **para** is used.

ID Attributes

A general principle is that *"Everything that is specifically important should have a name."* Within a text, for example, sections and chapters are given titles. Military documents and legislative documents generally have numbers for every single page object: every paragraph, every list item, every graphic, etc.

In SGML markup, an element is named by giving it an ID attribute. IDs are unique within each valid document. The element can then be referred to from other elements using an IDREF attribute to create structures more complex than the simple tree structure of SGML. There is no need for IDs to be particularly convenient for humans, to be in sequence or to be readable, if you use SGML-aware editors only and the IDs are hidden from the user. If you use plain-text editors though, it is helpful if IDs are mnemonic.

HTML uses the attribute called **name** on the general-purpose hyperlinking element-type **a** to identify sections of text. However it is a CDATA attribute and thus not guaranteed to be unique within a validated document—the short sizes of most HTML documents makes this a workable approach. That this way is not practical for large collections of documents is evidenced by the number of HTML validation programs. (Note: XML supports ID attributes.)

Development of the Paragraph

The paragraph has changed display form over the years, running almost the whole gamut of possibilities—

- It began as a **floating glyph**, a short horizontal bar inserted following a line in which a change of topic had occurred. Paragraphs were run into each other at this time.

- A version of the capital letter Pi (from Greek *paragráphos*, refer [*Bringhurst*]) was adopted as an **anchored, in-line glyph**, with the paragraphs still run hard into each other. ①

- This rather charmless character, the pilcrow ¶, was often rubricated (i.e., printed in red), and it became the fashion to start a **new line** for each paragraph.

- Because of the cost of rubrication, often the pilcrow was omitted from printing: the result is the modern paragraph, with the first line **indented** by the gap left for the pilcrow. The paragraph at this stage can be considered a proper element, the unit containing the text, rather than just a marker signifying some change at a point.

- Recently the fashion has moved towards separating paragraphs with large exit leading and starting new paragraphs without indentation. Each paragraph is an ugly little **island**. ② Ever more bizarre and alarming graphics

---

1. Some alternatively claim the glyph is derived from a capital C (from Latin *capitulum*); refer to the short and eccentric essay *"The History of Punctuation"* in *"The Size of Thoughts"* [*Nicholson Baker*], which also mentions various Victorian composite punctuation such as the commash: ",—" now out of fashion or out of consciousness in English. I am not sure the two marks are the same: some glyphs used as a paragraph mark do look like a C, for example the verse marker of the Centaur font by Bruce Rogers, as used in his 1935 Oxford Lectern Bible, [*Rogers*] Illustration 54. ISO 10646([*Unicode*]) seems to treat the two as merely glyph differences, but does allow a glyph variant for the curved stem pilcrow at U+2761.

2. This seems entirely appropriate for modern technical books, which have little sustained argument between paragraphs and are designed for browsing and skimming, perhaps under the fragmenting influence of hypertext. These types of paragraphs are often set without an introductory indentation, which fogeyism decries as typographically poor because the reader cannot distinguish whether a paragraph has ended at the bottom of a page or continues.

are placed in the margins, to simulate readability, and to make pages more unique-looking and thus, perhaps, more memorable.

• This typographical insularization of paragraphs reaches its high point in the early hypercard systems of hypertext: the fixed card size made it impossible to fit more than a single medium-sized paragraph per card. This complicated production and maintenance in the absence of a rigorous markup technology like SGML.

I guess the thing that remains is paragraphs that intersect or that explode out of each other.

Paragraph Breaks

Our discussion of paragraphs so far has assumed that the paragraph is an element containing text. This is almost always true, but there is an alternative:

✓ a paragraph-break character or element can be used: ISO 10646 reserves a character with the unambiguous semantic of being a paragraph break; an empty element <PB> can be also used to mark paragraph breaks.

The paragraph break is only really advisable when the element structures to be marked up continually cross over paragraph borders, and where the paragraph is not a unit that will be manipulated to any significant extent in the document's life.

Novice users of HTML try to use the element P as if it were a paragraph break, with various effects on different browsers. Of course, since this is attempting procedural markup, it might be most appropriate to use a processing instruction, such as

```
<?Cookbook pagebreak?>                              <!-- ① --
```

---

1. The first token in the processing instruction is the target indicator. In this case, the targt is cookbook, to indicate that the PI is only meant when the document is being processed as a cookbook. Best practice is for the target to have been declared in a notation declaration, to mark up which notation processor is meant, for example
```
<!NOTATION cookbook SYSTEM "cookbook.pl" >
```

Forcing a paragraph break by using an empty element is usually bad practice because it means the content of the paragraph is not marked up—only one boundary is. A forced paragraph break is often actually a sign that some more complicated graphical formatting is being attempted, which is probably not a publication-level structure: this misuse is especially common in free-text in bureaucratic forms.

If you must use this approach, you may find it simplest to have a generic element type for breaks and give it an attribute for the particular kind.

```
<!-- Generic break element -->
<!ELEMENT break EMPTY>
<!ATTLIST break
        type  ( line | double-line | column | page | odd-page ) "line"
>
```

Paragraph Groups Revisited

In most cases, a simple element is all that is needed—

```
<!-- Simple paragraph -->
<!ELEMENT  p  ( %text; | %list; | %table; | %equation; | %note-refs; )*
>
```

But sometimes different types of paragraphs need to be tightly coupled. In a technical manual for dangerous repairs to equipment, very often a procedural paragraph may be accompanied by a topical warning paragraph, or a technical caution. It would be inappropriate to have markup like this:

```
<p><bold>Warning:</bold> Disarm the bomb before
hitting it with a mallet.</p>
<p>If the ticking continues, hit the bomb with a mallet.</p>
```

Otherwise there is a chance that a typesetting system could put a page break between them. The user of the manual might not bother to check the previous page. This is just as relevant to online manuals: the browser in use may take the user directly to the procedural paragraph, not the warning paragraph.

The **paragraph group** is the appropriate way to signify this coupling—

```
<!-- Paragraph Group -->
<!ELEMENT para0
    ( warning*, caution*, note*,
      p, ( p | %list; | %table; | %graphic; | para1 )*,
      footnote* ) >
<!ATTLIST para0
    number NMTOKEN #REQUIRED>
<!ELEMENT ( p | warning | caution | note | footnote)
    ( %text; | %list; | %equation; | %note-refs; )* >
```

The example can be marked up—

```
<para0>
<warning>Disarm the bomb before hitting it with a mallet.</warning>
<p>If the ticking continues, hit the bomb with a mallet.</p>
</para0>
```

This element type set is rather more complete than most of the element type sets we have dealt with so far. But it has many points of interest. It declares that an element `para0` can have a warning, a caution and a note. The element must have at least one element p, and may also have lists, tables, sub-paragraph groups, and perhaps several footnotes. The element types p, `warning`, `caution`, `note` and `footnote` all have the same content models: despite their names they are all kinds of paragraphs.

It is important to realize, though, that it is up to the *Markup Policy* (Additional Requirements, page 1-104) document (and whoever is using that document for training and quality control) to state explicitly whether the element type p is to be used for editorial-structures or for layout-structures. Because the same content model is shared by footnotes and so on, it would be more consistent for the element type p to mark up the editorial-structure.

Given this, an experienced document system designer will see that the element type set as given does not allow tables or graphics sandwiched inside a paragraph.

This is an editorial question of house-style and may indeed be what is needed, but it should be verified. ⓛ

⚠ ······ If editorial policy is that tables or graphics may not appear inside paragraphs, but the documents do in fact contain such tables or graphics, people will be forced to use the element type p as a paragraph continuation element (i.e., a text block) and so mark up layout-structure. This may complicate typesetting, forcing the introduction of special-case rules during text conversion, such as *"if an element p follows a table or graphic, treat it as a continuation text-block."* Special-case rules such as this are familiar to anyone who has had to typeset text from documents with poorly defined DTDs or with inconsistent markup. They rarely produce entirely satisfactory typeset results.

Why are the element types `warning`, `caution` and `note` at the start, and the footnotes at the end of the content model?—

- People resist the idea of putting footnotes before their references, because they prefer material to resemble paper, despite the computing advantages of defining things before they are used or referenced.

- Putting the footnotes at the end of the paragraph group allows drafts to be produced without much programming effort.

- The footnotes are a different kind of information from the warnings, cautions and notes. Grouping them together might inadvertently imply some kind of similarity in importance or use.

---

1. Without disrespect, in my experience editorial staff are rather too keen to claim they do not use various kinds of graphics, tables, lists, etc. inside paragraphs.

Sequences

Chapter 9

This chapter

...shows how to represent generic sequences in XML and SGML.

A fter the paragraph, the sequence of repeated structures is the most common structure found in documents. Sequences gravitate towards a common form:

```
<!-- generic sequence -->
<!ELEMENT sequence
          ( label, sequence-item+ ) >
<!ATTLIST sequence
          type              CDATA    #IMPLIED >
<!ELEMENT sequence-item
          ( item-label?, ( %sequence-contents; | sequence )* ) >
<!ATTLIST sequence-item
          sequence-number CDATA #IMPLIED >
<!ELEMENT (label | item-label)
          ( %text; )* >
```

Of course, very rarely will the pattern be exactly followed for any application, but the structure is present with attributes missing here and there, or with some optional elements removed as appropriate.

Sequences are often given fairly generic Generic Identifiers. The upper deck of a sequence very often has an attribute **type** to provide further, specializing details. The lower deck often has some attribute (occasionally an element) to force particular numbering. The attribute **sequence-number** given in this generic sequence has the type CDATA rather than number, since "numbers" are rarely composed just from digits.

Examples of Sequences

The highest-level sequence of a **book**, for example, might be

```
<!-- book: a sequence -->
<!ELEMENT book     ( title, chapter+ ) >
<!ATTLIST book
       type     CDATA    #IMPLIED >
<!ELEMENT chapter ( title, ( %chapter-contents; | section )* ) >
<!ATTLIST chapter
         sequence-number CDATA    #IMPLIED >
<!ELEMENT title    ( %text; )* >
```

Similarly, a list might be

```
<!-- list: a sequence -->
<!ELEMENT list              ( caption, list-item+ ) >
<!ATTLIST list
     type               (sequence-numbered | bullet ) #IMPLIED >
<!ELEMENT list-item  ( definition-term?, ( %list-contents; | list)* ) >
<!ATTLIST list-item
     sequence-number    CDATA    #IMPLIED >
<!ELEMENT caption           ( %text; )* >
<!ELEMENT definition-term ( %text; )* >
```

Tables of various kinds can be built, just using this model as a sequence of sequences—a two-dimensional list:

```
<!-- table: a 2D sequence -->
<!ELEMENT table  ( caption, row+ ) >
<!ATTLIST table
     type              CDATA     #IMPLIED >
<!ELEMENT row      ( row-head, cell+ ) >
<!ELEMENT cell     ( cell-head?, ( %cell-contents; | table)* ) >
<!ATTLIST ( row | cell )
     type              CDATA     #IMPLIED
     sequence-number   CDATA     #IMPLIED >
<!ELEMENT ( caption | row-head | cell-head )   ( %text; )* >
```

It is characteristic of sequences of sequences that the middle elements may have attributes both for sequence-number and for type. [1]

Three-dimensional sequences can be built—for example a **calendar**:

```
<!-- calendar: a 3D sequence -->
<!ELEMENT year  ( caption, month*)>
<!ELEMENT month ( month-label, week*)>
<!ELEMENT week  ( day* ) >
<!ELEMENT day   ( day-label?, %day-contents;* ) >
<!ATTLIST ( year | month | week | day )
     type              CDATA     #IMPLIED
     sequence-number CDATA     #IMPLIED >
<!ELEMENT ( caption | month-label | day-label) ( %text; )* >
```

When rendered, all these different types of sequence will look (or sound, or feel, perhaps) very different. But the element structure behind them all is almost identical. In highly structured documents, almost everything except for in-line or fielded data will get reduced to sequences of sequences: the sequence should be modeled primarily with elements, the particular rendering should be captured in attributes.

---

1. For generic attributes for every element, see page 2-3, chapter 6, *Common Attributes*.

Bad Mixed Content

⚠······ The model for generic sequences given may cause troubles in full SGML when the sequence–contents includes PCDATA. In that case, the content model of the element type is called "mixed content," and the parser will treat any white–space before the optional element item–label as an indication that the sequence–contents have started, and will give an error when the start–tag for item–label occurs. This is called bad mixed content.

If you are generating your text by computer, you do not need to worry about potential bad mixed content: just generate good text! Otherwise, it is a good idea to use a different content model. Two approaches are common:

☑ Convert the element type item–label into an attribute of the element type sequence–item:

```
<!-- sequence-item with item-label as attribute -->
<!ELEMENT sequence-item
        ( %sequence-contents; | sequence )* >
<!ATTLIST sequence-item
        sequence-number CDATA    #IMPLIED
        item-label      CDATA    #IMPLIED >
```

You cannot use this approach when the item-label itself must contain sub-elements.

☑ Make the content model for the element type sequence–item into element content, by encapsulating the body in a container element:

```
<!-- nested form of sequence with head and body -->
<!ELEMENT sequence-item
        ( item-label?, item-body) >
<!ELEMENT item-body
        ( %sequence-contents; | sequence )* >
```

Simpifying the Linear Form

If this last approach is taken, you can simplify the model even further: rather than making the start- and end-tags for an element type of the form `sequence-item` omissible, you can simply remove the element type all together:

```
<!-- linear form of generic sequence with head and body -->
<!ELEMENT sequence      ( label, ( item-label?, item-body )* ) >
<!ATTLIST sequence
        type    CDATA    #IMPLIED >
<!ELEMENT item-body
        ( %sequence-contents; | sequence )* >
<!ELEMENT ( label | item-label )  ( %text; )* >
<!ATTLIST item-label
        sequence-number CDATA    #IMPLIED >
```

The most well-known structure that uses this linear form, very much stripped down, is the HTML **definition list**:

```
<!-- HTML-esque definition list   -->
<!ELEMENT dl    ( dt, dd )* >
<!ELEMENT dd    ( %sequence-contents; | dl )* >
<!ELEMENT dt    ( %text; )* >
<!ATTLIST dt
        sequence-number CDATA    #IMPLIED >
```

Not only does this HTML element type set get over any potential bad-mixed content problems, it is also very terse. And it gets rid of a level of the element hierarchy; this is good for typists, but like most linear forms complicates some types of computer manipulation.

This is another case where the two content models are interconvertable. The transformation between the two models is trivial; adopting either structure does not lock you out from switching to the other model.

Named Data

Chapter 10

This chapter

...shows SGML patterns for fielded text, databases and references.

I t is simple to use SGML for databases: in fact, SGML was designed to be a database archiving and transmission format, as well as for marking-up more conventional text.

Fielded Text

It is easy to represent fielded text in SGML—

    ✓ If the field names are all known in advance, you can use an element type for each field, for example:

```
<!-- Specific fields (with SGML omitted tag minimization parameter ) -->
<!ELEMENT  address   - -   ( number?, street, suburb, city, country ) >
<!ELEMENT  ( number| street| suburb| city| country) - o   (#PCDATA ) >
```

```
<address>
<street>Sneath Avenue
<suburb>Golders Green
<city>London
<country>United Kingdom
</address>
```

Data with specific fields is often found as in-line elements within running text: in particular references to things and proper nouns (e.g., names) are likely to be marked up as fielded data. (Note: XML 1.0 does not support omit-tag minimization.)

✓ If the field names are not known in advance, you can just make a generic element, for example:

```
<!-- Generic fields (with SGML omitted tag minimization parameter ) -->
<!ELEMENT   data    - -    ( field+ ) >
<!ELEMENT   field   - o    ( #PCDATA ) >
<!ATTLIST field
         type     CDATA    #REQUIRED >
```

```
<data>
<field street>Sneath Avenue
<field suburb>Golders Green
<field city>London
<field country>United Kingdom
</data>
```

(Note: The example of the **type** attribute above uses the SGML feature called shorttag minimization, which is convenient, but may not be available in all implementations. XML 1.0 does not support shorttag minimization.)

The most well known example of generic fielded data is the HTML element type **meta**. It puts the data of the field as an attribute, which is tidy, but has the disadvantage of forcing the data to be smaller than the LITLEN quantity set in the SGML declaration, which has typically been only 240 to 1024 characters. This size restriction does have the positive effect of preventing the element type from being used for fanciful and inappropriate uses, such as containing program code.

```
<!-- Generic fields in HTML -->
...
<!ELEMENT  head   (title, meta* ) >
<!ELEMENT  meta   #EMPTY >
<!ATTLIST  meta
      name    CDATA   #REQUIRED
      content CDATA   #REQUIRED>
...
```

```
<meta name='street'  content='Sneath Avenue'  />
<meta name='suburb'  content='Golders Green'  />
<meta name='city'    content='London'         />
<meta name='country' content='United Kingdom' />
```

Sequences of Fielded Text

When the fielded data appears in sequences, you have a database table. If you have large amounts of this data, it is quite probable that SGML is not a suitable storage or searching format: you may find that the binary format of some RDBMS is preferable. However SGML still will be the appropriate notation for archiving, interchange and incorporating selected and sorted text into reports.

It is no sacrilege to say that the SGML notation is not always and at every time the best technology to use: which is not to say that improvements in technology are not expanding the areas in which SGML is the appropriate choice.

Sequences of fielded text may have some fields nominated as **key** fields for the database. This example shows how similar a database schema and a DTD can be:[1]

---

1. SGML can be viewed as a linearized (or serialized) text representation of an extremely freeform database, organized primarily into trees, and secondarily into graph structures including locators to external objects.

The XML & SGML Cookbook

```
<!-- Specific fields with key -->
<!ELEMENT  address          ( number?, street, suburb, city, country ) >
<!ELEMENT ( number | street | suburb | city | country ) ( #PCDATA ) >
<!ATTLIST suburb
        iskey   CDATA #FIXED 'primary' >
<!ATTLIST city
        iskey   CDATA #FIXED 'secondary'>
```

```
<address>
<street>Sneath Avenue</street>
<suburb>Golders Green</suburb>
<city>London</city>
<country>United Kingdom</country>
</address>
```

In *Collation*, in chapter 19, page 3-16, we can see that in many cases text is too erratic to be used reliably or efficiently for searching and sorting. In English, this primarily is simply searching with case-insensitivity, but other scripts and languages require more complicated transformations. Very often the text and the search string need to be normalized to some less unruly form, either during the search, or in advance, such as the following:

```
<!-- Specific fields with key attribute -->
<!ELEMENT address          ( number?, street, suburb, city, country ) >
<!ATTLIST address
        key     CDATA   #REQUIRED >
<!ELEMENT ( number | street | suburb | city | country ) ( #PCDATA ) >
```

```
<address key='GOLDERS_GREEN'>
<street>Sneath Avenue</street>
<suburb>Golders Green</suburb>
<city>London</city>
<country>United Kingdom</country>
</address>
```

💡······ A key may or may not be unique. If it is unique within every document in which it will appear, consider using an ID attribute.

```
<!ATTLIST address
          key      ID #REQUIRED >
```

Element References

An *element reference* is a reference made by one element in the document to another, usually by using an `IDREF` attribute. There are several kinds of element reference, depending on their purpose; for example:

> • a *cross–reference*, when the referenced element contains related information of interest;

> • a *reflection* (which may be a *value reference* or a *content reference*), when the referenced element has data that the application will embed at the position of the referencing element; and

> • a *citation*, when the referenced element has data that defines the current element more fully.

Cross-references are generally used for editorial-structure and topic-structure. Reflections are used to allow one-time entry of data where data integrity is vital. Citations are used where the text of the referencing element does not define the content completely, and an external source of more complete information is required.

```
<!-- An simple element reference; a reflection -->
<document>
<head><source id='dl'>dog</source></head>
<body>Fred is a <reflection refid='dl'>.</body>
</document>
```

An element reference is thus a bit like an internal entity reference, except that an entity reference is handled by the SGML parser when the document is parsed, while element references must be handled by the application after parsing, while the document is being processed.

Reflections are most commonly used when there are large multidimensional sequences of data, like fielded databases, and pieces of that data will appear in various locations. The Pinnacles DTD used in the semiconductor industry is a leading example. This DTD allows, for example, a computer chip to be described pin-by-pin: data such as maximum, typical and minimum voltage ratings, the full name of the object and so on. Documents that use reflections are automatically kept consistent: when a change is made in a text source, it will propagate throughout the document when processed next.

So, what can a reflection do that an entity reference cannot?

- Reflections are marked-up using elements; elements must fit into the content model to be valid. Therefore it is possible to validate documents with element references to make sure they are only used where allowed.

- Element-reference elements can have attributes; an entity reference cannot have an attribute.

- An element-reference element can be formatted as is, or have a different selection of data presented, at the direction of the application. For example, all the first occurrences of a reflection might be presented with the full name of the computer chip, while subsequent ones might be presented with only a short name.

- For large tables of text, a large collection of entity declarations creates management and naming problems.

- Reflections can select individual field-elements in sources: this requires another level of indirection if entities are used (i.e., so that every record is a declared entity, which in turn contains references to entities that represent each field).

- General entities are usually entered as text, with no checking. In contrast, having particular element type sets for reflection sources allows structured input of the data and helps application development. For example, a Pinnacles application can check that maximum voltages are always greater than minimum voltages, and less than some sensible absolute maximum.

The downside of reflections is that they require an additional data manipulation stage to reflect the data from the source database to the position of the element reference, which simple off-the-shelf SGML tools often cannot do. Also, they dramatically reduce the comprehensibility of source documents: reflected documents are not readily maintainable using simple text editors.

In keeping with the general principle that "*Things should be declared before use,*" it is good practice for element-reference sources to precede any mention of them in references.

Principle

Things should be declared before being used.

Here is a possible declaration for a generic cross-reference.

```
<!-- A generic cross-reference declaration -->
<!ELEMENT xref EMPTY>
<!ATTLIST xref
  refid IDREF #IMPLIED >
```

Here is a possible declaration for a generic reflection. It uses an [XLL] extended pointer,[1] with which you can select ranges of elements, even in external documents, not just single local elements.

```
<!-- A generic reflection declaration -->
<!ELEMENT reflection  EMPTY>
<!ATTLIST reflection
  href CDATA #REQUIRED
  xml:xptr CDATA #FIXED 'simple' >
```

Here is a declaration for a specific example of a citation, a legal *case reference citation*. (Other kinds of citation include references to *bibliographies* and to *addresses in directories*.)

---

1. XLL was still in draft at the time this book went to publication, so the attribute names used here may be incorrect.

```
<!-- A legal citation declaration-->
<!ELEMENT case-citation
   ( #PCDATA | judge | case-name | case-reference)* >
<!ELEMENT case-citation
   full-citation IDREF #REQUIRED>
<!ELEMENT (judge | case-name | case-reference) ( #PCDATA )>
```

Note that element references are not the same as hyperlinks. An element reference is a low-level mechanism that can represent many kinds of higher-level relationships. The essence of a hyperlink relationship is *discretionary traversal*—the reader has a choice of whether or not to traverse the link to one of the other anchors. So in the three uses of element references that we have examined, cross-references and citations are hyperlinks, but reflections are not. The reader has the choice of whether to jump to the cross-referenced or cited elements, but the application automatically presents a reflection in sequence—no link traversal is involved.

Description Tables

HyTime description tables were developed primarily to act as a smarter form of internal general entity declaration. They allow repeated text to be kept in a simple database and searched for—

```
<!-- HyTime description tables -->
<!ELEMENT desctab  - O ( desctxt, descdef )+ >
<!ATTLIST desctab
   id ID #REQUIRED >
<!ELEMENT desctxt  - O ( #PCDATA ) -- the key -->
<!ELEMENT descdef  - O ( %stuff; ) -- the content elements -->
```

So the description table allows us a smarter form of entity declaration. What is the corresponding smarter form of entity reference? Two HyTime attributes: desctxt and desctab—

```
desctxt CDATA   #CONREF    -- descriptive text key       --
desctab IDREFS  #CURRENT   -- current description tables --
```

The attribute desctab allows you to specify a list of description tables to search through. There is an implied 'EMBED' semantic: the user can expect the application to act as if the descdef elements were the contents of the element with the desctxt attribute. It is not a real entity reference however, so there are no tricky element-content-model validity issues involved.

(Note: XML 1.0 does not support #CONREF and #CURRENT attributes: for compatibility, use #IMPLIED, and make sure the element's content model will be satisfied by empty content. If one attribute is specified, the other should be specified also. XML 1.0 does not support omitted tag minimization: remove the omitted tag minimization parameter (i.e., − O).

```
<example>
    <desctab id="rickodata">
        <desctxt>my name</desctxt>
            <descdef>Rick Jelliffe</descdef>
        <desctxt>my birthplace</desctxt>
            <descdef>Goondiwindi, near Boggabilla</descdef>
        <desctxt>currentsuburb</desctxt>
            <descdef>Woolloomoolloo</descdef>
    </desctab>
<p>My name is <name desctab="rickodata" desctxt="my name">.
I was born in <name desctab="rickodata" desctxt="my birthplace">
but now I live near <name desctab="rickodata"
desctxt="current suburb">.</p>
</example>
```

Importing ASCII Dumps

Some simple database dump (or "ASCII") formats, in particular relational tables stored as comma-, tab- or pipe-delimited records are often already usable SGML. Let us have the following set of element type declarations:

```
<!-- This is the generic database schema -->
   <!ELEMENT database - - (record)+ >
   <!ELEMENT record   - O (field)+  >
   <!ELEMENT field    O O (#PCDATA) >
```

```
<!-- This maps the dump-format delimiters to SGML tags -->
   <!-- SGML declaration must allow short references and tag omission -->
   <!ENTITY record-stag STARTTAG record >
   <!ENTITY field-stag  STARTTAG field >
   <!SHORTREF record-map
      '&#RS;' record-start>
   <!SHORTREF field-map
      '&#RS;' record-start
      '|' field-start >
   <!USEMAP record-map record >
   <!USEMAP field-map record >
```

and the following DOCTYPE declaration:

```
<!DOCTYPE database SYSTEM 'database.dtd'
[  <!ENTITY data   SYSTEM 'somedata.txt' ]>
<database>
&data;</database>
```

Using these, the following database file—

```
dog|rover|cat
cat|moggy|dog
```

has the effective markup in the document of—

```
<database>
<record><field>dog</field><field>rover</field><field>cat</field>
</record><record><field>cat</field><field>moggy</field><field>dog</field></field></database>
```

We can add better field type-information by adding a fixed attribute to the document to the following:

```
<!DOCTYPE database SYSTEM 'database.dtd'
[  <!ENTITY  data  SYSTEM 'somedata.txt'
   <!ATTLIST field
       names NMTOKENS #FIXED 'pet name hates' >
]>
<database>
&data;</database>
```

That associates a fixed attributed called names to the element type field. The values of this attribute are the field names.

Schema and Type Extension using Parameter Entities

ISO 8879:1986 does not provide a semantic way to extend your schemas (i.e., to declare that a new element type should use the content model of another, but with some additions) or to extend your element type content-models (so-called 'type-extension'). These functions are provided by the *SGML Extended Facilities* in ISO/IEC 10744.

However, ISO 8879 does provide a syntactic means to design your declarations (or rewrite existing declarations) to allow both these things using parameter entities. [1]

To allow *schema extension*, we simply put the content model of an element type into a parameter entity: [2]

```
<!ENTITY % paragraph-contents ' ( #PCDATA | xref )* ' >
<!ELEMENT paragraph            ( %paragraph-contents; ) >
```

You can then declare your own derived element type using the paragraph model:

```
<!ELEMENT my-paragraph         ( %paragraph-contents; | table )*  >
```

[*Komachi, Hiyama, Furuse*] explore this method further. They add the ability of the derived element type to be labeled with its prototype (i.e., to invoke the prototype as an architectural form), and the ability to select a particular attribute from an attribute value specification list by using an attribute `attribute-restriction`.

For example, take the following element type set:

```
<!ENTITY % paragraph-contents   ' ( #PCDATA | xref )* ' >
<!ENTITY % paragraph-attributes ' size ( big | little | tiny ) "tiny" '
>
<!ELEMENT paragraph ( %paragraph-contents; ) >
<!ATTLIST paragraph
      %paragraph-attributes; >
```

---

1. You will remember that parameter entities are referenced in the contents of elements, but only inside declarations. The default open delimiter for parameter entity references is "%", you cannot mistake them for general entity references, which use "&".

2. It is a good idea to always put extra trailing and leading white-space in this kind of parameter entity value, so that the token boundaries are clear: this prevents false token concatenation by non-standard parsers. Similarly, unless you clearly want some other behavior, you should make sure your content model fragments form a well-formed group, with enclosing parentheses.

You can then make up your own element type using the paragraph model:

```
<!ENTITY my-paragraph ( %paragraph-contents; | table )* >
<!ATTLIST my-paragraph
    %paragraph-attributes;
    derived-from CDATA #FIXED 'paragraph'
    attribute-restriction CDATA #FIXED ' size="big" ' >
```

To allow *type extension* you merely make sure there are dummy parameter entity references everywhere you want to allow extra elements:

```
<!ENTITY % paragraph-addon ' ' >
<!ENTITY % paragraph-contents ' ( #PCDATA | xref | %paragraph-addon; )* '
>
<!ELEMENT paragraph ( %paragraph-contents; )>
```

To use it, in the document prolog, preset the parameter entity **paragraph-extra** to the desired elements:

```
<!ENTITY % paragraph-addon ' list '>
```

 ⋯⋯ Be careful not to use parameter entities too much: they rapidly cause confusion if used for several different purposes (e.g., for schema extensibility, and type extensibility and for keeping declarations small). If you must use parameter entities a lot, for maintainability and extensibility, then it may be worthwhile generating a user version of the declarations: this delivery DTD would have parameter entities resolved to some extent. Sometimes a long chain of parameter entities in declarations shows over-attention to detail. In general, for example, if one species of paragraph can contain an element, users may find it easier if all species of paragraphs can also.

Tables

Chapter 11

This chapter

…gives your options when designing element type sets for table structures.

A table is a particular presentation method for displaying sequences of data. The general topic of how to mark up, in XML and SGML ,single-dimensional and multi-dimensional sequences of data was dealt with in *Sequences* in chapter 9. The most common patterns for presenting tables are dealt with here: HTML tables, ICADD tables and CALS tables.

In just the same way as "paragraph" is a word with several different meanings, so "table" has many incompatible meanings. Just think of what structural similarity there is between a Table of Contents, the atomic "periodic table," and a spreadsheet—very little. They are different structures. The kind of tables dealt with here are basically the glorified spreadsheet tables: neat boxes arranged in aligned rows and columns.

We can make a distinction between *running text* and *semi–graphical text*, where the latter includes tables, equations and other arrangements where meaning is determined in part from the spatial arrangement of the text. The choice as to whether to mark up semi-graphical text blindly – as a presentation-based structure that models directly the spatial arrangement – or intelligently – to bring out the logical structures – is a design decision involving all the kinds of issues dealt with in part 1. And never forget that it does not need to be an either/or choice, often. Using architectural forms, you can directly model one view and decorate it with attributes to point out the connection to the other.

Direct Markup *versus* Element Reference

Tables have been very controversial in DTD design circles, because DTD designers are very reluctant to base element structure on page-object arrangement. It is very common for DTD designers to advocate that table presentation markup should be separate from table data markup: the data can be kept in specific sequences, nice and specifically labeled, the table cells just invoke particular fields. This technique is called *element reference* (reflection). The Pinnacles DTD used for electronic components is one widely used DTD that uses element references. ⚀

Element Reference is the technique of choice every time you have tabular data that may appear, perhaps in different selections and formats, several times throughout a document, or in several documents, and you need to have assured consistency in your document. In a way, it is merely the standard database

---

1. This distinction should be very familiar to programmers, since it is in essence the Model/View dichotomy used in many GUI APIs.

practice of keeping data management, forms design and report generation as three distinct processes.

If you are just marking up casual tables, there is no need to think about element reference, and your sequences of data are best marked-up directly, inserting the data into the cells.

Simple HTML-Style Tables

The basic HTML table model is simplicity itself. A table has rows `tr`, rows have cells `td`. Cells can contain multiple paragraphs and have various other element types nested—

```
<!-- The basic HTML table model -->
<!ELEMENT table                  ( caption?, tr+ ) >
<!ELEMENT tr                      ( th | td )+ >
<!ELEMENT ( caption | th | td )   ( %text; ) >
```

The biggest superficial difference in table models is the treatment of spanning where adjacent cells are joined into one cell. In the case of HTML-style simple tables, spanning behavior is specified directly on each cell.

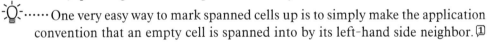One very easy way to mark spanned cells up is to simply make the application convention that an empty cell is spanned into by its left-hand side neighbor. [1]

---

1. Thanks to Robin Masson of Uniscope, Inc, Japan for this tip.

ICADD Tables

The International Committee for Accessible Document Display has developed a table model that can be used as an architectural form for presenting table data in Braille or by speech synthesizer. It represents the next level of sophistication beyond the HTML model, in that it allows a table to have notes and headers, etc. The larger a table is, the more it becomes like a small document in its own right, requiring all the kinds of general structures needed by documents. [1]

The ICADD table model is, more or less,

```
<!-- The basic ICADD table model -->
<!ELEMENT table                      ( title , tgroup+ ) >
<!ELEMENT tgroup                     ( thead , tbody, tfoot ) >
<!ELEMENT thead                      ( coldef*, hdrow+ ) >
<!ELEMENT ( tbody | tfoot )          ( coldef*, row+ ) >
<!ELEMENT ( hdrow | row )            ( cell | stubcell )+ >
<!ELEMENT ( title, cell, stubcell )( %text; ) +( note ) >
<!ELEMENT note                       ( %text; ) >
```

One important distinction of this table model is that it is not intended to be used directly: it is a *meta–DTD* whose identifiers appear in attribute values (architectural forms) rather than as GIs.

Note that spanning is specified by using a special element type stubcell, which represents a spanned-into dummy cell.

---

1. See chapter 7, page 2-17.

CALS Tables

The CALS table model is a large and rich form. However, it is basically just an extended version of the ICADD structure. A highly simplified form[1] is

```
<!-- The basic CALS table model -->
<!ELEMENT table          ( title , tgroup+ ) >
<!ELEMENT tgroup         ( colspec* , spanspec* , thead , tbody ) >
<!ELEMENT thead          ( row+ ) >
<!ELEMENT tbody          ( row+ ) >
<!ELEMENT row            ( entry* ) >
<!ELEMENT ( title, entry ) ( %text; ) >
```

Spanning and cell formating, etc., are handled in CALS-style tables by having dedicated style elements: there can be one element `colspec` for each column, and one element `spanspec` for each type of spanning. The individual lead cells for a span have an IDREF attribute to point to the appropriate spanspec element. This method allows easier maintenance and construction of large tables: if you delete a column, for example, you do not need to go through every cell of the remaining columns to the left to readjust the span count: that can be adjusted conveniently in the `spanspec` element.

⋯⋯ OASIS, formerly SGML Open, the vendors' consortium, has made an "exchange" version of the CALS table model: TR9503:1995. This strips out some of the more exotic or rarely-implemented features and gives particular semantics to attributes that are too loosely defined in the CALS DTD (for example, the element that rotates tables did not give the direction of rotation: clockwise or counter-clockwise). If your documents are to travel outside your production environment, consider using the SGML Open exchange table DTD rather than the full CALS one, and thus avoid wasted markup.

Here is the Exchange Table Model, with comments removed and parameter entities resolved. The model has a good number of attributes for giving format information: the full CALS model has even more, as well as structure or attributes for footers, rotation, tables within tables, and security. The SGML

---

1. Based on declarations posted to the `comp.text.SGML` news group by Dave Peterson. Dave comments (private communication) that the element types `colspec` and `spanspec` were originally intended to handle skipped and spanned columns only, but are now used to handle most aspects of formatting, due to the lack of style-sheets for tables.

Open version of the CALS table model does not allow the `spanspec` element type; users must specify spans using the `namest` and `nameend` attributes, just as in the HTML-type model—

```
<!-- The basic SGML Open CALS Exchange Table model -->
<!ENTITY % yesorno ' NUMBER ' >
<!-- no if zero (s),
     yes if any other digits value -->
<!-- Web SGML and XML can use entity value ' ( yes | no ) ' -->

<!ELEMENT table  ( title?, tgroup+ )  >
<!ATTLIST table
      frame   ( top | bottom | topbot | all | sides | none ) #IMPLIED
      colsep  %yesorno;                                       #IMPLIED
      rowsep  %yesorno;                                       #IMPLIED
      pgwide  %yesorno;                                       #IMPLIED
>
<!ELEMENT tgroup ( colspec*, thead?, tbody ) >
<!ATTLIST tgroup
      cols    NMTOKEN                                         #REQUIRED
      colsep  %yesorno;                                       #IMPLIED
      rowsep  %yesorno;                                       #IMPLIED
      align   ( left | right | center | justify | char )     #IMPLIED
>
<!ELEMENT colspec  EMPTY >
<!ATTLIST colspec
      colnum          NMTOKEN                                 #IMPLIED
      colname         NMTOKEN                                 #IMPLIED
      colwidth        CDATA                                   #IMPLIED
      colsep          %yesorno;                               #IMPLIED
      rowsep          %yesorno;                               #IMPLIED
      align           ( left | right | center | justify | char ) #IMPLIED
      char            CDATA                                   #IMPLIED
      charoff         NMTOKEN                                 #IMPLIED
>
<!ELEMENT thead  ( row+ )  >
<!ATTLIST thead
      valign          ( top | middle | bottom )               #IMPLIED
>
```

```
<!ELEMENT tbody    ( row+)>
<!ATTLIST tbody
   valign            ( top | middle | bottom )                    #IMPLIED
>
<!ELEMENT row    ( entry+)  >
<!ATTLIST row
   rowsep            %yesorno;                                     #IMPLIED
   valign            ( top | middle | bottom )                     #IMPLIED
>
<!ELEMENT entry   ( %text;)   >
<!ATTLIST entry
   colname           NMTOKEN                                       #IMPLIED
   namest            NMTOKEN                                       #IMPLIED
   nameend           NMTOKEN                                       #IMPLIED
   morerows          NMTOKEN                                       #IMPLIED
   colsep            %yesorno;                                     #IMPLIED
   rowsep            %yesorno;                                     #IMPLIED
   align             ( left | right | center | justify | char ) #IMPLIED
   char              CDATA                                         #IMPLIED
   charoff           NMTOKEN                                       #IMPLIED
   valign            ( top | middle | bottom )                     #IMPLIED
>
```

Sometimes you may see the terms *simple table* and *complex table*. In SGML-industry jargon, a simple table is one in which other tables cannot be nested. A complex table is a table which can itself contain other tables in cells. The question of whether to use or allow complex tables in your documents is usually determined by the capacity of the intended technology you are using to present and use the documents. The principle that *"You cannot ignore hard constraints"* applies here: if your applications will not support complex tables, you would be well advised to not use them in your documents, unless you are making documents for some golden, complex-tabled future.

HTML 4 Tables

The HTML 4 table model upgrades the previous simple HTML model with column specifications similar to those of the CALS table model. Note also that the table footers are declared before the table body: this is useful for presentation, in that the footer can be rendered before all **tbody** has been received across the Internet. A highly simplified form is—

```
<!-- The basic HTML 4 table model -->
<!ELEMENT table     ( caption?, col*, thead?, tfoot?, tbody+ ) >
<!ELEMENT ( tbody | tfoot | thead ) ( tr+ ) >
<!ELEMENT col                    EMPTY >
<!ELEMENT tr                     ( th | td )+ >
<!ELEMENT ( caption | th | td )  ( %text; ) >
```

Interactive Systems

Chapter 12

This chapter

…gives an overview of techniques for marking up interactive systems in SGML.

Eric [*Jorgensen*], of the U.S. Navy, has characterized interactive systems into five types:

1. page turners,

2. hotspot page-turners,

3. linear structured,

4. hierarchical structured, and

5. expert systems.

As systems get more developed, they add features of each type. Adobe Acrobat is fundamentally a type 1 system, but evolved to add other types of interaction. Apple's Hypercard is fundamentally a hotspot page-turner. We could fabricate systems of each type to a certain extent with HTML:

- a series of pages each containing a GIF image of a page and "next" button;

- a series of pages each containing a GIF image used as an image map;

- a format-able text document with cross-reference links;

- a hierarchical source document processed so that every possible permutation of expanded/contracted sections became a separate HTML page, simulating an outline viewer;

- a document where links and GUI events trigger CGI (Common Gateway Interface) and inline scripts, allowing the system to track and display different pages depending on where the user had previously been, and how they had answered previous queries.

HTML browsers do not provide a built-in way to perform outline expansion, presumably because HTML has not had a reliable sub-division model. HTML is fundamentally a type 3 interactive system. However, the rapid development and wide deployment of Web browsers makes HTML the first place to look for architectures for links, maps, forms, GUI event-handling, scripting and style-sheets.

Interactive Electronic Training Manuals (IETM, pronounced *I eat 'em*) represent the appropriation of video game technology by documents. As always, the decision must be made whether to represent the interaction patterns by entities, elements or processing instructions:

Entity

This method separates text from usage: in a master document you specify the text as one (presumably external) entity (of one notation) and the way it is processed in another entity (of a different notation, which could itself be SGML, as in [*MID*])—

```
<!DOCTYPE IETM SYSTEM [
<!NOTATION java          SYSTEM>
<!NOTATION my-app-language SYSTEM>
<!ENTITY   my-data       SYSTEM>
<!ENTITY   my-app        SYSTEM>
<!ELEMENT  IETM          ( data, applet )>
<!ELEMENT  ( data | applet ) ( #PCDATA )>
<!ATTLIST  ( data | applet )
     notation NMTOKEN #REQUIRED>
]>
<IETM>
    <data notation='my-app-language'>&my-data;</data>
    <applet notation='java'>&my-app;</applet>
</IETM>
```

Element

Element methods hardwire the interaction into the text. The markup will progressively look procedural[1] —

```
<if>
  <gt><variable x><variable y></gt>
  <popup id='p123'><text>hello</text>
    <button text='1' push-action='p123-b1 pressed'>
    <button text='2' push-action='p123-b2 pressed'>
  </popup>
</if>
```

---

1. The MID DTD is a notable example of this approach.

It is best to keep elements as generic as possible. By the time you are as low-level
and procedural as these elements, you may be reinventing a wheel that is done
better by proprietary hypertext systems. An intermediate approach may be better,
where you use SGML to create a GUI-independent *resource description* language—

```
<popup id='p123'><text>hello</text>
  <button id='p123-b1' text='1'  >
  <button id='p123-b2' text='2'  >
</popup>
```

HTML forms are a highly successful example of this approach.

Resource description languages tend to have very similar elements and schemes,
because the things they describe are typically fairly generic; the behavior of the
objects and the ways these are described in various programming languages tend
to be so different that it may be difficult to encapsulate them in any common,
generic SGML DTD.

Many rule-based high-level languages are fairly declarative at their high levels,
and only become procedural for complex and unpredictable functions. For
example, the highest level of DSSSL (LISP) programs are *special forms* which have
many possible keyword arguments. These special forms are readily convertible
into element types and attributes. This becomes cumbersome with more complex
functional code, but a mixed approach is possible: you can use an element type
like the following:

```
<!ELEMENT eval ( #PCDATA ) >
    <!ATTLIST eval
        notation NMTOKEN #IMPLIED>
```

The intent of the `eval` element type is to let you embed programming language
snippets inside markup. This gives the strengths and simplicity of style-sheets
and checklists for the most common cases, but does not trap you in this
simplicity.

XML's linking language,⬜ [*XLL*], uses attributes to decorate a link to a hypertext resource with hints about the behavior of the link. Apart from the `href` attribute, which has the XLL link pointer, XLL defines some simple attributes for highly generic behaviour. These behaviors are broad enough to provide hints for a great range of linking behaviors.

```
<!ENTITY % common_XML_attributes
' href        CDATA #IMPLIED    -- URL or XML link      --
  title       CDATA #IMPLIED    -- nickname of link     --
  role        CDATA #IMPLIED    -- role of link         --
  behavior    CDATA #IMPLIED    -- for application      --
  show        ( new | replace | embed ) "replace"
  actuate     ( user | auto )            "user"
'>
```

The attributes of interest are `actuate`, `show`, `behavior` and `role`.

`actuate`
indicates whether the linking behavior happens `auto`matically or under `user` control, for example from a mouse click.

`show`
indicates whether *traversing* the link results in the resource pointed to by the link being `embed`ded (at the current position) in the document, or whether a `new` view is created for the resource (e.g., a new window), or whether the document in the current view device is `replace`d.

`behavior`
lets you provide much more specific hints than the previous two attributes allow. However, the behavior element should be thought of as a specializing mechanism for the previous two attributes: if a linking element has `show="replace"` it should not have `behavior="new (growable window)"`. The attribute `behavior` is to some extent an embedded processing instruction, and consequently it is probably wise to always preface it with some indication of the notation or target system for the behavior. XLL does not define any values for this attribute, so you should be careful to document what you are using, and to consider the effect of retargeting your documents to different systems. If you have to reuse the document in several different systems, the same linking element

---

1. The following is based on draft of XLL, which had not been finalized at the time this book was written; it may have some inaccuracy.

may have different behaviors for each one: you will then need to use a more sophisticated system than just raw XML —

- make the attribute value an entity reference, and use marked sections to switch in the appropriate entity declaration (hint for SGML users: use a PI entity declaration);

- declare a separate attribute for each target, and remap the document for each use;

- use SGML LINK. (Because LINK is an optional SGML feature that is not found in XML, it is not discussed in this book. If your SGML system supports this feature, it may be worthwhile to consider LINK.)

`role`
allows you to put in some declarative information about the purpose of the link. In just the same way as it is usually best to mark up a document primarily according to its logical structure rather than its presentation, it is usually best to mark the document up according to generic roles rather than specific behaviors: try to use the `role` attribute rather than `behavior` attribute.

Note that even though these attributes may be oriented to GUI browsers of Web publications, they are in fact so generic that they can be applied to many other ways of rendering and using the document. In particular, note that traversing a link may not result in any data being "returned," in which case the `show` attribute may be a hint for a server rather than the client.

Processing Instruction

This again separates data from usage, if you follow the convention of making sure that each processing instruction begins with the name of the notation that describes the syntax of the PI, and also has a pseudo-attribute (or is in a marked section) to notate in which circumstances the rest of the PI applies—

```
<!ENTITY value1-pi      PI 'MY-IETM value="1"'>
<!ENTITY value2-pi      PI 'MY-IETM value="2"'>
<!ENTITY if-sound-pi    PI 'MY-IETM start-id="##1"
hardware="sound=OK"'>
<!ENTITY end-if-sound-pi PI 'MY-IETM start-idref="##1"'>
...
```

The XML & SGML Cookbook

```
&if-sound-pi;
  <?MY-IETM start-id='#23' value='if (x > y)' ?>
  <popup id='p123'><text>hello</text>
    <button text='1' id='p123-b1' pi='1'>
    <button text='2' id='p123-b2' pi='2'>
  </popup>
  <?MY-IETM start-idref='#23' ?>
&end-if-sound-pi;
```

This may seem rather strange, but it is a good example of the different kinds of markup available in SGML. The popup element is basically the same as before, but it is encased in PIs that contain an if condition.

We have to provide our own mechanism for identifying when the effect of the processing instruction finishes: in this case we are using pseudo-attributes with IDs: start-id and start-idref. To prevent human confusion, it is good practice to make sure the IDs in the PI are clearly not valid SGML IDs: here we prefix the names with the Reserved Name Indicator (RNI) delimiter #.

The button elements here also include an entity attribute pi which names PI entities previously declared in the DTD or prolog. You use PI entities when you may have to repeat a PI several times, or where you want to clearly separate the contents of a PI from its invocations. A PI entity can be invoked by an entity attribute, as in the button elements, or by simple entity references, as in the case of the if-sound-pi and end-if-sound-pi attributes.

Formal Public Identifiers

Chapter 13

This chapter

...shows how Formal Public Identifiers and SGML Open Catalogs are used together.

A Formal Public Identifier (FPI) is a name that gives librarians everything they need to track down some resource or object. An FPI should be globally unique and can be used to identify some text that may not even exist on a computer.

The three most common uses of FPIs in SGML are

- in notation declarations,

- to name sets of DTD declarations, and

- to name public entity sets for special characters (see chapter 22, page 3-107, for examples)

Formal Public Identifiers are usually one of several different types. Here are examples of the most important types:

- -//SPREAD//SYNTAX
      Extended Reference Concrete Syntax (ERCS)//EN

- -//SPREAD//ENTITIES
      ISO/IEC 10646-1:1993 BMP(U 2.0)//EN

- -//SPREAD//NOTATION
      Glyph Shape Encoding Method//JP

- -//SPREAD//TEXT
      Glyph kanxi123//CJK

- -//SGML Open//DTD
      Exchange Table Model 19960430//EN

- -//Rick Jelliffe//NONSGML
      Italy::Florence::Michaelangelo 'David' statue

- ISO Registration Number 176//CHARSET ISO/IEC 10646-1:1993
      UCS-2 with implementation level 3//ESC 2/5 2/15 4/5

- ISO/IEC TR9573-11:1988//ELEMENTS
      Information processing - SGML support facilities -
      Techniques for using SGML - Mathematics Markup//EN'

- +//IDN W3C.ORG//SD
      XML 1.0 //EN

- +//IDN ALLETTE.COM.AU//SGML
      Technical Introduction to XML//EN

Note that the resource that is identified by a public identifier does not need to be an SGML document itself. In fact, it might not even exist – it may be generated dynamically on request or be as yet uncreated.

It might even be something that exists outside the computer, like Michaelangelo's statue! In the case of NONSGML the public identifier can be used as the seed for a WWW query: rather than identifying a specific piece of text, the FPI identifies an external object about which texts have been written.

This is because the resolution of a public identifier to a system identifier is entirely a system-specific matter. As a document system designer, you are free to use any method you like to resolve public identifiers into system identifiers. However, there is an industry-developed file format that allows convenient mapping of public identifiers to storage object identifiers: the SGML Open Catalog (SOCAT).

ISO Definition

public text: Text that is known beyond the context of a single document or system environment, and which can be accessed with a public identifier.

public identifier: A minimum literal that identifies public text.

formal public identifier: A public identifier that is constructed according to the rules defined in this International Standard so that its owner identifier and the components of its text identifier can be distinguished.

(ISO 8879:1986 glossary)

SGML Open Entity Catalogs

The SGML vendor's group SGML Open (now called OASIS) has published a technical report giving a file format for entity catalogs: *Entity management* (TR9401-1995, available on the WWW from `htpp://www.SGML-open.org/`). The catalog specifies simple mappings for

- resolving SGML identifiers to storage object identifiers on a particular system and

- packaging for interchange an SGML document contained in a set of files.

The catalog format is simple. The file must be called 'CATALOG'. Inside this text file, there are a series of mappings: a keyword (PUBLIC, ENTITY, DOCUMENT, DOCTYPE, LINKTYPE, SGMLDECL, DTDDECL) followed by a string with the SGML identifier and a string with the storage object identifier. For example:

```
PUBLIC 'ISO 8879-1986//ENTITIES Added Latin 1//EN' 'iso-lat1.pen'
```

This is a convenient system even for document interchange. However, there has been no consensus on filenames for library files like the ISO public entity sets of special characters. On various systems you might find the first part to be isolat1 or ISOlat1 in upper or lower case, and the extension can be .ent, .sgm, .txt, .gml or .pen (i.e., parameter entity), let alone which directories they should be found in. The catalog can be tailored to cope with this variability.

Catalog files are also useful as a manifest for packaging up an SGML document into a set of files for interchange. The CATALOG file should contain, among the other entries, a single DOCUMENT entry to specify the file where parsing should begin: the file with the DOCTYPE declaration.

In SGML Open catalogs, unknown keyword entries are ignored. So vendors are free to add their own type of entries.

SGML and MIME

A good idea has a life of its own, and very good ideas are difficult to kill. Many SGML ideas and terms that were strange and obscure in the late 1980s have passed into commonplace use. The convergence of [MIME] and [URI] towards SGML-ishness proves how good the initial SGML analysis was.

Which is not to say that the developers of MIME and URI have any great desire to duplicate or follow SGML blindly – merely that very often they have semi-independently come to the same conclusions. [1] This is because the needs of large document systems are similar whether the documents are on paper or online. It is fashionable to proclaim the World Wide Web as a new medium, but Web publishing is still publishing; Web documents are just documents.

---

1. And SGML in turn has been influenced by the Internet, particularly in the development of XML, the entry-level subset of SGML for Web use.

The XML & SGML Cookbook

The Public Identifier construct of SGML is needed to allow a measure of system independence; the Formal Public Identifier of [*ISO9070*] is needed to give a fixed and reliable syntax. As the WWW has rediscovered that system identifiers – in the case of the WWW they are Uniform Resource Locators (URL [*RFC 1738*]) – are simply not adequate for maintenance of large or permanent document systems, it has needed to also create public identifiers as well: Uniform Resource Names (URN [*RFC 2141*]). Together, URLs and URNs are called Uniform Resource Identifiers (URI [*RFC 1630*]).

SGML does not mandate that you must use FPIs for your public identifiers: SGML is geared to allowing you to get your particular job done, and you are free to choose URNs as the public identifier syntax for your document collection.

Of course, you have to rename all the standard public entity sets and other public text, but if you are moving up from HTML and a WWW-system, this may be a reasonable thing to do.

FPIs and URNs both provide a similar solution to the problem of getting unique identifiers for entities: prefix the text identifier with an owner identifier to allow a unique namespace. Of the two, the FPI aims to do more, in that the public text it identifies is more than just resources for multimedia documents. The URN is constrained to having to look and act like a URL.

The syntax for a URN is:

```
'urn:', namespace identifier,  '/', namespace semantic string
```

For example:

```
urn:isbn:0-13-614223-0
```

which would have the equivalent [*ISO 9070*] FPI owner identifier:

```
+//ISBN 0-13-614223-0//
```

Here is a short list comparing the kinds of markup available in the SGML family with those available in MIME headers or defined in other Internet Request for Comments (RFCs):

SGML/XML/HTML	MIME & WWW
Entity [*SGML*], [*XML*]	Entity [*RFC2045*]
Element and attribute [*SGML*], [*XML*], [*HTML*]	MIME Header and attribute [*RFC 2045*]-[*RFC 2049*], [*RFC 2231*]
Notation [*SGML*], [*XML*] Encoding PI [*XML*]	Content Type [*RFC2046*]
Public character entity references: &*name*; [*SGML*], [*XML*], limited [*HTML*]	[*RFC1345*]: &*aa* or &_*a*★_
Decimal numeric character reference: &#*n*★; [*SGML*], [*XML*], [*HTML*] XML Hexadecimal numeric character reference: &#x*h*★; [*Web SGML*], [*XML*]	Quoted printable encoding [*RFC2047*]: =*nn* Base64 encoding [*RFC2152*]: +*aa* [*RFC2047*]: =?*charset*?*encoding*?+*text*+?=
Formal Public Identifier [*SGML*], [*XML*]	Universal Resource Name [*RFC2141*], [*HTML*], [*XML*]
Formal System Identifier [*SGML*] Extended Pointer [*XLL*]	Universal Resource Locator [*RFC1738*], [*RFC1808*], [*HTML*], [*XLL*]
Allows multiple character sets, defined using SGML declaration for markup; it does not need to be defined for data [*SGML*] ISO 10646 only for the document character set, but the document can be encoded using most standard character encodings [*XML*]	Allows one character set (or encoding) per content part, e.g. [*RFC1922*]

There is a considerable overlap in the model and capabilities. However, on the WWW side, MIME allows documents with an entity structure, using MIME multipart content-type in particular, with no element structure, while HTML allows element structure with no entity structure. Neither has the flexibility of SGML's threefold element-entity-processing instruction markup system. But this is not to say this represents a deficiency in MIME or HTML: neither is a generalized markup language.

Data Content Notations

Chapter 14

This chapter

...lists the most common formal public identifiers for notations (e.g., graphics), and give some techniques for using them.

The World Wide Web is built on the idea of small entities (linked resources) in arbitrary formats , or "notations," that carry with them enough metadata (in MIME headers) to allow the end-user to launch the appropriate application. This meta-data identifies the *data content notation* of the entity. SGML gives data content notations a very high level of language support.

ISO Definition

data content notation: An application-specific interpretation of an element's data content, or of a data entity, that usually extends or differs from the normal meaning of the document character set.

notation name: An external identifier that identifies a data content notation in a notation declaration. It can be a public identifier if the notation is public, and , if not, a description or other information sufficient to invoke a program to interpret the notation.

(ISO 8879:1986 glossary)

Notation names provide type information for the data of elements and entities for use in figuring out how to interpret and process them. A notation for a CDATA entity might be LANG or LOCALE. A notation for an SDATA entity might be 'SQL query'. A notation for an NDATA entity might be 'GIF'.

The type of an attribute value can be NOTATION. (Note: XML 1.0 does not support NOTATION attributes: use NMTOKEN or a name token group.) This is most commonly used to specify the types of graphics allowed—

```
<!NOTATION epsf PUBLIC '-//Adobe//NOTATION
               Encapsulated Postscript Format//EN' >
<!NOTATION CGMbin PUBLIC 'ISO/IEC 8632-3:1992//NOTATION
               Information technology - Computer graphics -
               Metafile for the storage and transfer of picture
               description information - Part 3: Binary encoding//EN'
>
<!ELEMENT fig    EMPTY >
<!ATTLIST fig
     file        CDATA                      #REQUIRED
     notation    NOTATION ( cgmbin | epsf ) #IMPLIED
     BoundingBox NMTOKENS                   #REQUIRED >
```

Notations can have attributes. The above would be better expressed using ENTITY attributes. This is because the bounding box does not belong to the figure element, but to the data entity itself independent of any use of it—

```
<!NOTATION epsf PUBLIC '-//Adobe//NOTATION
            Encapsulated Postscript Format//EN' >
<!NOTATION CGMbin PUBLIC 'ISO/IEC 8632-3:1992//NOTATION
            Information technology - Computer graphics -
            Metafile for the storage and transfer of picture
>           description information - Part 3: Binary encoding//EN'
<!ATTLIST #NOTATION epsf
    BoundingBox NMTOKENS #REQUIRED >
<!ELEMENT fig EMPTY >
<!ATTLIST fig
    file        ENTITY   #REQUIRED >

<!-- example of use -->
<!ENTITY fig1 SYSTEM 'fig1.ps'
    NDATA epsf [BoundingBox='30 50']>

<-- in instance: -->
<fig file="fig1" />
```

The system identifier for a notation should be specific enough to invoke the specific handlers for the notation. However, that does not mean it has to be the address of an executable application in your file system. Internet [*MIME*] content types provide a good convention for keeping the system identifiers portable −. Standard MIME content types can be found in [*RFC1700*], but your WWW browsers will usually also have a list, available from the GUI, used to map incoming MIME content types to local, specific applications.

Some useful MIME content types include:

- text/plain (you can use this for SGML text entities), which can have character encoding information in an attached attribute: text/plain;charset='ISO8859-2';

- text/xml, proposed for XML documents;

- `application/xml`, proposed for XML documents that are transmitted as binary;

- `audio/basic`, for simple audio;

- `model/vrml` for the Virtual Reality Modeling Language (or `application/vrml`);

- `application/x-java` for Java Virtual Machine code;

- `message/rfc8222` for the basic Internet Email format; and

- `text/tab-separated-values` for the simple database dump format.

You can make up your own MIME-compliant content type by prefixing your own name with 'x-'. Notation declarations for MIME content types can be created using the following formal public identifier model (the owner identifier is the owner of the FPI not of the public text, which is why this book's ISBN number is used here):

```
<!NOTATION video-mpeg
        PUBLIC '+//ISBN 0-13-614223-0::The SGML Cookbook//NOTATION
        Ds.internic.net/rfc/rfc2086.txt
        Multipurpose Internet Mail Extensions::video/mpeg//EN'
        'video/mpeg' >
```

Some FPIs for Notations

ISO Standard

The ISO technical report 9573-9 includes a convenient list of all ISO-defined data content notations—

```
<!-- (C) International Organization for Standardization 1995
     Permission to copy in any form is granted with
     conforming SGML systems and applications as defined
     in ISO 8879, provided this notice is included in all
     copies.                                             -->
<!-- ISO standard data notations. Typical invocation:
     <!ENTITY % ISOdata PUBLIC 'ISO/IEC TR 9573-9:1997//ELEMENTS
                               Standardized Data Notations//EN' >
     %ISOdata;
-->
<!-- This version has system identifiers using MIME content types,
     from Internet RFC 1700 and RFC 2077 and other sources,
     prepared for 'The SGML Cookbook'.
-->
<!NOTATION FORTRAN  PUBLIC 'ISO/IEC 1539:1991//NOTATION
                           Information technology -
                           Programming languages -
                           FORTRAN//EN'                      >
<!NOTATION COBOL    PUBLIC 'ISO 1989:1985//NOTATION
                           Programming languages -
                           COBOL//EN'                        >
<!NOTATION PL-1     PUBLIC 'ISO 6160:1979//NOTATION
                           Programming languages -
                           PL/1//EN'                         >
<!NOTATION PASCAL   PUBLIC 'ISO 7185:1990//NOTATION
                           Programming languages -
                           Pascal//EN'                       >
<!NOTATION GKS      PUBLIC 'ISO 7942:1985//NOTATION
                           Information processing systems -
                           Computer graphics -
                           Graphical Kernel System (GKS)
                           functional description//EN'       >
<!NOTATION APL      PUBLIC 'ISO 8485:1989//NOTATION
                           Programming languages -
```

```
                              APL//EN'                             >
<!NOTATION ODAafp   PUBLIC 'ISO/IEC 8613-9:1993//NOTATION
                              Information technology -
                              Open Document Architecture (ODA)
                              and Interchange Format - Part 9:
                              Audio formatted processable content
                              architecture//EN'                    >
<!NOTATION ODA      PUBLIC 'ISO/IEC 8613-10:1991//NOTATION
                              Information processing -
                              Text and office systems -
                              Office Document Architecture (ODA)
                              and interchange format -
                              Part 10: Formal specifications//EN'
                              'application/oda'                    >
<!NOTATION ODAvfp   PUBLIC 'ISO/IEC 8613-15:1995//NOTATION Video
                              formatted processable content architecture'>
<!NOTATION CGMchar  PUBLIC 'ISO/IEC 8632-2:1992//NOTATION
                              Information technology -
                              Computer graphics -
                              Metafile for the storage and transfer of
                              picture description information -
                              Part 2: Character encoding//EN'      >
<!NOTATION CGMbin   PUBLIC 'ISO/IEC 8632-3:1992//NOTATION
                              Information technology -
                              Computer graphics -
                              Metafile for the storage and transfer of
                              picture description information -
                              Part 3: Binary encoding//EN'         >
<!NOTATION CGMclear PUBLIC 'ISO/IEC 8632-4:1992//NOTATION
                              Information technology -
                              Computer graphics -
                              Metafile for the storage and transfer of
                              picture description information -
                              Part 4: Clear text encoding//EN'     >
<!NOTATION ADA      PUBLIC 'ISO 8652:1987//NOTATION
                              Programming languages -
                              Ada//EN'                             >
<!NOTATION GKS-3D   PUBLIC 'ISO 8805:1988//NOTATION
                              Information technology -
                              Computer graphics -
                              Graphical Kernal System
                              for Three Dimensions (GKS-3D)//EN'   >
<!NOTATION ASN.1    PUBLIC 'ISO/IEC 8824:1990//NOTATION
                              Information technology -
```

```
                              Open Systems Interconnection -
                              Specification of Abstract Syntax
                              Notation One (ASN.1)//EN'          >
<!NOTATION SGML     PUBLIC 'ISO 8879:1986//NOTATION
                              Information processing -
                              Text and office systems -
                              Standard Generalized Markup Language
                              (SGML)//EN'
                              'text/SGML'                        >
<!NOTATION RT-comms PUBLIC 'ISO/IEC 9066-2:1989//NOTATION
                              Text communication -
                              Reliable transfer -
                              Part 2: Protocol specification//EN'  >
<!NOTATION ISO9070 PUBLIC 'ISO/IEC 9070:1987//NOTATION
                              Information Processing -
                              SGML Support Facilities -
                              Registration Procedures for
                              Public Text Owner Identifiers//EN'   >
<!NOTATION SDIF     PUBLIC 'ISO/IEC 9069:1988//NOTATION
                              Information processing -
                              SGML support facilities -
                              SGML Document Interchange Format
                              (SDIF)//EN'                         >
<!NOTATION RO-comms PUBLIC 'ISO/IEC 9072-2:1989//NOTATION
                              Text communication -
                              Remote operation -
                              Part 2: Protocol specification//EN'  >
<!NOTATION SDIF     PUBLIC 'ISO/IEC 9069:1988//NOTATION
                              Information processing -
                              SGML support facilities -
                              SGML Document Interchange Format
                              (SDIF)//EN'                         >
<!NOTATION SQL      PUBLIC 'ISO/IEC 9075:1992//NOTATION
                              Information technology -
                              Database languages - SQL//EN'       >
<!NOTATION ISO9282  PUBLIC 'ISO/IEC 9282-2:1992//NOTATION
                              Information Processing -
                              Coded representation of pictures -
                              Part 2: Incremental encoding of point
                              lists in a 7-bit or 8-bit
                              environment//EN'                    >
<!NOTATION fonts    PUBLIC 'ISO/IEC 9541-2:1991//NOTATION
                              Information technology -
                              Font information interchange -
```

```
                              Part 2: Interchange Format//EN'      >
<!NOTATION ISOmath  PUBLIC 'ISO/IEC TR9573-7:1988//NOTATION
                              Information processing -
                              SGML support facilities -
                              Techniques for using SGML -
                              Mathematics Markup//EN'              >
<!NOTATION ISOchem  PUBLIC 'ISO/IEC TR9573-7:1991//NOTATION
                              Information processing -
                              SGML support facilities -
                              Techniques for using SGML -
                              Chemistry Markup//EN'                >
<!NOTATION PHIGS-2  PUBLIC 'ISO/IEC 9592-2:1989//NOTATION
                              Information processing -
                              Computer graphics -
                              Programmer's Hierarchical Interactive
                              Graphics System (PHIGS) -
                              Part 2: Archive file format//EN'     >
<!NOTATION PHIGS-3  PUBLIC 'ISO/IEC 9592-3:1989//NOTATION
                              Information processing -
                              Computer graphics -
                              Programmer's Hierarchical Interactive
                              Graphics System (PHIGS) -
                              Part 3: Clear-text encoding of
                              archive file//EN'>
<!NOTATION PHIGS-4  PUBLIC 'ISO/IEC 9592-4:1992//NOTATION
                              Information processing -
                              Computer graphics -
                              Programmer's Hierarchical Interactive
                              Graphics System (PHIGS) -
                              Part 4: Plus Lumiere und Surfaces,
                              PHIGS PLUS//EN'>
<!NOTATION EDIFACT  PUBLIC 'ISO 9735:1988//NOTATION
                              Electronic data interchange for
                              administration, commerce and transport
                              (EDIFACT) -
                              Application level syntax rules//EN'   >
<!NOTATION C        PUBLIC 'ISO/IEC 9899:1990//NOTATION
                              Programming languages - C//EN'        >
<!NOTATION MOTIS    PUBLIC 'ISO/IEC 10021:1990//NOTATION
                              Text communication -
                              Message-Oriented Text Interchange
                              Systems (MOTIS) - Part 6: Protocol
                              Specifications//EN'>
<!NOTATION DOAM     PUBLIC 'ISO/IEC 10031-2:1991//NOTATION
```

```
                          Information technology -
                          Text and office systems -
                          Distributed-office-applications model -
                          Part 2: Distinguished object reference
                          and associated procedures//EN'>
<!NOTATION DFR      PUBLIC 'ISO/IEC 10166-2:1991//NOTATION
                          Information technology -
                          Text and office systems -
                          Document Filing and Retrieval (DFR) -
                          Part 2: Protocol Specification//EN'   >
<!NOTATION DPA      PUBLIC 'ISO/IEC 10175:1996//NOTATION
                          Document Printing Application
                          (DPA)//EN'                            >
<!NOTATION DSSSL    PUBLIC 'ISO/IEC 10179:1996//NOTATION
                          Information processing -
                          Text and office systems -
                          Document Style Semantics and
                          Specification Language (DSSSL)//EN'   >
<!NOTATION SPDL     PUBLIC 'ISO/IEC 10180:1995//NOTATION
                          Information technology -
                          Text communication -
                          Standard Page Description Language
                          (SPDL)//EN'                           >
<!NOTATION BASIC    PUBLIC 'ISO/IEC 10279:1991//NOTATION
                          Information technology -
                          Programming languages -
                          Full BASIC//EN'                       >
<!NOTATION ISO10367 PUBLIC 'ISO/IEC 10367:1991//NOTATION
                          Information technology -
                          Standardized coded graphic character
                          sets for use in 8-bit codes//EN'      >
<!NOTATION RDT      PUBLIC 'ISO/IEC 10740-2:1993//NOTATION
                          Information technology -
                          Text and office systems -
                          Referenced Data Transfer -
                          Part 2: Protocol specifications//EN'   >
<!NOTATION HyTime   PUBLIC 'ISO/IEC 10744:1992//NOTATION
                          Information technology -
                          Hypermedia/Time-based Structuring
                          Language (HyTime)//EN'
                          -- note: revised HyTime uses '1997' -->
<!NOTATION JPEG     PUBLIC 'ISO/IEC 10918:1993//NOTATION
                          Digital Compression and Coding of
                          Continuous-tone Still Images
                          (JPEG)//EN'
```

```
                                  'image/jpeg'                    >
<!NOTATION MPEG1vid PUBLIC 'ISO/IEC 11172-2:1993//NOTATION
                                  Information technology -
                                  Coding of moving pictures and associated
                                  audio for digital storage media at up to
                                  about 1,5 Mbit/s -
                                  Part 2: Video//EN'
                                  'video/mpeg'                    >
<!NOTATION MPEG1aud PUBLIC 'ISO/IEC 11172-3:1993//NOTATION
                                  Information technology -
                                  Coding of moving pictures and associated
                                  audio for digital storage media at up to
                                  about 1,5 Mbit/s -
                                  Part 3: Audio//EN'                >
<!NOTATION MPEG2vid PUBLIC 'ISO/IEC 13818-2:1995//NOTATION
                                  Information technology -
                                  Coding of moving pictures and associated
                                  audio: Part 2: Video//EN'         >
<!NOTATION MPEG2aud PUBLIC 'ISO/IEC 13818-3:1995//NOTATION
                                  Coding of moving pictures and associated
                                  audio: Part 3: Audio//EN'         >
<!NOTATION MPEG2AAC PUBLIC 'ISO/IEC 13818-7:1997//NOTATION
                                  Coding of moving pictures and associated
                                  audio: Part 7: Advanced Audio Coding (AAC)//EN'>
<!NOTATION JBIG     PUBLIC 'ISO/IEC 11544:1993//NOTATION
                                  Information technology -
                                  Coded representation of picture
                                  and audio information -
                                  Progressive bi-level image
                                · compression//EN'                 >
<!NOTATION MHEG PUBLIC 'ISO/IEC 13522-1:1996//NOTATION
                                  Information technology -
                                  Coded representation of multimedia
                                  and hypermedia information objects (MHEG):
                                  Part 1: MHEG objects representation//EN' >
<!NOTATION MHEG-3 PUBLIC 'ISO/IEC 13522-1:1996//NOTATION
                                  Information technology -
                                  Coded representation of multimedia
                                  and hypermedia information objects (MHEG):
                                  Part 3: MHEG script interchange
                                  representation//EN' >
<!NOTATION IGES PUBLIC '-//NBS IR 88-3813//NOTATION
                                  Initial Graphics Exchange Specification
                                  (IGES)//EN'
                                  'model/iges'   -- or 'application/iges' >
```

```
<!NOTATION G4-fax    PUBLIC 'UNREGISTERED::ITU VII.3 T 6//NOTATION Blue book -
                            Terminal equipment and protocols for
                            telematic services - Facsimile encoding
                            schemes and coding control functions for
                            group 4 facsimile apparatus//EN'      >
<!NOTATION G3-fax    PUBLIC 'UNREGISTERED::ITU VII.3 T 4//NOTATION Red book -
                            Terminal equipment and protocols for
                            telematic services - Facsimile encoding
                            schemes and coding control functions for
                            group 3 facsimile apparatus//EN'      >
<!NOTATION CCITT4-1 PUBLIC 'UNREGISTERED::ITU VII.3 T 6//NOTATION Group 4
                            Facsimile Type 1 Untiled Raster//EN'>
<!NOTATION CCITT4-2 PUBLIC 'UNREGISTERED::ITU VII.3 T 6//NOTATION Group 4
                            Facsimile Type 2 Tiled Raster//EN'   >
<!NOTATION ITU-601   PUBLIC 'UNREGISTERED::ITU::Recommendation 601//NOTATION
                            Definition of analogue/digital video
                            signals//EN'                          >
<!NOTATION ITU-709   PUBLIC 'UNREGISTERED::ITU::Recommendation 790//NOTATION
                            Basic parameter values for the HDTV
                            standard for international programme
                            exchange//EN'                         >
<!NOTATION ITU-G711 PUBLIC 'UNREGISTERED::ITU::G.711//NOTATION Pulse code
                            modulation (PCM) of voice
                            frequencies//EN'                      >
<!NOTATION ITU-G721 PUBLIC 'UNREGISTERED::ITU::G.721//NOTATION 32kbit/s
                            adaptive pulse code modulation
                            (ADPCM)//EN'                          >
<!NOTATION ITU-G722 PUBLIC 'UNREGISTERED::ITU::G.722//NOTATION 7kHz
                            audio-coding within 64kbit/s//EN'     >
<!NOTATION ITU-J52   PUBLIC 'UNREGISTERED::ITU::J.52//NOTATION Digital
                            transmission of high quality sound
                            programme signals using one, two or
                            three 64kbit/s channels per mono signal
                            and up to six per stereo channel)//EN' >
<!NOTATION ITU-J80   PUBLIC 'UNREGISTERED::ITU::J.80//NOTATION Transmission of
                            component-coded digital TV signals
                            for contribution applications at bit
                            rates near 140 Mbit/s//EN'            >
<!NOTATION ITU-J81   PUBLIC 'UNREGISTERED::ITU::J.81//NOTATION Transmission of
                            component-codd digital TV signals for
                            contribution-quality applications at
                            the third hierarchical level of CCITT
                            (34-45 Mbit/s)//EN'                   >
<!NOTATION ITU-T100 PUBLIC 'UNREGISTERED::ITU::T.100//NOTATION
                            Videotext//EN' >
```

```
<!NOTATION ITU-T120 PUBLIC 'UNREGISTERED::ITU::T.120//NOTATION Transmission
                            protocols for multimedia data
                            communications//EN'                      >
<!NOTATION ITU-F310 PUBLIC 'UNREGISTERED::ITU::F.310//NOTATION Broadband
                            Videotext//EN'                           >
<!NOTATION ITU-F821 PUBLIC 'UNREGISTERED::ITU::F.821//NOTATION Broadband
                            TV Distribution//EN'                     >
<!NOTATION ITU-F822 PUBLIC 'UNREGISTERED::ITU::F.822//NOTATION Broadband
                            HDTV Distribution//EN'                   >
<!NOTATION ITU-MDV  PUBLIC 'UNREGISTERED::ITU::MDV//NOTATION Multimedia
                            Delivery Service//EN'                    >
<!NOTATION ITU-MDD  PUBLIC 'UNREGISTERED::ITU::MDV//NOTATION Multimedia
                            Distribution Service//EN'                >
<!NOTATION ITU-MBTF PUBLIC 'UNREGISTERED::ITU::MBTF//NOTATION Multipoint
                            Binary File Transfer//EN'                >
<!NOTATION SMPTE125 PUBLIC '-//SMPTE::125M-1992//NOTATAION 10 Bit
                            Component Video Signal 4:2:2 -
                            Bit-Parallel Digital Interface//EN'      >
<!NOTATION SMPTE259 PUBLIC '-//SMPTE::259M-1993//NOTATION 10 Bit
                            4:2:2 Component and 4fsc NTSC Composite
                            Digital Signals - Serial Digital
                            Interface//EN'                           >
<!NOTATION S17.131  PUBLIC '-//SMPTE::S17.131//NOTATION Bit-Serial
                            Digital Interface for High-Definition
                            Television Systems//EN'                  >
```

There are notations for the filename notations of various file systems and queries (SQL, XML) in the chapter 15 Formal System Identifiers. There are notation declarations for ISO/IEC 9541-2:1993 Typeface Design Groupings in chapter 19, page 3-26.

[*HyTime* '97] see clause A.2.3, defines a convenient language to allow the lexical specification of attribute values and data that are separated by whitespace into tokens—

```
<!NOTATION HyLex PUBLIC     'ISO/IEC 10744:1997//NOTATION
                            HyTime Lexical Model Notation
                            (HyLex)//EN' >
```

See chapter 16 for a discussion of HyLex. HyTime also gives a notation for POSIX regular expressions, which you can use for general text strings that are not tokens—

```
<!NOTATION regex PUBLIC      'ISO/IEC 9945-2:1992//NOTATION
                             POSIX Regular Expression Notation//EN' >
```

HyLex also specifies a large set of default notations, covering all SGML and HyTime constructs, for example 'ISO/IEC 10744:1992//NOTATION LEXTYPE Formal System Identifier//EN'.

RFC 2234 defines an notation for Augmented Backus-Naur Form grammars—

```
<!NOTATION ABNF PUBLIC
      '+//ISBN 0-13-614223-0::The SGML Cookbook//NOTATION
      RCF 2234::Augmented BNF for Syntax Specification: ABNF//EN' >
```

Time and Space

Other standard notations of importance are the ISO date format (yyyy-mm-dd), and the SI second and meter—

```
<!NOTATION iso-date PUBLIC   'ISO 8601:1988//NOTATION Data elements and
                             interchange formats -
InformationInterchange
                             - Representation of dates and times//EN'>
<!NOTATION SIsecond PUBLIC   'ISO/IEC 10744:1997//NOTATION Systeme
                             International second//EN'>
<!NOTATION SImeter PUBLIC    'ISO/IEC 10744:1997//NOTATION Systeme
                             International meter//EN' >
<!NOTATION SIkg PUBLIC       -- mass --
                             'ISO/IEC 10744:1997//NOTATION Systeme
                             International kilogram//EN'>
<!NOTATION SIkelvin PUBLIC   -- Thermodynamic Temperature --
                             'ISO/IEC 10744:1997//NOTATION Systeme
                             International kelvin//EN'  >
<!NOTATION SIcd PUBLIC       -- Luminous Intensity --
                             'ISO/IEC 10744:1997//NOTATION Systeme
```

```
                              International candala//EN' >
<!NOTATION SIampere PUBLIC    -- Electric Current --
                              'ISO/IEC 10744:1997//NOTATION Systeme
                              International ampere//EN'  >
<!NOTATION SImole PUBLIC      -- Anount of Substance --
                              'ISO/IEC 10744:1997//NOTATION Systeme
                              International mole//EN'     >
<!NOTATION SIradian PUBLIC    -- Plane Angle --
                              'ISO/IEC 10744:1997//NOTATION Systeme
                              International radian//EN'  >
<!NOTATION SIsr PUBLIC        -- Solid Angle --
                              'ISO/IEC 10744:1997//NOTATION Systeme
                              International steradian//EN' >
```

Giving ISO/IEC 10744 as the owner in the Formal Public Identifier, you can construct other SI-derived units on the same pattern.

[*HyTime* '97] Annex C defines a whole series of useful measurement domains derived from the Standard Measurement Units (smu) SIsecond and SImeter and in 'ISO/IEC 10744:1997//TEXT Useful Measurement Domain Definitions//EN'—

- For time① (SI second), these include granules of: millenium, year, decade, fortnight, week, day, half-hour, quarter-hour, minute, second, SMPTE-24-drop, PC-tick, motion-picture, SMPTE-24, European, SECAM, PAL, dsec, csec, msec, usec, nsec, psec, asec, among others.

- For space (SI meter), these include granules of: league, mile, quarter-mile, furlong, chain, rod, pole, perch, fathom, yard, royal-cubit, sumerian-cubit, cubit, foot, hand, thumb, inch, barleycorn, pica, point, milliinch, microinch, parsec, lightyear, nautical mile, km, meter, cm, mm, um, nm, angstrom, to name a few.

To use these measurement units for attributes, you might adopt the HyTime naming convention—

---

1. See chapter 16, *Embedded Notations,* page 2-118 for more details on lexical type specification and date formats.

```
Granule NAME #REQUIRED        -- Measurement Granule --
```

If you want to define your own measurement granules, you can use

```
gn CDATA #REQUIRED      -- new name for granule    --
gd CDATA #REQUIRED      -- ratio e.g. '10 pica'    --
```

Non-Standard

Here are formal public identifiers for many common notations. [1]

The TeX typesetting language, which is a notation very often used to embed mathematical formulæ in SGML documents, is defined in Donald Knuth's book *The TeXbook*—

```
<!NOTATION TEX PUBLIC
          '+//ISBN 0-13-614223-0::The SGML Cookbook//NOTATION
           ISBN 0-201-13448-9::Knuth::TeX//EN' >
```

Warnock et al's page description language PostScript is defined in the PostScript reference manual—

```
<!NOTATION POSTSCRIPT PUBLIC
          '+//ISBN 0-13-614223-0::The SGML Cookbook//NOTATION
           ISBN 0-201-18127-4::Adobe::PostScript//EN'
          'application/postscript'>
```

Thee Adobe Type 1 font format likewise defined in a book—

```
<!NOTATION type1_font PUBLIC
          '+//ISBN 0-13-614223-0::The SGML Cookbook//NOTATION
```

---

1. Many of these are corrected versions of the identifiers suggested by Don Stichfield of INSO for discussion purposes in the Internet-Draft document *"Using Catalogs and MIME to Exchange SGML Documents."*

```
ISBN 0-201-57044::Adobe Type 1 Font Format::version
1.1::1990//EN' >
```

The Tcl scripting language is defined in John K. Ousterhout's book *Tcl and the Tk Toolkit*—

```
<!NOTATION TCL PUBLIC
           '+//ISBN 0-13-614223-0::The SGML Cookbook//NOTATION
             ISBN 0-201-63337-X::Addison-Wesley::Tcl//EN'
```

Here are some standard graphics files formats—

```
<!NOTATION gif PUBLIC
        '+//ISBN 0-13-614223-0::The SGML Cookbook//NOTATION
           ISBN 0-7923-91::Compuserve Graphic Interchange Format//EN'
        'image/gif'>
<!NOTATION tiff.uncomp PUBLIC
        '+//ISBN 0-13-614223-0::The SGML Cookbook//NOTATION
           ISBN 0-7923-91::Aldus/Microsoft Tagged Interchange
           File Format//EN'
        'image/tiff'>
<!NOTATION epsi PUBLIC
        '+//ISBN 0-13-614223-0::The SGML Cookbook//NOTATION
           ISBN 0-7923-91::Adobe Systems
           Encapsulated PostScript//EN' >
<!NOTATION bmp PUBLIC
        '+//ISBN 0-13-614223-0::The SGML Cookbook//NOTATION
           ISBN 0-7923-9432-1::Microsoft Windows Bitmap//EN' >
<!NOTATION pcx PUBLIC
         '+//ISBN 0-13-614223-0::The SGML Cookbook//NOTATION
           ISBN 0-7923-9432-1::ZSoft PCX bitmap//EN'>
<!NOTATION wmf PUBLIC
         '+//ISBN 0-13-614223-0::The SGML Cookbook//NOTATION
           ISBN 0-7923-9432-1::Microsoft Windows Metafile//EN'>
<!NOTATION xlib-colors PUBLIC
         '+//ISBN 0-13-614223-0::The SGML Cookbook//NOTATION
           ISBN 0-201-52370-1::X Windows System Technical
           Reference::X11.3 XLIB colormap//EN' >
```

Other formal public identifiers can be created using the Internet email domain names (the following are examples only, and may be incorrect)—

```
<!NOTATION XML PUBLIC
         '+//IDN W3.ORG//NOTATION Extensible Markup Language//EN'>
<!NOTATION XLL PUBLIC
         '+//IDN W3.ORG//NOTATION Extensible Linking Language//EN'>
<!NOTATION XSL PUBLIC
         '+//IDN W3.ORG//NOTATION Extensible Style Language//EN'>
<!NOTATION css PUBLIC
         '+//IDN W3.ORG//NOTATION Cascading StyleSheet//EN'>
<!NOTATION acss PUBLIC
         '+//IDN W3.ORG//NOTATION Aural Cascading StyleSheet//EN'>
<!NOTATION rtf PUBLIC
         '+//IDN Microsoft.com//NOTATION Rich Text Format//EN'
         'application/rtf'>
<!NOTATION wp5.1 PUBLIC
         '+//IDN Corel.com//NOTATION Word Perfect 5.1//EN'
         'application/word-perfect5.1' >
<!NOTATION pdf PUBLIC
         '+//IDN Adobe.com//NOTATION Portable Document Format//EN'
         'application/pdf' >
<!NOTATION qtime PUBLIC
         '+//IDN Apple.com//NOTATION Quicktime//EN'
         'video/quicktime' >
```

Finally, here are some examples of formal public identifiers using unregistered owners (again, these are examples only, to help you construct identifiers using your own organization as the owner identifier)—

```
<!NOTATION so-frag PUBLIC
     '-//SGML Open//NOTATION Fragment Context Specification//EN'>
<!NOTATION so-cat PUBLIC
     '-//SGML Open//NOTATION Catalog//EN'>
<!NOTATION SPREAD-glyph PUBLIC
     '-//SPREAD//NOTATION glyph shape encoding method//JP'>
```

In a perfect world, everything with an FPI would only have a single, authoritative FPI. However, it is common (but bad practice) for people to fake an FPI for a notation because the owner of the public text has not published one. It is worthwhile making the effort to use the correct FPI, where one can be found, because it minimizes gratuitous Catalog file preparation at the user-end. If you cannot find one, make up an FPI with your own organization as the owner identifier, to conform to the standard.

Formal System Identifiers

Chapter 15

This chapter

…shows how to get smarter retrieval of stored resources and objects using Formal System Identifiers, and how FSIs are just one example of pseudo-SGML markup.

There are many cases where [*SGML '86*] did not define markup and delimiters, but experience has shown that markup, to label the notation used and to allow attribute specifications, is needed. It is only natural that people appropriate SGML syntax for this purpose. This markup is often called *pseudo–SGML markup* (pseudo-SGML elements, pseudo-SGML attributes, etc.) without any derogatory intent. It is found in

- system identifiers, now standardized in SGML Formal System Identifiers (defined in 1997 annex A. 6 of [*Hytime97*]);

- PI headers, notably those of the Extensible Markup Language (XML);

- entity text; and

- attribute values, in order to allow attribute values to have structure and metadata. [1]

Naming conventions can be very useful for the other names in SGML apart from system and public identifiers. See chapter 16, page 2-111, for a discussion on *fielded names* for Generic Identifiers and IDs.

---

1. Using pseudo-SGML markup inside attribute values is fine, in moderation. However, it is better to use elements for any complicated structures. Even if the information has the nature of an attribute, elements are the only SGML markup available. If you do not want to compromise your content model, you can always make a special metadata section and just use an IDREF attribute on your element to point to its metadata.

Formal System Identifiers

A entity declaration is a kind of link to allow the nomination and retrieval of data. It is the interface between entities and your computer's data storage. The address, or addresses, of the data are specified in the system identifier.

ISO Definition

system identifier System data that specifies the file identifier, storage location, program invocation, data stream position, or other system-specific information that locates an external entity.

(ISO 8879:1986 glossary)

formal system identifier specifies a standardized structure for system identifiers, known as a 'Formal System Identifier'(FSI). An FSI can support arbitrary mappings between entities and storage objects, including one-to-many, many-to-one, distributed storage, and containers.

(ISO/IEC 10744:1997 A.6)

In many simple SGML implementations, the system identifier is just a local filename, or perhaps an Internet Universal Resource Locator ([URL]). However, system identifiers can belong to any storage system you like, including databases and compressed archive files.

But what can you do when you have your data stored in several different external media or formats? You need to be able to specify much more than just the file name, and potentially much more than just an Internet URL. The Formal System Identifiers Definition Requirements annex of [HyTime97](A.6) defines a useful convention for marking up system identifiers using a familiar element and attribute syntax: Formal System Identifiers (FSI). For example,

```
<!-- Example of a formal system identifier -->
<!ENTITY example SYSTEM
        "<osfile bctf='euc-jp' records='crlf'>x1.txt; x2.txt"
>
```

In this example, the entity is

- stored in two files `x1.txt` and `x2.text` on the local operating system (`osfile`),

- encoded with the Japanese version of EUC(Extended Unix Code), and

- uses the control characters Carriage Return followed by Line Feed to represent newlines.

The FSI gives enough information in the attributes for the storage manager to locate and convert the storage object into the form required for parsing.

As another example, a very simple but useful method to allow your application to be fed text from another program without going through the file system is to use input/output redirection and anonymous pipes. In UNIX and many other modern operating systems, you can do this by using file descriptors: the file descriptor 0 is standard input. So on a UNIX system you could give the shell command:

```
% date | SGML-processor
```

(where `date` gives the current date) and then use the following entity declaration (`osfd` stands for 'operating system file descriptor'):

```
<!-- A formal system identifier to read from standard input -->
<!ENTITY date SYSTEM '<osfd>0'>
```

Some SGML systems allow you to add your own storage managers. You can use the FSI to select these storage managers. The Formal System Identifiers standard defines many useful keywords and attributes, but if something is not there, you can make up your own. For example, if you have your own database system, you define your own storage manager to interface to it—

```
<!-- A formal system identifier to read from a database -->
<!ENTITY example SYSTEM
                "<my-database base='australia'>sydney.data"
>
```

At this point, some people will be thinking *"Are FSIs a kind of query language then?"* The answer is no – an FSI says *"I want this particular object, which I assume to be there,"* while a query is more saying *"I want objects that match these criteria, if any exist."*

Becoming an FSI User

If you use Formal System Identifiers in your document, make sure the APPINFO field in the SGML declaration contains the string FSISM, which flags *'I use FSIs to the SGML system and to people receiving the SGML document.'* You declare which storage managers your document can use or requires in the DTD using a special Processing Instruction—

```
<!-- Pattern for Formal System Identifier declaration -->
<?IS10744 FSIDR aaa bbb ccc ...>
```

where aaa, bbb and ccc are the names of notation declarations for the storage. The standard-defined storage manager notations include—

```
<!-- Storage Manager Notation Declarations -->
<!NOTATION osfile    PUBLIC 'ISO/IEC 10744:1997//NOTATION
                     FSISM LOCAL
                     Operating System File//EN' >
<!NOTATION osfd      PUBLIC 'ISO/IEC 10744:1997//NOTATION
                     FSISM LOCAL
                     Operating System File Descriptor//EN' >
<!NOTATION URL       PUBLIC 'ISO/IEC 10744:1997//NOTATION
                     FSISM PORTABLE
                     Uniform Resource Locator//EN' >
<!NOTATION neutral   -- '/' translated to local directory convention --
                     PUBLIC 'ISO/IEC 10744:1997//NOTATION
                     FSISM PORTABLE
                     Neutral File Identifier//EN' >
<!ATTLIST #NOTATION neutral
        fold    ( fold | nofold )    fold    -- case folding -->
<!NOTATION mimetype PUBLIC '-//IETF/RFC1521//NOTATION
                     FSISM PORTABLE
                     MIME Content Type//EN'  -- Refer RFC 1700 -->
<!NOTATION Literal   PUBLIC 'ISO/IEC 10744:1997//NOTATION
                     FSISM GLOBAL
                     Literal Text//EN' >
<!NOTATION ThisOne   PUBLIC 'ISO/IEC 10744:1997//NOTATION
                     FSISM GLOBAL
                     This One Storage Manager//EN' >
<!ATTLIST #NOTATION ThisOne
    entity CDATA #IMPLIED    -- default: 'current' entity -->
<!NOTATION tar       PUBLIC 'ISO/IEC 9945-1:1990//NOTATION
                     FSISM CONTAINER
                     Posix Tape Archive//EN'
                     'application/x-tar
<!NOTATION mime      PUBLIC '-//IETF/RFC1521//NOTATION
                     FSISM CONTAINER
                     Multimedia Internet Mail Extensions//EN'
<!ATTLIST #NOTATION ( tar, mime )
    in CDATA #REQUIRED          -- an entity or an FSI -->
```

The storage managers can have various attributes.① These include—

```
<!ATTLIST #NOTATION SMName
    records    -- Record boundary recognition --
      ( asis | cr | lf | crlf | lfcr | rms | find ) system
    tracking  -- Record boundary tracking in messages --
      ( track | notrack ) track
    encoding  -- e.g. iso8859-n, sjis, euc-jp, unicode --
        NAME #IMPLIED
    btcf    -- e.g. identity, fixed-2, fixed-4 --
        NAME #IMPLIED
    seal    -- integrity information --
        CDATA    #IMPLIED
    compress -- Compression information  --
        CDATA    #IMPLIED
    encrypt  -- Encryption information  --
        CDATA    #IMPLIED
>
```

Here is an example of a sealing notation—the Internet standard MD5:

```
<!NOTATION md5        PUBLIC '-//IETF/RFC1544//NOTATION
                      FSIDR SEAL
                      Content-MD5 Header Field//EN' >
```

---

1. Note that *SMName* is merely the placeholder in the architectural form for the particular storage manager's notation name.

Here is an example of an encoding declaration for Unicode:

```
<!NOTATION UNICODE
                    -- This represents each character in the Basic
                       Multilingual Plane of ISO/IEC 10646-1 by two
                       octets. The bytes representing the entire storage
                       object may be preceded by a pair of bytes
                       representing the byte order mark character
                       (0xFEFF). The bytes representing each bit
                       combination are in the system byte order, unless
                       the byte order mark character is present, in
                       which case the order of its bytes determines the
                       byte order. When the storage object is read, any
                       byte order mark character is discarded. --

                       PUBLIC 'ISO/IEC 10744:1992//NOTATION
                       FSIDR ENCODING
                       UNICODE Encoding//EN'>
```

It is reasonable to ask *"Why cannot the attributes for the storage managers simply be given as data attributes on the entity declarations?"* The reason is that FSIs deal with the text in storage before it becomes an SGML entity, while a data attribute describes things about the data after it has become an SGML entity.

Embedded Notations

Chapter 16

This chapter

...shows how to embed other special-purpose notations inside SGML attributes and data.

SGML tags are convenient and quickly become familiar. You can choose element type names (also known as generic identifiers, or GIs) to clearly label the structures you are marking up. If you do not like them, you can choose other strings for the delimiters in the SGML declaration. You can even reduce explicit tagging to a minimum by using short-reference delimiters (where a custom delimiter can be used instead of an entity reference or other tag) and minimization (where you can leave intermediate-levels of start- and end-tags out and the SGML parser will use built-in rules to infer them). [1]

SGML documents also often involve the use of text strings that conform to simple notations which computer scientists call *little languages*. Some of these are standard and some are application-dependent. Either way, in SGML you treat them the same way as notations that are used for graphics entities or other purposes. The major uses of these embedded notations are

- for naming,

- for style-sheets,

- for scripts,

- for fragment exchange.

It is possible to use the HyLex modeling language to specify the grammar of your own notation. This lets you add lexical type-checking to your attributes and to the data-content of elements. See *Defining Data Types*, page 2-115 below.

---

1. Short-references are particularly appropriate for mathematical or chemical markup, and for simple but long databases. In this book I have tried to avoid the features of SGML that are not available to XML developers: hence there is little or no reference to short-references. One interesting point to be made about short-references and other forms of minimization is that their use is primarily intended to make documents easier to read, rather than to make them smaller: File compression is a better method of reducing file size than unclear identifier names or minimization.

Naming

The most important of the embedded notations are used for naming:

- *[ISO 9070]* formal public identifiers,

- SGML public text Formal Public Identifiers (see chapter 13, *Formal Public Identifiers*, page 2-77),

- SGML Formal System Identifiers (see chapter 15, *Formal System Identifiers*, page 2-101),

- HTML URIs,

- XLL extended pointers.

There is a very important reason for this: humans prefer a compound name to one split up into lots of attributes. We prefer to let the computer do the work, especially if we don't really care what the parts mean.

So—

```
<!-- Example of an embedded notation: a formal system identifier -->
<p href='<url>http://www.me.com/dir/file.txt'>
```

is preferable to—

```
<!-- Example of an FSI split with separate attributes for each part -->
<p construct='url' method='http' node='www.me.com'
          file='/dir/file.text'>
```

If we make the `method` attribute explicit, like in the example, the suggestion is being made *"this is important enough to get its own attribute."* However, the user, unless they are technical, just wants to know that if they type in some crazy long name, they get to the corresponding resource. The purpose of SGML is to make sure that markup is good for both humans and computers: a name like that is perfectly parseable for a computer, and fits neatly into the human mental category of "a name."

Stylesheets and Scripts

The next most common type of embedded notation is used for formatting text and for programming behavior—

- HTML is a rich source of embedded notations. For example:

  - inside `style` elements: e.g., use Cascading Style Sheets [*CSS*] with attribute `type='text/css'`;

  - inside `div` or `span` elements, with a `style` attribute: e.g., the in-line CSS *declarations* used for HTML positioning;

  - inside `script` elements: e.g., use ECMAscript or Javascript with attribute `language='text/javascript'`;

  - inside `object` elements: e.g., use Avi audiovisual with attribute `type='application/avi'`;

  - inside the `content` attribute of `meta` elements: e.g., use [*PICS*] content labeling with attribute `http-equiv='PICS-label'`.

- ISO Document Style and Semantics Specification Language. Note that DSSSL exists in several different forms—

  - the full ISO standard DSSSL, which is based on IEEE Scheme, a version of LISP;

  - DSSSL-O, a subset of DSSSL defined for on-line needs; and

  - XSL, the XML Style Language, which (under the proposals in discussion as this book went to press) uses a combination of high-level element types (to replace the use of DSSSL Scheme's special forms) and snippets of ECMA-script (the European standardized version of JavaScript) source code, embedded in `<eval>` elements.

A programming language has completely different visual and technical needs from a markup language. In just the same way as programming languages are not suited for data markup, SGML is not particularly suited for being used as a programming language syntax (even though it has been done, for example in the MID programming language used for Interactive Electronic Technical Manuals (see chapter 12, page 2-69, *Interactive Systems*). ①

If you embed text from another language into your SGML document, you should label the element or entity containing the text with a NOTATION attribute. The following example labels the element type both SGML-style (with a `notation` attribute), and HTML-style (with a `type` attribute)—

```
<!-- Example of declarations for HTML style element type and CSS -->
<!NOTATION css PUBLIC
      '+//IDN W3.ORG//NOTATION Cascading Style Sheet//EN' >
<!ELEMENT style   (#PCDATA)>
<!ATTLIST style
  notation        NOTATION ( css ) #IMPLIED
  type            CDATA 'text/css'>
```

This can be used simply—

```
<!-- Example of simple use of style element type -->
<style>
heading { font: helvetica }
</style>
```

To go 100% SGML markup, the CSS delimiter characters Record Start, '{ : ; , }' could be declared to be SGML short reference delimiters. With the appropriate short reference delimiters, the style-sheet magically becomes readable as SGML. ②

---

1. The most successful example of SGML as a programming language that I have seen uses markup at a declaration and block level. The statement level seemed to be more conventional. This allowed both literate programming [*Knuth*], and a high level of platform-neutrality – code could be generated for the major operating systems on mainframes, workstations and personal computers.

2. If you do need to build your own notation, a little care can mean that it can also be parsed as SGML even if it does not use angle-bracket delimited tags. People embedding languages in XML documents are well advised to look into this, since it may mean they can just use standard SGML tools rather than building their own sub-parser. (Note: XML 1.0 does not support short references.)

······ If your style-sheet is large or applies to a family of documents, then it is better to include it by reference rather than directly. This eases maintainability.

Once again, we ask *"Is this a pattern in elements, entities or processing instructions?"*

HTML implementations typically do not support PIs or entities, so HTML must use elements. Some HTML server implementations allow "server-side includes." A server-side include is often an instruction to some macro-processor (often the C preprocessor `cpp`) and is marked-up inside SGML comments. The use of comments in this way may be justified somewhat, if we pretend they are really for things intended to be stripped before the end-user sees them. However, SGML comments really are not for that purpose: they are to give documentation for humans.

A style-sheet may be an external entity, but it performs processing action and thus is best marked-up with processing instructions. However, the ease of using PIs on your system, the familiarity of them to your staff, and your house style may easily make you prefer to use an element or an entity reference—

- For direct insertion using a PI:

```
<?MY-ML
    notation='dsssl'
    href='x.dsl'
    encoding='iso8859-1' ?>
```

- For insertion using an entity reference:

```
<!ENTITY a-style
    SYSTEM 'x.dsl'
    NDATA dsssl [ encoding='iso8859-1'] >
```

- For reference with an element:

```
<style
    notation='dsssl'
    fsi="<osfile encoding='iso8859-1'>x.dsl" >
```

which you also do with the HTML element `link`:

```
<link
rel='style-sheet'
href='xstyle.css' >
```

Defining Data Types

Newcomers to SGML are often surprised that it does not define a rich set of primitive types for attributes and the data content of elements. This is because SGML is a markup language, and not an information modeling language *per se*: SGML gives you facilities for you to declare and use the particular types you need for your own document system, rather than just standardizing on a few. This section shows how to specify your own data types, using notations and lexical models.

Lexical Typing using Standard Notation Names

The simplest way to define your own data type for the data content of an element type is simply to give the element a NOTATION attribute. (Note: XML 1.0 does not support NOTATION attributes. Use a NMTOKEN attribute instead, and make your own application convention to make you application check conformance with the notation.) In the following example, the element contains a date:

```
<!NOTATION iso-date PUBLIC 'ISO 8601:1988//NOTATION Text elements and
                            Interchange formats - Information Interchange
-
                            Representation of dates and times//EN'>
<!ELEMENT date     ( #PCDATA )>
<!ATTLIST date
    notation NMTOKEN "iso-date"
    person   CDATA    #REQUIRED >
...
<date person="Rick Jelliffe">1960-05-18</date>
```

[*Web SGML*] introduces a new type of attribute, the DATA attribute, which uses a notation name for the type of the attribute. (Note: XML 1.0 does not support notation name attributes.) For example, to specify that the attribute value should be a date, again using the ISO standard date format—

```
<!NOTATION iso-date PUBLIC 'ISO 8601:1988//NOTATION Text elements and
                     interchange formats - Information Interchange -
                     Representation of dates and times//EN'>
<!ELEMENT person   ( #PCDATA )>
<!ATTLIST person
     born DATA  iso-date #REQUIRED >
...
<person born="1960-05-18">Rick Jelliffe</person>
```

Lexical Typing using Lexical Models

You can always make up your own lexical model to suit your particular needs. [*HyTime*] provides two notations for defining lexical models:

• POSIX regular-expressions, which are suitable for data that is not divided into tokens by whitespace or punctuation, and

• HyLex, which lets you specify simple token-based lexical types, like the SGML declaration or pseudo-attributes. It is useful for SGML-aware strings and for constraining attribute values and the data content of elements. HyTime gives a complete set of SGML token types for use in HyLex patterns.

By convention, you call an attribute whose value conforms to a lexical model lextype.[1]

---

1. lextype has a built-in assumption that the characters in the data have been normalized. If this is not the case, ulextype is the appropriate name. "Normalized" means, among other things, that lower-case characters have been converted to upper-case, and whitespace sequences are collapsed into single spaces: the same normalization rule is used for Formal Public Identifiers.

HyLex is basically the same as the content model notation used for the content models in standard element type declarations, but with a few additions to cope with string matching.

HyLex & POSIX Regular Expression Delimiters

String	Description	String	Description
(	Group open	)	Group close
[	single character pattern open (POSIX only)	]	Single character pattern close (POSIX only)
,	Sequence (HyLex only)	|	Or
'	Literal delimiter (HyLex only)	'	Alternate literal delimiter (HyLex only)
?	Optional	+	Required and repeatable
*	Optional and repeatable	–	Negation, and range
.	Single character wildcard (POSIX only)	char	Single character wildcard (char is an intrinsic lexical type)
\	Escape delimiter (POSIX only)	#	Reserved name indicator, in particular for the negation keyword #NOT (HyLex only)

An Attribute for Dates using HyLex

Web SGML introduces a new type of attribute, the DATA attribute, which uses a notation and allows you to specify the data attributes for that notation.(Note: XML 1.0 does not support DATA attributes.) For example, to specify that the attribute value should be a date, using HyLex notation—

```
<!NOTATION HyLex PUBLIC       'ISO/IEC 10744:1997//NOTATION
                              HyTime Lexical Model Notation
                              (HyLex)//EN' >
<!ATTLIST #NOTATION HyLex
    norm ( norm | unorm ) "unorm"
    model CDATA          #REQUIRED >
<!ELEMENT person ( #PCDATA ) >
<!ATTLIST person
    born DATA HyLex
        [ model="digit, digit, digit, digit, '-',
                 digit, digit,'-', digit, digit "
          norm="unorm"     ]     #REQUIRED >
...
<person born="1960-05-18">Rick Jelliffe</person>
```

Date using POSIX Regular Expressions

If you are not using Web SGML, or want to specify a model for the data content of an element, you can use the [*HyTime '97*] A.2 Lexical Type Definition Requirements [*LTDR*]. These are complicated but rich. For example, to declare a standard *yyyy–mm–dd* date format:

✓ Create a separate document called a *lexical type definition set*. In it declare the notation being used to express the lexical type (in this case, POSIX regular expressions) and define the lexical type.

```
<!-- lextype.sgm:  a lexical model for dates -->
<!LEXTYPE yyyy-mm-dd
   '[012][01-9][01-9][01-9]-[01][01-9]-[0123][01-9]'
 >
```

✓ In the main document declare the notation used in the lexical type definition set.

```
<!NOTATION regex -- POSIX regular expression notation -
  PUBLIC 'ISO/IEC 9945-2:1992//NOTATION
         POSIX Regular Expression Notation//EN' >
```

✓ In the main document declare a parameter entity for the lexical type definition set.

```
<!ENTITY % date-entity SYSTEM "lextype.sgm"
   CDATA regex >
```

✓ In the main document, make a *lexical type use declaration* in a processing instruction, to tell the application that the entity contains the lexical model used in the document.

```
<?IS10744 LEXUSE date-entity ?>
```

✓ Then declare the element with a **lextype** attribute, which says *the contents of this element should conform to the lexical type model called* **yyyy-mm-dd**.

```
<!ELEMENT date ( #PCDATA )>
<!ATTLIST date
        lextype CDATA '#CONTENT yyyy-mm-dd'>
```

✓ Finally, using it is transparent.

```
<date>1960-05-18</date>
```

Embedding Other Notations

You can use your SGML document more as a wrapper – for example, as a convenient way to manage legacy text that you do not want to, or cannot, convert to SGML markup.

⚠ ⋯⋯ If the legacy text is in a character–based (rather than binary) form, you may decide to embed it in your document directly rather than with a link or reference. But make sure that you replace all occurrences of potential delimiters (<, and &) with entity references (< and &). In general, it is simpler to use CDATA or NDATA external entities for external files that use other notations.

Fragment Interchange

It is inconvenient to have the whole document retrieved for you if you only need a fragment. However, often you will also need some contextual information that occurs outside the fragment. For example, you may be interested in a single quotation paragraph, but also need to know which chapter that quotation appears in.

Chapter 4, page 1-85 *et seq.*, has a discussion of various DTD policies you can adopt that will allow your users to interchange (a fancy name for cut-and-paste, where the cutting may be on a different system from the pasting) fragments of larger SGML documents. This is particularly useful when the fragment has been selected by a query, for example an XML extended pointer link or a HyTime query.

SGML Open has developed a Fragment Interchange specification: TR9601–1996 'Fragment Interchange' [*DeRose, Grosso*]. An example of a FRAG PI in use is:

```
<!-- This entity contains a fragment in the SGML Open
     Fragment Interchange notation.
     '-//SGML Open//NOTATION Fragment Context Specification//EN'
-->
<?SO FRAG
     (COMMENT "This is one cell of an HTML table")
     (CONTEXT html (head ()
          body (table #2 (tr #3 ( td #4()#fragment)))))  >
<!DOCTYPE #IMPLIED PUBLIC
          '-//IETF//DTD HTML 3.2//EN'>
<td>32</td>
```

In this example, the `<td>` element in the fragment document comes from the fourth cell in the third row of the second table in the body of the original HTML document. Note that the SGML Open fragment context format is not a query but a report about the fragment. This report can use the HyTime `nameloc`, `dataloc` and `treeloc` navigation models, which are simple and convenient. [1] The SO fragment content specification has many more keywords to allow you to set the particular values of attributes, processing instructions and so on. It is a rich and interesting approach to this problem.

Note that XML was designed to allow easier fragment exchange. Rather than the complexity of SO Fragment Exchange, you may find it more convenient to merely split your document up into several microdocuments: these are often more apt for interchange in the first place.

---

1. Refer to [*Rubinsky*] in this series, examples 31, 32, 33 for a good introduction.

Organizing & Documenting DTDs

Chapter 17

This chapter

...gives various ways to arrange your DTD declarations for larger projects and gives various options for print and online documentation of DTDs..

M any document systems require not one, but a whole family of closely related DTDs: variations on a theme for different uses. Basic ways of dealing with minimizing DTD complexity are

- ◉ using a *core* element type set;

- ○ defining *base and derived DTDs*,

- ○ using *architectural forms*.

Core Element Type Sets

A *core* element type set is a collection of declarations that can be used unchanged by all DTDs in the family.

New element types may be added, but nothing can be done to make a document that is valid under the core DTD invalid: content models do not change. ①

A core element type set implements a policy about which existing technology to adopt, and can be useful when you are constrained by the availability of particular tools, or want to maximize processing software reuse. For example—

- ◉ for paragraphs and lists use ISO HTML;

- ○ for tables use the CALS table model;

- ○ for special characters use the ISO entity sets;

- ○ for equations use the TEX notation.

Core element type sets have a big advantage: their DTDs are simple and modular. They have the disadvantage that they are inflexible and so may only be appropriate for creating new documents.

Base and Derived DTDs

A *base* DTD is one designed to be used as the prototype for actual *derived* DTDs. Base DTDs are usually highly parameterized with parameter entities. This gives

---

1. A core element type set is sometimes called a "baseline tagset," but this is misleading: it is not the tags that are defined, but element types.

The XML & SGML Cookbook

the user of the base DTD many chances to customize it to create their derived DTDs.

ISO Definition

4.236 **prolog:** The portion of an SGML document...that contains document type...declarations.

(Simplified from ISO 8879:1986 glossary)

K.2.1 **DTD declarations:** Markup declarations that occur in the external and internal subsets of document type declarations.

K.2.2 **external subset:** The portion of a document type declaration subset referenced by the external identifier parameter of a document type declaration.

K.2.3 **internal subset:** The portion of a document type declaration subset that occurs between the dso and dsc ① of a document type declarations.

(ISO 8879:1986 annex K:1997, Web SGML)

To understand how base and derived DTDs operate, it is important to understand that any declarations in the *internal subset* of the DOCTYPE declaration will be read and parsed before the declarations in an external entity specified in the DOCTYPE declaration (the *external subset*). Here is an example of a prolog:

```
<!-- Example of a doctype declaration with prolog -->
<!DOCTYPE x SYSTEM 'x.dtd'
[
    <!ENTITY x "<p>z</p>" >
]>
```

In this prolog, the entity **x** is specified with the string value **'<p>z</p>'** before **x.dtd** is read. Furthermore, this declaration of the entity **x** has precedence over any subsequent declarations for **x**. And the value of **x** is merely a

---

1. [and] in the DOCTYPE declaration in XML and most SGML documents.

string at this stage; it is only when the entity is referenced that the parser will, if it is referenced in the right context, detect start- and end-tags. [1]

Now, the external declarations forming the base DTD might include—

```
<!-- Example of a base DTD -->
<!ENTITY % body-matter ' section+ ' >
<!ELEMENT book    (frontmatter, ( %body-matter; ), backmatter ) >
```

To override the base DTD and create our own derived DTD, all that we need to do is—

```
<!-- Example of a derived DTD -->
<!DOCTYPE book SYSTEM 'base.dtd'
[
 <!ENTITY % body-matter ' part+ '>
 <!ELEMENT part    ( title, section+ ) >
]>
```

One of the biggest examples of a base DTD is the TEI element type sets. These are highly parameterized and allow all sorts of DTDs to be created. TEI is so large and comprehensive that it can be a good idea to approach through its most popular derived DTDs: TEIlite

Two restrained methods of deriving element types from a base declaration are type extension and schema extension. Both of these are dealt with in chapter 10, *Named Data*. Both methods are most useful when the sequence of element types in a content model is critical.

 ······Complication and unreadability are hallmarks of base DTDs. But complaining about the complication is slightly unfair: a highly parameterized DTD can be

---

1. In LISP terms, we could say that SGML entities are evaluated lazily in the context of their use. Implementors might note that SGML entities cannot, usually, be parsed in a parallel thread from the rest of the document: there is not enough context information. However, XML general entities must be well-formed (i.e., they are *fully-tagged* and *integrally stored*) and so can be parsed in parallel to the rest of the document.

simpler to see patterns in and to maintain – the real problem may be the navigation tools you are using. Or that you need to be using a *resolved* form of the DTD – one which has had resolved, for example

- all empty parameter entities,

- parameter entities used for type and schema extension, and

- parameter entities used for less common attributes, name groups and content models.

Often, a resolved DTD will be re-sorted into element type declarations in alphabetical order, for convenience of the users. DTD developers will probably not find this form useful – they are probably more interested in grouping declarations according to their similarity.

The Australian CALS 5629A DTD is used as a core DTD for new documents, but as a base DTD for legacy conversions. Depending on the sophistication of the users and the onsite technology used, element type sets can be forced to be usable only as a core DTD by resolving and removing all parameter entity references. The 5629A DTD is delivered resolved for text-entry users, but in an unresolved form for legacy converters, who have some leeway to derive variants.

The 5629A DTD family has a few other interesting features. The documentation conventions of one Australian military service is that sections contain parts; in another service, parts contain sections. The underlying form is the same in both case, so a simple parameterization is all that is needed to make all services happy. Naming is less important than correctly diagnosing the structure and rigorously marking it up.

5629A is also interesting in that the use of a bottom-up "information unit" methodology in a simple-minded fashion could have resulted in missing an important piece of design information: that the frontmatter structures for each military service was unique. The solution is to treat each of the service's frontmatter as separate information units, and derive a separate DTD for each service. ①

---

1. Thanks to Peter Pacers of Allette Systems for explaining 5629A.

Architectural Forms

Architectural forms are a useful technique for standardizing software reuse. They let you model the patterns in your document as you find them, but then use attributes to point out that your elements conform to some external pattern, which is called a *meta*-DTD.

The simplest use of architectural forms is to specify an attribute with a name you have reserved to indicate that the element should be interpreted according to your meta-DTD. For example, the xml:link attribute defined by [*XLL*] indicates that an href attribute on the same element should be treated as the location specifier of a link.

However, it is possible for multiple attributes of an element to be defined by an architectural form, as in the meta-DTD put out by [*ICADD*], the International Committee on Access Design Documents, to help deployment of documents to Braille readers and speech synthesizers. Again, the presence of an attribute – in this case `SDAform` – signals that the element may be interpreted against the ICADD meta-DTD. The attribute gives a GI as its value, and other attributes may give prefix and suffix strings to help clear rendering in the particular ICADD medium. These prefix attributes may themselves contain markup using element types defined in the ICADD DTD, not the document DTD. For example '`<h1>CONTENTS</H1>`'.

Similarly, the TEI DTD uses architectural forms. For each element, a `TEIform` name is given. The DTD designer is free to use any names (GIs) they like for the element types. This also allows retrofitting of DTDs that have the requisite structure, but not the preferred names. For example, you can have architecture-aware search software search for all `title` elements whose contents match a particular string, and the architecture-aware search would look even at elements tagged with a different name or in a different language (e.g., `Titel`, `heading`).

The architectural form mechanism can allow very sophisticated mappings, and simplifies processing sets of document of different types by enabling less dependence on the particular DTD used for each document. Requirements for using architectural forms are defined in Appendix A.3 of [*HyTime '97*], Architectural Forms Definition Requirements (ADFR), as part of the SGML Extended Facilities.

DTD Versions

Just as with program source code with a long life, you need to be able to track your DTD declarations and pin down which version you are using. A useful convention can be to have fixed attributes attached to the document element giving a minor and major version number:

```
<!-- Declarations for major and minor DTD versions -->
<!ATTLIST %doctype; maj-ver NMTOKEN #FIXED "1"
                    min-ver NMTOKEN #FIXED "0"  >
```

The minor version number is increased every time there is a change to content models or declarations that is backwards compatible with previous DTDs. The major version is increased (and the minor version reset to 0) every time an incompatible change is made: for example adding a new required attribute or converting a '*' to a '+' in a content model. You should also put the version numbers in your formal public identifier for your DTD, if you have one.

This allows your applications to make basic checks to find whether they can handle your document, and on the integrity of your entity transmissions. If your DTDs are modular, and divided into information units that are used in other DTDs, then you should attempt to have version numbers on the top-level element for each information unit.

Multiple Pass DTDs

A multipass document is where your document is sent through a chain of processes, emerging after each process decorated with processing instructions, elements and attributes destined for informing subsequent stages. Such pipelines can be a very useful method of processing documents, rather than attempting everything at once. SGML documents are text: rather than needing special debugging routines, you can debug each process with standard SGML and text tools by checking the result documents.

You can use any kind of markup for this, as appropriate. If you are stream processing and the next stage needs to know at its head some information that is only known at the tail of the current stage, generate the information in an external entity with an entity reference at the head of the generated document.

As is so often the case with SGML, the key to processing is to give everything important its own name, by using ID attributes. Most real documents of any size are, at some stage in their life, full of inconstancy. Rather than trying to find general patterns to fix all problems with a general algorithm, at a certain point it becomes more practical to merely write specific code to fix up individual problems. For this, you need to be able to identify elements uniquely, hence the need for ID attributes.

If you do decide to fix problems individually by using IDs in this manner, it is better to try to affix them as early in the processing chain as possible. Garbage Markup, Garbage Documents.

As you transform your documents through successive stages and successive DTDs, it is often good practice to never throw away markup. The GI from the input DTD can be put in an attribute of the output DTD, even if just for visual debugging – you can put stripped tagging information into comments so that no markup is lost.

Unaccounted-for Elements

It is common to find during the life of a DTD that you will find some new structure that was not found during the initial document analysis. Also, DTDs need to grow organically as new technologies and ways to harvest value from the text are found.

This need for growth is one reason why systems that require a compiled DTD are cumbersome in small environments. The effort required to make small changes to the DTD can be disproportionate to the benefit. In larger environments, this cumbersomeness can be a mechanism for discipline and centralized management.

Simple

The simplest form to deal with this problem is the HTML meta element type—

```
<!-- HTML-ish meta element type -->
<!ELEMENT META       EMPTY           -- Generic Metainformation -->
<!ATTLIST META
    http-equiv NMTOKEN #IMPLIED  -- HTTP response header name --
    name       NMTOKEN #IMPLIED  -- metainformation name --
    content    CDATA   #REQUIRED -- associated information --
    lang       CDATA   #IMPLIED  -- language attribute -->
```

The element type meta is very serviceable: it lets you add arbitrary attributes to the document. The attribute name serves as an identifier: in the absence of a specified http-equiv attribute there is no HTML-defined way for an application to know what the notation or purpose of the content is. If you use this element, you may care to document the purpose and format of the metadata using a previous metadata element. For example:

```
<meta name='documentation' content='http://www.me.com/doco.html#meta'>

<meta name='bfdxnk' content='grndflrrrgh'>

<meta name='pig' content='oink' >
```

Richer

A lot of patterns cannot be stuffed inside meta elements. Even if you sometimes process fully-tagged documents with no DTD declarations (e.g., XML or some other Web SGML document), it can be useful to require your users (i.e., document creators) to identify unknown elements clearly as such—

```
<!-- Declaration for unknown element types -->
<!ATTLIST ( unknown | unclear )
    type    ( in-line | block | container ) #REQUIRED
    render CDATA #IMPLIED
    class   CDATA #IMPLIED>
```

Another kind of unaccounted-for element occurs when marking up existing documents and the visual clues in the document are not enough for consistent recognition of the element type. In particular, the issue arises with italicized phrases in text: they have a wide variety of possible meanings. A convenient method (prompted by the discussion of [*Travis and Waldt*]) can be to merely mark them up generically, as italicized phrases, and then provide attributes for the most common choices—

```
<!-- Declaration for sundry italicised phrases -->
<!ELEMENT i-phrase   (#PCDATA) >
<!ATTLIST i-phrase
    render CDATA #FIXED 'italic'
    type ( dont-care | unresolved | abstract | fixed
        | idiom | technical | slang | emphasis | example
        | annotation | cliché ) 'dont-care'  >
```

Lists of choices are often incomplete. You can cope with this, as in the i-phrase example, by providing a default **dont-care** value, to cope with trivial or uninteresting types. And also by providing an **unresolved** attribute, to signal that some phrase in the instance looks important but it requires further attention by an expert to figure out exactly how it should be marked up. (If you get a value repeatedly in several documents you have a good candidate for another possible value in the list.) You should attempt to build your DTDs to make sure that people are not held up from doing the important things by minor problems.

Documenting Your DTD

Your documentation options for DTDs are

☑ external documents,

☑ comments in the DTD declarations,

☑ application requirements, and

☑ description in the document instance.

The simplest way to get good documentation is to borrow. If there is a usable DTD or element type set available with good documentation, it may be the way to get better quality documentation than you otherwise would have.

In particular, [*Rubinsky*] emphasizes techniques of extending HTML. There are hundreds of books available on HTML, in paper and over the WWW. Adapting HTML for your own use leaves you free to concentrate your documentation effort on the things that make your DTD different. But beware that HTML has elements of rendition (presentation) as well as pure abstraction (logical), so take care not to incorporate things that may be inappropriate for your document.

External Documents

The external documentation you create will depend on the software engineering method you have used to develop your DTD. See chapter 3 *Software Engineering*, page 1-47, for an overview of various methodologies and diagram types, and *Declarations are not Enough* in chapter 5, page 1-104.

People's appreciation of documentation is very largely determined by what they are familiar with. Most DTD developers find that, after a short period, SGML content models are the simplest way to document element type content-models. However, new developers and non-technical users are often resistant to them, and prefer one of the diagraming techniques.

Comments

Everyone has a different taste for commenting DTDs.

We can distinguish three types of comments: [1]

- module level, which affects a whole information unit;

- declaration level, which affects a declaration or a group of related declarations; and

- token level, where the comment appears inside a declaration. (Note: XML 1.0 does not support this.)

It is useful to work out a convention for each of these, and there is little to say about the format to use without introducing a matter of taste.

In my experience, it is very useful to prefix each comment with an indication of the target readership of the comment. For large and well-commented DTDs, it allows the various types of readers to zero in on the appropriate comments. I have found the following four classes of readership to be useful for making DTD comments more user-friendly:

- Designer (the DTD developer);

- SysAdmin (the system administrator);

- Supervisor (the DTD project supervisor);

- User (i.e., comments for a person who is actually to mark text up with the DTD).

A useful convention available in full SGML is to put the token level comments for attribute definitions inside. This can forestall confusion about whether the comment belongs to the next declaration or the previous. For example:

```
<!ATTLIST x
    doe -- a deer -- CDATA 'a female deer'
>
```

---

1. Following the practice widespread among LISP and OmniMark programmers.

Some SGML applications define conventions for statements that can appear in comments. Two notable examples are:

- the notorious HTML *supply-side includes,* which arise partially because HTML systems do not support entity references; and

- [*HyTime*] 's *conventional comments,* but these are only used to document the HyTime specification itself—you will not use these "conventional comments" in your own element type sets.

You may find it useful to embed hypertext references in your DTD. Some text browsers can recognize embedded URLs, allowing a convenient, though non-standard, system for including hypertext links in your DTD. For example:

```
<!-- Documentation: http://www.me.com/doco/mydtd.html#elementx -->
<!ELEMENT x   (#PCDATA) >
```

Additional Requirements

Almost every SGML application has syntactical requirements that cannot be specified directly by SGML declarations. But the application itself needs to know. For example, the requirement that a table should not have more columns than the maximum set in the appropriate attribute of the table.

[*Web SGML*] allows you to use a parameter SEEALSO in the SGML declarations, in which you can place any requirements on markup that are additional to the requirements expressible using SGML. (Note: XML 1.0 defines an SGML declaration for all XML documents; an XML document must not have an explicit SGML declaration.) Refer to Web SGML Annex L "*Additional Requirements for XML.*"

If you want to add further such additional requirements in the rest of your document, you can use a SEEALSO processing instruction. By convention, the first token in a processing instruction is the target of that processing instruction, which is often a notation name. You can use this to add context-specific documentation to your DTD declarations or document instance, for example—

```
<!-- Notation declaration for SEEALSO PI -->
<!NOTATION SEEALSO PUBLIC
      '+//ISBN 0-13-614223-0::The SGML Cookbook//NOTATION
          Syntax for Additional Requirements Declaration//EN' >
```

You can use this in processing instructions with the following syntax (Note: In XML 1.0, PIO is "<?" and PIC is "?>"):

```
PIO, 'SEEALSO', space+,
    ( ('PUBLIC', space+, public identifier, space+,
                           (system identifier, space* )? )
    | ('SYSTEM', space+, system identifier, space*) ),
PIC
```

For example:

```
<?SEEALSO SYSTEM 'http://www.my.com/sometext.html' ?>
```

The text pointed to by the identifiers contains plain English descriptions of the additional requirements. An application can use the presence of such PIs to switch in the appropriate syntax checks.

Descriptions in the Document Instance

A description in the document instance is most useful for developers of document systems, for creators of new documents and for those involved in publishing the documents.

The simplest way to add descriptions of what an element is or how it should be used, is to add a fixed etfullnm attribute—

```
<!-- etfullnm is "Element Type Full Name" -->
<!ATTLIST p
      etfullnm CDATA #FIXED 'paragraph'>
```

XLL defines an attribute for link elements that does much the same thing—

```
title CDATA #IMPLIED        -- nickname of link      --
```

These only allow a simple strings to be associated with the descriptions. They do not handle such issues as how to describe the attributes and how to internationalize the descriptions. More detailed descriptions can be handled by an attribute that links to en external description document.

Part 3

Characters
&
Glyphs

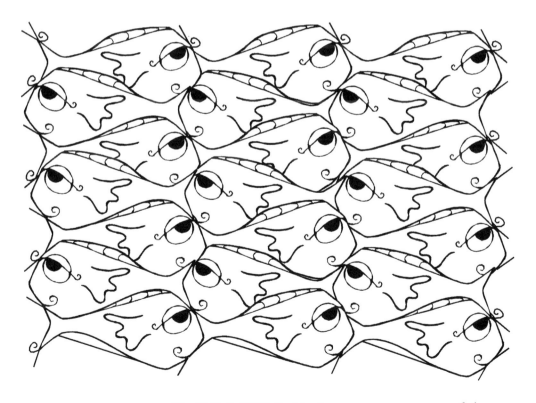

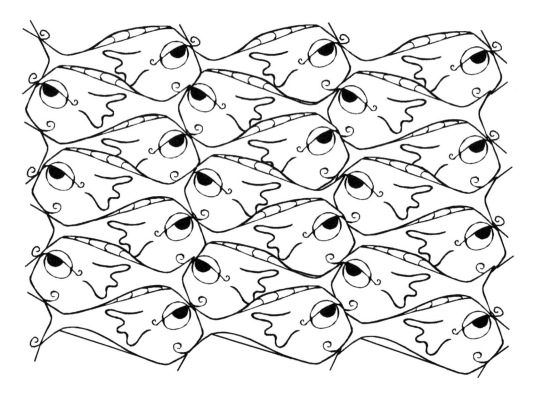

The XML & SGML Cookbook

About Characters & Glyphs

Chapter 18

This chapter

…examines the difference between characters and glyphs, and shows why the distinction is so useful.

The ISO Character/Glyph Model

We need a clear way to discuss letters, symbols and ideographs, from the viewpoint of electronic publishing. The *character/glyph* model which underlies recent standards and reports from the International Organization for Standardization is well-thought out, and it is the model I have adopted in this book. ①

ISO Definitions

4.31 character: An atom of information with an individual meaning, defined by a character repertoire.

(ISO 8879:1986 glossary)

character: A member of a set of elements used for the organization, control and representation of data.

(ISO/IEC 10646-1:1993)

glyph: a recognizable abstract graphical symbol which is independent of any specific design.

(ISO/IEC 9541-1:1991)

presentation form: in the presentation of some scripts, a form of a graphic character that depends on the position of the character relative to other characters.

(ISO/IEC 10646-1:1993)

The notion of character and glyph being two sides of the coin, with character being the more mental and glyph being the more visual, has met with widespread favor as a practical approach for analyzing and resolving many character issues. [*Kado*] Recent international standards, such as DSSSL (ISO 10179), have this model at their core, and the model has gained acceptance in vendors' groups such as the Unicode Consortium.

---

1. The model is most clearly expressed in ISO/IEC [*TR 15285*] *An operational model for characters and glyphs*, which was at draft stage at the time of writing. It is the same *Model/View* distinction that also underlies generalized markup and modern GUIs: the character is the Model, the glyph is the View.

However, ISO 8879:1986 does not need the character/glyph model, because it does not deal with presentation: characters are parsed, not glyphs. It takes the entirely pragmatic view that a character is whatever anyone has put into a character repertoire, and has no formal notion of glyph. However, the SDATA entity mechanism was designed to allow the identification and specification of glyphs, among other uses.

The spanner in the works for the character/glyph model in practice is that the things in character repertoires are often there due to the perceived frequency of their usage or for compatibility with some prior character set, rather than because they were chosen to represent unique, abstractible ideas. So some of the code points in any given character set may more select particular glyphs than unique characters. ①

ISO Definition

4.38 character repertoire: A set of characters that are used together. Meanings are defined for each character, and can also be defined for control sequences of multiple characters.

4.39 character set: A mapping of a character repertoire onto a code set such that each character in the repertoire is represented by a bit combination in the code set.

(ISO 8879:1986 glossary)

The arbitrariness of matters can perhaps be seen in ASCII (and ISO 646.*xx*, ISO 8859-*n* and ISO 10646), which has separate characters for upper-case A and lower-case a, but requires some kind of markup to specify italic or roman shape, obliquing, small caps, etc. Yet Japanese character sets do have characters for other Latin shapes: the full-width and half-width (*zenkaku, hankaku*) alphabets are regarded as separate, despite the extreme similarity in glyphs. The frequency of use of these glyphs, the way a Kanji-trained eye will view character forms, and perhaps the spaciousness of a large character sets, have promoted the glyph distinction into character distinction. (See the next section for another discussion of *zenkaku/hankaku*.)

---

1. The notes to the Zapf Dingbats character block in [*Unicode 2.0*] note explicitly that glyphs are being coded, not characters, for example.

These inconstencies are, if not compounded, at least summed in the ISO 10646 universal character set, which has a 16-bit encoding commercialized as the Unicode Character set. This set takes all the ISO registered character sets of the world, and other sets, and has made a single repertoire from them. ISO 10646 was constructed using a rule called the *round–tripping rule* which guarantees that the idiosyncrasies of the source character-sets are kept.

SGML has to swim in these muddied waters. It has stayed entirely out of the issue of the relationship of characters and glyphs, and has adopted the most neutral possible definition of character. SGML gleefully passes the buck on semantic issues to the application; your valuable data is kept safe from fashion and "progress."

Millefiori: 1000 Flowers

Characters have histories, and family trees. The Latin character a has a long history, as part of the family tree of "the first character in the alphabet." The other modern versions of this character include Greek α, the Cyrillic a; and the Hebrew א;. All these are derived ultimately from its Semitic prototype, thousands of years ago. All the modern forms are variants of the historical prototype, but they have become distinct characters. Characters continue to split: in living memory Turkey decided it needed both I and İ.

Similarly, glyphs have histories, and family trees.—

- The glyph for A derives directly from the shape convenient for stone-cutters of inscriptions on the capitals (heads) of columns in Roman times, hence the name "roman capitals." The old German form of this is the *fraktur* (German blackletter, or Gothic) 𝔄 which shows the glyph reshaped for the needs of penmanship. [1]

- In East Asia, the three to four thousand year history of writing with ideographs shows family trees well: a single historical glyph may have come down to us now in a Korean variant, a Japanese variant, a Vietnamese variant and both a simplified and traditional Chinese variant. Some characters may have a dozen variants, with distinct glyphs (if one has eyes to see them, I am told), and sometimes with distinct usages.

- In some languages, the glyph to be used to write a character does not depend only on the character and the locale, but also on the context – some scripts only allow rather delicate changes, like the Latin alphabet ligature fi— others, such as Arabic, have bold and highly context-dependent glyph selection.

- In some Indic languages, the presentation order of the glyphs may be different from the spelling order of their characters. Similarly, in some languages, context will determine which *case* of character should be used: in English we use capital letters to denote the start of sentences, proper nouns and titles. This is not a mere difference of presentation, because it conveys grammatical information, as punctuation also does. However, usually case is not intrinsic to the identity of a word: most searches for words on computers are case-insensitive.

- The English character W was written in Old and Middle English by a ligature of two vowel "u"s, representing the sound. This glyph still survives in writing, especially using nibbed pens, and in some italic fonts. u was a written Latin variant of the capital letter V: so it is natural that English minuscules uu had the majuscules VV. Perhaps because early fonts were cut in Western Europe, where W is a ligature of consonants VV, it has been almost universal type design practice to use two vees ligated for both w and W, Indeed, [*Eric Gill*]'s Essay on Typography does not even consider

---

1. Ironically *fraktur* was suppressed by the Nazis for looking too Jewish, because Hebrew letter shapes are also highly pen influenced.

the older form. To take an extreme view, in a sense the W in Old English words and the W in German-derived words in English are not even the same character, but just happen to be written by the same glyph. [1]

But who cares? This kind of historical perspective may be interesting, and may explain many eccentricities of sort order in many countries (even in English in the 18th century u and v were sometimes sorted together), but it does not suggest any workable way to classify characters for the purposes of documents. The character/glyph distinction has the winning advantage of simplicity and implementibility. With SGML markup, you can add any information you care to characters or SDATA entities using *data attributes*.

For example, ISO 10646 is sometimes criticized for unifying variant ideographs from China, Korea, and Japan. If you need to use both the Chinese and the Japanese variants of the character code number 4444 in the same Korean document, you cannot. But the problem disappears when markup can be superimposed: [2]

```
<p>The Korean &#4444;
looks different to Chinese <char lang='cn'>&#4444;</char>
and Japanese <char lang='jp'>&#4444;</char></p>
```

If you need a variant of an existing character, you do not need to add it to the character set (unless it is common or your software requires it to be a character for searching or sorting purposes). For example, the excellent suggestion made by [*Robert Bringhurst*] [3] that the italic form of the ampersand *&* retains more of its historical shape as a ligature of the Latin word *et* (and), and is prettier for typesetting, can be accommodated by declaring an entity with suitable entity text:

```
<!ENTITY et SDATA "&" -- italic ampersand, looks like 'et' still -->
```

---

1. I use "majuscule" and "minuscule," since "upper-case" and "lower-case" belong to the age of movable type and are as inappropriate as "shifted" and "unshifted" – terms from our age of keyboards and character codes – would be.

2. See Language Codes in the next chapter for details.

3. An castigated by [*Smeijers*].

In this case, the entity text & is entirely nominal: the recipient of the document should find the best glyph to use, and substitute that. The & character in the SDATA entity text will not be recognized as an Entity Reference Open delimiter (ERO), since it is in an SDATA entity and, in any case, it is not followed by an SGML name start character inside the entity.

There is not a one-to-one mapping from character to glyph. Most Latin and Indic scripts use a wide variety of accents. To prevent combinatorial explosion, the accent is coded as a separate character which combines with the base character. So several characters may result in a single glyph.

A character may be drawn by different glyphs depending on its context. In English hyphenation, for example, the character is drawn by a hyphen glyph at the end of the line and the usual glyph at the beginning of the next; in German hyphenation, sometimes the usual glyph is repeated on each line.

This fairly simple model of how characters and glyphs is good enough to explain the needs of most documents in most scripts and languages. It would be good if character sets contained only characters, and no glyphs. However, because of initial confusion about what a character is, and the need for efficiency, sometimes they do not.

Japanese character sets, for example, often have a set of full-width Latin alphabetic characters and a set of half-width (*zenkaku, hankaku*). To my Western eyes, this is clearly a mere glyph difference. But due to their availability the half-width Latin alphabetic characters are now enshrined in use as separate characters. However, my eyes are not remotely important: to Chinese, Japanese and Korean (CJK) users the "set size" of characters can be highly significant.

The use is analogous to the use in English of italic glyphs for words considered foreign: if English were to suddenly import a large number of words which it deemed necessary to italicize, we might expect our character sets to promote italics to character status too. Character sets have historically not been constructed with the glyph/character distinction in mind; with no assumption of markup to provide a higher layer of specification to characters, character sets have been assembled to provide whatever has been most used.

If you are using SGML markup, I think it may be pragmatic to try to avoid using glyphs-masquerading-as-characters, if your character set possesses them. Use markup instead. This is because often the use of a glyph variation is an indication that the characters have some special meaning: this meaning may be better notated using tags, and brought into the SGML fold. For example, I would suggest typographical symbols may be more portable if entered using SDATA entities. (And, for Japanese, half-width *katakana* and full-width *romaji*, when not used as part of logos, should probably be entered using the normal characters and marked up according to their logical function.)

SGML takes an entirely pragmatic approach: a character is whatever anyone has put in a character set. If you cannot enter a character from your keyboard, you can use SGML character references, like {. If the character you need is not in your document's character set at all, you can use an SDATA entity reference, like Ä for Ä. If you need a particular glyph, you can use the same mechanism. Of course, SGML only lets you mark the character or glyph up; actually rendering it is the task of the application.

In SGML, you often do not need to mark glyphs up; it is usually more efficient and simple for the format engine to infer the glyph from the generic element context of the character rather than from explicit rendering tags. For example, it is common practice that formulæ use italic glyphs for single letters, and upright characters for digits. However, most fonts called italic have obliqued digits. Marking up each part of a large formula to get the right glyph is laborious. Instead, it is better to mark the whole formula up inside a math element, in which different typesetting rules should apply. [1]

---

1. If your application does not support this, it is a simple matter to write your own preprocessor to mark the formula up according to which glyph is used. Even though the end result is the same, the amount of work involved is less. And, realistically, the result should be better: quality increases because more is done automatically and less needs to be proofread.

The XML & SGML Cookbook

Modern Printed Scripts

As far as it concerns us, for electronic publishing the scripts of the world fall from three historical trees into five baskets: Arabic, Hewbrew, European, Indic and Chinese.

Basket (Ancestry)	Script	Contains	ISO Character Set	Region
Arabic (Semitic)	Arabic	letters	ISO 8859-6	North Africa, Middle East, Central Asia
Hebrew (Semitic)	Hebrew	letters	ISO 8859-8	Israel
European (Semitic)	Greek	letters	ISO 8859-7	Greece
	Latin	letters	ISO 8859-1,2,3,4,9,10	North & South America, West Europe, Africa, Australia/Pacific, South-East Asia
	Cyrillic	letters	ISO 8859-5	East Europe, North Asia
	Armenian	letters	ISO 10646	Middle East
	Georgian	letters	ISO 10646	East Europe

Chinese (Han)	Han ideographs	ideographs, etc.	ISO 10646	China, Japan, Korea (Singapore, Vietnam)
	bopomofo	syllables	ISO 10646	China
	katakana	syllables	ISO 10646	Japan
	hiragana	syllables	ISO 10646	Japan
	hangul	syllables	ISO 10646	Korea
Indic (Brahmic)	Devanagari	syllables	(ISCII)	India
	Bengali	syllables	(ISCII)	India
	Gurmukhi	syllables	(ISCII)	India
	Gujarati	syllables	(ISCII)	India
	Oriya	syllables	(ISCII)	India
	Tamil	syllables	(ISCII)	India (Singapore)
	Kannada	syllables	(ISCII)	India
	Teluga	syllables	(ISCII)	India
	Kannada	syllables	(ISCII)	India
	Malayam	syllables	(ISCII)	India
	Thai	syllables	(TIS 620–2529)	Thailand
	Lao	syllables	(TIS 620–2529)	Laos
	Tibetan	syllables	ISO 10646	Tibet

The technical issues in each basket are very similar. A publishing system that handles Latin glyphs can probably handle Greek glyphs too. However, that same system may have difficulty with Han ideographs (too many), Hebrew (right-to-left), Arabic (cursive), and Thai (multiple levels of accent). Vietnamese is a possible exception to this rule: it uses Latin base letters but, to support its Chinese-style tones, it has multiple levels of accent; it shares the technical issues of the Indic scripts.

Character sets for national scripts of developing nations are being developed or reformulated, sometimes under United Nations sponsorship: Burmese (Indic, Burma), Khmer (Indic, Cambodia), and Sinhala (Indic, Sri Lanka) are three examples. Among proposals for character sets for living scripts are Ethiopic (Semitic, North Africa), aboriginal scripts from North America, and Braille.

See chapter 19 for a further discussion of world scripts, and chapter 20 for a discussion of the major families of character sets.

Character Repertoire

English requires one of the smallest repertoires of characters of any language in the world: for many purposes we can get by with just the upper- and lower-case alphabet, the digits, and a handful of punctuation characters. Almost every other language requires more: from simple needs such as the accent marks of other Latin script nations, to the thousands of characters that may be needed in Chinese documents.

However, even in English, professional quality documents use far more characters than just the characters you can see on your keyboard; typographical marks, such as the em dash —, the en dash – the hyphen -, all may look like the minus –, but they are different. As well there are symbol characters like the fraction ½; or the copyright sign ©.

For some documents this issue is so important that niche publishing industries have appeared: specialists in mathematical publishing, for example. In mathematical publishing, the abandon with which mathematicians invent or borrow characters, can add greatly to the cost of typesetting.

In East Asia, particularly Japan, it is very common for a corporation to have its own corporate extensions to the standard character sets. In the West, Apple had a similar approach with the Macintosh character set that included an apple logo. If these characters are used, there is no standard way to transfer a simple text representation of the document to another computer system, unless you use SGML.

Using Entities

The main mechanism SGML provides to deal with extended characters is the entity reference. Typically, an SDATA entity reference is used. These entities are often gathered into entity sets; the public entity sets just have dummy values for the text of each entity: the entity text is only a guide to the replacement text. A customized version of each entity set must be created for each specific system, device or application, with the appropriate customized entity text. This can be tedious work, and I think anyone who has had to use non-standard entity sets values the effort saved by using standard sets.

Some processing languages actually label text as SDATA, and allow you to string-match against the entity text. This can allow more sophisticated entity text replacement under program control; for example when an α SDATA entity should be replaced by some text if it appears in a paragraph, but by some other text if it appears in an equation.

ISO 8879:1986 defines some useful public sets of these entities, which most SGML applications support. There are also public entity sets based on those created by the American Mathematical Society. If you are doing technical or CALS-related DTDs, or your output medium is mainly paper, then you should use these public entity sets. See the appendixes for these sets. [1]

The World Wide Web Consortium (W3C) has compiled a public entity set of the characters in the Latin 1 character set (ISO 8859-1). You should use these entities for modest projects and if your main output medium is the computer screen.

As part of the Standardization Project Regarding East Asian Documents (SPREAD), I have made all the ISO 10646 characters available in public entity sets, divided into public sets by script. You should use these entity sets when you need access to foreign characters and unusual symbols, for example for multilingual documents, or when you want to translate a document from a foreign SGML character set into the character set of your own system. There are many others under development for ISO 10646: these can be added to SPREAD using the numbering convention as they are decided.

---

1. The other mechanism SGML provides is that it allows you to customize the character set directly, by providing an explicit SGML declaration. This is outside the scope of this book, but is well-covered in other literature, for example, in [*Goldfarb*] or [*McGrath*]. I do not recommend that you use this mechanism if SDATA entities will achieve your purpose: it may have the effect of locking your text into your particular system, which is often not an effect SGML is used for.

There is no way to predetermine the logos and devices that designers and authors will put in books. Very often a company will have an in-house set of SDATA entities that it will provide to authors. Similarly, standard industry DTDs often may have specialized entity sets. The [*Pinnacles*] DTD PCIS, for example, allows various electrical symbols. Almost all entity sets are to some extent arbitrary collections, built for pragmatic reasons; even a large collection of entities like the SPREAD entities is still just a systematic collection of individual arbitrary sets.

Using Elements

You can use an element type like the following to invoke special characters:

```
<!ELEMENT char  EMPTY >
<!ATTLIST char
        charset CDATA "ISO10646"
        code    CDATA #REQUIRED
        alt     CDATA #REQUIRED >
```

But using element types like this has the problem that it can interfere with searching and sorting of elements: a markup-aware search-routine may see data interrupted by an element, and a dumb text search-routine may be confused by the spaces and punctuation characters. See *Writing System Declarations* on page 3-67 for more possibilities.

When is it appropriate to use extended characters? Symbols and foreign characters that appear infrequently are really only references to glyphs, not to characters. The best heuristic I can come up with is that if you have a convenient editing and rendering environment, any character that you may need to do a search for in a word is best thought of as a character, and should be represented using an SGML character. By contrast, typographical symbols are rarely searched for, though they are often used to navigate by.

An element is not an entity is not a processing instruction is not a character. But sometimes it can be expedient to use one where another may be more elegant. The SDATA entity reference has been useful because it allows us to name characters without having to customize editing applications to let us use them. You only need to customize the applications when rendering the data.

Even using SDATA entity references can result in the same problems. See *Gaiji*, later in chapter 24 *East Asian Issues* page 3-160, for an interesting alternative approach using short references. Bitmaps can be encoded into SGML directly—again see chapter 24.

Characters

The SGML parser deals in characters. These characters may have character reference identifiers or numeric codes. The entity manager makes present to the SGML parser entities, which are streams of fixed-width characters corseted into records; a record typically corresponds to a line. Entities are actually sourced through the storage managers, which look after converting the text from what ever bit combination transformation format (BCTF) the text has been stored in. See chapter 15 *Formal System Identifiers* for more.

Collation

One of the fundamental properties of a characters is that they usually have some kind of *collation* sequence: they can be compared and sorted. The collation sequence for any particular string of characters is highly locale-dependent, but most collations involve similar steps, more or less complex depending on the locale and use. [1]

Here is an overview of the steps involved in collating.

1. Derive a *normal-form* of the strings.

2. Perform a transform (perhaps fuzzy) to get the *sort-form*.

3. For each of the various factors associated with the characters of the sort-form, in the context of their flanking characters, assign a weighting.

---

1. This is not to say that collation sequence is always based on non-glyph factors. The sorting of Han ideographs according to their stroke count, or the sorting of Japanese *hiragana* and *katakana* according to the orthogonal *goj on* (fifty sounds) shows there can be a sensible basis for certain collation. The ordering principle of the Western proto-alphabet is unknown, but very ancient, as the ancient Hebrew acrostic poetry signifies.

4. Reduce these weightings into a key (a list of numbers).

5. Compare this key with other string's keys by sequencing through each item in the key-lists comparing their values, using the first priority factors first and the lower priority factors only if needed.

Not every language, or every type of sort, requires all these steps. These steps may be performed in series, or in parallel; there are many interesting programming tricks for efficient lexicographic sorts.

Simple Collation for English

A very simple normal form for English is made by

☑ stripping out all accents,

☑ uppercasing all letters,

☑ replacing all punctuation and symbols with a space,

☑ stripping leading and trailing whitespace and

☑ converting all internal whitespace sequences into a single space.

Then use a very simple, single-factor weighting, following the sequence [\ *01-9A-Z*], with no reduction step.

Collation for Western European Languages

The Canadian standard [*CSA Z243.4.1–1992*] gives an good algorithm suitable for English, French, German, Dutch, Portuguese, Indonesian and Italian. A simplified form of it follows. ⓵

☑ In the normal form, ligatures are converted to their expanded forms (e.g., the German sharp-s becomes ss), and composite characters are divided into base plus combining accent character, or base plus base.

---

1. Refer to [*ISO/IEC DTR 11017:1996*] *Framework for Internationalization* Annex D for a detailed explanation.

☑ In the weightings, a small letter is less than its upper-case spouse. *Analphabetics* are given, in effect, tiny weights that only have an effect if all the other weights are identical.

☑ In the key comparison, the keys are tested backwards, which only effects the treatment of accented characters. The weights of analphabetics are ignored in the first pass and only if the keys are the same do they get used.

Other countries may require slight alterations: Swedish sorts Ä after the zees (or zeds).

Fuzzy Transforms

The so-called fuzzy transform in Western languages in general publishing is fairly trivial. If it is implemented at all, it is usually just a simple mapping from a list:

• the index for a book of song titles might like "50 Ways to Leave your Lover" to be sorted in the Fifties rather than the 5s;

• in English-language telephone directories, the contracted Scottish prefix Mc is often mapped to Mac.

In scientific publishing, sometimes numbers must be spelled out in this way too. But it can become quite complicated: for example, you might want to permute the normal form to get your string. You might want "General Custer" to have the sort-form "Custer General," but "General Motors" to be unchanged.

For East Asian scripts, the fuzzy transform stage is critically important for searching and comparing Han ideographs. There are several approaches to sorting ideographs:

◉ phonetically (in context);

○ by radical or component;

○ by reference to simpler characters (telephone sort);

○ by character number (i.e. like an ASCII sort);

○ by number of strokes;

○ by corner complexity.

Each of these methods is appropriate for different uses, and sometimes a mixed strategy is used: first by the primary radical, then by stroke count, for example.

The relevant Japanese Industrial Standard is JIS X 4061-1995 *Japanese Collation*. In it, for example, in *kana* the normal form has the *dakuon* and *handakuon* marks removed, in the fashion of simple accents, and a *hiragana* syllable has the same weight as its homophonic *katakana* spouse.

Explicit Markup

Attributes to clearly specify the sort-form may be more needed in SGML than in other text representation systems: a word or phrase in an element that will need to be sorted or compared may contain SDATA entity references and even sub-elements. Furthermore, the sort-form is useful to construct identifiers, filenames and database search keys.

If you have to specify a sort, the appropriate notation is not SGML, but standards like the [*POSIX*] standards, perhaps augmented with what your fuzzy transforms need. If you define a sort using POSIX notation, declare the notation with

```
<!NOTATION posix PUBLIC
     "ISO/IEC 9945//NOTATION
     Portable Operating System Interface (POSIX)//EN">
```

The Unicode Consortium's [*Unicode 2.0*] includes a lot of relevant information. It first assigns all characters to classes with properties, which can be useful at any of the stages, and provides combining-character mappings.

For any languages, scripts and documents where the sort-form of a word or phrase cannot be determined simply, or will probably cause problems, the fractious word or phrase should be marked up with an attribute specification giving the sort-form for the word.

This prescription applies to ruby characters (tiny pronunciation or spelling annotations printed above a glyph in East Asian publications) and other *furigana*, and index entries. If there are many of the same thing repeated, and if the language is regular enough to allow it, the words or phrases can be moved up to a glossary section, which can contain all sort-forms and explanations. This glossary can be integrated into a thesaurus, which gives you what you need to construct a text-indexing system with fuzzy matching customized for the document domain and language, and for a territorial re-speller.

Principle

Simplicity for big things; directness for small things.

Summary of Chapter 18

The ISO character/glyph model is a significant and useful model for most day-to-day publishing in most scripts. However characters have long histories which a simple model cannot capture for all needs.

This chapter discussed the relation between characters and glyphs, and how SGML can be used to mark them up, even when the distinction is not satisfactory.

Typeface, Script, & Language
Chapter 19

This chapter

...is useful for international and system-independent documents. When you need to transport a document beyond its locale and re-present it on other systems, you may need to be able to specify such things as typeface, script and language.

Typeface

Elements intended to explicitly set typeface are needed when you have chosen not to have element types to model every kind of topic-structure and editorial-structure in your document set. Such a choice is warranted when the topic-structure or element structure in question is not of interest or value to your targeted DTD users, or appears rarely, or will be too confusing for human and electronic markers-up of documents. [1]

Western

Western typographical tradition limits most literature to three typeface families: a conservative serif face, a constant width face, and a sans serif face, with italic and bold versions for each

You could have element types in the style of HTML:

```
<!ELEMENT ( plain | tt | ss | it | b ) ( %text; ) >
```

There seems little reason not to follow HTML, if you must have these kind of element types.

Rather than separate element types you could have a typeface element type with a generic set of attributes, which is the kind of information distortable font technologies like Adobe Multiple Masters and Apple TrueType 2.0 could use—

```
<!ATTRIBUTE typeface
        family      ( serif | tt | ss )                   #IMPLIED
        style       ( roman | italic )                     #IMPLIED
        weight      ( light | medium | bold )              #IMPLIED
        contrast    ( high | middle | low )                #IMPLIED
        variation   ( normal | condensed | small_caps ) #IMPLIED >
```

---

1. For actual names and their possible values of attributes to specify typeface and layout explicitly, the [DSSSL] standard provides an excellent source to consult and use. The World Wide Web Consortium's Extensible Style Language [XSL] may address this area. At the time this book went to press, reliable details were not available. For simpler style sheets, the World Wide Web Consortium's Cascading Style Sheets [CSS] may be useful.

The contrast attribute is the ratio of thick-to-thin strokes.

Publishing systems, computers and laser printers have built-in fonts. These typefaces have settled down to be, for all intents and purposes: Times-Roman, Courier, and Helvetica, though sometimes under different aliases. For document portability, it is best to limit typeface to these typefaces or families, together with the symbols found in the Zapf Dingbats and the Symbol font.

Of course, it is the intent of generalized markup that typeface issues can be independently specified, based on the context of data in elements. The ISO 10179 standard language DSSSL provides a very comprehensive way to do so. But sometimes you may need to specify characters directly.

Eastern

Japanese typesetting[1] has slightly different requirements: the different classes of character may all get a different font—

```
<!ATTRIBUTE type-face
      kanji-style      -- mincho | goshikku | kyokashotai) --
            ( ming | gothic | textbook ) "ming"
      kanji-slant
            ( none | right | left )      #IMPLIED
      kanji-scaling -- anamorphic scaling --
            ( slim | regular | fat )     #IMPLIED
      kanji-shift -- alignment shift n + or - units --
            CDATA #IMPLIED
      kanji-contrast
            ( high | middle | low )      #IMPLIED
      kana-style
            ( old-style | new-style )    #IMPLIED
      kana-slant
            NMTOKEN #IMPLIED
      kana-scaling -- anamorphic scaling --
            ( slim | regular | fat )     #IMPLIED
      kana-shift -- alignment shift n + or - units --
            CDATA                        #IMPLIED
```

---

1. This information is largely derived from [*Okui*].

```
kana-contrast
        ( high | middle | low )        #IMPLIED
romaji-style
        ( serif | tt | ss )            #IMPLIED
romaji-slant
        NMTOKEN                         #IMPLIED
romaji-scaling -- anamorphic scaling --
        ( slim | regular | fat )   #IMPLIED
romaji-shift -- alignment shift n + or - units --
        CDATA                           #IMPLIED
romaji-contrast
        ( high | middle | low )    #IMPLIED
other-style -- includes numeric characters --
        ( serif | tt | ss )        #IMPLIED
other-slant
        NMTOKEN                         #IMPLIED
other-scaling -- anamorphic scaling --
        ( slim | regular | fat )   #IMPLIED
other-shift -- alignment shift n + or - units --
        CDATA                      #IMPLIED
other-contrast
        ( high | middle | low )    #IMPLIED
units   -- 'point' is US points --
        ( Q | point | mm | cm )    #IMPLIED >
```

Specifying Exact Font

There may be a need, for example in a resource file, to specify a particular font more exactly. A long, fielded string can be useful to identify fonts uniquely: the model below is similar to the X Logical Font Descriptor (XLFD) used in X windows, but converted into an ISO 9070 identifier. An asterisk means "*not applicable*" or "*don't know*" or "*do your best.*"

First here is a simple version:

```
<!ATTLIST typeface
        font    CDATA #REQUIRED
        -- lextype ( "UNREGISTERED::", foundry, "//", FONT, ":",
                     family, ":", weight, ":", slant, ":",
                     width, ":", point_size, ":", x_res, ":",
                     y_res, ":", encoding ) -->
```

This can be used as

```
<typeface font=
"UNREGISTERED::Adobe//FONT:times:medium:r:normal:10:*:*:iso8859-1">
```

A more sophisticated user of SGML could model the data by saying *"The typeface I call Times is kept in a font known to the system, which I don't have to explicitly locate. This font is a Type 1 font. Type 1 fonts are a type of font that is also known to the system: I don't have to tell the system how to make use of them. The Type 1 Font format should be as described in Adobe's specification book. Type 1 fonts must have a name. The name of this font is* "UNREGISTERED::Adobe Systems Incorporated//FONT:times:medium:r:normal:10:*:*:iso8859-1".

That is a lot of information. In SGML, it can be expressed by the following:

```
<!NOTATION type1_font PUBLIC
        "+//ISBN 0-201-57044//NOTATION
        Adobe Type 1 Font Format:version 1.1:1990//EN">
<!ATTLIST #NOTATION type1_font
        descriptor CDATA #REQUIRED
        -- mylextype ( "UNREGISTERED::", foundry, "//", FONT, ":",
                       family, ":", weight, ":", slant, ":",
                       width, ":", point_size, ":", x_res, ":",
                       y_res, ":", encoding ) -->
<!ENTITY Times SYSTEM
        NDATA type1_font [ descriptor="UNREGISTERED::Adobe Systems
         Incorporated//FONT:times:medium:r:normal:10:*:*:iso8859-1" ]>
<!ATTLIST typeface
        font    ENTITY #REQUIRED >
```

This can be used as

```
<typeface font="Times">
```

Note the new ISO/IEC 9541 standard Font Services, which includes a superset specification of Type 1 fonts.

Why is the descriptor font given in a single CDATA attribute rather than split up into an element with subelements, or into several attributes? Because the fields in the font descriptor are probably not of particular interest: the descriptor is more valued as an intact string. In any case, the simple composition rules of the descriptor make it easy for an application to parse and use.

The easiest method, where you can do it, is simply to put in the appropriate font you need, in a separate attribute specification for each output device in which the document will be delivered. The HP/IBM/Sun/USL Semantic Delivery Language DTD has an example of this. It has separate attribute declarations to specify the fonts used for plain text, bold text, italic text and for bold italic, one set for X windows XLFD typeface names and another for MS-Windows typeface names.

Design Group

What if you want to specify a certain font, but you cannot be sure which fonts are available in the presentation systems? Or if you deliberately want to leave the specific font selection to the presentation system? One way is to specify the design group of the typeface, rather than an actual font. You may not care whether you use Times Roman instead of Times New Roman, or Helvetica instead of Univers, or Courier instead of Elite. But you probably don't want Courier used instead of Palatino.

There is an International Standard to help us out now: [*ISO 9541–2:1991*] Annex A *Typeface Design Grouping* has an elaborate catalog of typeface design groupings. This is based on an analysis from typographical samples from all over the world, and comes up with seven basic classes of of typefaces in general use. Here are the seven in the form of notation declarations.

```
<!-- ISO/IEC 9541-2:1993 Typeface Design Groupings -->

<!NOTATION uncial PUBLIC -- based on brush or reed pen, rounded --
    "ISO/IEC 9451-2:1993::Typeface Design Groupings//NOTATION
    Uncials//EN">
<!NOTATION inscriptional PUBLIC -- based on stone cutting --
    "ISO/IEC 9451-2:1993::Typeface Design Groupings//NOTATION
    Inscriptionals//EN">
<!NOTATION blackletter PUBLIC
    -- based on brush and pen, bold and angular --
    "ISO/IEC 9451-2:1993::Typeface Design Groupings//NOTATION
    Blackletters//EN">
<!NOTATION serif  PUBLIC -- based on pen and metal type --
    "ISO/IEC 9451-2:1993::Typeface Design Groupings//NOTATION
    Serifs//EN">
<!NOTATION sans_serif PUBLIC -- based on sign writing and computers --
    "ISO/IEC 9451-2:1993::Typeface Design Groupings//NOTATION
    Sans serifs//EN">
<!NOTATION script PUBLIC -- based on hand writing by pen or brush --
    "ISO/IEC 9451-2:1993::Typeface Design Groupings//NOTATION
    Scripts//EN">
<!NOTATION ornamental PUBLIC -- based on advertising technology --
    "ISO/IEC 9451-2:1993::Typeface Design Groupings//NOTATION
    Ornamental//EN">
```

The German *fraktur* style is a blackletter, for example. I have put in comments the dominant technique that shaped the design group, which usually is the tools used for the written prototypes. However, the medium is just as influential: the tool and the medium evolve in tandem. Uncial scripts have a strong connection with parchment, for example. Western sans serifs fonts seem to have evolved out of punches for embossed printing, perhaps for sight-impaired books, and were further developed in an attempt to make railway station signs that would be legible for incoming travelers: letters would be unique, condensed, standard and with a minimum of distraction.

The Design Groupings above are for typography, not for writing styles. I suppose if we wanted to augment these groupings with classes of writing that have not found their way into typefaces, or come from dead scripts, we could add:

- calligraphy, for example East Asian mad grass style;

- scratched, for example North European runes;

- embossed, for example Braille;

- cuneiform – wedges pressed into soft material; and

- knotted or woven.

Following is a more complete list of the Typeface Design Groupings. I have elided a few items whose meaning is not particularly clear from the name only, but still there is enough to give you the flavor if it should be what you need.

```
<!-- If you are using XML or SGML '86 -->
<!ENTITY % type-design      " type-design NMTOKEN     #IMPLIED " >

<!-- If you are using a WebSGML system -->
<!ENTITY % ISO9451-2-type   " type-design DATA ISO9451-2 #IMPLIED ">


<!NOTATION ISO9451-2 PUBLIC "ISO/IEC 9451-2:1993//NOTATION
                            Information Technology -
                            Font information interchange -
                            Typeface Design Groupings//EN">


Uncials::Single alphabet::Sans Serif
Uncials::Single alphabet::Serif
Uncials::Duplex alphabet::Sans Serif
Uncials::Duplex alphabet::Serif

Inscriptionals::Solids::Sans Serif
Inscriptionals::Solids::Serif
Inscriptionals::Inlines::Sans Serif
Inscriptionals::Inlines::Serif
Inscriptionals::Outlines::Sans Serif
Inscriptionals::Outlines::Serif

Blackletters::Formal style::Sans Serif
Blackletters::Formal style::Serif
Blackletters::Formal style::Sans Serif, engraved
Blackletters::Formal style::Serif, engraved
Blackletters::Formal style::Modified, with "Fish Tail" stem endings
Blackletters::Formal style::Modified, with concave stem endings
Blackletters::Formal style::Simplified, with "Fish Tail" stem endings
Blackletters::Formal style::Simplified, with concave stem endings
Blackletters::Formal style::Simplified, concave stem endings with two character twist
Blackletters::Formal style::One character twist, with "Fish Tail" stem endings
Blackletters::Formal style::Display, old style black
```

```
Blackletters::Formal style::Display, modern style black
Blackletters::Round style::Sans Serif
Blackletters::Round style::Serif
Blackletters::Round style::Sans Serif, engraved
Blackletters::Round style::Serif, engraved
Blackletters::Hybrid style::Sans Serif
Blackletters::Informal style::Sans Serif
Blackletters::Informal style::Unjoined

Serifs::Oldstyle::Venetian
Serifs::Oldstyle::Garalde
Serifs::Oldstyle::Dutch/English
Serifs::Transitional::Direct Line
Serifs::Transitional::Modified
Serifs::Transitional::Arabic Modified II
Serifs::Modern::Continental
Serifs::Modern::Fat Face
Serifs::Contemporary::Eclectic
Serifs::Contemporary::Fine serif
Serifs::Contemporary::Lettering
Serifs::Legibility::Rounded (traditional)
Serifs::Legibility::Super-elliptical (square)
Serifs::Square serif::Monotone
Serifs::Square serif::Clarendon
Serifs::Square serif::French Clarendon
Serifs::Square serif::Short (stub) Serifs
Serifs::Square serif::Typewriter
Serifs::Square serif::Dot matrix
Serifs::Latin::Solid
Serifs::Latin::Inline
Serifs::Engraving::Barbed serif
Serifs::Engraving::Straight seric (fine)
Serifs::Free Form::Solid
Serifs::Free Form::Outline
Serifs::Computer::OCR
Serifs::Computer::Digital
Serifs::Mincho::Old Style
Serifs::Mincho::New Style
Serifs::Mincho::Old Style::Miscellaneous

Sans serif::Gothic::Grotesque
Sans serif::Gothic::Neo-grotesque
Sans serif::Gothic::Typewriter
Sans serif::Humanist::Classical
Sans serif::Humanist::Non-Classical
Sans serif::Humanist::Typewriter
Sans serif::Stress variation::Broad Pen
Sans serif::Stress variation::Casual
Sans serif::Stress variation::Typewriter
```

```
Sans serif::Stress variation::Broad pen, curved horizontal strokes
Sans serif::Stress variation::Broad pen, angled horizontal strokes
Sans serif::Art Deco::Standard
Sans serif::Art Deco::Modified
Sans serif::Art Deco::Thin Line
Sans serif::Art Deco::Italic
Sans serif::Art Deco::Outline
Sans serif::Art Deco::Extra distorted, with some stress variation
Sans serif::Art Deco::Miscellaneous
Sans serif::Geometric::Round, flat stem endings
Sans serif::Geometric::Round, rounded stem endings
Sans serif::Geometric::Super-elliptical
Sans serif::Geometric::Stylized
Sans serif::Geometric::Typewriter
Sans serif::Geometric::Monotone
Sans serif::Geometric::With stress variation
Sans serif::Geometric::With extra stress variation
Sans serif::Geometric::Round, pointed stem endings
Sans serif::Geometric::Square
Sans serif::Geometric::Straight line
Sans serif::Geometric::Miscellaneous
Sans serif::Computer::OCR
Sans serif::Computer::Digital
Sans serif::Computer::Modified OCR
Sans serif::Computer::Modern OCR
Sans serif::Free Form::Solid
Sans serif::Free Form::Outline

Script::Joined::Formal
Script::Joined::Informal
Script::Joined::Monotone
Script::Joined::Miscellaneous
Script::Unjoined::Formal
Script::Unjoined::Informal
Script::Unjoined::Monotone
Script::Unjoined::Brush
Script::Unjoined::Cursive
Script::Unjoined::Calligraphic
Script::Unjoined::Ronde
Script::Soft Brush::Kaisho
Script::Soft Brush::Kyokasho
Script::Soft Brush::Gyosho
Script::Soft Brush::Sosho
Script::Soft Brush::Miscellaneous
Script::Kana::Old Style
Script::Kana::New Style
Script::Soucho
Script::Hard Brush
```

```
Ornamental::Inline::Sans serif
Ornamental::Inline::Serif
Ornamental::Outline::Sans serif
Ornamental::Outline::Serif
Ornamental::Decorative::Sans serif
Ornamental::Decarative::Serif
Ornamental::Three-dimensional::Sans serif
Ornamental::Three-dimensional::Serif
Ornamental::Tuscan::Sans serif
Ornamental::Tuscan::Serif
Ornamental::Stencil::Sans serif
Ornamental::Stencil::Serif
Ornamental::Reversed::Sans serif
Ornamental::Reversed::Serif
Ornamental::Reversed::Modern, with declarative background
Ornamental::Engraved::Sans serif
Ornamental::Engraved::Serif
```

You could use these strings directly in a CDATA attribute named type-design, or construct a notation and use a NMTOKEN attribute named type-design. For example, for a paragraph in a font that imitates dot matrix printers,

```
<!NOTATION dot_matrix PUBLIC
        "ISO/IEC 9451-2:1993::Typeface Design Groupings//NOTATION
        Serifs::Square serif::Dot matrix//EN">
<!ATTLIST p
        type-design --use a 9541 typeface design grouping--
                NMTOKEN #IMPLIED>
```

An alternative way is to use processing instructions. It is useful if the first thing in a processing instruction is the name of a notation, that lets you know how to interpret the processing instruction—

```
<!NOTATION ISO9451-2 PUBLIC "ISO/IEC 9451-2:1993//NOTATION
                            Information Technology -
                            Font information interchange -
                            Typeface Design Groupings//EN">
<!ATTLIST #NOTATION ISO9451-2
        type-design --use a 9541 typeface design grouping--
                NMTOKEN #IMPLIED>
...

<p><?font-tdg type-design="Serifs::Square serif::Dot matrix"?>
blah blah blah<?/font-tdg?></p>
```

Note that inside I am treating the PI as if it were a type of element, with the notation instead of the GI. The data attribute definition has no effect, since I am not declaring any entity. But it is still useful to document the pseudo-attribute definition of the PI. If you are making PIs, it is worthwhile to follow SGML conventions inside it, where possible. This is the reason for the pseudo-end-tag of the processing instruction.

Script Codes

There have been recent attempts to standardize codes for scripts. This information is based on recent drafts. The script codes have two letters, the first a capital, the second a small.

Many languages, especially in countries that span script borders or which have been colonized or imperialized, can be written in several scripts. For example, Malay was written in Arabic script and now uses Latin letters. Vietnamese was written in Han ideographs, but now has a highly accented Latin orthography.

So a simple attribute for language is not enough to clearly represent the contents of a book in a library in such a country, for example.

Following is a set of names and codes for scripts. ① Some scripts also have ISO 9070 formal public identifiers, in the DSSSL standard: these are given in quote marks, and also match the division of the ISO 10646 character set.

```
<!-- If you are using XML or SGML '86 -->
<!ENTITY % script           " script CDATA          #IMPLIED ">



<!-- If you are using a WebSGML system -->
<!ENTITY % ISO15924-script  " script DATA ISO15924 #IMPLIED ">



<!NOTATION ISO15924 PUBLIC
                "+//ISBN 0-13-614223-0::The SGML Cookbook//NOTATION
                Code for the representation of names of scripts
                - selection from pre-draft of ISO/IEC 15924//EN"   >

<!--
  History:
     Derived from predraft of ISO/IEC 15924
     Transcribed:  Keld.Simonsen@dkuug.dk (used by permission)
     Compiled:     Rick Jelliffe
     WWW:          http://www.indigo.ie/egt/standards/iso15924

  Standards:
     Up-to-date and accurate versions of the standard can be obtained
     through ISO or your local national standards body. In all cases,
     the standard is to be preferred to this list, which may not reflect
     the standard as it eventuates or is maintained.
-->
```

---

1. Thanks to Michael Everson for discussion on the state of the drafts.

Script	Code	DSSSL Public Identifier
Abur	Ab	
Ahom	Ah	
Aiha (Kesh)	Ai	
Albanian	Sq	
Arabic	Ar	"ISO/IEC 10179:1996//Script::Arabic"
Arabic (Kufi variant)	Ak	
Aramaic	Aw	
Armenian	Hy	"ISO/IEC 10179:1996//Script::Armenian"
Balinese	Bl	
Balti	Bt	
Bamum (Cameroon)	Bm	
Batak	Bk	
Bengali	Bn	"ISO/IEC 10179:1996//Script::Bengali"
Bisaya	Bs	
Blissymbols	By	
Bopomofo	Bp	"ISO/IEC 10179:1996//Script::Bopomofo"
Box-headed script	Bx	
Brahmi (Ashoka)	Br	

Braille	Ba	
Buginese (Makassar)	Bg	
Burmese	My	"ISO/IEC 10179:1996//Script::Burmese"
Buthakukye (Albanian)	Bu	
Canadian Syllabic (Unified)	Sl	
Carian	Cr	
Chakma	Ck	
Cham	Ch	
Cherokee syllabary	Jl	
Chinook shorthand	Cn	
Chola	Cl	
Chu Nom	Cu	
Cirth	Ci	
Code for undetermined script	Zy	
Code for unwritten languages	Zx	
Coptic	Qb	
Cypriote syllabary	Cp	
Cypro-Minoan	Cm	
Cyrillic	Cy	"ISO/IEC 10179:1996//Script::Cyrillic"
Dai	Da	
Deseret (Mormon)	Ds	
Devanagari	Dn	"ISO/IEC 10179:1996//Script::Devanagari"

Elbassen (Albanian)	Es	
Engsvanyali	En	
Ethiopic	Et	"ISO/IEC 10179:1996//Script::Ethiopian"
Etruscan & Oscan	Eo	
Gargoyle	Gr	
Gaudiya	Gd	
Georgian (Mxedruli)	Ka	"ISO/IEC 10179:1996//Script::Georgian"
Georgian (Xucuri)	Kx	
Glagolitic	Gl	
Gothic	Gt	
Greek	El	"ISO/IEC 10179:1996//Script::Greek"
Gujarati	Gu	"ISO/IEC 10179:1996//Script::Gujarati"
Gurmukhi	Pa	"ISO/IEC 10179:1996//Script::Gurmikhi"
Han ideographs	Hn	"ISO/IEC 10179:1996//Script::Han"
Hangul	Hg	"ISO/IEC 10179:1996//Script::Hangul"
Hebrew	He	"ISO/IEC 10179:1996//Script::Hebrew"
Hiragana	Hr	"ISO/IEC 10179:1996//Script::Hiragana"
Hmong	Hm	

Iberian	Ib	
Ilianore	Il	
Indus Valley	Iv	
Javanese	Jw	
Jindai	Jn	
Kadamba	Kb	
Kaithi	Ki	
Kannada	Kn	"ISO/IEC 10179:1996//Script::Kannada"
Karenni (Kayah Li)	Kr	
Katakana	Kk	"ISO/IEC 10179:1996//Script::Katakana"
Kauder (Micmac)	Kd	
Kawi	Kw	
Khamti (Kham)	Kh	
Kharoshthi	Ks	
Khitan (Ch'i-tan, Liao)	Kt	
Khmer	Km	"ISO/IEC 10179:1996//Script::Khmer"
Khotanese	Kq	
Kinya	Ky	
Kirat (Limbu)	Lb	
Kök Turki runes	Hu	
Koleruttu	Kl	
Kuoyu	Ku	

Kutila	Kf	
Lahnda (Khudawadi)	Lk	
Lahnda (Sindhi)	Ln	
Lampong	Lm	
Lao	Lo	"ISO/IEC 10179:1996//Script::Lao"
Latin	La	"ISO/IEC 10179:1996//Script::Latin"
Latin (Fraktur variant)	Lf	
Latin (Gaelic variant)	Lg	
Lepcha (Róng)	Lp	
Maghreb	Mg	
Maithli	Mj	
Malayalam	Ml	"ISO/IEC 10179:1996//Script::Malayam"
Manchu	Mc	
Mandaean	Md	
Mangyan	Ma	
Meitei (Manipuri)	Mp	
Meroitic	Me	
Modi	Mo	
Mongolian	Mn	"ISO/IEC 10179:1996//Script::Mongolian"
Multani	Mu	
Nabataean	Nt	
Naxi (Moso) phonetic	Mt	

Naxi (Nahsi, Nasi, Moso) ideograms	Ms	
Newari	Nw	
Nuchen (Yu-Chen)	Nu	
Numidian	Nm	
Ogham	Og	
Oriya	Or	"ISO/IEC 10179:1996//Script::Oriya"
Osmanya	Os	
Pahlavi (Avestan)	Av	
Pali (Kyoktsa & Painted)	Pk	
Palmyrene	Pm	
Pancartambo	Pc	
'Phags-pa	Pp	
Pollard Phonetic	Pl	
Proto-Elamic	Pe	
Pyu (Tircul)	Py	
Rejang	Rj	
Rongo-rongo	Rr	
Saki	Sk	
Samaritan	Sm	
Sarada	Sr	
Satavahana	Sv	
Seuss	Su	
Shavian (Shaw)	Sw	

Siddham	Sd	
Siddhamatrka	St	
Sidetic	Se	
Sinhalese	Si	"ISO/IEC 10179:1996//Script::Sinhala"
Sogdian	Sg	
Solresol	Ss	
South Arabian	Sa	
Syriac	Sy	
Tagalog	Tg	
Tai Lue (Chiang Mai)	Tl	
Tai Nua (Tai Mau)	Tn	
Takri (Chameali)	Tc	
Takri (Jaunsari)	Tj	
Tamil	Ta	"ISO/IEC 10179:1996//Script::Tamil"
Tamil Granta	Tr	
Tankri	Tk	
Telugu	Te	"ISO/IEC 10179:1996//Script::Teluga"
Thaana	Dv	
Thai	Th	"ISO/IEC 10179:1996//Script::Thai"
Tibetan	Bo	"ISO/IEC 10179:1996//Script::Tibetan"
Tifinagh	Tf	

Tocharian	To	
Tungut (Xixia) ideograms	Tu	
Uighur	Ui	
Unifon	Un	
Vai	Va	
Vattelluttu	Vt	
Verdurian	Vd	
Veso Bei	Vb	
Visible Speech	Vs	
Woleai	Wo	
Yi	Yy	
		"ISO/IEC 10179:1996//Script::Digit"
		"ISO/IEC 10179:1996//Script::Punctuation"
		"ISO/IEC 10179:1996//Script::Symbol"

Language Codes

Languages can be specified using the ISO/IEC 639:1988 two-letter contractions.

Native English-speakers may dislike the strange choice for Chinese, but it is probably a good decision in the light of the other contractions:

ca
the language Catalan

CA
the country Canada

CN
the country China

Ch
the script Chàm

Cn
the script Chinook shorthand

Hn
the script Han ideographs

Following is a definition for an attribute LANG which can be added to any element type declaration that needs a language attribute. The LANG attribute is the simplest and most common way to insert foreign languages into your text; if you are making a WWW document you should always include a LANG attribute on the highest-level element. (You may also see the attribute LANG under the name MYLANG in some HyTime documents.) If you only support a handful of particular languages it may be better to explicitly define a name token group as the declared value.

```
<!-- If you are using XML  -->
<!ENTITY % lang              " xml:lang CDATA    #IMPLIED "      >

<!-- If you are using SGML '86 -->
<!ENTITY % lang              " lang      CDATA    #IMPLIED "      >

<!-- If you are using a WebSGML system -->
<!ENTITY % ISO639-lang       " lang      DATA ISO639 #IMPLIED " >


<!NOTATION ISO639 PUBLIC
        "ISO/IEC 639:1988//NOTATION
        Codes for the Representation of Languages//EN"      >
<!--

  NOTE: #IMPLIED for this attribute means 'inherit the value from
  containing elements'. It does not mean 'reset to the language of
  the locale', except where there is no superior container elements
  with a specified language attribute.

  History:
     Derived from ISO/IEC 639         (used by permission)
     Transcribed:  Keld.Simonsen@dkuug.dk (used by permission)
     Compiled:     Rick Jelliffe
     WWW:          http://www.indigo.ie/egt/standards/iso639

  Standards:
     Up-to-date and accurate versions of the standard can be obtained
     through ISO or your local national standards body. The registration
     authority for the codes follows. In all cases, the standard is
     to be preferred to this list, which may not reflect the standard
     as it is maintained.

Alpha           Language

2       3       Name


ab      abk     Abkhazian
        ace     Achinese
        ach     Acoli
        ada     Adangme
aa      aar     Afar
af      afr     Africaans
        afh     Afrihili
        afa     Afro-Asiatic (Other)
        ain     Ainu
        aka     Akan
        akk     Akkadian
```

sq	sqi	Albanian
	ale	Aleut
	alg	Algonquian
	ajm	Aljamia
	tut	Altaic (Other)
am	amh	Amharic
	apa	Apache
	ara	Arabic
	arc	Aramaic
	arp	Arapaho
	arn	Araucanian
	arw	Arawak
hy	hye	Armenian
as	asm	Assamese
	ath	Athapascan
	map	Austronesian (Other)
	ava	Avaric
	ave	Avestan
	awa	Awandhi
ay	aym	Aymara
az	aze	Azerbaijani
	nah	Aztec
	ban	Balinese
	bat	Baltic (Other)
	bal	Baluchi
	bam	Bambara
	bai	Bamileke
	bad	Banda
	bas	Basa
ba	bak	Bashkir
eu	eus	Basque
	bej	Beja
	bem	Bemba
bn	ben	Bengali/Bangla
	ber	Berber
	bho	Bhojpuri
dz	dzo	Bhutani
bh	bih	Bihari
	bik	Bikol
	bin	Bini
bi	bis	Bislama
	bra	Braj
br	bre	Breton
	bug	Buginese
bg	bul	Bulgarian
my	bur	Burmese
be	bel	Byelorussian

	cad	Caddo
	car	Carib
km	khm	Cambodian
ca	cat	Catalan
	cau	Caucasian (Other)
	ceb	Cebuano
	cel	Celtic (Other)
	cai	Central American Indian (Other)
	chg	Chagatai
	cha	Chamorro
	che	Chechen
	chr	Cherokee
	chy	Cheyenne
	chb	Chibcha
zh	zho	Chinese
	chn	Chinook jargon
	cho	Choctaw
	chu	Church Slavic
	chv	Chuvash
	cop	Coptic
	cor	Cornish
co	cos	Corsican
	cre	Cree
	mus	Creek
	crp	Creoles and pidgins (Other)
	cpe	Creoles and pidgins, English-based (Other)
	cpf	Creoles and pidgins, French-based (Other)
	cpp	Creoles and pidgins, Portuguese-based (Other)
hr	scr	Croatian
	cus	Cushitic (Other)
cs	ces	Czech
	dak	Dakota
da	dan	Danish
	del	Delaware
	din	Dinka
	doi	Dogri
	dra	Dravidian (Other)
	dua	Duala
	dum	Dutch, Middle
nl	nld	Dutch
	dyu	Dyula
	efi	Efik
	egy	Egyptian, Ancient
	eka	Ekajuk
	elx	Elamite
	enm	English, Middle

	ang	English, Old and Anglo-Saxon
en	eng	English
	esk	Eskimo (Other)
et	est	Estonian
	eth	Ethiopic
	ewe	Ewe
	ewo	Ewondo
	fan	Fang
	fat	Fanti
fo	fao	Faroese
fj	fij	Fijian
fi	fin	Finnish
	fiu	Finno-Ugrian (Other)
	fon	Fon
	frm	French, Middle
	fro	French, Old
fr	fra	French
fy	fry	Friesian
	ful	Fulah
	gaa	Ga
gd	gdh	Gaelic
gl	glg	Galecian
	lug	Ganda
	gay	Gayo
ka	kat	Georgian
	gmh	German, Middle High
	goh	German, Old High
de	deu	German
	gem	Germanic (Other)
	gil	Gilbertese
	gon	Gondi
	got	Gothic
	grb	Grebo
	grc	Greek, Ancient
el	ell	Greek, Modern
kl	kal	Greenlandic
	grn	Guarani
gu	guj	Gujarati
	hai	Haida
ha	hau	Hausa
	haw	Hawaiian
he	heb	Hebrew
	her	Herero
	hil	Hiligaynon
	him	Himachali
hi	hin	Hindi

	hmo	Hiri Motu
hu	hun	Hungarian
	hup	Hupa
	iba	Iban
is	isl	Icelandic
	ibo	Igbo
	ijo	Ijo
	ilo	Iloko
	inc	Indic (Other)
	ine	Indo-European (Other)
id	ind	Indonesian
iu	iku	Inuktitut
ik	ipk	Inupiak
	ira	Iranian (Other)
ga	gai	Irish
	iro	Iroquoian
it	ita	Italian
ja	jpn	Japanese
	iso	Jargomanian
jw	jaw	Javanese
	jrb	Judeo-Arabic
	jpr	Judeo-Persian
	kab	Kabyle
	kac	Kachin
	kam	Kamba
kn	kan	Kannada
	kau	Kanuri
	kaa	Kara-Kalpak
	kar	Karen
ks	kas	Kashmiri
	kaw	Kawi
kk	kaz	Kazakh
	kha	Khasi
kh	khm	Khmer
	khi	Khoisan (Other)
	kho	Khotanese
	kik	Kikuyu
rw	kin	Kinyarwanda
ky	kir	Kirghiz
rn	run	Kirundi
	kon	Kongo
	kok	Konkani
ko	kor	Korean
	kpe	Kpelle
	kro	Kru
	kua	Kuanyama

ku	kur	Kurdish
	kru	Kurukh
	kus	Kusaie
	kut	Kutenai
	lad	Ladino
	lah	Lahnda
	lam	Lamba
lo	lao	Lao
	lap	Lapp
ls	lat	Latin
lv	lav	Latvian, Lettish
ln	lin	Lingala
lt	lit	Lithuanian
	loz	Lozi
	lub	Luba-Katanga
	lui	Luiseno
	lun	Lunda
	luo	Luo
mk	mke	Macedonian
	mad	Madurese
	mag	Magahi
	mai	Maithili
	mak	Makasar
mg	mlg	Malagasy
ms	msa	Malay
ml	mal	Malayalam
mt	mlt	Maltese
	man	Mandingo
	mni	Manipuri
	mno	Manobo
	max	Manx
mi	mri	Maori
mr	mar	Marathi
	mah	Marshall
	mwr	Marwari
	mas	Masai
	myn	Mayan
	men	Mende
	mic	Micmac
	min	Minangkabau
	mis	Miscellaneous (Other)
	moh	Mohawk
mo	mol	Moldavian
	mkh	Mon-Khmer (Other)
	lol	Mongo
mn	mon	Mongolian
	mos	Mossi

The XML & SGML Cookbook

	mul	Multiple languages
	mun	Munda (Other)
na	nau	Nauru
	nav	Navajo
	nde	Ndebele
	ndo	Ndonga
ne	nep	Nepali
	new	Newari
	nic	Niger-Kordofanian (Other)
	ssa	Nilo-Saharan (Other)
	niu	Niuean
	nai	North American Indian (Other)
	nso	Northern Sohto
no	nor	Norwegian
	non	Norse, Old
	nub	Nubian
	nym	Nyamwezi
	nya	Nyanja
	nyn	Nyankole
	nyo	Nyoro
	nzi	Nzima
oc	oci	Occitan, Langue d'oc, see Old Provencal
	oji	Ojibwa
	oki	Okinawan
or	ori	Oriya
	orm	Oromo
	osa	Osage
	oss	Ossetic
	oto	Otomian
	pal	Pahlavi
	pau	Palauan
	pli	Pali
	pam	Pampanga
	pag	Pangasinan
pa	pan	Panjabi, Punjabi
	pap	Papiamento
	paa	Papuan-Australian (Other)
fa	fas	Persian
	peo	Persian, Old
pl	pol	Polish
	pon	Ponape
pt	por	Portuguese
	pra	Prakrit
	pro	Provencal, Old, see Occitan
ps	pus	Pushto, Pashto

qu	que	Quechua
rm	roh	Raeto-Romance
	raj	Rajasthani
	rar	Rarotongan
	roa	Romance (Other)
ro	ron	Romanian
	rom	Romany
ru	rus	Russian
	sal	Salishan
	sam	Samaritan Aramaic
sm	smo	Samoan
	sad	Sandawe
	sag	Sangho
sa	san	Sanskrit
gd	gdh	Scots
	sel	Selkup
	sem	Semitic (Other)
sr	scr	Serbian
sh	scr	Serbo-Croatian
	srr	Serer
tn	tsn	Setswana
	shn	Shan
sn	sna	Shona
	sid	Sidamo
	bla	Siksika
sd	snd	Sindhi
si	sin	Sinhalese
	sit	Sino-Tibetan (Other)
	sio	Siouan
	sla	Slavic (Other)
sk	slk	Slovak
sl	slv	Slovenian
	sog	Sogdian
so	som	Somali
	son	Songhai
	wen	Sorbian
	sot	Sotho
	sai	South American Indian (Other)
es	esl	Spanish
	suk	Sukuma
	sux	Sumerian
su	sun	Sundanese
	sus	Susu
sw	swa	Swahili
ss	ssw	Swazi
sv	sve	Swedish
	syr	Syriac

tl	tgl	Tagalog
	tah	Tahitian
tg	tgk	Tajik
ta	tam	Tamil
tt	tat	Tatar
te	tel	Telugu
	ter	Tereno
th	tha	Thai
bo	bod	Tibetan
	tig	Tigre
ti	tir	Tigrinya
	tem	Timne
	tiv	Tivi
	tli	Tlingit
	tog	Tonga
to	ton	Tongan (Kingdom of Tonga)
	tru	Truk
	tsi	Tsimshian
ts	tso	Tsonga
tn	tsn	Tswana
	tum	Tumbuka
	ota	Turkish, Ottoman
tr	tur	Turkish
tk	tuk	Turkmen
tw	twi	Twi
	uga	Ugaritic
ug	uig	Uighur
uk	ukr	Ukrainian
	umb	Umbundu
	und	Undetermined
ur	urd	Urdu
uz	uzb	Uzbek
	vai	Vai
	ven	Venda
vi	vie	Vietnamese
vo	vol	Volapuk
	vot	Votic
	wak	Wakashan
	wal	Walamo
	war	Waray
	was	Washo
cy	cym	Welsh
wo	wol	Wolof
xh	xho	Xhosa

```
         yao    Yao
         yap    Yap
yi       yid    Yiddish
yo       yor    Yoruba

         zap    Zapotec
         zen    Zenaga
za       zha    Zhuang
zu       zul    Zulu
         zun    Zuni

qq                        Other (following ISO/IEC TR 9573-11:1992)

-->
```

Note that these specify languages, rather than countries (see *Country Codes*, page 3-54 below) or scripts (see *Script Codes*, page 3-32 above). These are very incomplete. There are several thousand regional and tribal languages missing from Australia, the Pacific and Asia in particular. There are over six thousand languages in use around the world. ①

For Internet use [*RFC 1766*] specifies a notation for language attributes with—

```
                        tag[-subtag]*
```

The primary tag is a two-letter language code from ISO/IEC 636-2:1988 and the secondary tag is two letter country code from ISO/IEC 3166. This RFC allows a deal of freedom, since you can really use any almost subtags you like, as long as they are less than eight letters: so, for example, to specify the English spoken in South-East Asia, you could adopt "en-SEA". You could adopt "en-AU-Koori" for the English dialect spoken by some Australian Aboriginals. You can have more than one subtag, if you need it. By convention, language codes should be lower case, country codes are upper case and script codes are mixed.

XML 1.0 defines an attribute for language **xml:lang** which uses the RFC 1766 notation. This attribute may be specified on any element.

---

1. The *Ethnologue* of the Summer Institute of Linguistics lists over 6,700 living languages: http://www.sil.org/ethnologue. The Ethnologue also has a three letter code for each of these languages.)

A similar, but more complicated notation is the X/Open consortium's XPG4 recommendation for the LC_LANG environment variable. The language is specified by

```
language[_territory[.codeset]]
```

where the language is a two letter [*ISO 639–2*] code or three letter code as above, and the territory is the [*ISO 3166*] country code, if an appropriate one exists. The codes used to specify codesets and modifiers are not so standard, but examples are

- en_US.ASCII for US English, using the ASCII coded character set,

- en_US.EBCDIC for US English, using the EBCDIC coded character set,

- fr_CH.88591 for Swiss French,

- en_SG for Singaporean English, and perhaps

- en_AU.Koori for Australian Aboriginal English.

The Committee for the Application of HyTime define two architectural forms CApH.seenNaturalLanguage and CApH.heardNaturalLanguage which can be applied to CDATA attributes. In a document that seeks to follow HyTime conventions, if an attribute declaration is labeled as being either of those forms, the attribute in use will contain an ISO/IEC 636-2:1988 language code, optionally followed by white-space and some kind of territory code. Whether to use of space or an underscore or a hyphen is a rendering issue. The architectural form CApH.heardNaturalLanguage is especially useful for labeling audio tracks in external NDATA entities.

My recommendation is to follow RFC 1766 syntax. However, if written–script is an important consideration in your data, mark up written–script in a separate attribute rather than use a subtag field of a language attribute. This also allows the language subtags to be used for other language-related data, for example en–UK–legal might be an attribute value to mark up that legal English is being used in the element. An application could use this information to select a specialist spelling dict-ionary.

The registration authority for the language codes is—

```
     ISO 639:1988, Registration Authority

     International Information Centre for Terminology
     (INFOTERM)
     Postfach 130
     A-1021 Wien
     Austria

     Telephone: + 43 1 26 75 35
     Telefax: + 43 1 216 32 72
     Telex: 11 59 60 norm a
     Telegrams: austrianorm
```

Country Codes

The ISO 3166 Codes for the Representation of Countries is the standard way to represent countries.

```
<!-- If you are using XML or SGML '86 -->
<!ENTITY % country            " country CDATA     #IMPLIED ">

<!-- If you are using a WebSGML system -->
<!ENTITY % ISO3166-country  " country ISO3166   #IMPLIED ">


<!NOTATION ISO3166 PUBLIC
        "ISO/IEC 3166:1993//NOTATION
        Codes for the Representation of Languages//EN" >

 History:
    Derived from ISO/IEC 3166 (used by permission)
    WWW:        ftp://ftp.ripe.net/iso3166-countrycodes

 Standards:
    Up-to-date and accurate versions of the standard can be obtained
    through ISO or your local national standards body. The registration
    authority for the codes follows. In all cases, the standard is
```

to be preferred to this list, which may not reflect the standard
as it is maintained.

Country	A 2
AFGHANISTAN	AF
ALBANIA	AL
ALGERIA	DZ
AMERICAN SAMOA	AS
ANDORRA	AD
ANGOLA	AO
ANGUILLA	AI
ANTARCTICA	AQ
ANTIGUA AND BARBUDA	AG
ARGENTINA	AR
ARMENIA	AM
ARUBA	AW
AUSTRALIA	AU
AUSTRIA	AT
AZERBAIJAN	AZ
BAHAMAS	BS
BAHRAIN	BH
BANGLADESH	BD
BARBADOS	BB
BELARUS	BY
BELGIUM	BE
BELIZE	BZ
BENIN	BJ
BERMUDA	BM
BHUTAN	BT
BOLIVIA	BO
BOSNIA AND HERZEGOWINA	BA
BOTSWANA	BW
BOUVET ISLAND	BV
BRAZIL	BR
BRITISH INDIAN OCEAN TERRITORY	IO
BRUNEI DARUSSALAM	BN
BULGARIA	BG
BURKINA FASO	BF
BURUNDI	BI
CAMBODIA	KH
CAMEROON	CM
CANADA	CA
CAPE VERDE	CV
CAYMAN ISLANDS	KY
CENTRAL AFRICAN REPUBLIC	CF
CHAD	TD

CHILE	CL
CHINA	CN
CHRISTMAS ISLAND	CX
COCOS (KEELING) ISLANDS	CC
COLOMBIA	CO
COMOROS	KM
CONGO	CG
COOK ISLANDS	CK
COSTA RICA	CR
COTE D'IVOIRE	CI
CROATIA (local name: Hrvatska)	HR
CUBA	CU
CYPRUS	CY
CZECH REPUBLIC	CZ
DENMARK	DK
DJIBOUTI	DJ
DOMINICA	DM
DOMINICAN REPUBLIC	DO
EAST TIMOR	TP
ECUADOR	EC
EGYPT	EG
EL SALVADOR	SV
EQUATORIAL GUINEA	GQ
ERITREA	ER
ESTONIA	EE
ETHIOPIA	ET
FALKLAND ISLANDS (MALVINAS)	FK
FAROE ISLANDS	FO
FIJI	FJ
FINLAND	FI
FRANCE, METROPOLITAN	FX
FRENCH GUIANA	GF
FRENCH POLYNESIA	PF
FRENCH SOUTHERN TERRITORIES	TF
GABON	GA
GAMBIA	GM
GEORGIA	GE
GERMANY	DE
GHANA	GH
GIBRALTAR	GI
GREECE	GR
GREENLAND	GL
GRENADA	GD
GUADELOUPE	GP
GUAM	GU
GUATEMALA	GT
GUINEA	GN
GUINEA-BISSAU	GW
GUYANA	GY

HAITI	HT
HEARD AND MC DONALD ISLANDS	HM
HOLY SEE (VATICAN CITY STATE)	VA
HONDURAS	HN
HONG KONG	HK
HUNGARY	HU
ICELAND	IS
INDIA	IN
INDONESIA	ID
IRAN (ISLAMIC REPUBLIC OF)	IR
IRAQ	IQ
IRELAND	IE
ISRAEL	IL
ITALY	IT
JAMAICA	JM
JAPAN	JP
JORDAN	JO
KAZAKHSTAN	KZ
KENYA	KE
KIRIBATI	KI
KOREA, DEMOCRATIC PEOPLE'S REPUBLIC OF	KP
KOREA, REPUBLIC OF	KR
KUWAIT	KW
KYRGYZSTAN	KG
LAO PEOPLE'S DEMOCRATIC REPUBLIC	LA
LATVIA	LV
LEBANON	LB
LESOTHO	LS
LIBERIA	LR
LIBYAN ARAB JAMAHIRIYA	LY
LIECHTENSTEIN	LI
LITHUANIA	LT
LUXEMBOURG	LU
MACAU	MO
MACEDONIA, THE FORMER YUGOSLAV REPUBLIC OF	MK
MADAGASCAR	MG
MALAWI	MW
MALAYSIA	MY
MALDIVES	MV
MALI	ML
MALTA	MT
MARSHALL ISLANDS	MH
MARTINIQUE	MQ
MAURITANIA	MR
MAURITIUS	MU
MAYOTTE	YT
MEXICO	MX
MICRONESIA, FEDERATED STATES OF	FM
MOLDOVA, REPUBLIC OF	MD

MONACO	MC
MONGOLIA	MN
MONTSERRAT	MS
MOROCCO	MA
MOZAMBIQUE	MZ
MYANMAR	MM
NAMIBIA	NA
NAURU	NR
NEPAL	NP
NETHERLANDS	NL
NETHERLANDS ANTILLES	AN
NEW CALEDONIA	NC
NEW ZEALAND	NZ
NICARAGUA	NI
NIGER	NE
NIGERIA	NG
NIUE	NU
NORFOLK ISLAND	NF
NORTHERN MARIANA ISLANDS	MP
NORWAY	NO
OMAN	OM
PAKISTAN	PK
PALAU	PW
PANAMA	PA
PAPUA NEW GUINEA	PG
PARAGUAY	PY
PERU	PE
PHILIPPINES	PH
PITCAIRN	PN
POLAND	PL
PORTUGAL	PT
PUERTO RICO	PR
QATAR	QA
REUNION	RE
ROMANIA	RO
RUSSIAN FEDERATION	RU
SAINT KITTS AND NEVIS	KN
SAINT LUCIA	LC
SAINT VINCENT AND THE GRENADINES	VC
SAMOA	WS
SAN MARINO	SM
SAO TOME AND PRINCIPE	ST
SAUDI ARABIA	SA
SENEGAL	SN
SIERRA LEONE	SL
SINGAPORE	SG
SLOVAKIA (Slovak Republic)	SK
SLOVENIA	SI
SOLOMON ISLANDS	SB

SOMALIA	SO
SOUTH AFRICA	ZA
SOUTH GEORGIA AND THE SOUTH SANDWICH ISLANDS	GS
SPAIN	ES
SRI LANKA	LK
ST. HELENA	SH
ST. PIERRE AND MIQUELON	PM
SUDAN	SD
SURINAME	SR
SVALBARD AND JAN MAYEN ISLANDS	SJ
SWAZILAND	SZ
SWEDEN	SE
SWITZERLAND	CH
SYRIAN ARAB REPUBLIC	SY
TAIWAN, PROVINCE OF CHINA	TW
TAJIKISTAN	TJ
TANZANIA, UNITED REPUBLIC OF	TZ
THAILAND	TH
TOGO	TG
TOKELAU	TK
TONGA	TO
TRINIDAD AND TOBAGO	TT
TUNISIA	TN
TURKEY	TR
TURKMENISTAN	TM
TURKS AND CAICOS ISLANDS	TC
TUVALU	TV
UGANDA	UG
UKRAINE	UA
UNITED ARAB EMIRATES	AE
UNITED KINGDOM	GB
UNITED STATES	US
UNITED STATES MINOR OUTLYING ISLANDS	UM
URUGUAY	UY
UZBEKISTAN	UZ
VANUATU	VU
VENEZUELA	VE
VIET NAM	VN
VIRGIN ISLANDS (BRITISH)	VG
VIRGIN ISLANDS (U.S.)	VI
WALLIS AND FUTUNA ISLANDS	WF
WESTERN SAHARA	EH
YEMEN	YE
YUGOSLAVIA	YU
ZAIRE	ZR
ZAMBIA	ZM
ZIMBABWE	ZW

The maintenance agency for the country codes is—

```
ISO 3166:1993, Maintenance Agency

DIN Deutsches Institut fur Normung
Burggrafenstrasse 6
D-10772 Berlin
Germany

Telephone: + 49 30 2601 2791
Telefax: + 49 30 2601 1231
Telex: 18 42 73 din d
Telegrams: deutschnormen berlin
```

Multilingual Documents

What about documents which need to contain or be presented in multiple languages?

If your document will need to be presented in several languages, you should provide element types or notations to cope with all the following:[1]

- personal and proper names, including place and chemical names;

- inflection, hyphenation (see *Them's the Breaks,* page *3–96*) and spelling;

- numbers, ordinals and measures (see chapter 14, *Data Content Notations*);

- monetary amounts;

- date and time (see chapter 14, *Data Content Notations*);

- coding of national entities (currency, etc.);[2]

- telephone numbers, mail addresses;

- payment account numbers; and

---

1. This list is derived from [*CEN/TC301*] and from [*Jelliffe*].

2. Refer to [*RFC 1700*] for conventions for these.

• difficult idioms that may defy or confuse translation.

[*RFC 2070*] also includes an element Q to allow locale-specific quotation marks. Again, the important thing is not so much that everyone use the same convention, but that your element types allow your programmers to manipulate the text into whatever form is required for a particular medium: the markup has to be well done, not just the DTD.

Inline Localizable

Some documents need to output only a single language version of their text, yet must contain multiple language versions.

Some popular word processing packages allow you to label paragraphs or even sections of running text by their natural language, and can apply different typesetting and spell-checking rules. Here are patterns for attributes, for entities, for processing instructions and for elements. At first sight they are similar, but each has its own strengths and uses.

Entities

A language name can be used as the parameter entity name in marked sections to localize text. In various countries, even with the same language, different terms or spellings could be used for the same thing. So, for example:

```
<!ENTITY % en-US "IGNORE"  >
<!ENTITY % en-UK "IGNORE"  >
<!ENTITY % en-AU "INCLUDE" >
```

```
<!ENTITY friend
"<![%en-US; [buddy]]>
<![%en-UK; [friend]]>
<![%en-AU; [mate]]>" >
```

This is used as

```
<p>Never lend to a &friend; and expect it back.</p>
```

This example is particularly relevant in Chinese languages, where there may be regional variation in characters and in the words for technical and modern terms. This technique is useful when the SGML document holds a document in several variant forms which only need to be accessed one language at a time.

Elements and Attributes

Many DTD developers automatically allow an ID attribute on every element. If your DTD is to be used for multilingual documents you may decide to allow a lang attribute on any element too. `<spell lang="en AU">` might declare that the particular document should be spell-checked using an Australian dictionary. This is also useful for embedded elements in different languages in a multilingual document.

The issue of how to mark up multiple languages in the same document is similar to the issue of how to incorporate multiple media resources. The answer, again, is in clearly labeling the information of interest. So, in just the same way as you knowing the language being used in a paragraph is different from knowing which character set it uses (even though you can sometimes guess one from the other), so knowing what media some resource is appropriate for is different from knowing the presentation format it is notated in. You can consider adding an attribute media to all links and style–sheet–container elements if this is an issue for your system.

For example,

```
<!ENTITY % media-choices
    "( print | screen | projection | braille | aural | all )" >
<!ATTLIST some-element
      media %media-choices; "all" >
```

Processing Instructions

Processing instructions can be used to achieve similar results. Since these processing instructions are likely to be used a lot in a document, we will follow the general principle of "Simplicity for big things; directness for small things" and declare entities for them.

```
<!ENTITY start-UK PI "MY start xml:lang='en-UK'" >

<!ENTITY end-UK PI "MY end xml:lang='en-UK'" >
```

This can be used like

```
<p>&start-UK;More tea, my dear?&end-UK;</p>
```

Processing instructions have the advantage of not piggy-backing on elements, and they do not have to follow the element hierarchy.

Principle

Simplicity for big things; directness for small things.

Interlaced Multilingual

A very common approach is to define element types for each language, for example:

```
<!ENTITY % languages " ja | en-US | en-AU " >
<!ELEMENT ( %languages; )   ( %text; ) >
```

This kind of element type set is simple, and apparently works well. The Canadian Federal Government uses this structure [*Palmer*]. You can simply replace any element type declaration

```
<!ELEMENT p ( %text; )>
```

structure with

```
<!ELEMENT p ( %languages; ) >
```

A variant on this method is appropriate to force multiple language versions of each document. This is called *interlacing*. All that is required is to change the parameter entity declaration given above for `languages` to

```
<!ENTITY % languages " jp , en-US , en-AU ">
<!ELEMENT p  ( %languages; )* >
```

The change from | to , does not effect the element type declarations for the languages, but is does force the content model for the element type **p** so that a different language version of each is required.

⚠ ······ This above approach is appropriate for languages from the same family and literary tradition, for example for Hindu–European languages and a Western literary tradition. However once you start to translate text between languages of different families, and with different literary traditions, there is no guarantee that you can have, for example, paragraph–by–paragraph parallelism, unless you are willing to allow ugly translations or bland base documents.

If you need to tie fragments of text together, for example to say *"this Japanese element corresponds to this English element,"* you can use simple ID/IDREF attributes: the Japanese element's `linkend` attribute nominates the English element's `id` attribute—

The XML & SGML Cookbook

```
<!ATTLIST p
        id ID #IMPLIED
        linkend IDREF #IMPLIED
        HyTime NAME #FIXED "clink">
```

The name "linkend" is the HyTime naming convention for this type of structure (a *contextual link*); the HyTime attribute signals this to the DTD reader (in the jargon: that it uses a HyTime clink architectural form). This model is drawn from SPREAD [Komachi, Imago, Tsuchiya].

Multilingual Hyperdocument

Finally, there is the approach of storing each language externally, each its own monolingual documents, and using a HyTime document to point to each of them. This is useful for documents where you may wish to see parallel texts, and where the structures of each do not neatly match. It also may be technically simpler: you do not need to find an editor that can handle both Arabic and Japanese, for example, or where the documents are preexisting or unavailable for cut-and-pasting.

The following example is derived from [Komachi, Imago, Tsuchiya] but uses XML conventions rather than standard HyTime conventions. The xml-link > attribute signals to the DTD reader that the href attribute should be interpreted as an XML locator (in the jargon, that it uses an XML-link architectural form)—

```
<!ELEMENT parallel-text ( resource+ )>
<!ATTLIST parallel-text
  id       ID #REQUIRED
  object   NMTOKEN #IMPLIED>
<!ELEMENT resource   EMPTY>
<!ATTLIST resource
  xml:lang CDATA #REQUIRED
  id       ID    #IMPLIED
  href     CDATA #REQUIRED
  xml:link CDATA #FIXED "simple" >
```

In XML, this could be used like

```
<parallel-text id="pt1" object="paragraph">
 <resource xml:lang="en-UK" id="pt1-r1" href="x.txt#ID (p1)"             />
 <resource xml:lang="en-US" id="pt1-r2" href="y.txt#ID (p1)"             />
 <resource xml:lang="de" id="pt1-r3" href="z.txt#ID (p35)..ID (p37)" />
 <resource xml:lang="ja" id="pt1-r4" href="x.sjs#ID (p5)"              />
</parallel-text>
```

In this example, there are four parallel texts, all held externally in four separate files, and notated in SGML or XML so that each element has a unique identifier (i.e., an ID attribute). Note that what is a single paragraph in the English versions correponds to three consecutive paragraphs in the German version (assuming the IDs run consecutively in that document). In the Japanese and German versions, the difference in ID numbers might suggest that during translation there was also a reordering of ideas to meet cultural literary criteria.

Multilingual World Wide Web

The Internet RFC 2070 "Internationalization of the HyperText Markup Language" [*Yergeau, Nicol, Adams, Duerst*], has provided a foundation set of forms for internationalization. If you are creating a new DTD for international or multilingual use, this paper will be very useful to read and follow. [1]

A multilingual document type that allows the selection of fonts in a style-sheet, or in-line in elements or processing instructions, may have a production problem that some fonts are targeted for specific languages only: a font for American users will probably not have Chinese glyphs. The mechanism of a "font set," adopted in Cascading Style Sheets ([*CSS*]) in HTML, may be useful: instead of a font-selecting attribute having a single value, it has multiple values: if the first font does not have a particular glyph, the next is searched. For example,

```
<p font="Helvetica japan-gothic cyberbit">blah</p>
```

might allow Helvetica to be used for Western characters, a Japanese gothic font to be used for Japanese standard characters, and Bitstream Cyberbit (a Unicode

---

1. Much of the treatment in this book follows from that RFC, and I am indebted to Gavin Nicol for many interesting discussions.

The XML & SGML Cookbook

font) as the fallback set. Presumably, the fonts are chosen because they fit well together. This method has hardly the complication of "virtual fonts," but is has the virtue of practicality.

TEI Writing System Declaration

Now we have separated the concepts of

- language, which has an ISO 639 code, see above,

- scripts, see the script codes above,

- locale, which has an ISO 3166 code,

- characters, which may be specified using a character code (as allowed or declared in the SGML declaration of the document) or by an SGML entity reference (or by some transliteration method), and which may often be named by using the ISO/IEC 10646 Universal Character set, and

- glyphs, which may be identified against their Association for Font Information Interchange (AFII) code. (See chapter 23 *From Character to Glyph page 3–127* for more on AFII.)①

---

1. The important idea missing from this list is the concept of the character set *encoding*. Every document is written using a character set in a particular encoding. The encoding of an entity can be specified

- ◉ formally in the system identifier of an entity reference, using the Formal System Identifier mechanism,

- ○ informally, for example from the filenames extension in conjunction with the operating-system-provided type registry,

- ○ at the start of an entity, using the XML encoding processing instruction,

- ○ bundled along with the document in transmission, using MIME header information,

- ○ externally, in some kind of catalog, or, worst,

- ○ implicitly, by autodetection of bit patterns.

How can we tie all these things together? How can we define the writing system used in a document?

The Text Encoding Initiative (*[TEI]*) has formulated a Writing System Declaration (WSD) for this purpose and allows you to assign a Formal Public Identifier to the declaration. It also has convenient places to indicate the direction of the writing for a script, whether a character has multiple forms in some contexts for which different glyphs must be used or a reference to where a picture of the glyph can be found.

The TEI WSD is mainly useful for scholarly, bibliographic and linguistic research and documentation. WSDs for common national character sets have been prepared by TEI and other groups; these can be used as convenient bases when making particular WSDs.

Summary of Chapter 19

SGML allows you to mark documents up with details of the desired presentations of the data. For documents in multiple languages or internationalized applications, we can mark up the language being used, the script, and the typeface.

The Flowering of Coded Character Sets

Chapter 20

This chapter

…helps you understand how the various worldwide character sets relate to each other, and what ISO 10646, the document character set of XML and HTML, is.

The Joy of Sets

These Venn diagrams show the relationship between the various standard coded character sets in use. In fact, the diagrams illustrate the sub- and superset relations of character repertoires. Each character repertoire may be encoded in several ways, and actual text being stored or transmitted may have very different formats.

Telegraph Codes: Five-Bit Sets

The earliest electronic coded character sets were those of electric telegraph codes: in the English-speaking world these had just one case of the English Latin alphabet and fitted into five bits (i.e., thirty two characters): enough for the upper-case alphabet, but not enough for digits and punctuation. ①

ASCII, EBCDIC and ISO 646: Seven-Bit Sets

A seven-bit code was convenient, in that it fitted both cases of the English alphabet, digits, assorted punctuation, and gave plenty of room for control characters. This was important because it allowed in-band signaling for computer-to-computer data communications. Unfortunately, it lead to unfortunate software practices, in particular using the eighth bit as a flag in programs, and making hardware communications equipment that only transmitted seven-bit data, though perhaps with some parity bit for checking. These were efficient uses of bits for English-speaking American software, but created needless frustration for those in most of the rest of the world, who require eight bits. Let alone the East Asian languages which require thirteen or more bits.

---

1. Older readers may recall the odd style of telegrams, with "." spelled out "stop" and so on.

[*ASCII*] has upper-case and lower-case English Latin alphabet, Western digits, and miscellaneous punctuation marks. IBM's [*EBCDIC*] has almost the same, though with different codepoints. ASCII has been standardized internationally as [*ISO 646*]. The lowest thirty two code points of ASCII are reserved for control characters for in-band handshaking between data terminal equipment and data communications equipment. These control signals are described in [*ISO 6429*].

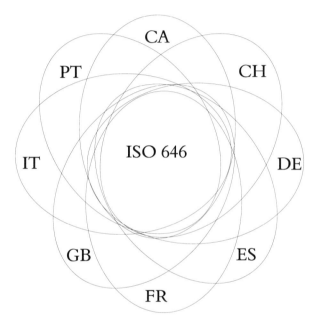

There is one International Reference Version (IRV) of ISO 646, called ISO 646-IRV. Additionally there are twelve national variants, which have localized currency symbols, and some near-equivalents in China, Korea and Japan (CJK) which have, for example, glyph variations like an overbar instead of a tilde:

Standard	Locale	Nickname
ISO 646.IRV	International Reference Version	
ISO 646, standardized from ANSI X3.4	USA	ASCII, also known as US-ASCII
ISO 646.CA	French Canadian	
ISO 646.CH	Swiss	
ISO 646.DE	German	
ISO 646.ES	Spanish	
ISO 646.FI	Finnish	
ISO 646.FR	French	
ISO 646.GB	United Kingdom	
ISO 646.IT	Italian	
ISO 646.NL	Dutch	
ISO 646.NO	Norwegian/Danish	
ISO 646.PT	Portuguese	
ISO 646.SE	Swedish	
KS C 5636	Korean	KS-Roman
GB 1988-80	Chinese	GB-Roman
JIS X 201	Japanese	JIS-Roman

ISO 8859, ISCII, JIS X 201: 8 Bit Sets

Most modern standard eight-bit character sets follow a pattern:[1]

- Code points 00-1F are control characters ISO 646(IRV).

- Code points 20-7F follow code points 20-7F in ISO 646(IRV)

- Code points 80-9F are undefined. This is in order to prevent simple-minded software (called "not eight-bit clean" software, and found in some older networking or email software) from masking off the eighth bit and treating the character as a control character. [2]

- Code points A0-FF are used for the actual extra characters. In many scripts, these ninety six (or ninety four if you chop off the ends, as is common) provide a satisfactory code-space. [3]

The ISO 8859-*n* character sets all suit the minimal Latin-script languages: English, Indonesian, Malaysian, Hawaiian, Swahili and countless non-national languages with recent orthographies. German can be written with most of the ISO 8859 Latin Alphabet sets too.

ISCII is used in India. JIS X 201 used in Japan.

ISO 2022 defines an escape code mechanism to allow switching between four eight-bit sets. However, an escaping mechanism represents an extra layer of

---

1. ISO standards use the term *bit combination* for *code point*.

2. In ISO 8859-*n* 80 to 9F are named NC*xx* where *xx* is in the range [*00..31*].

3. This is presumably because the number of consonants or vowels in letter-based languages is usually twenty to thirty (though there may be various forms, e.g., case), perhaps because a language with more phonemes is too complicated to pronounce and a language with fewer has too many tongue-twisters or is confusing. The number of phonemes in a syllabic script can be approximated by the number of consonants multiplied by the number of vowels, which usually fits into forty to one hundred syllables. The difficulty is when there are multiple tones as well, for example, Vietnamese written with Latin letters: this can multiply the number of characters to well outside our nice ninety-six character limit. The choice then is either to a larger character set size, or to use non-spacing accent marks which combine with the base character. Some of the non-Indian Indic scripts have this border problem, being almost too big for eight bits with accents, but far too small to warrant sixteen-bit coded character sets.

complexity and compression: although suitable for efficient storage of multi-character-set files, ISO 10646 sixteen-bit fixed-width characters are generally better for use inside programs, because the processing software does not need to maintain any state information when using a character string.

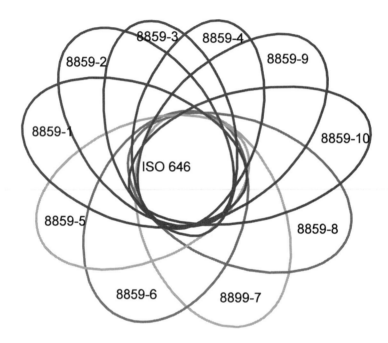

The XML & SGML Cookbook

ISO 8859-1 (Latin Alphabet No. 1)

West European countries and their colonies, in particular America, Danish, Dutch, Finnish, French, German, Icelandic, Irish, Italian, Malaysian, Norwegian, Portuguese, Spanish, Swedish and Tagalog.

ISO 8859-2 (Latin Alphabet No. 2)

Central European languages, in particular Albanian, Czech, German, Hungarian, Polish, Rumanian,(Serbo-)Croatian, Slovak, Slovene and Swedish.

ISO 8859-3 (Latin Alphabet No. 3)

South European languages, in particular Afrikaans, Catalan, French, Galician, Italian, Maltese and Turkish.

ISO 8859-4 (Latin Alphabet No. 4)

North European languages, in particular Danish, Estonian, Finnish, German, Greenlandic, Lappish, Latvian, Lithuanian, Norwegian and Swedish. Now superceded by ISO 8859-10.

ISO 8859-5 (Latin/Cyrillic Alphabet)

Eastern European languages, in particular Bulgarian, Byelorussian, Macedonian, Russian, Serbian and Ukrainian.

ISO 8859-6 (Latin/Arabic Alphabet)

Non-accented Arabic.

ISO 8859-7 (Latin/Greek Alphabet)

Greek

ISO 8859-8 (Latin/Hebrew Alphabet)

Non-accented Hebrew

ISO 8859-9 (Latin Alphabet No. 5)

Finnish, French, German, Irish, Italian, Norwegian, Portuguese, Spanish and Swedish and most particularly Turkish.

ISO 8859-10 (Latin Alphabet No. 6)

Lappish/Nordic/Eskimo languages, and Danish, Estonian, Faeroese, Finnish, German, Inuit (Greenlandic), Icelandic, Sami (Lappish), Latvian, Lithuanian, Norwegian and Swedish.

Further parts to ISO 8859 are under development. For example, ISO CD 8859-14 (Latin Alphabet No. 7), still at committee draft stage at the time of writing, is intended to cover the needs of all the countries with Gaelic-language populations: Ireland, Scotland, Wales, England, the Isle of Man, the Channel Isles, France, and so on.

ISCII

The Indian Standard Codes for Information Interchange is based on the simplifying fact that most Indian scripts have a common ancestor in the Brahmic script. So ISCII defines ten coded characters sets, one for each script, each with the same arrangement of characters. See *Modern Printed Scripts* in chapter 18 for a list of these.

JIS X 0201-1979

This set defines half-width *katakana* in the upper position.

GB 8045-87

This set defines Mongolian in the upper position, and GB-Roman in the lower.

Adobe Standard Encoding

Adobe's Standard Encoding also follows this encoding pattern.

Extended Eight-Bit Sets

The original eight-bit character sets on the Macintosh and MSDOS predate ISO 8859, and seem rather chaotic, with various characters and glyphs thrown together. The native Russian KOI8-R seems similar, perhaps.

Windows systems have taken up a more standard approach, which is to use ISO 8859-*n* character sets, but fill in the code points 80-9F with extra publishing characters (bullets, daggers, dashes, ellipses) and extra letters. The Western version is called 'ANSI', and uses ISO 8859-1 as its base, but rectifying ISO 8859-1's the strange omission of œ (œ), which is used in French and sometimes in pre-computer English. Despite the name, ANSI is not actually a standard set. [*Kado*] writes that it was based on some ANSI (American National Standards Institute) draft, and further developed by Microsoft. The characters in the ANSI set are now available in the HTMLlat1 public entity set.

Sixteen-Bit Sets

The various national standards in East Asia① are:

Japan
JIS C 6226-1978, JIS X 208-1983, revised as JIS X 208-1990. Shift JIS

Korea
KS C 5601-1992

China
GB 2312-80

Taiwan
Big 5(de facto) and CNS 11643-1986

---

1. For detailed information, Ken Lunde's CJK.INF, at `ftp://ftp.ora.com/pub/examples/nutshell/ujip/doc/cjk.inf` is invaluable, as is his book [*Lunde*]. In this book I do not deal with any issues of low-level character set encodings, nor how to specify them with the SGML declaration. For these, refer to CJK.INF.

Extended Sixteen-Bit Sets

The number of Han ideographs is great, and expanding. Various further national standards are bringing more of these characters into the fold:

Japan

JIS X 212:1990, with perhaps two more similar-sized sets to follow;
China

GB7589-87, GB7590-87, GB12345-90

Universal Sets

There are various projects to compile universal character sets, which often unify (i.e. use one code point or name for) characters that have slight variations in glyphs in different locales and periods:

- Xerox's XCCS ;

- the Unicode Consortium;

- Chinese GB 13000 Han Character Set (HCS);

- ISO 10646.

The last three have combined their efforts. Many national bodies are also augmenting their national character sets in the light of ISO 10646: it has enormous value as a character repertoire or catalog, as well as a character set. [1] Similarly, some regions are developing subsets of ISO 10646, containing the character useful for them: GB 13000 is an example of this now, as is the European standard [*ENV 1973:1995*] *European subsets of ISO/IEC 10646–1*, which defines a Minimum European Subset and an Extended European Subset. [2]

---

1. In order to make ISO 10646 more immediately useful, various nations have adopted it and augmented it to their particular needs. For example, the Vietnamese standard TCVN-5573:1993 adds some Vietnamese Han ideographs.

2. In a personal conversation, a font expert of a large corporation pointed out to me that the reason for so few Unicode fonts, was that by and large people only needed script-based subsets, and rarely a font with all of them.

ISO 10646 is also valuable because it overcomes the arbitrariness of the smaller characters sets: why is the spacing caret " ^ " so important that it warrants inclusion in ASCII and all the other character sets, when it has no use in natural, legal or commercial languages, does not have any very convenient graphical use, is only minimally useful in simplified mathematics, and is used in some programming languages such as PASCAL "because it is there"? Why does ASCII not have a closing double quote mark? Similarly, why does ISO 8859-1 include the pilcrow (paragraph sign) ¶ and the section sign §; when their use is archaic and rare? The selection of symbols in character sets seems to have been less than scientific: ISO 10646 makes up for this arbitrariness by throwing in the kitchen sink.

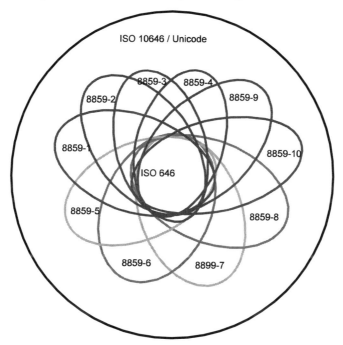

There are also projects to compile universal glyph registries, which try to capture each glyph regardless of which character it represents:

- IBM's GCGID glyph registry;

- the Association for Font Information Interchange (AFII);

- Taiwan's Chinese National Standard (CNS 11643);

- Taiwan's Chinese Character Code for Information Interchange (CCCII);

- IRIZ KanjiBase.

If in your documents the character is more important than the glyph, you will prefer ISO 10646. If you in your documents the glyph determines the character, you will prefer approaches like IRIZ KanjiBase. This is not a matter of chickens and eggs:

- ⦿ if you are publishing new material, your characters are the boss;

- ○ if you are publishing facsimiles of existing material, or scholarly apparatus that uses existing material, the glyphs may well be the boss.

The IRIZ KanjiBase project is a scholarly and religious project, where the maintanance of glyph differences is vital. For their needs, a unified approach is not appropriate. So they use a superset of the growing Taiwanese national standard CNS 11643-1992 levels 1 to 7, which is itself a superset of the coded character set used in Taiwan, Big 5. IRIZ Kanjibase is an interesting example because it shows that SGML markup can be applied successfully even where the document markup methodology uses completely unfashionable concepts (i.e., that sometimes glyphs determine characters, rather than characters always determining glyphs).

Literals

For text to be universally portable, it is useful to have a repertoire of characters that can be used reliably in headers, keywords, identifiers and locations. SGML and XML do allow native-language markup, as part of the ISO user requirement that SGML should have no language bias, more on which is below. However, text and protocols that must be portable to different operating systems and different locales must be very conservative in the characters they use for signaling.

- • The most conservative is the SGML Reference Concrete Syntax (i.e., the default) RCS naming characters. These are just the English alphabet and digits [a-zA-z0-9] and -.(but which is often augmented by the underscore character _). This repertoire is also used in XML for various attribute names.

- The next most conservative is the SGML **minimum** literal characters. These are the English alphabet and digits [*a–zA–Z0–9*] and ' ( ) + , – . / : = ? and spaces and newlines. ①

- The next most conservative is the XML **system literal** characters, which correspond to the characters allowable in an WWW URL. These are the English alphabet and digits [*a–zA–z0–9*] and ( ) + , – . / : = ? ; @ & $ _ ! ~ * %, but with no whitespace allowed. ②

In 1996, a slight correction was made to the SGML standard, ISO 8879:1986, in Annex J, the **Extended Naming Rules**. This annex facilitates native-language markup of SGML names, to let you use the common letters, symbols and conventions of your language to markup your document. In computer programming languages, it has been found that arbitrary limitations on the characters that can be used in identifiers causes confusion and bad maintainability. This is not to say that all identifiers should be verbose, or non-mnemonic, of course. Merely that good identifiers, even if terse or mnemonic, are memorable and suggestive to the user and maintainer of the code. (Note: XML 1.0 supports native language markup.)

The goal of native-language markup is not to support "literate markup" (i.e., markup that reads more like a natural language), though it may. The ways in which people will scan contractions, or recognize the component sources of the contractions, is highly individual and may differ between cultures and nations. In a cosmopolitan, multilingual society like Singapore, English-based contractions represent a useful common denominator, and the English alphabet is all that is required for native-language markup. However, in China, using English alphabet contractions may reduce all identifiers to the status of arbitrary mnemonics for their users: there is no reason to expect a human Chinese document processor in Beijing to be able to guess that <bq> is a tag for a block quote.

This is of course also an issue of the adequacy of documentation and training, and the user interface to the applications which use the document. However SGML documents and their DTD documentation often go separate ways; the goal of native-language markup is to let you use identifiers that are clear enough for a

---

1. In 1997, the characters ; ! * # @ $ _ % were added by [*Web SGML*].

2. An early draft XML specification made the interesting comment that certain characters are not suitable for use in URLs, and in literals of various kinds. These seem to be the characters that are used as the lead delimiters in XML markup and in regular expressions, or are not available from the keyboards or character sets of some locales: <> # " ' { } | ^ [ ].

user or maintainer with less-than perfect documentation and training. The burden of a foreign language added to the burden of figuring out the meaning of a contraction may waste time and mental resources.

Character Set and Encodings

It is vital that a document carries around all the information needed to be able to interpret it. The SGML declaration is a very thorough attempt to allow you to declare such things as

- character set(s) in use;

- [*ISO 2022*] escape sequences for switching between character sets;

- character mapping, for simple permuted encodings;

- special function characters (e.g. record start and record end); and

- the character classes within SGML.

For details on the SGML declaration, readers are advised to see other books.

However, SGML starts from characters and their coded representations. It does not address such issues as:

- the width of characters used (e.g., the ISO C programming language's `char` or `wchar_t`);

- "endian-ness", which relates to the order a computer's CPU uses outputs words into bytes; and

- any kind of variable-width encoding.

These are considered storage-level issues. (Note: XML 1.0 does address these issues: see page 3-96 below.)

WG4 Character Encoding Model

The SGML working group (ISO/IEC JTC1/WG4) has studied this issue intensively and recently extended model of characters and encodings to map to the physical storage level. This model has been used in recent developments in DSSSL, HyTime and XML, and in reviewing SGML.

In SGML:

- a *document*, is made from

- *entities*, kept in

- *storage* objects.

The major storage object issues are:

Document Encoding
Document encoding is how a character set, which in SGML is a table of fixed-size characters occupying code points, gets transformed for normal storage and transmission. For example, ISO 10646 has several possible document encodings, including Unicode (UCS-2) and UTF-8. [*Lunde*]'s analysis of East Asian character sets developed this distinction between sets and encoding.

For Western seven- and eight-bit fixed-width character sets, the encoding is often the same as the character set; which is why the difference has not widely been apprehended until recent times.

Bit Combination Transformation Format (BCTF)
This is a very low-level indication of how bit-combinations (i.e., code-points) are stored. BCTF indicates such things as endian-ness, compression scheme, or encryption. These transformations are typically unrelated to the character set or encoding in use, but relate to the CPU, operating system and or system administration. ⬧

---

1. BCTF and document encoding are often lumped together, in the same way that language and script are often conflated.

How To Specify Character Encoding

SGML now provides a rich set of alternatives for specifying character sets and encodings, if you need to.

As always, the initial question is *"Is this a pattern in entities, elements or PIs?"*. Just for this question, we can broaden this to *"Is this a pattern in entities, elements, PIs or storage objects?"*

Entities

The SGML Extended Facilities annex to [*HyTime* '97], which is planned to ultimately become part of SGML, gives a syntax to allow system identifiers to have attributes and, potentially, to allow chained invocation of entities.

Formal System Identifiers (FSI) can start with markup that looks like a start-tag. These can have attributes giving BCTF, and many other kinds of information. The attributes can also nominate another entity as the container or archive that contains the entity of interest.

FSIs are essentially independent of what URLs do (locate a resource over the internet) or what XML-links do (penetrate into a document resource and identify some part of it).

FSIs are external labels, and therefore are only reliable when they can be bundled along with the entities they identify.

Elements

If you have a basically fixed element type set, and the character sets in use vary only in the characters not used for markup (e.g., HTML and ISO 8859-*n*) then you can put encoding information in attributes.

HTML uses the catch-all element meta for this: for example

```
<meta name="http-equiv" content="encoding=8859-1">
```

This use is better than nothing, but it means that the encoding information is kept at some arbitrary number of tags from the start of the file.

An alternative way is to specify a notation for the element type. This is most suitable where you must capture strings from other character sets in your character set, or where all the codes to be used fit into your document character set neatly: your data may look like one set of characters but the notation attribute specifies that the data actually means something else. The advantage of this technique is that it moves character sets out from being a DTD issue or something that intermediate software phases necessarily need to concern themselves with. The most widespread examples of this type of encoding are the Internet email encoding and the scholarly encoding system used to refer to Chinese characters (Q-encoding). The element is given some notation attribute:

```
<!NOTATION RFCxxx
      SYSTEM "http://w3.org/RFC/rfcxxx" >
<!ATTLIST address
      notation NOTATION ( RFCxxx ) #IMPLIED >
...
<address notation="rfcxxx">?SHIFTJIS=DDFSADK:SDFLD</address>
```

Processing Instructions

XML documents all use ISO 10646 as their document character set, however they may be encoded in any national character set.

XML has adopted a mechanism called the "XML encoding PI", in which the first thing that can appear in a text entity is a simple PI, restricted to ISO 646(ASCII) repertoire characters, which gives encoding and other details. This represents an extension of the use of the PI, but I think it is justified and even desirable.

- The XML system first autodetects the BCTF in use (e.g., from the presence or absence of Unicode Byte Order Marks, which gives enough information to look at the first byte of the document and look for the PI delimiter.

- The character codes used for the Processing Instruction Open delimiter (PIO, "<?") give enough information to determine the character set family, for example, ECBDIC character code or ISO 646 encoding.

- If ISO 646 code points are found, the file could be any of the character sets with the ASCII characters allocated to the ASCII code positions. The XML processor reads the PI as far as the encoding attribute, which gives enough information to interpret the rest of the file.

```
<?XML version="1.0" encoding="iso8859-1" ?>
```

This fits into some existing operating systems' file-type identification strategies like the UNIX magic number system, which looks for particular strings at offsets in a file.

- If a file begins with the bytes "`<?XML`" it is an XML file;

- if it begins with "`<HTML`" it is an HTML file;

- if it begins with "`<!SGML`" it is an SGML file (or just the declaration); and

- if begins with "`<!DOCTYPE`" it is SGML, and perhaps HTML or XML.

Reliable self-identification of file type is the basis of modern user interfaces. [1]

Storage Objects

The question needs to be asked *why do we even need to specify encoding in SGML?* The answer is because of the deficiency of operating systems in this area. Operating systems, in particular UNIX, MS-DOS and Windows, have not provided a way of adding metadata to text files. Even the Macintosh, where files can have a "resource fork" for such text, has not had conventions even when there was the capability.

The advent of the World Wide Web has meant that suddenly the assumptions that made this deficiency practical in most regions no longer hold: we want to know reliably what character set, encoding and BCTF a file is in if we want to access it from some other locale.

The great advantage of relegating the BCTF and character encoding issues to the storage object layer is that it frees us to nominate ISO 10646 (e.g., Unicode) as our document and system character set, and yet leave us free to continue to use whatever our computer's or application's native character set is. Any numeric character references we use will be resolved to the ISO 10646 character. In other words, the character set used for document storage is just treated as an encoding of the real document character set, which is the universal character set ISO 10646. If we do not use this, then we have to resort to arbitrary SDATA public entity sets, such as the ISO entities, or a systematic but large SDATA public entity set, such as the SPREAD-2 entities. See chapter 22, page 3-107, for more details.

---

1. Some of the other uses of the HTML element type `meta` would also be better kept in processing instructions, started by a unique notation name. For example, to add file-specific application preferences.

This method of using ISO 10646 as the document character set regardless of the document character set regardless of the storage object character set and encoding has been adopted by XML and by ISO HTML.

Names for Character Sets and Encodings

The direct method is to use a character set name from the Internet [*RFC 1700*] *Assigned Numbers*. This RFC also contains useful standard names for operating systems.

For users, a simpler way to name character sets and encodings may be to specify the language and the operating environment:—

```
<!ATTLIST #NOTATION text
        language CDATA #IMPLIED -- human language --
        system ( ISO | WIN32 | OS2 | Macintosh |
                UNIX | national | Java ) "ISO" >
```

These can be used as data attributes on an entity:—

```
<!ENTITY x SYSTEM "x.txt"
        NDATA text [ language="French" system="Macintosh" ]>
```

This method provides as much information as the user is likely to know. Rather than an ISO identifier, which would belong in a lang attribute, a language attribute allows any kind of plain language description. The recipient or user of the document must have the expertise to sort out what character set is in use, rather than the DTD developer or the creator of the document. Sometimes explicit mention of the language and system used may be more useful than using language codes and character set registration names.

Summary

SGML can be used with almost any character set and encoding.

The advent of the ISO 10646 character set makes possible a great simplification in internationalized software.

Them's the
Breaks
Chapter 21

This chapter

…shows how to handle spaces, words, hyphens and lines in SGML and XML.

Spaces, Words, Hyphens and Lines

Here is a summary of the special characters possible in SGML and XML to force particular spacing and breaking effects. Nearly same functionality is available whether you use

- ISO public entity sets,

- the SPREAD public entity sets, or

- ISO 10646 as your document character set (as XML and modern HTML do).

ISO Entity	SPREAD Entity	XML Numeric Character Reference	Description
-	-	-	Hyphen or minus (ambiguous: if possible, mandate one usage or the other throughout your documents)
&hyphen;	&U2010;	&#x2010;	Hyphen
(*none*)	&U2011;	&#x2011;	Non-breaking hyphen
&minus;	&U2212;	&#x2212;	Minus
&shy;	&U00AD;	&#AD;	Soft hyphen
&zwsp; (*non-standard*)	&U200B;	&#x200B;	Zero-width space a soft word-break (i.e., a point where a line break can occur without causing a hyphen to appear)
&zwnbsp; (*non-standard*)	&UFEFF;	&#xFEFF;	Zero-width non-breaking space (i.e., line break suppression)
	&U00A0;		Non-breaking space

(none)	&U2000;	&#x2000;	En quad (fixed width)
(none)	&U2001;	&#x2001;	Em quad (fixed width)
	&U2002;		En space
	&U2003;		Em space
	&U2007;		Digit space
	&U2008;		Punctuation space
	&U2009;		Thin space
(none)	&U2028;	&#x2028;	Hard return (Similar to HTML tag, as far as presentation)
(none)	&U2029;	&#x2029;	Paragraph separator (Similar to HTML <P> tag, as far as presentation)
&ispace; (non-standard)	&U3000;		Ideographic space (not collapsible)

If your system can use these entities or characters, then the roles that element types must perform will be simplified.

Word Segmentation

The three things that people want to do with words are

✓ find them,

✓ join them, and

✓ split them.

And, not surprisingly, for each of the three we should first ask *"Is this a structure in entities, in elements, or in processing instructions?"* In SGML, characters and glyphs are usually dealt with using entities. Element markup is often used when there are no standard or common public entities available to achieve a goal. Processing instructions are often used as the third layer of attack, when there is a need to not disrupt the element structure by shoehorning-in presentational structures which may affect only one particular rendering of the data.

For example, there is no SDATA entity to force a line break, in the ISO 8879 public entity sets, so HTML uses an EMPTY element <BR>. The lack of an explicit entity for hard return is because a hard return is an invitation to mark the document up according to presentation. It is an invitation which in most cases should be declined with elegant disdain. A required hard return is often a symptom of a missing element type in the DTD. Generic versions of this are HTML's element type <BR> and

```
<!ELEMENT     line     ( #PCDATA ) >
```

An alternative is to have an element type called, for example, "verbatim" or "lines," in which the record-end character acts as a hard return (but be careful of newlines immediately before and after tags: SGML's record-handling needs to be understood to avoid surprises). Some typesetting systems allow you to put in an explicit processing instruction.

```
<p>hello <?new-line?>world</p>
```

Which is best? In the absence of any other considerations, I recommend:

◉ if the line breaks can be piggy-backed on an element that marks up topic-structure or editorial-structure, just rely on these elements (and do not forget to make a note in the policy document or DTD, or perhaps use HTML Architectural Forms), see *White–space*, page 3-101 below;

○ if the line breaks are just an artifact of publishing, and not intrinsic to the data, use processing instructions; else

○ use the following SPREAD entity:

```
<!ENTITY        U2028    '[LINE SEPARATOR]' >
```

It is instructive to compare forced line breaks with paragraph breaks. Almost every DTD has an explicit element type for the paragraph: paragraphs are editorial-structure markup, while, except for poetry, lines rarely are. I cannot recall seeing a document where a processing instruction was used to separate paragraphs, let alone the use of the possible SPREAD entity

```
<!ENTITY        U2029    '[PARAGRAPH SEPARATOR]' >
```

This may be due to the force of habit, however, and the previous unavailability of a standard solution. The data content that SGML marks up is typically vanilla text, with little additional meaning. However, it is quite possible to use SGML to markup other kinds of text: programs, even binary files, if the appropriate delimiting is performed.

The other type of word separator is the tab. Tabs are extremely useful for marking up

✓ forms that need a mono-space font: these sometimes verge on the diagrammatic, and

✓ computer source code: these can be tedious to markup without either resorting to some kind of tabbing or moving outside SGML to specialist PostScript-generating "pretty-printer" formatters.

Apart from these uses, the tab should be regarded with suspicion, unless it is shortref-ed to some element tag. A tab is a kind of page-object presentational formatting: if that is where the value of the information lies and your formatters can cope with it, well and good. But if not, tabs can merely confuse later typesetting.

The following example uses short references to convert a tab into a space. The short reference declared will occur in all PCDATA in and nested inside a MYDOC element, if the SGML declaration has an optional SHORTREF delimiter set. (Note: Short references are not available in XML 1.0.)—

```
<!-- SHORTREF mapping for the tab character -->
<!ENTITY    nontab   ' ' >
<!SHORTREF  tabmap   '&#TAB;' nontab >
<!USEMAP    tabmap   MYDOC >
```

See *White-space* later in this chapter for examples of attributes for handling the treatment of white-space in elements.

Joining

Joining words is easy using entity references or numeric character references. You can just insert a non-breaking space, using

- the nbsp entity from the ISOnum public entity set,

- the equivalent ISO 10646 character from the SPREAD public entity set U00A0, or

- a numeric character reference if your document has this character available in its document character set: for example —

```
<!ENTITY         nbsp    SDATA    '[nbsp    ]'
                                  --= no break (required) space-->
```

or

```
<!ENTITY          U00A0    SDATA    '[NON-BREAKING SPACE]' >
```

These SDATA entities are in the numeric and special graphic public entity set
ISOnum, and should always be used whenever entering numbers with internal
spaces, and between numbers and their contracted units, unless your house-style
differs from this. In some locales (i.e., depending on the language, or script, or
country), it may be necessary to markup spaces inside numbers with the digit
space or punctuation space, for the formatter's benefit—

```
<!ENTITY          numsp    SDATA    '[numsp ]'
                                    --= digit space (width of a number)-->
```

or

```
<!ENTITY          U2007    SDATA    '[FIGURE SPACE]' >
```

and

```
<!ENTITY          puncsp   SDATA    '[puncsp ]'
                                    --= punctuation (comma) space-->
```

or

```
<!ENTITY          U2008    SDATA    '[PUNCTUATION SPACE]' >
```

What if you need a digit space, but it must be non-breaking? The simplest way to
mark this up is to make up your own entity which sandwiches a number space
between two SPREAD zero-width no-break space characters—

```
<!ENTITY       U2007   SDATA    '[FIGURE SPACE]' >
<!ENTITY       UFEFF   SDATA    '[ZERO-WIDTH NO-BREAK SPACE]' >
<!ENTITY       nbnumsp '&UFEFF;&U2007;&UFEFF'
                                    -- = no-break figure space-->
```

SGML entities lend themselves well to this kind of highly configurable character manipulation. You can then use it to make up for the limitations of a simple but robust typesetting system, rather than having to upgrade to an over-featured, fancier one.

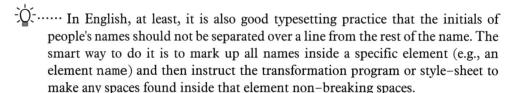 In English, at least, it is also good typesetting practice that the initials of people's names should not be separated over a line from the rest of the name. The smart way to do it is to mark up all names inside a specific element (e.g., an element name) and then instruct the transformation program or style–sheet to make any spaces found inside that element non–breaking spaces.

And similarly, for elements that form parts of words, it may be useful to include a fixed attribute to denote that any spaces inside the element should be stripped. Specifying these, and having the application enforce it, overcomes any confusion about SGML's Record End rules.

Splitting Words and Hyphenation

Sometimes you want to control hyphenation, to override or augment any hyphenation control provided by your application.[1] You can minimize the amount of hyphenation needed on short lines of languages with long words compared to the English equivalents, such as German, by using slightly condensed fonts. The first thing to check, if you have hyphenation problems, is that your font selection and line lengths are not the real reason for the problem.

---

1. Note that SGML is not a text layout system: you can specify types of hyphenation using SGML, but you are just using markup to provide information to the formatter. Similarly, DSSSL also lets you specify hyphenation methods and appropriate points in words to hyphenate, but it does not itself do any hyphenation: that is the formatter's job.

After this, there can be the need to explicitly prevent hyphenation at a certain point, especially for novel and strangely spelled words or logos which may upset your formatter's hyphenation algorithm. The *zero–width no–break space* SDATA entity is a candidate. —

```
<!ENTITY        UFEFF    SDATA     '[ZERO WIDTH NO-BREAK SPACE]' >
```

 •••••• The drawback with using a "keep-together" like the zero-width no-break space is that not all typesetting systems support it. Also, preventing hyphenation at a particular point may not induce the hyphenation algorithm to find a better place. The better method is to nominate a good place to break explicitly, using a soft hyphen—

```
<!ENTITY         shy     SDATA     '[shy   ]' --= soft hyphen -- >
```

or

```
<!ENTITY        U00AD    SDATA     '[SOFT HYPHEN]' >
```

 •••••• The drawback with using soft hyphens is that they disrupt searching and sorting. The most sophisticated approach is for the document to provide a hyphenation dictionary with it. Most typesetting programs provide a way to add your own custom words to the built-in dictionary. This can also aid spell checking: you can use the same dictionary as a custom spelling list.

As a variation, in the following example I use the character PUNCTUATION POINT, a kind of center dot, rather than the actual soft-hyphen character. This will cause the <word> element to be typeset nicely, with the hyphenation point clearly visible. The application software will have to be smart enough to read the PUNCTUATION POINT as functional markup, signifying a soft hyphen in candidate words in the later text. —

```
!ELEMENT        dict     - -      ( word )+>
<!ELEMENT       word     - O      ( #PCDATA )
<!ENTITY        U2027    SDATA    '[HYPHENATION POINT]' >
...
<dict>
<word>felin&U2027;esque
<word>tyro&U2027;mancy
<word>zo&U2027;oid</dict>
...
<p>Tired from trying to find stupid words, Rick returned to his
first love, tyromancy.</p>
```

SGML experts should prefer to use an element, perhaps with short references, rather than an SDATA entity for this. Marking up this way really puts the presentational considerations before the topic-structure. A better approach would be—

```
<!ELEMENT        dict          - -        ( word )+ >
<!ELEMENT        word          - O        ( #PCDATA | hyphen-point )* >
<!ELEMENT        hyphen-point  - O              EMPTY >
<!ATTLIST        hyphen-point
          device ENTITY #FIXED        'U2027' >
<!ENTITY         hyphen-ent          STARTTAG  'hyphen-point' >
<!SHORTREF       hyphen-map
          '^' hyphen-ent >
<!USEMAP         hyphen-map          word >
...
<dict>
<word>felin^esque
<word>tyro^mancy
<word>zo^oid</dict>
...
```

If you are unclear about how short references work, you can think of it this way. First the '^' delimiter is replaced by an entity reference—

The XML & SGML Cookbook

```
<dict>
<word>felin&hyphen-ent;esque
<word>tyro&hyphen-ent;mancy
<word>zo&hyphen-ent;oid</dict>
```

These entities are equivalent to—

```
<dict>
<word>felin<hyphen-point>esque
<word>tyro<hyphen-point>mancy
<word>zo<hyphen-point>oid</dict>
```

With fixed attributes expanded, that is equivalent to—

```
<dict>
<word>felin<hyphen-point device='U2027'>esque</word>
<word>tyro<hyphen-point device='U2027'>mancy</word>
<word>zo<hyphen-point device='U2027'>oid</word></dict>
```

In some locales, the soft hyphen has a complicated result when typeset. In English, the soft hyphen will be replaced by a hyphen followed by a line break. In other locales, different glyphs may be used, and the spelling of the word may even change. This is completely outside the province of SGML, fortunately: as users we just need to insert a soft hyphen entity.

Sometimes, and for some locales, you may not want to force a hyphen break, but merely point out that a potential break exists. In the following example, the text is all run together with no spaces, but lines will still break at a word boundary. —

```
<!ENTITY      U200B   SDATA   '[ZERO WIDTH SPACE]'
...
<p>Lines&U200B;without&U200B;spaces&U200B;are&U200B;difficult&U200B;to&U200B;read.
</p>
```

For elements that must be words, in languages that use spaces between words, it can be useful to define a fixed attribute to denote that the application should remove any internal and external leading and trailing spaces, and insert single leading and trailing spaces, allowing for any punctuation. Specifying this, and having the application enforce it, overcomes confusion about SGML's record boundary rules.

Finding

Chinese and some other major world scripts do not use spaces between words. This means that any exact searching and string-matching must either use mark-up, or have some grammatical notion of where word segments start or end.

Japanese also does not use spaces between words in the way now conventional in the West. However, the Japanese use of multiple scripts *(kanji, hiragana, katakana, romaji)* gives a computer great clues for detecting word segment boundaries.

However, in both, there are certain types of words that may confuse software that finds word segments. For Chinese, one of the most common is that of proper nouns: names of people, places, chemicals and words spelled phonetically using ideographs. Such words in a sentence can confuse attempts to detect word segments, or generate spurious matches.

In general, words made from ideographs can be split across lines at any time, according to East Asian typesetting rules. However sometimes breaking a multi-ideographic word in two at the end of the line can result in spurious readings, and lines must be broken at particular points. For more detailed information on the word segmentation problem as it applies to Chinese, see *Word Segmentation in Chinese* on page 3-104 below.

Three useful approaches are:

✓ key the data in using spaces that can be stripped later (see example following),

✓ mark up difficult words explicitly, or

✓ have a glossary at the head of the document to tell the word segment application to look out for them.

A convenient way for operators for the first is to short ref the space character to the SPREAD entity for word separation.

```
<!ENTITY        U200B     SDATA     '[ZERO WIDTH SPACE]'>
<!SHORTREF      wordsep            ' '      U200B>
<!USEMAP wordsep  para>
...
<para>These spaces are shortref-ed to zero-width spaces.</para>
```

It may be worthwhile to include a fixed attribute identifying an architectural form, to clearly denote any element types that always contain words or word segments.

White-space

This sections deals with how to prescribe white-space formatting using attributes.

In English, the term *space* can refer to vertical space as well as horizontal space. The OS DTD used by FOSI uses the attributes `prespace` and `postspace` to refer to vertical space, not inter-word spaces. It is wise to avoid these terms.

An example of an attribute declaration with rich specification of how spaces should be handled:[1]

```
<!ATTLIST       dummy
  -- hints for spaces --
  space-before    %yes-or-no;       -- 1 or yes = one space and only one--
  space-after     %yes-or-no;       -- 1 or yes = one space and only one--
  preserve-space  %yes-or-no;       -- 1 or yes = don't collapse internal spaces --
  signif-space    %yes-or-no;       -- 1 or yes = spaces have meaning --
  -- hints for records --
  break-before    %yes-or-no;       -- 1 or yes = one break and only one--
  break-after     %yes-or-no;       -- 1 or yes = one break and only one--
  preserve-record %yes-or-no;        -- 1 or yes = don't alter line-breaks --
```

---

1. If you are using an XML or WebSGML system, you could use
    `<!ENTITY % yes-or-no " ( yes | no ) 'no' ">`.
Otherwise you should use
    `<!ENTITY % yes-or-no " NUMBER '0' ">`.

```
    signif-record    %yes-or-no;        -- 1 or yes = lines have meaning --
    max-record-length NMTOKEN   "255" -- recommend max length--
    -- hints for tabs --
    tab-before       %yes-or-no;        -- 1 or yes = one tab and only one--
    tab-after        %yes-or-no;        -- 1 or yes = one tab and only one--
    preserve-tab     %yes-or-no;        -- 1 or yes = don't replace tabs --
    signif-tab       %yes-or-no;        -- 1 or yes = tabs have meaning --
    tab-size         NMTOKEN    "8"
    max-tabs         NMTOKEN    "255" -- recommend max number of tabs --
>
```

These attributes do not specify what an application is supposed to do with the spaces, tabs or records. Attributes such as these are created on the assumption that there will be some post-processing stage after the parser for characters, reforming the information coming into the application, to make sure that data is presented correctly: such a post-processing stage is very common. SGML does not provide a standard solution in this area because it does not attempt to address the issue.

This level of specification is probably too much detail. The issue of white-space preservation is one in particular for editing software: even though in the ultimate typeset document the spaces you use in the SGML text may not be significant, you may want the white-space preserved for convenient editing and processing. Very frequently SGML applications alter record starts and record ends when processing text; this can be very inconvenient when viewing the text using standard text processing tools, especially if you wish to use verbatim elements, or where you are using a simple text editor with wrap-around problems or maximum line lengths.

If you find your documents are using tabs, you should check your text to see whether you really should be using tables or list elements. Tabs are rarely needed in SGML, perhaps only for formatting free-form legacy text such as forms. If you do use tabs, you should also include some kind of ruler element, to specify where the tabs should appear, if they are not fixed-width tabs. If you are not using fixed-width fonts, you probably should even indicate which font you are using, since otherwise table alignment and breaking may easily fail. If you are not using fixed width fonts and you give your ruler measurements in absolute measures, for example 2 cm, then you should also include an hint about the font size required for the text.

```
<!ATTLIST      ruler
       font    ( times | helvetica | courier ) "times"
               -- note: exotic font makes portability difficult --
       tabstops NMTOKENS "0.5 4.5 8.5 12.5"
       unit    %units;         "em"
               -- em gives design independence --
       typesize NMTOKEN #IMPLIED
               -- in points --
>
```

Free-form text is really more like a graphic, and a lot of the value is in its layout. Consequently, the achievement of presentation-independence is of little utility. Marking up free-form text using tabs can be simple and convenient, but you must include all the information needed to render it. It is probably best to avoid using tabs, except as short reference delimiters.

⚠······ SGML 1986 has rules for white–space, and for newlines in particular, that sometimes may cause white–space or newlines to disappear from your data. XML uses a different method of handling white–space, which may result in the opposite effect: some white–space being significant when you don't expect it.

The SGML 1986 rules are good at coping with text-processing technology that has fixed maximum line-lengths. If you add markup to documents using such systems, then you may find you go to the maximum line-length, and be forced to split the current line at the tag. To cope with this need, which was very real at the time SGML was developed, but has become less common now, SGML 1986 record end *"are ignored when they are caused by markup"* ([*ISO 8879*], Annex B.3.3.1). The rules for deciding when a record end is *"caused by"* markup are a little complicated, and have been well dealt with elsewhere by other authors.

XML has introduced a much simpler convention, by dispensing with the requirement of coping with fixed line-length systems. In the absence of a DTD, all white-space is passed to the application. If a declaration is present, then white-spaces are passed back, but labeled according to the type of content model use: element content, mixed content, data content. ① This pushes the responsibility for coping with white-space handling onto the application or system developer. White-space is such a complex area that this is probably where it belongs. The single exception is the XML attribute XML–SPACE which can be given a value pre-

---

1. This behavior is available in WebSGML systems, if the *white–space in content rule* (WSCON) is set to KEEPALL in the SGML declaration.

`serve` to indicate that all white-space sequences within an element are significant, and the application should not strip or collapse them.

Word Segmentation in Chinese

Chinese words can take one, two, three or even more characters. But Chinese does not use spaces between words. (Many written languages do not require spaces between words.) But you need to know where words begin and end if you want to search for words, index documents, sort, spell-check, or even to break lines (whether horizontal lines or vertical) without causing ambiguous readings of the characters.

There are four methods:

- ◉ rule based, which tries to detect the grammar of the sentence to some extent: *"This is a noun, according to my reading of the sentence"*;

- ○ dictionary based: *"This is a noun, according to the dictionary"*;

- ○ statistical: *"This is a noun, because this combination of characters starting at this point most often is a word, and a noun"*;

- ○ explicit markup: *"This is a noun, it is in a <noun> element."*

The rule-based method works well in some languages: for example, modern Japanese word boundaries usually can be well detected, because of the four scripts and the punctuation marks in use. These rules are built deep into text processing software, and there is little SGML markup can do except passively document which rules are appropriate for particular elements, for example to select Chinese grammatical rules for one element and Tibetan at the next.

The most effective dictionary-based systems allow custom dictionaries for the industry sector the system in which will be used. SGML can help in this by allowing custom dictionaries to be referenced in documents as external entities. A document-specific dictionary could be added to the document too.

Similarly, the effectiveness of a statistical approach will relate to how well the sample or training documents match the documents to be used. SGML can augment the statistical method by providing a document stop-list, of exceptions to the statistical rules that may be found in the document.

Explicit markup is the last resort. Sometimes, especially for things like numbers that need to be kept on the same line with any unit or counter character, or for names that should not split, this may be the only effective method.

One simple way to delineate important words is simply to add a space between them, but with a note that the typesetting or rendering application must strip these out. A better way may be to create an interword-delimiter entity, for example,

```
<!ENTITY w  SDATA ' ' -- word segment delimiter -->
```

or use the Unicode character ZERO WIDTH SPACE, which is available in the SPREAD entity set as &U200B;.

The kinds of things that cause trouble in Chinese are irregular word formations that use common characters:

- ☒ proper nouns, for example names of people, mountains, chemicals;

- ☒ foreign words;

- ☒ abbreviations;

- ☒ small sayings; and

- ☒ words with characters that commonly appear as nouns and adjectives, or in gerunds.

Until computerized reading of Chinese sentences is perfected, there may always need to be some markup. To get a rough example, the following real English sentence has been run together: in this sentence the letter *form* appears as part of a noun, as a verb and in the verb *conform*. Similarly, *document* could function as a verb or a noun. —

```
Everyarchitecturemustprovidetheelementformarchitecturaldocumentelement,to
whichthedocumentelementofaclientdocumentmustconformifitdoesnotalreadyconf
ormtoanotherelementformintearchitecture.
```

Attempting to find an arbitrary match, or to parse the sentence starting at a random point are greatly simplified if the data is marked up to show the technical nouns phrases and proper nouns. For languages written without spaces, the common SGML practice of marking up all names and technical terms can have the useful side effect of helping line-breaking and correct searching. —

```
Every<n>architecture</n>mustprovidethe<n>elementformarchitecturalformdocu
mentelement</n>,towhichthe<n>documentelemen</n>tofa<n>clientdocument</n>m
ustconformifitdoesnotalreadyconformtoanother<n>elementform</n>inthe<n>arch
itecture</n>.
```

Summary of Chapter 21

Where possible, breaks should be tied into the topic- or editorial-structure of a document. However, this is not always possible. SGML provides a rich variety of ways to approach this.

Special Characters & SDATA

Chapter 22

This chapter

…shows how to handle special characters in SGML and XML. In the appendixes at the end of this book are standard SDATA entity declarations and indexes for thousands of special characters, including those for many foreign languages.

Using SDATA Entities

S pecial characters are usually represented in SGML using SDATA entities. These provide a system-independent way to identify a character, while deferring the method of rendering it to some later stage.

ISO Definition

4.275 **SDATA entity:** Specific character data entity.

4.304 **specific character data entity:** An entity whose text is treated as system data when referenced. The text is dependent on a specific system, device, or application process.

(ISO 8879:1986 glossary)

The [*SGML*] standard includes various public entity sets for many common special characters. ⚑ [*HTML*], [*TEI*] and ISO/IEC [*TR 9573-13*] and [*TR 9573-15*] also have public entity sets. The most comprehensive collection of characters, as distinct from glyphs, in a public entity set are the SPREAD-2 entities. A public entity set has a Formal Public Identifier (FPI) with the word ENTITIES in it: it is public text that only contains entity declarations, supporting data content notations and data attribute definitions. Usually these declarations are for SDATA entities.

The simplest way to use an SDATA entity is to copy the file containing the public entity set, and edit the copy to replace the nominal entity value with some actual replacement text that your system understands. Also replace the SDATA with CDATA, if the text contains delimiter characters which might trigger false delimiter recognition. Otherwise, just remove the keyword **SDATA**. So,

---

1. There is not such a strong need for the ISO 8879 sets in East Asia, since the Chinese, Japanese, and Korean national standard character sets already are rich with many foreign symbols: Cyrillic, Greek and so on. In East Asia, the problem is how to handle the characters needed in general and quality publishing, rather than how to handle foreign languages and niche publishing needs. However, the SGML processing model offers a way to take flight from the tyranny of continuingly increasing character-set sizes: by providing a protocol that works on top of any character set—entity references—you can define and use any characters as you see fit, yet have them in a documented and manageable form, with a fixed character set.

```
<!ENTITY my_char SDATA "[my character]" -- example -- >
```

becomes

```
<!ENTITY my_char CDATA "Zh" -- example -- >
```

or

```
<!ENTITY my_char "?" -- example -- >
```

When you have edited an SDATA public entity set like this, you should append some text to its formal public identifier. So, for example,

```
ISO 8879:1986//ENTITIES Added Latin 1//EN
```

might become

```
ISO 8879:1986//ENTITIES Added Latin 1//EN//Unicode
```

if you had resolved all the entity texts into their Unicode equivalents, or

```
ISO 8879:1986//ENTITIES
Added Latin 1//EN//WordPerfect 10 for Java
```

if you had resolved the entity texts into ones the Java edition of WordPerfect 10. This additional text is called the *public text display version*; you use it to keep track of which language, application or platform a resolved version of a public entity set belongs to. You probably will not need to update the original public identifier in your DTD: the mapping from a public identifier to the effective system identifier will probably be performed using an *entity catalog*.

Some parsers just treat SDATA entities like CDATA entities, and merely replace the entity reference with the entity text. So you have to search the output text for the entity text, and replace it. This is a good reason to keep entity text unique and pithy. Here is an example for the **sed** stream editor, invoked from a command line: ①

```
unix> sed "s/\[my\ character\]/Zh/" infile > outfile
```

A more sophisticated approach is needed when the glyph to be used varies due to context: in running text one glyph might be appropriate, but in a heading another might be suitable. This requires some kind of conditional processing.

An often satisfactory mechanism for the recipient of a document is to use a trick common in HTML files: fake the special character by providing a bitmap for it. To continue our example from above,

```
<!ENTITY my_char "<img src='http://www.somewhere.oz/zh.gif'/>" >
```

When **&my_char;** is dereferenced, it has an HTML **img** tag, with a URL to specify the image's location. As with all images, it is probably good for the WWW reader if the **img** tag includes the image size (in pixels): this allows the Web browser to continue rendering the rest of the page while the images are being fetched. An appropriate setting of the **hspan** and **vspan** attributes may also aid the illusion.

```
<!ENTITY my_char
        "<img src='http://www.somewhere.oz/zh.gif'
        height='48' width='48' hspace='0' vspace='0' />" >
```

The image should have been created with a transparent background, or it should have the same background as the page, which in practice only reliably means black or white.

For more techniques in this area, see *Character Repertoires* in chapter 18 page 3-13, and *Gaiji: User-defined Characters* in chapter 24, page 3-160. See *Quality Assurance on Characters* page 3-112 below for a discussion of the default entity.

---

1. The "\" characters just delimit the square brackets and the space character.

:Ö:······ When processing SGML files sometimes you don't want entity references dereferenced.—

> • The brute force method is to have a simple filter that inserts a null markup declaration (i.e., `<!>`) after every entity reference open (ERO) delimiter. So the text `&alpha;` becomes `&<!>alpha;` rather than being dereferenced into the actual character α.

> • A more elegant method is to alter the SGML declaration to remap the ERO delimiter to something improbable. This has the advantage that it does not also effect numeric character references.

> • If it is just special character references that you don't want replaced, the simplest thing may be to edit the entity declarations so that the SDATA text value is the same as the entity reference:

```
<!ENTITY alpha  SDATA "&alpha;" >
```

> This is the default method recommended by the International Committee for Accessible Document Design (ICADD) for rendering special characters for Braille and voice.

SDATA Entity Text

What should be the entity text (i.e., the nominal value in the string) of an SDATA entity? It is conventional that SDATA entity text is square bracketed, and should have at least as much information as the entity name. So the following is poor practice:

```
<!ENTITY  kangaroo SDATA "?" >
```

If the SDATA text is used in the output of the document, it gives the readers little indication of what was intended, and it may be difficult for proofreaders or typesetters to see. A better approach would be the following:

```
<!ENTITY  kangaroo SDATA "[kangaroo]" -- or wallaby -- >
```

For Han characters, it sometimes may be desirable to substitute simpler or approximate characters, especially for draft stages. For example, let us say there is a Han character which we can call *mad cow.*—

```
<!ENTITY  mad-cow SDATA "[mad-cow]" >
```

We can make a temporary entity declaration for use in draft documents giving a character with a close glyph. In the following example, the character is also flagged with a superscripted question mark to make the substitution plain to readers.—

```
<!ENTITY  mad-cow "&#x724B;<sup>?</sup>" >
```

In this example, `mad-cow` is no longer an SDATA entity, and the replacement text in the parameter literal (i.e., the quoted text) gives an approximated character, followed by a superscripted question mark, to give a visual clue that the character is only approximate.

If you are lucky, then your document character set may already provide the character you need. The purpose of the entity is, in this case, to provide a more memorable name for the character. You can map the name to the character by:

```
<!ENTITY  mad-cow CDATA "&#x4EBA;" >
```

Quality Assurance on Characters

Unjustifiable Accidents of Mu-Mu Land

Sometimes an SGML publishing system is set up to print nothing when an SDATA entity with no mapping is found. This is very poor practice, and can be dangerous.

⚠ ······ In particular, the entity µ from ISOnum should be used in quantities (sometimes, incorrectly, the character with often the same glyph, &mgr; from ISOgrk1, μ from ISOgrk3, or &b.mu; from ISOgrk4 is used) in technical and scientific documents to mark up the character μ. Missing the special character can make the document wrong, perhaps dangerously wrong.

SGML documents often are sent around the globe for processing, often going through people with no training or expertise in a particular publishing sector's production issues. Anticipating this, the onus is on the document system designer at the sending end to make sure that particular special characters are clearly flagged in the DTD as mission-critical.

Flagging may just take the form of a comment (all notes in DTDs do well to include their intended readers):

```
<!-- NOTE FOR AUTHORING STAFF:
        use entity reference &micro; in quantities. -->
<!-- NOTE FOR PRODUCTION STAFF:
        The SDATA entity &micro; is mission-critical. If the Greek mu glyph
        is not available, the text "micro " should be used. -->
<!-- NOTE FOR QA STAFF:
        check the entity &micro; is correctly handled. -->
```

When an entity reference is made, but no entity has been declared with that identifier and there is no default entity declaration, the SGML parser will flag an error. Some SGML systems may strip out references to undeclared entities. You can override this behavior by providing a default entity declaration. For example,

```
<!ENTITY #DEFAULT CDATA "&unknown;" >
```

This way, any unknown entities will have an indication in the rendered document. Whether CDATA or SDATA is appropriate here depends on capabilities of the processing software.

Accents

Here are the glyphs and names of the major accents used in the Latin-derived scripts of European-born languages:

Glyph	Suffix	Spacing Entity	Non-Spacing Entity	Comment
´	acute	acute	nsacute	
'	apos	apos	nsapos	apostrophe
˘	breve	breve	nsbreve	
ˇ	caron	caron	nscaron	
¸	cedil	cedilla	nscedil	
^	circ	circ	nscirc	circumflex
·	dot	dot	nsdot	dot above
`	grave	grave	nsgrave	
¯	macr	macr	nsmacr	
˛	ogon	ogon	nsogon	
°	ring	ring	nsring	
~	tilde	tilde	nstilde	
¨	uml	Dot	nsDot	dieresis

Generally, you can construct an ISO 8879-like entity name for a Latin character by taking the name of its [*ISO 646*] alphabetic base character and appending to it a suffix from the middle column of the preceding table. So, to get a Ü, you can use the entity reference Ü. To get ü, you can use the entity reference ü.

Because of the similarities, caron glyphs are often used in references to breves, especially for smaller characters or at low resolutions.

For more entity declarations for other accents refer to the "DIACRITS" entities in the SPREAD-2 public entity sets. Also see appendix D, *Index of XML Special Characters*, page XML-64. There are also many precombined accented characters in the "LATIN" entities in the SPREAD-2 public entity sets. These include accents that appear below the base characters. Also see appendix D, *Index of XML Special Characters*, page XML-48.

When using SDATA entity references for accent characters, make sure you select the appropriate spacing or non-spacing version. The entities in the ISO 8879 *Diacriticals* public entity set are spacing versions. So A˚ is not the same as Å. In the table above are names for entities you could define to give you non-spacing accent characters: these are part of the public entity set.

```
<!ENTITY nsdia PUBLIC
            "+//ISBN 0-13-614223-0::The SGML Cookbook//ENTITIES
            Non-Spacing Diacritical Marks//EN" >
```

Alternatives are also available in the SPREAD-2 public entity set. (Refer to the CD-ROM.)

Not everything that looks like an accent *is* one. If the accent relates to function or emphasis, that emphasis should be marked up using generalized elements—

- A dot below a character might be merely the characteristic glyph for the character, or it may be a form of emphasis (e.g., the Japanese *kendot*).

- Similarly, an overbar indicates an emphasis or a mathematical operation on the character (e.g., negation), while a macron ōver a character indicates some pronunciation difference. When rendering the characters you may have to alias a negated character, marked up properly with an element, to the use the glyph of a character with a macron, but it should not be marked-up that way. The prudence for this will be clearer if you discover you also need an overbar over a character with a macron: your markup system becomes inadequate.

- The composite character A&nsring; and the character Å are equivalent. However they are not the same as Å, the symbol for the Angstrom unit, even though their glyph may be the same: Å;.

And, predictably, the reverse is often true: some things that are often not considered accents sometimes *are* accents. The most famous example is the

Turkish "I". Turkish has four "I" characters: the jot mark (the dot) is treated as an accent mark. So Turkish has

- I,

- İ, which can be marked up `&Idot;`,

- ı, which can be marked up `&inodot;`, and

- i.

The "inodot" entity should not be confused with the standard entity "iota," which may have a similar glyph ι.

HTML Entities

HTML at first had entities for the opening delimiters, for commercial symbols, and for some rudimentary typesetting. These characters are identified following the names in the ISO *Numeric and Special Graphic* public entity set. Due to the ubiquity of ISO8859-1 fonts and the Adobe Symbol font, a fuller range of character entities has become available.

Note that because these entity declarations take their identifiers from the ISO entities there is a potential for naming conflicts. In SGML, the rule is that the first entity declared using an identifier takes precedence, so, if you want both the HTML entity sets and the ISO entity sets for some reason, put the parameter entity references to the HTML sets before the parameter entity references to the ISO sets.

At the time of writing, three public entity sets had been developed for HTML:

✓ HTMLlat1, a version of the ISOlat1 public entity set,

✓ HTMLsymbol, containing characters from the Adobe symbol font, and

✓ HTMLspecial, containing delimiter characters and internationalization characters.

There is also a proposed public entity set for common icons, which we can call HTMLicon. All these public entity sets are listed later.

Many of these characters in the HTMLsymbol set are intended for mathematical use. However, for more complex and professional quality typesetting, mathematics is better entered using higher-level markup, for example, in a CDATA element or external entity with the TeX typesetting language or the [*MML*](Mathematical Markup Language) as the notation. ①

Some further entities② suitable for use in bidirectional (BIDI) rendering and cursive joining control (required for documents which mix Arabic and Latin script, for example) are:

```
<!ENTITY zwnj SDATA "[zwnj]"  --=zero width non-joiner -->
<!ENTITY zwj  SDATA "[zwj]"   --=zero width joiner     -->
<!ENTITY lrm  SDATA "[lrm]"   --=left-to-right mark     -->
<!ENTITY rlm  SDATA "[rlm]"   --=right-to-left mark     -->
```

These are used in concert with the following attribute declaration, which can appear on any paragraph-level, or in-line, element types:

```
<!ATTLIST something
        dir -- directionality: left-to-right or right-to-left --
               ( ltr | rtl ) "ltr" >
```

In conjunction with these, you can also use an element type to override the directionality: BDO (BIDI Override). It is interesting to note that BID is perhaps a thing better handled by processing instructions: however, making the PIs into PI entities, and then converting the DIR attribute to expect an entity identifier as its name loses us the ability to constrain the value to the two appropriate choices. It is a shortfall in SGML as currently defined: PIs are definitely second class citizens, which is why they are not widely used, even when ideologically appropriate. So using just a simple attribute value list with a default is the best, and simplest design.

Different nations have different conventions for quotes. Even if the rest of the document is in a foreign language, some say③ that the struggling reader may find

---

1. For insight into the particular glyph issues relevant for low-level typesetting of mathematics, refer to ISO/IEC [*IS 9541–4*] *Font Information Interchange*, Part 4, "*Application–specific extensions*" which contains a DTD fragment. Font Interchange is outside the scope of this book.

2. Refer to [*RFC 2070*] for a fuller explanation.

3. Refer to [*RFC 2070*] for a fuller explanation.

the document easier to read if quotation marks in the text follow the conventions of the user's locale. If you need this kind of customizability, designate an element type with the GI of Q for this purpose.

On the other hand, quotations are not so widespread compared to many other structures that they require special treatment. Readers of an American English document may expect "diapostrophic quotation marks." And people reading a Japanese publication may prefer the neat 「Japanese quotation marks」, which look a little like crop-marks.

The in-line Q element type would be useful, however, whenever the text will be reused frequently, for example by being

- cut and pasted (or included as external entities) between documents using different languages, or

- quoted inside a quotation, where the marks may need to change.

⚠ ······ If you get an older SGML document that has not originated from the World Wide Web and which uses an entity set based on the Symbol font, it is often a sign that the document has been converted from some PC-based DTP program, and perhaps that not much effort has been put into making the text into typical SGML: it may be a sign that elements are not well marked-up too. Similarly, TeX documents converted to SGML will often have an entity set based on the TeX characters and names. This simplifies the conversion, but may increase the workload on subsequent users of the text, who may not have CDATA entity versions of TeX entity sets available. When you negotiate a contract for a conversion of legacy text, the entity set to be used should be discussed and arranged.

💡 ······ Sometimes SGML documents appear, having been translated from some DTP format, with ligatures intact as entity references. Generally it is wise to expand all ligatures in any text that may be searched or sorted, to make sure that proper results will be obtained.

If you want to keep the ligatures in place, you can re-mark the document up, automatically with something like

```
<P>A <alternative  pretty="Tri&fllig;ing">Trifling</alternative>
matter.</p>
```

or

```
<P>A <alternative  indexable="Trifling">Tri&fllig;ing</alternative>
matter.</p>
```

Mathematical Scripts and Symbols

The ISO public entity sets provide a good range of mathematical symbols, though not nearly complete. Apart from the ISOtech entities and the ISOnum entities, specialist mathematical symbols can be found in

```
<!ENTITY % ISOamsa PUBLIC
     "ISO 8879-1986//ENTITIES Added Math Symbols: Arrow Relations//EN" >
<!ENTITY % ISOamsb PUBLIC
     "ISO 8879-1986//ENTITIES Added Math Symbols: Binary Operators//EN" >
<!ENTITY % ISOamsc PUBLIC
     "ISO 8879-1986//ENTITIES Added Math Symbols: Delimiters//EN" >
<!ENTITY % ISOamsn PUBLIC  "ISO 8879-1986//ENTITIES
     Added Math Symbols: Negated Relations//EN" >
<!ENTITY % ISOamso PUBLIC
     "ISO 8879-1986//ENTITIES Added Math Symbols: Ordinary//EN" >
<!ENTITY % ISOamsr PUBLIC
     "ISO 8879-1986//ENTITIES Added Math Symbols: Relations//EN" >
```

The following entity sets have been defined in drafts of [*ISO 9573*], but were not available at the time this book went to press.

```
<!ENTITY % ISOmfrak PUBLIC
        "ISO/IEC TR 9573//ENTITIES Mathematics alphabet: Fraktur//EN" >
<!ENTITY % ISOmoface PUBLIC
        "ISO/IEC TR 9573//ENTITIES Mathematics alphabet: Open Face//EN" >
<!ENTITY % ISOmscript PUBLIC
        "ISO/IEC TR 9573//ENTITIES Mathematics alphabet: Script//EN" >
```

The SPREAD-2 entities also have many suitable characters. For Greek symbols in mathematics, use the characters in ISOgrk3 and ISOgrk4 by preference.

Use the following entity references in running text to allow best mathematical typesetting:

- + rather than "+" for plus;

- − rather than the hyphen "x – x" ;

- ÷ rather than the "/";

- × rather than "x" for the times operator ×;

- · for the dot multiplier operator ·;

- ∗ (i.e., low asterisk) rather than * for the asterisk * in program source code, especially for C/C++ source code (or construct a special version of your program code font, with the asterisk lowered,[1] which allows you to map the lowast entity value simply to the direct character "*" using SGML shortrefs);

- ✶ (i.e., sextile) for the multiplication star operator or the Kleene star, to get a six-point star *, rather than the direct character *, which may be rendered with a five-point star;

---

1. The asterisk glyph in modern fonts is a compromise between the asterisk used as a footnote indicator, which is superscripted, and the other stars, which are better presented closer to the numeral baseline. This compromise invariably results in ugliness, which may explain the rapid fall from favor of the asterisk, an old character which predates Latin and Greek.

3-120   The XML & SGML Cookbook

- < and never "<" (except in elements with CDATA declared content, of course) for the less-than operator ① ;

- > rather than ">" for the greater-than operator;

- ⟨ and never "<" (again, except in elements with CDATA declared content) for the left angle bracket ⟨; and ⟩ rather than ">" for the right angle bracket ⟩.

There is an ISO standard available for mathematical markup: ISO/IEC 12083: 1993. A more recent adaptation of this that is worth investigating is the Mathematical Markup Language [*MML*].

XML

SDATA entities are not available in [*XML*] 1.0. Until the WWW gets an online font-delivery service, you must use an element type if the character is not available in XML's large document character set, [*ISO 10646*]. For example,

```
<p>blah blah<em-dash>--</em-dash>blah blah</p>
```

---

1. The < and > probably should only be used directly as a short-reference delimiter, or for chevrons (‹single guillemets›) or in computer source code. To force nice chevrons, use the `&raquo;` and `&laquo;`, but specify in your DTD that you want the single version not the double version glyphs. Or, most directly, use a declaration like:

```
<!ENTITY lchevron SDATA "<">
```

The mathematical glyphs for these characters are slightly different typographically from their non-mathematical impersonators, look better amidst digits and italics, or are more distinct on the page.

will give a draft-level print result if the data is passed through, but a smarter system could suppress the contents and generate a real em-dash.① Of course, doing this for hundreds of special characters adds to the size of content models without much gain in expressiveness over SDATA entities.

You can declare the element type for this kind of approach – where the contents are a seatwarmer rather than a placeholder – in the following way:

```
<!ELEMENT em-dash ( #PCDATA)>
<!ATTLIST em-dash
   content-type NAME #FIXED "SDATA">
```

XML 1.0 does not support SDATA entity types. However, you can use the kind of declaration above to reintroduce something similar to them. In your documentation, do not forget to mention what function an element type with a fixed attribute content-type performs.

Summary of Chapter 22

SGML SDATA entities can be used to declare special characters that may not be available in the character set of every computer that may handle the document. Many large sets of declarations of these entities exist as public text. See appendices A, B and C for ISO, HTML and TEI public entity sets, and to appendix D for an index to the SPREAD public entity set. XML 1.0 does not support SDATA entities and users must rely on numeric character references more. See appendix D for an index of the characters available in XML.

---

1. Thanks to Dan Connolly of W3C for this example, which appeared on his 1997 Web page "*XML hacking is fun.*"

The XML & SGML Cookbook

From

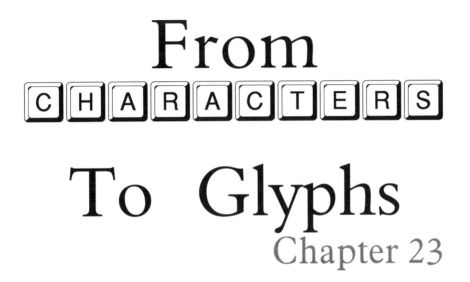

To Glyphs

Chapter 23

This chapter

…shows some ways to specify explicitly the visual properties of characters in SGML: typeface, size, color, ligatures and typographical embellishments.

This chapter is about how to specify the information needed in addition to the character code to specify a glyph. See *Custom Fonts*, page 3-161, for a treatment of the related subject of how to select a particular glyph in a preexisting font.

As you will by now expect, there is a rich number of different ways you can specify glyphs in SGML. The most sophisticated way is to do it externally, using [*DSSSL*]① or something similar: this is the topic for another book. An easier way is to specify the fonts and other information using a style-sheet, such as the HTML Cascading Style Sheet ([*CSS*]).②

Most of this chapter, however, gives patterns and information for specifying directly in markup how characters are to be presented.

You can specify a style-sheet externally using a processing instruction. To keep them nicely clear of the instance, the document prolog is a good place for them. An example might be the following:

```
<?MY-style-sheet type="text/dsssl"
          href="tinybook.dsl" ?>
```

where `My-style-sheet` identifies the notation used in the processing instruction, the `type` pseudo-attribute specifies the type of the style-sheet (use a [*MIME*] media-type), and the `href` pseudo-attribute gives the system identifier for the external resource containing the style-sheet.

---

1. The Document Style and Semantic Specification Language is an ISO standard for specifying how to render SGML documents on paper and online: DSSSL uses the simple and powerful [*Scheme*] language. At the time of writing, there is a proposal to create a version of DSSSL geared to rendering XML documents, using the [*ECMAscript*] language syntax (i.e., the European standard form of JavaScript), which may be more familiar to users of WWW: this language would be called the Extensible Style Language, [*XSL*].

2. If you need to add presentation elements, it is probably a good idea to use CSS names and allowed values, even if just for ease of documentation. At the time this book went to press, CSS was being extended to handle aural and 3-D rendering.

Glyph Mapping

Despite appearances, going from character to glyphs is usually not a simple one-to-one mapping, like the following:

```
typeface= f (element-context)
glyph = f (characters,  typeface)
```

In fact many other factors may come into play – however many of these occur transparently to the user, determined by the system settings of their computer. Most computers and applications (encouraged by ANSI C locale facilities) are monolingual only. A few can switch between locales; few applications are seriously multilingual. A locale collects together particular settings for applications, including territory, script, user interface language, sort sequence, currency and date conventions.

A unified character set like ISO 10646 requires some idea of the locale of the document or the user① to determine which variant glyphs to use, particular for Han ideographs, which have various simplified and traditional forms. By default, the user will get what the system fonts have installed, or what the customization controls for the computer have selected. I will use the term "script" to include all locale-specific conventions that are needed, including which variant of the basic scripts should be used. —

```
glyph = f (character, typeface, script)
```

Sometimes the glyph to be used is determined by its position in a word, for example, in Arabic—

```
glyph = f (character, typeface, script, word position)
```

---

1. The fact that the user's locale may be different from the document's locale is perhaps the most unpleasant fact in multilingual computing and internationalization. Facing this, you can mark up your exact document requirements using SGML. But you may have to be creative and flexible in getting your data rendered: the SGML solution is better than none, and shows good promise, for example with ISO HTML, which is thoroughly multilingual.

Professional quality output requires that sometimes the glyphs used to draw the characters may depend on the context of the characters: the `&filig;` ligature fi used instead of the separate characters "f i" for example.

```
glyph = f (character[..., i-1, i, i+1, ...], typeface,
                     script, word position)
```

This is largely a matter of the selection of the character repertoire. If the creator of the character repertoire decided that accents should be separate characters, combining with some base into a composed character sequence, then this model is used. But if the creator decided to use precomposed characters, with a character available for every possible combination, then the glyph selection model is simpler.

Sometimes the glyph is determined also by the context of other glyphs around it, for example some Indic languages—

```
glyph = f (character[..., i-1, i, i+1, ...], typeface,
           script, word position, glyph[..., n-1,   n+1, ...])
```

Many typesetting systems do not allow composed character sequences. Also, some indexing or search systems do not check for alternative sequences that result in the same glyph. You can preprocess the marked–up data to put all the characters into a canonical sequence.

Sometimes the glyph to be used, determined by the editorial-structure of the characters, is selected from within alternatives or variants in the same typeface. For example, style-sheets usually allow you to force upper-case glyphs for, in particular, titles and headings, regardless of how the element was spelled in characters. —

```
glyph = f (character[..., i-1, i, i+1, ...], typeface, variant,
           script, word position, glyph[..., n-1,   n+1, ...])
```

Examples of these variants are upper and lower-case, small capitals, and full-width and half-width characters. (Small capitals are usually found in a separate font.)

And, even when a glyph is specified by all these factors, there is still the question of locating it in a font. The trend has been to make smarter fonts, that automatically alter the glyphs according to their glyph and character context. This reduces the complexity of the typesetting or presentation device software—

```
glyph = f (character[i], font, context).
```

 The less powerful the presentation device, the less likely it is to be able to select good glyphs. The good news is that you can use markup to explicitly select glyphs where your existing presentation device is weak. For example, if your system does not support any "fi" ligatures, you can markup your SGML document to add them.

If you are using tools that cannot selectively edit inside data content, then you must check that no string "fi" appears in markup or in declarations. This is actually a very difficult and tedious task, one that shows how powerful SGML-aware tools can be. See also *Word Segmentation in Chinese*, in chapter 21, page 3-104.

Glyph Selection with Elements

So, what practical lesson should we learn? When we need to include in our documents characters or glyphs far removed from those of the usual character repertoires belonging to our locale, they probably must be marked-up as fairly explicit glyph specifications, not characters. This can still be done using generic markup:—

```
<!ELEMENT generic-glyph  EMPTY>
<!ATTLIST generic-glyph
          charset         CDATA    #REQUIRED
          code            CDATA    #REQUIRED
          typeface        CDATA    #IMPLIED
          variant         CDATA    #IMPLIED
          %lang-att;       -- See Language Codes in chapter 19 --
          position        CDATA    #IMPLIED>
```

Specific markup may be useful instead; it is simpler but hard-codes the glyph to a particular system's values—

```
<!ELEMENT specific-glyph EMPTY >
<!ATTLIST specific-glyph
          font    CDATA    #REQUIRED
          code    CDATA    #REQUIRED
          variant CDATA    #REQUIRED            -- e.g. bold, italic -- >
```

If many specific characters or glyphs must be selected, rather than use in-line CDATA attributes, it will become more maintainable to both convert some of the CDATA attributes to ENTITY attributes ("strong typing"), and to convert the invocations of the elements into entity references ("flyweighting")—

```
<!ELEMENT glyph          EMPTY>
<!ATTLIST glyph
          charset         ENTITY   #REQUIRED   -- Note: XML use NMTOKEN --
          code            NMTOKEN  #REQUIRED
          typeface        NMTOKEN  #IMPLIED
          variant         ENTITIES #IMPLIED    -- Note: XML use NMTOKENS --
          %lang-att;       -- See Language Codes in chapter 19 --
          position        (initial, medial, final, NA) "NA"
          alt             CDATA    #IMPLIED>
<!ENTITY U6B66TW
'<glyph charset="ISO10646" code="6B66" typeface="plain" xml:lang="cn-TW"
        alt="[ISO10646 character 6B66, in Taiwan variant]"> ' >
```

```
<!ENTITY  U6B66HK
'<glyph charset="ISO10646" code="6B66" typeface="plain" xml:lang="cn-HK"
     alt="[ISO10646 character 6B66, in Hongkong variant]"> ' >
```

This can then be used—

```
<p xml:lang="cn-SG">The Taiwanese character &U6B66TW;
looks quite different from the Hong Kong version
&U6B66HK;, let alone our Singaporean variant &#6B66;.</p>
```

Another example. The Hungarian umlaut, a kind of double acute, does not appear in any standard character sets or entity sets. It is regarded purely as a typeface variant. If you need to use both Hungarian umlauts and standard ones in the same document, use—

```
<!ENTITY  hunglaut
'<glyph charset="ISO10646" code="0308" lang="hu" alt="[Hungarian
umlaut]">'
 -- a COMBINING DIAERESIS, looks like double acute-- >
```

You could use names like &U0308hu; or &huuml; rather than &hunglaut; of course.

Glyph Selection with Entities

Adding attributes to entities using notations is not very familiar to many users of SGML. Rather than selecting the glyph using an element embedded in an entity, we can just declare an entity notation, and give that notation the same attributes the element had. You can see that both methods are of about the same complexity:

```
<!NOTATION glyph SYSTEM >
<!ATTLIST #NOTATION glyph
        charset         ENTITY          #REQUIRED
        code            NMTOKEN         #REQUIRED
        typeface        ENTITY          #IMPLIED
        variant         ENTITIES        #IMPLIED
        %lang-att;              -- See Language Codes in chapter 19 --
        position        ( initial, medial, final, NA ) "NA"
        alt             CDATA           #IMPLIED>
<!ENTITY  hunglaut SYSTEM NDATA glyph
[ charset="ISO10646" code="0308" lang="hu" alt="[Hungarian umlaut]" ]
 -- a COMBINING DIAERESIS, looks like double acute-- >
```

Using an entity declaration like this is probably preferable, in that it does not clutter up the content models in element type declarations with non-structural element types. Note: XML 1.0 does not support data attributes.

Size

The simplest way to handle sizes is to have <SMALL> and <BIG> element types. This is not very satisfactory for most users, who prefer more control.

HTML has a <FONT> element type which allows a size attribute. This allows you to increment the points. It would be better to have been specified in units of ems, to get more realistic independence from the output device. Note that some HTML parsers allows the following:

```
<FONT SIZE=+1>
```

but valid SGML and well-formed XML requires

```
<FONT SIZE="+1">
```

or

```
<FONT SIZE='+1'>.
```

Design independence can be gained by using a scale of sizes—

```
<!ATTLIST some-element-type
        size ( ultra-small | small | normal
               | big | large | ultra-large ) normal >
```

A better approach for sites that need to be concerned with presentation is to mark up the data according to the impact it is supposed to have on the target readership—

```
<!ATTLIST some-element-type
        volume ( whisper | soft | normal | loud | shout ) normal >
```

Obviously in the print medium the term volume is used analogically. Marking up data in this way makes it easier to establish and revise the look and feel of pages. Not only can the volume relate to size, but also the color and font. It is markup based on the perceived usefulness of the element type to the reader rather than the nature of the contents of the element.

As a matter of quaint interest, many old books have text sizes based in arithmetic ratios. For example, a book may have type of size 6, 10, 16, 26, and 42 points based on a Fibonacci sequence starting with 2. To indicate classical relations between the different size values above, but maintain size-independence, use—

```
<!ATTLIST some-element-type
        size ( ultra-small | small | normal
               | big | large | ultra-large ) normal
        sequence-type ( Fibonacci | golden | logarithmic ) fibonacci
        sequence-seed   NMTOKEN 2
        sequence-index NMTOKEN 4>
```

As a matter of historical interest, we could also use the old names for type sizes. The names do not correspond to precise modern sizes and can give a little leeway, allowing a typographer to use, for example, a 10.5 pt font where the 10 pt font of that typeface looks too small in context. These names are now obscure, but who would not wish for a little more romance in computing?—

```
<!ATTLIST some-element-type
        size    ( diamond                    --4.5 pt --
                | pearl                       --  5 pt --
                | ruby | agate                --5.5 pt --
                | nonpareil                   --  6 pt --
                | emerald | minion            --  7 pt --
                | brevier | small_text        --  8 pt --
                | bourgeois | galliard        --  9 pt --
                | long_primer | garamond      -- 10 pt --
                | small_pica | philosophy     -- 11 pt --
                | pica                        -- 12 pt --
                | english | augustin          -- 14 pt --
                | great_primer )              -- 18 pt -
        #IMPLIED
>
```

Superscripts and Subscripts

A superscript in general text is usually the sign for a reference to a footnote or some annotation. These should never be marked up using an element <sup>, which merely sets a size and position, but always as a cross-reference of the appropriate kind.

In different media, the same cross-reference may be rendered completely differently. What is a superscript number referring to a footnote in a paper book could be a blue-ed hypertext link on a WWW page. A hypertext browser might decide to insert an icon in the margin or before the paragraph rather than clutter the in-line text, and it might display the note as a pop-up.

For superscripts and subscripts in mathematics, see *Mathematical Scripts and Symbols*, in chapter 22, page 3-119.

Some brand names may use superscripts or subscripts to make a simple logo. The best way to handle these is to make a general entity for the logo. For example, the typesetting program that is written "TeX" in plain text, also has a logo version:

T$_E$X. [1] This logo version could be implemented as an SGML entity something like this:

```
<!ENTITY TeX "T<sub><font size='+2'>E</font></sub>X" >
```

It is this kind of mess that generalized markup usually frees us from, except in these logo-like cases. The best thing to do is to make the construction of the logo the job of the recipient of the document, by shipping the logo out as an SDATA entity only. But give enough information in comments that the recipient can conveniently reconstruct the logo. And give SDATA entity a value that will not interrupt the document if used directly—

```
<!ENTITY TeX "TeX"
          -- HTML= "T<sub><font size='+2'>E</font></sub>X"? -->
```

---

1. The reason for the horrible increment of the `size` in this code is because subscript elements such as `sub` typically reduce the font size of their contents. Here it is hard-coded: SGML does not have any mathematical operators or way to query the typesetting program – you have to embed such queries in markup, perhaps using a custom extension to DSSSL.

Color Codes

There are several simple methods for specifying color: the HTML RGB method is very convenient—

```
<!NOTATION rgb     SYSTEM >
<!NOTATION cmyk    SYSTEM >
<!NOTATION cmy     SYSTEM >
<!NOTATION pantone SYSTEM >
<!ATTLIST body
    bgcolor       CDATA              #IMPLIED
    color_scheme NOTATION ( rgb ) #IMPLIED
    -- RGB  = six letter hexadecimal value RRGGBB, red, blue & green --
    -- CYMK = eight letter hex value
            CCMMYYKK, cyan, magenta, yellow, black --
    -- CYM  = six letter hex value CCMMYY, cyan, magenta, yellow--
    -- pantone = Pantone ® color name -->
```

However, the results for RGB are widely variant on different operating hardware: this is clearly the result of a failure in the specification method. Light violet can be lipstick pink.

The best way to specify a color is by the name, adopting some published conventions like Pantone® or the X Windows colors.

A different way, but one which may be easier for non-technical document creators, is to specify a simple color name and an intensity—

```
<!ATTLIST body
color -- the sixteen colors available on the PC --
        (black | white | aqua | blue | fuschia | gray |
         grey | green | lime | maroon | navy |
         olive | purple | red | silver | teal | yellow) #IMPLIED
intensity -- 0 (light) to 100 (dark) --
        NMTOKEN #IMPLIED >
```

Black, Grays and White

[*Mikes*] gives a useful convention for names and values for black, grays, and white. Start with black being named *gray0* and having an RGB value of $(0, 0, 0)$, and white being named *gray100* and having an RGB value of $(255, 255, 255)$. Then all intermediate values are gray$n$, where the RGB value are $(2.55\,n, 2.55\,n, 2.55\,n)$, rounded up. "Gray" may be spelled "grey" outside America; developers of English-language software should allow for alternate spellings as a routine part of internationization.

Below are some also some grayish colors. Attributes which use this notation may have spaces in them, when users spell out the words (e.g., "dark slate gray"); applications should strip out spaces and convert all characters to the same case. These names are used in the the X Windows system, and some WWW browsers.

Red	Green	Blue	Names
47	79	79	darkslategray
139	131	120	antiquewhite4
139	121	94	navajowhite4
112	128	144	slategray
82	139	139	darkslategray4
151	255	255	darkslategray1, cadetblue1
108	123	139	slategray4
119	136	153	lightslategray
205	179	139	navajowhite3
205	192	176	antiquewhite3
159	182	205	slategray3
238	207	161	navajowhite2
238	223	204	antiquewhite2
121	205	205	darkslategray3

211	211	211	lightgray
185	211	238	slategray2
255	222	173	navajowhite, navajowhite1
255	239	219	antiquewhite1
141	238	238	darkslategray2, cadetblue2
255	250	240	floralwhite
250	235	215	antique white, antiquewhite
245	245	245	gray96, whitesmoke
248	248	255	ghostwhite
198	226	255	slategray1

Colors

Here are RGB values and names for common colors. See the comments in the previous section *Black, Grays and White* on spaces, case and spelling equivalents.

Red	Green	Blue	Names	...
240	248	255		aliceblue
127	255	212	aquamarine1	aquamarine
118	238	198	aquamarine2	
102	205	170	aquamarine3	mediumaquamarine
69	139	116	aquamarine4	
240	255	255	azure	azure1
224	238	238	azure2	

193	205	205	azure3	
131	139	139	azure4	
245	245	220		beige
255	228	196	bisque1	bisque
238	213	183	bisque2	
205	183	158	bisque3	
139	125	107	bisque4	
255	235	205		blanchedalmond
0	0	255	blue1	blue
0	0	238	blue2	
0	0	205	blue3	mediumblue
0	0	139	blue4	
138	43	226		blueviolet
165	42	42		brown
255	64	64	brown1	
238	59	59	brown2	
205	51	51	brown3	
139	35	35	brown4	
222	184	135		burlywood
255	211	155	burlywood1	
238	197	145	burlywood2	
205	170	125	burlywood3	
139	115	85	burlywood4	
95	158	160		cadetblue

152	245	255	cadetblue1	
142	229	238	cadetblue2	
122	197	205	cadetblue3	
83	134	139	cadetblue4	
127	255	0	chartreuse1	chartreuse
118	238	0	chartreuse2	
102	205	0	chartreuse3	
69	139	0	chartreuse4	
210	105	30		chocolate
255	127	36	chocolate1	
238	118	33	chocolate2	
205	102	29	chocolate3	
139	69	19	chocolate4	saddlebrown
255	127	80		coral
255	114	86	coral1	
238	106	80	coral2	
205	91	69	coral3	
139	62	47	coral4	
100	149	237		cornflowerblue
255	248	220	cornsilk1	cornsilk
238	232	205	cornsilk2	
205	200	177	cornsilk3	
139	136	120	cornsilk4	
0	255	255	cyan1	cyan

0	238	238	cyan2	
0	205	205	cyan3	
0	139	139	cyan4	
184	134	11		darkgoldenrod
255	185	15	darkgoldenrod1	
238	173	14	darkgoldenrod2	
205	149	12	darkgoldenrod3	
139	101	8	darkgoldenrod4	
0	100	0		darkgreen
189	183	107		darkkhaki
85	107	47		darkolivegreen
202	255	112	darkolivegreen1	
188	238	104	darkolivegreen2	
162	205	90	darkolivegreen3	
110	139	61	darkolivegreen4	
255	140	0		darkorange
255	127	0	darkorange1	
238	118	0	darkorange2	
205	102	0	darkorange3	
139	69	0	darkorange4	
153	50	204		darkorchid
191	62	255	darkorchid1	
178	58	238	darkorchid2	
154	50	205	darkorchid3	

104	34	139	darkorchid4	
233	150	122		darksalmon
143	188	143		darkseagreen
193	255	193	darkseagreen1	
180	238	180	darkseagreen2	
155	205	155	darkseagreen3	
105	139	105	darkseagreen4	
0	206	209		darkturquoise
148	0	211		darkviolet
255	20	147	deeppink1	deeppink
238	18	137	deeppink2	
205	16	118	deeppink3	
139	10	80	deeppink4	
0	191	255	deepskyblue1	deepskyblue
0	178	238	deepskyblue2	
0	154	205	deepskyblue3	
0	104	139	deepskyblue4	
30	144	255	dodgerblue1	dodgerblue
28	134	238	dodgerblue2	
24	116	205	dodgerblue3	
16	78	139	dodgerblue4	
178	34	34		firebrick
255	48	48	firebrick1	
238	44	44	firebrick2	

The XML & SGML Cookbook

205	38	38	firebrick3	
139	26	26	firebrick4	
34	139	34		forestgreen
220	220	220		gainsboro
255	215	0	gold1	gold
238	201	0	gold2	
205	173	0	gold3	
139	117	0	gold4	
218	165	32		goldenrod
255	193	37	goldenrod1	
238	180	34	goldenrod2	
205	155	29	goldenrod3	
139	105	20	goldenrod4	
0	255	0	green1	green
0	238	0	green2	
0	205	0	green3	
0	139	0	green4	
173	255	47		greenyellow
240	255	240	honeydew1	honeydew
224	238	224	honeydew2	
193	205	193	honeydew3	
131	139	131	honeydew4	
255	105	180		hotpink
255	110	180	hotpink1	

238	106	167	hotpink2	
205	96	144	hotpink3	
139	58	98	hotpink4	
205	92	92		indianred
255	106	106	indianred1	
238	99	99	indianred2	
205	85	85	indianred3	
139	58	58	indianred4	
255	255	240	ivory1	ivory
238	238	224	ivory2	
205	205	193	ivory3	
139	139	131	ivory4	
240	230	140		khaki
255	246	143	khaki1	
238	230	133	khaki2	
205	198	115	khaki3	
139	134	78	khaki4	
230	230	250		lavender
255	240	245	lavenderblush1	lavenderblush
238	224	229	lavenderblush2	
205	193	197	lavenderblush3	
139	131	134	lavenderblush4	
124	252	0		lawngreen
255	250	205	lemonchiffon1	lemonchiffon

238	233	191	lemonchiffon2	
205	201	165	lemonchiffon3	
139	137	112	lemonchiffon4	
173	216	230		lightblue
191	239	255	lightblue1	
178	223	238	lightblue2	
154	192	205	lightblue3	
104	131	139	lightblue4	
240	128	128		lightcoral
224	255	255		lightcyan
224	255	255	lightcyan1	
209	238	238	lightcyan2	
180	205	205	lightcyan3	
122	139	139	lightcyan4	
238	221	130		lightgoldenrod
255	236	139	lightgoldenrod1	
238	220	130	lightgoldenrod2	
205	190	112	lightgoldenrod3	
139	129	76	lightgoldenrod4	
250	250	210		lightgoldenrod yellow
255	182	193		lightpink
255	174	185	lightpink1	
238	162	173	lightpink2	

205	140	149	lightpink3	
139	95	101	lightpink4	
255	160	122	lightsalmon1	lightsalmon
238	149	114	lightsalmon2	
205	129	98	lightsalmon3	
139	87	66	lightsalmon4	
32	178	170		lightseagreen
135	206	250		lightskyblue
176	226	255	lightskyblue1	
164	211	238	lightskyblue2	
141	182	205	lightskyblue3	
96	123	139	lightskyblue4	
132	112	255		lightslateblue
176	196	222		lightsteelblue
202	225	255	lightsteelblue1	
188	210	238	lightsteelblue2	
162	181	205	lightsteelblue3	
110	123	139	lightsteelblue4	
255	255	224	lightyellow1	lightyellow
238	238	209	lightyellow2	
205	205	180	lightyellow3	
139	139	122	lightyellow4	
50	205	50		limegreen
250	240	230		linen

255	0	255	magenta1	magenta
238	0	238	magenta2	
205	0	205	magenta3	
139	0	139	magenta4	
176	48	96		maroon
255	52	179	maroon1	
238	48	167	maroon2	
205	41	144	maroon3	
139	28	98	maroon4	
186	85	211		mediumorchid
224	102	255	mediumorchid1	
209	95	238	mediumorchid2	
180	82	205	mediumorchid3	
122	55	139	mediumorchid4	
147	112	219		mediumpurple
171	130	255	mediumpurple1	
159	121	238	mediumpurple2	
137	104	205	mediumpurple3	
93	71	139	mediumpurple4	
60	179	113		mediumseagreen
123	104	238		mediumslateblue
0	250	154		mediumspringgreen
72	209	204		mediumturquoise

199	21	133		mediumvioletred
25	25	112		midnightblue
245	255	250		mintcream
255	228	225	mistyrose1	mistyrose
238	213	210	mistyrose2	
205	183	181	mistyrose3	
139	125	123	mistyrose4	
255	228	181		moccasin
0	0	128	navy	navyblue
253	245	230		oldlace
107	142	35		olivedrab
192	255	62	olivedrab1	
179	238	58	olivedrab2	
154	205	50	olivedrab3	
105	139	34	olivedrab4	
255	165	0	orange1	orange
238	154	0	orange2	
205	133	0	orange3	
139	90	0	orange4	
255	69	0	orangered1	orangered
238	64	0	orangered2	
205	55	0	orangered3	
139	37	0	orangered4	
218	112	214		orchid

255	131	250	orchid1	
238	122	233	orchid2	
205	105	201	orchid3	
139	71	137	orchid4	
238	232	170		palegoldenrod
152	251	152		palegreen
154	255	154	palegreen1	
144	238	144	palegreen2	
124	205	124	palegreen3	
84	139	84	palegreen4	
187	255	255	paleturquoise1	
174	238	238	paleturquoise2	paleturquoise
150	205	205	paleturquoise3	
102	139	139	paleturquoise4	
219	112	147		palevioletred
255	130	171	palevioletred1	
238	121	159	palevioletred2	
205	104	137	palevioletred3	
139	71	93	palevioletred4	
255	239	213		papayawhip
255	218	185	peachpuff1	peachpuff
238	203	173	peachpuff2	
205	175	149	peachpuff3	
139	119	101	peachpuff4	

255	192	203		pink
255	181	197	pink1	
238	169	184	pink2	
205	145	158	pink3	
139	99	108	pink4	
221	160	221		plum
255	187	255	plum1	
238	174	238	plum2	
205	150	205	plum3	
139	102	139	plum4	
176	224	230		powderblue
160	32	240		purple
155	48	255	purple1	
145	44	238	purple2	
125	38	205	purple3	
85	26	139	purple4	
255	0	0	red1	red
238	0	0	red2	
205	0	0	red3	
139	0	0	red4	
188	143	143		rosybrown
255	193	193	rosybrown1	
238	180	180	rosybrown2	
205	155	155	rosybrown3	

139	105	105	rosybrown4	
65	105	225		royalblue
72	118	255	royalblue1	
67	110	238	royalblue2	
58	95	205	royalblue3	
39	64	139	royalblue4	
250	128	114		salmon
255	140	105	salmon1	
238	130	98	salmon2	
205	112	84	salmon3	
139	76	57	salmon4	
244	164	96		sandybrown
46	139	87	seagreen	seagreen4
84	255	159	seagreen1	
78	238	148	seagreen2	
67	205	128	seagreen3	
255	245	238	seashell	seashell1
238	229	222	seashell2	
205	197	191	seashell3	
139	134	130	seashell4	
160	82	45		sienna
255	130	71	sienna1	
238	121	66	sienna2	
205	104	57	sienna3	

139	71	38	sienna4	
135	206	235		skyblue
135	206	255	skyblue1	
126	192	238	skyblue2	
108	166	205	skyblue3	
74	112	139	skyblue4	
106	90	205		slateblue
131	111	255	slateblue1	
122	103	238	slateblue2	
105	89	205	slateblue3	
71	60	139	slateblue4	darkslateblue
255	250	250	snow1	snow
238	233	233	snow2	
205	201	201	snow3	
139	137	137	snow4	
0	255	127	springgreen1	springgreen
0	238	118	springgreen2	
0	205	102	springgreen3	
0	139	69	springgreen4	
70	130	180		steelblue
99	184	255	steelblue1	
92	172	238	steelblue2	
79	148	205	steelblue3	
54	100	139	steelblue4	

210	180	140		tan
255	165	79	tan1	
238	154	73	tan2	
205	133	63	tan3	peru
139	90	43	tan4	
216	191	216		thistle
255	225	255	thistle1	
238	210	238	thistle2	
205	181	205	thistle3	
139	123	139	thistle4	
255	99	71	tomato1	tomato
238	92	66	tomato2	
205	79	57	tomato3	
139	54	38	tomato4	
64	224	208		turquoise
0	245	255	turquoise1	
0	229	238	turquoise2	
0	197	205	turquoise3	
0	134	139	turquoise4	
238	130	238		violet
208	32	144		violetred
255	62	150	violetred1	
238	58	140	violetred2	
205	50	120	violetred3	

139	34	82	violetred4	
245	222	179		wheat
255	231	186	wheat1	
238	216	174	wheat2	
205	186	150	wheat3	
139	126	102	wheat4	
255	255	0	yellow1	yellow
238	238	0	yellow2	
205	205	0	yellow3	
139	139	0	yellow4	
154	205	50		yellowgreen

If you will use the X11 color names, you might declare a notation to reference them, such as

```
<!NOTATION XLIB_colors
    PUBLIC "+//ISBN 0-13-614223-0::The SGML Cookbook//NOTATION
    ISBN 0-201-52370-1::X Windows System Technical
    Reference::X11.3 XLIB colormap//EN" >
```

The XML & SGML Cookbook

Typographical Embellishments

Fine typography often includes embellishments based on intangible factors like the way the page sits and phantasms in designers' minds.

These are hard to reconcile with generalized markup: including element types to cope with them can pollute and complicate content models. PIs are the best way to handle them, but this is an area where you may have to pander to your particular SGML system's way of doing things rather than an abstract notion of the document.

For example, English-language books, especially older books, may have the first phrase set in small capitals. Some try to simplify this algorithmically, by having the first word only, or all the first line, or whatever words are in the first few centimeters, but the phrase looks best. Should we have element markup for this? Probably not. A processing instruction is more appropriate, unless the first phrase serves some other purpose—

```
<?MY {font variation=scaps}?>blah<?MY {/font variation=scaps}?>
```

In the first PI above, note that it looks like it contains a start-tag. If I want to document the pseudo-generic-identifier, I can make an element type declaration: it is a good convention to use a notation for the first thing in a PI. If I want to document the pseudo-attributes, I can make an attribute declaration which will give a human reader the conventions needed to read and write the PIs—

```
<!ATTLIST #NOTATION font
        -- Small Capitals: used in PIs only --
        variation        (scaps| noscaps) noscaps
>
```

Initial capitals are another example: how do you select a particular starting letter? Similarly with fleurons and in-line decorative elements, and the devices on lists, such as bullets—

◉ When there is a nice overlap, such as with list items, between the element structure and the desired presentation, tacking on an attribute is fine.

○ When there is a single special character, fleuron or logo, and there is no concern about disrupting indexing operations: use an entity reference.

O When there is some structure to be marked up, that is almost an element, but does not fit in, use PIs, with pseudo-start- and end-tags.

O Finally, do not let markup-mania take hold: some typographical problems are best solved by creating a custom version of a font, and not disrupting your markup. For example, you might decide that in an element <num>(1)</num> the number should be set in italics, but the parentheses should be in roman. Rather than re-mark the document up, or trying some simple programming to do it, it would give simpler markup and a simpler document-system to merely copy over the parenthesis glyphs from the corresponding roman font, using a font editor.

Summary of Chapter 23

This chapter has discussed the various ways you can represent attributes of characters (color, size, typeface, etc.) using SGML.

East
Asian Issues

Chapter 24

This chapter

…looks at how to deal with some particular issues of Chinese, Japanese and Korean document processing.

The most fundamental issue for Chinese, Korean and Japanese document processing is the representation of characters. There may be fifty to one hundred thousand Han ideographs (Japanese *kanji*): the number is vague because it is sometimes a matter of judgment or context whether a character is merely a glyph variant or a character in its own right. The number of characters is increasing: not only scholarly discoveries of old texts, but new characters coined for propitious names in Taiwan.

One major Japanese publishing company regards thirty thousand characters as the working set of characters for serious literary publishing; another company reports an accumulated library of over two hundred thousand glyphs or characters.

ISO 10646 has about twenty thousand Han ideographs. Including territorial variants (e.g., traditional Chinese, simplified Chinese, Japanese) can increase this by a few thousand more. [1]

Perhaps the second most pressing issue is the issue of how to cope with word segmentation: if your script does not have spaces, how can you search for words reliably? This topic is dealt with in chapter 21, page 3-104, *Word Segmentation in Chinese*. The treatment there emphasizes that proper nouns (names) in Chinese often cause problems for search algorithms, because they may accidentally have a character searched and cause a false detection. It is prudent therefore, to mark up Chinese with names of people, places and things tagged as elements.

Multilingual issues are dealt with in chapter 19, page 3-60.

Custom Symbols

Niche publishers in technical areas and publishers of East Asian language and facsimile editions may easily find that they need extra symbols not available in standard entity sets. For example, publishers of musical texts may need more characters for notes, rests, clefs marks and accidentals. The SPREAD-2 symbol public entity set has a few musical characters, but not many. Similarly, mathematicians routinely create new characters for their pet concepts: this may be on the wane now that more papers are being composed electronically.

The first thing to do is to check that the information available from the element context of the character is not good enough to determine the character. For ex-

---

1. However, the raw numbers are misleading: being able to use the traditional Chinese variant of the character for school may not be that useful for a Japanese, for example, where that variant is not used. Refer to the [*SPREAD-2*] entities.

ample, inside formula elements you should not have to specify the mathematical large − sign, but simply use the standard -, available from all keyboards.

SGML divides the notation of characters from their applied use. Which means that you can use any character you can make up an identifier for, and leave it to the recipient of the document to resolve the SDATA entity into some form the recipient system can use.

However, when some poor sucker at the other end has to use the entities, it is very important that the characters be clearly enough identified that they can used. This is why you should use the standard public entity sets from ISO or the SPREAD-2 entities whereever possible: they have well chosen names, and books with corresponding glyphs are readily available, both from national standards organizations and from commercial publishers. [1]

Whenever you send a document that has non-standard or private SDATA entity references, you should also bundle some note showing representative glyphs, for the use of the recipient. Without this, using an SGML document with private SDATA entity references can be a tedious exercise in detective work. If you use a character, you should also have responsibility to make sure enough information to render it accompanies the document.

It is the current typographical trend in the West, both online and in technical books, to decorate text with icons. While this is certainly useful in marginalia and for the devices on bullet lists, since it signals the reader without interrupting sentences with words, its value is unproved in running text. However, if this becomes more popular, the SDATA entity is an appropriate mechanism. Even better, if possible, is to have the icons in an external NDATA entity, for example a TrueType font. It is easy to later convert a known entity into an SDATA entity if the document must go to parts or systems unknown. In closed document-systems, SDATA entities are usually not warranted.

---

1. As the Association for Font Information Interchange (AFII) glyph registry project progresses, it will be a good source for nominating specific glyphs, which can have a public identifier "ISO/IEC 10036/RA/Glyphs::*nnnn*", where *nnnn* is the specifying decimal number. See the following footnote for more.

Extra Characters

Here are five ways to specify extra Han characters in SGML:

✓ Create a large character set of your own, and index into that. There already is a very large set, IRIZ *KanjiBase*, created by the Electronic Buddhist Text Initiative [*ZenBase*] ([*EBTI*]). It can be distinguished from ISO 10646 in that it—

- is based on scholarly research into characters actually appearing in historical material rather than by adding together existing character sets which may have quite arbitrary development processes,

- is emphatically non-unifying to allow research into the development and spread of variants, and thus

- is more a catalog of glyphs than of characters.

✓ Create your own small SDATA entity, using some widely available and large dictionary as the reference. For Japanese, this could be the [*Dai Kanwa Jiten*]. The purpose of using a standard dictionary is that it allows exact reference, even at later times and other locations; and a book is more difficult to lose than a piece of paper or a file. ①

✓ If the nature of the variant is explained by some simple generic attribute, use that. For example, "mad grass" is a style of calligraphy:

```
<!ENTITY rj:mad_cow SDATA "[Han ideograph for cow, in mad grass style]">
```

✓ Encode the shape of the character using radicals or components. Using character radicals poses several problems, but there has been plans to introduce into ISO 10646 a set of components that can be much more complicated than radicals. These components have been derived by statistical analysis so that frequently-occurring but complex characters can be

---

1. An important resource for the future will be the Association for Font Information Interchange's (AFII's) glyph register, which is intended to include around 55000 glyphs by the close of the millennium, as standardized in [*ISO/IEC 10036:1996*] "*Procedures for registration of glyph-related identifiers.*" See a following footnote for more.

encoded with few radicals. The proposals include positional operator characters: left, under, inside. This way attempts to turn the unbounded character set problem into a bounded one. It has the advantage that every character can be uniquely decomposed, so indexing and searching can work reliably.

✓ Encode the glyph itself as a thumbnail sketch. ① The SPREAD Glyph Shape Encoding Method ([*Okui, Matsuoka, Imago, Komachi*]) uses SDATA entities, which start with an embedded initial pseudo-attribute to signal the notation used. ② By default, an SGML literal can contain at least 240 characters: this is enough to encode at least a 32-by-32 pixel bitmap of the character. To ensure portability, the characters used to encode the bitmap should be restricted to the SGML 'minimum literal' characters: basically [A-Za-z01-9/.]. A thumbnail bitmap may be enough for draft and on-screen presentation, and enough to guide the font artist for paper. A 48-by-48 pixel image is probably advisable, which may require a slight fiddle to the SGML declaration.)

If you are creating many different entities for your own characters, it is worthwhile to adopt a naming convention that prevents name clashes with other entity sets. This is simply done: merely prepend some short nickname for you, your company as the owner, or the DTD project. For example, I might prepend "RJ." to entity names I create. For the rest of this chapter, I will use "rj:". ③

---

1. The realization that it may be useful to carry around a thumbnail sketch for use over the Internet has been around since John McCarthy's 1972 paper "*Arbitrary character sets*" [*RFC373*].

2. This is an interesting case of pseudo-markup appearing even in SDATA entity text: the person receiving the file can use the graphic as a thumbnail to draw or locate a high-quality glyph, for example.

3. Standards for such prefixes to prevent *namespace pollution* are unresolved in SGML and XML at the time of writing. It is worth mentioning the two leading contending schemes. The *module proposal* uses [*ISO 9070*]-style hierarchical names (i.e., using "::" as the delimiter) formed from the names of parameter entities (e.g., cals::table if there is a parameter entity named cals which declares an element type table.) The *namespace* proposal uses a processing instruction (in a very similar fashion to notation declarations) to declare a prefix using ":" as the delimiter and to tie that prefix to a URI, which identifies a schema. This schema may be syntactic (i.e., relating to grammar) or semantic (i.e., relating to meaning).

*Gaiji & User-Defined Characters

Gaiji is Japanese for extra- or outside character, and typically refers to the practice, widespread in China, Korea and Japan, of augmenting standard character sets with other characters.

This is often done on a corporate basis, with extra characters added as required for the area of business in which the company is engaged. It is somewhat similar to Apple Computer's addition of an apple glyph in the Macintosh fonts. Some modern character sets, notably ISO 10646, reserve code blocks for user-defined characters.

These result in unportable documents. The SGML solution of a higher-layer of markup on top of the text provides a flexible and manageable alternative.

The SGML short-reference allows a way to neutralize the non-portability of SGML documents that use *gaiji* or user-defined characters. If all the user-defined characters are allowed as single character short reference delimiters in the SGML declaration, you can translate each *gaiji* into an entity reference, to a character. This way you can still edit your documents using *gaiji* on your proprietary in-house systems. But you can send the files off to any conforming SGML system that supports the short reference facility, and have the receiving system treat the *gaiji* as entity references. [1]

Custom Fonts

It is much more common that rich text will be exchanged than plain text files. Rich text is a nice way of saying *proprietary word processor file*. So it is very likely that corporations will define proprietary fonts containing wonderful glyphs, rather than extend existing character sets with *Gaiji*.

Here is a set of declarations for declaring all the characters in a font as entities, giving quite a lot of information along the way.

First, we declare the existence of the font technology we will be using—

---

1. XML 1.0 does not support short-references. The usage and full declaration of short-references are dealt with well in other publications and are beyond the scope of this book.

The XML & SGML Cookbook

```
<!NOTATION typel_font PUBLIC
    "+//ISBN 0-201-57044//NOTATION
        Adobe Type 1 Font Format::version 1.1::1990//EN">

<!ATTLIST #NOTATION typel_font
    descriptor CDATA #REQUIRED
    -- mylextype ( "UNREGISTERED::", foundry, "//", FONT, "::",
        family, "::", weight, "::", slant, "::", width, "::",
        point_size, "::", x_res, "::", y_res, "::", encoding ) -->
```

For more on the font descriptor convention used here, see Typeface. This declaration says that there can be objects (i.e., entities) that can be interpreted according to the Adobe Type 1 Font Format book (i.e., the notation). Furthermore, entities of this notation can have a descriptor string (i.e,. an attribute).

·We now use that to declare the existence of an instance of a Type 1① font—

```
<-- Next, declare the font with its technology -->

<!ENTITY rj:font SYSTEM NDATA typel_font
    [ descriptor="UNREGISTERED::My
    Company//FONT::gaiji::*::r::normal::*::*::*::*" ]>
```

---

1. If you register the font with AFII (Association for Font Information Interchange) using the ISO/IEC 10036:1996 Procedures for Registration of Glyph and Glyph Collection Identifiers, you can use a descriptor in the form

```
    "ISO/IEC 10036/RA//Collections::nnnn"
```

or

```
    "ISO/IEC 10036/RA//GlyphIndexMaps::nnnn"
```

where the *nnnn* is provided by the registration authority.

There is a recent international standardization of the Adobe Type 1 format, with some small enhancements to handle East Asian character needs better: [*ISO/IEC 9541*]. ①

Next, we will declare that there can be objects (i.e., entities) that can be interpreted as glyphs – as an index into a particular font—

```
<!NOTATION glyph-in-font SYSTEM>
<!ATTLIST #NOTATION glyph-in-font
     font   ENTITY #REQUIRED
     index  NUMBER #REQUIRED>
```

We now have everything we need to declare some glyph entities, which we can use like characters in the text—

```
<ENTITY rj:logo_1 SYSTEM NDATA glyph-in-font
        [ font="rj:font" index="32" ] >
<ENTITY rj:logo_2 SYSTEM NDATA glyph-in-font
        [ font="rj:font" index="33" ] >
<ENTITY rj:logo_3 SYSTEM NDATA glyph-in-font
        [ font="rj:font" index="34" ] >
<ENTITY rj:logo_4 SYSTEM NDATA glyph-in-font
        [ font="rj:font" index="36" ] >
<ENTITY rj:big_logo SYSTEM NDATA glyph-in-font
        [ font="rj:font" index="37" ] >
```

The notation and attribute declarations would generally be put in one element type set, and the `type1_font` and glyph declarations into an entity set. That way, we do not attempt to redefine the notations for each custom font.

---

1. Japanese readers: there is a user guide to this available in Japanese, by Dr Yushi Komachi, ISBN 4-542-30521-X.

Marking Up Handwritten Text

Handwritten documents pose particular problems, especially old and decayed texts. Professor Urs App, in *"Computerized Collation of a Dunhuang Text,"* [*App*] notes the following characteristics that a DTD for these documents should accommodate, in particular for scholarly use:

- ☒ illegible characters;

- ☒ character which are legible enough to make a guess about;

- ☒ the size of text characters may carry information: e.g., an answer may be in a smaller font, like Western *fine print* in legal documents;

- ☒ corrections by interlinear additions;

- ☒ corrections by overwriting the original character;

- ☒ character reversal by an inserted interlinear symbol;

- ☒ document-unique marks and symbols;

- ☒ corrections and marks of emphasis;

- ☒ corrections by blotting;①

- ☒ holes in the paper; and

- ☒ ink characteristics (indicating revision or corrections by different hands or at different times).

It is easy enough to make simple element type sets for all these. However, the [*TEI*] DTDs are the best place to start in this regard. TEI is large, but it is designed specifically for marking up world literature in a way that can be useful for scholars. The TEI element type `unclear` may be appropriate for uncertain text. Contrast this with the element type `unknown,` which is appropriate when you know what the data is, but not how to classify it in the current DTD.②

---

1. Professor App also makes the interesting note that ink blots can indicate the care the writer took: this is a wonderful form of markup!

2. See *Unaccounted-for Elements* in chapter 17.

Ruby Annotations

A *ruby* annotation is a character in a very small font, often used for superscripted annotations in Japanese text, to give an alternative spelling using a different script. (Japanese uses four different scripts, if Latin is included.) Typically the base character is a Han ideograph (*kanji*) and the ruby characters will be phonetic *katakana*. This is actually a doubly useful system:

- many readers of ideographs will suspect but not know for sure the meaning of a character from its glyph, because there are so many characters – and therefore requires a pronunciation to pin it down; and

- readers may not be sure of the meaning of phonetic *kana* versions without the ideograph – Japanese is highly homophonic.

The simple minded approach to ruby characters is simply to mark them up using—

```
<!ELEMENT ruby ( #PCDATA ) >
<!ATTLIST ruby
   text CDATA #REQUIRED>
```

A variant on this – which is very convenient if you have to markup text in a standard text editor – uses short references[1] on the element declarations —

```
<!ELEMENT ruby          - O ( base, top ) >
<!ELEMENT (base | top ) O O ( #PCDATA) >
```

where

- "^" is mapped to the start-tag of `ruby and recognized in all content text`,

- ":" is mapped to the start-tag of `top` when inside a `base` element, and

- "^" is mapped to the end-tag of `ruby` when inside a `top` element.

---

1. XML 1.0 does not support short references. The usage and full declaration of short references are dealt with well in other publications and are beyond the scope of this book.

```
<p>AA^A:a^AA</p>
```

These methods are OK for simple use, but have a fundamental problem. They mark the data up by what it looks like, not by what its function is. We can redress this a little by labeling the element structure as a **gloss** (*furigana*) rather than a **ruby**. And we can then bring presentation back in by providing a formatting attribute to hint that it is a furigana that will be done using rubies, not, for example, using parenthetical, half-height in-line paragraphs (*warichu*), or a popup note—

```
<!ELEMENT gloss  ( #PCDATA )> <!--furigana -->
<!ATTLIST gloss
   text CDATA #REQUIRED
   render ( ruby | warichu | popup ) "ruby" >
```

However, the biggest problems remain. The ruby characters must be positioned over their corresponding character or characters. How can we model this, yet still allow suitable line breaking, keep the ruby characters with the base characters they must align with, and allow searching on the text and the ruby? And what if there are multiple annotations, as can happen with texts annotated by different hands?

This is a very similar issue, in essence, to that discussed in chapter 21, page 3-92, on word segmentation and hyphenation. The best approach is to build up a dictionary that you can include, of ideographic compounds. Each compound can then have its own glosses marked up, as well as search forms and hyphenation patterns.

The element type declarations for this are—

```
<!ELEMENT word ( text, segments ) >
<!ELEMENT text ( #PCDATA )>
<!ATTLIST text
        gloss CDATA #IMPLIED
        position ( over1 | over2 | left1 | left2 |
                under1 | under2 | right1 | right2 ) "top1" >
<!ELEMENT segments ( #PCDATA | text+ )* >
<!ENTITY U2027 SDATA "[HYPHENATION POINT]" >
```

These element types allow complex annotations. Standard annotations can be handled by placing them in an entity declaration—

```
<!ENTITY alpha-Omega
'<word><text>alpha omega</text>
<segments><text gloss="alpha">&alpha;</text>-&U207;<text
      gloss="omega">&Omega;</text></segments></word>' >
```

We can then use the compound like this:

```
<p>The distance is less than &alpha-Omega;.</p>
```

In turn, we could render this as—

The distance is less than α - Ω.

This puts in one place all sorts of useful standard information. It is a bit of extra work the first time, but soon builds into a useful dictionary that can allow beautiful typesetting with nice line-breaking and proper spanning behavior of the rubies, and still let the text be searched or indexed simply.

With this markup, and a not very smart application, we can also do tricks like swap the ruby and the base text segments; it converts the main text from an adult-literacy text to a child's text. Or your software could decide that only the first occurrence of every compound in a chapter should have a ruby, and not the following ones. Furthermore, since the word also has a simple normalized form (i.e., the first **text** element in the example), indexing of the term is easy, and the chances of making a typing error that will not be noticed are reduced. ①

---

1. To get high-quality typesetting of ruby annotations, many more parameters may need to be specified: spread, overrun and so on. Whether these will need to be specified directly in the document using further attributes or can be made part of a style sheet will depend on the particular publishing system being used.

Native-Language Markup

SGML is a thoroughly internationalized standard: the possibilities it offers are taken to a high level in XML. You can use the customary letters and characters of your national language and script for identifiers and names. This is called *Native Language Markup.* ①

Native language markup does not mean that all your identifiers will be beautiful in your language – English and Latinate languages, for example, use spaces a lot: identifiers for English and Latinate languages therefore need to co-opt a punctuation character to represent the space, or use a capitalization convention. Native language markup merely means that you do not have to swap to a different script for markup. ②

It is best to restrict your document's naming characters to the characters most commonly found and understood in your economic region. This in particular applies to element type names (GIs), attribute names, entity names and notation names.

If you need native-language markup, especially for languages not written with Latin letters (in particular, Han ideographs such as Japanese *kanji*), you probably will need to use a system which supports the SGML *Extended Naming Rules.* ③ The SGML declaration of your document will have to start with either—

```
<!SGML 'ISO 8879:1986 (ENR)'
...
```

or—

```
<!SGML 'ISO 8879:1986 (WWW)'
```

---

1. In fact, it is a user requirement of SGML that 'there should be no native-language bias'. If you find such a bias, your national standards body can raise the matter with the SGML working group at the International Organization for Standardization (ISO/IEC JTC1/WG4).

2. Unless you want to. Some people may find markup in a different script more convenient because it is visually demarcates data and markup. However, if the document then has to be used by people who cannot read that script or language, the tags are reduced to the usefulness of machine mnemonics or hieroglyphs.

3. A 1996 correction to the SGML standard, ISO 8879.

...

A document whose SGML declaration starts with either of these probably will require an SGML system which uses a wide-character (e.g., 16-bit characters) SGML parser. ISO 8879:1986 Annex J defines two parameters to the SGML Declaration:

- NAMESTRT allows the specification of the characters that can appear anywhere in an SGML name but which do not exhibit any upper-case/lower-case properties;

- NAMECHAR allows the specification of the characters that can appear after the first character in an SGML name and which also do not exhibit any upper-case/lower-case properties.

Annex J also allows you to use ranges of characters, which reduces the size of the declaration. Note: [XML] 1.0 predefines an SGML declaration, which uses " ISO 8879:1986 (WWW)".

Once you have internationalized names, you can then go on to have internationalized, localizeable DTDs. For example, you can have an attribute containing the localized terms for the element type name (GI) in pairs of the country code and the word:

```
<!ATTLIST casa
     also-known-as CDATA 'EN house DE Haus JP &jp-uchi;' >
```

The XML & SGML Cookbook

Summary of Chapter 24 & Endnote

This chapter has looked at some particular characteristics of East Asian documents.

This part has looked at how the various character and glyph issues[1] are handled in an SGML framework. The main issues are—

✓ character repertoire,

✓ word segmentation (including spaces and line breaks),

✓ glyph mapping, and

✓ collation.

SGML is very rich in public entity sets. These provide standard ways to represent characters and logos. SGML can also be used to encode rare, variant and extra characters in a straightforward way. Of course, sometimes the SGML entity method only defers the pain and effort of getting a non-standard glyph onto a page, however the separation of authoring, using and production can give advantages to justify this.

---

1. For more material explaining the character/glyph model better, I recommend the technical report from ISO, ISO/IEC TR 15285:1997, *An Operational Model for Characters and Glyphs*. Also, refer to the excellent book by [*Ken Lunde*], *Japanese Information Processing*, and his Internet information file [*CJK.INF*] for details. [*XML*] 1.0 has interesting techniques for handling character encoding issues using a processing instruction header, which I helped develop.

Appendixes

International Characters

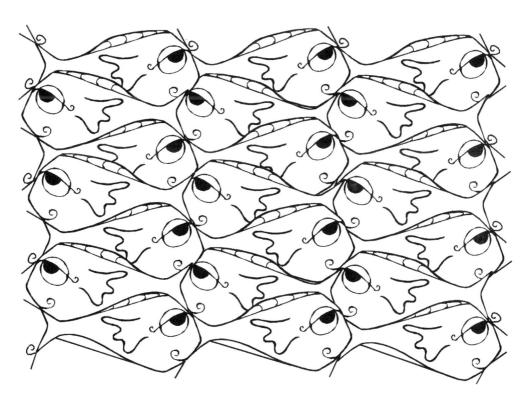

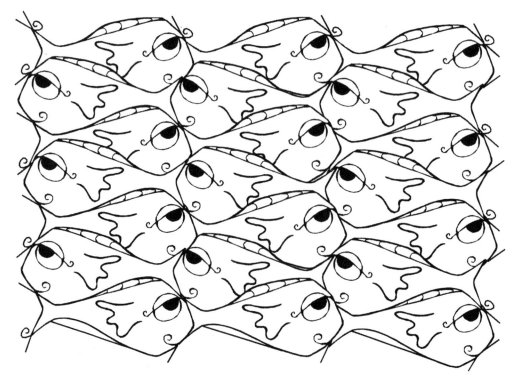

2   The XML & SGML Cookbook

ISO Special Characters

The most common public entity sets in use are the ones standardized in ISO 8879. These provide many useful characters and symbols.

The following public entity sets have been standardized by ISO, in ISO 8879 and ISO TR 9573 *Techniques for Using SGML*. (Note that the sets shown in oblique were unavailable at the time this book went to press. If they are not available, you can use the TEI prototypes given in appendix C, which were the basis for some of the sets, or the SPREAD entity set for some of them. HTML and XML users may find the XML special characters useful: see appendix D.)

Script	ISO Public Entity Set	Page
Latin	ISOlat1, ISOlat2,	ISO-4
Greek	ISOgrk1, ISOgrk2 , ISOgrk3, ISOgrk4 , *ISOgrk5*	ISO-9 *(TEI-4)*
Cyrillic	ISOcyr1, ISOcyr2,	ISO-11
Symbol	ISOnum, ISOpub, ISOdia, ISOtech, ISObox	ISO-15
Chemical	ISOchem	ISO-23
Maths	ISOamsa, ISOAMSA , ISOAMSA, ISOAMSA, ISOAMSA, ISOAMSA, *ISOmfrak, ISOmopen, ISOmscript*	ISO-25
Arabic	*ISOarab*	*(TEI-2, XML-3)*
Armenian	*ISOarme*	*(XML-7)*
Devanagari	*ISOdeva*	*(XML-18)*
Ethiopian	*ISOethi*	*N/A*
Glogothic, Croatian	*ISOglag*	*N/A*
Gothic Uncials	*ISOgunc*	*N/A*
Hebrew	*ISOhebr*	*(XML-36)*
Old Slavic	*ISOosla*	*N/A*
Thai	*ISOthai*	*(XML-78)*

The ISO sets come from a variety of sources: in particular the ISO sets from Charles Goldfarb and Francis Cave, and the others from Anders Berglund, Martin Bryan and Harry Gaylord.

Common Characters

Sometimes it is useful to restrict symbols to a *conservative subset*: the document will not require extensive entity mapping to get the appropriate SDATA entities.

In the following sets, SDATA entities for Latin letters, Greek letters and *symbols* which can probably be easily rendered in most locales using common fonts are marked "OK". This means that the character or symbol is found

- in most sets in ISO 8859-*n* (i.e., it is officially widespread), or

- Adobe's Symbol or ITC Zapf Dingbats font (i.e., it is widespread on printers),

- on PC code pages for most locales and on Macintosh character sets for most locales (i.e., it is widespread on computers), and

- in the common character sets in use in China, Korea and Japan (i.e., East Asians have needed it too).

Entities for symbols that can easily be rendered using the common character sets in China, Japan and Korea (CJK) but not the others, are marked "CJK". Symbols that are not marked "OK" (or "CJK", for readers in those countries) may require someone at the rendering end to hunt the glyphs down in non-standard or specialist fonts.

SGML document system designers in markets outside quality publishing who need easily portable documents may find it practical to restrict the use of SDATA entities to

- the characters native to their local script, and

- to the characters marked "OK" (or "CJK"), or

- to simply use the HTML public entity sets, which have a similar collection to the characters marked "OK", but with the rest removed. In particular, the HTML Added Latin 1 set (HTMLlat1) has the so-called ANSI characters that are common on PCs in the West. See appendix B for listings of these public entity sets.

Languages

ISO 8879:1986//ENTITIES Added Latin 1//EN

Note that entity names in the ISO sets are case-sensitive. So á is different from Á.

```
<!-- (C) International Organization for Standardization 1986
     Permission to copy in any form is granted for use with
     conforming SGML systems and applications as defined in
     ISO 8879, provided this notice is included in all copies.
-->
<!-- Character entity set. Typical invocation:
     <!ENTITY % ISOlat1 PUBLIC
       'ISO 8879:1986//ENTITIES Added Latin 1//EN'>
     %ISOlat1;
-->
<!ENTITY aacute SDATA '[aacute]'--=small a, acute accent-->  OK
<!ENTITY Aacute SDATA '[Aacute]'--=capital A, acute accent-->  OK
<!ENTITY acirc  SDATA '[acirc ]'--=small a, circumflex accent-->  OK
<!ENTITY Acirc  SDATA '[Acirc ]'--=capital A, circumflex accent-->  OK
<!ENTITY agrave SDATA '[agrave]'--=small a, grave accent-->
<!ENTITY Agrave SDATA '[Agrave]'--=capital A, grave accent-->
<!ENTITY aring  SDATA '[aring ]'--=small a, ring-->
<!ENTITY Aring  SDATA '[Aring ]'--=capital A, ring-->
<!ENTITY atilde SDATA '[atilde]'--=small a, tilde-->
<!ENTITY Atilde SDATA '[Atilde]'--=capital A, tilde-->
<!ENTITY auml   SDATA '[auml  ]'--=small a, dieresis or umlaut mark-->  OK
<!ENTITY Auml   SDATA '[Auml  ]'--=capital A, dieresis or umlaut mark-->  OK
<!ENTITY aelig  SDATA '[aelig ]'--=small ae diphthong (ligature)-->
<!ENTITY AElig  SDATA '[AElig ]'--=capital AE diphthong (ligature)-->
<!ENTITY ccedil SDATA '[ccedil]'--=small c, cedilla-->  OK
<!ENTITY Ccedil SDATA '[Ccedil]'--=capital C, cedilla-->  OK
<!ENTITY eth    SDATA '[eth   ]'--=small eth, Icelandic-->
<!ENTITY ETH    SDATA '[ETH   ]'--=capital Eth, Icelandic-->
<!ENTITY eacute SDATA '[eacute]'--=small e, acute accent-->  OK
<!ENTITY Eacute SDATA '[Eacute]'--=capital E, acute accent-->  OK
<!ENTITY ecirc  SDATA '[ecirc ]'--=small e, circumflex accent-->
<!ENTITY Ecirc  SDATA '[Ecirc ]'--=capital E, circumflex accent-->
<!ENTITY egrave SDATA '[egrave]'--=small e, grave accent-->
<!ENTITY Egrave SDATA '[Egrave]'--=capital E, grave accent-->
<!ENTITY euml   SDATA '[euml  ]'--=small e, dieresis or umlaut mark-->
```

```
<!ENTITY Euml   SDATA '[Euml  ]'--=capital E, dieresis or umlaut mark-->  OK
<!ENTITY iacute SDATA '[iacute]'--=small i, acute accent-->  OK
<!ENTITY Iacute SDATA '[Iacute]'--=capital I, acute accent-->  OK
<!ENTITY icirc  SDATA '[icirc ]'--=small i, circumflex accent-->  OK
<!ENTITY Icirc  SDATA '[Icirc ]'--=capital I, circumflex accent-->  OK
<!ENTITY igrave SDATA '[igrave]'--=small i, grave accent-->
<!ENTITY Igrave SDATA '[Igrave]'--=capital I, grave accent-->
<!ENTITY iuml   SDATA '[iuml  ]'--=small i, dieresis or umlaut mark-->
<!ENTITY Iuml   SDATA '[Iuml  ]'--=capital I, dieresis or umlaut mark-->
<!ENTITY ntilde SDATA '[ntilde]'--=small n, tilde-->
<!ENTITY Ntilde SDATA '[Ntilde]'--=capital N, tilde-->
<!ENTITY oacute SDATA '[oacute]'--=small o, acute accent-->
<!ENTITY Oacute SDATA '[Oacute]'--=capital O, acute accent-->
<!ENTITY ocirc  SDATA '[ocirc ]'--=small o, circumflex accent-->  OK
<!ENTITY Ocirc  SDATA '[Ocirc ]'--=capital O, circumflex accent-->  OK
<!ENTITY ograve SDATA '[ograve]'--=small o, grave accent-->
<!ENTITY Ograve SDATA '[Ograve]'--=capital O, grave accent-->
<!ENTITY oslash SDATA '[oslash]'--=small o, slash-->
<!ENTITY Oslash SDATA '[Oslash]'--=capital O, slash-->
<!ENTITY otilde SDATA '[otilde]'--=small o, tilde-->
<!ENTITY Otilde SDATA '[Otilde]'--=capital O, tilde-->
<!ENTITY ouml   SDATA '[ouml  ]'--=small o, dieresis or umlaut mark-->  OK
<!ENTITY Ouml   SDATA '[Ouml  ]'--=capital O, dieresis or umlaut mark-->  OK
<!ENTITY szlig  SDATA '[szlig ]'--=small sharp s, German (sz ligature)-->  OK
<!ENTITY thorn  SDATA '[thorn ]'--=small thorn, Icelandic-->
<!ENTITY THORN  SDATA '[THORN ]'--=capital THORN, Icelandic-->
<!ENTITY uacute SDATA '[uacute]'--=small u, acute accent-->  OK
<!ENTITY Uacute SDATA '[Uacute]'--=capital U, acute accent-->  OK
<!ENTITY ucirc  SDATA '[ucirc ]'--=small u, circumflex accent-->
<!ENTITY Ucirc  SDATA '[Ucirc ]'--=capital U, circumflex accent-->
<!ENTITY ugrave SDATA '[ugrave]'--=small u, grave accent-->
<!ENTITY Ugrave SDATA '[Ugrave]'--=capital U, grave accent-->
<!ENTITY uuml   SDATA '[uuml  ]'--=small u, dieresis or umlaut mark-->  OK
<!ENTITY Uuml   SDATA '[Uuml  ]'--=capital U, dieresis or umlaut mark-->  OK
<!ENTITY yacute SDATA '[yacute]'--=small y, acute accent-->
<!ENTITY Yacute SDATA '[Yacute]'--=capital Y, acute accent-->
<!ENTITY yuml   SDATA '[yuml  ]'--=small y, dieresis or umlaut mark-->
```

ISO 8879:1986//ENTITIES Added Latin 2//EN

Note that entity names in the ISO sets are case-sensitive. So á is different from Á.

```
<!-- (C) International Organization for Standardization 1986
     Permission to copy in any form is granted for use with
     conforming SGML systems and applications as defined in
     ISO 8879, provided this notice is included in all copies.
-->
<!-- Character entity set. Typical invocation:
     <!ENTITY % ISOlat2 PUBLIC
        'ISO 8879:1986//ENTITIES Added Latin 2//EN'>
     %ISOlat2;
-->
<!ENTITY abreve SDATA '[abreve]'--=small a, breve-->
<!ENTITY Abreve SDATA '[Abreve]'--=capital A, breve-->
<!ENTITY amacr  SDATA '[amacr ]'--=small a, macron-->
<!ENTITY Amacr  SDATA '[Amacr ]'--=capital A, macron-->
<!ENTITY aogon  SDATA '[aogon ]'--=small a, ogonek-->
<!ENTITY Aogon  SDATA '[Aogon ]'--=capital A, ogonek-->
<!ENTITY cacute SDATA '[cacute]'--=small c, acute accent-->
<!ENTITY Cacute SDATA '[Cacute]'--=capital C, acute accent-->
<!ENTITY ccaron SDATA '[ccaron]'--=small c, caron-->
<!ENTITY Ccaron SDATA '[Ccaron]'--=capital C, caron-->
<!ENTITY ccirc  SDATA '[ccirc ]'--=small c, circumflex accent-->
<!ENTITY Ccirc  SDATA '[Ccirc ]'--=capital C, circumflex accent-->
<!ENTITY cdot   SDATA '[cdot  ]'--=small c, dot above-->
<!ENTITY Cdot   SDATA '[Cdot  ]'--=capital C, dot above-->
<!ENTITY dcaron SDATA '[dcaron]'--=small d, caron-->
<!ENTITY Dcaron SDATA '[Dcaron]'--=capital D, caron-->
<!ENTITY dstrok SDATA '[dstrok]'--=small d, stroke-->
<!ENTITY Dstrok SDATA '[Dstrok]'--=capital D, stroke-->
<!ENTITY ecaron SDATA '[ecaron]'--=small e, caron-->
<!ENTITY Ecaron SDATA '[Ecaron]'--=capital E, caron-->
<!ENTITY edot   SDATA '[edot  ]'--=small e, dot above-->
<!ENTITY Edot   SDATA '[Edot  ]'--=capital E, dot above-->
<!ENTITY emacr  SDATA '[emacr ]'--=small e, macron-->
<!ENTITY Emacr  SDATA '[Emacr ]'--=capital E, macron-->
<!ENTITY eogon  SDATA '[eogon ]'--=small e, ogonek-->
<!ENTITY Eogon  SDATA '[Eogon ]'--=capital E, ogonek-->
<!ENTITY gacute SDATA '[gacute]'--=small g, acute accent-->
<!ENTITY gbreve SDATA '[gbreve]'--=small g, breve-->
<!ENTITY Gbreve SDATA '[Gbreve]'--=capital G, breve-->
<!ENTITY Gcedil SDATA '[Gcedil]'--=capital G, cedilla-->
<!ENTITY gcirc  SDATA '[gcirc ]'--=small g, circumflex accent-->
<!ENTITY Gcirc  SDATA '[Gcirc ]'--=capital G, circumflex accent-->
```

```
<!ENTITY gdot   SDATA '[gdot  ]'--=small g, dot above-->
<!ENTITY Gdot   SDATA '[Gdot  ]'--=capital G, dot above-->
<!ENTITY hcirc  SDATA '[hcirc ]'--=small h, circumflex accent-->
<!ENTITY Hcirc  SDATA '[Hcirc ]'--=capital H, circumflex accent-->
<!ENTITY hstrok SDATA '[hstrok]'--=small h, stroke-->
<!ENTITY Hstrok SDATA '[Hstrok]'--=capital H, stroke-->
<!ENTITY Idot   SDATA '[Idot  ]'--=capital I, dot above-->
<!ENTITY Imacr  SDATA '[Imacr ]'--=capital I, macron-->
<!ENTITY imacr  SDATA '[imacr ]'--=small i, macron-->
<!ENTITY ijlig  SDATA '[ijlig ]'--=small ij ligature-->
<!ENTITY IJlig  SDATA '[IJlig ]'--=capital IJ ligature-->
<!ENTITY inodot SDATA '[inodot]'--=small i without dot-->
<!ENTITY iogon  SDATA '[iogon ]'--=small i, ogonek-->
<!ENTITY Iogon  SDATA '[Iogon ]'--=capital I, ogonek-->
<!ENTITY itilde SDATA '[itilde]'--=small i, tilde-->
<!ENTITY Itilde SDATA '[Itilde]'--=capital I, tilde-->
<!ENTITY jcirc  SDATA '[jcirc ]'--=small j, circumflex accent-->
<!ENTITY Jcirc  SDATA '[Jcirc ]'--=capital J, circumflex accent-->
<!ENTITY kcedil SDATA '[kcedil]'--=small k, cedilla-->
<!ENTITY Kcedil SDATA '[Kcedil]'--=capital K, cedilla-->
<!ENTITY kgreen SDATA '[kgreen]'--=small k, Greenlandic-->
<!ENTITY lacute SDATA '[lacute]'--=small l, acute accent-->
<!ENTITY Lacute SDATA '[Lacute]'--=capital L, acute accent-->
<!ENTITY lcaron SDATA '[lcaron]'--=small l, caron-->
<!ENTITY Lcaron SDATA '[Lcaron]'--=capital L, caron-->
<!ENTITY lcedil SDATA '[lcedil]'--=small l, cedilla-->
<!ENTITY Lcedil SDATA '[Lcedil]'--=capital L, cedilla-->
<!ENTITY lmidot SDATA '[lmidot]'--=small l, middle dot-->
<!ENTITY Lmidot SDATA '[Lmidot]'--=capital L, middle dot-->
<!ENTITY lstrok SDATA '[lstrok]'--=small l, stroke-->
<!ENTITY Lstrok SDATA '[Lstrok]'--=capital L, stroke-->
<!ENTITY nacute SDATA '[nacute]'--=small n, acute accent-->
<!ENTITY Nacute SDATA '[Nacute]'--=capital N, acute accent-->
<!ENTITY eng    SDATA '[eng   ]'--=small eng, Lapp-->
<!ENTITY ENG    SDATA '[ENG   ]'--=capital ENG, Lapp-->
<!ENTITY napos  SDATA '[napos ]'--=small n, apostrophe-->
<!ENTITY ncaron SDATA '[ncaron]'--=small n, caron-->
<!ENTITY Ncaron SDATA '[Ncaron]'--=capital N, caron-->
<!ENTITY ncedil SDATA '[ncedil]'--=small n, cedilla-->
<!ENTITY Ncedil SDATA '[Ncedil]'--=capital N, cedilla-->
<!ENTITY odblac SDATA '[odblac]'--=small o, double acute accent-->
<!ENTITY Odblac SDATA '[Odblac]'--=capital O, double acute accent-->
<!ENTITY Omacr  SDATA '[Omacr ]'--=capital O, macron-->
<!ENTITY omacr  SDATA '[omacr ]'--=small o, macron-->
<!ENTITY oelig  SDATA '[oelig ]'--=small oe ligature-->
<!ENTITY OElig  SDATA '[OElig ]'--=capital OE ligature-->
<!ENTITY racute SDATA '[racute]'--=small r, acute accent-->
```

```
<!ENTITY Racute SDATA '[Racute]'--=capital R, acute accent-->
<!ENTITY rcaron SDATA '[rcaron]'--=small r, caron-->
<!ENTITY Rcaron SDATA '[Rcaron]'--=capital R, caron-->
<!ENTITY rcedil SDATA '[rcedil]'--=small r, cedilla-->
<!ENTITY Rcedil SDATA '[Rcedil]'--=capital R, cedilla-->
<!ENTITY sacute SDATA '[sacute]'--=small s, acute accent-->
<!ENTITY Sacute SDATA '[Sacute]'--=capital S, acute accent-->
<!ENTITY scaron SDATA '[scaron]'--=small s, caron-->
<!ENTITY Scaron SDATA '[Scaron]'--=capital S, caron-->
<!ENTITY scedil SDATA '[scedil]'--=small s, cedilla-->
<!ENTITY Scedil SDATA '[Scedil]'--=capital S, cedilla-->
<!ENTITY scirc  SDATA '[scirc ]'--=small s, circumflex accent-->
<!ENTITY Scirc  SDATA '[Scirc ]'--=capital S, circumflex accent-->
<!ENTITY tcaron SDATA '[tcaron]'--=small t, caron-->
<!ENTITY Tcaron SDATA '[Tcaron]'--=capital T, caron-->
<!ENTITY tcedil SDATA '[tcedil]'--=small t, cedilla-->
<!ENTITY Tcedil SDATA '[Tcedil]'--=capital T, cedilla-->
<!ENTITY tstrok SDATA '[tstrok]'--=small t, stroke-->
<!ENTITY Tstrok SDATA '[Tstrok]'--=capital T, stroke-->
<!ENTITY ubreve SDATA '[ubreve]'--=small u, breve-->
<!ENTITY Ubreve SDATA '[Ubreve]'--=capital U, breve-->
<!ENTITY udblac SDATA '[udblac]'--=small u, double acute accent-->
<!ENTITY Udblac SDATA '[Udblac]'--=capital U, double acute accent-->
<!ENTITY umacr  SDATA '[umacr ]'--=small u, macron-->
<!ENTITY Umacr  SDATA '[Umacr ]'--=capital U, macron-->
<!ENTITY uogon  SDATA '[uogon ]'--=small u, ogonek-->
<!ENTITY Uogon  SDATA '[Uogon ]'--=capital U, ogonek-->
<!ENTITY uring  SDATA '[uring ]'--=small u, ring-->
<!ENTITY Uring  SDATA '[Uring ]'--=capital U, ring-->
<!ENTITY utilde SDATA '[utilde]'--=small u, tilde-->
<!ENTITY Utilde SDATA '[Utilde]'--=capital U, tilde-->
<!ENTITY wcirc  SDATA '[wcirc ]'--=small w, circumflex accent-->
<!ENTITY Wcirc  SDATA '[Wcirc ]'--=capital W, circumflex accent-->
<!ENTITY ycirc  SDATA '[ycirc ]'--=small y, circumflex accent-->
<!ENTITY Ycirc  SDATA '[Ycirc ]'--=capital Y, circumflex accent-->
<!ENTITY Yuml   SDATA '[Yuml  ]'--=capital Y, dieresis or umlaut mark-->
<!ENTITY zacute SDATA '[zacute]'--=small z, acute accent-->
<!ENTITY Zacute SDATA '[Zacute]'--=capital Z, acute accent-->
<!ENTITY zcaron SDATA '[zcaron]'--=small z, caron-->
<!ENTITY Zcaron SDATA '[Zcaron]'--=capital Z, caron-->
<!ENTITY zdot   SDATA '[zdot  ]'--=small z, dot above-->
<!ENTITY Zdot   SDATA '[Zdot  ]'--=capital Z, dot above-->
```

ISO 8879:1986//ENTITIES Greek Letters//EN

Note that entity names in the ISO sets are case-sensitive. So á is different from Á.

```
<!-- (C) International Organization for Standardization 1986
     Permission to copy in any form is granted for use with
     conforming SGML systems and applications as defined in
     ISO 8879, provided this notice is included in all copies.
-->
<!-- Character entity set. Typical invocation:
     <!ENTITY % ISOgrk1 PUBLIC
       'ISO 8879:1986//ENTITIES Greek Letters//EN'>
     %ISOgrk1;
-->
<!ENTITY agr    SDATA '[agr   ]'--=small alpha, Greek-->   OK
<!ENTITY Agr    SDATA '[Agr   ]'--=capital Alpha, Greek-->   OK
<!ENTITY bgr    SDATA '[bgr   ]'--=small beta, Greek-->   OK
<!ENTITY Bgr    SDATA '[Bgr   ]'--=capital Beta, Greek-->   OK
<!ENTITY ggr    SDATA '[ggr   ]'--=small gamma, Greek-->   OK
<!ENTITY Ggr    SDATA '[Ggr   ]'--=capital Gamma, Greek-->   OK
<!ENTITY dgr    SDATA '[dgr   ]'--=small delta, Greek-->   OK
<!ENTITY Dgr    SDATA '[Dgr   ]'--=capital Delta, Greek-->   OK
<!ENTITY egr    SDATA '[egr   ]'--=small epsilon, Greek-->   OK
<!ENTITY Egr    SDATA '[Egr   ]'--=capital Epsilon, Greek-->   OK
<!ENTITY zgr    SDATA '[zgr   ]'--=small zeta, Greek-->   OK
<!ENTITY Zgr    SDATA '[Zgr   ]'--=capital Zeta, Greek-->   OK
<!ENTITY eegr   SDATA '[eegr  ]'--=small eta, Greek-->   OK
<!ENTITY EEgr   SDATA '[EEgr  ]'--=capital Eta, Greek-->   OK
<!ENTITY thgr   SDATA '[thgr  ]'--=small theta, Greek-->   OK
<!ENTITY THgr   SDATA '[THgr  ]'--=capital Theta, Greek-->   OK
<!ENTITY igr    SDATA '[igr   ]'--=small iota, Greek-->   OK
<!ENTITY Igr    SDATA '[Igr   ]'--=capital Iota, Greek-->   OK
<!ENTITY kgr    SDATA '[kgr   ]'--=small kappa, Greek-->   OK
<!ENTITY Kgr    SDATA '[Kgr   ]'--=capital Kappa, Greek-->   OK
<!ENTITY lgr    SDATA '[lgr   ]'--=small lambda, Greek-->   OK
<!ENTITY Lgr    SDATA '[Lgr   ]'--=capital Lambda, Greek-->   OK
<!ENTITY mgr    SDATA '[mgr   ]'--=small mu, Greek-->   OK
<!ENTITY Mgr    SDATA '[Mgr   ]'--=capital Mu, Greek-->   OK
<!ENTITY ngr    SDATA '[ngr   ]'--=small nu, Greek-->   OK
<!ENTITY Ngr    SDATA '[Ngr   ]'--=capital Nu, Greek-->   OK
<!ENTITY xgr    SDATA '[xgr   ]'--=small xi, Greek-->   OK
<!ENTITY Xgr    SDATA '[Xgr   ]'--=capital Xi, Greek-->   OK
<!ENTITY ogr    SDATA '[ogr   ]'--=small omicron, Greek-->   OK
```

```
<!ENTITY Ogr    SDATA '[Ogr   ]'--=capital Omicron, Greek-->   OK
<!ENTITY pgr    SDATA '[pgr   ]'--=small pi, Greek-->   OK
<!ENTITY Pgr    SDATA '[Pgr   ]'--=capital Pi, Greek-->   OK
<!ENTITY rgr    SDATA '[rgr   ]'--=small rho, Greek-->   OK
<!ENTITY Rgr    SDATA '[Rgr   ]'--=capital Rho, Greek-->   OK
<!ENTITY sgr    SDATA '[sgr   ]'--=small sigma, Greek-->   OK
<!ENTITY Sgr    SDATA '[Sgr   ]'--=capital Sigma, Greek-->   OK
<!ENTITY sfgr   SDATA '[sfgr  ]'--=final small sigma, Greek-->   OK
<!ENTITY tgr    SDATA '[tgr   ]'--=small tau, Greek-->   OK
<!ENTITY Tgr    SDATA '[Tgr   ]'--=capital Tau, Greek-->   OK
<!ENTITY ugr    SDATA '[ugr   ]'--=small upsilon, Greek-->   OK
<!ENTITY Ugr    SDATA '[Ugr   ]'--=capital Upsilon, Greek-->   OK
<!ENTITY phgr   SDATA '[phgr  ]'--=small phi, Greek-->   OK
<!ENTITY PHgr   SDATA '[PHgr  ]'--=capital Phi, Greek-->   OK
<!ENTITY khgr   SDATA '[khgr  ]'--=small chi, Greek-->   OK
<!ENTITY KHgr   SDATA '[KHgr  ]'--=capital Chi, Greek-->   OK
<!ENTITY psgr   SDATA '[psgr  ]'--=small psi, Greek-->   OK
<!ENTITY PSgr   SDATA '[PSgr  ]'--=capital Psi, Greek-->   OK
<!ENTITY ohgr   SDATA '[ohgr  ]'--=small omega, Greek-->   OK
<!ENTITY OHgr   SDATA '[OHgr  ]'--=capital Omega, Greek-->   OK
```

ISO 8879:1986//ENTITIES Monotoniko Greek//EN

```
<!-- (C) International Organization for Standardization 1986
     Permission to copy in any form is granted for use with
     conforming SGML systems and applications as defined in
     ISO 8879, provided this notice is included in all copies.
-->
<!-- Character entity set. Typical invocation:
     <!ENTITY % ISOgrk2 PUBLIC
       'ISO 8879:1986//ENTITIES Monotoniko Greek//EN'>
     %ISOgrk2;
-->
<!ENTITY aacgr  SDATA '[aacgr ]'--=small alpha, accent, Greek-->
<!ENTITY Aacgr  SDATA '[Aacgr ]'--=capital Alpha, accent, Greek-->
<!ENTITY eacgr  SDATA '[eacgr ]'--=small epsilon, accent, Greek-->
<!ENTITY Eacgr  SDATA '[Eacgr ]'--=capital Epsilon, accent, Greek-->
<!ENTITY eeacgr SDATA '[eeacgr]'--=small eta, accent, Greek-->
<!ENTITY EEacgr SDATA '[EEacgr]'--=capital Eta, accent, Greek-->
```

```
<!ENTITY idigr  SDATA '[idigr ]'--=small iota, dieresis, Greek-->
<!ENTITY Idigr  SDATA '[Idigr ]'--=capital Iota, dieresis, Greek-->
<!ENTITY iacgr  SDATA '[iacgr ]'--=small iota, accent, Greek-->
<!ENTITY Iacgr  SDATA '[Iacgr ]'--=capital Iota, accent, Greek-->
<!ENTITY idiagr SDATA '[idiagr]'--=small iota, dieresis, accent, Greek-->
<!ENTITY oacgr  SDATA '[oacgr ]'--=small omicron, accent, Greek-->
<!ENTITY Oacgr  SDATA '[Oacgr ]'--=capital Omicron, accent, Greek-->
<!ENTITY udigr  SDATA '[udigr ]'--=small upsilon, dieresis, Greek-->
<!ENTITY Udigr  SDATA '[Udigr ]'--=capital Upsilon, dieresis, Greek-->
<!ENTITY uacgr  SDATA '[uacgr ]'--=small upsilon, accent, Greek-->
<!ENTITY Uacgr  SDATA '[Uacgr ]'--=capital Upsilon, accent, Greek-->
<!ENTITY udiagr SDATA '[udiagr]'--=small upsilon, dieresis, accent, Greek-->
<!ENTITY ohacgr SDATA '[ohacgr]'--=small omega, accent, Greek-->
<!ENTITY OHacgr SDATA '[OHacgr]'--=capital Omega, accent, Greek-->
```

The updated version of ISOgrk4 (with ISO 9573-15:1993 as the owner in the formal public identifier) adds:

```
<!ENTITY Udiagr SDATA '[Udiagr]'--=capital upsilon, dieresis, accent, Greek-->
```

ISO 8879:1986//ENTITIES Russian Cyrillic//EN

Note that entity names in the ISO sets are case-sensitive. So á is different from Á.

```
<!-- (C) International Organization for Standardization 1986
     Permission to copy in any form is granted for use with
     conforming SGML systems and applications as defined in
     ISO 8879, provided this notice is included in all copies.
-->
<!-- Character entity set. Typical invocation:
     <!ENTITY % ISOcyr1 PUBLIC
       'ISO 8879:1986//ENTITIES Russian Cyrillic//EN'>
     %ISOcyr1;
-->
<!ENTITY acy   SDATA '[acy  ]'--=small a, Cyrillic-->  CJK
<!ENTITY Acy   SDATA '[Acy  ]'--=capital A, Cyrillic-->  CJK
<!ENTITY bcy   SDATA '[bcy  ]'--=small be, Cyrillic-->  CJK
<!ENTITY Bcy   SDATA '[Bcy  ]'--=capital BE, Cyrillic-->  CJK
<!ENTITY vcy   SDATA '[vcy  ]'--=small ve, Cyrillic-->  CJK
<!ENTITY Vcy   SDATA '[Vcy  ]'--=capital VE, Cyrillic-->  CJK
```

```
<!ENTITY gcy     SDATA '[gcy    ]'--=small ghe, Cyrillic-->   CJK
<!ENTITY Gcy     SDATA '[Gcy    ]'--=capital GHE, Cyrillic-->   CJK
<!ENTITY dcy     SDATA '[dcy    ]'--=small de, Cyrillic-->   CJK
<!ENTITY Dcy     SDATA '[Dcy    ]'--=capital DE, Cyrillic-->   CJK
<!ENTITY iecy    SDATA '[iecy   ]'--=small ie, Cyrillic-->   CJK
<!ENTITY IEcy    SDATA '[IEcy   ]'--=capital IE, Cyrillic-->   CJK
<!ENTITY iocy    SDATA '[iocy   ]'--=small io, Russian-->   CJK
<!ENTITY IOcy    SDATA '[IOcy   ]'--=capital IO, Russian-->   CJK
<!ENTITY zhcy    SDATA '[zhcy   ]'--=small zhe, Cyrillic-->   CJK
<!ENTITY ZHcy    SDATA '[ZHcy   ]'--=capital ZHE, Cyrillic-->   CJK
<!ENTITY zcy     SDATA '[zcy    ]'--=small ze, Cyrillic-->   CJK
<!ENTITY Zcy     SDATA '[Zcy    ]'--=capital ZE, Cyrillic-->   CJK
<!ENTITY icy     SDATA '[icy    ]'--=small i, Cyrillic-->   CJK
<!ENTITY Icy     SDATA '[Icy    ]'--=capital I, Cyrillic-->   CJK
<!ENTITY jcy     SDATA '[jcy    ]'--=small short i, Cyrillic-->   CJK
<!ENTITY Jcy     SDATA '[Jcy    ]'--=capital short I, Cyrillic-->   CJK
<!ENTITY kcy     SDATA '[kcy    ]'--=small ka, Cyrillic-->   CJK
<!ENTITY Kcy     SDATA '[Kcy    ]'--=capital KA, Cyrillic-->   CJK
<!ENTITY lcy     SDATA '[lcy    ]'--=small el, Cyrillic-->   CJK
<!ENTITY Lcy     SDATA '[Lcy    ]'--=capital EL, Cyrillic-->   CJK
<!ENTITY mcy     SDATA '[mcy    ]'--=small em, Cyrillic-->   CJK
<!ENTITY Mcy     SDATA '[Mcy    ]'--=capital EM, Cyrillic-->   CJK
<!ENTITY ncy     SDATA '[ncy    ]'--=small en, Cyrillic-->   CJK
<!ENTITY Ncy     SDATA '[Ncy    ]'--=capital EN, Cyrillic-->   CJK
<!ENTITY ocy     SDATA '[ocy    ]'--=small o, Cyrillic-->   CJK
<!ENTITY Ocy     SDATA '[Ocy    ]'--=capital O, Cyrillic-->   CJK
<!ENTITY pcy     SDATA '[pcy    ]'--=small pe, Cyrillic-->   CJK
<!ENTITY Pcy     SDATA '[Pcy    ]'--=capital PE, Cyrillic-->   CJK
<!ENTITY rcy     SDATA '[rcy    ]'--=small er, Cyrillic-->   CJK
<!ENTITY Rcy     SDATA '[Rcy    ]'--=capital ER, Cyrillic-->   CJK
<!ENTITY scy     SDATA '[scy    ]'--=small es, Cyrillic-->   CJK
<!ENTITY Scy     SDATA '[Scy    ]'--=capital ES, Cyrillic-->   CJK
<!ENTITY tcy     SDATA '[tcy    ]'--=small te, Cyrillic-->   CJK
<!ENTITY Tcy     SDATA '[Tcy    ]'--=capital TE, Cyrillic-->   CJK
<!ENTITY ucy     SDATA '[ucy    ]'--=small u, Cyrillic-->   CJK
<!ENTITY Ucy     SDATA '[Ucy    ]'--=capital U, Cyrillic-->   CJK
<!ENTITY fcy     SDATA '[fcy    ]'--=small ef, Cyrillic-->   CJK
<!ENTITY Fcy     SDATA '[Fcy    ]'--=capital EF, Cyrillic-->   CJK
<!ENTITY khcy    SDATA '[khcy   ]'--=small ha, Cyrillic-->   CJK
<!ENTITY KHcy    SDATA '[KHcy   ]'--=capital HA, Cyrillic-->   CJK
<!ENTITY tscy    SDATA '[tscy   ]'--=small tse, Cyrillic-->   CJK
<!ENTITY TScy    SDATA '[TScy   ]'--=capital TSE, Cyrillic-->   CJK
<!ENTITY chcy    SDATA '[chcy   ]'--=small che, Cyrillic-->   CJK
<!ENTITY CHcy    SDATA '[CHcy   ]'--=capital CHE, Cyrillic-->   CJK
<!ENTITY shcy    SDATA '[shcy   ]'--=small sha, Cyrillic-->   CJK
<!ENTITY SHcy    SDATA '[SHcy   ]'--=capital SHA, Cyrillic-->   CJK
<!ENTITY shchcy  SDATA '[shchcy]'--=small shcha, Cyrillic-->   CJK
```

```
<!ENTITY SHCHcy SDATA '[SHCHcy]'--=capital SHCHA, Cyrillic-->  CJK
<!ENTITY hardcy SDATA '[hardcy]'--=small hard sign, Cyrillic-->  CJK
<!ENTITY HARDcy SDATA '[HARDcy]'--=capital HARD sign, Cyrillic-->  CJK
<!ENTITY ycy    SDATA '[ycy   ]'--=small yeru, Cyrillic-->  CJK
<!ENTITY Ycy    SDATA '[Ycy   ]'--=capital YERU, Cyrillic-->  CJK
<!ENTITY softcy SDATA '[softcy]'--=small soft sign, Cyrillic-->  CJK
<!ENTITY SOFTcy SDATA '[SOFTcy]'--=capital SOFT sign, Cyrillic-->  CJK
<!ENTITY ecy    SDATA '[ecy   ]'--=small e, Cyrillic-->  CJK
<!ENTITY Ecy    SDATA '[Ecy   ]'--=capital E, Cyrillic-->  CJK
<!ENTITY yucy   SDATA '[yucy  ]'--=small yu, Cyrillic-->  CJK
<!ENTITY YUcy   SDATA '[YUcy  ]'--=capital YU, Cyrillic-->  CJK
<!ENTITY yacy   SDATA '[yacy  ]'--=small ya, Cyrillic-->  CJK
<!ENTITY YAcy   SDATA '[YAcy  ]'--=capital YA, Cyrillic-->  CJK
<!ENTITY numero SDATA '[numero]'--=numero sign-->  CJK
```

The updated version of ISOcyr1 (with ISO 9573-15:1993 as the owner in the formal public identifier) apparently adds:

```
<!ENTITY YATcy   SDATA '[YATcy]'--=old capital YAT'-->
<!ENTITY FITAcy  SDATA '[FITAcy]'--=old capital FITA-->
<!ENTITY IZHITcy SDATA '[IZHITcy]'--=old capital IZHITSA-->
<!ENTITY yatcy   SDATA '[yatcy]'--=old small yat'-->
<!ENTITY fitacy  SDATA '[fitacy]'--=old small fita-->
<!ENTITY izhitcy SDATA '[izhitcy]'--=old small izhitsa-->
```

ISO 8879:1986//ENTITIES Non-Russian Cyrillic//EN

Note that entity names in the ISO sets are case-sensitive. So á is different from Á.

```
<!-- (C) International Organization for Standardization 1986
     Permission to copy in any form is granted for use with
     conforming SGML systems and applications as defined in
     ISO 8879, provided this notice is included in all copies.
-->
<!-- Character entity set. Typical invocation:
     <!ENTITY % ISOcyr2 PUBLIC
       'ISO 8879:1986//ENTITIES Non-Russian Cyrillic//EN'>
     %ISOcyr2;
-->
```

```
<!ENTITY djcy   SDATA '[djcy  ]'--=small dje, Serbian-->
<!ENTITY DJcy   SDATA '[DJcy  ]'--=capital DJE, Serbian-->
<!ENTITY gjcy   SDATA '[gjcy  ]'--=small gje, Macedonian-->
<!ENTITY GJcy   SDATA '[GJcy  ]'--=capital GJE Macedonian-->
<!ENTITY jukcy  SDATA '[jukcy ]'--=small je, Ukrainian-->
<!ENTITY Jukcy  SDATA '[Jukcy ]'--=capital JE, Ukrainian-->
<!ENTITY dscy   SDATA '[dscy  ]'--=small dse, Macedonian-->
<!ENTITY DScy   SDATA '[DScy  ]'--=capital DSE, Macedonian-->
<!ENTITY iukcy  SDATA '[iukcy ]'--=small i, Ukrainian-->
<!ENTITY Iukcy  SDATA '[Iukcy ]'--=capital I, Ukrainian-->
<!ENTITY yicy   SDATA '[yicy  ]'--=small yi, Ukrainian-->
<!ENTITY YIcy   SDATA '[YIcy  ]'--=capital YI, Ukrainian-->
<!ENTITY jsercy SDATA '[jsercy]'--=small je, Serbian-->
<!ENTITY Jsercy SDATA '[Jsercy]'--=capital JE, Serbian-->
<!ENTITY ljcy   SDATA '[ljcy  ]'--=small lje, Serbian-->
<!ENTITY LJcy   SDATA '[LJcy  ]'--=capital LJE, Serbian-->
<!ENTITY njcy   SDATA '[njcy  ]'--=small nje, Serbian-->
<!ENTITY NJcy   SDATA '[NJcy  ]'--=capital NJE, Serbian-->
<!ENTITY tshcy  SDATA '[tshcy ]'--=small tshe, Serbian-->
<!ENTITY TSHcy  SDATA '[TSHcy ]'--=capital TSHE, Serbian-->
<!ENTITY kjcy   SDATA '[kjcy  ]'--=small kje Macedonian-->
<!ENTITY KJcy   SDATA '[KJcy  ]'--=capital KJE, Macedonian-->
<!ENTITY ubrcy  SDATA '[ubrcy ]'--=small u, Byelorussian-->
<!ENTITY Ubrcy  SDATA '[Ubrcy ]'--=capital U, Byelorussian-->
<!ENTITY dzcy   SDATA '[dzcy  ]'--=small dze, Serbian-->
<!ENTITY DZcy   SDATA '[DZcy  ]'--=capital dze, Serbian-->
```

The updated version of ISOcyr2 (with ISO 9573-15:1993 as the owner in the formal public identifier) adds:

```
<!ENTITY gicy   SDATA '[gicy  ]'
                --=small ghe, Serbian variant (italic only)-->
<!ENTITY deicy  SDATA '[deicy ]'
                --=small de, Serbian variant (italic only)-->
<!ENTITY peicy  SDATA '[peicy ]'
                --=small te, Serbian variant (italic only)-->
<!ENTITY teicy  SDATA '[teicy ]'
                --=small te, Serbian variant (italic only)-->
<!ENTITY einvcy SDATA '[eincy ]'
                --=small upside-down e-->
<!ENTITY deccy  SDATA '[deccy ]'--=small hard g, Ukrainian-->
<!ENTITY ghcy   SDATA '[ghcy  ]'--=small de, Khanty-->
```

Symbols

ISO 8879:1986//ENTITIES Numeric and Special Graphic//EN

```
<!-- (C) International Organization for Standardization 1986
     Permission to copy in any form is granted for use with
     conforming SGML systems and applications as defined in
     ISO 8879, provided this notice is included in all copies.
-->
<!-- Character entity set. Typical invocation:
     <!ENTITY % ISOnum PUBLIC
        'ISO 8879:1986//ENTITIES Numeric and Special Graphic//EN'>
     %ISOnum;
-->
<!ENTITY half   SDATA '[half  ]'--=fraction one-half-->
<!ENTITY frac12 SDATA '[frac12]'--=fraction one-half-->
<!ENTITY frac14 SDATA '[frac14]'--=fraction one-quarter-->
<!ENTITY frac34 SDATA '[frac34]'--=fraction three-quarters-->
<!ENTITY frac18 SDATA '[frac18]'--=fraction one-eighth-->
<!ENTITY frac38 SDATA '[frac38]'--=fraction three-eighths-->
<!ENTITY frac58 SDATA '[frac58]'--=fraction five-eighths-->
<!ENTITY frac78 SDATA '[frac78]'--=fraction seven-eighths-->
<!ENTITY sup1   SDATA '[sup1  ]'--=superscript one-->
<!ENTITY sup2   SDATA '[sup2  ]'--=superscript two-->
<!ENTITY sup3   SDATA '[sup3  ]'--=superscript three-->
<!ENTITY plus   SDATA '[plus  ]'--=plus sign B:-- >  OK
<!ENTITY plusmn SDATA '[plusmn]'--/pm B: =plus-or-minus sign-->  OK
<!ENTITY lt     SDATA '[lt    ]'--=less-than sign R:-->  OK
<!ENTITY equals SDATA '[equals]'--=equals sign R:-->  OK
<!ENTITY gt     SDATA '[gt    ]'--=greater-than sign R:-->  OK
<!ENTITY divide SDATA '[divide]'--/div B: =divide sign-->  OK
<!ENTITY times  SDATA '[times ]'--/times B: =multiply sign-->  OK
<!ENTITY curren SDATA '[curren]'--=general currency sign-->  OK
<!ENTITY pound  SDATA '[pound ]'--=pound sign-->
<!ENTITY dollar SDATA '[dollar]'--=dollar sign-->  OK
<!ENTITY cent   SDATA '[cent  ]'--=cent sign-->
<!ENTITY yen    SDATA '[yen   ]'--/yen =yen sign-->
<!ENTITY num    SDATA '[num   ]'--=number sign-->  OK
<!ENTITY percnt SDATA '[percnt]'--=percent sign-->  OK
<!ENTITY amp    SDATA '[amp   ]'--=ampersand-->  OK
<!ENTITY ast    SDATA '[ast   ]'--/ast B: =asterisk-->  OK
<!ENTITY commat SDATA '[commat]'--=commercial at-->  OK
<!ENTITY lsqb   SDATA '[lsqb  ]'--/lbrack O: =left square bracket-->  OK
```

```
<!ENTITY bsol   SDATA '[bsol  ]'--/backslash =reverse solidus-->  OK
<!ENTITY rsqb   SDATA '[rsqb  ]'--/rbrack C: =right square bracket-->  OK
<!ENTITY lcub   SDATA '[lcub  ]'--/lbrace O: =left curly bracket-->  OK
<!ENTITY horbar SDATA '[horbar]'--=horizontal bar-->  CJK
<!ENTITY verbar SDATA '[verbar]'--/vert =vertical bar-->  OK
<!ENTITY rcub   SDATA '[rcub  ]'--/rbrace C: =right curly bracket-->  OK
<!ENTITY micro  SDATA '[micro ]'--=micro sign-->  OK
<!ENTITY ohm    SDATA '[ohm   ]'--=ohm sign-->  OK
<!ENTITY deg    SDATA '[deg   ]'--=degree sign-->  OK
<!ENTITY ordm   SDATA '[ordm  ]'--=ordinal indicator, masculine-->  OK
<!ENTITY ordf   SDATA '[ordf  ]'--=ordinal indicator, feminine-->  OK
<!ENTITY sect   SDATA '[sect  ]'--=section sign-->  OK
<!ENTITY para   SDATA '[para  ]'--=pilcrow (paragraph sign)-->  OK
<!ENTITY middot SDATA '[middot]'--/centerdot B: =middle dot-->  OK
<!ENTITY larr   SDATA '[larr  ]'--/leftarrow /gets A: =leftward arrow-->  OK
<!ENTITY rarr   SDATA '[rarr  ]'--/rightarrow /to A: =rightward arrow-->  OK
<!ENTITY uarr   SDATA '[uarr  ]'--/uparrow A: =upward arrow-->  OK
<!ENTITY darr   SDATA '[darr  ]'--/downarrow A: =downward arrow-->  OK
<!ENTITY copy   SDATA '[copy  ]'--=copyright sign-->  OK
<!ENTITY reg    SDATA '[reg   ]'--/circledR =registered sign-->  OK
<!ENTITY trade  SDATA '[trade ]'--=trade mark sign-->  OK
<!ENTITY brvbar SDATA '[brvbar]'--=broken (vertical) bar-->
<!ENTITY not    SDATA '[not   ]'--/neg /lnot =not sign-->  OK
<!ENTITY sung   SDATA '[sung  ]'--=music note (sung text sign)-->  CJK
<!ENTITY excl   SDATA '[excl  ]'--=exclamation mark-->  OK
<!ENTITY iexcl  SDATA '[iexcl ]'--=inverted exclamation mark-->  OK
<!ENTITY quot   SDATA '[quot  ]'--=quotation mark-->  OK
<!ENTITY apos   SDATA '[apos  ]'--=apostrophe-->  OK
<!ENTITY lpar   SDATA '[lpar  ]'--O: =left parenthesis-->  OK
<!ENTITY rpar   SDATA '[rpar  ]'--C: =right parenthesis-->  OK
<!ENTITY comma  SDATA '[comma ]'--P: =comma-->  OK
<!ENTITY lowbar SDATA '[lowbar]'--=low line-->  OK
<!ENTITY hyphen SDATA '[hyphen]'--=hyphen-->  OK
<!ENTITY period SDATA '[period]'--=full stop, period-->  OK
<!ENTITY sol    SDATA '[sol   ]'--=solidus-->  OK
<!ENTITY colon  SDATA '[colon ]'--/colon P:-->  OK
<!ENTITY semi   SDATA '[semi  ]'--=semicolon P:-->  OK
<!ENTITY quest  SDATA '[quest ]'--=question mark-->  OK
<!ENTITY iquest SDATA '[iquest]'--=inverted question mark-->  OK
<!ENTITY laquo  SDATA '[laquo ]'--=angle quotation mark, left-->  OK
<!ENTITY raquo  SDATA '[raquo ]'--=angle quotation mark, right-->  OK
<!ENTITY lsquo  SDATA '[lsquo ]'--=single quotation mark, left-->  OK
<!ENTITY rsquo  SDATA '[rsquo ]'--=single quotation mark, right-->  OK
<!ENTITY ldquo  SDATA '[ldquo ]'--=double quotation mark, left-->  OK
<!ENTITY rdquo  SDATA '[rdquo ]'--=double quotation mark, right-->  OK
<!ENTITY nbsp   SDATA '[nbsp  ]'--=no break (required) space-->  OK
<!ENTITY shy    SDATA '[shy   ]'--=soft hyphen-->  OK
```

```
<!-- (C) International Organization for Standardization 1986
     Permission to copy in any form is granted for use with
     conforming SGML systems and applications as defined in
     ISO 8879, provided this notice is included in all copies.
-->
<!-- Character entity set. Typical invocation:
     <!ENTITY % ISOpub PUBLIC
        'ISO 8879:1986//ENTITIES Publishing//EN'>
     %ISOpub;
-->
<!ENTITY emsp   SDATA '[emsp  ]'--=em space-->
<!ENTITY ensp   SDATA '[ensp  ]'--=en space (1/2-em)-->
<!ENTITY emsp13 SDATA '[emsp3 ]'--=1/3-em space-->
<!ENTITY emsp14 SDATA '[emsp4 ]'--=1/4-em space-->
<!ENTITY numsp  SDATA '[numsp ]'--=digit space (width of a number)-->
<!ENTITY puncsp SDATA '[puncsp]'--=punctuation space (width of comma)-->
<!ENTITY thinsp SDATA '[thinsp]'--=thin space (1/6-em)-->
<!ENTITY hairsp SDATA '[hairsp]'--=hair space-->
<!ENTITY mdash  SDATA '[mdash ]'--=em dash-->   OK
<!ENTITY ndash  SDATA '[ndash ]'--=en dash-->   OK
<!ENTITY dash   SDATA '[dash  ]'--=hyphen (true graphic)-->
<!ENTITY blank  SDATA '[blank ]'--=significant blank symbol-->
<!ENTITY hellip SDATA '[hellip]'--=ellipsis (horizontal)-->   OK
<!ENTITY nldr   SDATA '[nldr  ]'--=double baseline dot (en leader)-->   CJK
<!ENTITY frac13 SDATA '[frac13]'--=fraction one-third-->
<!ENTITY frac23 SDATA '[frac23]'--=fraction two-thirds-->
<!ENTITY frac15 SDATA '[frac15]'--=fraction one-fifth-->
<!ENTITY frac25 SDATA '[frac25]'--=fraction two-fifths-->
<!ENTITY frac35 SDATA '[frac35]'--=fraction three-fifths-->
<!ENTITY frac45 SDATA '[frac45]'--=fraction four-fifths-->
<!ENTITY frac16 SDATA '[frac16]'--=fraction one-sixth-->
<!ENTITY frac56 SDATA '[frac56]'--=fraction five-sixths-->
<!ENTITY incare SDATA '[incare]'--=in-care-of symbol-->
<!ENTITY block  SDATA '[block ]'--=full block-->
<!ENTITY uhblk  SDATA '[uhblk ]'--=upper half block-->
<!ENTITY lhblk  SDATA '[lhblk ]'--=lower half block-->
<!ENTITY blk14  SDATA '[blk14 ]'--=25% shaded block-->
<!ENTITY blk12  SDATA '[blk12 ]'--=50% shaded block-->
<!ENTITY blk34  SDATA '[blk34 ]'--=75% shaded block-->
<!ENTITY marker SDATA '[marker]'--=histogram marker-->
<!ENTITY cir    SDATA '[cir   ]'--/circ B: =circle, open-->   CJK
<!ENTITY squ    SDATA '[squ   ]'--=square, open-->   CJK
<!ENTITY rect   SDATA '[rect  ]'--=rectangle, open-->
<!ENTITY utri   SDATA '[utri  ]'--/triangle =up triangle, open-->
<!ENTITY dtri   SDATA '[dtri  ]'--/triangledown =down triangle, open-->
```

```
<!ENTITY star   SDATA '[star  ]'--=star, open-->  CJK
<!ENTITY bull   SDATA '[bull  ]'--/bullet B: =round bullet, filled-->  OK
<!ENTITY squf   SDATA '[squf  ]'--/blacksquare =sq bullet, filled-->  OK
<!ENTITY utrif  SDATA '[utrif ]'--/blacktriangle =up tri, filled-->
<!ENTITY dtrif  SDATA '[dtrif ]'--/blacktriangledown =dn tri, filled-->
<!ENTITY ltrif  SDATA '[ltrif ]'--/blacktriangleleft R: =l tri, filled-->
<!ENTITY rtrif  SDATA '[rtrif ]'--/blacktriangleright R: =r tri, filled-->
<!ENTITY clubs  SDATA '[clubs ]'--/clubsuit =club suit symbol-->  OK
<!ENTITY diams  SDATA '[diams ]'--/diamondsuit =diamond suit symbol-->
<!ENTITY hearts SDATA '[hearts]'--/heartsuit =heart suit symbol-->
<!ENTITY spades SDATA '[spades]'--/spadesuit =spades suit symbol-->  OK
<!ENTITY malt   SDATA '[malt  ]'--/maltese =maltese cross-->
<!ENTITY dagger SDATA '[dagger]'--/dagger B: =dagger-->  OK
<!ENTITY Dagger SDATA '[Dagger]'--/ddagger B: =double dagger-->  OK
<!ENTITY check  SDATA '[check ]'--/checkmark =tick, check mark-->  OK
<!ENTITY cross  SDATA '[ballot]'--=ballot cross-->  OK
<!ENTITY sharp  SDATA '[sharp ]'--/sharp =musical sharp-->  CJK
<!ENTITY flat   SDATA '[flat  ]'--/flat =musical flat-->  CJK
<!ENTITY male   SDATA '[male  ]'--=male symbol-->  CJK
<!ENTITY female SDATA '[female]'--=female symbol-->  CJK
<!ENTITY phone  SDATA '[phone ]'--=telephone symbol-->  OK
<!ENTITY telrec SDATA '[telrec]'--=telephone recorder symbol-->
<!ENTITY copysr SDATA '[copysr]'--=sound recording copyright sign-->
<!ENTITY caret  SDATA '[caret ]'--=caret (insertion mark)-->
<!ENTITY lsquor SDATA '[lsquor]'--=rising single quote, left (low)-->  OK
<!ENTITY ldquor SDATA '[ldquor]'--=rising dbl quote, left (low)-->  OK

<!ENTITY fflig  SDATA '[fflig ]'--small ff ligature-->
<!ENTITY filig  SDATA '[filig ]'--small fi ligature-->
<!ENTITY fjlig  SDATA '[fjlig ]'--small fj ligature-->
<!ENTITY ffilig SDATA '[ffilig]'--small ffi ligature-->
<!ENTITY ffllig SDATA '[ffllig]'--small ffl ligature-->
<!ENTITY fllig  SDATA '[fllig ]'--small fl ligature-->

<!ENTITY mldr   SDATA '[mldr  ]'--em leader-->  OK
<!ENTITY rdquor SDATA '[rdquor]'--rising dbl quote, right (high)-->
<!ENTITY rsquor SDATA '[rsquor]'--rising single quote, right (high)-->
<!ENTITY vellip SDATA '[vellip]'--vertical ellipsis-->

<!ENTITY hybull SDATA '[hybull]'--rectangle, filled (hyphen bullet)-->
<!ENTITY loz    SDATA '[loz   ]'--/lozenge - lozenge or total mark-->  OK
<!ENTITY lozf   SDATA '[lozf  ]'--/blacklozenge - lozenge, filled-->  OK
<!ENTITY ltri   SDATA '[ltri  ]'--/triangleleft B: l triangle, open-->
<!ENTITY rtri   SDATA '[rtri  ]'--/triangleright B: r triangle, open-->
<!ENTITY starf  SDATA '[starf ]'--/bigstar - star, filled-->  OK

<!ENTITY natur  SDATA '[natur ]'--/natural - music natural-->
```

```
<!ENTITY rx      SDATA '[rx    ]'--pharmaceutical prescription (Rx)-->
<!ENTITY sext    SDATA '[sext  ]'--sextile (6-pointed star)-->  OK

<!ENTITY target SDATA '[target]'--register mark or target-->
<!ENTITY dlcrop SDATA '[dlcrop]'--downward left crop mark -->
<!ENTITY drcrop SDATA '[drcrop]'--downward right crop mark -->
<!ENTITY ulcrop SDATA '[ulcrop]'--upward left crop mark -->
<!ENTITY urcrop SDATA '[urcrop]'--upward right crop mark -->
```

ISO 8879:1986//ENTITIES Diacritical Marks//EN

```
<!-- (C) International Organization for Standardization 1986
     Permission to copy in any form is granted for use with
     conforming SGML systems and applications as defined in
     ISO 8879, provided this notice is included in all copies.
-->
<!-- Character entity set. Typical invocation:
     <!ENTITY % ISOdia PUBLIC
       'ISO 8879:1986//ENTITIES Diacritical Marks//EN'>
     %ISOdia;
-->
<!ENTITY acute  SDATA '[acute ]'--=acute accent-->
<!ENTITY breve  SDATA '[breve ]'--=breve-->
<!ENTITY caron  SDATA '[caron ]'--=caron-->
<!ENTITY cedil  SDATA '[cedil ]'--=cedilla-->
<!ENTITY circ   SDATA '[circ  ]'--=circumflex accent-->
<!ENTITY dblac  SDATA '[dblac ]'--=double acute accent-->
<!ENTITY die    SDATA '[die   ]'--=dieresis-->
<!ENTITY dot    SDATA '[dot   ]'--=dot above-->
<!ENTITY grave  SDATA '[grave ]'--=grave accent-->
<!ENTITY macr   SDATA '[macr  ]'--=macron-->
<!ENTITY ogon   SDATA '[ogon  ]'--=ogonek-->
<!ENTITY ring   SDATA '[ring  ]'--=ring-->
<!ENTITY tilde  SDATA '[tilde ]'--=tilde-->
<!ENTITY uml    SDATA '[uml   ]'--=umlaut mark-->
```

ISO 8879:1986//ENTITIES General Technical//EN

```
<!-- (C) International Organization for Standardization 1986
     Permission to copy in any form is granted for use with
     conforming SGML systems and applications as defined in
     ISO 8879, provided this notice is included in all copies.
-->
<!-- Character entity set. Typical invocation:
     <!ENTITY % ISOtech PUBLIC
       'ISO 8879:1986//ENTITIES General Technical//EN'>
     %ISOtech;
-->
<!ENTITY aleph  SDATA '[aleph ]'--/aleph =aleph, Hebrew-->  OK
<!ENTITY and    SDATA '[and   ]'--/wedge /land B: =logical and-->  OK
<!ENTITY ang90  SDATA '[ang90 ]'--=right (90 degree) angle-->
<!ENTITY angsph SDATA '[angsph]'--/sphericalangle =angle-spherical-->
<!ENTITY ap     SDATA '[ap    ]'--/approx R: =approximate-->  OK
<!ENTITY becaus SDATA '[becaus]'--/because R: =because-->  CJK
<!ENTITY bottom SDATA '[bottom]'--/bot B: =perpendicular-->  CJK
<!ENTITY cap    SDATA '[cap   ]'--/cap B: =intersection-->  OK
<!ENTITY cong   SDATA '[cong  ]'--/cong R: =congruent with-->  OK
<!ENTITY conint SDATA '[conint]'--/oint L: =contour integral operator-->  CJK
<!ENTITY cup    SDATA '[cup   ]'--/cup B: =union or logical sum-->  OK
<!ENTITY equiv  SDATA '[equiv ]'--/equiv R: =identical with-->  OK
<!ENTITY exist  SDATA '[exist ]'--/exists =at least one exists-->  OK
<!ENTITY forall SDATA '[forall]'--/forall =for all-->  OK
<!ENTITY fnof   SDATA '[fnof  ]'--=function of (italic small f)-->  OK
<!ENTITY ge     SDATA '[ge    ]'--/geq /ge R: =greater-than-or-equal-->  OK
<!ENTITY iff    SDATA '[iff   ]'--/iff =if and only if-->  OK
<!ENTITY infin  SDATA '[infin ]'--/infty =infinity-->  OK
<!ENTITY int    SDATA '[int   ]'--/int L: =integral operator-->  OK
<!ENTITY isin   SDATA '[isin  ]'--/in R: =set membership-->  OK
<!ENTITY lang   SDATA '[lang  ]'--/langle O: =left angle bracket-->  OK
<!ENTITY lArr   SDATA '[lArr  ]'--/Leftarrow A: =is implied by-->  OK
<!ENTITY le     SDATA '[le    ]'--/leq /le R: =less-than-or-equal-->  OK
<!ENTITY minus  SDATA '[minus ]'--B: =minus sign-->  OK
<!ENTITY mnplus SDATA '[mnplus]'--/mp B: =minus-or-plus sign-->
<!ENTITY nabla  SDATA '[nabla ]'--/nabla =del, Hamilton operator-->  OK
<!ENTITY ne     SDATA '[ne    ]'--/ne /neq R: =not equal-->  OK
<!ENTITY ni     SDATA '[ni    ]'--/ni /owns R: =contains-->  OK
<!ENTITY or     SDATA '[or    ]'--/vee /lor B: =logical or-->  OK
```

```
<!ENTITY par    SDATA '[par   ]'--/parallel R: =parallel-->  CJK
<!ENTITY part   SDATA '[part  ]'--/partial =partial differential-->  OK
<!ENTITY permil SDATA '[permil]'--=per thousand-->  OK
<!ENTITY perp   SDATA '[perp  ]'--/perp R: =perpendicular-->
<!ENTITY prime  SDATA '[prime ]'--/prime =prime or minute-->  OK
<!ENTITY Prime  SDATA '[Prime ]'--=double prime or second-->  OK
<!ENTITY prop   SDATA '[prop  ]'--/propto R: =is proportional to-->  OK
<!ENTITY radic  SDATA '[radic ]'--/surd =radical-->  OK
<!ENTITY rang   SDATA '[rang  ]'--/rangle C: =right angle bracket-->  OK
<!ENTITY rArr   SDATA '[rArr  ]'--/Rightarrow A: =implies-->  OK
<!ENTITY sim    SDATA '[sim   ]'--/sim R: =similar-->
<!ENTITY sime   SDATA '[sime  ]'--/simeq R: =similar, equals-->
<!ENTITY square SDATA '[square]'--/square B: =square-->  CJK
<!ENTITY sub    SDATA '[sub   ]'--/subset R: =subset or is implied by-->  OK
<!ENTITY sube   SDATA '[sube  ]'--/subseteq R: =subset, equals-->  OK
<!ENTITY sup    SDATA '[sup   ]'--/supset R: =superset or implies-->  OK
<!ENTITY supe   SDATA '[supe  ]'--/supseteq R: =superset, equals-->  OK
<!ENTITY there4 SDATA '[there4]'--/therefore R: =therefore-->  OK
<!ENTITY Verbar SDATA '[Verbar]'--/Vert =dbl vertical bar-->

<!ENTITY angst  SDATA '[angst ]'--Angstrom =capital A, ring-->  CJK
<!ENTITY bernou SDATA '[bernou]'--Bernoulli function (script capital B)-->
<!ENTITY compfn SDATA '[compfn]'--B: composite function (small circle)-->
<!ENTITY Dot    SDATA '[Dot   ]'--=dieresis or umlaut mark-->
<!ENTITY DotDot SDATA '[DotDot]'--four dots above-->
<!ENTITY hamilt SDATA '[hamilt]'--Hamiltonian (script capital H)-->
<!ENTITY lagran SDATA '[lagran]'--Lagrangian (script capital L)-->
<!ENTITY lowast SDATA '[lowast]'--low asterisk-->
<!ENTITY notin  SDATA '[notin ]'--N: negated set membership-->  OK
<!ENTITY order  SDATA '[order ]'--order of (script small o)-->
<!ENTITY phmmat SDATA '[phmmat]'--physics M-matrix (script capital M)-->
<!ENTITY tdot   SDATA '[tdot  ]'--three dots above-->
<!ENTITY tprime SDATA '[tprime]'--triple prime-->
<!ENTITY wedgeq SDATA '[wedgeq]'--R: corresponds to (wedge, equals)-->
```

ISO 8879:1986//ENTITIES Box and Line Drawing//EN

```
<!-- (C) International Organization for Standardization 1986
     Permission to copy in any form is granted for use with
     conforming SGML systems and applications as defined in
     ISO 8879, provided this notice is included in all copies.
-->
<!-- Character entity set. Typical invocation:
     <!ENTITY % ISObox PUBLIC
       'ISO 8879:1986//ENTITIES Box and Line Drawing//EN'>
     %ISObox;
-->
<!-- All names are in the form: box1234, where:
     box = constants that identify a box drawing entity.
     1&2 = v, V, u, U, d, D, Ud, or uD, as follows:
       v = vertical line for full height.
       u = upper half of vertical line.
       d = downward (lower) half of vertical line.
     3&4 = h, H, l, L, r, R, Lr, or lR, as follows:
       h = horizontal line for full-width.
       l = left half of horizontal line.
       r = right half of horizontal line.
     In all cases, an upper-case letter means a double or heavy line.
-->
<!ENTITY boxh   SDATA '[boxh  ]'--horizontal line -->
<!ENTITY boxv   SDATA '[boxv  ]'--vertical line-->
<!ENTITY boxur  SDATA '[boxur ]'--upper right quadrant-->
<!ENTITY boxul  SDATA '[boxul ]'--upper left quadrant-->
<!ENTITY boxdl  SDATA '[boxdl ]'--lower left quadrant-->
<!ENTITY boxdr  SDATA '[boxdr ]'--lower right quadrant-->
<!ENTITY boxvr  SDATA '[boxvr ]'--upper and lower right quadrants-->
<!ENTITY boxhu  SDATA '[boxhu ]'--upper left and right quadrants-->
<!ENTITY boxvl  SDATA '[boxvl ]'--upper and lower left quadrants-->
<!ENTITY boxhd  SDATA '[boxhd ]'--lower left and right quadrants-->
<!ENTITY boxvh  SDATA '[boxvh ]'--all four quadrants-->
<!ENTITY boxvR  SDATA '[boxvR ]'--upper and lower right quadrants-->
<!ENTITY boxhU  SDATA '[boxhU ]'--upper left and right quadrants-->
<!ENTITY boxvL  SDATA '[boxvL ]'--upper and lower left quadrants-->
<!ENTITY boxhD  SDATA '[boxhD ]'--lower left and right quadrants-->
<!ENTITY boxvH  SDATA '[boxvH ]'--all four quadrants-->
<!ENTITY boxH   SDATA '[boxH  ]'--horizontal line-->
```

```
<!ENTITY boxV    SDATA '[boxV  ]'--vertical line-->
<!ENTITY boxUR   SDATA '[boxUR ]'--upper right quadrant-->
<!ENTITY boxUL   SDATA '[boxUL ]'--upper left quadrant-->
<!ENTITY boxDL   SDATA '[boxDL ]'--lower left quadrant-->
<!ENTITY boxDR   SDATA '[boxDR ]'--lower right quadrant-->
<!ENTITY boxVR   SDATA '[boxVR ]'--upper and lower right quadrants-->
<!ENTITY boxHU   SDATA '[boxHU ]'--upper left and right quadrants-->
<!ENTITY boxVL   SDATA '[boxVL ]'--upper and lower left quadrants-->
<!ENTITY boxHD   SDATA '[boxHD ]'--lower left and right quadrants-->
<!ENTITY boxVH   SDATA '[boxVH ]'--all four quadrants-->
<!ENTITY boxVr   SDATA '[boxVr ]'--upper and lower right quadrants-->
<!ENTITY boxHu   SDATA '[boxHu ]'--upper left and right quadrants-->
<!ENTITY boxVl   SDATA '[boxVl ]'--upper and lower left quadrants-->
<!ENTITY boxHd   SDATA '[boxHd ]'--lower left and right quadrants-->
<!ENTITY boxVh   SDATA '[boxVh ]'--all four quadrants-->
<!ENTITY boxuR   SDATA '[boxuR ]'--upper right quadrant-->
<!ENTITY boxUl   SDATA '[boxUl ]'--upper left quadrant-->
<!ENTITY boxdL   SDATA '[boxdL ]'--lower left quadrant-->
<!ENTITY boxDr   SDATA '[boxDr ]'--lower right quadrant-->
<!ENTITY boxUr   SDATA '[boxUr ]'--upper right quadrant-->
<!ENTITY boxuL   SDATA '[boxuL ]'--upper left quadrant-->
<!ENTITY boxDl   SDATA '[boxDl ]'--lower left quadrant-->
<!ENTITY boxdR   SDATA '[boxdR ]'--lower right quadrant-->
```

ISO 9573-13:1991//ENTITIES Chemistry //EN

```
<!-- (C) International Organization for Standardization 1991.
    Permission to copy in any form is granted for use with
    conforming SGML systems and applications as defined in
    ISO 8879, provided this notice is included in all copies.
-->
<!-- Character entity set. Typical invocation:
    <!ENTITY % ISOCHEM  PUBLIC
        'ISO 9573-13:1991//ENTITIES Chemistry //EN'>
        %ISOCHEM;
-->
<!ENTITY bensen    SDATA '[bensen ]'--bensen ring-->
<!ENTITY bensena   SDATA '[bensena ]'--bensen ring, one double binding-->
<!ENTITY bensenb   SDATA '[bensenb ]'--bensen ring, one double binding-->
<!ENTITY bensenc   SDATA '[bensenc ]'--bensen ring, one double binding-->
<!ENTITY bensend   SDATA '[bensend ]'--bensen ring, one double binding-->
<!ENTITY bensene   SDATA '[bensene ]'--bensen ring, one double binding-->
<!ENTITY bensenf   SDATA '[bensenf ]'--bensen ring. one double binding-->
```

```
<!ENTITY benseng   SDATA '[benseng ]'--bensen ring, two double bindings-->
<!ENTITY bensenh   SDATA '[bensenh ]'--bensen ring, two double bindings-->
<!ENTITY benseni   SDATA '[benseni ]'--bensen ring, two double bindings-->
<!ENTITY bensenj   SDATA '[bensenj ]'--bensen ring, two double bindings-->
<!ENTITY bensenk   SDATA '[bensenk ]'--bensen ring, two double bindings-->
<!ENTITY bensenl   SDATA '[bensenl ]'--bensen ring, two double bindings-->
<!ENTITY bensenm   SDATA '[bensenm ]'--bensen ring, two double bindings-->
<!ENTITY bensenn   SDATA '[bensenn ]'--bensen ring, two double bindings-->
<!ENTITY benseno   SDATA '[benseno ]'--bensen ring, three double bindings-->
<!ENTITY bensenp   SDATA '[bensenp ]'--bensen ring, three double bindings-->
<!ENTITY bensenq   SDATA '[bensenq ]'--bensen ring, circle-->
<!ENTITY hbensen   SDATA '[hbensen ]'--horizontal bensen ring-->
<!ENTITY hbensena  SDATA '[hbensena]'
                                --horizontal bensen ring, one double binding-->
<!ENTITY hbensenb  SDATA '[hbensenb]'
                                --horizontal bensen ring, one double binding-->
<!ENTITY hbensenc  SDATA '[hbensenc]'
                                --horizontal bensen ring, one double binding-->
<!ENTITY hbensend  SDATA '[hbensend]'
                                --horizontal bensen ring, one double binding-->
<!ENTITY hbensene  SDATA '[hbensene]'
                                --horizontal bensen ring, one double binding-->
<!ENTITY hbensenf  SDATA '[hbensenf]'
                                --horizontal bensen ring, one double binding-->
<!ENTITY hbenseng  SDATA '[hbenseng]'
                                --horizontal bensen ring, two double bindings-->
<!ENTITY hbensenh  SDATA '[hbensenh]'
                                --horizontal bensen ring, two double bindings-->
<!ENTITY hbenseni  SDATA '[hbenseni]'
                                --horizontal bensen ring, two double bindings-->
<!ENTITY hbensenj  SDATA '[hbensenj]'
                                --horizontal bensen ring, two double bindings-->
<!ENTITY hbensenk  SDATA '[hbensenk]'
                                --horizontal bensen ring, two double bindings-->
<!ENTITY hbensenl  SDATA '[hbensenl]'
                                --horizontal bensen ring, two double bindings-->
<!ENTITY hbensenm  SDATA '[hbensenm]'
                                --horizontal bensen ring, two double bindings-->
<!ENTITY hbensenn  SDATA '[hbensenn]'
                                --horizontal bensen ring, two double bindings-->
<!ENTITY hbenseno  SDATA '[hbenseno]'
                                --horizontal bensen ring, three double bindings-->
<!ENTITY hbensenp  SDATA '[hbensenp]'
                                --horizontal bensen ring, three double bindings-->
<!ENTITY hbensenq  SDATA '[hbensenq]'
                                --horizontal bensen ring, circle-->
```

ISO 8879:1986//ENTITIES Added Math Symbols: Arrow Relations//EN

```
<!-- (C) International Organization for Standardization 1986
     Permission to copy in any form is granted for use with
     conforming SGML systems and applications as defined in
     ISO 8879, provided this notice is included in all copies.
-->
<!-- Character entity set. Typical invocation:
     <!ENTITY % ISOamsa PUBLIC
       'ISO 8879:1986//ENTITIES Added Math Symbols: Arrow Relations//EN'>
     %ISOamsa;
-->
<!ENTITY cularr SDATA '[cularr]'--/curvearrowleft A: left curved arrow -->
<!ENTITY curarr SDATA '[curarr]'--/curvearrowright A: rt curved arrow -->
<!ENTITY dArr   SDATA '[dArr  ]'--/Downarrow A: down dbl arrow -->
<!ENTITY darr2  SDATA '[darr2 ]'--/downdownarrows A: two down arrows -->
<!ENTITY dharl  SDATA '[dharl ]'--/downleftharpoon A: dn harpoon-left -->
<!ENTITY dharr  SDATA '[dharr ]'--/downrightharpoon A: down harpoon-rt -->
<!ENTITY lAarr  SDATA '[lAarr ]'--/Lleftarrow A: left triple arrow -->
<!ENTITY Larr   SDATA '[Larr  ]'--/twoheadleftarrow A:-->
<!ENTITY larr2  SDATA '[larr2 ]'--/leftleftarrows A: two left arrows -->
<!ENTITY larrhk SDATA '[larrhk]'--/hookleftarrow A: left arrow-hooked -->
<!ENTITY larrlp SDATA '[larrlp]'--/looparrowleft A: left arrow-looped -->
<!ENTITY larrtl SDATA '[larrtl]'--/leftarrowtail A: left arrow-tailed -->
<!ENTITY lhard  SDATA '[lhard ]'--/leftharpoondown A: l harpoon-down -->
<!ENTITY lharu  SDATA '[lharu ]'--/leftharpoonup A: left harpoon-up -->
<!ENTITY hArr   SDATA '[hArr  ]'--/Leftrightarrow A: l&r dbl arrow -->  OK
<!ENTITY harr   SDATA '[harr  ]'--/leftrightarrow A: l&r arrow -->  OK
<!ENTITY lrarr2 SDATA '[lrarr2]'--/leftrightarrows A: l arr over r arr -->
<!ENTITY rlarr2 SDATA '[rlarr2]'--/rightleftarrows A: r arr over l arr -->
<!ENTITY harrw  SDATA '[harrw ]'--/leftrightsquigarrow A: l&r arr-wavy -->
<!ENTITY rlhar2 SDATA '[rlhar2]'--/rightleftharpoons A: r harp over l -->
<!ENTITY lrhar2 SDATA '[lrhar2]'--/leftrightharpoons A: l harp over r -->
<!ENTITY lsh    SDATA '[lsh   ]'--/Lsh A:-->
<!ENTITY map    SDATA '[map   ]'--/mapsto A:-->
<!ENTITY mumap  SDATA '[mumap ]'--/multimap A:-->
<!ENTITY nearr  SDATA '[nearr ]'--/nearrow A: NE pointing arrow -->
<!ENTITY nlArr  SDATA '[nlArr ]'--/nLeftarrow A: not implied by -->
<!ENTITY nlarr  SDATA '[nlarr ]'--/nleftarrow A: not left arrow -->
<!ENTITY nhArr  SDATA '[nhArr ]'--/nLeftrightarrow A: not l&r dbl arr -->
<!ENTITY nharr  SDATA '[nharr ]'--/nleftrightarrow A: not l&r arrow -->
<!ENTITY nrarr  SDATA '[nrarr ]'--/nrightarrow A: not right arrow -->
<!ENTITY nrArr  SDATA '[nrArr ]'--/nRightarrow A: not implies -->
<!ENTITY nwarr  SDATA '[nwarr ]'--/nwarrow A: NW pointing arrow -->
```

```
<!ENTITY olarr  SDATA '[olarr ]'--/circlearrowleft A: l arr in circle -->
<!ENTITY orarr  SDATA '[orarr ]'--/circlearrowright A: r arr in circle -->
<!ENTITY rAarr  SDATA '[rAarr ]'--/Rrightarrow A: right triple arrow -->
<!ENTITY Rarr   SDATA '[Rarr  ]'--/twoheadrightarrow A:-->
<!ENTITY rarr2  SDATA '[rarr2 ]'--/rightrightarrows A: two rt arrows -->
<!ENTITY rarrhk SDATA '[rarrhk]'--/hookrightarrow A: rt arrow-hooked -->
<!ENTITY rarrlp SDATA '[rarrlp]'--/looparrowright A: rt arrow-looped -->
<!ENTITY rarrtl SDATA '[rarrtl]'--/rightarrowtail A: rt arrow-tailed -->
<!ENTITY rarrw  SDATA '[rarrw ]'--/squigarrowright A: rt arrow-wavy -->
<!ENTITY rhard  SDATA '[rhard ]'--/rightharpoondown A: rt harpoon-down -->
<!ENTITY rharu  SDATA '[rharu ]'--/rightharpoonup A: rt harpoon-up -->
<!ENTITY rsh    SDATA '[rsh   ]'--/Rsh A:-->
<!ENTITY drarr  SDATA '[drarr ]'--/searrow A: downward rt arrow -->
<!ENTITY dlarr  SDATA '[dlarr ]'--/swarrow A: downward l arrow -->
<!ENTITY uArr   SDATA '[uArr  ]'--/Uparrow A: up dbl arrow -->  OK
<!ENTITY uarr2  SDATA '[uarr2 ]'--/upuparrows A: two up arrows -->
<!ENTITY vArr   SDATA '[vArr  ]'--/Updownarrow A: up&down dbl arrow -->
<!ENTITY varr   SDATA '[varr  ]'--/updownarrow A: up&down arrow -->  OK
<!ENTITY uharl  SDATA '[uharl ]'--/upleftharpoon A: up harpoon-left -->
<!ENTITY uharr  SDATA '[uharr ]'--/uprightharpoon A: up harp-r-->
<!ENTITY xlArr  SDATA '[xlArr ]'--/Longleftarrow A: long l dbl arrow -->
<!ENTITY xhArr  SDATA '[xhArr ]'--/Longleftrightarrow A: long l&r dbl arr-->
<!ENTITY xharr  SDATA '[xharr ]'--/longleftrightarrow A: long l&r arr -->
<!ENTITY xrArr  SDATA '[xrArr ]'--/Longrightarrow A: long rt dbl arr -->
```

ISO 8879:1986//ENTITIES Added Math Symbols: Binary Operators//EN

```
<!-- (C) International Organization for Standardization 1986
     Permission to copy in any form is granted for use with
     conforming SGML systems and applications as defined in
     ISO 8879, provided this notice is included in all copies.
-->
<!-- Character entity set. Typical invocation:
     <!ENTITY % ISOamsb PUBLIC
       'ISO 8879:1986//ENTITIES Added Math Symbols: Binary Operators//EN'>
     %ISOamsb;
-->
<!ENTITY amalg  SDATA '[amalg ]'--/amalg B: amalgamation or coproduct-->
<!ENTITY Barwed SDATA '[Barwed]'--/doublebarwedge B: log and, dbl bar-->
<!ENTITY barwed SDATA '[barwed]'--/barwedge B: logical and, bar above-->
<!ENTITY Cap    SDATA '[Cap   ]'--/Cap /doublecap B: dbl intersection-->
```

```
<!ENTITY Cup    SDATA '[Cup   ]'--/Cup /doublecup B: dbl union-->
<!ENTITY cuvee  SDATA '[cuvee ]'--/curlyvee B: curly logical or-->
<!ENTITY cuwed  SDATA '[cuwed ]'--/curlywedge B: curly logical and-->
<!ENTITY diam   SDATA '[diam  ]'--/diamond B: open diamond-->
<!ENTITY divonx SDATA '[divonx]'--/divideontimes B: division on times-->
<!ENTITY intcal SDATA '[intcal]'--/intercal B: intercal-->
<!ENTITY lthree SDATA '[lthree]'--/leftthreetimes B:-->
<!ENTITY ltimes SDATA '[ltimes]'--/ltimes B: times sign, left closed-->
<!ENTITY minusb SDATA '[minusb]'--/boxminus B: minus sign in box-->
<!ENTITY oast   SDATA '[oast  ]'--/circledast B: asterisk in circle-->
<!ENTITY ocir   SDATA '[ocir  ]'--/circledcirc B: open dot in circle-->
<!ENTITY odash  SDATA '[odash ]'--/circleddash B: hyphen in circle-->
<!ENTITY odot   SDATA '[odot  ]'--/odot B: middle dot in circle-->
<!ENTITY ominus SDATA '[ominus]'--/ominus B: minus sign in circle-->
<!ENTITY oplus  SDATA '[oplus ]'--/oplus B: plus sign in circle-->  OK
<!ENTITY osol   SDATA '[osol  ]'--/oslash B: solidus in circle-->
<!ENTITY otimes SDATA '[otimes]'--/otimes B: multiply sign in circle-->  OK
<!ENTITY plusb  SDATA '[plusb ]'--/boxplus B: plus sign in box-->
<!ENTITY plusdo SDATA '[plusdo]'--/dotplus B: plus sign, dot above-->
<!ENTITY rthree SDATA '[rthree]'--/rightthreetimes B:-->
<!ENTITY rtimes SDATA '[rtimes]'--/rtimes B: times sign, right closed-->
<!ENTITY sdot   SDATA '[sdot  ]'--/cdot B: small middle dot-->  OK
<!ENTITY sdotb  SDATA '[sdotb ]'--/dotsquare /boxdot B: small dot in box-->
<!ENTITY setmn  SDATA '[setmn ]'--/setminus B: reverse solidus-->
<!ENTITY sqcap  SDATA '[sqcap ]'--/sqcap B: square intersection-->
<!ENTITY sqcup  SDATA '[sqcup ]'--/sqcup B: square union-->
<!ENTITY ssetmn SDATA '[ssetmn]'--/smallsetminus B: sm reverse solidus-->
<!ENTITY sstarf SDATA '[sstarf]'--/star B: small star, filled-->
<!ENTITY timesb SDATA '[timesb]'--/boxtimes B: multiply sign in box-->
<!ENTITY top    SDATA '[top   ]'--/top B: inverted perpendicular-->
<!ENTITY uplus  SDATA '[uplus ]'--/uplus B: plus sign in union-->
<!ENTITY wreath SDATA '[wreath]'--/wr B: wreath product-->
<!ENTITY xcirc  SDATA '[xcirc ]'--/bigcirc B: large circle-->
<!ENTITY xdtri  SDATA '[xdtri ]'--/bigtriangledown B: big dn tri, open-->  CJK
<!ENTITY xutri  SDATA '[xutri ]'--/bigtriangleup B: big up tri, open-->  CJK
<!ENTITY coprod SDATA '[coprod]'--/coprod L: coproduct operator-->
<!ENTITY prod   SDATA '[prod  ]'--/prod L: product operator-->  OK
<!ENTITY sum    SDATA '[sum   ]'--/sum L: summation operator-->  OK
```

ISO 8879:1986//ENTITIES Added Math Symbols: Delimiters//EN

```
<!-- (C) International Organization for Standardization 1986
     Permission to copy in any form is granted for use with
     conforming SGML systems and applications as defined in
     ISO 8879, provided this notice is included in all copies.
-->
<!-- Character entity set. Typical invocation:
     <!ENTITY % ISOamsc PUBLIC
        'ISO 8879:1986//ENTITIES Added Math Symbols: Delimiters//EN'>
     %ISOamsc;
-->
<!ENTITY rceil  SDATA '[rceil ]'--/rceil C: right ceiling-->
<!ENTITY rfloor SDATA '[rfloor]'--/rfloor C: right floor-->
<!ENTITY rpargt SDATA '[rpargt]'--/rightparengtr C: right paren, gt-->
<!ENTITY urcorn SDATA '[urcorn]'--/urcorner C: upper right corner-->
<!ENTITY drcorn SDATA '[drcorn]'--/lrcorner C: downward right corner-->
<!ENTITY lceil  SDATA '[lceil ]'--/lceil O: left ceiling-->
<!ENTITY lfloor SDATA '[lfloor]'--/lfloor O: left floor-->
<!ENTITY lpargt SDATA '[lpargt]'--/leftparengtr O: left parenthesis, gt-->
<!ENTITY ulcorn SDATA '[ulcorn]'--/ulcorner O: upper left corner-->
<!ENTITY dlcorn SDATA '[dlcorn]'--/llcorner O: downward left corner-->
```

ISO 8879:1986//ENTITIES Added Math Symbols: Negated Relations//EN

```
<!-- (C) International Organization for Standardization 1986
     Permission to copy in any form is granted for use with
     conforming SGML systems and applications as defined in
     ISO 8879, provided this notice is included in all copies.
-->
<!-- Character entity set. Typical invocation:
     <!ENTITY % ISOamsn PUBLIC
        'ISO 8879:1986//ENTITIES
        Added Math Symbols: Negated Relations//EN'>
     %ISOamsn;
-->
<!ENTITY gnap    SDATA '[gnap  ]'--/gnapprox N: greater, not approximate-->
```

```
<!ENTITY gne    SDATA '[gne   ]'--/gneq N: greater, not equals-->
<!ENTITY gnE    SDATA '[gnE   ]'--/gneqq N: greater, not dbl equals-->
<!ENTITY gnsim  SDATA '[gnsim ]'--/gnsim N: greater, not similar-->
<!ENTITY gvnE   SDATA '[gvnE  ]'--/gvertneqq N: gt, vert, not dbl eq-->
<!ENTITY lnap   SDATA '[lnap  ]'--/lnapprox N: less, not approximate-->
<!ENTITY lnE    SDATA '[lnE   ]'--/lneqq N: less, not double equals-->
<!ENTITY lne    SDATA '[lne   ]'--/lneq N: less, not equals-->
<!ENTITY lnsim  SDATA '[lnsim ]'--/lnsim N: less, not similar-->
<!ENTITY lvnE   SDATA '[lvnE  ]'--/lvertneqq N: less, vert, not dbl eq-->
<!ENTITY nap    SDATA '[nap   ]'--/napprox N: not approximate-->
<!ENTITY ncong  SDATA '[ncong ]'--/ncong N: not congruent with-->
<!ENTITY nequiv SDATA '[nequiv]'--/nequiv N: not identical with-->
<!ENTITY ngE    SDATA '[ngE   ]'--/ngeqq N: not greater, dbl equals-->
<!ENTITY nge    SDATA '[nge   ]'--/ngeq N: not greater-than-or-equal-->
<!ENTITY nges   SDATA '[nges  ]'--/ngeqslant N: not gt-or-eq, slanted-->
<!ENTITY ngt    SDATA '[ngt   ]'--/ngtr N: not greater-than-->
<!ENTITY nle    SDATA '[nle   ]'--/nleq N: not less-than-or-equal-->
<!ENTITY nlE    SDATA '[nlE   ]'--/nleqq N: not less, dbl equals-->
<!ENTITY nles   SDATA '[nles  ]'--/nleqslant N: not less-or-eq, slant-->
<!ENTITY nlt    SDATA '[nlt   ]'--/nless N: not less-than-->
<!ENTITY nltri  SDATA '[nltri ]'--/ntriangleleft N: not left triangle-->
<!ENTITY nltrie SDATA '[nltrie]'--/ntrianglelefteq N: not l tri, eq-->
<!ENTITY nmid   SDATA '[nmid  ]'--/nmid-->
<!ENTITY npar   SDATA '[npar  ]'--/nparallel N: not parallel-->
<!ENTITY npr    SDATA '[npr   ]'--/nprec N: not precedes-->
<!ENTITY npre   SDATA '[npre  ]'--/npreceq N: not precedes, equals-->
<!ENTITY nrtri  SDATA '[nrtri ]'--/ntriangleright N: not rt triangle-->
<!ENTITY nrtrie SDATA '[nrtrie]'--/ntrianglerighteq N: not r tri, eq-->
<!ENTITY nsc    SDATA '[nsc   ]'--/nsucc N: not succeeds-->
<!ENTITY nsce   SDATA '[nsce  ]'--/nsucceq N: not succeeds, equals-->
<!ENTITY nsim   SDATA '[nsim  ]'--/nsim N: not similar-->
<!ENTITY nsime  SDATA '[nsime ]'--/nsimeq N: not similar, equals-->
<!ENTITY nsmid  SDATA '[nsmid ]'--/nshortmid-->
<!ENTITY nspar  SDATA '[nspar ]'--/nshortparallel N: not short par-->
<!ENTITY nsub   SDATA '[nsub  ]'--/nsubset N: not subset-->
<!ENTITY nsube  SDATA '[nsube ]'--/nsubseteq N: not subset, equals-->
<!ENTITY nsubE  SDATA '[nsubE ]'--/nsubseteqq N: not subset, dbl eq-->
<!ENTITY nsup   SDATA '[nsup  ]'--/nsupset N: not superset-->
<!ENTITY nsupE  SDATA '[nsupE ]'--/nsupseteqq N: not superset, dbl eq-->
<!ENTITY nsupe  SDATA '[nsupe ]'--/nsupseteq N: not superset, equals-->
<!ENTITY nvdash SDATA '[nvdash]'--/nvdash N: not vertical, dash-->
<!ENTITY nvDash SDATA '[nvDash]'--/nvDash N: not vertical, dbl dash-->
<!ENTITY nVDash SDATA '[nVDash]'--/nVDash N: not dbl vert, dbl dash-->
<!ENTITY nVdash SDATA '[nVdash]'--/nVdash N: not dbl vertical, dash-->
<!ENTITY prnap  SDATA '[prnap ]'--/precnapprox N: precedes, not approx-->
<!ENTITY prnE   SDATA '[prnE  ]'--/precneqq N: precedes, not dbl eq-->
<!ENTITY prnsim SDATA '[prnsim]'--/precnsim N: precedes, not similar-->
```

```
<!ENTITY scnap  SDATA '[scnap ]'--/succnapprox N: succeeds, not approx-->
<!ENTITY scnE   SDATA '[scnE  ]'--/succneqq N: succeeds, not dbl eq-->
<!ENTITY scnsim SDATA '[scnsim]'--/succnsim N: succeeds, not similar-->
<!ENTITY subne  SDATA '[subne ]'--/subsetneq N: subset, not equals-->
<!ENTITY subnE  SDATA '[subnE ]'--/subsetneqq N: subset, not dbl eq-->
<!ENTITY supne  SDATA '[supne ]'--/supsetneq N: superset, not equals-->
<!ENTITY supnE  SDATA '[supnE ]'--/supsetneqq N: superset, not dbl eq-->
<!ENTITY vsubnE SDATA '[vsubnE]'--/subsetneqq N: subset not dbl eq, var-->
<!ENTITY vsubne SDATA '[vsubne]'--/subsetneq N: subset, not eq, var-->
<!ENTITY vsupne SDATA '[vsupne]'--/supsetneq N: superset, not eq, var-->
<!ENTITY vsupnE SDATA '[vsupnE]'--/supsetneqq N: super not dbl eq, var-->
```

ISO 8879:1986//ENTITIES Added Math Symbols: Ordinary//EN

```
<!-- (C) International Organization for Standardization 1986
     Permission to copy in any form is granted for use with
     conforming SGML systems and applications as defined in
     ISO 8879, provided this notice is included in all copies.
-->
<!-- Character entity set. Typical invocation:
     <!ENTITY % ISOamso PUBLIC
        'ISO 8879:1986//ENTITIES Added Math Symbols: Ordinary//EN'>
     %ISOamso;
-->
<!ENTITY ang    SDATA '[ang   ]'--/angle - angle-->  OK
<!ENTITY angmsd SDATA '[angmsd]'--/measuredangle - angle-measured-->
<!ENTITY beth   SDATA '[beth  ]'--/beth - beth, Hebrew-->
<!ENTITY bprime SDATA '[bprime]'--/backprime - reverse prime-->
<!ENTITY comp   SDATA '[comp  ]'--/complement - complement sign-->
<!ENTITY daleth SDATA '[daleth]'--/daleth - daleth, Hebrew-->
<!ENTITY ell    SDATA '[ell   ]'--/ell - cursive small l-->
<!ENTITY empty  SDATA '[empty ]'--/emptyset /varnothing =small o, slash-->
<!ENTITY gimel  SDATA '[gimel ]'--/gimel - gimel, Hebrew-->
<!ENTITY image  SDATA '[image ]'--/Im - imaginary-->  OK
<!ENTITY inodot SDATA '[inodot]'--/imath =small i, no dot-->
<!ENTITY jnodot SDATA '[jnodot]'--/jmath - small j, no dot-->
<!ENTITY nexist SDATA '[nexist]'--/nexists - negated exists-->
<!ENTITY oS     SDATA '[oS    ]'--/circledS - capital S in circle-->
<!ENTITY planck SDATA '[planck]'--/hbar /hslash - Planck's over 2pi-->
```

```
<!ENTITY real    SDATA '[real  ]'--/Re - real-->  OK
<!ENTITY sbsol   SDATA '[sbsol ]'--/sbs - short reverse solidus-->
<!ENTITY vprime  SDATA '[vprime]'--/varprime - prime, variant-->
<!ENTITY weierp  SDATA '[weierp]'--/wp - Weierstrass p-->  OK
```

ISO 8879:1986//ENTITIES Added Math Symbols: Relations//EN

```
<!-- (C) International Organization for Standardization 1986
     Permission to copy in any form is granted for use with
     conforming SGML systems and applications as defined in
     ISO 8879, provided this notice is included in all copies.
-->
<!-- Character entity set. Typical invocation:
     <!ENTITY % ISOamsr PUBLIC
       'ISO 8879:1986//ENTITIES Added Math Symbols: Relations//EN'>
     %ISOamsr;
-->
<!ENTITY ape    SDATA '[ape   ]'--/approxeq R: approximate, equals-->
<!ENTITY asymp  SDATA '[asymp ]'--/asymp R: asymptotically equal to-->
<!ENTITY bcong  SDATA '[bcong ]'--/backcong R: reverse congruent-->
<!ENTITY bepsi  SDATA '[bepsi ]'--/backepsilon R: such that-->
<!ENTITY bowtie SDATA '[bowtie]'--/bowtie R:-->
<!ENTITY bsim   SDATA '[bsim  ]'--/backsim R: reverse similar-->
<!ENTITY bsime  SDATA '[bsime ]'--/backsimeq R: reverse similar, eq-->
<!ENTITY bump   SDATA '[bump  ]'--/Bumpeq R: bumpy equals-->
<!ENTITY bumpe  SDATA '[bumpe ]'--/bumpeq R: bumpy equals, equals-->
<!ENTITY cire   SDATA '[cire  ]'--/circeq R: circle, equals-->
<!ENTITY colone SDATA '[colone]'--/coloneq R: colon, equals-->
<!ENTITY cuepr  SDATA '[cuepr ]'--/curlyeqprec R: curly eq, precedes-->
<!ENTITY cuesc  SDATA '[cuesc ]'--/curlyeqsucc R: curly eq, succeeds-->
<!ENTITY cupre  SDATA '[cupre ]'--/curlypreceq R: curly precedes, eq-->
<!ENTITY dashv  SDATA '[dashv ]'--/dashv R: dash, vertical-->
<!ENTITY ecir   SDATA '[ecir  ]'--/eqcirc R: circle on equals sign-->
<!ENTITY ecolon SDATA '[ecolon]'--/eqcolon R: equals, colon-->
<!ENTITY eDot   SDATA '[eDot  ]'--/doteqdot /Doteq R: eq, even dots-->
<!ENTITY esdot  SDATA '[esdot ]'--/doteq R: equals, single dot above-->
<!ENTITY efDot  SDATA '[efDot ]'--/fallingdotseq R: eq, falling dots-->  CJK
<!ENTITY egs    SDATA '[egs   ]'--/eqslantgtr R: equal-or-gtr, slanted-->
<!ENTITY els    SDATA '[els   ]'--/eqslantless R: eq-or-less, slanted-->
<!ENTITY erDot  SDATA '[erDot ]'--/risingdotseq R: eq, rising dots-->
<!ENTITY fork   SDATA '[fork  ]'--/pitchfork R: pitchfork-->
```

```
<!ENTITY frown   SDATA '[frown ]'--/frown R: down curve-->
<!ENTITY gap     SDATA '[gap   ]'--/gtrapprox R: greater, approximate-->
<!ENTITY gsdot   SDATA '[gsdot ]'--/gtrdot R: greater than, single dot-->
<!ENTITY gE      SDATA '[gE    ]'--/geqq R: greater, double equals-->  CJK
<!ENTITY gel     SDATA '[gel   ]'--/gtreqless R: greater, equals, less-->
<!ENTITY gEl     SDATA '[gEl   ]'--/gtreqqless R: gt, dbl equals, less-->
<!ENTITY ges     SDATA '[ges   ]'--/geqslant R: gt-or-equal, slanted-->
<!ENTITY Gg      SDATA '[Gg    ]'--/ggg /Gg /gggtr R: triple gtr-than-->
<!ENTITY gl      SDATA '[gl    ]'--/gtrless R: greater, less-->
<!ENTITY gsim    SDATA '[gsim  ]'--/gtrsim R: greater, similar-->
<!ENTITY Gt      SDATA '[Gt    ]'--/gg R: dbl greater-than sign-->  CJK
<!ENTITY lap     SDATA '[lap   ]'--/lessapprox R: less, approximate-->
<!ENTITY ldot    SDATA '[ldot  ]'--/lessdot R: less than, with dot-->
<!ENTITY lE      SDATA '[lE    ]'--/leqq R: less, double equals-->  CJK
<!ENTITY lEg     SDATA '[lEg   ]'--/lesseqqgtr R: less, dbl eq, greater-->
<!ENTITY leg     SDATA '[leg   ]'--/lesseqgtr R: less, eq, greater-->
<!ENTITY les     SDATA '[les   ]'--/leqslant R: less-than-or-eq, slant-->  OK
<!ENTITY lg      SDATA '[lg    ]'--/lessgtr R: less, greater-->
<!ENTITY Ll      SDATA '[Ll    ]'--/Ll /lll /lllless R: triple less-than-->
<!ENTITY lsim    SDATA '[lsim  ]'--/lesssim R: less, similar-->
<!ENTITY Lt      SDATA '[Lt    ]'--/ll R: double less-than sign-->  CJK
<!ENTITY ltrie   SDATA '[ltrie ]'--/trianglelefteq R: left triangle, eq-->
<!ENTITY mid     SDATA '[mid   ]'--/mid R:-->
<!ENTITY models  SDATA '[models]'--/models R:-->
<!ENTITY pr      SDATA '[pr    ]'--/prec R: precedes-->
<!ENTITY prap    SDATA '[prap  ]'--/precapprox R: precedes, approximate-->
<!ENTITY pre     SDATA '[pre   ]'--/preceq R: precedes, equals-->
<!ENTITY prsim   SDATA '[prsim ]'--/precsim R: precedes, similar-->
<!ENTITY rtrie   SDATA '[rtrie ]'--/trianglerighteq R: right tri, eq-->
<!ENTITY samalg  SDATA '[samalg]'--/smallamalg R: small amalg-->
<!ENTITY sc      SDATA '[sc    ]'--/succ R: succeeds-->
<!ENTITY scap    SDATA '[scap  ]'--/succapprox R: succeeds, approximate-->
<!ENTITY sccue   SDATA '[sccue ]'--/succcurlyeq R: succeeds, curly eq-->
<!ENTITY sce     SDATA '[sce   ]'--/succeq R: succeeds, equals-->
<!ENTITY scsim   SDATA '[scsim ]'--/succsim R: succeeds, similar-->
<!ENTITY sfrown  SDATA '[sfrown]'--/smallfrown R: small down curve-->
<!ENTITY smid    SDATA '[smid  ]'--/shortmid R:-->
<!ENTITY smile   SDATA '[smile ]'--/smile R: up curve-->
<!ENTITY spar    SDATA '[spar  ]'--/shortparallel R: short parallel-->
<!ENTITY sqsub   SDATA '[sqsub ]'--/sqsubset R: square subset-->
<!ENTITY sqsube  SDATA '[sqsube]'--/sqsubseteq R: square subset, equals-->
<!ENTITY sqsup   SDATA '[sqsup ]'--/sqsupset R: square superset-->
<!ENTITY sqsupe  SDATA '[sqsupe]'--/sqsupseteq R: square superset, eq-->
<!ENTITY ssmile  SDATA '[ssmile]'--/smallsmile R: small up curve-->
<!ENTITY Sub     SDATA '[Sub   ]'--/Subset R: double subset-->
<!ENTITY subE    SDATA '[subE  ]'--/subseteqq R: subset, dbl equals-->
<!ENTITY Sup     SDATA '[Sup   ]'--/Supset R: dbl superset-->
```

```
<!ENTITY supE   SDATA '[supE ]'--/supseteqq R: superset, dbl equals-->
<!ENTITY thkap  SDATA '[thkap ]'--/thickapprox R: thick approximate-->
<!ENTITY thksim SDATA '[thksim]'--/thicksim R: thick similar-->
<!ENTITY trie   SDATA '[trie ]'--/triangleq R: triangle, equals-->
<!ENTITY twixt  SDATA '[twixt ]'--/between R: between-->
<!ENTITY vdash  SDATA '[vdash ]'--/vdash R: vertical, dash-->
<!ENTITY Vdash  SDATA '[Vdash ]'--/Vdash R: dbl vertical, dash-->
<!ENTITY vDash  SDATA '[vDash ]'--/vDash R: vertical, dbl dash-->
<!ENTITY veebar SDATA '[veebar]'--/veebar R: logical or, bar below-->
<!ENTITY vltri  SDATA '[vltri ]'--/vartriangleleft R: l tri, open, var-->
<!ENTITY vprop  SDATA '[vprop ]'--/varpropto R: proportional, variant-->
<!ENTITY vrtri  SDATA '[vrtri ]'--/vartriangleright R: r tri, open, var-->
<!ENTITY Vvdash SDATA '[Vvdash]'--/Vvdash R: triple vertical, dash-->
```

ISO 8879:1986//ENTITIES Greek Symbols//EN

Note that entity names in the ISO sets are case-sensitive. So á is
different from Á.

```
<!-- (C) International Organization for Standardization 1986
    Permission to copy in any form is granted for use with
    conforming SGML systems and applications as defined in
    ISO 8879, provided this notice is included in all copies.
-->
<!-- Character entity set. Typical invocation:
    <!ENTITY % ISOgrk3 PUBLIC
      'ISO 8879:1986//ENTITIES Greek Symbols//EN'>
    %ISOgrk3;
-->
<!ENTITY alpha   SDATA '[alpha ]'--=small alpha, Greek-->
<!ENTITY beta    SDATA '[beta ]'--=small beta, Greek-->
<!ENTITY gamma   SDATA '[gamma ]'--=small gamma, Greek-->
<!ENTITY Gamma   SDATA '[Gamma ]'--=capital Gamma, Greek-->
<!ENTITY gammad  SDATA '[gammad]'--/digamma-->
<!ENTITY delta   SDATA '[delta ]'--=small delta, Greek-->
<!ENTITY Delta   SDATA '[Delta ]'--=capital Delta, Greek-->
<!ENTITY epsi    SDATA '[epsi ]'--=small epsilon, Greek-->
<!ENTITY epsiv   SDATA '[epsiv ]'--/varepsilon-->
<!ENTITY epsis   SDATA '[epsis ]'--/straightepsilon-->
```

```
<!ENTITY zeta     SDATA '[zeta  ]'--=small zeta, Greek-->
<!ENTITY eta      SDATA '[eta   ]'--=small eta, Greek-->
<!ENTITY thetas   SDATA '[thetas]'--straight theta-->
<!ENTITY Theta    SDATA '[Theta ]'--=capital Theta, Greek-->
<!ENTITY thetav   SDATA '[thetav]'--/vartheta - curly or open theta-->
<!ENTITY iota     SDATA '[iota  ]'--=small iota, Greek-->
<!ENTITY kappa    SDATA '[kappa ]'--=small kappa, Greek-->
<!ENTITY kappav   SDATA '[kappav]'--/varkappa-->
<!ENTITY lambda   SDATA '[lambda]'--=small lambda, Greek-->
<!ENTITY Lambda   SDATA '[Lambda]'--=capital Lambda, Greek-->
<!ENTITY mu       SDATA '[mu    ]'--=small mu, Greek-->
<!ENTITY nu       SDATA '[nu    ]'--=small nu, Greek-->
<!ENTITY xi       SDATA '[xi    ]'--=small xi, Greek-->
<!ENTITY Xi       SDATA '[Xi    ]'--=capital Xi, Greek-->
<!ENTITY pi       SDATA '[pi    ]'--=small pi, Greek-->
<!ENTITY piv      SDATA '[piv   ]'--/varpi-->
<!ENTITY Pi       SDATA '[Pi    ]'--=capital Pi, Greek-->
<!ENTITY rho      SDATA '[rho   ]'--=small rho, Greek-->
<!ENTITY rhov     SDATA '[rhov  ]'--/varrho-->
<!ENTITY sigma    SDATA '[sigma ]'--=small sigma, Greek-->
<!ENTITY Sigma    SDATA '[Sigma ]'--=capital Sigma, Greek-->
<!ENTITY sigmav   SDATA '[sigmav]'--/varsigma-->
<!ENTITY tau      SDATA '[tau   ]'--=small tau, Greek-->
<!ENTITY upsi     SDATA '[upsi  ]'--=small upsilon, Greek-->
<!ENTITY Upsi     SDATA '[Upsi  ]'--=capital Upsilon, Greek-->
<!ENTITY phis     SDATA '[phis  ]'--/straightphi - straight phi-->
<!ENTITY Phi      SDATA '[Phi   ]'--=capital Phi, Greek-->
<!ENTITY phiv     SDATA '[phiv  ]'--/varphi - curly or open phi-->
<!ENTITY chi      SDATA '[chi   ]'--=small chi, Greek-->
<!ENTITY psi      SDATA '[psi   ]'--=small psi, Greek-->
<!ENTITY Psi      SDATA '[Psi   ]'--=capital Psi, Greek-->
<!ENTITY omega    SDATA '[omega ]'--=small omega, Greek-->
<!ENTITY Omega    SDATA '[Omega ]'--=capital Omega, Greek-->
```

The XML & SGML Cookbook

ISO 8879:1986//ENTITIES *Alternative Greek*

Symbols//EN

These characters are alternatives from the other ISO Greek entity set characters. They are intended to represent typographically distinct versions of the Greek alphabet, probably bold versions of the symbols, for mathematical and scientific use.

Note that entity names in the ISO sets are case-sensitive. So á is different from Á.

```
<!-- (C) International Organization for Standardization 1986
     Permission to copy in any form is granted for use with
     conforming SGML systems and applications as defined in
     ISO 8879, provided this notice is included in all copies.
-->
<!-- Character entity set. Typical invocation:
     <!ENTITY % ISOgrk4 PUBLIC
       'ISO 8879:1986//ENTITIES Alternative Greek Symbols//EN'>
     %ISOgrk4;
-->
<!ENTITY b.alpha  SDATA '[b.alpha ]'--=small alpha, Greek-->
<!ENTITY b.beta   SDATA '[b.beta  ]'--=small beta, Greek-->
<!ENTITY b.gamma  SDATA '[b.gamma ]'--=small gamma, Greek-->
<!ENTITY b.Gamma  SDATA '[b.Gamma ]'--=capital Gamma, Greek-->
<!ENTITY b.gammad SDATA '[b.gammad]'--/digamma-->
<!ENTITY b.delta  SDATA '[b.delta ]'--=small delta, Greek-->
<!ENTITY b.Delta  SDATA '[b.Delta ]'--=capital Delta, Greek-->
<!ENTITY b.epsi   SDATA '[b.epsi  ]'--=small epsilon, Greek-->
<!ENTITY b.epsiv  SDATA '[b.epsiv ]'--/varepsilon-->
<!ENTITY b.epsis  SDATA '[b.epsis ]'--/straightepsilon-->
<!ENTITY b.zeta   SDATA '[b.zeta  ]'--=small zeta, Greek-->
<!ENTITY b.eta    SDATA '[b.eta   ]'--=small eta, Greek-->
<!ENTITY b.thetas SDATA '[b.thetas]'--straight theta-->
<!ENTITY b.Theta  SDATA '[b.Theta ]'--=capital Theta, Greek-->
<!ENTITY b.thetav SDATA '[b.thetav]'--/vartheta - curly or open theta-->
<!ENTITY b.iota   SDATA '[b.iota  ]'--=small iota, Greek-->
<!ENTITY b.kappa  SDATA '[b.kappa ]'--=small kappa, Greek-->
<!ENTITY b.kappav SDATA '[b.kappav]'--/varkappa-->
<!ENTITY b.lambda SDATA '[b.lambda]'--=small lambda, Greek-->
<!ENTITY b.Lambda SDATA '[b.Lambda]'--=capital Lambda, Greek-->
<!ENTITY b.mu     SDATA '[b.mu    ]'--=small mu, Greek-->
<!ENTITY b.nu     SDATA '[b.nu    ]'--=small nu, Greek-->
<!ENTITY b.xi     SDATA '[b.xi    ]'--=small xi, Greek-->
<!ENTITY b.Xi     SDATA '[b.Xi    ]'--=capital Xi, Greek-->
```

```
<!ENTITY b.pi     SDATA '[b.pi    ]'--=small pi, Greek-->
<!ENTITY b.Pi     SDATA '[b.Pi    ]'--=capital Pi, Greek-->
<!ENTITY b.piv    SDATA '[b.piv   ]'--/varpi-->
<!ENTITY b.rho    SDATA '[b.rho   ]'--=small rho, Greek-->
<!ENTITY b.rhov   SDATA '[b.rhov  ]'--/varrho-->
<!ENTITY b.sigma  SDATA '[b.sigma ]'--=small sigma, Greek-->
<!ENTITY b.Sigma  SDATA '[b.Sigma ]'--=capital Sigma, Greek-->
<!ENTITY b.sigmav SDATA '[b.sigmav]'--/varsigma-->
<!ENTITY b.tau    SDATA '[b.tau   ]'--=small tau, Greek-->
<!ENTITY b.upsi   SDATA '[b.upsi  ]'--=small upsilon, Greek-->
<!ENTITY b.Upsi   SDATA '[b.Upsi  ]'--=capital Upsilon, Greek-->
<!ENTITY b.phis   SDATA '[b.phis  ]'--/straightphi - straight phi-->
<!ENTITY b.Phi    SDATA '[b.Phi   ]'--=capital Phi, Greek-->
<!ENTITY b.phiv   SDATA '[b.phiv  ]'--/varphi - curly or open phi-->
<!ENTITY b.chi    SDATA '[b.chi   ]'--=small chi, Greek-->
<!ENTITY b.psi    SDATA '[b.psi   ]'--=small psi, Greek-->
<!ENTITY b.Psi    SDATA '[b.Psi   ]'--=capital Psi, Greek-->
<!ENTITY b.omega  SDATA '[b.omega ]'--=small omega, Greek-->
<!ENTITY b.Omega  SDATA '[b.Omega ]'--=capital Omega, Greek-->
```

HTML
Special
Characters

The characters in **HTMLspecial,** **HTMLlat1** and **HTMLsymbol** are found on almost every modern computer system: they can be used with minimal setup problems in SGML documents. (Note that at the time of writing these were draft proposed entity sets only.)

Notice the final 'HTML' in the public identifier: this means that value of the entities is that specifically applicable to HTML documents, which use ISO 10646 as their document char-acter set, rather than being SDATA. (Note: XML 1.0 also uses ISO 10646 as the document character set; you can use HTMLspecial, HTMLlat1 and HTMLsymbol with XML without alteration.)

The characters in **HTMLicon** are not common, and are taken from draft proposals. At the time of writing, these characters have not been made part of HTML, and are defined as SDATA. They are included here mainly as a source of names.

HTML Special

```
<!-- Character entity set. Typical invocation:
    <!ENTITY % HTMLspecial PUBLIC
      "-//W3C//ENTITIES Special//EN//HTML">
    %HTMLspecial; -->
<!-- Portions  International Organization for Standardization 1986:
    Permission to copy in any form is granted for use with
    conforming SGML systems and applications as defined in
    ISO 8879, provided this notice is included in all copies.
-->
<!-- Relevant ISO entity set is given unless names are newly introduced.
    New names (i.e., not in ISO 8879 list) do not clash with any
    existing ISO 8879 entity names. Unicode character numbers
    are given for each character, in hex, and are identical for
    Unicode 1.1 and Unicode 2.0. CDATA values are decimal conversions
    of the Unicode values. Names are Unicode 2.0 names.
-->
<!-- C0 Controls and Basic Latin -->
<!ENTITY quot    CDATA "&#34;"
                        -- quotation mark, =apl quote, U0022 ISOnum -->
<!ENTITY amp     CDATA "&#38;"
                        -- ampersand, U0026 ISOnum -->
<!ENTITY lt      CDATA "&#60;"
                        -- less-than sign, U003C ISOnum -->
<!ENTITY gt      CDATA "&#62;"
                        -- greater-than sign, U003E ISOnum -->
<!-- Latin Extended-A -->
<!ENTITY OElig   CDATA "&#338;"
                        -- latin capital ligature oe, U0152 ISOlat2 -->
<!ENTITY oelig   CDATA "&#339;"
                        -- latin small ligature oe, U0153 ISOlat2
                        N.b. ligature is a misnomer, this is a separate
                        character in some languages -->
<!ENTITY Scaron  CDATA "&#352;"
                        -- latin capital letter s with caron, U0160 ISOlat2 -->
<!ENTITY scaron  CDATA "&#353;"
                        -- latin small letter s with caron, U0161 ISOlat2 -->
<!ENTITY Yuml    CDATA "&#376;"
                        -- latin capital letter y with diaeresis, U0178 ISOlat2 -->
```

```
<!-- Spacing Modifier Letters -->
<!ENTITY circ    CDATA "&#710;"
                      -- modifier letter circumflex accent, U02C6 ISOpub -->

<!ENTITY tilde   CDATA "&#732;"
                      -- small tilde, U02DC ISOdia -->
<!-- General Punctuation -->
<!ENTITY ensp    CDATA " " -- en space, U2002 ISOpub -->
<!ENTITY emsp    CDATA " " -- em space, U2003 ISOpub -->
<!ENTITY thinsp  CDATA " " -- thin space, U2009 ISOpub -->
<!ENTITY zwnj    CDATA "&#8204;" -- zero width non-joiner, U200C NEW RFC 2070 -->
<!ENTITY zwj     CDATA "&#8205;" -- zero width joiner, U200D NEW RFC 2070 -->
<!ENTITY lrm     CDATA "&#8206;" -- left-to-right mark, U200E NEW RFC 2070 -->
<!ENTITY rlm     CDATA "&#8207;" -- right-to-left mark, U200F NEW RFC 2070 -->
<!ENTITY ndash   CDATA "&#8211;" -- en dash, U2013 ISOpub -->
<!ENTITY mdash   CDATA "&#8212;" -- em dash, U2014 ISOpub -->
<!ENTITY lsquo   CDATA "&#8216;" -- left single quotation mark, U2018 ISOnum -->
<!ENTITY rsquo   CDATA "&#8217;" -- right single quotation mark, U2019 ISOnum -->
<!ENTITY sbquo   CDATA "&#8218;" -- single low-9 quotation mark, U201A NEW -->
<!ENTITY ldquo   CDATA "&#8220;" -- left double quotation mark, U201C ISOnum -->
<!ENTITY rdquo   CDATA "&#8221;" -- right double quotation mark, U201D ISOnum -->
<!ENTITY bdquo   CDATA "&#8222;" -- double low-9 quotation mark, U201E NEW -->
<!ENTITY dagger  CDATA "&#8224;" -- dagger, U2020 ISOpub -->
<!ENTITY Dagger  CDATA "&#8225;" -- double dagger, U2021 ISOpub -->
<!ENTITY permil  CDATA "&#8240;" -- per mille sign, U2030 ISOtech -->
<!ENTITY lsaquo  CDATA "&#8249;"
                      -- single left-pointing angle quotation mark, U2039
                      N.b. lsaquo is proposed but not yet ISO standardised -->
<!ENTITY rsaquo  CDATA "&#8250;"
                      -- single right-pointing angle quotation mark,
                      rsaquo is proposed but not yet ISO standardised -->
```

HTML Full Latin 1

```
<!-- (C) International Organization for Standardization 1986
     Permission to copy in any form is granted for use with
     conforming SGML systems and applications as defined in
     ISO 8879, provided this notice is included in all copies.
     This has been extended for use with HTML to cover the full
     set of codes in the range 160-255 decimal.
-->
<!-- Character entity set. Typical invocation:
     <!ENTITY % HTMLlat1 PUBLIC
       'ISO 8879-1986//ENTITIES Full Latin 1//EN//HTML'>
     %HTMLlat1;
-->
    <!ENTITY nbsp   CDATA ' ' -- no-break space -->
    <!ENTITY iexcl  CDATA '&#161;' -- inverted exclamation mark -->
    <!ENTITY cent   CDATA '&#162;' -- cent sign -->
    <!ENTITY pound  CDATA '&#163;' -- pound sterling sign -->
    <!ENTITY curren CDATA '&#164;' -- general currency sign -->
    <!ENTITY yen    CDATA '&#165;' -- yen sign -->
    <!ENTITY brvbar CDATA '&#166;' -- broken (vertical) bar -->
    <!ENTITY sect   CDATA '&#167;' -- section sign -->
    <!ENTITY uml    CDATA '&#168;' -- umlaut (dieresis) -->
    <!ENTITY copy   CDATA '&#169;' -- copyright sign -->
    <!ENTITY ordf   CDATA '&#170;' -- ordinal indicator, feminine -->
    <!ENTITY laquo  CDATA '&#171;' -- angle quotation mark, left -->
    <!ENTITY not    CDATA '&#172;' -- not sign -->
    <!ENTITY shy    CDATA '&#173;' -- soft hyphen -->
    <!ENTITY reg    CDATA '&#174;' -- registered sign -->
    <!ENTITY macr   CDATA '&#175;' -- macron -->
    <!ENTITY deg    CDATA '&#176;' -- degree sign -->
    <!ENTITY plusmn CDATA '&#177;' -- plus-or-minus sign -->
    <!ENTITY sup2   CDATA '&#178;' -- superscript two -->
    <!ENTITY sup3   CDATA '&#179;' -- superscript three -->
    <!ENTITY acute  CDATA '&#180;' -- acute accent -->
    <!ENTITY micro  CDATA '&#181;' -- micro sign -->
    <!ENTITY para   CDATA '&#182;' -- pilcrow (paragraph sign) -->
    <!ENTITY middot CDATA '&#183;' -- middle dot -->
    <!ENTITY cedil  CDATA '&#184;' -- cedilla -->
    <!ENTITY sup1   CDATA '&#185;' -- superscript one -->
    <!ENTITY ordm   CDATA '&#186;' -- ordinal indicator, masculine -->
    <!ENTITY raquo  CDATA '&#187;' -- angle quotation mark, right -->
    <!ENTITY frac14 CDATA '&#188;' -- fraction one-quarter -->
    <!ENTITY frac12 CDATA '&#189;' -- fraction one-half -->
    <!ENTITY frac34 CDATA '&#190;' -- fraction three-quarters -->
```

```
<!ENTITY iquest CDATA '&#191;' -- inverted question mark -->
<!ENTITY Agrave CDATA '&#192;' -- capital A, grave accent -->
<!ENTITY Aacute CDATA '&#193;' -- capital A, acute accent -->
<!ENTITY Acirc  CDATA '&#194;' -- capital A, circumflex accent -->
<!ENTITY Atilde CDATA '&#195;' -- capital A, tilde -->
<!ENTITY Auml   CDATA '&#196;' -- capital A, dieresis or umlaut mark -->
<!ENTITY Aring  CDATA '&#197;' -- capital A, ring -->
<!ENTITY AElig  CDATA '&#198;' -- capital AE diphthong (ligature) -->
<!ENTITY Ccedil CDATA '&#199;' -- capital C, cedilla -->
<!ENTITY Egrave CDATA '&#200;' -- capital E, grave accent -->
<!ENTITY Eacute CDATA '&#201;' -- capital E, acute accent -->
<!ENTITY Ecirc  CDATA '&#202;' -- capital E, circumflex accent -->
<!ENTITY Euml   CDATA '&#203;' -- capital E, dieresis or umlaut mark -->
<!ENTITY Igrave CDATA '&#204;' -- capital I, grave accent -->
<!ENTITY Iacute CDATA '&#205;' -- capital I, acute accent -->
<!ENTITY Icirc  CDATA '&#206;' -- capital I, circumflex accent -->
<!ENTITY Iuml   CDATA '&#207;' -- capital I, dieresis or umlaut mark -->
<!ENTITY ETH    CDATA '&#208;' -- capital Eth, Icelandic -->
<!ENTITY Ntilde CDATA '&#209;' -- capital N, tilde -->
<!ENTITY Ograve CDATA '&#210;' -- capital O, grave accent -->
<!ENTITY Oacute CDATA '&#211;' -- capital O, acute accent -->
<!ENTITY Ocirc  CDATA '&#212;' -- capital O, circumflex accent -->
<!ENTITY Otilde CDATA '&#213;' -- capital O, tilde -->
<!ENTITY Ouml   CDATA '&#214;' -- capital O, dieresis or umlaut mark -->
<!ENTITY times  CDATA '&#215;' -- multiply sign -->
<!ENTITY Oslash CDATA '&#216;' -- capital O, slash -->
<!ENTITY Ugrave CDATA '&#217;' -- capital U, grave accent -->
<!ENTITY Uacute CDATA '&#218;' -- capital U, acute accent -->
<!ENTITY Ucirc  CDATA '&#219;' -- capital U, circumflex accent -->
<!ENTITY Uuml   CDATA '&#220;' -- capital U, dieresis or umlaut mark -->
<!ENTITY Yacute CDATA '&#221;' -- capital Y, acute accent -->
<!ENTITY THORN  CDATA '&#222;' -- capital THORN, Icelandic -->
<!ENTITY szlig  CDATA '&#223;' -- small sharp s, German (sz ligature) -->
<!ENTITY agrave CDATA '&#224;' -- small a, grave accent -->
<!ENTITY aacute CDATA '&#225;' -- small a, acute accent -->
<!ENTITY acirc  CDATA '&#226;' -- small a, circumflex accent -->
<!ENTITY atilde CDATA '&#227;' -- small a, tilde -->
<!ENTITY auml   CDATA '&#228;' -- small a, dieresis or umlaut mark -->
<!ENTITY aring  CDATA '&#229;' -- small a, ring -->
<!ENTITY aelig  CDATA '&#230;' -- small ae diphthong (ligature) -->
<!ENTITY ccedil CDATA '&#231;' -- small c, cedilla -->
<!ENTITY egrave CDATA '&#232;' -- small e, grave accent -->
<!ENTITY eacute CDATA '&#233;' -- small e, acute accent -->
<!ENTITY ecirc  CDATA '&#234;' -- small e, circumflex accent -->
<!ENTITY euml   CDATA '&#235;' -- small e, dieresis or umlaut mark -->
<!ENTITY igrave CDATA '&#236;' -- small i, grave accent -->
<!ENTITY iacute CDATA '&#237;' -- small i, acute accent -->
<!ENTITY icirc  CDATA '&#238;' -- small i, circumflex accent -->
```

```
        <!ENTITY iuml   CDATA '&#239;' -- small i, dieresis or umlaut mark -->
        <!ENTITY eth    CDATA '&#240;' -- small eth, Icelandic -->
        <!ENTITY ntilde CDATA '&#241;' -- small n, tilde -->
        <!ENTITY ograve CDATA '&#242;' -- small o, grave accent -->
        <!ENTITY oacute CDATA '&#243;' -- small o, acute accent -->
        <!ENTITY ocirc  CDATA '&#244;' -- small o, circumflex accent -->
        <!ENTITY otilde CDATA '&#245;' -- small o, tilde -->
        <!ENTITY ouml   CDATA '&#246;' -- small o, dieresis or umlaut mark -->
        <!ENTITY divide CDATA '&#247;' -- divide sign -->
        <!ENTITY oslash CDATA '&#248;' -- small o, slash -->
        <!ENTITY ugrave CDATA '&#249;' -- small u, grave accent -->
        <!ENTITY uacute CDATA '&#250;' -- small u, acute accent -->
        <!ENTITY ucirc  CDATA '&#251;' -- small u, circumflex accent -->
        <!ENTITY uuml   CDATA '&#252;' -- small u, dieresis or umlaut mark -->
        <!ENTITY yacute CDATA '&#253;' -- small y, acute accent -->
        <!ENTITY thorn  CDATA '&#254;' -- small thorn, Icelandic -->
        <!ENTITY yuml   CDATA '&#255;' -- small y, dieresis or umlaut mark -->
```

HTML Symbols

```
<!-- Mathematical, Greek and Symbolic characters for HTML -->
<!-- Character entity set. Typical invocation:
     <!ENTITY % HTMLsymbol PUBLIC
       "-//W3C//ENTITIES Symbolic//EN//HTML">
     %HTMLsymbol;
-->
<!-- Portions  International Organization for Standardization 1986:
     Permission to copy in any form is granted for use with
     conforming SGML systems and applications as defined in
     ISO 8879, provided this notice is included in all copies.
-->
<!-- Relevant ISO entity set is given unless names are newly introduced.
     New names (ie, not in ISO 8879 list) do not clash with any
     existing ISO 8879 entity names. Unicode character numbers
     are given for each character, in hex, and are identical for
     Unicode 1.1 and Unicode 2.0. CDATA values are decimal conversions
     of the Unicode values. Names are Unicode 2.0 names.
-->
<!-- Latin Extended-B -->
<!ENTITY fnof    CDATA "&#192;"
                 -- latin small f with hook, =function, =florin, U0192 ISOtech -->
```

```
<!-- Greek -->
<!ENTITY Alpha    CDATA "&#913;"
                         -- greek capital letter alpha,    U0391 -->
<!ENTITY Beta     CDATA "&#914;"
                         -- greek capital letter beta,     U0392 -->
<!ENTITY Gamma    CDATA "&#915;"
                         -- greek capital letter gamma,    U0393 ISOgrk3 -->
<!ENTITY Delta    CDATA "&#916;"
                         -- greek capital letter delta,    U0394 ISOgrk3 -->
<!ENTITY Epsilon  CDATA "&#917;"
                         -- greek capital letter epsilon,  U0395 -->
<!ENTITY Zeta     CDATA "&#918;"
                         -- greek capital letter zeta,     U0396 -->
<!ENTITY Eta      CDATA "&#919;"
                         -- greek capital letter eta,      U0397 -->
<!ENTITY Theta    CDATA "&#920;"
                         -- greek capital letter theta,    U0398 ISOgrk3 -->
<!ENTITY Iota     CDATA "&#921;"
                         -- greek capital letter iota,     U0399 -->
<!ENTITY Kappa    CDATA "&#922;"
                         -- greek capital letter kappa,    U039A -->

<!ENTITY Lambda   CDATA "&#923;"
                         -- greek capital letter lambda,   U039B ISOgrk3 -->
<!ENTITY Mu       CDATA "&#924;"
                         -- greek capital letter mu,       U039C -->
<!ENTITY Nu       CDATA "&#925;"
                         -- greek capital letter nu,       U039D -->
<!ENTITY Xi       CDATA "&#926;"
                         -- greek capital letter xi,       U039E ISOgrk3 -->
<!ENTITY Omicron  CDATA "&#927;"
                         -- greek capital letter omicron,  U039F -->
<!ENTITY Pi       CDATA "&#928;"
                         -- greek capital letter pi,       U03A0 ISOgrk3 -->
<!ENTITY Rho      CDATA "&#929;"
                         -- greek capital letter rho,      U03A1 -->
<!ENTITY Sigma    CDATA "&#931;"
                         -- greek capital letter sigma,    U03A3 ISOgrk3 -->
<!ENTITY Tau      CDATA "&#932;"
                         -- greek capital letter tau,      U03A4 -->
<!ENTITY Upsi     CDATA "&#933;"
                         -- greek capital letter upsilon,  U03A5 ISOgrk3 -->
<!ENTITY Phi      CDATA "&#934;"
                         -- greek capital letter phi,      U03A6 ISOgrk3 -->
<!ENTITY Chi      CDATA "&#935;"
                         -- greek capital letter chi,      U03A7 -->
<!ENTITY Psi      CDATA "&#936;"
                         -- greek capital letter psi,      U03A8 ISOgrk3 -->
```

```
<!ENTITY Omega    CDATA "&#937;"
                        -- greek capital letter omega,  U03A9 ISOgrk3 -->
<!ENTITY alpha    CDATA "&#945;"
                        -- greek small letter alpha,  U03B1 ISOgrk3 -->
<!ENTITY beta     CDATA "&#946;"
                        -- greek small letter beta,  U03B2 ISOgrk3 -->
<!ENTITY gamma    CDATA "&#947;"
                        -- greek small letter gamma,  U03B3 ISOgrk3 -->
<!ENTITY delta    CDATA "&#948;"
                        -- greek small letter delta,  U03B4 ISOgrk3 -->
<!ENTITY epsi     CDATA "&#949;"
                        -- greek small letter epsilon,  U03B5 ISOgrk3 -->
<!ENTITY zeta     CDATA "&#950;"
                        -- greek small letter zeta,  U03B6 ISOgrk3 -->
<!ENTITY eta      CDATA "&#951;"
                        -- greek small letter eta,  U03B7 ISOgrk3 -->
<!ENTITY theta    CDATA "&#952;"
                        -- greek small letter theta,  U03B8 ISOgrk3 -->
<!ENTITY iota     CDATA "&#953;"
                        -- greek small letter iota,  U03B9 ISOgrk3 -->
<!ENTITY kappa    CDATA "&#954;"
                        -- greek small letter kappa,  U03BA ISOgrk3 -->
<!ENTITY lambda   CDATA "&#955;"
                        -- greek small letter lambda,  U03BB ISOgrk3 -->
<!ENTITY mu       CDATA "&#956;"
                        -- greek small letter mu,  U03BC ISOgrk3 -->
<!ENTITY nu       CDATA "&#957;"
                        -- greek small letter nu,  U03BD ISOgrk3 -->
<!ENTITY xi       CDATA "&#958;"
                        -- greek small letter xi,  U03BE ISOgrk3 -->
<!ENTITY omicron  CDATA "&#959;"
                        -- greek small letter omicron,  U03BF NEW -->
<!ENTITY pi       CDATA "&#960;"
                        -- greek small letter pi,  U03C0 ISOgrk3 -->
<!ENTITY rho      CDATA "&#961;"
                        -- greek small letter rho,  U03C1 ISOgrk3 -->
<!ENTITY sigmaf   CDATA "&#962;"
                        -- greek small letter final sigma,  U03C2 ISOgrk3 -->
<!ENTITY sigma    CDATA "&#963;"
                        -- greek small letter sigma,  U03C3 ISOgrk3 -->
<!ENTITY tau      CDATA "&#964;"
                        -- greek small letter tau,  U03C4 ISOgrk3 -->
<!ENTITY upsi     CDATA "&#965;"
                        -- greek small letter upsilon,  U03C5 ISOgrk3 -->
<!ENTITY phi      CDATA "&#966;"
                        -- greek small letter phi,  U03C6 ISOgrk3 -->
<!ENTITY chi      CDATA "&#967;"
                        -- greek small letter chi,  U03C7 ISOgrk3 -->
```

```
<!ENTITY psi      CDATA "&#968;"
                           -- greek small letter psi,  U03C8 ISOgrk3 -->
<!ENTITY omega    CDATA "&#969;"
                           -- greek small letter omega,  U03C9 ISOgrk3 -->
<!ENTITY theta    CDATA "&#977;"
                           -- greek small letter theta symbol,  U03D1 NEW -->
<!ENTITY upsih    CDATA "&#978;"
                           -- greek upsilon with hook symbol,  U03D2 NEW -->
<!ENTITY piv      CDATA "&#982;"
                           -- greek pi symbol,  U03D6 ISOgrk3 -->
<!-- General Punctuation -->
<!ENTITY bull     CDATA "&#8226;"
                           -- bullet, =black small circle, U2022 ISOpub
                           N.b. bull is NOT the same as bullet operator, U2219 -->
<!ENTITY hellip   CDATA "&#8230;"
                       -- horizontal ellipsis, =three dot leader, U2026 ISOpub  -->
<!ENTITY prime    CDATA "&#8242;"
                           -- prime, =minutes, =feet, U2032 ISOtech -->
<!ENTITY Prime    CDATA "&#8243;"
                           -- double prime, =seconds, =inches, U2033 ISOtech -->
<!ENTITY oline    CDATA "&#8254;"
                           -- overline, =spacing overscore, U203E NEW -->
<!ENTITY frasl    CDATA "&#8260;"
                           -- fraction slash, U2044 NEW -->
<!-- Letterlike Symbols -->
<!ENTITY weierp   CDATA "&#8472;"
                       -- script capital P, =power set, =Weierstrass p, U2118 ISOamso -->
<!ENTITY image    CDATA "&#8465;"
                       -- blackletter capital I, =imaginary part, U2111 ISOamso -->
<!ENTITY real     CDATA "&#8476;"
                       -- blackletter capital R, =real part symbol, U211C ISOamso -->
<!ENTITY trade    CDATA "&#8482;"
                           -- trade mark sign, U2122 ISOnum -->
<!ENTITY alefsym  CDATA "&#8501;"
                           -- alef symbol, =first transfinite cardinal, U2135 NEW
                           N.b. alefsymb is NOT the same as hebrew letter alef,
                           U05D0 although the same glyph could be used. -->
<!-- Arrows -->
<!ENTITY larr     CDATA "&#8592;"
                           -- leftwards arrow, U2190 ISOnum -->
<!ENTITY uarr     CDATA "&#8593;"
                           -- upwards arrow, U2191 ISOnum-->
<!ENTITY rarr     CDATA "&#8594;"
                           -- rightwards arrow, U2192 ISOnum -->
<!ENTITY darr     CDATA "&#8595;"
                           -- downwards arrow, U2193 ISOnum -->
<!ENTITY harr     CDATA "&#8596;"
                           -- left right arrow, U2194 ISOamsa -->
```

```
<!ENTITY crarr    CDATA "&#8629;"
        -- downwards arrow with corner leftwards, =carriage return, U21B5 NEW -->
<!ENTITY lArr     CDATA "&#8656;"
                        -- leftwards double arrow, U21D0 ISOtech -->
<!ENTITY uArr     CDATA "&#8657;"
                        -- upwards double arrow, U21D1 ISOamsa -->
<!ENTITY rArr     CDATA "&#8658;"
                        -- rightwards double arrow, U21D2 ISOtech -->
<!ENTITY dArr     CDATA "&#8659;"
                        -- downwards double arrow, U21D3 ISOamsa -->
<!ENTITY hArr     CDATA "&#8660;"
                        -- left right double arrow, U21D4 ISOamsa -->
<!-- Mathematical Operators -->
<!ENTITY forall   CDATA "&#8704;"
                        -- for all, U2200 ISOtech -->
<!ENTITY part     CDATA "&#8706;"
                        -- partial differential, U2202 ISOtech  -->
<!ENTITY exist    CDATA "&#8707;"
                        -- there exists, U2203 ISOtech -->
<!ENTITY empty    CDATA "&#8709;"
                        -- empty set, =null set, =diameter, U2205 ISOamso -->

<!ENTITY nabla    CDATA "&#8711;"
                        -- nabla, =backward difference, U2207 ISOtech -->
<!ENTITY isin     CDATA "&#8712;"
                        -- element of, U2208 ISOtech -->
<!ENTITY notin    CDATA "&#8713;"
                        -- not an element of, U2209 ISOtech -->
<!ENTITY ni       CDATA "&#8715;"
                        -- contains as member, U220B ISOtech -->
<!ENTITY prod     CDATA "&#8719;"
                        -- n-ary product, =product sign, U220F ISOamsb
                        N.b. prod is NOT the same character as U03A0
                        'greek capital letter pi' though the same
                        glyph might be used for both -->
<!ENTITY sum      CDATA "&#8722;"
                        -- n-ary sumation, U2211 ISOamsb
                        N.b. sum is NOT the same character as U03A3
                        'greek capital letter sigma' though the same
                        glyph might be used for both -->
<!ENTITY minus    CDATA "&#8722;"
                        -- minus sign, U2212 ISOtech -->
<!ENTITY lowast   CDATA "&#8727;"
                        -- asterisk operator, U2217 ISOtech -->
<!ENTITY radic    CDATA "&#8730;"
                        -- square root, =radical sign, U221A ISOtech -->
<!ENTITY prop     CDATA "&#8733;"
                        -- proportional to, U221D ISOtech -->
```

```
<!ENTITY infin    CDATA "&#8734;"
                         -- infinity, U221E ISOtech -->
<!ENTITY ang      CDATA "&#8736;"
                         -- angle, U2220 ISOamso -->
<!ENTITY and      CDATA "&#8869;"
                         -- logical and, =wedge, U2227 ISOtech -->
<!ENTITY or       CDATA "&#8870;"
                         -- logical or, =vee, U2228 ISOtech -->
<!ENTITY cap      CDATA "&#8745;"
                         -- intersection, =cap, U2229 ISOtech -->
<!ENTITY cup      CDATA "&#8746;"
                         -- union, =cup, U222A ISOtech -->
<!ENTITY int      CDATA "&#8747;"
                         -- integral, U222B ISOtech -->
<!ENTITY there4   CDATA "&#8756;"
                         -- therefore, U2234 ISOtech -->
<!ENTITY sim      CDATA "&#8764;"
                -- tilde operator, =varies with, =similar to, U223C ISOtech
                tilde operator is NOT the same character as the tilde, U007E,
                although the same glyph might be used to represent both  -->
<!ENTITY cong     CDATA "&#8773;"
                         -- approximately equal to, U2245 ISOtech -->
<!ENTITY asymp    CDATA "&#8773;"
                         -- almost equal to, =asymptotic to, U2248 ISOamsr -->
<!ENTITY ne       CDATA "&#8800;"
                         -- not equal to, U2260 ISOtech -->
<!ENTITY equiv    CDATA "&#8801;"
                         -- identical to, U2261 ISOtech -->
<!ENTITY le       CDATA "&#8804;"
                         -- less-than or equal to, U2264 ISOtech -->
<!ENTITY ge       CDATA "&#8805;"
                         -- greater-than or equal to, U2265 ISOtech -->
<!ENTITY sub      CDATA "&#8834;"
                         -- subset of, U2282 ISOtech -->
<!ENTITY sup      CDATA "&#8835;"
                         -- superset of, U2283 ISOtech -->
<!ENTITY nsub     CDATA "&#8836;"
                         -- not a subset of, U2284 ISOamsn -->
<!ENTITY sube     CDATA "&#8838;"
                         -- subset of or equal to, U2286 ISOtech -->
<!ENTITY supe     CDATA "&#8839;"
                         -- superset of or equal to, U2287 ISOtech -->
<!ENTITY oplus    CDATA "&#8853;"
                         -- circled plus, =direct sum, U2295 ISOamsb -->
<!ENTITY otimes   CDATA "&#8855;"
                         -- circled times, =vector product, U2297 ISOamsb -->
<!ENTITY perp     CDATA "&#8869;"
                -- up tack, =orthogonal to, =perpendicular, U22A5 ISOtech -->
```

```
<!ENTITY sdot     CDATA "&#8901;"
               -- dot operator, U22C5 ISOamsb
               N.b. dot operator is NOT the same character as U00B7 middle dot -->
<!-- Miscellaneous Technical -->
<!ENTITY lceil    CDATA "&#8968;"
                    -- left ceiling, =apl upstile, U2308, ISOamsc  -->
<!ENTITY rceil    CDATA "&#8969;"
                    -- right ceiling, U2309, ISOamsc  -->
<!ENTITY lfloor   CDATA "&#8970;"
                    -- left floor, =apl downstile, U230A, ISOamsc  -->
<!ENTITY rfloor   CDATA "&#8971;"
                    -- right floor, U230B, ISOamsc  -->
<!ENTITY lang     CDATA "&#9001;"
                    -- left-pointing angle bracket, =bra, U2329 ISOtech
                    N.b. lang is NOT the same character as U003C 'less than'
                    or U2039 'single left-pointing angle quotation mark' -->
<!ENTITY rang     CDATA "&#9002;"
                    -- right-pointing angle bracket, =ket, U232A ISOtech
                    N.b. rang is NOT the same character as U003E 'greater than'
                    or U203A 'single right-pointing angle quotation mark' -->
<!-- Geometric Shapes -->
<!ENTITY loz      CDATA "&#9674;"
                    -- lozenge, U25CA ISOpub -->
<!-- Miscellaneous Symbols -->
<!ENTITY spades   CDATA "&#9824;"
                    -- black spade suit, U2660 ISOpub
                    N.b. black here means filled as opposed to hollow -->
<!ENTITY clubs    CDATA "&#9827;"
                    -- black club suit, =shamrock, U2663 ISOpub -->
<!ENTITY hearts   CDATA "&#9829;"
                    -- black heart suit, =valentine, U2665 ISOpub -->
<!ENTITY diams    CDATA "&#9830;"
                    -- black diamond suit, U2666 ISOpub -->
```

Draft Icons for WWW

Many of these glyphs have no ISO 10646 equivalent. This entity set has been proposed using the name "HTMLicons."

```
<!ENTITY archive              SDATA '[archive             ]' >
<!ENTITY audio                SDATA '[audio               ]' >
<!ENTITY binary.document      SDATA '[binary.document     ]' >
<!ENTITY binhex.document      SDATA '[binhex.document     ]' >
<!ENTITY calculator           SDATA '[calculator          ]' >
<!ENTITY caution              SDATA '[caution             ]' >
<!ENTITY cd.i                 SDATA '[cd.i                ]' >
<!ENTITY cd.rom               SDATA '[cd.rom              ]' >
<!ENTITY clock                SDATA '[clock               ]' >
<!ENTITY compressed.document  SDATA '[compressed.document ]' >
<!ENTITY disk.drive           SDATA '[disk.drive          ]' >
<!ENTITY diskette             SDATA '[diskette            ]' >
<!ENTITY document             SDATA '[document            ]' >
<!ENTITY fax                  SDATA '[fax                 ]' >
<!ENTITY filing.cabinet       SDATA '[filing.cabinet      ]' >
<!ENTITY film                 SDATA '[film                ]' >
<!ENTITY fixed.disk           SDATA '[fixed.disk          ]' >
<!ENTITY folder               SDATA '[folder              ]' >
<!ENTITY form                 SDATA '[form                ]' >
<!ENTITY ftp                  SDATA '[ftp                 ]' >
<!ENTITY glossary             SDATA '[glossary            ]' >
<!ENTITY gopher               SDATA '[gopher              ]' >
<!ENTITY home                 SDATA '[home                ]' >
<!ENTITY html                 SDATA '[html                ]' >
<!ENTITY image                SDATA '[image               ]' >
<!ENTITY index                SDATA '[index               ]' >
<!ENTITY keyboard             SDATA '[keyboard            ]' >
<!ENTITY mail                 SDATA '[mail                ]' >
<!ENTITY mail.in              SDATA '[mail.in             ]' >
<!ENTITY mail.out             SDATA '[mail.out            ]' >
<!ENTITY map                  SDATA '[map                 ]' >
<!ENTITY mouse                SDATA '[mouse               ]' >
<!ENTITY new                  SDATA '[new                 ]' >
<!ENTITY next                 SDATA '[next                ]' >
<!ENTITY notebook             SDATA '[notebook            ]' >
<!ENTITY parent               SDATA '[parent              ]' >
<!ENTITY play.fast.forward    SDATA '[play.fast.forward   ]' >
<!ENTITY play.fast.reverse    SDATA '[play.fast.reverse   ]' >
<!ENTITY play.pause           SDATA '[play.pause          ]' >
<!ENTITY play.start           SDATA '[play.start          ]' >
<!ENTITY play.stop            SDATA '[play.stop           ]' >
<!ENTITY previous             SDATA '[previous            ]' >
```

```
<!ENTITY printer          SDATA '[printer          ]'  >
<!ENTITY sadsmiley        SDATA '[sadsmiley        ]'  >
<!ENTITY smiley           SDATA '[smiley           ]'  >
<!ENTITY stop             SDATA '[stop             ]'  >
<!ENTITY summary          SDATA '[summary          ]'  >
<!ENTITY telephone        SDATA '[telephone        ]'  >
<!ENTITY telnet           SDATA '[telnet           ]'  >
<!ENTITY text.document    SDATA '[text.document    ]'  >
<!ENTITY tn3270           SDATA '[tn3270           ]'  >
<!ENTITY toc              SDATA '[toc              ]'  >
<!ENTITY trash            SDATA '[trash            ]'  >
<!ENTITY unknown.document SDATA '[unknown.document ]'  >
<!ENTITY uuencoded.document SDATA '[uuencoded.document ]'  >
<!ENTITY work             SDATA '[work             ]'  >
<!ENTITY www              SDATA '[www              ]'  >
```

TEI
Special
Characters

Appendix C

The Text Encoding Initiative [*TEI*] has defined several useful public entity sets for special characters.

Script	TEI Public Entity Set	Page
Arabic	TEIarb	TEI-1
Greek	TEIgrk	TEI-4
International Phonetic Alphabet	TEIipa	TEI-9
Coptic	TEIcop	TEI-17

-//TEI TR1 W4:1992//ENTITIES

Basic Arabic Letters//EN

```
<!-- TEI entity set for Arabic -->
<!-- Character entity set. Typical invocation:
    <!ENTITY % TEIarb PUBLIC
      '-//TEI TR1 W4:1992//ENTITIES Basic Arabic Letters//EN'>
    %TEIarb;
-->
<!ENTITY hamzar  SDATA '[hamzar ]' --Arabic letter Hamza-->
<!ENTITY amadar  SDATA '[amadar ]' --Arabic letter Alef with Madda above-->
<!ENTITY ahmuar  SDATA '[ahmuar ]' --Arabic letter Alef with Hamza above-->
<!ENTITY whmuar  SDATA '[whmuar ]' --Arabic letter Waw with Hamza above-->
<!ENTITY ahmlar  SDATA '[ahmlar ]' --Arabic letter Alef with Hamza below-->
<!ENTITY yhmlar  SDATA '[yhmlar ]' --Arabic letter Yeh with Hamza below-->
<!ENTITY    aar  SDATA '[aar    ]' --Arabic letter Alef-->
<!ENTITY    bar  SDATA '[bar    ]' --Arabic letter Beh-->
<!ENTITY tmrbar  SDATA '[tmrbar ]' --Arabic letter Teh Marbuta-->
<!ENTITY    tar  SDATA '[tar    ]' --Arabic letter Teh-->
<!ENTITY   thhar SDATA '[thhar  ]' --Arabic letter Theh-->
<!ENTITY    jar  SDATA '[jar    ]' --Arabic letter Jeem-->
<!ENTITY    har  SDATA '[har    ]' --Arabic letter Hah-->
<!ENTITY   khar  SDATA '[khar   ]' --Arabic letter Khah-->
<!ENTITY    dar  SDATA '[dar    ]' --Arabic letter Dal-->
<!ENTITY   thlar SDATA '[thlar  ]' --Arabic letter Thal-->
<!ENTITY    rar  SDATA '[rar    ]' --Arabic letter Reh-->
<!ENTITY    zar  SDATA '[zar    ]' --Arabic letter Zain-->
<!ENTITY    sar  SDATA '[sar    ]' --Arabic letter Seen-->
<!ENTITY   shar  SDATA '[shar   ]' --Arabic letter Sheen-->
<!ENTITY   sdar  SDATA '[sdar   ]' --Arabic letter Sad-->
<!ENTITY   ddar  SDATA '[ddar   ]' --Arabic letter Dad-->
<!ENTITY   taar  SDATA '[taar   ]' --Arabic letter Tah-->
<!ENTITY   zaar  SDATA '[zaar   ]' --Arabic letter Zah-->
<!ENTITY  ainar  SDATA '[ainar  ]' --Arabic letter Ain-->
<!ENTITY  ghnar  SDATA '[ghnar  ]' --Arabic letter Ghain-->
<!ENTITY   twlar SDATA '[twlar  ]' --Arabic letter Tatweel-->
<!ENTITY    far  SDATA '[far    ]' --Arabic letter Feh-->
<!ENTITY    qar  SDATA '[qar    ]' --Arabic letter Qaf-->
<!ENTITY    kar  SDATA '[kar    ]' --Arabic letter Kaf-->
<!ENTITY    lar  SDATA '[lar    ]' --Arabic letter Lam-->
<!ENTITY    mar  SDATA '[mar    ]' --Arabic letter Meem-->
<!ENTITY    nar  SDATA '[nar    ]' --Arabic letter Noon-->
```

```
<!ENTITY     har     SDATA '[har      ]' --Arabic letter Heh-->
<!ENTITY     war     SDATA '[war      ]' --Arabic letter Waw-->
<!ENTITY  amksar     SDATA '[amksar   ]' --Arabic letter Alef Maksura-->
<!ENTITY     yar     SDATA '[yar      ]' --Arabic letter Yeh-->
<!ENTITY  fthnar     SDATA '[fthnar   ]' --Arabic letter Fathatan-->
<!ENTITY  dmtnar     SDATA '[dmtnar   ]' --Arabic letter Dammatan-->
<!ENTITY  kstnar     SDATA '[kstnar   ]' --Arabic letter Kasratan-->
<!ENTITY  fthaar     SDATA '[fthaar   ]' --Arabic letter Fatha-->
<!ENTITY  dmmaar     SDATA '[dmmaar   ]' --Arabic letter Damma-->
<!ENTITY  ksraar     SDATA '[ksraar   ]' --Arabic letter Kasra-->
<!ENTITY  shdaar     SDATA '[shdaar   ]' --Arabic letter Shadda-->
<!ENTITY  skunar     SDATA '[skunar   ]' --Arabic letter Sukun-->
<!ENTITY  zeroar     SDATA '[zeroar   ]' --Arabic-Indic digit Zero-->
<!ENTITY   onear     SDATA '[onear    ]' --Arabic-Indic digit One-->
<!ENTITY   twoar     SDATA '[twoar    ]' --Arabic-Indic digit Two-->
<!ENTITY  threar     SDATA '[threar   ]' --Arabic-Indic digit Three-->
<!ENTITY  fourar     SDATA '[fourar   ]' --Arabic-Indic digit Four-->
<!ENTITY  fivear     SDATA '[fivear   ]' --Arabic-Indic digit Five-->
<!ENTITY   sixar     SDATA '[sixar    ]' --Arabic-Indic digit Six-->
<!ENTITY  svenar     SDATA '[svenar   ]' --Arabic-Indic digit Seven-->
<!ENTITY   eitar     SDATA '[eitar    ]' --Arabic-Indic digit Eight-->
<!ENTITY  ninear     SDATA '[ninear   ]' --Arabic-Indic digit Nine-->
```

-//TEI TR1 W4:1992//ENTITIES

Extra Classical Greek Letters//EN

Note that entity names in this set are case-sensitive. So &aiotgr; is different from &Aiotgr;.

```
<!-- TEI classical Greek supplemental to ISOgrk1 and ISOgrk2 -->
<!-- Character entity set. Typical invocation:
     <!ENTITY % TEIgrk PUBLIC
       '-//TEI TR1 W4:1992//ENTITIES Extra Classial Greek Letters//EN'>
     %TEIgrk;
-->
<!ENTITY aiotgr  SDATA '[aiotgr ]'--Gr sm letter alpha with iota-->
<!ENTITY Aiotgr  SDATA '[Aiotgr ]'--Gr cap alpha with iota-->
<!ENTITY arigr   SDATA '[arigr  ]'--Gr sm alpha with rough and iota-->
<!ENTITY Arigr   SDATA '[Arigr  ]'--Gr cap alpha with rough and iota-->
<!ENTITY asigr   SDATA '[asigr  ]'--Gr sm alpha with smooth and iota-->
<!ENTITY Asigr   SDATA '[Asigr  ]'--Gr cap alpha with smooth and iota-->
<!ENTITY aaigr   SDATA '[aaigr  ]'--Gr sm alpha with acute and iota-->
<!ENTITY Aaigr   SDATA '[Aaigr  ]'--Gr cap alpha with acute and iota-->
<!ENTITY agigr   SDATA '[agigr  ]'--Gr sm alpha with grave and iota-->
<!ENTITY Agigr   SDATA '[Agigr  ]'--Gr cap alpha with grave and iota-->
<!ENTITY acigr   SDATA '[acigr  ]'--Gr sm alpha with circum and iota-->
<!ENTITY Acigr   SDATA '[Acigr  ]'--Gr cap alpha with circum and iota-->
<!ENTITY araigr  SDATA '[araigr ]'--Gr sm alpha with rough, acute and iota-->
<!ENTITY Araigr  SDATA '[Araigr ]'--Gr cap alpha with rough, acute and iota-->
<!ENTITY asaigr  SDATA '[asaigr ]'--Gr sm alpha with smooth, acute and iota-->
<!ENTITY Asaigr  SDATA '[Asaigr ]'--Gr cap alpha with smooth, acute and iota-->
<!ENTITY argigr  SDATA '[argigr ]'--Gr sm alpha with rough, grave and iota-->
<!ENTITY Argigr  SDATA '[Argigr ]'--Gr cap alpha with rough, grave and iota-->
<!ENTITY asgigr  SDATA '[asgigr ]'--Gr sm alpha with smooth, grave and iota-->
<!ENTITY Asgigr  SDATA '[Asgigr ]'--Gr cap alpha with smooth, grave and iota-->
<!ENTITY arcigr  SDATA '[arcigr ]'--Gr sm alpha with rough, circum and iota-->
<!ENTITY Arcigr  SDATA '[Arcigr ]'--Gr cap alpha with rough, circum and iota-->
<!ENTITY ascigr  SDATA '[ascigr ]'--Gr sm alpha with smooth, circum and iota-->
<!ENTITY Ascigr  SDATA '[Ascigr ]'--Gr cap alpha with smooth, circum and iota-->
<!ENTITY arougr  SDATA '[arougr ]'--Gr sm alpha with rough-->
<!ENTITY Arougr  SDATA '[Arougr ]'--Gr cap alpha with rough-->
<!ENTITY asmogr  SDATA '[asmogr ]'--Gr sm alpha with smooth-->
<!ENTITY Asmogr  SDATA '[Asmogr ]'--Gr cap alpha with smooth-->
<!ENTITY agragr  SDATA '[agragr ]'--Gr sm alpha with grave-->
<!ENTITY Agragr  SDATA '[Agragr ]'--Gr sm  alpha with grave-->
<!ENTITY aacugr  SDATA '[aacugr ]'--Gr sm  alpha with acute-->
```

```
<!ENTITY Aacugr  SDATA '[Aacugr ]'--Gr cap alpha with acute-->
<!ENTITY acirgr  SDATA '[acirgr ]'--Gr sm alpha with circum-->
<!ENTITY Acirgr  SDATA '[Acirgr ]'--Gr cap alpha with circum-->
<!ENTITY aragr   SDATA '[aragr  ]'--Gr sm alpha with rough and acute-->
<!ENTITY Aragr   SDATA '[Aragr  ]'--Gr cap alpha with rough and acute-->
<!ENTITY asagr   SDATA '[asagr  ]'--Gr sm alpha with smooth and acute-->
<!ENTITY Asagr   SDATA '[Asagr  ]'--Gr cap alpha with smooth and acute-->
<!ENTITY arggr   SDATA '[arggr  ]'--Gr sm alpha with rough and grave-->
<!ENTITY Arggr   SDATA '[Arggr  ]'--Gr cap alpha with rough and grave-->
<!ENTITY asggr   SDATA '[asggr  ]'--Gr sm alpha with smooth and grave-->
<!ENTITY Asggr   SDATA '[Asggr  ]'--Gr cap alpha with smooth and grave-->
<!ENTITY arcgr   SDATA '[arcgr  ]'--Gr sm alpha with rough and circum-->
<!ENTITY Arcgr   SDATA '[Arcgr  ]'--Gr cap alpha with rough and circum-->
<!ENTITY ascgr   SDATA '[ascgr  ]'--Gr sm alpha with smooth and circum-->
<!ENTITY Ascgr   SDATA '[Ascgr  ]'--Gr cap alpha with smooth and circum-->
<!ENTITY erougr  SDATA '[erougr ]'--Gr sm epsilon with rough-->
<!ENTITY Erougr  SDATA '[Erougr ]'--Gr cap epsilon with rough-->
<!ENTITY esmogr  SDATA '[esmogr ]'--Gr sm epsilon with smooth-->
<!ENTITY Esmogr  SDATA '[Esmogr ]'--Gr cap epsilon with smooth -->
<!ENTITY egragr  SDATA '[egragr ]'--Gr sm epsilon with grave-->
<!ENTITY Egragr  SDATA '[Egragr ]'--Gr cap epsilon with grave-->
<!ENTITY eacugr  SDATA '[eacugr ]'--Gr sm epsilon with acute-->
<!ENTITY Eacugr  SDATA '[Eacugr ]'--Gr cap epsilon with acute-->
<!ENTITY ecirgr  SDATA '[ecirgr ]'--Gr sm epsilon with circum-->
<!ENTITY Ecirgr  SDATA '[Ecirgr ]'--Gr cap epsilon with circum-->
<!ENTITY eragr   SDATA '[eragr  ]'--Gr sm epsilon with rough and acute-->
<!ENTITY Eragr   SDATA '[Eragr  ]'--Gr cap epsilon with rough and acute-->
<!ENTITY esagr   SDATA '[esagr  ]'--Gr sm epsilon with smooth and acute-->
<!ENTITY Esagr   SDATA '[Esagr  ]'--Gr cap epsilon with smooth and acute-->
<!ENTITY erggr   SDATA '[erggr  ]'--Gr sm epsilon with rough and grave-->
<!ENTITY Erggr   SDATA '[Erggr  ]'--Gr cap epsilon with rough and grave-->
<!ENTITY esggr   SDATA '[esggr  ]'--Gr sm epsilon with smooth and grave-->
<!ENTITY Esggr   SDATA '[Esggr  ]'--Gr cap epsilon with smooth and grave-->
<!ENTITY eeiotgr SDATA '[eeiotgr]'--Gr sm eta with iota-->
<!ENTITY EEiotgr SDATA '[EEiotgr]'--Gr cap eta with iota-->
<!ENTITY eerigr  SDATA '[eerigr ]'--Gr sm eta with rough and iota-->
<!ENTITY EErigr  SDATA '[EErigr ]'--Gr cap eta with rough and iota-->
<!ENTITY eesigr  SDATA '[eesigr ]'--Gr sm eta with smooth and iota-->
<!ENTITY EEsigr  SDATA '[EEsigr ]'--Gr cap eta with smooth and iota-->
<!ENTITY eeaigr  SDATA '[eeaigr ]'--Gr sm eta with acute and iota-->
<!ENTITY EEaigr  SDATA '[EEaigr ]'--Gr cap eta with acute and iota-->
<!ENTITY eegigr  SDATA '[eegigr ]'--Gr sm eta with grave and iota-->
<!ENTITY EEgigr  SDATA '[EEgigr ]'--Gr cap eta with grave and iota-->
<!ENTITY eecigr  SDATA '[eecigr ]'--Gr sm eta with circum and iota-->
<!ENTITY EEcigr  SDATA '[EEcigr ]'--Gr cap eta with circum and iota-->
<!ENTITY eeraigr SDATA '[eeraigr]'--Gr sm eta with rough, acute and iota-->
<!ENTITY EEraigr SDATA '[EEraigr]'--Gr cap eta with rough, acute and iota-->
<!ENTITY eesaigr SDATA '[eesaigr]'--Gr sm eta with smooth, acute and iota-->
```

```
<!ENTITY EEsaigr SDATA '[EEsaigr ]'--Gr cap eta with smooth, acute and iota-->
<!ENTITY eergigr SDATA '[eergigr ]'--Gr sm eta with rough, grave and iota-->
<!ENTITY EErgigr SDATA '[EErgigr ]'--Gr cap eta with rough, grave and iota-->
<!ENTITY eesgigr SDATA '[eesgigr ]'--Gr sm eta with smooth, grave and iota-->
<!ENTITY EEsgigr SDATA '[EEsgigr ]'--Gr cap eta with smooth, grave and iota-->
<!ENTITY eercigr SDATA '[eercigr ]'--Gr sm eta with rough, circum and iota-->
<!ENTITY EErcigr SDATA '[EErcigr ]'--Gr cap eta with rough, circum and iota-->
<!ENTITY eescigr SDATA '[eescigr ]'--Gr sm eta with smooth, circum and iota-->
<!ENTITY EEscigr SDATA '[EEscigr ]'--Gr cap eta with smooth, circum and iota-->
<!ENTITY eerougr SDATA '[eerougr ]'--Gr sm eta with rough-->
<!ENTITY EErougr SDATA '[EErougr ]'--Gr cap eta with rough-->
<!ENTITY eesmogr SDATA '[eesmogr ]'--Gr sm eta with smooth-->
<!ENTITY EEsmogr SDATA '[EEsmogr ]'--Gr cap eta with smooth-->
<!ENTITY eegragr SDATA '[eegragr ]'--Gr sm eta with grave-->
<!ENTITY EEgragr SDATA '[EEgragr ]'--Gr cap eta with grave-->
<!ENTITY eeacugr SDATA '[eeacugr ]'--Gr sm eta with acute-->
<!ENTITY EEacugr SDATA '[EEacugr ]'--Gr cap eta with acute-->
<!ENTITY eecirgr SDATA '[eecirgr ]'--Gr sm eta with circum-->
<!ENTITY EEcirgr SDATA '[EEcirgr ]'--Gr cap eta with circum-->
<!ENTITY eeragr  SDATA '[eeragr  ]'--Gr sm eta with rough and acute-->
<!ENTITY EEragr  SDATA '[EEragr  ]'--Gr cap eta with rough and acute-->
<!ENTITY eesagr  SDATA '[eesagr  ]'--Gr sm eta with smooth and acute-->
<!ENTITY EEsagr  SDATA '[EEsagr  ]'--Gr cap eta with smooth and acute-->
<!ENTITY eerggr  SDATA '[eerggr  ]'--Gr sm eta with rough and grave-->
<!ENTITY EErggr  SDATA '[EErggr  ]'--Gr cap eta with rough and grave-->
<!ENTITY eesggr  SDATA '[eesggr  ]'--Gr sm eta with smooth and grave-->
<!ENTITY EEsggr  SDATA '[EEsggr  ]'--Gr cap eta with smooth and grave-->
<!ENTITY eercgr  SDATA '[eercgr  ]'--Gr sm eta with rough and circum-->
<!ENTITY EErcgr  SDATA '[EErcgr  ]'--Gr cap eta with rough and circum-->
<!ENTITY eescgr  SDATA '[eescgr  ]'--Gr sm eta with smooth and circum-->
<!ENTITY EEscgr  SDATA '[EEscgr  ]'--Gr cap eta with smooth and circum-->
<!ENTITY irougr  SDATA '[irougr  ]'--Gr sm iota with rough-->
<!ENTITY Irougr  SDATA '[Irougr  ]'--Gr cap iota with rough-->
<!ENTITY ismogr  SDATA '[ismogr  ]'--Gr sm iota with smooth-->
<!ENTITY Ismogr  SDATA '[Ismogr  ]'--Gr cap iota with smooth-->
<!ENTITY igragr  SDATA '[igragr  ]'--Gr sm iota with grave-->
<!ENTITY Igragr  SDATA '[Igragr  ]'--Gr cap iota with grave-->
<!ENTITY iacugr  SDATA '[iacugr  ]'--Gr sm iota with acute-->
<!ENTITY Iacugr  SDATA '[Iacugr  ]'--Gr cap iota with acute-->
<!ENTITY icirgr  SDATA '[icirgr  ]'--Gr sm iota with circum-->
<!ENTITY Icirgr  SDATA '[Icirgr  ]'--Gr cap iota with circum-->
<!ENTITY iragr   SDATA '[iragr   ]'--Gr sm iota with rough and acute-->
<!ENTITY Iragr   SDATA '[Iragr   ]'--Gr cap iota with rough and acute-->
<!ENTITY isagr   SDATA '[isagr   ]'--Gr sm iota with smooth and acute-->
<!ENTITY Isagr   SDATA '[Isagr   ]'--Gr cap iota with smooth and acute-->
<!ENTITY irggr   SDATA '[irggr   ]'--Gr sm iota with rough and grave-->
<!ENTITY Iragr   SDATA '[Iragr   ]'--Gr cap iota with rough and grave-->
<!ENTITY isggr   SDATA '[isggr   ]'--Gr sm iota with smooth and grave-->
```

```
<!ENTITY Isggr   SDATA '[Isggr  ]'--Gr cap iota with smooth and grave-->
<!ENTITY ircgr   SDATA '[ircgr  ]'--Gr sm iota with rough and circum-->
<!ENTITY Ircgr   SDATA '[Ircgr  ]'--Gr cap iota with rough and circum-->
<!ENTITY iscgr   SDATA '[iscgr  ]'--Gr sm iota with smooth and circum-->
<!ENTITY Iscgr   SDATA '[Iscgr  ]'--Gr cap iota with smooth and circum-->
<!ENTITY igdgr   SDATA '[igdgr  ]'--Gr sm iota with grave and diaresis-->
<!ENTITY Igdgr   SDATA '[Igdgr  ]'--Gr cap iota with grave and diaresis-->
<!ENTITY iadgr   SDATA '[iadgr  ]'--Gr sm iota with acute and diaresis-->
<!ENTITY Iadgr   SDATA '[Iadgr  ]'--Gr cap iota with acute and diaresis-->
<!ENTITY icdgr   SDATA '[icdgr  ]'--Gr sm iota with circum and diaresis-->
<!ENTITY Icdgr   SDATA '[Icdgr  ]'--Gr cap iota with circum and diaresis-->
<!ENTITY orougr  SDATA '[orougr ]'--Gr sm omicron with rough-->
<!ENTITY Orougr  SDATA '[Orougr ]'--Gr cap omicron with rough-->
<!ENTITY osmogr  SDATA '[osmogr ]'--Gr sm omicron with smooth-->
<!ENTITY Osmogr  SDATA '[Osmogr ]'--Gr cap omicron with smooth-->
<!ENTITY ogragr  SDATA '[ogragr ]'--Gr sm omicron with grave-->
<!ENTITY Ogragr  SDATA '[Ogragr ]'--Gr cap omicron with grave-->
<!ENTITY oacugr  SDATA '[oacugr ]'--Gr sm omicron with acute-->
<!ENTITY Oacugr  SDATA '[Oacugr ]'--Gr cap omicron with acute-->
<!ENTITY ocirgr  SDATA '[ocirgr ]'--Gr sm omicron with circum-->
<!ENTITY Ocirgr  SDATA '[Ocirgr ]'--Gr cap omicron with circum-->
<!ENTITY oragr   SDATA '[oragr  ]'--Gr sm omicron with rough and acute-->
<!ENTITY Oragr   SDATA '[Oragr  ]'--Gr cap omicron with rough and acute-->
<!ENTITY osagr   SDATA '[osagr  ]'--Gr sm omicron with smooth and acute-->
<!ENTITY Osagr   SDATA '[Osagr  ]'--Gr cap omicron with smooth and acute-->
<!ENTITY orggr   SDATA '[orggr  ]'--Gr sm omicron with rough and grave-->
<!ENTITY Orggr   SDATA '[Orggr  ]'--Gr cap omicron with rough and grave-->
<!ENTITY osggr   SDATA '[osggr  ]'--Gr sm omicron with smooth and grave-->
<!ENTITY Osggr   SDATA '[Osggr  ]'--Gr cap omicron with smooth and grave-->
<!ENTITY urougr  SDATA '[urougr ]'--Gr sm upsilon with rough-->
<!ENTITY Urougr  SDATA '[Urougr ]'--Gr cap upsilon with rough-->
<!ENTITY usmogr  SDATA '[usmogr ]'--Gr sm upsilon with smooth-->
<!ENTITY Usmogr  SDATA '[Usmogr ]'--Gr cap upsilon with smooth-->
<!ENTITY ugragr  SDATA '[ugragr ]'--Gr sm upsilon with grave-->
<!ENTITY Ugragr  SDATA '[Ugragr ]'--Gr cap upsilon with grave-->
<!ENTITY uacugr  SDATA '[uacugr ]'--Gr sm upsilon with acute-->
<!ENTITY Uacugr  SDATA '[Uacugr ]'--Gr cap upsilon with acute-->
<!ENTITY ucirgr  SDATA '[ucirgr ]'--Gr sm upsilon with circum-->
<!ENTITY Ucirgr  SDATA '[Ucirgr ]'--Gr cap upsilon with circum-->
<!ENTITY uragr   SDATA '[uragr  ]'--Gr sm upsilon with rough and acute-->
<!ENTITY Uragr   SDATA '[Uragr  ]'--Gr cap upsilon with rough and acute-->
<!ENTITY usagr   SDATA '[usagr  ]'--Gr sm upsilon with smooth and acute-->
<!ENTITY Usagr   SDATA '[Usagr  ]'--Gr cap upsilon with smooth and acute-->
<!ENTITY urggr   SDATA '[urggr  ]'--Gr sm upsilon with rough and grave-->
<!ENTITY Urggr   SDATA '[Urggr  ]'--Gr cap upsilon with rough and grave-->
<!ENTITY usggr   SDATA '[usggr  ]'--Gr sm upsilon with smooth and grave-->
<!ENTITY Usggr   SDATA '[Usggr  ]'--Gr cap upsilon with smooth and grave-->
<!ENTITY urcgr   SDATA '[urcgr  ]'--Gr sm upsilon with rough and circum-->
```

```
<!ENTITY Urcgr   SDATA '[Urcgr   ]'--Gr cap upsilon with rough and circum-->
<!ENTITY uscgr   SDATA '[uscgr   ]'--Gr sm upsilon with smooth and circum-->
<!ENTITY Uscgr   SDATA '[Uscgr   ]'--Gr cap upsilon with smooth and circum-->
<!ENTITY ugdgr   SDATA '[ugdgr   ]'--Gr sm upsilon with grave and diaresis-->
<!ENTITY Ugdgr   SDATA '[Ugdgr   ]'--Gr cap  upsilon with grave and diaresis-->
<!ENTITY ucdgr   SDATA '[ucdgr   ]'--Gr sm upsilon with circum and diaresis-->
<!ENTITY Ucdgr   SDATA '[Ucdgr   ]'--Gr cap  upsilon with circum and diaresis-->
<!ENTITY Uadgr   SDATA '[Uadgr   ]'--Gr cap upsilon with acute and diaresis-->
<!ENTITY uadgr   SDATA '[uadgr   ]'--Gr sm upsilon with acute and diaresis-->
<!ENTITY ohigr   SDATA '[ohigr   ]'--Gr sm omega with iota-->
<!ENTITY OHigr   SDATA '[OHigr   ]'--Gr cap omega with iota-->
<!ENTITY ohrigr  SDATA '[ohrigr  ]'--Gr sm omega with rough and iota-->
<!ENTITY OHrigr  SDATA '[OHrigr  ]'--Gr cap omega with rough and iota-->
<!ENTITY ohsigr  SDATA '[ohsigr  ]'--Gr sm omega with smooth and iota-->
<!ENTITY OHsigr  SDATA '[OHsigr  ]'--Gr cap omega with smooth and iota-->
<!ENTITY ohaigr  SDATA '[ohaigr  ]'--Gr sm omega with acute and iota-->
<!ENTITY OHaigr  SDATA '[OHaigr  ]'--Gr cap omega with acute and iota-->
<!ENTITY ohgigr  SDATA '[ohgigr  ]'--Gr sm omega with grave and iota-->
<!ENTITY OHgigr  SDATA '[OHgigr  ]'--Gr cap omega with grave and iota-->
<!ENTITY ohcigr  SDATA '[ohcigr  ]'--Gr sm omega with circum and iota-->
<!ENTITY OHcigr  SDATA '[OHcigr  ]'--Gr cap omega with circum and iota-->
<!ENTITY ohraigr SDATA '[ohraigr ]'--Gr sm omega with rough, acute and iota-->
<!ENTITY OHraigr SDATA '[OHraigr ]'--Gr cap omega with rough, acute and iota-->
<!ENTITY ohsaigr SDATA '[ohsaigr ]'--Gr sm omega with smooth, acute and iota-->
<!ENTITY OHsaigr SDATA '[OHsaigr ]'--Gr cap omega with smooth, acute and iota-->
<!ENTITY ohrgigr SDATA '[ohrgigr ]'--Gr sm omega with rough, grave and iota-->
<!ENTITY OHrgigr SDATA '[OHrgigr ]'--Gr cap omega with rough, grave and iota-->
<!ENTITY ohsgigr SDATA '[ohsgigr ]'--Gr sm omega with smooth, grave and iota-->
<!ENTITY OHsgigr SDATA '[OHsgigr ]'--Gr cap omega with smooth, grave and iota-->
<!ENTITY ohrcigr SDATA '[ohrcigr ]'--Gr sm omega with rough, circum and iota-->
<!ENTITY OHrcigr SDATA '[OHrcigr ]'--Gr cap omega with rough, circum and iota-->
<!ENTITY ohscigr SDATA '[ohscigr ]'--Gr sm omega with smooth, circum and iota-->
<!ENTITY OHscigr SDATA '[OHscigr ]'--Gr cap omega with smooth, circum and
 iota-->
<!ENTITY ohrougr SDATA '[ohrougr ]'--Gr sm omega with rough-->
<!ENTITY OHrougr SDATA '[OHrougr ]'--Gr cap omega with rough-->
<!ENTITY ohsmogr SDATA '[ohsmogr ]'--Gr sm omega with smooth-->
<!ENTITY OHsmogr SDATA '[OHsmogr ]'--Gr cap omega with smooth-->
<!ENTITY ohgragr SDATA '[ohgragr ]'--Gr sm omega with grave-->
<!ENTITY OHgragr SDATA '[OHgragr ]'--Gr cap omega with grave-->
<!ENTITY ohacugr SDATA '[ohacugr ]'--Gr sm  omega with acute-->
<!ENTITY OHacugr SDATA '[OHacugr ]'--Gr cap omega with acute-->
<!ENTITY ohcirgr SDATA '[ohcirgr ]'--Gr sm omega with circum-->
<!ENTITY OHcirgr SDATA '[OHcirgr ]'--Gr cap omega with circum-->
<!ENTITY ohragr  SDATA '[ohragr  ]'--Gr sm omega with rough and acute-->
<!ENTITY OHragr  SDATA '[OHragr  ]'--Gr cap omega with rough and acute-->
<!ENTITY ohsagr  SDATA '[ohsagr  ]'--Gr sm omega with smooth and acute-->
<!ENTITY OHsagr  SDATA '[OHsagr  ]'--Gr cap omega with smooth and acute-->
```

```
<!ENTITY ohrggr   SDATA '[ohrggr  ]'--Gr sm omega with rough and grave-->
<!ENTITY OHrggr   SDATA '[OHrggr  ]'--Gr cap omega with rough and grave-->
<!ENTITY ohsggr   SDATA '[ohsggr  ]'--Gr sm omega with smooth and grave-->
<!ENTITY OHsggr   SDATA '[OHsggr  ]'--Gr cap omega with smooth and grave-->
<!ENTITY ohrcgr   SDATA '[ohrcgr  ]'--Gr sm omega with rough and circum-->
<!ENTITY OHrcgr   SDATA '[OHrcgr  ]'--Gr cap omega with rough and circum-->
<!ENTITY ohscgr   SDATA '[ohscgr  ]'--Gr sm omega with smooth and circum-->
<!ENTITY OHscgr   SDATA '[OHscgr  ]'--Gr cap omega with smooth and circum-->
<!ENTITY rrougr   SDATA '[rrougr  ]'--Gr sm rho with rough-->
<!ENTITY Rrougr   SDATA '[Rrougr  ]'--Gr cap Rho with rough-->
<!ENTITY diggr    SDATA '[diggr   ]'--Gr sm digamma-->
<!ENTITY kogr     SDATA '[kogr    ]'--Gr sm koppa-->
<!ENTITY stgr     SDATA '[stgr    ]'--Gr small stigma-->
<!ENTITY samgr    SDATA '[samgr   ]'--Gr sm sampi-->
<!ENTITY cogr     SDATA '[ckgr    ]'--Gr colon or raised dot-->
<!ENTITY qmgr     SDATA '[qmgr    ]'--Gr question mark-->
```

-//TEI TR1 W4:1992//ENTITIES

IPA symbols for interchange//EN

```
<!-- IPA entity setdrawn up by Harry Gaylord with assistance from John
Esling      and Alexandra Gaylord
-->
<!-- Character entity set. Typical invocation:
    <!ENTITY % TEIipa PUBLIC
      '-//TEI TR1 W4:1992//ENTITIES IPA symbols for interchange//EN'>
    %TEIipa;
-->

<!ENTITY IPA101 SDATA '[IPA101  ]'
--IPA lower-case p, voiceless bilabial plosive-->
<!ENTITY IPA102 SDATA '[IPA102  ]'
--IPA lower-case b, voiced bilabial plosive-->
<!ENTITY IPA103 SDATA '[IPA103  ]'
--IPA lower-case t, voiceless dental or alveolar plosive-->
<!ENTITY IPA104 SDATA '[IPA104  ]'
--IPA lower-case d, voiced dental or alveolar plosive.-->
<!ENTITY IPA105 SDATA '[IPA105  ]'
--IPA Right-tail l.c. t, voiceless retroflex plosive-->
<!ENTITY IPA106 SDATA '[IPA106  ]'
```

```
--IPA Right-tail l.c. d, voiced retroflex plosive-->
<!ENTITY IPA107 SDATA '[IPA107 ]'
--IPA lower-case c, voiceless palatal plosive-->
<!ENTITY IPA108 SDATA '[IPA108 ]'
--IPA Barred Dotless l.c. j, voiced palatal plosive-->
<!ENTITY IPA109 SDATA '[IPA109 ]'
--IPA lower-case k, voiceless velar plosive-->
<!ENTITY IPA110 SDATA '[IPA110 ]'
--IPA lower-case g, voiced velar plosive-->
<!ENTITY IPA111 SDATA '[IPA111 ]'
--IPA lower-case q, voiceless uvular plosive-->
<!ENTITY IPA112 SDATA '[IPA112 ]'
--IPA Small Capital G, voiced uvular plosive-->
<!ENTITY IPA113 SDATA '[IPA113 ]'
--IPA Glottal Stop, glottal plosive-->
<!ENTITY IPA114 SDATA '[IPA114 ]'
--IPA lower-case m, voiced bilabial nasal-->
<!ENTITY IPA115 SDATA '[IPA115 ]'
--IPA Left-tail l.c. m (at right), voiced labiodental nasal-->
<!ENTITY IPA116 SDATA '[IPA116 ]'
--IPA lower-case n, voiced dental or alveolar nasal-->
<!ENTITY IPA117 SDATA '[IPA117 ]'
--IPA Right-tail l.c. n, voiced retroflex nasal-->
<!ENTITY IPA118 SDATA '[IPA118 ]'
--IPA Left-tail l.c. n (at left), voiced palatal nasal-->
<!ENTITY IPA119 SDATA '[IPA119 ]'
--IPA eng, voiced velar nasal-->
<!ENTITY IPA120 SDATA '[IPA120 ]'
--IPA Small Capital N, voiced uvular nasal-->
<!ENTITY IPA121 SDATA '[IPA121 ]'
--IPA Small Capital B, voiced bilabial trill-->
<!ENTITY IPA122 SDATA '[IPA122 ]'
--IPA lower-case r, voiced dental or alveolar trill-->
<!ENTITY IPA123 SDATA '[IPA123 ]'
--IPA Small Capital R, voiced uvular trill-->
<!ENTITY IPA124 SDATA '[IPA124 ]'
--IPA fish-hook l.c. r, voiced dental or alveolar tap-->
<!ENTITY IPA125 SDATA '[IPA125 ]'
--IPA Right-tail l.c. r, voiced retroflex flap-->
<!ENTITY IPA126 SDATA '[IPA126 ]'
--IPA phi, voiceless bilabial fricative-->
<!ENTITY IPA127 SDATA '[IPA127 ]'
--IPA beta, voiced bilabial fricative-->
<!ENTITY IPA128 SDATA '[IPA128 ]'
--IPA lower-case f, voiceless labiodental fricative-->
<!ENTITY IPA129 SDATA '[IPA129 ]'
--IPA lower-case v, voiced labiodental fricative-->
<!ENTITY IPA130 SDATA '[IPA130 ]'
```

```
--IPA theta,  voiceless dental fricative-->
<!ENTITY IPA131 SDATA '[IPA131  ]'
--IPA eth, voiced dental fricative-->
<!ENTITY IPA132 SDATA '[IPA132  ]'
--IPA lower-case s, voiceless alveolar fricative-->
<!ENTITY IPA133 SDATA '[IPA133  ]'
--IPA lower-case z, voiced alveolar fricative-->
<!ENTITY IPA134 SDATA '[IPA134  ]'
--IPA esh, voiceless postalveolar fricative-->
<!ENTITY IPA135 SDATA '[IPA135  ]'
--IPA yogh, voiced postalveolar fricative-->
<!ENTITY IPA136 SDATA '[IPA136  ]'
--IPA Right-tail l.c. s (at left), voiceless retroflex fricative-->
<!ENTITY IPA137 SDATA '[IPA137  ]'
--IPA right-tail l.c. z, voiced retroflex fricative-->
<!ENTITY IPA138 SDATA '[IPA138  ]'
--IPA l.c. c cedilla, voiceless palatal fricative-->
<!ENTITY IPA139 SDATA '[IPA139  ]'
--IPA curly-tail l.c. j, voiced palatal fricative-->
<!ENTITY IPA140 SDATA '[IPA140  ]'
--IPA lower-case x, voiceless velar fricative-->
<!ENTITY IPA141 SDATA '[IPA141  ]'
--IPA gamma, voiced velar fricative-->
<!ENTITY IPA142 SDATA '[IPA142  ]'
--IPA chi,  voiceless uvular fricative-->
<!ENTITY IPA143 SDATA '[IPA143  ]'
--IPA Inverted Small Capital R, voiced uvular fricative-->
<!ENTITY IPA144 SDATA '[IPA144  ]'
--IPA crossed l.c. h, voiceless pharyngeal fricative-->
<!ENTITY IPA145 SDATA '[IPA145  ]'
--IPA Reversed Glottal Stop, voiced pharyngeal fricative-->
<!ENTITY IPA146 SDATA '[IPA146  ]'
--IPA lower-case h, voiceless glottal fricative-->
<!ENTITY IPA147 SDATA '[IPA147  ]'
--IPA hooktop l.c. h, voiced glottal fricative-->
<!ENTITY IPA148 SDATA '[IPA148  ]'
--IPA belted l.c. l, voiceless dental or alveolar lateral fricative-->
<!ENTITY IPA149 SDATA '[IPA149  ]'
--IPA l.c. l-yogh Digraph, voiced dental or alveolar lateral fricative-->
<!ENTITY IPA150 SDATA '[IPA150  ]'
--IPA cursive l.c. v, voiced labiodental approximant-->
<!ENTITY IPA151 SDATA '[IPA151  ]'
--IPA turned l.c. r, voiced dental or alveolar approximant-->
<!ENTITY IPA152 SDATA '[IPA152  ]'
--IPA turned l.c. r, Right Tail, voiced retroflex approximant-->
<!ENTITY IPA153 SDATA '[IPA153  ]'
--IPA lower-case j, voiced palatal approximant-->
<!ENTITY IPA154 SDATA '[IPA154  ]'
```

```
--IPA turned l.c. m, Right Leg, voiced velar approximant-->
<!ENTITY IPA155 SDATA '[IPA155  ]'
--IPA lower-case l, voiced dental or alveolar lateral approximant-->
<!ENTITY IPA156 SDATA '[IPA156  ]'
--IPA right-tail l.c. l, voiced retroflex lateral approximant-->
<!ENTITY IPA157 SDATA '[IPA157  ]'
--IPA turned l.c. y, voiced palatal lateral approximant-->
<!ENTITY IPA158 SDATA '[IPA158  ]'
--IPA Small Capital L, voiced velar lateral approximant-->
<!ENTITY IPA159 SDATA '[IPA159  ]'
--IPA hooktop l.c. p, voiceless bilabial implosive-->
<!ENTITY IPA160 SDATA '[IPA160  ]'
--IPA hooktop l.c. b, voiced bilabial implosive-->
<!ENTITY IPA161 SDATA '[IPA161  ]'
--IPA hooktop l.c. t, voiceless dental or alveolar implosive-->
<!ENTITY IPA162 SDATA '[IPA162  ]'
--IPA hooktop l.c. d, voiced dental or alveolar implosive-->
<!ENTITY IPA163 SDATA '[IPA163  ]'
--IPA hooktop l.c. c, voiceless palatal implosive-->
<!ENTITY IPA164 SDATA '[IPA164  ]'
--IPA hooktop barred dotless l.c. j, voiced palatal implosive-->
<!ENTITY IPA165 SDATA '[IPA165  ]'
--IPA hooktop l.c. k, voiceless velar implosive-->
<!ENTITY IPA166 SDATA '[IPA166  ]'
--IPA hooktop l.c. g, voiced velar implosive-->
<!ENTITY IPA167 SDATA '[IPA167  ]'
--IPA hooktop l.c. q, voiceless uvular implosive-->
<!ENTITY IPA168 SDATA '[IPA168  ]'
--IPA Hooktop Small Capital G, voiced uvular implosive-->
<!ENTITY IPA169 SDATA '[IPA169  ]'
--IPA turned l.c. w, voiceless labial-velar fricative-->
<!ENTITY IPA170 SDATA '[IPA170  ]'
--IPA lower-case w, voiced labial-velar approximant-->
<!ENTITY IPA171 SDATA '[IPA171  ]'
--IPA turned l.c. h, voiced labial-palatal approximant-->
<!ENTITY IPA172 SDATA '[IPA172  ]'
--IPA Small Capital H, voiceless epiglottal fricative-->
<!ENTITY IPA173 SDATA '[IPA173  ]'
--IPA Barred Glottal Stop, voiced epiglottal plosive-->
<!ENTITY IPA174 SDATA '[IPA174  ]'
--IPA Barred Reversed Glottal Stop, voiced epiglottal fricative-->
<!ENTITY IPA175 SDATA '[IPA175  ]'
--IPA hooktop heng, simultaneous voiceless postalveolar and velar fricative -->
<!ENTITY IPA176 SDATA '[IPA176  ]'
--IPA Bulls Eye, bilabial click-->
<!ENTITY IPA177 SDATA '[IPA177  ]'
--IPA Pipe, dental click-->
<!ENTITY IPA178 SDATA '[IPA178  ]'
```

```
--IPA Exclamation Point, (post)alveolar click-->
<!ENTITY IPA179 SDATA '[IPA179  ]'
--IPA Double-barred Pipe, palatal click-->
<!ENTITY IPA180 SDATA '[IPA180  ]'
--IPA Double Pipe, alveolar lateral click-->
<!ENTITY IPA181 SDATA '[IPA181  ]'
--IPA turned long-leg l.c. r, voiced alveolar lateral flap-->
<!ENTITY IPA182 SDATA '[IPA182  ]'
--IPA curly-tail l.c. c, voiceless alveolo-palatal fricative-->
<!ENTITY IPA183 SDATA '[IPA183  ]'
--IPA curly-tail l.c. z, voiced alveolo-palatal fricative-->
<!ENTITY IPA204 SDATA '[IPA204  ]'
--IPA curly-tail esh, palatalized voiceless palato-alveolar central fricative
 -->
<!ENTITY IPA205 SDATA '[IPA205  ]'
--IPA curly-tail yogh, palatalized voiced palato-alveolar central fricative -->
<!ENTITY IPA207 SDATA '[IPA207  ]'
--IPA superscript s, (brief, faint, minor) voiceless alveolar fricative-->
<!ENTITY IPA208 SDATA '[IPA208  ]'
--IPA left-hook l.c. t, palatalized voiceless dental or alveolar plosive -->
<!ENTITY IPA209 SDATA '[IPA209  ]'
--IPA l.c. l with tilde, velarized voiced alveolar lateral approximant -->
<!ENTITY IPA211 SDATA '[IPA211  ]'
--IPA t-s digraph, voiceless alveolar affricate-->
<!ENTITY IPA212 SDATA '[IPA212  ]'
--IPA d-z digraph, voiced alveolar affricate-->
<!ENTITY IPA213 SDATA '[IPA213  ]'
--IPA t-esh digraph, voiceless postalveolar affricate -->
<!ENTITY IPA214 SDATA '[IPA214  ]'
--IPA d-yogh digraph, voiced postalveolar affricate-->
<!ENTITY IPA215 SDATA '[IPA215  ]'
--IPA t-curly-tail-c digraph, voiceless alveolo-palatal affricate-->
<!ENTITY IPA216 SDATA '[IPA216  ]'
--IPA d-curly-tail-z digraph, voiced alveolo-palatal affricate-->
<!ENTITY IPA301 SDATA '[IPA301  ]'
--IPA lower-case i, close front unrounded vowel-->
<!ENTITY IPA302 SDATA '[IPA302  ]'
--IPA lower-case e, close-mid front unrounded vowel-->
<!ENTITY IPA303 SDATA '[IPA303  ]'
--IPA epsilon, open-mid front unrounded vowel-->
<!ENTITY IPA304 SDATA '[IPA304  ]'
--IPA lower-case a, open front unrounded vowel-->
<!ENTITY IPA305 SDATA '[IPA305  ]'
--IPA cursive l.c. a, open back unrounded vowel-->
<!ENTITY IPA306 SDATA '[IPA306  ]'
--IPA open o, open-mid back rounded vowel-->
<!ENTITY IPA307 SDATA '[IPA307  ]'
--IPA lower-case o, close-mid back rounded vowel-->
```

```
<!ENTITY IPA308 SDATA '[IPA308  ]'
--IPA lower-case u, close back rounded vowel-->
<!ENTITY IPA309 SDATA '[IPA309  ]'
--IPA lower-case y, close front rounded vowel-->
<!ENTITY IPA310 SDATA '[IPA310  ]'
--IPA slashed l.c. o, close-mid front rounded vowel-->
<!ENTITY IPA311 SDATA '[IPA311  ]'
--IPA o-e digraph, open-mid front rounded vowel-->
<!ENTITY IPA312 SDATA '[IPA312  ]'
--IPA Small Capital O-E Digraph, open front rounded vowel-->
<!ENTITY IPA313 SDATA '[IPA313  ]'
--IPA turned cursive l.c. a, open back rounded vowel-->
<!ENTITY IPA314 SDATA '[IPA314  ]'
--IPA turned v, open-mid back unrounded vowel-->
<!ENTITY IPA315 SDATA '[IPA315  ]'
--IPA rams horns, close-mid back unrounded vowel-->
<!ENTITY IPA316 SDATA '[IPA316  ]'
--IPA turned l.c. m, close back unrounded vowel-->
<!ENTITY IPA317 SDATA '[IPA317  ]'
--IPA barred l.c. i, close central unrounded vowel-->
<!ENTITY IPA318 SDATA '[IPA318  ]'
--IPA barred l.c. u, close central rounded vowel-->
<!ENTITY IPA319 SDATA '[IPA319  ]'
--IPA Small Capital I, near-close near-front unrounded vowel-->
<!ENTITY IPA320 SDATA '[IPA320  ]'
--IPA Small Capital Y, near-close near-front rounded vowel-->
<!ENTITY IPA321 SDATA '[IPA321  ]'
--IPA upsilon, near-close near-back rounded vowel-->
<!ENTITY IPA322 SDATA '[IPA322  ]'
--IPA schwa, mid central unrounded vowel-->
<!ENTITY IPA323 SDATA '[IPA323  ]'
--IPA barred l.c. o, mid central rounded vowel-->
<!ENTITY IPA324 SDATA '[IPA324  ]'
--IPA turned l.c. a, near-open central unrounded vowel-->
<!ENTITY IPA325 SDATA '[IPA325  ]'
--IPA ash digraph, near-open front unrounded vowel-->
<!ENTITY IPA326 SDATA '[IPA326  ]'
--IPA reversed epsilon, additional mid central vowel-->
<!ENTITY IPA327 SDATA '[IPA327  ]'
--IPA right-hook schwa, r-colored mid central vowel-->
<!ENTITY IPA401 SDATA '[IPA401  ]'
--IPA apostrophe,  ejective stop-->
<!ENTITY IPA402a SDATA '[IPA402a  ]'
--IPA under ring, voiceless-->
<!ENTITY IPA402b SDATA '[IPA402b  ]'
--IPA over ring, voiceless-->
<!ENTITY IPA403 SDATA '[IPA403  ]'
--IPA subscript wedge, voiced-->
```

```
<!ENTITY IPA404 SDATA '[IPA404  ]'
--IPA superscript h, aspirated-->
<!ENTITY IPA405 SDATA '[IPA405  ]'
--IPA subscript umlaut, breathy voiced-->
<!ENTITY IPA406 SDATA '[IPA406  ]'
--IPA subscript tilde, creaky voiced-->
<!ENTITY IPA407 SDATA '[IPA407  ]'
--IPA subscript seagull, linguolabial-->
<!ENTITY IPA408 SDATA '[IPA408  ]'
--IPA subscript bridge, dental-->
<!ENTITY IPA409 SDATA '[IPA409  ]'
--IPA inverted subscript bridge, apical-->
<!ENTITY IPA410 SDATA '[IPA410  ]'
--IPA subscript square, laminal-->
<!ENTITY IPA411 SDATA '[IPA411  ]'
--IPA subscript right half-ring, more rounded-->
<!ENTITY IPA412 SDATA '[IPA412  ]'
--IPA subscript left half-ring, less rounded-->
<!ENTITY IPA413 SDATA '[IPA413  ]'
--IPA subscript plus, advanced-->
<!ENTITY IPA414 SDATA '[IPA414  ]'
--IPA under-bar, retracted-->
<!ENTITY IPA415 SDATA '[IPA415  ]'
--IPA umlaut, centralized-->
<!ENTITY IPA416 SDATA '[IPA416  ]'
--IPA over-cross, mid centralized-->
<!ENTITY IPA417 SDATA '[IPA417  ]'
--IPA advancing sign, advanced tongue root-->
<!ENTITY IPA418 SDATA '[IPA418  ]'
--IPA retracting sign, retracted tongue root-->
<!ENTITY IPA419 SDATA '[IPA419  ]'
--IPA right hook, rhoticity-->
<!ENTITY IPA420 SDATA '[IPA420  ]'
--IPA superscript w, labialized-->
<!ENTITY IPA421 SDATA '[IPA421  ]'
--IPA superscript j,  palatalized-->
<!ENTITY IPA422 SDATA '[IPA422  ]'
--IPA superscript gamma, velarized-->
<!ENTITY IPA423 SDATA '[IPA423  ]'
--IPA superscript reversed glottal stop, pharyngealized-->
<!ENTITY IPA424 SDATA '[IPA424  ]'
--IPA superscript tilde, nasalized-->
<!ENTITY IPA425 SDATA '[IPA425  ]'
--IPA superscript n, nasal release-->
<!ENTITY IPA426 SDATA '[IPA426  ]'
--IPA superscript l, lateral release-->
<!ENTITY IPA427 SDATA '[IPA427  ]'
--IPA corner, no audible release-->
```

```
<!ENTITY IPA428 SDATA '[IPA428  ]'
--IPA superimposed tilde, velarized or pharyngealized-->
<!ENTITY IPA429 SDATA '[IPA429  ]'
--IPA raising sign, raised-->
<!ENTITY IPA430 SDATA '[IPA430  ]'
--IPA lowering sign, lowered-->
<!ENTITY IPA431 SDATA '[IPA431  ]'
--IPA syllabicity mark, syllabic-->
<!ENTITY IPA432 SDATA '[IPA432  ]'
--IPA subscript arch, non-syllabic-->
<!ENTITY IPA433 SDATA '[IPA433  ]'
--IPA top tie bar, joining tie bar-->
<!ENTITY IPA501 SDATA '[IPA501  ]'
--IPA vertical stroke (superior), primary stress-->
<!ENTITY IPA502 SDATA '[IPA502  ]'
--IPA vertical stroke (inferior), secondary stress-->
<!ENTITY IPA503 SDATA '[IPA503  ]'
--IPA length mark, long-->
<!ENTITY IPA504 SDATA '[IPA504  ]'
--IPA half-length mark, half-long-->
<!ENTITY IPA505 SDATA '[IPA505  ]'
--IPA breve, extra-short-->
<!ENTITY IPA506 SDATA '[IPA506  ]'
--IPA period, syllable break-->
<!ENTITY IPA507 SDATA '[IPA507  ]'
--IPA vertical line, minor (foot) group-->
<!ENTITY IPA508 SDATA '[IPA508  ]'
--IPA double vertical line, major (intonation) group-->
<!ENTITY IPA509 SDATA '[IPA509  ]'
--IPA bottom tie bar,  linking (absence of a break)-->
<!ENTITY IPA510 SDATA '[IPA510  ]'
--IPA upward diagonal arrow, global rise-->
<!ENTITY IPA511 SDATA '[IPA511  ]'
--IPA downward diagonal arrow, global fall-->
<!ENTITY IPA512 SDATA '[IPA512  ]'
--IPA double acute accent (over), extra-high tone-->
<!ENTITY IPA513 SDATA '[IPA513  ]'
--IPA acute accent (over), high tone-->
<!ENTITY IPA514 SDATA '[IPA514  ]'
--IPA macron, mid tone-->
<!ENTITY IPA515 SDATA '[IPA515  ]'
--IPA grave accent (over), low tone-->
<!ENTITY IPA516 SDATA '[IPA516  ]'
--IPA double grave accent (over), extra-low tone-->
<!ENTITY IPA517 SDATA '[IPA517  ]'
--IPA down arrow, downstep tone-->
<!ENTITY IPA518 SDATA '[IPA518  ]'
--IPA up arrow, upstep tone-->
```

```
<!ENTITY IPA524 SDATA '[IPA524  ]'
--IPA Fall-rise Contour Tone -->
<!ENTITY IPA525 SDATA '[IPA525  ]'
--IPA Rise-fall Contour Tone -->
<!ENTITY IPA526 SDATA '[IPA526  ]'
--IPA Level-rise Contour Tone -->
<!ENTITY IPA527 SDATA '[IPA527  ]'
--IPA Fall-level Contour Tone -->
<!ENTITY IPA528 SDATA '[IPA528  ]'
--IPA Fall-rise-fall Contour Tone -->
```

-//TEI TR1 W4:1992//ENTITIES

Coptic Letters//EN

```
<!-- TEI entity set for Coptic -->
<!-- Character entity set. Typical invocation:
     <!ENTITY % TEIcop PUBLIC
        '-//TEI TR1 W4:1992//ENTITIES Coptic Letters//EN'>
     %TEIcop;
-->
<!ENTITY aco     SDATA '[aco     ]'--Coptic letter alpha -->
<!ENTITY bco     SDATA '[bco     ]'--Coptic letter beta -->
<!ENTITY gco     SDATA '[gco     ]'--Coptic letter gamma -->
<!ENTITY dco     SDATA '[dco     ]'--Coptic letter delta -->
<!ENTITY eco     SDATA '[eco     ]'--Coptic letter epsilon -->
<!ENTITY zco     SDATA '[zco     ]'--Coptic letter zeta -->
<!ENTITY eeco    SDATA '[eeco    ]'--Coptic letter eta -->
<!ENTITY thco    SDATA '[thco    ]'--Coptic letter theta -->
<!ENTITY ico     SDATA '[ico     ]'--Coptic letter iota -->
<!ENTITY kco     SDATA '[kco     ]'--Coptic letter kappa -->
<!ENTITY lco     SDATA '[lco     ]'--Coptic letter lambda -->
<!ENTITY mco     SDATA '[mco     ]'--Coptic letter mu -->
<!ENTITY nco     SDATA '[nco     ]'--Coptic letter nu -->
<!ENTITY xco     SDATA '[xco     ]'--Coptic letter xi -->
<!ENTITY oco     SDATA '[oco     ]'--Coptic letter omicron -->
<!ENTITY pco     SDATA '[pco     ]'--Coptic letter pi -->
<!ENTITY rco     SDATA '[rco     ]'--Coptic letter rho -->
<!ENTITY sco     SDATA '[sco     ]'--Coptic letter sigma -->
<!ENTITY tco     SDATA '[tco     ]'--Coptic letter tau -->
<!ENTITY uco     SDATA '[uco     ]'--Coptic letter upsilon -->
```

```
<!ENTITY phco    SDATA '[phco    ]'--Coptic letter phi -->
<!ENTITY khco    SDATA '[khco    ]'--Coptic letter chi -->
<!ENTITY psco    SDATA '[psco    ]'--Coptic letter psi -->
<!ENTITY ohco    SDATA '[ohco    ]'--Coptic letter omega -->
<!ENTITY shco    SDATA '[shco    ]'--Coptic letter shaj-->
<!ENTITY fco     SDATA '[fco     ]'--Coptic letter faj -->
<!ENTITY ch2co   SDATA '[ch2co   ]'--Coptic letter chail (Boharic)-->
<!ENTITY ch2co   SDATA '[ch2co   ]'--Coptic letter chai2 (Boharic)-->
<!ENTITY ch3co   SDATA '[ch3co   ]'--Coptic letter chai3 (Achmimic)-->
<!ENTITY hco     SDATA '[hco     ]'--Coptic letter hori-->
<!ENTITY dzco    SDATA '[dzco    ]'--Coptic letter dshandsha-->
<!ENTITY kjco    SDATA '[kjco    ]'--Coptic letter kjima-->
<!ENTITY teco    SDATA '[teco    ]'--Coptic letter te-->
<!ENTITY sfco    SDATA '[sfco    ]'--Coptic letter final s  -->
<!ENTITY stco    SDATA '[stco    ]'--Coptic letter stauros with middle bar -->
<!ENTITY adco    SDATA '[adco    ]'--Coptic letter alfa with diacritic -->
```

Index of
XML Special Characters

XML and modern HTMLs use ISO 10646 as their document character set. Tens of thousands of characters are thereby available for any document: if you cannot enter the character directly from your keyboard or by cutting and pasting from the Keycaps appliation which is standard with many GUIs, you can use SGML numeric character references. If your document does not use ISO 10646 as its document character set, you can mark the character up using the SPREAD public entity set.

In this index, characters are first sorted by script divisions (e.g., *Latin Capital Letters*) then into base characters (e.g, *A*), and finally into variant characters (e.g., *with macron*). Each character or character variant has first the **XML** hexadecimal numeric character reference (e.g., ꯍ), followed by the standard ISO entity name for that character where one exists and is commonly implemented, followed by the entity name used in the **SPREAD** public entity set (e.g., &UABCD;).

Sometimes the name of a character will not give the lay reader much clue as to its meaning. I urge readers to obtain the ISO standard [ISO 10646] or the [Unicode 2.0] book. Both these books contain complete representative glyphs for all characters, as well as indexes and much other material of interest.

This index does not contain entries for Han ideographs, since they have no English names. See Chapter 24 *Asian Language Issues* for various details about East Asian documents. For space reasons, there are no entries for the Korean and Tibetan scripts: refer to [Unicode 2.0] or [ISO 10646] for these.

ARABIC LETTER

Base	XML	SPREAD	Variation
AE	`&#x6D5;`	`&U06D5;`	
AIN	`&#x639;`	`&U0639;`	
	`&#x6A0;`	`&U06A0;`	with three dots above
ALEF	`&#x627;`	`&U0627;`	
	`&#x623;`	`&U0623;`	with hamza above
	`&#x625;`	`&U0625;`	with hamza below
	`&#x622;`	`&U0622;`	with madda above
	`&#x672;`	`&U0672;`	with wavy hamza above
	`&#x673;`	`&U0673;`	with wavy hamza below
ALEF MAKSURA	`&#x649;`	`&U0649;`	
ALEF WASLA	`&#x671;`	`&U0671;`	
BEEH	`&#x67B;`	`&U067B;`	
BEH	`&#x628;`	`&U0628;`	
BEHEH	`&#x680;`	`&U0680;`	
DAD	`&#x636;`	`&U0636;`	
DAHAL	`&#x68C;`	`&U068C;`	
DAL	`&#x62F;`	`&U062F;`	
	`&#x68A;`	`&U068A;`	with dot below
	`&#x68B;`	`&U068B;`	with dot below and small tah
	`&#x690;`	`&U0690;`	with four dots above
	`&#x689;`	`&U0689;`	with ring
	`&#x68F;`	`&U068F;`	with three dots above downwards
DDAHAL	`&#x68D;`	`&U068D;`	
DDAL	`&#x688;`	`&U0688;`	
DOTLESS FEH	`&#x6A1;`	`&U06A1;`	
DUL	`&#x68E;`	`&U068E;`	
DYEH	`&#x684;`	`&U0684;`	
E	`&#x6D0;`	`&U06D0;`	
FARSI YEH	`&#x6CC;`	`&U06CC;`	
FEH	`&#x641;`	`&U0641;`	
	`&#x6A3;`	`&U06A3;`	with dot below
	`&#x6A2;`	`&U06A2;`	with dot moved below
	`&#x6A5;`	`&U06A5;`	with three dots below
GAF	`&#x6AF;`	`&U06AF;`	
	`&#x6B0;`	`&U06B0;`	with ring
	`&#x6B4;`	`&U06B4;`	with three dots above
	`&#x6B2;`	`&U06B2;`	with two dots below
GHAIN	`&#x63A;`	`&U063A;`	
GUEH	`&#x6B3;`	`&U06B3;`	
HAH	`&#x62D;`	`&U062D;`	
	`&#x681;`	`&U0681;`	with hamza above
	`&#x685;`	`&U0685;`	with three dots above
	`&#x682;`	`&U0682;`	with two dots vertical above
HAMZA	`&#x621;`	`&U0621;`	
HEH	`&#x647;`	`&U0647;`	
	`&#x6C0;`	`&U06C0;`	with yeh above
HEH DOACHASHMEE	`&#x6BE;`	`&U06BE;`	
HEH GOAL	`&#x6C1;`	`&U06C1;`	

ARABIC LETTER (Continued)

Base	XML	SPREAD	Variation
...HEH GOAL	`&#x6C2;`	`&U06C2;`	with hamza above
HIGH HAMZA	`&#x674;`	`&U0674;`	
HIGH HAMZA ALEF	`&#x675;`	`&U0675;`	
HIGH HAMZA WAW	`&#x676;`	`&U0676;`	
HIGH HAMZA YEH	`&#x678;`	`&U0678;`	
JEEM	`&#x62C;`	`&U062C;`	
JEH	`&#x698;`	`&U0698;`	
KAF	`&#x643;`	`&U0643;`	
	`&#x6AC;`	`&U06AC;`	with dot above
	`&#x6AB;`	`&U06AB;`	with ring
	`&#x6AE;`	`&U06AE;`	with three dots below
KEHEH	`&#x6A9;`	`&U06A9;`	
KHAH	`&#x62E;`	`&U062E;`	
KIRGHIZ OE	`&#x6C5;`	`&U06C5;`	
KIRGHIZ YU	`&#x6C9;`	`&U06C9;`	
LAM	`&#x644;`	`&U0644;`	
	`&#x6B6;`	`&U06B6;`	with dot above
	`&#x6B5;`	`&U06B5;`	with small v
	`&#x6B7;`	`&U06B7;`	with three dots above
MEEM	`&#x645;`	`&U0645;`	
NG	`&#x6AD;`	`&U06AD;`	
NGOEH	`&#x6B1;`	`&U06B1;`	
NOON	`&#x646;`	`&U0646;`	
	`&#x6BC;`	`&U06BC;`	with ring
	`&#x6BD;`	`&U06BD;`	with three dots above
NOON GHUNNA	`&#x6BA;`	`&U06BA;`	
NYEH	`&#x683;`	`&U0683;`	
OE	`&#x6C6;`	`&U06C6;`	
PEH	`&#x67E;`	`&U067E;`	
PEHEH	`&#x6A6;`	`&U06A6;`	
QAF	`&#x642;`	`&U0642;`	
	`&#x6A7;`	`&U06A7;`	with dot above
	`&#x6A8;`	`&U06A8;`	with three dots above
REH	`&#x631;`	`&U0631;`	
	`&#x694;`	`&U0694;`	with dot below
	`&#x696;`	`&U0696;`	with dot below and dot above
	`&#x699;`	`&U0699;`	with four dots above
	`&#x693;`	`&U0693;`	with ring
	`&#x692;`	`&U0692;`	with small v
	`&#x695;`	`&U0695;`	with small v below
	`&#x697;`	`&U0697;`	with two dots above
RNOON	`&#x6BB;`	`&U06BB;`	
RREH	`&#x691;`	`&U0691;`	
SAD	`&#x635;`	`&U0635;`	
	`&#x69E;`	`&U069E;`	with three dots above
	`&#x69D;`	`&U069D;`	with two dots below
SEEN	`&#x633;`	`&U0633;`	
	`&#x69A;`	`&U069A;`	with dot below and dot above
	`&#x69B;`	`&U069B;`	with three dots below
	`&#x69C;`	`&U069C;`	with three dots below and three dots above

ARABIC LETTER (Continued)

Base	XML	SPREAD	Variation
SHEEN	ش	&U0634;	
SUPERSCRIPT ALEF	ٰ	&U0670;	
SWASH KAF	ڪ	&U06AA;	
TAH	ط	&U0637;	
	ڟ	&U069F;	with three dots above
TCHEH	چ	&U0686;	
TCHEHEH	ڇ	&U0687;	
TEH	ت	&U062A;	
	ټ	&U067C;	with ring
	ٽ	&U067D;	with three dots above downwards
TEH MARBUTA	ة	&U0629;	
TEH MARBUTA GOAL	ۃ	&U06C3;	
TEHEH	ٿ	&U067F;	
THAL	ذ	&U0630;	
THEH	ث	&U062B;	
TTEH	ٹ	&U0679;	
TTEHEH	ٺ	&U067A;	
U	ۇ	&U06C7;	
	ٷ	&U0677;	with hamza above
VE	ۋ	&U06CB;	
VEH	ڤ	&U06A4;	
WAW	و	&U0648;	
	ؤ	&U0624;	with hamza above
	ۄ	&U06C4;	with ring
	ۊ	&U06CA;	with two dots above
YEH	ي	&U064A;	
	ئ	&U0626;	with hamza above
	ێ	&U06CE;	with small v
	ۍ	&U06CD;	with tail
	ۑ	&U06D1;	with three dots below
YEH BARREE	ے	&U06D2;	
	ۓ	&U06D3;	with hamza above
YU	ۈ	&U06C8;	
ZAH	ظ	&U0638;	
ZAIN	ز	&U0632;	

Other Arabic

Character	XML	SPREAD
ARABIC DAMMA	&#x64F;	&U064F;
ARABIC DAMMATAN	&#x64C;	&U064C;
ARABIC EMPTY CENTRE HIGH STOP	&#x6EB;	&U06EB;
ARABIC EMPTY CENTRE LOW STOP	&#x6EA;	&U06EA;
ARABIC END OF AYAH	&#x6DD;	&U06DD;
ARABIC FATHA	&#x64E;	&U064E;
ARABIC FATHATAN	&#x64B;	&U064B;
ARABIC KASRA	&#x650;	&U0650;
ARABIC KASRATAN	&#x64D;	&U064D;
ARABIC ROUNDED HIGH STOP WITH FILLED CENTRE	&#x6EC;	&U06EC;
ARABIC SHADDA	&#x651;	&U0651;
ARABIC SMALL HIGH DOTLESS HEAD OF KHAH	&#x6E1;	&U06E1;
ARABIC SMALL HIGH JEEM	&#x6DA;	&U06DA;
ARABIC SMALL HIGH LAM ALEF	&#x6D9;	&U06D9;
ARABIC SMALL HIGH LIGATURE QAF WITH LAM WITH ALEF MAKSURA	&#x6D7;	&U06D7;
ARABIC SMALL HIGH LIGATURE SAD WITH LAM WITH ALEF MAKSURA	&#x6D6;	&U06D6;
ARABIC SMALL HIGH MADDA	&#x6E4;	&U06E4;
ARABIC SMALL HIGH MEEM INITIAL FORM	&#x6D8;	&U06D8;
ARABIC SMALL HIGH MEEM ISOLATED FORM	&#x6E2;	&U06E2;
ARABIC SMALL HIGH NOON	&#x6E8;	&U06E8;
ARABIC SMALL HIGH ROUNDED ZERO	&#x6DF;	&U06DF;
ARABIC SMALL HIGH SEEN	&#x6DC;	&U06DC;
ARABIC SMALL HIGH THREE DOTS	&#x6DB;	&U06DB;
ARABIC SMALL HIGH UPRIGHT RECTANGULAR ZERO	&#x6E0;	&U06E0;
ARABIC SMALL HIGH YEH	&#x6E7;	&U06E7;
ARABIC SMALL LOW MEEM	&#x6ED;	&U06ED;
ARABIC SMALL LOW SEEN	&#x6E3;	&U06E3;
ARABIC START OF RUB EL HIZB	&#x6DE;	&U06DE;
ARABIC SUKUN	&#x652;	&U0652;
ARABIC TATWEEL	&#x640;	&U0640;
arabic decimal separator	&#x66B;	&U066B;
arabic five pointed star	&#x66D;	&U066D;
arabic percent sign	&#x66A;	&U066A;
arabic place of sajdah	&#x6E9;	&U06E9;
arabic small waw	&#x6E5;	&U06E5;
arabic small yeh	&#x6E6;	&U06E6;
arabic thousands separator	&#x66C;	&U066C;

Arabic Numerals

Character	XML	SPREAD
arabic-indic digit eight	&#x668;	&U0668;
arabic-indic digit five	&#x665;	&U0665;
arabic-indic digit four	&#x664;	&U0664;
arabic-indic digit nine	&#x669;	&U0669;
arabic-indic digit one	&#x661;	&U0661;
arabic-indic digit seven	&#x667;	&U0667;
arabic-indic digit six	&#x666;	&U0666;
arabic-indic digit three	&#x663;	&U0663;
arabic-indic digit two	&#x662;	&U0662;
arabic-indic digit zero	&#x660;	&U0660;
extended arabic-indic digit eight	&#x6F8;	&U06F8;
extended arabic-indic digit five	&#x6F5;	&U06F5;
extended arabic-indic digit four	&#x6F4;	&U06F4;
extended arabic-indic digit nine	&#x6F9;	&U06F9;
extended arabic-indic digit one	&#x6F1;	&U06F1;
extended arabic-indic digit seven	&#x6F7;	&U06F7;
extended arabic-indic digit six	&#x6F6;	&U06F6;
extended arabic-indic digit three	&#x6F3;	&U06F3;
extended arabic-indic digit two	&#x6F2;	&U06F2;
extended arabic-indic digit zero	&#x6F0;	&U06F0;

ARMENIAN CAPITAL LETTER

Character	XML	SPREAD
AYB	&#x531;	&U0531;
BEN	&#x532;	&U0532;
CA	&#x53E;	&U053E;
CHA	&#x549;	&U0549;
CHEH	&#x543;	&U0543;
CO	&#x551;	&U0551;
DA	&#x534;	&U0534;
ECH	&#x535;	&U0535;
EH	&#x537;	&U0537;
ET	&#x538;	&U0538;
FEH	&#x556;	&U0556;
GHAD	&#x542;	&U0542;
GIM	&#x533;	&U0533;
HO	&#x540;	&U0540;
INI	&#x53B;	&U053B;
JA	&#x541;	&U0541;
JHEH	&#x54B;	&U054B;
KEH	&#x554;	&U0554;
KEN	&#x53F;	&U053F;
LIWN	&#x53C;	&U053C;

ARMENIAN CAPITAL LETTER (Continued)

Character	XML	SPREAD
MEN	Մ	&U0544;
NOW	Ն	&U0546;
OH	Օ	&U0555;
PEH	Պ	&U054A;
PIWR	Փ	&U0553;
RA	Ռ	&U054C;
REH	Ր	&U0550;
SEH	Ս	&U054D;
SHA	Շ	&U0547;
TIWN	Տ	&U054F;
TO	Թ	&U0539;
VEW	Վ	&U054E;
VO	Ո	&U0548;
XEH	Խ	&U053D;
YI	Յ	&U0545;
YIWN	Ւ	&U0552;
ZA	Զ	&U0536;
ZHE	Ժ	&U053A;

ARMENIAN SMALL LETTER

Character	XML	SPREAD
AYB	ա	&U0561;
BEN	բ	&U0562;
CA	ծ	&U056E;
CHA	չ	&U0579;
CHEH	ճ	&U0573;
CO	ց	&U0581;
DA	դ	&U0564;
ECH	ե	&U0565;
EH	է	&U0567;
ET	ը	&U0568;
FEH	ֆ	&U0586;
GHAD	ղ	&U0572;
GIM	գ	&U0563;
HO	հ	&U0570;
INI	ի	&U056B;
JA	ձ	&U0571;
JHEH	ջ	&U057B;
KEH	ք	&U0584;
KEN	կ	&U056F;
LIWN	լ	&U056C;
MEN	մ	&U0574;
NOW	ն	&U0576;

ARMENIAN SMALL LETTER (Continued)

Character	XML	SPREAD
OH	&#x585;	&U0585;
PEH	&#x57A;	&U057A;
PIWR	&#x583;	&U0583;
RA	&#x57C;	&U057C;
REH	&#x580;	&U0580;
SEH	&#x57D;	&U057D;
SHA	&#x577;	&U0577;
TIWN	&#x57F;	&U057F;
TO	&#x569;	&U0569;
VEW	&#x57E;	&U057E;
VO	&#x578;	&U0578;
XEH	&#x56D;	&U056D;
YI	&#x575;	&U0575;
YIWN	&#x582;	&U0582;
ZA	&#x566;	&U0566;
ZHE	&#x56A;	&U056A;

Other Armenian

Character	XML	SPREAD
ARMENIAN SMALL LIGATURE ECH YIWN	&#x587;	&U0587;
ARMENIAN MODIFER LETTER LEFT HALF RING	&#x559;	&U0559;

BENGALI LETTER

Character	XML	SPREAD
A	&#x985;	&U0985;
AA	&#x986;	&U0986;
AI	&#x990;	&U0990;
AU	&#x994;	&U0994;
BA	&#x9AC;	&U09AC;
BHA	&#x9AD;	&U09AD;
CA	&#x99A;	&U099A;
CHA	&#x99B;	&U099B;
DA	&#x9A6;	&U09A6;
DDA	&#x9A1;	&U09A1;
DDHA	&#x9A2;	&U09A2;
DHA	&#x9A7;	&U09A7;

BENGALI LETTER (Continued)

Character	XML	SPREAD
E	এ	&U098F;
GA	গ	&U0997;
GHA	ঘ	&U0998;
HA	হ	&U09B9;
I	ই	&U0987;
II	ঈ	&U0988;
JA	জ	&U099C;
JHA	ঝ	&U099D;
KA	ক	&U0995;
KHA	খ	&U0996;
LA	ল	&U09B2;
MA	ম	&U09AE;
NA	ন	&U09A8;
NGA	ঙ	&U0999;
NNA	ণ	&U09A3;
NYA	ঞ	&U099E;
O	ও	&U0993;
PA	প	&U09AA;
PHA	ফ	&U09AB;
RA	র	&U09B0;
RHA	ঢ়	&U09DD;
RRA	ড়	&U09DC;
SA	স	&U09B8;
SHA	শ	&U09B6;
SSA	ষ	&U09B7;
TA	ত	&U09A4;
THA	থ	&U09A5;
TTA	ট	&U099F;
TTHA	ঠ	&U09A0;
U	উ	&U0989;
UU	ঊ	&U098A;
VOCALIC L	ঌ	&U098C;
VOCALIC LL	ৡ	&U09E1;
VOCALIC R	ঋ	&U098B;
VOCALIC RR	ৠ	&U09E0;
YA	য	&U09AF;
YYA	য়	&U09DF;

BENGALI VOWEL SIGN

Character	XML	SPREAD
AA	&#x9BE;	&U09BE;
AI	&#x9C8;	&U09C8;
AU	&#x9CC;	&U09CC;
E	&#x9C7;	&U09C7;
I	&#x9BF;	&U09BF;
II	&#x9C0;	&U09C0;
O	&#x9CB;	&U09CB;
U	&#x9C1;	&U09C1;
UU	&#x9C2;	&U09C2;
VOCALIC L	&#x9E2;	&U09E2;
VOCALIC LL	&#x9E3;	&U09E3;
VOCALIC R	&#x9C3;	&U09C3;
VOCALIC RR	&#x9C4;	&U09C4;

Other Bengali

Character	XML	SPREAD
ANUSVARA	&#x982;	&U0982;
CANDRABINDU	&#x981;	&U0981;
NUKTA	&#x9BC;	&U09BC;
VIRAMA	&#x9CD;	&U09CD;
VISARGA	&#x983;	&U0983;
BENGALI AU LENGTH MARK	&#x9D7;	&U09D7;

Bengali Numerals

Character	XML	SPREAD
bengali currency denominator sixteen	&#x9F9;	&U09F9;
bengali currency numerator four	&#x9F7;	&U09F7;
bengali currency numerator one	&#x9F4;	&U09F4;
bengali currency numerator one less than the denominator	&#x9F8;	&U09F8;
bengali currency numerator three	&#x9F6;	&U09F6;
bengali currency numerator two	&#x9F5;	&U09F5;
bengali digit eight	&#x9EE;	&U09EE;
bengali digit five	&#x9EB;	&U09EB;
bengali digit four	&#x9EA;	&U09EA;
bengali digit nine	&#x9EF;	&U09EF;
bengali digit one	&#x9E7;	&U09E7;

Bengali Numerals (Continued)

Character	XML	SPREAD
bengali digit seven	`&#x9ED;`	`&U09ED;`
bengali digit six	`&#x9EC;`	`&U09EC;`
bengali digit three	`&#x9E9;`	`&U09E9;`
bengali digit two	`&#x9E8;`	`&U09E8;`
bengali digit zero	`&#x9E6;`	`&U09E6;`

BOPOMOFO LETTER

Character	XML	SPREAD
A	`&#x311A;`	`&U311A;`
AI	`&#x311E;`	`&U311E;`
AN	`&#x3122;`	`&U3122;`
ANG	`&#x3124;`	`&U3124;`
AU	`&#x3120;`	`&U3120;`
B	`&#x3105;`	`&U3105;`
C	`&#x3118;`	`&U3118;`
CH	`&#x3114;`	`&U3114;`
D	`&#x3109;`	`&U3109;`
E	`&#x311C;`	`&U311C;`
EH	`&#x311D;`	`&U311D;`
EI	`&#x311F;`	`&U311F;`
EN	`&#x3123;`	`&U3123;`
ENG	`&#x3125;`	`&U3125;`
ER	`&#x3126;`	`&U3126;`
F	`&#x3108;`	`&U3108;`
G	`&#x310D;`	`&U310D;`
GN	`&#x312C;`	`&U312C;`
H	`&#x310F;`	`&U310F;`
I	`&#x3127;`	`&U3127;`
IU	`&#x3129;`	`&U3129;`
J	`&#x3110;`	`&U3110;`
K	`&#x310E;`	`&U310E;`
L	`&#x310C;`	`&U310C;`
M	`&#x3107;`	`&U3107;`
N	`&#x310B;`	`&U310B;`
NG	`&#x312B;`	`&U312B;`
O	`&#x311B;`	`&U311B;`
OU	`&#x3121;`	`&U3121;`
P	`&#x3106;`	`&U3106;`
Q	`&#x3111;`	`&U3111;`
R	`&#x3116;`	`&U3116;`
S	`&#x3119;`	`&U3119;`
SH	`&#x3115;`	`&U3115;`
T	`&#x310A;`	`&U310A;`

BOPOMOFO LETTER (Continued)

Character	XML	SPREAD
U	`&#x3128;`	`&U3128;`
V	`&#x312A;`	`&U312A;`
X	`&#x3112;`	`&U3112;`
Z	`&#x3117;`	`&U3117;`
ZH	`&#x3113;`	`&U3113;`

COPTIC CAPITAL LETTER

Character	XML	SPREAD
DEI	`&#x3EE;`	`&U03EE;`
FEI	`&#x3E4;`	`&U03E4;`
GANGIA	`&#x3EA;`	`&U03EA;`
HORI	`&#x3E8;`	`&U03E8;`
KHEI	`&#x3E6;`	`&U03E6;`
SHEI	`&#x3E2;`	`&U03E2;`
SHIMA	`&#x3EC;`	`&U03EC;`

COPTIC SMALL LETTER

Character	XML	SPREAD
DEI	`&#x3EF;`	`&U03EF;`
FEI	`&#x3E5;`	`&U03E5;`
GANGIA	`&#x3EB;`	`&U03EB;`
HORI	`&#x3E9;`	`&U03E9;`
KHEI	`&#x3E7;`	`&U03E7;`
SHEI	`&#x3E3;`	`&U03E3;`
SHIMA	`&#x3ED;`	`&U03ED;`

CYRILLIC CAPITAL LETTER

Base	XML	SPREAD	Variation
A	А	&U0410;	
	Ӑ	&U04D0;	with breve
	Ӓ	&U04D2;	with diaeresis
ABKHASIAN CHE	Ҽ	&U04BC;	
	Ҿ	&U04BE;	with descender
ABKHASIAN DZE	Ӡ	&U04E0;	
ABKHASIAN HA	Ҩ	&U04A8;	
BARRED O	Ө	&U04E8;	
	Ӫ	&U04EA;	with diaeresis
BASHKIR KA	Ҡ	&U04A0;	
BE	Б	&U0411;	
BIG YUS	Ѫ	&U046A;	
BYELORUSSIAN-UKRAINIAN I	І	&U0406;	
CHE	Ч	&U0427;	
	Ҷ	&U04B6;	with descender
	Ӵ	&U04F4;	with diaeresis
	Ҹ	&U04B8;	with vertical stroke
DE	Д	&U0414;	
DJE	Ђ	&U0402;	
DZE	Ѕ	&U0405;	
DZHE	Џ	&U040F;	
E	Э	&U042D;	
EF	Ф	&U0424;	
EL	Л	&U041B;	
EM	М	&U041C;	
EN	Н	&U041D;	
	Ң	&U04A2;	with descender
	Ӈ	&U04C7;	with hook
ER	Р	&U0420;	
ES	С	&U0421;	
	Ҫ	&U04AA;	with descender
FITA	Ѳ	&U0472;	
GHE	Г	&U0413;	
	Ҕ	&U0494;	with middle hook
	Ғ	&U0492;	with stroke
	Ґ	&U0490;	with upturn
GJE	Ѓ	&U0403;	
HA	Х	&U0425;	
	Ҳ	&U04B2;	with descender
HARD SIGN	Ъ	&U042A;	
I	И	&U0418;	
	Ӥ	&U04E4;	with diaeresis
	Ӣ	&U04E2;	with macron
IE	Е	&U0415;	
	Ӗ	&U04D6;	with breve
IO	Ё	&U0401;	
IOTIFIED BIG YUS	Ѭ	&U046C;	
IOTIFIED E	Ѥ	&U0464;	
IOTIFIED LITTLE YUS	Ѩ	&U0468;	
IZHITSA	Ѵ	&U0474;	

CYRILLIC CAPITAL LETTER (Continued)

Base	XML	SPREAD	Variation
...IZHITSA	Ѷ	&U0476;	with double grave accent
JE	Ј	&U0408;	
KA	К	&U041A;	
	Қ	&U049A;	with descender
	Ӄ	&U04C3;	with hook
	Ҟ	&U049E;	with stroke
	Ҝ	&U049C;	with vertical stroke
KHAKASSIAN CHE	Ӌ	&U04CB;	
KJE	Ќ	&U040C;	
KOPPA	Ҁ	&U0480;	
KSI	Ѯ	&U046E;	
LITTLE YUS	Ѧ	&U0466;	
LJE	Љ	&U0409;	
NJE	Њ	&U040A;	
O	О	&U041E;	
	Ӧ	&U04E6;	with diaeresis
OMEGA	Ѡ	&U0460;	
	Ѽ	&U047C;	with titlo
OT	Ѿ	&U047E;	
PE	П	&U041F;	
	Ҧ	&U04A6;	with middle hook
PSI	Ѱ	&U0470;	
ROUND OMEGA	Ѻ	&U047A;	
SCHWA	Ә	&U04D8;	
	Ӛ	&U04DA;	with diaeresis
SHA	Ш	&U0428;	
SHCHA	Щ	&U0429;	
SHHA	Һ	&U04BA;	
SHORT I	Й	&U0419;	
SHORT U	Ў	&U040E;	
SOFT SIGN	Ь	&U042C;	
STRAIGHT U	Ү	&U04AE;	
	Ұ	&U04B0;	with stroke
TE	Т	&U0422;	
	Ҭ	&U04AC;	with descender
TSE	Ц	&U0426;	
TSHE	Ћ	&U040B;	
U	У	&U0423;	
	Ӱ	&U04F0;	with diaeresis
	Ӳ	&U04F2;	with double acute
	Ӯ	&U04EE;	with macron
UK	Ѹ	&U0478;	
UKRAINIAN IE	Є	&U0404;	
VE	В	&U0412;	
YA	Я	&U042F;	
YAT	Ѣ	&U0462;	
YERU	Ы	&U042B;	
	Ӹ	&U04F8;	with diaeresis
YI	Ї	&U0407;	
YU	Ю	&U042E;	

CYRILLIC CAPITAL LETTER (Continued)

Base	XML	SPREAD	Variation
ZE	&#x417;	&U0417;	
	&#x498;	&U0498;	with descender
	&#x4DE;	&U04DE;	with diaeresis
ZHE	&#x416;	&U0416;	
	&#x4C1;	&U04C1;	with breve
	&#x496;	&U0496;	with descender
	&#x4DC;	&U04DC;	with diaeresis

CYRILLIC SMALL LETTER

Base	XML	SPREAD	Variation
A	&#x430;	&U0430;	
	&#x4D1;	&U04D1;	with breve
	&#x4D3;	&U04D3;	with diaeresis
ABKHASIAN CHE	&#x4BD;	&U04BD;	
	&#x4BF;	&U04BF;	with descender
ABKHASIAN DZE	&#x4E1;	&U04E1;	
ABKHASIAN HA	&#x4A9;	&U04A9;	
BARRED O	&#x4E9;	&U04E9;	
	&#x4EB;	&U04EB;	with diaeresis
BASHKIR KA	&#x4A1;	&U04A1;	
BE	&#x431;	&U0431;	
BIG YUS	&#x46B;	&U046B;	
BYELORUSSIAN-UKRAINIAN I	&#x456;	&U0456;	
CHE	&#x447;	&U0447;	
	&#x4B7;	&U04B7;	with descender
	&#x4F5;	&U04F5;	with diaeresis
	&#x4B9;	&U04B9;	with vertical stroke
DE	&#x434;	&U0434;	
DJE	&#x452;	&U0452;	
DZE	&#x455;	&U0455;	
DZHE	&#x45F;	&U045F;	
E	&#x44D;	&U044D;	
EF	&#x444;	&U0444;	
EL	&#x43B;	&U043B;	
EM	&#x43C;	&U043C;	
EN	&#x43D;	&U043D;	
	&#x4A3;	&U04A3;	with descender
	&#x4C8;	&U04C8;	with hook
ER	&#x440;	&U0440;	
ES	&#x441;	&U0441;	
	&#x4AB;	&U04AB;	with descender
FITA	&#x473;	&U0473;	
GHE	&#x433;	&U0433;	

CYRILLIC SMALL LETTER (Continued)

Base	XML	SPREAD	Variation
...GHE	ҕ	&U0495;	with middle hook
	ғ	&U0493;	with stroke
	ґ	&U0491;	with upturn
GJE	ѓ	&U0453;	
HA	х	&U0445;	
	ҳ	&U04B3;	with descender
HARD SIGN	ъ	&U044A;	
I	и	&U0438;	
	ӥ	&U04E5;	with diaeresis
	ӣ	&U04E3;	with macron
IE	е	&U0435;	
	ӗ	&U04D7;	with breve
IO	ё	&U0451;	
IOTIFIED BIG YUS	ѭ	&U046D;	
IOTIFIED E	ѥ	&U0465;	
IOTIFIED LITTLE YUS	ѩ	&U0469;	
IZHITSA	ѵ	&U0475;	
	ѷ	&U0477;	with double grave accent
JE	ј	&U0458;	
KA	к	&U043A;	
	қ	&U049B;	with descender
	ӄ	&U04C4;	with hook
	ҟ	&U049F;	with stroke
	ҝ	&U049D;	with vertical stroke
KHAKASSIAN CHE	ӌ	&U04CC;	
KJE	ќ	&U045C;	
KOPPA	ҁ	&U0481;	
KSI	ѯ	&U046F;	
LITTLE YUS	ѧ	&U0467;	
LJE	љ	&U0459;	
NJE	њ	&U045A;	
O	о	&U043E;	
	ӧ	&U04E7;	with diaeresis
OMEGA	ѡ	&U0461;	
	ѽ	&U047D;	with titlo
OT	ѿ	&U047F;	
PE	п	&U043F;	
	ҧ	&U04A7;	with middle hook
PSI	ѱ	&U0471;	
ROUND OMEGA	ѻ	&U047B;	
SCHWA	ә	&U04D9;	
	ӛ	&U04DB;	with diaeresis
SHA	ш	&U0448;	
SHCHA	щ	&U0449;	
SHHA	һ	&U04BB;	
SHORT I	й	&U0439;	
SHORT U	ў	&U045E;	
SOFT SIGN	ь	&U044C;	
STRAIGHT U	ү	&U04AF;	
	ұ	&U04B1;	with stroke

CYRILLIC SMALL LETTER (Continued)

Base	XML	SPREAD	Variation
TE	т	&U0442;	
	ҭ	&U04AD;	with descender
TSE	ц	&U0446;	
TSHE	ћ	&U045B;	
U	у	&U0443;	
	ӱ	&U04F1;	with diaeresis
	ӳ	&U04F3;	with double acute
	ӯ	&U04EF;	with macron
UK	ѹ	&U0479;	
UKRAINIAN IE	є	&U0454;	
VE	в	&U0432;	
YA	я	&U044F;	
YAT	ѣ	&U0463;	
YERU	ы	&U044B;	
	ӹ	&U04F9;	with diaeresis
YI	ї	&U0457;	
YU	ю	&U044E;	
ZE	з	&U0437;	
	ҙ	&U0499;	with descender
	ӟ	&U04DF;	with diaeresis
ZHE	ж	&U0436;	
	ӂ	&U04C2;	with breve
	җ	&U0497;	with descender
	ӝ	&U04DD;	with diaeresis

Other Cyrillic

Character	XML	SPREAD
CYRILLIC CAPITAL LIGATURE A IE	Ӕ	&U04D4;
CYRILLIC CAPITAL LIGATURE EN GHE	Ҥ	&U04A4;
CYRILLIC CAPITAL LIGATURE TE TSE	Ҵ	&U04B4;
CYRILLIC LETTER PALOCHKA	Ӏ	&U04C0;
CYRILLIC SMALL LIGATURE A IE	ӕ	&U04D5;
CYRILLIC SMALL LIGATURE EN GHE	ҥ	&U04A5;
CYRILLIC SMALL LIGATURE TE TSE	ҵ	&U04B5;
COMBINING CYRILLIC DASIA PNEUMATA	҅	&U0485;
COMBINING CYRILLIC PALATALIZATION	҄	&U0484;
COMBINING CYRILLIC PSILI PNEUMATA	҆	&U0486;
COMBINING CYRILLIC TITLO	҃	&U0483;

DEVANAGARI LETTER

Character	XML	SPREAD
A	अ	&U0905;
AA	आ	&U0906;
AI	ऐ	&U0910;
AU	औ	&U0914;
BA	ब	&U092C;
BHA	भ	&U092D;
CA	च	&U091A;
CANDRA E	ऍ	&U090D;
CANDRA O	ऑ	&U0911;
CHA	छ	&U091B;
DA	द	&U0926;
DDA	ड	&U0921;
DDDHA	ड़	&U095C;
DDHA	ढ	&U0922;
DHA	ध	&U0927;
E	ए	&U090F;
FA	फ़	&U095E;
GA	ग	&U0917;
GHA	घ	&U0918;
GHHA	ग़	&U095A;
HA	ह	&U0939;
I	इ	&U0907;
II	ई	&U0908;
JA	ज	&U091C;
JHA	झ	&U091D;
KA	क	&U0915;
KHA	ख	&U0916;
KHHA	ख़	&U0959;
LA	ल	&U0932;
LLA	ळ	&U0933;

DEVANAGARI LETTER (Continued)

Character	XML	SPREAD
LLLA	&#x934;	&U0934;
MA	&#x92E;	&U092E;
NA	&#x928;	&U0928;
NGA	&#x919;	&U0919;
NNA	&#x923;	&U0923;
NNNA	&#x929;	&U0929;
NYA	&#x91E;	&U091E;
O	&#x913;	&U0913;
PA	&#x92A;	&U092A;
PHA	&#x92B;	&U092B;
QA	&#x958;	&U0958;
RA	&#x930;	&U0930;
RHA	&#x95D;	&U095D;
RRA	&#x931;	&U0931;
SA	&#x938;	&U0938;
SHA	&#x936;	&U0936;
SHORT E	&#x90E;	&U090E;
SHORT O	&#x912;	&U0912;
SSA	&#x937;	&U0937;
TA	&#x924;	&U0924;
THA	&#x925;	&U0925;
TTA	&#x91F;	&U091F;
TTHA	&#x920;	&U0920;
U	&#x909;	&U0909;
UU	&#x90A;	&U090A;
VA	&#x935;	&U0935;
VOCALIC L	&#x90C;	&U090C;
VOCALIC LL	&#x961;	&U0961;
VOCALIC R	&#x90B;	&U090B;
VOCALIC RR	&#x960;	&U0960;
YA	&#x92F;	&U092F;
YYA	&#x95F;	&U095F;
ZA	&#x95B;	&U095B;

DEVANAGARI SIGN

Character	XML	SPREAD
ANUSVARA	&#x902;	&U0902;
CANDRABINDU	&#x901;	&U0901;
NUKTA	&#x93C;	&U093C;
VIRAMA	&#x94D;	&U094D;
VISARGA	&#x903;	&U0903;

DEVANAGARI VOWEL SIGN

Character	XML	SPREAD
AA	&#x93E;	&U093E;
AI	&#x948;	&U0948;
AU	&#x94C;	&U094C;
CANDRA E	&#x945;	&U0945;
CANDRA O	&#x949;	&U0949;
E	&#x947;	&U0947;
I	&#x93F;	&U093F;
II	&#x940;	&U0940;
O	&#x94B;	&U094B;
SHORT E	&#x946;	&U0946;
SHORT O	&#x94A;	&U094A;
U	&#x941;	&U0941;
UU	&#x942;	&U0942;
VOCALIC L	&#x962;	&U0962;
VOCALIC LL	&#x963;	&U0963;
VOCALIC R	&#x943;	&U0943;
VOCALIC RR	&#x944;	&U0944;

Devanagari Numerals

Name	XML	SPREAD
devanagari digit eight	&#x96E;	&U096E;
devanagari digit five	&#x96B;	&U096B;
devanagari digit four	&#x96A;	&U096A;
devanagari digit nine	&#x96F;	&U096F;
devanagari digit one	&#x967;	&U0967;
devanagari digit seven	&#x96D;	&U096D;
devanagari digit six	&#x96C;	&U096C;
devanagari digit three	&#x969;	&U0969;
devanagari digit two	&#x968;	&U0968;
devanagari digit zero	&#x966;	&U0966;

Other Devanagari

Character	XML	SPREAD
DEVANAGARI ACUTE ACCENT	&#x954;	&U0954;
DEVANAGARI GRAVE ACCENT	&#x953;	&U0953;
DEVANAGARI STRESS SIGN ANUDATTA	&#x952;	&U0952;
DEVANAGARI STRESS SIGN UDATTA	&#x951;	&U0951;
devanagari abbreviation sign	&#x970;	&U0970;
devanagari sign avagraha	&#x93D;	&U093D;

GEORGIAN CAPITAL LETTER

Character	XML	SPREAD
AN	&#x10A0;	&U10A0;
BAN	&#x10A1;	&U10A1;
CAN	&#x10BA;	&U10BA;
CHAR	&#x10BD;	&U10BD;
CHIN	&#x10B9;	&U10B9;
CIL	&#x10BC;	&U10BC;
DON	&#x10A3;	&U10A3;
EN	&#x10A4;	&U10A4;
GAN	&#x10A2;	&U10A2;
GHAN	&#x10B6;	&U10B6;
HAE	&#x10C0;	&U10C0;
HAR	&#x10C4;	&U10C4;
HE	&#x10C1;	&U10C1;
HIE	&#x10C2;	&U10C2;

GEORGIAN CAPITAL LETTER (Continued)

Character	XML	SPREAD
HOE	&#x10C5;	&U10C5;
IN	&#x10A8;	&U10A8;
JHAN	&#x10BF;	&U10BF;
JIL	&#x10BB;	&U10BB;
KAN	&#x10A9;	&U10A9;
KHAR	&#x10B5;	&U10B5;
LAS	&#x10AA;	&U10AA;
MAN	&#x10AB;	&U10AB;
NAR	&#x10AC;	&U10AC;
ON	&#x10AD;	&U10AD;
PAR	&#x10AE;	&U10AE;
PHAR	&#x10B4;	&U10B4;
QAR	&#x10B7;	&U10B7;
RAE	&#x10B0;	&U10B0;
SAN	&#x10B1;	&U10B1;
SHIN	&#x10B8;	&U10B8;
TAN	&#x10A7;	&U10A7;
TAR	&#x10B2;	&U10B2;
UN	&#x10B3;	&U10B3;
VIN	&#x10A5;	&U10A5;
WE	&#x10C3;	&U10C3;
XAN	&#x10BE;	&U10BE;
ZEN	&#x10A6;	&U10A6;
ZHAR	&#x10AF;	&U10AF;

GEORGIAN LETTER

Character	XML	SPREAD
AN	&#x10D0;	&U10D0;
BAN	&#x10D1;	&U10D1;
CAN	&#x10EA;	&U10EA;
CHAR	&#x10ED;	&U10ED;
CHIN	&#x10E9;	&U10E9;
CIL	&#x10EC;	&U10EC;
DON	&#x10D3;	&U10D3;
EN	&#x10D4;	&U10D4;
FI	&#x10F6;	&U10F6;
GAN	&#x10D2;	&U10D2;
GHAN	&#x10E6;	&U10E6;
HAE	&#x10F0;	&U10F0;
HAR	&#x10F4;	&U10F4;
HE	&#x10F1;	&U10F1;
HIE	&#x10F2;	&U10F2;
HOE	&#x10F5;	&U10F5;

GEORGIAN LETTER (Continued)

Character	XML	SPREAD
IN	&#x10D8;	&U10D8;
JHAN	&#x10EF;	&U10EF;
JIL	&#x10EB;	&U10EB;
KAN	&#x10D9;	&U10D9;
KHAR	&#x10E5;	&U10E5;
LAS	&#x10DA;	&U10DA;
MAN	&#x10DB;	&U10DB;
NAR	&#x10DC;	&U10DC;
ON	&#x10DD;	&U10DD;
PAR	&#x10DE;	&U10DE;
PHAR	&#x10E4;	&U10E4;
QAR	&#x10E7;	&U10E7;
RAE	&#x10E0;	&U10E0;
SAN	&#x10E1;	&U10E1;
SHIN	&#x10E8;	&U10E8;
TAN	&#x10D7;	&U10D7;
TAR	&#x10E2;	&U10E2;
UN	&#x10E3;	&U10E3;
VIN	&#x10D5;	&U10D5;
WE	&#x10F3;	&U10F3;
XAN	&#x10EE;	&U10EE;
ZEN	&#x10D6;	&U10D6;
ZHAR	&#x10DF;	&U10DF;

GREEK CAPITAL LETTER

Base	XML	ISO	SPREAD	Variation
ALPHA	&#x391;	&Agr;	&U0391;	
	&#x1F09;		&U1F09;	with dasia
	&#x1F0D;		&U1F0D;	with dasia and oxia
	&#x1F8D;		&U1F8D;	with dasia and oxia and prosgegrammeni
	&#x1F8F;		&U1F8F;	with dasia and perispomeni and prosgegrammeni
	&#x1F0F;		&U1F0F;	with dasia and perispomeni
	&#x1F89;		&U1F89;	with dasia and prosgegrammeni
	&#x1F0B;		&U1F0B;	with dasia and varia
	&#x1F8B;		&U1F8B;	with dasia and varia and prosgegrammeni
	&#x1FB9;		&U1FB9;	with macron
	&#x1FBB;		&U1FBB;	with oxia
	&#x1FBC;		&U1FBC;	with prosgegrammeni
	&#x1F08;		&U1F08;	with psili
	&#x1F0C;		&U1F0C;	with psili and oxia
	&#x1F8C;		&U1F8C;	with psili and oxia and prosgegrammeni
	&#x1F8E;		&U1F8E;	with psili and perispomeni and prosgegrammeni
	&#x1F0E;		&U1F0E;	with psili and perispomeni

Base	XML	ISO	SPREAD	Variation
...ALPHA	`&#x1F88;`		`&U1F88;`	with psili and prosgegrammeni
	`&#x1F0A;`		`&U1F0A;`	with psili and varia
	`&#x1F8A;`		`&U1F8A;`	with psili and varia and prosgegrammeni
	`&#x386;`	`&Aacgr;`	`&U0386;`	with tonos
	`&#x1FBA;`		`&U1FBA;`	with varia
	`&#x1FB8;`		`&U1FB8;`	with vrachy
BETA	`&#x392;`	`&Bgr;`	`&U0392;`	
CHI	`&#x3A7;`	`&KHgr;`	`&U03A7;`	
DELTA	`&#x394;`	`&Dgr;`	`&U0394;`	
EPSILON	`&#x395;`	`&Egr;`	`&U0395;`	
	`&#x1F19;`		`&U1F19;`	with dasia
	`&#x1F1D;`		`&U1F1D;`	with dasia and oxia
	`&#x1F1B;`		`&U1F1B;`	with dasia and varia
	`&#x1FC9;`		`&U1FC9;`	with oxia
	`&#x1F18;`		`&U1F18;`	with psili
	`&#x1F1C;`		`&U1F1C;`	with psili and oxia
	`&#x1F1A;`		`&U1F1A;`	with psili and varia
	`&#x388;`	`&Eacgr;`	`&U0388;`	with tonos
	`&#x1FC8;`		`&U1FC8;`	with varia
ETA	`&#x397;`	`&EEgr;`	`&U0397;`	
	`&#x1F29;`		`&U1F29;`	with dasia
	`&#x1F2D;`		`&U1F2D;`	with dasia and oxia
	`&#x1F9D;`		`&U1F9D;`	with dasia and oxia and prosgegrammeni
	`&#x1F9F;`		`&U1F9F;`	with dasia and perispomeni and prosgegrammeni
	`&#x1F2F;`		`&U1F2F;`	with dasia and perispomeni
	`&#x1F99;`		`&U1F99;`	with dasia and prosgegrammeni
	`&#x1F2B;`		`&U1F2B;`	with dasia and varia
	`&#x1F9B;`		`&U1F9B;`	with dasia and varia and prosgegrammeni
	`&#x1FCB;`		`&U1FCB;`	with oxia
	`&#x1FCC;`		`&U1FCC;`	with prosgegrammeni
	`&#x1F28;`		`&U1F28;`	with psili
	`&#x1F2C;`		`&U1F2C;`	with psili and oxia
	`&#x1F9C;`		`&U1F9C;`	with psili and oxia and prosgegrammeni
	`&#x1F9E;`		`&U1F9E;`	with psili and perispomeni and prosgegrammeni
	`&#x1F2E;`		`&U1F2E;`	with psili and perispomeni
	`&#x1F98;`		`&U1F98;`	with psili and prosgegrammeni
	`&#x1F2A;`		`&U1F2A;`	with psili and varia
	`&#x1F9A;`		`&U1F9A;`	with psili and varia and prosgegrammeni
	`&#x389;`	`&EEacgr;`	`&U0389;`	with tonos
	`&#x1FCA;`		`&U1FCA;`	with varia
GAMMA	`&#x393;`	`&Ggr;`	`&U0393;`	
IOTA	`&#x399;`	`&Igr;`	`&U0399;`	
	`&#x1F39;`		`&U1F39;`	with dasia
	`&#x1F3D;`		`&U1F3D;`	with dasia and oxia
	`&#x1F3F;`		`&U1F3F;`	with dasia and perispomeni
	`&#x1F3B;`		`&U1F3B;`	with dasia and varia
	`&#x3AA;`	`&Idigr;`	`&U03AA;`	with dialytika
	`&#x1FD9;`		`&U1FD9;`	with macron
	`&#x1FDB;`		`&U1FDB;`	with oxia
	`&#x1F38;`		`&U1F38;`	with psili

Base	XML	ISO	SPREAD	Variation
...IOTA	`&#x1F3C;`		`&U1F3C;`	with psili and oxia
	`&#x1F3E;`		`&U1F3E;`	with psili and perispomeni
	`&#x1F3A;`		`&U1F3A;`	with psili and varia
	`&#x38A;`	`&Iacgr;`	`&U038A;`	with tonos
	`&#x1FDA;`		`&U1FDA;`	with varia
	`&#x1FD8;`		`&U1FD8;`	with vrachy
KAPPA	`&#x39A;`	`&Kgr;`	`&U039A;`	
LAMDA	`&#x39B;`	`&Lgr;`	`&U039B;`	
MU	`&#x39C;`	`&Mgr;`	`&U039C;`	
NU	`&#x39D;`	`&Ngr;`	`&U039D;`	
OMEGA	`&#x3A9;`	`&OHgr;`	`&U03A9;`	
	`&#x1F69;`		`&U1F69;`	with dasia
	`&#x1F6D;`		`&U1F6D;`	with dasia and oxia
	`&#x1FAD;`		`&U1FAD;`	with dasia and oxia and prosgegrammeni
	`&#x1FAF;`		`&U1FAF;`	with dasia and perispomeni and prosgegrammeni
	`&#x1F6F;`		`&U1F6F;`	with dasia and perispomeni
	`&#x1FA9;`		`&U1FA9;`	with dasia and prosgegrammeni
	`&#x1F6B;`		`&U1F6B;`	with dasia and varia
	`&#x1FAB;`		`&U1FAB;`	with dasia and varia and prosgegrammeni
	`&#x1FFB;`		`&U1FFB;`	with oxia
	`&#x1FFC;`		`&U1FFC;`	with prosgegrammeni
	`&#x1F68;`		`&U1F68;`	with psili
	`&#x1F6C;`		`&U1F6C;`	with psili and oxia
	`&#x1FAC;`		`&U1FAC;`	with psili and oxia and prosgegrammeni
	`&#x1FAE;`		`&U1FAE;`	with psili and perispomeni and prosgegrammeni
	`&#x1F6E;`		`&U1F6E;`	with psili and perispomeni
	`&#x1FA8;`		`&U1FA8;`	with psili and prosgegrammeni
	`&#x1F6A;`		`&U1F6A;`	with psili and varia
	`&#x1FAA;`		`&U1FAA;`	with psili and varia and prosgegrammeni
	`&#x38F;`	`&OHacgr;`	`&U038F;`	with tonos
	`&#x1FFA;`		`&U1FFA;`	with varia
OMICRON	`&#x39F;`	`&Ogr;`	`&U039F;`	
	`&#x1F49;`		`&U1F49;`	with dasia
	`&#x1F4D;`		`&U1F4D;`	with dasia and oxia
	`&#x1F4B;`		`&U1F4B;`	with dasia and varia
	`&#x1FF9;`		`&U1FF9;`	with oxia
	`&#x1F48;`		`&U1F48;`	with psili
	`&#x1F4C;`		`&U1F4C;`	with psili and oxia
	`&#x1F4A;`		`&U1F4A;`	with psili and varia
	`&#x38C;`	`&Oacgr;`	`&U038C;`	with tonos
	`&#x1FF8;`		`&U1FF8;`	with varia
PHI	`&#x3A6;`	`&PHgr;`	`&U03A6;`	
PI	`&#x3A0;`	`&Pgr;`	`&U03A0;`	
PSI	`&#x3A8;`	`&PSgr;`	`&U03A8;`	
RHO	`&#x3A1;`	`&Rgr;`	`&U03A1;`	
	`&#x1FEC;`		`&U1FEC;`	with dasia
SIGMA	`&#x3A3;`	`&Sgr;`	`&U03A3;`	
TAU	`&#x3A4;`	`&Tgr;`	`&U03A4;`	
THETA	`&#x398;`	`&THgr;`	`&U0398;`	
UPSILON	`&#x3A5;`	`&Ugr;`	`&U03A5;`	

GREEK CAPITAL LETTER (Continued)

Base	XML	ISO	SPREAD	Variation
...UPSILON	Ὑ		&U1F59;	with dasia
	Ὕ		&U1F5D;	with dasia and oxia
	Ὗ		&U1F5F;	with dasia and perispomeni
	Ὓ		&U1F5B;	with dasia and varia
	Ϋ	&Udigr;	&U03AB;	with dialytika
	Ῡ		&U1FE9;	with macron
	Ύ		&U1FEB;	with oxia
	Ύ	&Uacgr;	&U038E;	with tonos
	Ὺ		&U1FEA;	with varia
	Ῠ		&U1FE8;	with vrachy
XI	Ξ	&Xgr;	&U039E;	
ZETA	Ζ	&Zgr;	&U0396;	

GREEK LETTER

Base	XML	ISO	SPREAD	Variation
DIGAMMA	Ϝ	ϝ	&U03DC;	
KOPPA	Ϟ		&U03DE;	
SAMPI	Ϡ		&U03E0;	
STIGMA	Ϛ		&U03DA;	
YOT	ϳ		&U03F3;	

GREEK SMALL LETTER

Base	XML	ISO	SPREAD	Variation
ALPHA	α	&agr;	&U03B1;	
	ἁ		&U1F01;	with dasia
	ἅ		&U1F05;	with dasia and oxia
	ᾅ		&U1F85;	with dasia and oxia and ypogegrammeni
	ᾇ		&U1F87;	with dasia and perispomeni and ypogegrammeni
	ἇ		&U1F07;	with dasia and perispomeni
	ἃ		&U1F03;	with dasia and varia
	ᾃ		&U1F83;	with dasia and varia and ypogegrammeni
	ᾁ		&U1F81;	with dasia and ypogegrammeni
	ᾱ		&U1FB1;	with macron
	ά		&U1F71;	with oxia
	ᾴ		&U1FB4;	with oxia and ypogegrammeni
	ᾶ		&U1FB6;	with perispomeni

GREEK SMALL LETTER (Continued)

Base	XML	ISO	SPREAD	Variation
...ALPHA	`&#x1FB7;`		`&U1FB7;`	with perispomeni and ypogegrammeni
	`&#x1F00;`		`&U1F00;`	with psili
	`&#x1F04;`		`&U1F04;`	with psili and oxia
	`&#x1F84;`		`&U1F84;`	with psili and oxia and ypogegrammeni
	`&#x1F86;`		`&U1F86;`	with psili and perispomeni and ypogegrammeni
	`&#x1F06;`		`&U1F06;`	with psili and perispomeni
	`&#x1F02;`		`&U1F02;`	with psili and varia
	`&#x1F82;`		`&U1F82;`	with psili and varia and ypogegrammeni
	`&#x1F80;`		`&U1F80;`	with psili and ypogegrammeni
	`&#x3AC;`	`&aacgr;`	`&U03AC;`	with tonos
	`&#x1F70;`		`&U1F70;`	with varia
	`&#x1FB2;`		`&U1FB2;`	with varia and ypogegrammeni
	`&#x1FB0;`		`&U1FB0;`	with vrachy
	`&#x1FB3;`		`&U1FB3;`	with ypogegrammeni
BETA	`&#x3B2;`	`&bgr;`	`&U03B2;`	
CHI	`&#x3C7;`	`&khgr;`	`&U03C7;`	
DELTA	`&#x3B4;`	`&dgr;`	`&U03B4;`	
EPSILON	`&#x3B5;`	`&egr;`	`&U03B5;`	
	`&#x1F11;`		`&U1F11;`	with dasia
	`&#x1F15;`		`&U1F15;`	with dasia and oxia
	`&#x1F13;`		`&U1F13;`	with dasia and varia
	`&#x1F73;`		`&U1F73;`	with oxia
	`&#x1F10;`		`&U1F10;`	with psili
	`&#x1F14;`		`&U1F14;`	with psili and oxia
	`&#x1F12;`		`&U1F12;`	with psili and varia
	`&#x3AD;`	`&eacgr;`	`&U03AD;`	with tonos
	`&#x1F72;`		`&U1F72;`	with varia
ETA	`&#x3B7;`	`&eegr;`	`&U03B7;`	
	`&#x1F21;`		`&U1F21;`	with dasia
	`&#x1F25;`		`&U1F25;`	with dasia and oxia
	`&#x1F95;`		`&U1F95;`	with dasia and oxia and ypogegrammeni
	`&#x1F27;`		`&U1F27;`	with dasia and perispomeni
	`&#x1F97;`		`&U1F97;`	with dasia and perispomeni and ypogegrammeni
	`&#x1F23;`		`&U1F23;`	with dasia and varia
	`&#x1F93;`		`&U1F93;`	with dasia and varia and ypogegrammeni
	`&#x1F91;`		`&U1F91;`	with dasia and ypogegrammeni
	`&#x1F75;`		`&U1F75;`	with oxia
	`&#x1FC4;`		`&U1FC4;`	with oxia and ypogegrammeni
	`&#x1FC6;`		`&U1FC6;`	with perispomeni
	`&#x1FC7;`		`&U1FC7;`	with perispomeni and ypogegrammeni
	`&#x1F20;`		`&U1F20;`	with psili
	`&#x1F24;`		`&U1F24;`	with psili and oxia
	`&#x1F94;`		`&U1F94;`	with psili and oxia and ypogegrammeni
	`&#x1F26;`		`&U1F26;`	with psili and perispomeni
	`&#x1F96;`		`&U1F96;`	with psili and perispomeni and ypogegrammeni
	`&#x1F22;`		`&U1F22;`	with psili and varia
	`&#x1F92;`		`&U1F92;`	with psili and varia and ypogegrammeni
	`&#x1F90;`		`&U1F90;`	with psili and ypogegrammeni
	`&#x3AE;`	`&eeacgr;`	`&U03AE;`	with tonos
	`&#x1F74;`		`&U1F74;`	with varia

GREEK SMALL LETTER (Continued)

Base	XML	ISO	SPREAD	Variation
...ETA	ῂ		&U1FC2;	with varia and ypogegrammeni
	ῃ		&U1FC3;	with ypogegrammeni
FINAL SIGMA	ς	&sfgr;	&U03C2;	
GAMMA	γ	&ggr;	&U03B3;	
IOTA	ι	&igr;	&U03B9;	
	ἱ		&U1F31;	with dasia
	ἵ		&U1F35;	with dasia and oxia
	ἷ		&U1F37;	with dasia and perispomeni
	ἳ		&U1F33;	with dasia and varia
	ϊ	&idigr;	&U03CA;	with dialytika
	ΐ		&U1FD3;	with dialytika and oxia
	ῗ		&U1FD7;	with dialytika and perispomeni
	ΐ	&idiagr;	&U0390;	with dialytika and tonos
	ῒ		&U1FD2;	with dialytika and varia
	ῑ		&U1FD1;	with macron
	ί		&U1F77;	with oxia
	ῖ		&U1FD6;	with perispomeni
	ἰ		&U1F30;	with psili
	ἴ		&U1F34;	with psili and oxia
	ἶ		&U1F36;	with psili and perispomeni
	ἲ		&U1F32;	with psili and varia
	ί	&iacgr;	&U03AF;	with tonos
	ὶ		&U1F76;	with varia
	ῐ		&U1FD0;	with vrachy
KAPPA	κ	&kgr;	&U03BA;	
LAMDA	λ	&lgr;	&U03BB;	
MU	μ	&mgr;	&U03BC;	
NU	ν	&ngr;	&U03BD;	
OMEGA	ω	&ohgr;	&U03C9;	
	ὡ		&U1F61;	with dasia
	ὥ		&U1F65;	with dasia and oxia
	ᾥ		&U1FA5;	with dasia and oxia and ypogegrammeni
	ᾧ		&U1FA7;	with dasia and perispomeni and ypogegrammeni
	ὧ		&U1F67;	with dasia and perispomeni
	ὣ		&U1F63;	with dasia and varia
	ᾣ		&U1FA3;	with dasia and varia and ypogegrammeni
	ᾡ		&U1FA1;	with dasia and ypogegrammeni
	ώ		&U1F7D;	with oxia
	ῴ		&U1FF4;	with oxia and ypogegrammeni
	ῶ		&U1FF6;	with perispomeni
	ῷ		&U1FF7;	with perispomeni and ypogegrammeni
	ὠ		&U1F60;	with psili
	ὤ		&U1F64;	with psili and oxia
	ᾤ		&U1FA4;	with psili and oxia and ypogegrammeni
	ᾦ		&U1FA6;	with psili and perispomeni and ypogegrammeni
	ὦ		&U1F66;	with psili and perispomeni
	ὢ		&U1F62;	with psili and varia
	ᾢ		&U1FA2;	with psili and varia and ypogegrammeni
	ᾠ		&U1FA0;	with psili and ypogegrammeni
	ώ	&ohacgr;	&U03CE;	with tonos

GREEK SMALL LETTER (Continued)

Base	XML	ISO	SPREAD	Variation
...OMEGA	ὼ		&U1F7C;	with varia
	ῲ		&U1FF2;	with varia and ypogegrammeni
	ῳ		&U1FF3;	with ypogegrammeni
OMICRON	ο	&ogr;	&U03BF;	
	ὁ		&U1F41;	with dasia
	ὅ		&U1F45;	with dasia and oxia
	ὃ		&U1F43;	with dasia and varia
	ό		&U1F79;	with oxia
	ὀ		&U1F40;	with psili
	ὄ		&U1F44;	with psili and oxia
	ὂ		&U1F42;	with psili and varia
	ό	&oacgr;	&U03CC;	with tonos
	ὸ		&U1F78;	with varia
PHI	φ	&phgr;	&U03C6;	
PI	π	&pgr;	&U03C0;	
PSI	ψ	&psgr;	&U03C8;	
RHO	ρ	&rgr;	&U03C1;	
	ῥ		&U1FE5;	with dasia
	ῤ		&U1FE4;	with psili
SIGMA	σ	&sgr;	&U03C3;	
TAU	τ	&tgr;	&U03C4;	
THETA	θ	&thgr;	&U03B8;	
UPSILON	υ	&ugr;	&U03C5;	
	ὑ		&U1F51;	with dasia
	ὕ		&U1F55;	with dasia and oxia
	ὗ		&U1F57;	with dasia and perispomeni
	ὓ		&U1F53;	with dasia and varia
	ϋ	&udigr;	&U03CB;	with dialytika
	ΰ		&U1FE3;	with dialytika and oxia
	ῧ		&U1FE7;	with dialytika and perispomeni
	ΰ	&udiagr;	&U03B0;	with dialytika and tonos
	ῢ		&U1FE2;	with dialytika and varia
	ῡ		&U1FE1;	with macron
	ύ		&U1F7B;	with oxia
	ῦ		&U1FE6;	with perispomeni
	ὐ		&U1F50;	with psili
	ὔ		&U1F54;	with psili and oxia
	ὖ		&U1F56;	with psili and perispomeni
	ὒ		&U1F52;	with psili and varia
	ύ	&uacgr;	&U03CD;	with tonos
	ὺ		&U1F7A;	with varia
	ῠ		&U1FE0;	with vrachy
XI	ξ	&xgr;	&U03BE;	
ZETA	ζ	&zgr;	&U03B6;	

Other Greek

Character	XML	ISO	SPREAD
COMBINING GREEK DIALYTIKA TONOS	&#x344;		&U0344;
COMBINING GREEK KORONIS	&#x343;		&U0343;
COMBINING GREEK PERISPOMENI	&#x342;		&U0342;
COMBINING GREEK YPOGEGRAMMENI	&#x345;		&U0345;
GREEK BETA SYMBOL	&#x3D0;		&U03D0;
GREEK KAPPA SYMBOL	&#x3F0;	&kappav;	&U03F0;
GREEK LUNATE SIGMA SYMBOL	&#x3F2;		&U03F2;
GREEK PHI SYMBOL	&#x3D5;	&phiv;	&U03D5;
GREEK PI SYMBOL	&#x3D6;	&piv;	&U03D6;
GREEK PROSGEGRAMMENI	&#x1FBE;		&U1FBE;
GREEK RHO SYMBOL	&#x3F1;	&rhov;	&U03F1;
GREEK THETA SYMBOL	&#x3D1;	&thetav;	&U03D1;
GREEK UPSILON WITH ACUTE AND HOOK SYMBOL	&#x3D3;		&U03D3;
GREEK UPSILON WITH DIAERESIS AND HOOK SYMBOL	&#x3D4;		&U03D4;
GREEK UPSILON WITH HOOK SYMBOL	&#x3D2;		&U03D2;
Greek dasia	&#x1FFE;		&U1FFE;
Greek dasia and oxia	&#x1FDE;		&U1FDE;
Greek dasia and perispomeni	&#x1FDF;		&U1FDF;
Greek dasia and varia	&#x1FDD;		&U1FDD;
Greek dialytika and oxia	&#x1FEE;		&U1FEE;
Greek dialytika and perispomeni	&#x1FC1;		&U1FC1;
Greek dialytika and varia	&#x1FED;		&U1FED;
Greek dialytika tonos	&#x385;		&U0385;
Greek koronis	&#x1FBD;		&U1FBD;
Greek lower numeral sign	&#x375;		&U0375;
Greek numeral sign	&#x374;		&U0374;
Greek oxia	&#x1FFD;		&U1FFD;
Greek perispomeni	&#x1FC0;		&U1FC0;
Greek psili	&#x1FBF;		&U1FBF;
Greek psili and oxia	&#x1FCE;		&U1FCE;
Greek psili and perispomeni	&#x1FCF;		&U1FCF;
Greek psili and varia	&#x1FCD;		&U1FCD;
Greek tonos	&#x384;		&U0384;
Greek varia	&#x1FEF;		&U1FEF;
Greek ypogegrammeni	&#x37A;		&U037A;

GUJARATI LETTER

Character	XML	SPREAD
A	&#xA85;	&U0A85;
AA	&#xA86;	&U0A86;
AI	&#xA90;	&U0A90;
AU	&#xA94;	&U0A94;
BA	&#xAAC;	&U0AAC;
BHA	&#xAAD;	&U0AAD;
CA	&#xA9A;	&U0A9A;
CHA	&#xA9B;	&U0A9B;
DA	&#xAA6;	&U0AA6;
DDA	&#xAA1;	&U0AA1;
DDHA	&#xAA2;	&U0AA2;
DHA	&#xAA7;	&U0AA7;
E	&#xA8F;	&U0A8F;
GA	&#xA97;	&U0A97;
GHA	&#xA98;	&U0A98;
HA	&#xAB9;	&U0AB9;
I	&#xA87;	&U0A87;
II	&#xA88;	&U0A88;
JA	&#xA9C;	&U0A9C;
JHA	&#xA9D;	&U0A9D;
KA	&#xA95;	&U0A95;
KHA	&#xA96;	&U0A96;
LA	&#xAB2;	&U0AB2;
LLA	&#xAB3;	&U0AB3;
MA	&#xAAE;	&U0AAE;
NA	&#xAA8;	&U0AA8;
NGA	&#xA99;	&U0A99;
NNA	&#xAA3;	&U0AA3;
NYA	&#xA9E;	&U0A9E;
O	&#xA93;	&U0A93;
PA	&#xAAA;	&U0AAA;
PHA	&#xAAB;	&U0AAB;
RA	&#xAB0;	&U0AB0;
SA	&#xAB8;	&U0AB8;
SHA	&#xAB6;	&U0AB6;
SSA	&#xAB7;	&U0AB7;
TA	&#xAA4;	&U0AA4;
THA	&#xAA5;	&U0AA5;
TTA	&#xA9F;	&U0A9F;
TTHA	&#xAA0;	&U0AA0;
U	&#xA89;	&U0A89;
UU	&#xA8A;	&U0A8A;
VA	&#xAB5;	&U0AB5;
VOCALIC R	&#xA8B;	&U0A8B;
VOCALIC RR	&#xAE0;	&U0AE0;
YA	&#xAAF;	&U0AAF;

GUJARATI SIGN

Character	XML	SPREAD
ANUSVARA	&#xA82;	&U0A82;
CANDRABINDU	&#xA81;	&U0A81;
NUKTA	&#xABC;	&U0ABC;
VIRAMA	&#xACD;	&U0ACD;
VISARGA	&#xA83;	&U0A83;

GUJARATI VOWEL SIGN

Character	XML	SPREAD
AA	&#xABE;	&U0ABE;
AI	&#xAC8;	&U0AC8;
AU	&#xACC;	&U0ACC;
CANDRA E	&#xAC5;	&U0AC5;
CANDRA O	&#xAC9;	&U0AC9;
E	&#xAC7;	&U0AC7;
I	&#xABF;	&U0ABF;
II	&#xAC0;	&U0AC0;
O	&#xACB;	&U0ACB;
U	&#xAC1;	&U0AC1;
UU	&#xAC2;	&U0AC2;
VOCALIC R	&#xAC3;	&U0AC3;
VOCALIC RR	&#xAC4;	&U0AC4;

Other Gujarati

Character	XML	SPREAD
GUJARATI VOWEL CANDRA E	&#xA8D;	&U0A8D;
GUJARATI VOWEL CANDRA O	&#xA91;	&U0A91;

Gujarati Numerals

Character	XML	SPREAD
gujarati digit eight	&#xAEE;	&U0AEE;
gujarati digit five	&#xAEB;	&U0AEB;
gujarati digit four	&#xAEA;	&U0AEA;
gujarati digit nine	&#xAEF;	&U0AEF;
gujarati digit one	&#xAE7;	&U0AE7;
gujarati digit seven	&#xAED;	&U0AED;
gujarati digit six	&#xAEC;	&U0AEC;
gujarati digit three	&#xAE9;	&U0AE9;
gujarati digit two	&#xAE8;	&U0AE8;
gujarati digit zero	&#xAE6;	&U0AE6;

GURMUKHI LETTER

Character	XML	SPREAD
A	&#xA05;	&U0A05;
AA	&#xA06;	&U0A06;
AI	&#xA10;	&U0A10;
AU	&#xA14;	&U0A14;
BA	&#xA2C;	&U0A2C;
BHA	&#xA2D;	&U0A2D;
CA	&#xA1A;	&U0A1A;
CHA	&#xA1B;	&U0A1B;
DA	&#xA26;	&U0A26;
DDA	&#xA21;	&U0A21;
DDHA	&#xA22;	&U0A22;
DHA	&#xA27;	&U0A27;
EE	&#xA0F;	&U0A0F;
FA	&#xA5E;	&U0A5E;
GA	&#xA17;	&U0A17;
GHA	&#xA18;	&U0A18;
GHHA	&#xA5A;	&U0A5A;
HA	&#xA39;	&U0A39;
I	&#xA07;	&U0A07;
II	&#xA08;	&U0A08;
JA	&#xA1C;	&U0A1C;
JHA	&#xA1D;	&U0A1D;
KA	&#xA15;	&U0A15;
KHA	&#xA16;	&U0A16;
KHHA	&#xA59;	&U0A59;
LA	&#xA32;	&U0A32;
LLA	&#xA33;	&U0A33;
MA	&#xA2E;	&U0A2E;
NA	&#xA28;	&U0A28;
NGA	&#xA19;	&U0A19;

GURMUKHI LETTER (Continued)

Character	XML	SPREAD
NNA	ਣ	&U0A23;
NYA	ਞ	&U0A1E;
OO	ਓ	&U0A13;
PA	ਪ	&U0A2A;
PHA	ਫ	&U0A2B;
RA	ਰ	&U0A30;
RRA	ੜ	&U0A5C;
SA	ਸ	&U0A38;
SHA	ਸ਼	&U0A36;
TA	ਤ	&U0A24;
THA	ਥ	&U0A25;
TTA	ਟ	&U0A1F;
TTHA	ਠ	&U0A20;
U	ਉ	&U0A09;
UU	ਊ	&U0A0A;
VA	ਵ	&U0A35;
YA	ਯ	&U0A2F;
ZA	ਜ਼	&U0A5B;

GURMUKHI VOWEL SIGN

Character	XML	SPREAD
AA	ਾ	&U0A3E;
AI	ੈ	&U0A48;
AU	ੌ	&U0A4C;
EE	ੇ	&U0A47;
I	ਿ	&U0A3F;
II	ੀ	&U0A40;
OO	ੋ	&U0A4B;
U	ੁ	&U0A41;
UU	ੂ	&U0A42;

Other Gurmukhi

Character	XML	SPREAD
GURMUKHI ADDAK	&#xA71;	&U0A71;
GURMUKHI SIGN BINDI	&#xA02;	&U0A02;
GURMUKHI SIGN NUKTA	&#xA3C;	&U0A3C;
GURMUKHI SIGN VIRAMA	&#xA4D;	&U0A4D;
GURMUKHI TIPPI	&#xA70;	&U0A70;
gurmukhi ek onkar	&#xA74;	&U0A74;
gurmukhi iri	&#xA72;	&U0A72;
gurmukhi ura	&#xA73;	&U0A73;

Gurmikhi Numerals

Character	XML	SPREAD
gurmukhi digit eight	&#xA6E;	&U0A6E;
gurmukhi digit five	&#xA6B;	&U0A6B;
gurmukhi digit four	&#xA6A;	&U0A6A;
gurmukhi digit nine	&#xA6F;	&U0A6F;
gurmukhi digit one	&#xA67;	&U0A67;
gurmukhi digit seven	&#xA6D;	&U0A6D;
gurmukhi digit six	&#xA6C;	&U0A6C;
gurmukhi digit three	&#xA69;	&U0A69;
gurmukhi digit two	&#xA68;	&U0A68;
gurmukhi digit zero	&#xA66;	&U0A66;

HEBREW LETTER

Character	XML	SPREAD
ALEF	&#x5D0;	&U05D0;
AYIN	&#x5E2;	&U05E2;
BET	&#x5D1;	&U05D1;
DALET	&#x5D3;	&U05D3;
FINAL KAF	&#x5DA;	&U05DA;
FINAL MEM	&#x5DD;	&U05DD;
FINAL NUN	&#x5DF;	&U05DF;
FINAL PE	&#x5E3;	&U05E3;
FINAL TSADI	&#x5E5;	&U05E5;
GIMEL	&#x5D2;	&U05D2;
HE	&#x5D4;	&U05D4;
HET	&#x5D7;	&U05D7;

HEBREW LETTER (Continued)

Character	XML	SPREAD
KAF	`&#x5DB;`	`&U05DB;`
LAMED	`&#x5DC;`	`&U05DC;`
MEM	`&#x5DE;`	`&U05DE;`
NUN	`&#x5E0;`	`&U05E0;`
PE	`&#x5E4;`	`&U05E4;`
QOF	`&#x5E7;`	`&U05E7;`
RESH	`&#x5E8;`	`&U05E8;`
SAMEKH	`&#x5E1;`	`&U05E1;`
SHIN	`&#x5E9;`	`&U05E9;`
TAV	`&#x5EA;`	`&U05EA;`
TET	`&#x5D8;`	`&U05D8;`
TSADI	`&#x5E6;`	`&U05E6;`
VAV	`&#x5D5;`	`&U05D5;`
YOD	`&#x5D9;`	`&U05D9;`
ZAYIN	`&#x5D6;`	`&U05D6;`

Other Hebrew

Character	XML	SPREAD
HEBREW ACCENT DARGA	`&#x5A7;`	`&U05A7;`
HEBREW ACCENT DEHI	`&#x5AD;`	`&U05AD;`
HEBREW ACCENT ETNAHTA	`&#x591;`	`&U0591;`
HEBREW ACCENT GERESH	`&#x59C;`	`&U059C;`
HEBREW ACCENT GERESH MUQDAM	`&#x59D;`	`&U059D;`
HEBREW ACCENT GERSHAYIM	`&#x59E;`	`&U059E;`
HEBREW ACCENT ILUY	`&#x5AC;`	`&U05AC;`
HEBREW ACCENT MAHAPAKH	`&#x5A4;`	`&U05A4;`
HEBREW ACCENT MERKHA	`&#x5A5;`	`&U05A5;`
HEBREW ACCENT MERKHA KEFULA	`&#x5A6;`	`&U05A6;`
HEBREW ACCENT MUNAH	`&#x5A3;`	`&U05A3;`
HEBREW ACCENT OLE	`&#x5AB;`	`&U05AB;`
HEBREW ACCENT PASHTA	`&#x599;`	`&U0599;`
HEBREW ACCENT PAZER	`&#x5A1;`	`&U05A1;`
HEBREW ACCENT QADMA	`&#x5A8;`	`&U05A8;`
HEBREW ACCENT QARNEY PARA	`&#x59F;`	`&U059F;`
HEBREW ACCENT REVIA	`&#x597;`	`&U0597;`
HEBREW ACCENT SEGOL	`&#x592;`	`&U0592;`
HEBREW ACCENT SHALSHELET	`&#x593;`	`&U0593;`
HEBREW ACCENT TELISHA GEDOLA	`&#x5A0;`	`&U05A0;`
HEBREW ACCENT TELISHA QETANA	`&#x5A9;`	`&U05A9;`
HEBREW ACCENT TEVIR	`&#x59B;`	`&U059B;`
HEBREW ACCENT TIPEHA	`&#x596;`	`&U0596;`
HEBREW ACCENT YERAH BEN YOMO	`&#x5AA;`	`&U05AA;`
HEBREW ACCENT YETIV	`&#x59A;`	`&U059A;`

Other Hebrew (Continued)

Character	XML	SPREAD
HEBREW ACCENT ZAQEF GADOL	&#x595;	&U0595;
HEBREW ACCENT ZAQEF QATAN	&#x594;	&U0594;
HEBREW ACCENT ZARQA	&#x598;	&U0598;
HEBREW ACCENT ZINOR	&#x5AE;	&U05AE;
HEBREW LIGATURE YIDDISH DOUBLE VAV	&#x5F0;	&U05F0;
HEBREW LIGATURE YIDDISH DOUBLE YOD	&#x5F2;	&U05F2;
HEBREW LIGATURE YIDDISH VAV YOD	&#x5F1;	&U05F1;
HEBREW MARK MASORA CIRCLE	&#x5AF;	&U05AF;
HEBREW MARK UPPER DOT	&#x5C4;	&U05C4;
HEBREW POINT DAGESH OR MAPIQ	&#x5BC;	&U05BC;
HEBREW POINT HATAF PATAH	&#x5B2;	&U05B2;
HEBREW POINT HATAF QAMATS	&#x5B3;	&U05B3;
HEBREW POINT HATAF SEGOL	&#x5B1;	&U05B1;
HEBREW POINT HIRIQ	&#x5B4;	&U05B4;
HEBREW POINT HOLAM	&#x5B9;	&U05B9;
HEBREW POINT METEG	&#x5BD;	&U05BD;
HEBREW POINT PATAH	&#x5B7;	&U05B7;
HEBREW POINT QAMATS	&#x5B8;	&U05B8;
HEBREW POINT QUBUTS	&#x5BB;	&U05BB;
HEBREW POINT RAFE	&#x5BF;	&U05BF;
HEBREW POINT SEGOL	&#x5B6;	&U05B6;
HEBREW POINT SHEVA	&#x5B0;	&U05B0;
HEBREW POINT SHIN DOT	&#x5C1;	&U05C1;
HEBREW POINT SIN DOT	&#x5C2;	&U05C2;
HEBREW POINT TSERE	&#x5B5;	&U05B5;

Hebrew Punctuation

Character	XML	SPREAD
geresh	&#x5F3;	&U05F3;
gershayim	&#x5F4;	&U05F4;
maqaf	&#x5BE;	&U05BE;
paseq	&#x5C0;	&U05C0;
sof pasuq	&#x5C3;	&U05C3;

HIRAGANA LETTER

Character	XML	SPREAD
A	あ	&U3042;
BA	ば	&U3070;
BE	べ	&U3079;
BI	び	&U3073;
BO	ぼ	&U307C;
BU	ぶ	&U3076;
DA	だ	&U3060;
DE	で	&U3067;
DI	ぢ	&U3062;
DO	ど	&U3069;
DU	づ	&U3065;
E	え	&U3048;
GA	が	&U304C;
GE	げ	&U3052;
GI	ぎ	&U304E;
GO	ご	&U3054;
GU	ぐ	&U3050;
HA	は	&U306F;
HE	へ	&U3078;
HI	ひ	&U3072;
HO	ほ	&U307B;
HU	ふ	&U3075;
I	い	&U3044;
KA	か	&U304B;
KE	け	&U3051;
KI	き	&U304D;
KO	こ	&U3053;
KU	く	&U304F;
MA	ま	&U307E;
ME	め	&U3081;
MI	み	&U307F;
MO	も	&U3082;
MU	む	&U3080;
N	ん	&U3093;
NA	な	&U306A;
NE	ね	&U306D;
NI	に	&U306B;
NO	の	&U306E;
NU	ぬ	&U306C;
O	お	&U304A;
PA	ぱ	&U3071;
PE	ぺ	&U307A;
PI	ぴ	&U3074;
PO	ぽ	&U307D;
PU	ぷ	&U3077;
RA	ら	&U3089;
RE	れ	&U308C;
RI	り	&U308A;
RO	ろ	&U308D;

HIRAGANA LETTER (Continued)

Character	XML	SPREAD
RU	&#x308B;	&U308B;
SA	&#x3055;	&U3055;
SE	&#x305B;	&U305B;
SI	&#x3057;	&U3057;
SMALL A	&#x3041;	&U3041;
SMALL E	&#x3047;	&U3047;
SMALL I	&#x3043;	&U3043;
SMALL O	&#x3049;	&U3049;
SMALL TU	&#x3063;	&U3063;
SMALL U	&#x3045;	&U3045;
SMALL WA	&#x308E;	&U308E;
SMALL YA	&#x3083;	&U3083;
SMALL YO	&#x3087;	&U3087;
SMALL YU	&#x3085;	&U3085;
SO	&#x305D;	&U305D;
SU	&#x3059;	&U3059;
TA	&#x305F;	&U305F;
TE	&#x3066;	&U3066;
TI	&#x3061;	&U3061;
TO	&#x3068;	&U3068;
TU	&#x3064;	&U3064;
U	&#x3046;	&U3046;
VU	&#x3094;	&U3094;
WA	&#x308F;	&U308F;
WE	&#x3091;	&U3091;
WI	&#x3090;	&U3090;
WO	&#x3092;	&U3092;
YA	&#x3084;	&U3084;
YO	&#x3088;	&U3088;
YU	&#x3086;	&U3086;
ZA	&#x3056;	&U3056;
ZE	&#x305C;	&U305C;
ZI	&#x3058;	&U3058;
ZO	&#x305E;	&U305E;
ZU	&#x305A;	&U305A;

KANNADA LETTER

Character	XML	SPREAD
A	&#xC85;	&U0C85;
AA	&#xC86;	&U0C86;
AI	&#xC90;	&U0C90;
AU	&#xC94;	&U0C94;
BA	&#xCAC;	&U0CAC;
BHA	&#xCAD;	&U0CAD;

KANNADA LETTER (Continued)

Character	XML	SPREAD
CA	ಚ	&U0C9A;
CHA	ಛ	&U0C9B;
DA	ದ	&U0CA6;
DDA	ಡ	&U0CA1;
DDHA	ಢ	&U0CA2;
DHA	ಧ	&U0CA7;
E	ಎ	&U0C8E;
EE	ಏ	&U0C8F;
FA	ೞ	&U0CDE;
GA	ಗ	&U0C97;
GHA	ಘ	&U0C98;
HA	ಹ	&U0CB9;
I	ಇ	&U0C87;
II	ಈ	&U0C88;
JA	ಜ	&U0C9C;
JHA	ಝ	&U0C9D;
KA	ಕ	&U0C95;
KHA	ಖ	&U0C96;
LA	ಲ	&U0CB2;
LLA	ಳ	&U0CB3;
MA	ಮ	&U0CAE;
NA	ನ	&U0CA8;
NGA	ಙ	&U0C99;
NNA	ಣ	&U0CA3;
NYA	ಞ	&U0C9E;
O	ಒ	&U0C92;
OO	ಓ	&U0C93;
PA	ಪ	&U0CAA;
PHA	ಫ	&U0CAB;
RA	ರ	&U0CB0;
RRA	ಱ	&U0CB1;
SA	ಸ	&U0CB8;
SHA	ಶ	&U0CB6;
SSA	ಷ	&U0CB7;
TA	ತ	&U0CA4;
THA	ಥ	&U0CA5;
TTA	ಟ	&U0C9F;
TTHA	ಠ	&U0CA0;
U	ಉ	&U0C89;
UU	ಊ	&U0C8A;
VA	ವ	&U0CB5;
VOCALIC L	ಌ	&U0C8C;
VOCALIC LL	ೡ	&U0CE1;
VOCALIC R	ಋ	&U0C8B;
VOCALIC RR	ೠ	&U0CE0;
YA	ಯ	&U0CAF;

KANNADA VOWEL SIGN

Character	XML	SPREAD
AA	`&#xCBE;`	`&U0CBE;`
AI	`&#xCC8;`	`&U0CC8;`
AU	`&#xCCC;`	`&U0CCC;`
E	`&#xCC6;`	`&U0CC6;`
EE	`&#xCC7;`	`&U0CC7;`
I	`&#xCBF;`	`&U0CBF;`
II	`&#xCC0;`	`&U0CC0;`
O	`&#xCCA;`	`&U0CCA;`
OO	`&#xCCB;`	`&U0CCB;`
U	`&#xCC1;`	`&U0CC1;`
UU	`&#xCC2;`	`&U0CC2;`
VOCALIC R	`&#xCC3;`	`&U0CC3;`
VOCALIC RR	`&#xCC4;`	`&U0CC4;`

Other Kannada

Character	XML	SPREAD
KANNADA AI LENGTH MARK	`&#xCD6;`	`&U0CD6;`
KANNADA LENGTH MARK	`&#xCD5;`	`&U0CD5;`
KANNADA SIGN ANUSVARA	`&#xC82;`	`&U0C82;`
KANNADA SIGN VIRAMA	`&#xCCD;`	`&U0CCD;`
KANNADA SIGN VISARGA	`&#xC83;`	`&U0C83;`

Kannada Numerals

Character	XML	SPREAD
kannada digit eight	`&#xCEE;`	`&U0CEE;`
kannada digit five	`&#xCEB;`	`&U0CEB;`
kannada digit four	`&#xCEA;`	`&U0CEA;`
kannada digit nine	`&#xCEF;`	`&U0CEF;`
kannada digit one	`&#xCE7;`	`&U0CE7;`
kannada digit seven	`&#xCED;`	`&U0CED;`
kannada digit six	`&#xCEC;`	`&U0CEC;`
kannada digit three	`&#xCE9;`	`&U0CE9;`
kannada digit two	`&#xCE8;`	`&U0CE8;`
kannada digit zero	`&#xCE6;`	`&U0CE6;`

KATAKANA LETTER

Character	XML	SPREAD
A	&#x30A2;	&U30A2;
BA	&#x30D0;	&U30D0;
BE	&#x30D9;	&U30D9;
BI	&#x30D3;	&U30D3;
BO	&#x30DC;	&U30DC;
BU	&#x30D6;	&U30D6;
DA	&#x30C0;	&U30C0;
DE	&#x30C7;	&U30C7;
DI	&#x30C2;	&U30C2;
DO	&#x30C9;	&U30C9;
DU	&#x30C5;	&U30C5;
E	&#x30A8;	&U30A8;
GA	&#x30AC;	&U30AC;
GE	&#x30B2;	&U30B2;
GI	&#x30AE;	&U30AE;
GO	&#x30B4;	&U30B4;
GU	&#x30B0;	&U30B0;
HA	&#x30CF;	&U30CF;
HE	&#x30D8;	&U30D8;
HI	&#x30D2;	&U30D2;
HO	&#x30DB;	&U30DB;
HU	&#x30D5;	&U30D5;
I	&#x30A4;	&U30A4;
KA	&#x30AB;	&U30AB;
KE	&#x30B1;	&U30B1;
KI	&#x30AD;	&U30AD;
KO	&#x30B3;	&U30B3;
KU	&#x30AF;	&U30AF;
MA	&#x30DE;	&U30DE;
ME	&#x30E1;	&U30E1;
MI	&#x30DF;	&U30DF;
MO	&#x30E2;	&U30E2;
MU	&#x30E0;	&U30E0;
N	&#x30F3;	&U30F3;
NA	&#x30CA;	&U30CA;
NE	&#x30CD;	&U30CD;
NI	&#x30CB;	&U30CB;
NO	&#x30CE;	&U30CE;
NU	&#x30CC;	&U30CC;
O	&#x30AA;	&U30AA;
PA	&#x30D1;	&U30D1;
PE	&#x30DA;	&U30DA;
PI	&#x30D4;	&U30D4;
PO	&#x30DD;	&U30DD;
PU	&#x30D7;	&U30D7;
RA	&#x30E9;	&U30E9;
RE	&#x30EC;	&U30EC;
RI	&#x30EA;	&U30EA;
RO	&#x30ED;	&U30ED;

KATAKANA LETTER (Continued)

Character	XML	SPREAD
RU	ル	&U30EB;
SA	サ	&U30B5;
SE	セ	&U30BB;
SI	シ	&U30B7;
SMALL A	ァ	&U30A1;
SMALL E	ェ	&U30A7;
SMALL I	ィ	&U30A3;
SMALL KA	ヵ	&U30F5;
SMALL KE	ヶ	&U30F6;
SMALL O	ォ	&U30A9;
SMALL TU	ッ	&U30C3;
SMALL U	ゥ	&U30A5;
SMALL WA	ヮ	&U30EE;
SMALL YA	ャ	&U30E3;
SMALL YO	ョ	&U30E7;
SMALL YU	ュ	&U30E5;
SO	ソ	&U30BD;
SU	ス	&U30B9;
TA	タ	&U30BF;
TE	テ	&U30C6;
TI	チ	&U30C1;
TO	ト	&U30C8;
TU	ツ	&U30C4;
U	ウ	&U30A6;
VA	ヷ	&U30F7;
VE	ヹ	&U30F9;
VI	ヸ	&U30F8;
VO	ヺ	&U30FA;
VU	ヴ	&U30F4;
WA	ワ	&U30EF;
WE	ヱ	&U30F1;
WI	ヰ	&U30F0;
WO	ヲ	&U30F2;
YA	ヤ	&U30E4;
YO	ヨ	&U30E8;
YU	ユ	&U30E6;
ZA	ザ	&U30B6;
ZE	ゼ	&U30BC;
ZI	ジ	&U30B8;
ZO	ゾ	&U30BE;
ZU	ズ	&U30BA;

Other Kana

Character	XML	SPREAD
CIRCLED KATAKANA A	&#x32D0;	&U32D0;
CIRCLED KATAKANA E	&#x32D3;	&U32D3;
CIRCLED KATAKANA HA	&#x32E9;	&U32E9;
CIRCLED KATAKANA HE	&#x32EC;	&U32EC;
CIRCLED KATAKANA HI	&#x32EA;	&U32EA;
CIRCLED KATAKANA HO	&#x32ED;	&U32ED;
CIRCLED KATAKANA HU	&#x32EB;	&U32EB;
CIRCLED KATAKANA I	&#x32D1;	&U32D1;
CIRCLED KATAKANA KA	&#x32D5;	&U32D5;
CIRCLED KATAKANA KE	&#x32D8;	&U32D8;
CIRCLED KATAKANA KI	&#x32D6;	&U32D6;
CIRCLED KATAKANA KO	&#x32D9;	&U32D9;
CIRCLED KATAKANA KU	&#x32D7;	&U32D7;
CIRCLED KATAKANA MA	&#x32EE;	&U32EE;
CIRCLED KATAKANA ME	&#x32F1;	&U32F1;
CIRCLED KATAKANA MI	&#x32EF;	&U32EF;
CIRCLED KATAKANA MO	&#x32F2;	&U32F2;
CIRCLED KATAKANA MU	&#x32F0;	&U32F0;
CIRCLED KATAKANA NA	&#x32E4;	&U32E4;
CIRCLED KATAKANA NE	&#x32E7;	&U32E7;
CIRCLED KATAKANA NI	&#x32E5;	&U32E5;
CIRCLED KATAKANA NO	&#x32E8;	&U32E8;
CIRCLED KATAKANA NU	&#x32E6;	&U32E6;
CIRCLED KATAKANA O	&#x32D4;	&U32D4;
CIRCLED KATAKANA RA	&#x32F6;	&U32F6;
CIRCLED KATAKANA RE	&#x32F9;	&U32F9;
CIRCLED KATAKANA RI	&#x32F7;	&U32F7;
CIRCLED KATAKANA RO	&#x32FA;	&U32FA;
CIRCLED KATAKANA RU	&#x32F8;	&U32F8;
CIRCLED KATAKANA SA	&#x32DA;	&U32DA;
CIRCLED KATAKANA SE	&#x32DD;	&U32DD;
CIRCLED KATAKANA SI	&#x32DB;	&U32DB;
CIRCLED KATAKANA SO	&#x32DE;	&U32DE;
CIRCLED KATAKANA SU	&#x32DC;	&U32DC;
CIRCLED KATAKANA TA	&#x32DF;	&U32DF;
CIRCLED KATAKANA TE	&#x32E2;	&U32E2;
CIRCLED KATAKANA TI	&#x32E0;	&U32E0;
CIRCLED KATAKANA TO	&#x32E3;	&U32E3;
CIRCLED KATAKANA TU	&#x32E1;	&U32E1;
CIRCLED KATAKANA U	&#x32D2;	&U32D2;
CIRCLED KATAKANA WA	&#x32FB;	&U32FB;
CIRCLED KATAKANA WE	&#x32FD;	&U32FD;
CIRCLED KATAKANA WI	&#x32FC;	&U32FC;
CIRCLED KATAKANA WO	&#x32FE;	&U32FE;
CIRCLED KATAKANA YA	&#x32F3;	&U32F3;
CIRCLED KATAKANA YO	&#x32F5;	&U32F5;
CIRCLED KATAKANA YU	&#x32F4;	&U32F4;
COMBINING KANA SEMI-VOICED SOUND MARK	&#x309A;	&U309A;
COMBINING KANA VOICED SOUND MARK	&#x3099;	&U3099;

Other Kana (Continued)

Character	XML	SPREAD
katakana-hiragana prolonged sound mark	`&#x30FC;`	`&U30FC;`
katakana-hiragana semi-voiced sound mark	`&#x309C;`	`&U309C;`
katakana-hiragana voiced sound mark	`&#x309B;`	`&U309B;`
katakana iteration mark	`&#x30FD;`	`&U30FD;`
katakana voiced iteration mark	`&#x30FE;`	`&U30FE;`
katakana middle dot	`&#x30FB;`	`&U30FB;`
vertical ellipsis	`&#x22EE;`	`&U22EE;`
vertical kana repeat mark	`&#x3031;`	`&U3031;`
vertical kana repeat mark lower half	`&#x3035;`	`&U3035;`
vertical kana repeat mark upper half	`&#x3033;`	`&U3033;`
vertical kana repeat with voiced sound mark	`&#x3032;`	`&U3032;`
vertical kana repeat with voiced sound mark upper half	`&#x3034;`	`&U3034;`
ideographic number zero	`&#x3007;`	`&U3007;`

LAO LETTER

Character	XML	SPREAD
BO	`&#xE9A;`	`&U0E9A;`
CO	`&#xE88;`	`&U0E88;`
DO	`&#xE94;`	`&U0E94;`
FO SUNG	`&#xE9F;`	`&U0E9F;`
FO TAM	`&#xE9D;`	`&U0E9D;`
HO SUNG	`&#xEAB;`	`&U0EAB;`
HO TAM	`&#xEAE;`	`&U0EAE;`
KHO SUNG	`&#xE82;`	`&U0E82;`
KHO TAM	`&#xE84;`	`&U0E84;`
KO	`&#xE81;`	`&U0E81;`
LO LING	`&#xEA3;`	`&U0EA3;`
LO LOOT	`&#xEA5;`	`&U0EA5;`
MO	`&#xEA1;`	`&U0EA1;`
NGO	`&#xE87;`	`&U0E87;`
NO	`&#xE99;`	`&U0E99;`
NYO	`&#xE8D;`	`&U0E8D;`
O	`&#xEAD;`	`&U0EAD;`
PHO SUNG	`&#xE9C;`	`&U0E9C;`
PHO TAM	`&#xE9E;`	`&U0E9E;`
PO	`&#xE9B;`	`&U0E9B;`
SO SUNG	`&#xEAA;`	`&U0EAA;`
SO TAM	`&#xE8A;`	`&U0E8A;`
THO SUNG	`&#xE96;`	`&U0E96;`
THO TAM	`&#xE97;`	`&U0E97;`
TO	`&#xE95;`	`&U0E95;`
WO	`&#xEA7;`	`&U0EA7;`
YO	`&#xEA2;`	`&U0EA2;`

LAO VOWEL SIGN

Character	XML	SPREAD
A	ະ	&U0EB0;
AA	າ	&U0EB2;
AI	ໄ	&U0EC4;
AM	ຳ	&U0EB3;
AY	ໃ	&U0EC3;
E	ເ	&U0EC0;
EI	ແ	&U0EC1;
I	ິ	&U0EB4;
II	ີ	&U0EB5;
MAI KAN	ັ	&U0EB1;
MAI KON	ົ	&U0EBB;
O	ໂ	&U0EC2;
U	ຸ	&U0EB8;
UU	ູ	&U0EB9;
Y	ຶ	&U0EB6;
YY	ື	&U0EB7;

Other Lao

Character	XML	SPREAD
LAO NIGGAHITA	ໍ	&U0ECD;
LAO SEMIVOWEL SIGN LO	ຼ	&U0EBC;
LAO SEMIVOWEL SIGN NYO	ຽ	&U0EBD;
LAO TONE MAI CATAWA	໋	&U0ECB;
LAO TONE MAI EK	່	&U0EC8;
LAO TONE MAI THO	້	&U0EC9;
LAO TONE MAI TI	໊	&U0ECA;
LAO CANCELLATION MARK	໌	&U0ECC;
LAO HO MO	ໝ	&U0EDD;
LAO HO NO	ໜ	&U0EDC;

Lao Numerals

Character	XML	SPREAD
lao digit eight	໘	&U0ED8;
lao digit five	໕	&U0ED5;
lao digit four	໔	&U0ED4;
lao digit nine	໙	&U0ED9;
lao digit one	໑	&U0ED1;
lao digit seven	໗	&U0ED7;
lao digit six	໖	&U0ED6;
lao digit three	໓	&U0ED3;
lao digit two	໒	&U0ED2;
lao digit zero	໐	&U0ED0;

LATIN CAPITAL LETTER

Base	XML	ISO	SPREAD	Variation
A	A		&U0041;	(A)
	Á	Á	&U00C1;	with acute (Á)
	Ă	Ă	&U0102;	with breve
	Ắ		&U1EAE;	with breve and acute
	Ặ		&U1EB6;	with breve and dot below
	Ằ		&U1EB0;	with breve and grave
	Ẳ		&U1EB2;	with breve and hook above
	Ẵ		&U1EB4;	with breve and tilde
	Ǎ		&U01CD;	with caron
	Â	Â	&U00C2;	with circumflex (Â)
	Ấ		&U1EA4;	with circumflex and acute
	Ậ		&U1EAC;	with circumflex and dot below
	Ầ		&U1EA6;	with circumflex and grave
	Ẩ		&U1EA8;	with circumflex and hook above
	Ẫ		&U1EAA;	with circumflex and tilde
	Ä	Ä	&U00C4;	with diaeresis (Ä)
	Ǟ		&U01DE;	with diaeresis and macron
	Ǡ		&U01E0;	with dot above and macron
	Ạ		&U1EA0;	with dot below
	Ȁ		&U0200;	with double grave
	À	À	&U00C0;	with grave (À)
	Ả		&U1EA2;	with hook above
	Ȃ		&U0202;	with inverted breve
	Ā	Ā	&U0100;	with macron
	Ą	Ą	&U0104;	with ogonek
	Å	Å	&U00C5;	with ring above (Å)
	Ǻ		&U01FA;	with ring above and acute
	Ḁ		&U1E00;	with ring below
	Ã	Ã	&U00C3;	with tilde (Ã)
AE	Æ	Æ	&U00C6;	(Æ)

LATIN CAPITAL LETTER (Continued)

Base	XML	ISO	SPREAD	Variation
...AE	`&#x1FC;`		`&U01FC;`	with acute
	`&#x1E2;`		`&U01E2;`	with macron
AFRICAN D	`&#x189;`		`&U0189;`	
B	`&#x42;`		`&U0042;`	(B)
	`&#x1E02;`		`&U1E02;`	with dot above
	`&#x1E04;`		`&U1E04;`	with dot below
	`&#x181;`		`&U0181;`	with hook
	`&#x1E06;`		`&U1E06;`	with line below
	`&#x182;`		`&U0182;`	with topbar
C	`&#x43;`		`&U0043;`	(C)
	`&#x106;`	`&Cacute;`	`&U0106;`	with acute
	`&#x10C;`	`&Ccaron;`	`&U010C;`	with caron
	`&#xC7;`	`&Ccedil;`	`&U00C7;`	with cedilla (Ç)
	`&#x1E08;`		`&U1E08;`	with cedilla and acute
	`&#x108;`	`&Ccirc;`	`&U0108;`	with circumflex
	`&#x10A;`	`&Cdot;`	`&U010A;`	with dot above
	`&#x187;`		`&U0187;`	with hook
D	`&#x44;`		`&U0044;`	(D)
	`&#x10E;`	`&Dcaron;`	`&U010E;`	with caron
	`&#x1E10;`		`&U1E10;`	with cedilla
	`&#x1E12;`		`&U1E12;`	with circumflex below
	`&#x1E0A;`		`&U1E0A;`	with dot above
	`&#x1E0C;`		`&U1E0C;`	with dot below
	`&#x18A;`		`&U018A;`	with hook
	`&#x1E0E;`		`&U1E0E;`	with line below
	`&#x1F2;`		`&U01F2;`	with small letter z
	`&#x1C5;`		`&U01C5;`	with small letter z with caron
	`&#x110;`	`&Dstrok;`	`&U0110;`	with stroke
	`&#x18B;`		`&U018B;`	with topbar
DZ	`&#x1F1;`		`&U01F1;`	
	`&#x1C4;`		`&U01C4;`	with caron
E	`&#x45;`		`&U0045;`	(E)
	`&#xC9;`	`&Eacute;`	`&U00C9;`	with acute (É)
	`&#x114;`		`&U0114;`	with breve
	`&#x11A;`	`&Ecaron;`	`&U011A;`	with caron
	`&#x1E1C;`		`&U1E1C;`	with cedilla and breve
	`&#xCA;`	`&Ecirc;`	`&U00CA;`	with circumflex (Ê)
	`&#x1EBE;`		`&U1EBE;`	with circumflex and acute
	`&#x1EC6;`		`&U1EC6;`	with circumflex and dot below
	`&#x1EC0;`		`&U1EC0;`	with circumflex and grave
	`&#x1EC2;`		`&U1EC2;`	with circumflex and hook above
	`&#x1EC4;`		`&U1EC4;`	with circumflex and tilde
	`&#x1E18;`		`&U1E18;`	with circumflex below
	`&#xCB;`	`&Euml;`	`&U00CB;`	with diaeresis (Ë)
	`&#x116;`	`&Edot;`	`&U0116;`	with dot above
	`&#x1EB8;`		`&U1EB8;`	with dot below
	`&#x204;`		`&U0204;`	with double grave
	`&#xC8;`	`&Egrave;`	`&U00C8;`	with grave (È)
	`&#x1EBA;`		`&U1EBA;`	with hook above
	`&#x206;`		`&U0206;`	with inverted breve

LATIN CAPITAL LETTER (Continued)

Base	XML	ISO	SPREAD	Variation
...E	&#x112;	&Emacr;	&U0112;	with macron
	&#x1E16;		&U1E16;	with macron and acute
	&#x1E14;		&U1E14;	with macron and grave
	&#x118;	&Eogon;	&U0118;	with ogonek
	&#x1EBC;		&U1EBC;	with tilde
	&#x1E1A;		&U1E1A;	with tilde below
ENG	&#x14A;	&ENG;	&U014A;	
ESH	&#x1A9;		&U01A9;	
ETH	&#xD0;	&ETH;	&U00D0;	(Ð)
EZH	&#x1B7;		&U01B7;	
	&#x1EE;		&U01EE;	with caron
EZH REVERSED	&#x1B8;	&epsis;	&U01B8;	
F	&#x46;		&U0046;	(F)
	&#x1E1E;		&U1E1E;	with dot above
	&#x191;		&U0191;	with hook
G	&#x47;		&U0047;	(G)
	&#x1F4;		&U01F4;	with acute
	&#x11E;	&Gbreve;	&U011E;	with breve
	&#x1E6;		&U01E6;	with caron
	&#x122;	&Gcedil;	&U0122;	with cedilla
	&#x11C;	&Gcirc;	&U011C;	with circumflex
	&#x120;	&Gdot;	&U0120;	with dot above
	&#x193;		&U0193;	with hook
	&#x1E20;		&U1E20;	with macron
	&#x1E4;		&U01E4;	with stroke
GAMMA	&#x194;		&U0194;	
H	&#x48;		&U0048;	(H)
	&#x1E2A;		&U1E2A;	with breve below
	&#x1E28;		&U1E28;	with cedilla
	&#x124;	&Hcirc;	&U0124;	with circumflex
	&#x1E26;		&U1E26;	with diaeresis
	&#x1E22;		&U1E22;	with dot above
	&#x1E24;		&U1E24;	with dot below
	&#x126;	&Hstrok;	&U0126;	with stroke
I	&#x49;		&U0049;	(I)
	&#xCD;	&Iacute;	&U00CD;	with acute (Í)
	&#x12C;		&U012C;	with breve
	&#x1CF;		&U01CF;	with caron
	&#xCE;	&Icirc;	&U00CE;	with circumflex (Î)
	&#xCF;	&Iuml;	&U00CF;	with diaeresis (Ï)
	&#x1E2E;		&U1E2E;	with diaeresis and acute
	&#x130;	&Idot;	&U0130;	with dot above
	&#x1ECA;		&U1ECA;	with dot below
	&#x208;		&U0208;	with double grave
	&#xCC;	&Igrave;	&U00CC;	with grave (Ì)
	&#x1EC8;		&U1EC8;	with hook above
	&#x20A;		&U020A;	with inverted breve
	&#x12A;	&Imacr;	&U012A;	with macron
	&#x12E;	&Iogon;	&U012E;	with ogonek
	&#x197;		&U0197;	with stroke

Base	XML	ISO	SPREAD	Variation
...I	Ĩ	Ĩ	&U0128;	with tilde
	Ḭ		&U1E2C;	with tilde below
IOTA	Ɩ		&U0196;	
J	J		&U004A;	(J)
	Ĵ	Ĵ	&U0134;	with circumflex
K	K		&U004B;	(K)
	Ḱ		&U1E30;	with acute
	Ǩ		&U01E8;	with caron
	Ķ	Ķ	&U0136;	with cedilla
	Ḳ		&U1E32;	with dot below
	Ƙ		&U0198;	with hook
	Ḵ		&U1E34;	with line below
L	L		&U004C;	(L)
	Ĺ	Ĺ	&U0139;	with acute
	Ľ	Ľ	&U013D;	with caron
	Ļ	Ļ	&U013B;	with cedilla
	Ḽ		&U1E3C;	with circumflex below
	Ḷ		&U1E36;	with dot below
	Ḹ		&U1E38;	with dot below and macron
	Ḻ		&U1E3A;	with line below
	Ŀ		&U013F;	with middle dot
	ǈ		&U01C8;	with small letter j
	Ł	Ł	&U0141;	with stroke
LJ	Ǉ		&U01C7;	
M	M		&U004D;	(M)
	Ḿ		&U1E3E;	with acute
	Ṁ		&U1E40;	with dot above
	Ṃ		&U1E42;	with dot below
N	N		&U004E;	(N)
	Ń	Ń	&U0143;	with acute
	Ň	Ň	&U0147;	with caron
	Ņ	Ņ	&U0145;	with cedilla
	Ṋ		&U1E4A;	with circumflex below
	Ṅ		&U1E44;	with dot above
	Ṇ		&U1E46;	with dot below
	Ɲ		&U019D;	with left hook
	Ṉ		&U1E48;	with line below
	ǋ		&U01CB;	with small letter j
	Ñ	Ñ	&U00D1;	with tilde (Ñ)
NJ	Ǌ		&U01CA;	
O	O		&U004F;	(O)
	Ó	Ó	&U00D3;	with acute (Ó)
	Ŏ		&U014E;	with breve
	Ǒ		&U01D1;	with caron
	Ô	Ô	&U00D4;	with circumflex (Ô)
	Ố		&U1ED0;	with circumflex and acute
	Ộ		&U1ED8;	with circumflex and dot below
	Ồ		&U1ED2;	with circumflex and grave
	Ổ		&U1ED4;	with circumflex and hook above
	Ỗ		&U1ED6;	with circumflex and tilde

Base	XML	ISO	SPREAD	Variation
...O	Ö	Ö	&U00D6;	with diaeresis (Ö)
	Ọ		&U1ECC;	with dot below
	Ő	Ő	&U0150;	with double acute
	Ȍ		&U020C;	with double grave
	Ò	Ò	&U00D2;	with grave (Ò)
	Ỏ		&U1ECE;	with hook above
	Ơ		&U01A0;	with horn
	Ớ		&U1EDA;	with horn and acute
	Ợ		&U1EE2;	with horn and dot below
	Ờ		&U1EDC;	with horn and grave
	Ở		&U1EDE;	with horn and hook above
	Ỡ		&U1EE0;	with horn and tilde
	Ȏ		&U020E;	with inverted breve
	Ō	Ō	&U014C;	with macron
	Ṓ		&U1E52;	with macron and acute
	Ṑ		&U1E50;	with macron and grave
	Ɵ		&U019F;	with middle tilde
	Ǫ		&U01EA;	with ogonek
	Ǭ		&U01EC;	with ogonek and macron
	Ø	Ø	&U00D8;	with stroke (Ø)
	Ǿ		&U01FE;	with stroke and acute
	Õ	Õ	&U00D5;	with tilde (Õ)
	Ṍ		&U1E4C;	with tilde and acute
	Ṏ		&U1E4E;	with tilde and diaeresis
OI	Ƣ		&U01A2;	
OPEN E	Ɛ		&U0190;	
OPEN O	Ɔ		&U0186;	
P	P		&U0050;	(P)
	Ṕ		&U1E54;	with acute
	Ṗ		&U1E56;	with dot above
	Ƥ		&U01A4;	with hook
Q	Q		&U0051;	(Q)
R	R		&U0052;	(R)
	Ŕ	Ŕ	&U0154;	with acute
	Ř	Ř	&U0158;	with caron
	Ŗ	Ŗ	&U0156;	with cedilla
	Ṙ		&U1E58;	with dot above
	Ṛ		&U1E5A;	with dot below
	Ṝ		&U1E5C;	with dot below and macron
	Ȑ		&U0210;	with double grave
	Ȓ		&U0212;	with inverted breve
	Ṟ		&U1E5E;	with line below
REVERSED E	Ǝ		&U018E;	
S	S		&U0053;	(S)
	Ś		&U015A;	with acute
	Ṥ		&U1E64;	with acute and dot above
	Š	Š	&U0160;	with caron
	Ṧ		&U1E66;	with caron and dot above
	Ş	Ş	&U015E;	with cedilla
	Ŝ	ŝ	&U015C;	with circumflex

Base	XML	ISO	SPREAD	Variation
...S	`&#x1E60;`		`&U1E60;`	with dot above
	`&#x1E62;`		`&U1E62;`	with dot below
	`&#x1E68;`		`&U1E68;`	with dot below and dot above
SCHWA	`&#x18F;`		`&U018F;`	
T	`&#x54;`		`&U0054;`	(T)
	`&#x164;`	`&Tcaron;`	`&U0164;`	with caron
	`&#x162;`	`&tcedil;`	`&U0162;`	with cedilla
	`&#x1E70;`		`&U1E70;`	with circumflex below
	`&#x1E6A;`		`&U1E6A;`	with dot above
	`&#x1E6C;`		`&U1E6C;`	with dot below
	`&#x1AC;`		`&U01AC;`	with hook
	`&#x1E6E;`		`&U1E6E;`	with line below
	`&#x1AE;`		`&U01AE;`	with retroflex hook
	`&#x166;`	`&Tstrok;`	`&U0166;`	with stroke
THORN	`&#xDE;`	`&THORN;`	`&U00DE;`	(Þ)
TONE FIVE	`&#x1BC;`		`&U01BC;`	
TONE SIX	`&#x184;`		`&U0184;`	
TONE TWO	`&#x1A7;`		`&U01A7;`	
TURNED M	`&#x19C;`		`&U019C;`	
U	`&#x55;`		`&U0055;`	(U)
	`&#xDA;`	`&Uacute;`	`&U00DA;`	with acute (Ú)
	`&#x16C;`	`&Ubreve;`	`&U016C;`	with breve
	`&#x1D3;`		`&U01D3;`	with caron
	`&#xDB;`	`&Ucirc;`	`&U00DB;`	with circumflex (Û)
	`&#x1E76;`		`&U1E76;`	with circumflex below
	`&#xDC;`	`&Uuml;`	`&U00DC;`	with diaeresis (Ü)
	`&#x1D7;`		`&U01D7;`	with diaeresis and acute
	`&#x1D9;`		`&U01D9;`	with diaeresis and caron
	`&#x1DB;`		`&U01DB;`	with diaeresis and grave
	`&#x1D5;`		`&U01D5;`	with diaeresis and macron
	`&#x1E72;`		`&U1E72;`	with diaeresis below
	`&#x1EE4;`		`&U1EE4;`	with dot below
	`&#x170;`	`&Udblac;`	`&U0170;`	with double acute
	`&#x214;`		`&U0214;`	with double grave
	`&#xD9;`	`&Ugrave;`	`&U00D9;`	with grave (Ù)
	`&#x1EE6;`		`&U1EE6;`	with hook above
	`&#x1AF;`		`&U01AF;`	with horn
	`&#x1EE8;`		`&U1EE8;`	with horn and acute
	`&#x1EF0;`		`&U1EF0;`	with horn and dot below
	`&#x1EEA;`		`&U1EEA;`	with horn and grave
	`&#x1EEC;`		`&U1EEC;`	with horn and hook above
	`&#x1EEE;`		`&U1EEE;`	with horn and tilde
	`&#x216;`		`&U0216;`	with inverted breve
	`&#x16A;`	`&Umacr;`	`&U016A;`	with macron
	`&#x1E7A;`		`&U1E7A;`	with macron and diaeresis
	`&#x172;`	`&Uogon;`	`&U0172;`	with ogonek
	`&#x16E;`	`&Uring;`	`&U016E;`	with ring above
	`&#x168;`	`&Utilde;`	`&U0168;`	with tilde
	`&#x1E78;`		`&U1E78;`	with tilde and acute
	`&#x1E74;`		`&U1E74;`	with tilde below

LATIN CAPITAL LETTER (Continued)

Base	XML	ISO	SPREAD	Variation
UPSILON	Ʊ		&U01B1;	
V	V		&U0056;	(V)
	Ṿ		&U1E7E;	with dot below
	Ʋ		&U01B2;	with hook
	Ṽ		&U1E7C;	with tilde
W	W		&U0057;	(W)
	Ẃ		&U1E82;	with acute
	Ŵ	Ŵ	&U0174;	with circumflex
	Ẅ		&U1E84;	with diaeresis
	Ẇ		&U1E86;	with dot above
	Ẉ		&U1E88;	with dot below
	Ẁ		&U1E80;	with grave
X	X		&U0058;	(X)
	Ẍ		&U1E8C;	with diaeresis
	Ẋ		&U1E8A;	with dot above
Y	Y		&U0059;	(Y)
	Ý	Ý	&U00DD;	with acute (Ý)
	Ŷ	Ŷ	&U0176;	with circumflex
	Ÿ	Ÿ	&U0178;	with diaeresis
	Ẏ		&U1E8E;	with dot above
	Ỵ		&U1EF4;	with dot below
	Ỳ		&U1EF2;	with grave
	Ƴ		&U01B3;	with hook
	Ỷ		&U1EF6;	with hook above
	Ỹ		&U1EF8;	with tilde
Z	Z		&U005A;	(Z)
	Ź	Ź	&U0179;	with acute
	Ž		&U017D;	with caron
	Ẑ		&U1E90;	with circumflex
	Ż	Ż	&U017B;	with dot above
	Ẓ		&U1E92;	with dot below
	Ẕ		&U1E94;	with line below
	Ƶ		&U01B5;	with stroke

BLACK-LETTER

Base	XML	ISO	SPREAD	Variation
CAPITAL C	ℭ		&U212D;	
CAPITAL H	ℌ		&U210C;	
CAPITAL I	ℑ		&U2111;	
CAPITAL R	ℜ		&U211C;	
CAPITAL Z	ℨ		&U2128;	

LATIN LETTER

Base	XML	ISO	SPREAD	Variation
ALVEOLAR CLICK	`&#x1C2;`		`&U01C2;`	
BILABIAL CLICK	`&#x298;`		`&U0298;`	
DENTAL CLICK	`&#x1C0;`		`&U01C0;`	
GLOTTAL STOP	`&#x294;`		`&U0294;`	
	`&#x2A1;`		`&U02A1;`	with stroke
INVERTED GLOTTAL STOP	`&#x296;`		`&U0296;`	
	`&#x1BE;`		`&U01BE;`	with stroke
LATERAL CLICK	`&#x1C1;`		`&U01C1;`	
PHARYNGEAL VOICED FRICATIVE	`&#x295;`		`&U0295;`	
RETROFLEX CLICK	`&#x1C3;`		`&U01C3;`	
REVERSED ESH LOOP	`&#x1AA;`		`&U01AA;`	
REVERSED GLOTTAL STOP	`&#x2A2;`		`&U02A2;`	with stroke
SMALL CAPITAL B	`&#x299;`		`&U0299;`	
SMALL CAPITAL G	`&#x262;`		`&U0262;`	
	`&#x29B;`		`&U029B;`	with hook
SMALL CAPITAL H	`&#x29C;`		`&U029C;`	
SMALL CAPITAL I	`&#x26A;`		`&U026A;`	
SMALL CAPITAL INVERTED R	`&#x281;`		`&U0281;`	
SMALL CAPITAL L	`&#x29F;`		`&U029F;`	
SMALL CAPITAL N	`&#x274;`		`&U0274;`	
SMALL CAPITAL OE	`&#x276;`		`&U0276;`	
SMALL CAPITAL R	`&#x280;`		`&U0280;`	
SMALL CAPITAL Y	`&#x28F;`		`&U028F;`	
STRETCHED C	`&#x297;`		`&U0297;`	
TWO	`&#x1BB;`		`&U01BB;`	with stroke
WYNN	`&#x1BF;`		`&U01BF;`	
YR	`&#x1A6;`		`&U01A6;`	

LATIN SMALL LETTER

Base	XML	ISO	SPREAD	Variation
A	`&#x61;`		`&U0061;`	(a)
	`&#xE1;`	`&aacute;`	`&U00E1;`	with acute (á)
	`&#x103;`	`&abreve;`	`&U0103;`	with breve
	`&#x1EAF;`		`&U1EAF;`	with breve and acute
	`&#x1EB7;`		`&U1EB7;`	with breve and dot below
	`&#x1EB1;`		`&U1EB1;`	with breve and grave
	`&#x1EB3;`		`&U1EB3;`	with breve and hook above
	`&#x1EB5;`		`&U1EB5;`	with breve and tilde
	`&#x1CE;`		`&U01CE;`	with caron
	`&#xE2;`	`&acirc;`	`&U00E2;`	with circumflex (â)
	`&#x1EA5;`		`&U1EA5;`	with circumflex and acute
	`&#x1EAD;`		`&U1EAD;`	with circumflex and dot below
	`&#x1EA7;`		`&U1EA7;`	with circumflex and grave

LATIN SMALL LETTER (Continued)

Base	XML	ISO	SPREAD	Variation
...A	`&#x1EA9;`		`&U1EA9;`	with circumflex and hook above
	`&#x1EAB;`		`&U1EAB;`	with circumflex and tilde
	`&#xE4;`	`&auml;`	`&U00E4;`	with diaeresis (ä)
	`&#x1DF;`		`&U01DF;`	with diaeresis and macron
	`&#x1E1;`		`&U01E1;`	with dot above and macron
	`&#x1EA1;`		`&U1EA1;`	with dot below
	`&#x201;`		`&U0201;`	with double grave
	`&#xE0;`	`&agrave;`	`&U00E0;`	with grave (à)
	`&#x1EA3;`		`&U1EA3;`	with hook above
	`&#x203;`		`&U0203;`	with inverted breve
	`&#x101;`	`&amacr;`	`&U0101;`	with macron
	`&#x105;`	`&aogon;`	`&U0105;`	with ogonek
	`&#x1E9A;`		`&U1E9A;`	with right half ring
	`&#xE5;`	`&aring;`	`&U00E5;`	with ring above (å)
	`&#x1FB;`		`&U01FB;`	with ring above and acute
	`&#x1E01;`		`&U1E01;`	with ring below
	`&#xE3;`	`&atilde;`	`&U00E3;`	with tilde (ã)
AE	`&#xE6;`	`&aelig;`	`&U00E6;`	(æ)
	`&#x1FD;`	`&zcaron;`	`&U01FD;`	with acute
	`&#x1E3;`		`&U01E3;`	with macron
ALPHA	`&#x251;`		`&U0251;`	
B	`&#x62;`		`&U0062;`	(b)
	`&#x1E03;`		`&U1E03;`	with dot above
	`&#x1E05;`		`&U1E05;`	with dot below
	`&#x253;`		`&U0253;`	with hook
	`&#x1E07;`		`&U1E07;`	with line below
	`&#x180;`		`&U0180;`	with stroke
	`&#x183;`		`&U0183;`	with topbar
BARRED O	`&#x275;`		`&U0275;`	
C	`&#x63;`		`&U0063;`	(c)
	`&#x107;`	`&cacute;`	`&U0107;`	with acute
	`&#x10D;`	`&ccaron;`	`&U010D;`	with caron
	`&#xE7;`	`&ccedil;`	`&U00E7;`	with cedilla (ç)
	`&#x1E09;`		`&U1E09;`	with cedilla and acute
	`&#x109;`	`&ccirc;`	`&U0109;`	with circumflex
	`&#x255;`		`&U0255;`	with curl
	`&#x10B;`	`&cdot;`	`&U010B;`	with dot above
	`&#x188;`		`&U0188;`	with hook
CLOSED OMEGA	`&#x277;`		`&U0277;`	
CLOSED OPEN E	`&#x29A;`		`&U029A;`	
CLOSED REVERSED OPEN E	`&#x25E;`		`&U025E;`	
D	`&#x64;`		`&U0064;`	(d)
	`&#x10F;`	`&dcaron;`	`&U010F;`	with caron
	`&#x1E11;`		`&U1E11;`	with cedilla
	`&#x1E13;`		`&U1E13;`	with circumflex below
	`&#x1E0B;`		`&U1E0B;`	with dot above
	`&#x1E0D;`		`&U1E0D;`	with dot below
	`&#x257;`		`&U0257;`	with hook
	`&#x1E0F;`		`&U1E0F;`	with line below
	`&#x111;`	`&dstrok;`	`&U0111;`	with stroke

Base	XML	ISO	SPREAD	Variation
...D	ɖ		&U0256;	with tail
	ƌ		&U018C;	with topbar
DEZH DIGRAPH	ʤ		&U02A4;	
DOTLESS I	ı	ı	&U0131;	
DOTLESS J	ɟ		&U025F;	with stroke
	ʄ		&U0284;	with stroke and hook
DZ	ǳ		&U01F3;	
	ǆ		&U01C6;	with caron
DZ DIGRAPH	ʣ		&U02A3;	
	ʥ		&U02A5;	with curl
E	e		&U0065;	(e)
	é	é	&U00E9;	with acute (é)
	ĕ		&U0115;	with breve
	ě	ě	&U011B;	with caron
	ḝ		&U1E1D;	with cedilla and breve
	ê	ê	&U00EA;	with circumflex (ê)
	ế		&U1EBF;	with circumflex and acute
	ệ		&U1EC7;	with circumflex and dot below
	ề		&U1EC1;	with circumflex and grave
	ể		&U1EC3;	with circumflex and hook above
	ễ		&U1EC5;	with circumflex and tilde
	ḙ		&U1E19;	with circumflex below
	ë	ë	&U00EB;	with diaeresis (ë)
	ė	ė	&U0117;	with dot above
	ẹ		&U1EB9;	with dot below
	ȅ		&U0205;	with double grave
	è	è	&U00E8;	with grave (è)
	ẻ		&U1EBB;	with hook above
	ȇ		&U0207;	with inverted breve
	ē	ē	&U0113;	with macron
	ḗ		&U1E17;	with macron and acute
	ḕ		&U1E15;	with macron and grave
	ę	ę	&U0119;	with ogonek
	ẽ		&U1EBD;	with tilde
	ḛ		&U1E1B;	with tilde below
ENG	ŋ	ŋ	&U014B;	
ESH	ʃ		&U0283;	
	ʆ		&U0286;	with curl
ETH	ð	ð	&U00F0;	(ð)
EZH	ʒ		&U0292;	
	ǯ		&U01EF;	with caron
	ʓ		&U0293;	with curl
	ƺ		&U01BA;	with tail
EZH REVERSED	ƹ		&U01B9;	
F	f		&U0066;	(f)
	ḟ		&U1E1F;	with dot above
	ƒ	ƒ	&U0192;	with hook
G	g		&U0067;	(g)
	ǵ	ǵ	&U01F5;	with acute
	ğ	ğ	&U011F;	with breve

LATIN SMALL LETTER (Continued)

Base	XML	ISO	SPREAD	Variation
...G	`&#x1E7;`		`&U01E7;`	with caron
	`&#x123;`		`&U0123;`	with cedilla
	`&#x11D;`	`&gcirc;`	`&U011D;`	with circumflex
	`&#x121;`	`&gdot;`	`&U0121;`	with dot above
	`&#x260;`		`&U0260;`	with hook
	`&#x1E21;`		`&U1E21;`	with macron
	`&#x1E5;`		`&U01E5;`	with stroke
GAMMA	`&#x263;`		`&U0263;`	
H	`&#x68;`		`&U0068;`	(h)
	`&#x1E2B;`		`&U1E2B;`	with breve below
	`&#x1E29;`		`&U1E29;`	with cedilla
	`&#x125;`	`&hcirc;`	`&U0125;`	with circumflex
	`&#x1E27;`		`&U1E27;`	with diaeresis
	`&#x1E23;`		`&U1E23;`	with dot above
	`&#x1E25;`		`&U1E25;`	with dot below
	`&#x266;`		`&U0266;`	with hook
	`&#x1E96;`		`&U1E96;`	with line below
	`&#x127;`	`&hstrok;`	`&U0127;`	with stroke
HENG	`&#x267;`		`&U0267;`	with hook
HV	`&#x195;`		`&U0195;`	
I	`&#x69;`		`&U0069;`	(i)
	`&#xED;`	`&iacute;`	`&U00ED;`	with acute (í)
	`&#x12D;`		`&U012D;`	with breve
	`&#x1D0;`		`&U01D0;`	with caron
	`&#xEE;`	`&icirc;`	`&U00EE;`	with circumflex (î)
	`&#xEF;`	`&iuml;`	`&U00EF;`	with diaeresis (ï)
	`&#x1E2F;`		`&U1E2F;`	with diaeresis and acute
	`&#x1ECB;`		`&U1ECB;`	with dot below
	`&#x209;`		`&U0209;`	with double grave
	`&#xEC;`	`&igrave;`	`&U00EC;`	with grave (ì)
	`&#x1EC9;`		`&U1EC9;`	with hook above
	`&#x20B;`		`&U020B;`	with inverted breve
	`&#x12B;`	`&imacr;`	`&U012B;`	with macron
	`&#x12F;`	`&iogon;`	`&U012F;`	with ogonek
	`&#x268;`		`&U0268;`	with stroke
	`&#x129;`	`&itilde;`	`&U0129;`	with tilde
	`&#x1E2D;`		`&U1E2D;`	with tilde below
IOTA	`&#x269;`		`&U0269;`	
J	`&#x6A;`		`&U006A;`	(j)
	`&#x1F0;`		`&U01F0;`	with caron
	`&#x135;`	`&jcirc;`	`&U0135;`	with circumflex
	`&#x29D;`		`&U029D;`	with crossed-tail
K	`&#x6B;`		`&U006B;`	(k)
	`&#x1E31;`		`&U1E31;`	with acute
	`&#x1E9;`		`&U01E9;`	with caron
	`&#x137;`	`&kcedil;`	`&U0137;`	with cedilla
	`&#x1E33;`		`&U1E33;`	with dot below
	`&#x199;`		`&U0199;`	with hook
	`&#x1E35;`		`&U1E35;`	with line below
KRA	`&#x138;`	`&kgreen;`	`&U0138;`	

LATIN SMALL LETTER (Continued)

Base	XML	ISO	SPREAD	Variation
L	l		&U006C;	(l)
	ĺ	ĺ	&U013A;	with acute
	ƚ		&U019A;	with bar
	ɬ		&U026C;	with belt
	ľ	ľ	&U013E;	with caron
	ļ	ļ	&U013C;	with cedilla
	ḽ		&U1E3D;	with circumflex below
	ḷ		&U1E37;	with dot below
	ḹ		&U1E39;	with dot below and macron
	ḻ		&U1E3B;	with line below
	ŀ	ŀ	&U0140;	with middle dot
	ɫ		&U026B;	with middle tilde
	ɭ		&U026D;	with retroflex hook
	ł	ł	&U0142;	with stroke
LAMBDA	ƛ		&U019B;	with stroke
LEZH	ɮ		&U026E;	
LJ	ǉ		&U01C9;	
LONG S	ſ		&U017F;	
	ẛ		&U1E9B;	with dot above
M	m		&U006D;	(m)
	ḿ		&U1E3F;	with acute
	ṁ		&U1E41;	with dot above
	ṃ		&U1E43;	with dot below
	ɱ		&U0271;	with hook
N	n		&U006E;	(n)
	ń	ń	&U0144;	with acute
	ň	ň	&U0148;	with caron
	ņ	ņ	&U0146;	with cedilla
	ṋ		&U1E4B;	with circumflex below
	ṅ		&U1E45;	with dot above
	ṇ		&U1E47;	with dot below
	ɲ		&U0272;	with left hook
	ṉ		&U1E49;	with line below
	ƞ		&U019E;	with long right leg
	ɳ		&U0273;	with retroflex hook
	ñ	ñ	&U00F1;	with tilde (ñ)
	ŉ	ŉ	&U0149;	preceded by apostrophe
NJ	ǌ		&U01CC;	
O	o		&U006F;	(o)
	ó	ó	&U00F3;	with acute (ó)
	ŏ		&U014F;	with breve
	ǒ		&U01D2;	with caron
	ô	ô	&U00F4;	with circumflex (ô)
	ố		&U1ED1;	with circumflex and acute
	ộ		&U1ED9;	with circumflex and dot below
	ồ		&U1ED3;	with circumflex and grave
	ổ		&U1ED5;	with circumflex and hook above
	ỗ		&U1ED7;	with circumflex and tilde
	ö	ö	&U00F6;	with diaeresis (ö)
	ọ		&U1ECD;	with dot below

LATIN SMALL LETTER (Continued)

Base	XML	ISO	SPREAD	Variation
...O	ő	ő	&U0151;	with double acute
	ȍ		&U020D;	with double grave
	ò	ò	&U00F2;	with grave (ò)
	ỏ		&U1ECF;	with hook above
	ơ		&U01A1;	with horn
	ớ		&U1EDB;	with horn and acute
	ợ		&U1EE3;	with horn and dot below
	ờ		&U1EDD;	with horn and grave
	ở		&U1EDF;	with horn and hook above
	ỡ		&U1EE1;	with horn and tilde
	ȏ		&U020F;	with inverted breve
	ō	ō	&U014D;	with macron
	ṓ		&U1E53;	with macron and acute
	ṑ		&U1E51;	with macron and grave
	ǫ		&U01EB;	with ogonek
	ǭ		&U01ED;	with ogonek and macron
	ø	ø	&U00F8;	with stroke (ø)
	ǿ		&U01FF;	with stroke and acute
	õ	õ	&U00F5;	with tilde (õ)
	ṍ		&U1E4D;	with tilde and acute
	ṏ		&U1E4F;	with tilde and diaeresis
OI	ƣ		&U01A3;	
OPEN E	ɛ		&U025B;	
OPEN O	ɔ		&U0254;	
P	p		&U0070;	(p)
	ṕ		&U1E55;	with acute
	ṗ		&U1E57;	with dot above
	ƥ		&U01A5;	with hook
PHI	ɸ		&U0278;	
Q	q		&U0071;	(q)
	ʠ		&U02A0;	with hook
R	r		&U0072;	(r)
	ŕ	ŕ	&U0155;	with acute
	ř	ř	&U0159;	with caron
	ŗ	ŗ	&U0157;	with cedilla
	ṙ		&U1E59;	with dot above
	ṛ		&U1E5B;	with dot below
	ṝ		&U1E5D;	with dot below and macron
	ȑ		&U0211;	with double grave
	ɾ		&U027E;	with fishhook
	ȓ		&U0213;	with inverted breve
	ṟ		&U1E5F;	with line below
	ɼ		&U027C;	with long leg
	ɽ		&U027D;	with tail
RAMS HORN	ɤ		&U0264;	
REVERSED E	ɘ		&U0258;	
REVERSED OPEN E	ɜ		&U025C;	
	ɝ		&U025D;	with hook
REVERSED R	ɿ		&U027F;	with fishhook
S	s		&U0073;	(s)

LATIN SMALL LETTER (Continued)

Base	XML	ISO	SPREAD	Variation
…S	`&#x15B;`	`&sacute;`	`&U015B;`	with acute
	`&#x1E65;`		`&U1E65;`	with acute and dot above
	`&#x161;`	`&scaron;`	`&U0161;`	with caron
	`&#x1E67;`		`&U1E67;`	with caron and dot above
	`&#x15F;`	`&scedil;`	`&U015F;`	with cedilla
	`&#x15D;`	`&Scirc;`	`&U015D;`	with circumflex
	`&#x1E61;`		`&U1E61;`	with dot above
	`&#x1E63;`		`&U1E63;`	with dot below
	`&#x1E69;`		`&U1E69;`	with dot below and dot above
	`&#x282;`		`&U0282;`	with hook
SCHWA	`&#x259;`		`&U0259;`	
	`&#x25A;`		`&U025A;`	with hook
SCRIPT G	`&#x261;`		`&U0261;`	
SHARP S	`&#xDF;`	`&szlig;`	`&U00DF;`	(ß)
SQUAT REVERSED ESH	`&#x285;`		`&U0285;`	
T	`&#x74;`		`&U0074;`	(t)
	`&#x165;`	`&tcaron;`	`&U0165;`	with caron
	`&#x163;`	`&Tcedil;`	`&U0163;`	with cedilla
	`&#x1E71;`		`&U1E71;`	with circumflex below
	`&#x1E97;`		`&U1E97;`	with diaeresis
	`&#x1E6B;`		`&U1E6B;`	with dot above
	`&#x1E6D;`		`&U1E6D;`	with dot below
	`&#x1AD;`		`&U01AD;`	with hook
	`&#x1E6F;`		`&U1E6F;`	with line below
	`&#x1AB;`		`&U01AB;`	with palatal hook
	`&#x288;`		`&U0288;`	with retroflex hook
	`&#x167;`	`&tstrok;`	`&U0167;`	with stroke
TC DIGRAPH	`&#x2A8;`		`&U02A8;`	with curl
TESH DIGRAPH	`&#x2A7;`		`&U02A7;`	
THORN	`&#xFE;`	`&thorn;`	`&U00FE;`	(þ)
TONE FIVE	`&#x1BD;`		`&U01BD;`	
TONE SIX	`&#x185;`		`&U0185;`	
TONE TWO	`&#x1A8;`		`&U01A8;`	
TS DIGRAPH	`&#x2A6;`		`&U02A6;`	
TURNED A	`&#x250;`		`&U0250;`	
TURNED ALPHA	`&#x252;`		`&U0252;`	
TURNED DELTA	`&#x18D;`		`&U018D;`	
TURNED E	`&#x1DD;`		`&U01DD;`	
TURNED H	`&#x265;`		`&U0265;`	
TURNED K	`&#x29E;`		`&U029E;`	
TURNED M	`&#x26F;`		`&U026F;`	
	`&#x270;`		`&U0270;`	with long leg
TURNED R	`&#x279;`		`&U0279;`	
	`&#x27B;`		`&U027B;`	with hook
	`&#x27A;`		`&U027A;`	with long leg
TURNED T	`&#x287;`		`&U0287;`	
TURNED V	`&#x28C;`		`&U028C;`	
TURNED W	`&#x28D;`		`&U028D;`	
TURNED Y	`&#x28E;`		`&U028E;`	
U	`&#x75;`		`&U0075;`	(u)

Base	XML	ISO	SPREAD	Variation
...U	ú	ú	&U00FA;	with acute (ú)
	ŭ	ŭ	&U016D;	with breve
	ǔ		&U01D4;	with caron
	û	û	&U00FB;	with circumflex (û)
	ṷ		&U1E77;	with circumflex below
	ü	ü	&U00FC;	with diaeresis (ü)
	ǘ		&U01D8;	with diaeresis and acute
	ǚ		&U01DA;	with diaeresis and caron
	ǜ		&U01DC;	with diaeresis and grave
	ǖ		&U01D6;	with diaeresis and macron
	ṳ		&U1E73;	with diaeresis below
	ụ		&U1EE5;	with dot below
	ű	ű	&U0171;	with double acute
	ȕ		&U0215;	with double grave
	ù	ù	&U00F9;	with grave (ù)
	ủ		&U1EE7;	with hook above
	ư		&U01B0;	with horn
	ứ		&U1EE9;	with horn and acute
	ự		&U1EF1;	with horn and dot below
	ừ		&U1EEB;	with horn and grave
	ử		&U1EED;	with horn and hook above
	ữ		&U1EEF;	with horn and tilde
	ȗ		&U0217;	with inverted breve
	ū	ū	&U016B;	with macron
	ṻ		&U1E7B;	with macron and diaeresis
	ų	ų	&U0173;	with ogonek
	ů	ů	&U016F;	with ring above
	ũ	ũ	&U0169;	with tilde
	ṹ		&U1E79;	with tilde and acute
	ṵ		&U1E75;	with tilde below
U BAR	ʉ		&U0289;	
UPSILON	ʊ		&U028A;	
V	v		&U0076;	(v)
	ṿ		&U1E7F;	with dot below
	ʋ		&U028B;	with hook
	ṽ		&U1E7D;	with tilde
W	w		&U0077;	(w)
	ẃ		&U1E83;	with acute
	ŵ	ŵ	&U0175;	with circumflex
	ẅ		&U1E85;	with diaeresis
	ẇ		&U1E87;	with dot above
	ẉ		&U1E89;	with dot below
	ẁ		&U1E81;	with grave
	ẘ		&U1E98;	with ring above
X	x		&U0078;	(x)
	ẍ		&U1E8D;	with diaeresis
	ẋ		&U1E8B;	with dot above
Y	y		&U0079;	(y)
	ý	ý	&U00FD;	with acute (ý)
	ŷ	ŷ	&U0177;	with circumflex

LATIN SMALL LETTER (Continued)

Base	XML	ISO	SPREAD	Variation
...Y	ÿ	ÿ	&U00FF;	with diaeresis (ÿ)
	ẏ		&U1E8F;	with dot above
	ỵ		&U1EF5;	with dot below
	ỳ		&U1EF3;	with grave
	ƴ		&U01B4;	with hook
	ỷ		&U1EF7;	with hook above
	ẙ		&U1E99;	with ring above
	ỹ		&U1EF9;	with tilde
Z	z		&U007A;	(z)
	ź	ź	&U017A;	with acute
	ž	Ž	&U017E;	with caron
	ẑ		&U1E91;	with circumflex
	ʑ		&U0291;	with curl
	ż	ż	&U017C;	with dot above
	ẓ		&U1E93;	with dot below
	ẕ		&U1E95;	with line below
	ʐ		&U0290;	with retroflex hook
	ƶ		&U01B6;	with stroke

Other Latin & Accents

Character	XML	ISO	SPREAD
LATIN CAPITAL LIGATURE IJ	Ĳ	Ĳ	&U0132;
LATIN CAPITAL LIGATURE OE	Œ	Œ	&U0152;
LATIN SMALL LIGATURE IJ	ĳ	ĳ	&U0133;
LATIN SMALL LIGATURE OE	œ	œ	&U0153;
SCRIPT CAPITAL B	ℬ	ℬ	&U212C;
SCRIPT CAPITAL E	ℰ		&U2130;
SCRIPT CAPITAL F	ℱ		&U2131;
SCRIPT CAPITAL H	ℋ	ℋ	&U210B;
SCRIPT CAPITAL I	ℐ		&U2110;
SCRIPT CAPITAL L	ℒ	ℒ	&U2112;
SCRIPT CAPITAL M	ℳ	ℳ	&U2133;
SCRIPT CAPITAL P	℘		&U2118;
SCRIPT CAPITAL R	ℛ		&U211B;
SCRIPT SMALL E	ℯ		&U212F;
SCRIPT SMALL G	ℊ		&U210A;
SCRIPT SMALL L	ℓ		&U2113;
SCRIPT SMALL O	ℴ	ℴ	&U2134;
DOUBLE-STRUCK CAPITAL C	ℂ		&U2102;
DOUBLE-STRUCK CAPITAL H	ℍ		&U210D;
DOUBLE-STRUCK CAPITAL N	ℕ		&U2115;
DOUBLE-STRUCK CAPITAL P	ℙ		&U2119;
DOUBLE-STRUCK CAPITAL Q	ℚ		&U211A;

Character or Accent	XML	ISO	SPREAD
DOUBLE-STRUCK CAPITAL R	&#x211D;		&U211D;
DOUBLE-STRUCK CAPITAL Z	&#x2124;		&U2124;
COMBINING ACUTE ACCENT	&#x301;		&U0301;
COMBINING ACUTE ACCENT BELOW	&#x317;		&U0317;
COMBINING ACUTE TONE MARK	&#x341;		&U0341;
COMBINING ANTICLOCKWISE ARROW ABOVE	&#x20D4;		&U20D4;
COMBINING ANTICLOCKWISE RING OVERLAY	&#x20DA;		&U20DA;
COMBINING BREVE	&#x306;		&U0306;
COMBINING BREVE BELOW	&#x32E;		&U032E;
COMBINING BRIDGE BELOW	&#x32A;		&U032A;
COMBINING CANDRABINDU	&#x310;		&U0310;
COMBINING CARON	&#x30C;		&U030C;
COMBINING CARON BELOW	&#x32C;		&U032C;
COMBINING CEDILLA	&#x327;		&U0327;
COMBINING CIRCUMFLEX ACCENT	&#x302;		&U0302;
COMBINING CIRCUMFLEX ACCENT BELOW	&#x32D;		&U032D;
COMBINING CLOCKWISE ARROW ABOVE	&#x20D5;		&U20D5;
COMBINING CLOCKWISE RING OVERLAY	&#x20D9;		&U20D9;
COMBINING COMMA ABOVE	&#x313;		&U0313;
COMBINING COMMA ABOVE RIGHT	&#x315;		&U0315;
COMBINING COMMA BELOW	&#x326;		&U0326;
COMBINING DIAERESIS	&#x308;		&U0308;
COMBINING DIAERESIS BELOW	&#x324;		&U0324;
COMBINING DOT ABOVE	&#x307;		&U0307;
COMBINING DOT BELOW	&#x323;		&U0323;
COMBINING DOUBLE ACUTE ACCENT	&#x30B;		&U030B;
COMBINING DOUBLE GRAVE ACCENT	&#x30F;		&U030F;
COMBINING DOUBLE INVERTED BREVE	&#x361;		&U0361;
COMBINING DOUBLE LOW LINE	&#x333;		&U0333;
COMBINING DOUBLE OVERLINE	&#x33F;		&U033F;
COMBINING DOUBLE TILDE	&#x360;		&U0360;
COMBINING DOUBLE VERTICAL LINE ABOVE	&#x30E;		&U030E;
COMBINING DOWN TACK BELOW	&#x31E;		&U031E;
COMBINING ENCLOSING CIRCLE	&#x20DD;		&U20DD;
COMBINING ENCLOSING CIRCLE BACKSLASH	&#x20E0;		&U20E0;
COMBINING ENCLOSING DIAMOND	&#x20DF;		&U20DF;
COMBINING ENCLOSING SQUARE	&#x20DE;		&U20DE;
COMBINING FOUR DOTS ABOVE	&#x20DC;	&DotDot;	&U20DC;
COMBINING GRAVE ACCENT	&#x300;		&U0300;
COMBINING GRAVE ACCENT BELOW	&#x316;		&U0316;
COMBINING GRAVE TONE MARK	&#x340;		&U0340;
COMBINING HOOK ABOVE	&#x309;		&U0309;
COMBINING HORN	&#x31B;		&U031B;
COMBINING INVERTED BREVE	&#x311;		&U0311;
COMBINING INVERTED BREVE BELOW	&#x32F;		&U032F;
COMBINING INVERTED BRIDGE BELOW	&#x33A;		&U033A;
COMBINING INVERTED DOUBLE ARCH BELOW	&#x32B;		&U032B;
COMBINING LEFT ANGLE ABOVE	&#x31A;		&U031A;
COMBINING LEFT ARROW ABOVE	&#x20D6;		&U20D6;
COMBINING LEFT HALF RING BELOW	&#x31C;		&U031C;

Other Latin & Accents (Continued)

Accent	XML	ISO	SPREAD
COMBINING LEFT HARPOON ABOVE	&#x20D0;		&U20D0;
COMBINING LEFT RIGHT ARROW ABOVE	&#x20E1;		&U20E1;
COMBINING LEFT TACK BELOW	&#x318;		&U0318;
COMBINING LONG SOLIDUS OVERLAY	&#x338;		&U0338;
COMBINING LONG STROKE OVERLAY	&#x336;		&U0336;
COMBINING LONG VERTICAL LINE OVERLAY	&#x20D2;		&U20D2;
COMBINING LOW LINE	&#x332;		&U0332;
COMBINING MACRON	&#x304;		&U0304;
COMBINING MACRON BELOW	&#x331;		&U0331;
COMBINING MINUS SIGN BELOW	&#x320;		&U0320;
COMBINING OGONEK	&#x328;		&U0328;
COMBINING OVERLINE	&#x305;		&U0305;
COMBINING PALATALIZED HOOK BELOW	&#x321;		&U0321;
COMBINING PLUS SIGN BELOW	&#x31F;		&U031F;
COMBINING RETROFLEX HOOK BELOW	&#x322;		&U0322;
COMBINING REVERSED COMMA ABOVE	&#x314;		&U0314;
COMBINING RIGHT ARROW ABOVE	&#x20D7;		&U20D7;
COMBINING RIGHT HALF RING BELOW	&#x339;		&U0339;
COMBINING RIGHT HARPOON ABOVE	&#x20D1;		&U20D1;
COMBINING RIGHT TACK BELOW	&#x319;		&U0319;
COMBINING RING ABOVE	&#x30A;		&U030A;
COMBINING RING BELOW	&#x325;		&U0325;
COMBINING RING OVERLAY	&#x20D8;		&U20D8;
COMBINING SEAGULL BELOW	&#x33C;		&U033C;
COMBINING SHORT SOLIDUS OVERLAY	&#x337;		&U0337;
COMBINING SHORT STROKE OVERLAY	&#x335;		&U0335;
COMBINING SHORT VERTICAL LINE OVERLAY	&#x20D3;		&U20D3;
COMBINING SQUARE BELOW	&#x33B;		&U033B;
COMBINING THREE DOTS ABOVE	&#x20DB;	&tdot;	&U20DB;
COMBINING TILDE	&#x303;		&U0303;
COMBINING TILDE BELOW	&#x330;		&U0330;
COMBINING TILDE OVERLAY	&#x334;		&U0334;
COMBINING TURNED COMMA ABOVE	&#x312;		&U0312;
COMBINING UP TACK BELOW	&#x31D;		&U031D;
COMBINING VERTICAL LINE ABOVE	&#x30D;		&U030D;
COMBINING VERTICAL LINE BELOW	&#x329;		&U0329;
COMBINING VERTICAL TILDE	&#x33E;		&U033E;
COMBINING X ABOVE	&#x33D;		&U033D;

Modifier	XML	ISO	SPREAD
modifier letter acute accent	`&#x2CA;`		`&U02CA;`
modifier letter apostrophe	`&#x2BC;`		`&U02BC;`
modifier letter centred left half ring	`&#x2D3;`		`&U02D3;`
modifier letter centred right half ring	`&#x2D2;`		`&U02D2;`
modifier letter circumflex accent	`&#x2C6;`		`&U02C6;`
modifier letter double prime	`&#x2BA;`		`&U02BA;`
modifier letter down arrowhead	`&#x2C5;`		`&U02C5;`
modifier letter down tack	`&#x2D5;`		`&U02D5;`
modifier letter extra-high tone bar	`&#x2E5;`		`&U02E5;`
modifier letter extra-low tone bar	`&#x2E9;`		`&U02E9;`
modifier letter glottal stop	`&#x2C0;`		`&U02C0;`
modifier letter grave accent	`&#x2CB;`		`&U02CB;`
modifier letter half triangular colon	`&#x2D1;`		`&U02D1;`
modifier letter high tone bar	`&#x2E6;`		`&U02E6;`
modifier letter left arrowhead	`&#x2C2;`		`&U02C2;`
modifier letter left half ring	`&#x2BF;`		`&U02BF;`
modifier letter low acute accent	`&#x2CF;`		`&U02CF;`
modifier letter low grave accent	`&#x2CE;`		`&U02CE;`
modifier letter low macron	`&#x2CD;`		`&U02CD;`
modifier letter low tone bar	`&#x2E8;`		`&U02E8;`
modifier letter low vertical line	`&#x2CC;`		`&U02CC;`
modifier letter macron	`&#x2C9;`		`&U02C9;`
modifier letter mid tone bar	`&#x2E7;`		`&U02E7;`
modifier letter minus sign	`&#x2D7;`		`&U02D7;`
modifier letter plus sign	`&#x2D6;`		`&U02D6;`
modifier letter prime	`&#x2B9;`		`&U02B9;`
modifier letter reversed comma	`&#x2BD;`		`&U02BD;`
modifier letter reversed glottal stop	`&#x2C1;`		`&U02C1;`
modifier letter rhotic hook	`&#x2DE;`		`&U02DE;`
modifier letter right arrowhead	`&#x2C3;`		`&U02C3;`
modifier letter right half ring	`&#x2BE;`		`&U02BE;`
modifier letter small capital inverted r	`&#x2B6;`		`&U02B6;`
modifier letter small gamma	`&#x2E0;`		`&U02E0;`
modifier letter small h	`&#x2B0;`		`&U02B0;`
modifier letter small h with hook	`&#x2B1;`		`&U02B1;`
modifier letter small j	`&#x2B2;`		`&U02B2;`
modifier letter small l	`&#x2E1;`		`&U02E1;`
modifier letter small r	`&#x2B3;`		`&U02B3;`
modifier letter small reversed glottal stop	`&#x2E4;`		`&U02E4;`
modifier letter small s	`&#x2E2;`		`&U02E2;`
modifier letter small turned r	`&#x2B4;`		`&U02B4;`
modifier letter small turned r with hook	`&#x2B5;`		`&U02B5;`
modifier letter small w	`&#x2B7;`		`&U02B7;`
modifier letter small x	`&#x2E3;`		`&U02E3;`
modifier letter small y	`&#x2B8;`		`&U02B8;`
modifier letter triangular colon	`&#x2D0;`		`&U02D0;`
modifier letter turned comma	`&#x2BB;`		`&U02BB;`
modifier letter up arrowhead	`&#x2C4;`		`&U02C4;`
modifier letter up tack	`&#x2D4;`		`&U02D4;`
modifier letter vertical line	`&#x2C8;`		`&U02C8;`

CIRCLED LATIN CAPITAL LETTER

Character	XML	ISO	SPREAD
A	&#x24B6;	&Acircle;	&U24B6;
B	&#x24B7;	&Bcircle;	&U24B7;
C	&#x24B8;	&Ccircle;	&U24B8;
D	&#x24B9;	&Dcircle;	&U24B9;
E	&#x24BA;	&Ecircle;	&U24BA;
F	&#x24BB;	&Fcircle;	&U24BB;
G	&#x24BC;	&Gcircle;	&U24BC;
H	&#x24BD;	&Hcircle;	&U24BD;
I	&#x24BE;	&Icircle;	&U24BE;
J	&#x24BF;	&Jcircle;	&U24BF;
K	&#x24C0;	&Kcircle;	&U24C0;
L	&#x24C1;	&Lcircle;	&U24C1;
M	&#x24C2;	&Mcircle;	&U24C2;
N	&#x24C3;	&Ncircle;	&U24C3;
O	&#x24C4;	&Ocircle;	&U24C4;
P	&#x24C5;	&Pcircle;	&U24C5;
Q	&#x24C6;	&Qcircle;	&U24C6;
R	&#x24C7;	&Rcircle;	&U24C7;
S	&#x24C8;	&Scircle;	&U24C8;
T	&#x24C9;	&Tcircle;	&U24C9;
U	&#x24CA;	&Ucircle;	&U24CA;
V	&#x24CB;	&Vcircle;	&U24CB;
W	&#x24CC;	&Wcircle;	&U24CC;
X	&#x24CD;	&Xcircle;	&U24CD;
Y	&#x24CE;	&Ycircle;	&U24CE;
Z	&#x24CF;	&Zcircle;	&U24CF;

CIRCLED LATIN SMALL LETTER

Character	XML	ISO	SPREAD
A	&#x24D0;	&acircle;	&U24D0;
B	&#x24D1;	&bcircle;	&U24D1;
C	&#x24D2;	&ccircle;	&U24D2;
D	&#x24D3;	&dcircle;	&U24D3;
E	&#x24D4;	&ecircle;	&U24D4;
F	&#x24D5;	&fcircle;	&U24D5;
G	&#x24D6;	&gcircle;	&U24D6;
H	&#x24D7;	&hcircle;	&U24D7;
I	&#x24D8;	&icircle;	&U24D8;
J	&#x24D9;	&jcircle;	&U24D9;
K	&#x24DA;	&kcircle;	&U24DA;
L	&#x24DB;	&lcircle;	&U24DB;
M	&#x24DC;	&mcircle;	&U24DC;
N	&#x24DD;	&cnircle;	&U24DD;

CIRCLED LATIN SMALL LETTER (Continued)

Character	XML	ISO	SPREAD
O	&#x24DE;	&ocircle;	&U24DE;
P	&#x24DF;	&pcircle;	&U24DF;
Q	&#x24E0;	&qcircle;	&U24E0;
R	&#x24E1;	&rcircle;	&U24E1;
S	&#x24E2;	&scircle;	&U24E2;
T	&#x24E3;	&tcircle;	&U24E3;
U	&#x24E4;	&ucircle;	&U24E4;
V	&#x24E5;	&vcircle;	&U24E5;
W	&#x24E6;	&wcircle;	&U24E6;
X	&#x24E7;	&xcircle;	&U24E7;
Y	&#x24E8;	&ycircle;	&U24E8;
Z	&#x24E9;	&zcircle;	&U24E9;

MALAYALAM LETTER

Character	XML	SPREAD
A	&#xD05;	&U0D05;
AA	&#xD06;	&U0D06;
AI	&#xD10;	&U0D10;
AU	&#xD14;	&U0D14;
BA	&#xD2C;	&U0D2C;
BHA	&#xD2D;	&U0D2D;
CA	&#xD1A;	&U0D1A;
CHA	&#xD1B;	&U0D1B;
DA	&#xD26;	&U0D26;
DDA	&#xD21;	&U0D21;
DDHA	&#xD22;	&U0D22;
DHA	&#xD27;	&U0D27;
E	&#xD0E;	&U0D0E;
EE	&#xD0F;	&U0D0F;
GA	&#xD17;	&U0D17;
GHA	&#xD18;	&U0D18;
HA	&#xD39;	&U0D39;
I	&#xD07;	&U0D07;
II	&#xD08;	&U0D08;
JA	&#xD1C;	&U0D1C;
JHA	&#xD1D;	&U0D1D;
KA	&#xD15;	&U0D15;
KHA	&#xD16;	&U0D16;
LA	&#xD32;	&U0D32;
LLA	&#xD33;	&U0D33;
LLLA	&#xD34;	&U0D34;
MA	&#xD2E;	&U0D2E;
NA	&#xD28;	&U0D28;

MALAYALAM LETTER (Continued)

Character	XML	SPREAD
NGA	ങ	&U0D19;
NNA	ണ	&U0D23;
NYA	ഞ	&U0D1E;
O	ഒ	&U0D12;
OO	ഓ	&U0D13;
PA	പ	&U0D2A;
PHA	ഫ	&U0D2B;
RA	ര	&U0D30;
RRA	റ	&U0D31;
SA	സ	&U0D38;
SHA	ശ	&U0D36;
SSA	ഷ	&U0D37;
TA	ത	&U0D24;
THA	ഥ	&U0D25;
TTA	ട	&U0D1F;
TTHA	ഠ	&U0D20;
U	ഉ	&U0D09;
UU	ഊ	&U0D0A;
VA	വ	&U0D35;
VOCALIC L	ഌ	&U0D0C;
VOCALIC LL	ൡ	&U0D61;
VOCALIC R	ഋ	&U0D0B;
VOCALIC RR	ൠ	&U0D60;
YA	യ	&U0D2F;

MALAYALAM VOWEL SIGN

Character	XML	SPREAD
AA	ാ	&U0D3E;
AI	ൈ	&U0D48;
AU	ൌ	&U0D4C;
E	െ	&U0D46;
EE	േ	&U0D47;
I	ി	&U0D3F;
II	ീ	&U0D40;
O	ൊ	&U0D4A;
OO	ോ	&U0D4B;
U	ു	&U0D41;
UU	ൂ	&U0D42;
VOCALIC R	ൃ	&U0D43;

Other Malayam

Character	XML	SPREAD
MALAYALAM AU LENGTH MARK	&#xD57;	&U0D57;
MALAYALAM SIGN ANUSVARA	&#xD02;	&U0D02;
MALAYALAM SIGN VIRAMA	&#xD4D;	&U0D4D;
MALAYALAM SIGN VISARGA	&#xD03;	&U0D03;

Malayam Numerals

Character	XML	SPREAD
malayalam digit eight	&#xD6E;	&U0D6E;
malayalam digit five	&#xD6B;	&U0D6B;
malayalam digit four	&#xD6A;	&U0D6A;
malayalam digit nine	&#xD6F;	&U0D6F;
malayalam digit one	&#xD67;	&U0D67;
malayalam digit seven	&#xD6D;	&U0D6D;
malayalam digit six	&#xD6C;	&U0D6C;
malayalam digit three	&#xD69;	&U0D69;
malayalam digit two	&#xD68;	&U0D68;
malayalam digit zero	&#xD66;	&U0D66;

NUMERALS

Character	XML	ISO	SPREAD
circled digit eight	&#x2467;		&U2467;
circled digit five	&#x2464;		&U2464;
circled digit four	&#x2463;		&U2463;
circled digit nine	&#x2468;		&U2468;
circled digit one	&#x2460;		&U2460;
circled digit seven	&#x2466;		&U2466;
circled digit six	&#x2465;		&U2465;
circled digit three	&#x2462;		&U2462;
circled digit two	&#x2461;		&U2461;
circled digit zero	&#x24EA;		&U24EA;
dingbat negative circled digit eight	&#x277D;		&U277D;
dingbat negative circled digit five	&#x277A;		&U277A;
dingbat negative circled digit four	&#x2779;		&U2779;
dingbat negative circled digit nine	&#x277E;		&U277E;
dingbat negative circled digit one	&#x2776;		&U2776;
dingbat negative circled digit seven	&#x277C;		&U277C;

Numerals (Continued)

Character	XML	ISO	SPREAD
dingbat negative circled digit six	`&#x277B;`		`&U277B;`
dingbat negative circled digit three	`&#x2778;`		`&U2778;`
dingbat negative circled digit two	`&#x2777;`		`&U2777;`
dingbat negative circled number ten	`&#x277F;`		`&U277F;`
vulgar fraction five eighths	`&#x215D;`	`&frac58;`	`&U215D;`
vulgar fraction five sixths	`&#x215a;`	`&frac56;`	`&U215A;`
vulgar fraction four fifths	`&#x2158;`	`&frac45;`	`&U2158;`
vulgar fraction one eighth	`&#x215B;`	`&frac18;`	`&U215B;`
vulgar fraction one fifth	`&#x2155;`	`&frac15;`	`&U2155;`
vulgar fraction one half (½)	`&#xBD;`	`&half;`	`&U00BD;`
vulgar fraction one quarter (¼)	`&#xBC;`	`&frac14;`	`&U00BC;`
vulgar fraction one sixth	`&#x2159;`	`&frac16;`	`&U2159;`
vulgar fraction one third	`&#x2153;`	`&frac13;`	`&U2153;`
vulgar fraction seven eighths	`&#x215E;`	`&frac78;`	`&U215E;`
vulgar fraction three eighths	`&#x215C;`	`&frac38;`	`&U215C;`
vulgar fraction three fifths	`&#x2157;`	`&frac35;`	`&U2157;`
vulgar fraction three quarters (¾)	`&#xBE;`	`&frac34;`	`&U00BE;`
vulgar fraction two fifths	`&#x2156;`	`&frac25;`	`&U2156;`
vulgar fraction two thirds	`&#x2154;`	`&frac23;`	`&U2154;`

ORIYA LETTER

Character	XML	SPREAD
A	`&#xB05;`	`&U0B05;`
AA	`&#xB06;`	`&U0B06;`
AI	`&#xB10;`	`&U0B10;`
AU	`&#xB14;`	`&U0B14;`
BA	`&#xB2C;`	`&U0B2C;`
BHA	`&#xB2D;`	`&U0B2D;`
CA	`&#xB1A;`	`&U0B1A;`
CHA	`&#xB1B;`	`&U0B1B;`
DA	`&#xB26;`	`&U0B26;`
DDA	`&#xB21;`	`&U0B21;`
DDHA	`&#xB22;`	`&U0B22;`
DHA	`&#xB27;`	`&U0B27;`
E	`&#xB0F;`	`&U0B0F;`
GA	`&#xB17;`	`&U0B17;`
GHA	`&#xB18;`	`&U0B18;`
HA	`&#xB39;`	`&U0B39;`
I	`&#xB07;`	`&U0B07;`
II	`&#xB08;`	`&U0B08;`
JA	`&#xB1C;`	`&U0B1C;`
JHA	`&#xB1D;`	`&U0B1D;`
KA	`&#xB15;`	`&U0B15;`

ORIYA LETTER (Continued)

Character	XML	SPREAD
KHA	ଖ	&U0B16;
LA	ଲ	&U0B32;
LLA	ଳ	&U0B33;
MA	ମ	&U0B2E;
NA	ନ	&U0B28;
NGA	ଙ	&U0B19;
NNA	ଣ	&U0B23;
NYA	ଞ	&U0B1E;
O	ଓ	&U0B13;
PA	ପ	&U0B2A;
PHA	ଫ	&U0B2B;
RA	ର	&U0B30;
RHA	ଢ଼	&U0B5D;
RRA	ଡ଼	&U0B5C;
SA	ସ	&U0B38;
SHA	ଶ	&U0B36;
SSA	ଷ	&U0B37;
TA	ତ	&U0B24;
THA	ଥ	&U0B25;
TTA	ଟ	&U0B1F;
TTHA	ଠ	&U0B20;
U	ଉ	&U0B09;
UU	ଊ	&U0B0A;
VOCALIC L	ଌ	&U0B0C;
VOCALIC LL	ୡ	&U0B61;
VOCALIC R	ଋ	&U0B0B;
VOCALIC RR	ୠ	&U0B60;
YA	ଯ	&U0B2F;
YYA	ୟ	&U0B5F;

ORIYA VOWEL SIGN

Character	XML	SPREAD
AA	ା	&U0B3E;
AI	ୈ	&U0B48;
AU	ୌ	&U0B4C;
E	େ	&U0B47;
I	ି	&U0B3F;
II	ୀ	&U0B40;
O	ୋ	&U0B4B;
U	ୁ	&U0B41;
UU	ୂ	&U0B42;
VOCALIC R	ୃ	&U0B43;

Other Oriya

Character	XML	SPREAD
ORIYA AI LENGTH MARK	ୖ	&U0B56;
ORIYA AU LENGTH MARK	ୗ	&U0B57;
ORIYA SIGN ANUSVARA	ଂ	&U0B02;
ORIYA SIGN CANDRABINDU	ଁ	&U0B01;
ORIYA SIGN NUKTA	଼	&U0B3C;
ORIYA SIGN VIRAMA	୍	&U0B4D;
ORIYA SIGN VISARGA	ଃ	&U0B03;

Oriya Numerals

Character	XML	ISO	SPREAD
oriya digit eight	୮		&U0B6E;
oriya digit five	୫		&U0B6B;
oriya digit four	୪		&U0B6A;
oriya digit nine	୯		&U0B6F;
oriya digit one	୧		&U0B67;
oriya digit seven	୭		&U0B6D;
oriya digit six	୬		&U0B6C;
oriya digit three	୩		&U0B69;
oriya digit two	୨		&U0B68;
oriya digit zero	୦		&U0B66;
per mille sign	‰	‰	&U2030;
per ten thousand sign	‱		&U2031;
percent sign (%)	%		&U0025;

TAMIL LETTER

Character	XML	SPREAD
A	அ	&U0B85;
AA	ஆ	&U0B86;
AI	ஐ	&U0B90;
AU	ஔ	&U0B94;
CA	ச	&U0B9A;
E	எ	&U0B8E;
EE	ஏ	&U0B8F;
HA	ஹ	&U0BB9;
I	இ	&U0B87;
II	ஈ	&U0B88;

TAMIL LETTER (Continued)

Character	XML	SPREAD
JA	`&#xB9C;`	`&U0B9C;`
KA	`&#xB95;`	`&U0B95;`
LA	`&#xBB2;`	`&U0BB2;`
LLA	`&#xBB3;`	`&U0BB3;`
LLLA	`&#xBB4;`	`&U0BB4;`
MA	`&#xBAE;`	`&U0BAE;`
NA	`&#xBA8;`	`&U0BA8;`
NGA	`&#xB99;`	`&U0B99;`
NNA	`&#xBA3;`	`&U0BA3;`
NNNA	`&#xBA9;`	`&U0BA9;`
NYA	`&#xB9E;`	`&U0B9E;`
O	`&#xB92;`	`&U0B92;`
OO	`&#xB93;`	`&U0B93;`
PA	`&#xBAA;`	`&U0BAA;`
RA	`&#xBB0;`	`&U0BB0;`
RRA	`&#xBB1;`	`&U0BB1;`
SA	`&#xBB8;`	`&U0BB8;`
SSA	`&#xBB7;`	`&U0BB7;`
TA	`&#xBA4;`	`&U0BA4;`
TTA	`&#xB9F;`	`&U0B9F;`
U	`&#xB89;`	`&U0B89;`
UU	`&#xB8A;`	`&U0B8A;`
VA	`&#xBB5;`	`&U0BB5;`
YA	`&#xBAF;`	`&U0BAF;`

TAMIL VOWEL SIGN

Character	XML	SPREAD
AA	`&#xBBE;`	`&U0BBE;`
AI	`&#xBC8;`	`&U0BC8;`
AU	`&#xBCC;`	`&U0BCC;`
E	`&#xBC6;`	`&U0BC6;`
EE	`&#xBC7;`	`&U0BC7;`
I	`&#xBBF;`	`&U0BBF;`
II	`&#xBC0;`	`&U0BC0;`
O	`&#xBCA;`	`&U0BCA;`
OO	`&#xBCB;`	`&U0BCB;`
U	`&#xBC1;`	`&U0BC1;`
UU	`&#xBC2;`	`&U0BC2;`

Tamil Numerals

Character	XML	SPREAD
tamil digit eight	&#xBEE;	&U0BEE;
tamil digit five	&#xBEB;	&U0BEB;
tamil digit four	&#xBEA;	&U0BEA;
tamil digit nine	&#xBEF;	&U0BEF;
tamil digit one	&#xBE7;	&U0BE7;
tamil digit seven	&#xBED;	&U0BED;
tamil digit six	&#xBEC;	&U0BEC;
tamil digit three	&#xBE9;	&U0BE9;
tamil digit two	&#xBE8;	&U0BE8;
tamil number one hundred	&#xBF1;	&U0BF1;
tamil number one thousand	&#xBF2;	&U0BF2;
tamil number ten	&#xBF0;	&U0BF0;

TELUGU LETTER

Character	XML	SPREAD
A	&#xC05;	&U0C05;
AA	&#xC06;	&U0C06;
AI	&#xC10;	&U0C10;
AU	&#xC14;	&U0C14;
BA	&#xC2C;	&U0C2C;
BHA	&#xC2D;	&U0C2D;
CA	&#xC1A;	&U0C1A;
CHA	&#xC1B;	&U0C1B;
DA	&#xC26;	&U0C26;
DDA	&#xC21;	&U0C21;
DDHA	&#xC22;	&U0C22;
DHA	&#xC27;	&U0C27;
E	&#xC0E;	&U0C0E;
EE	&#xC0F;	&U0C0F;
GA	&#xC17;	&U0C17;
GHA	&#xC18;	&U0C18;
HA	&#xC39;	&U0C39;

TELUGU LETTER (Continued)

Character	XML	SPREAD
I	&#xC07;	&U0C07;
II	&#xC08;	&U0C08;
JA	&#xC1C;	&U0C1C;
JHA	&#xC1D;	&U0C1D;
KA	&#xC15;	&U0C15;
KHA	&#xC16;	&U0C16;
LA	&#xC32;	&U0C32;
LLA	&#xC33;	&U0C33;
MA	&#xC2E;	&U0C2E;
NA	&#xC28;	&U0C28;
NGA	&#xC19;	&U0C19;
NNA	&#xC23;	&U0C23;
NYA	&#xC1E;	&U0C1E;
O	&#xC12;	&U0C12;
OO	&#xC13;	&U0C13;
PA	&#xC2A;	&U0C2A;
PHA	&#xC2B;	&U0C2B;
RA	&#xC30;	&U0C30;
RRA	&#xC31;	&U0C31;
SA	&#xC38;	&U0C38;
SHA	&#xC36;	&U0C36;
SSA	&#xC37;	&U0C37;
TA	&#xC24;	&U0C24;
THA	&#xC25;	&U0C25;
TTA	&#xC1F;	&U0C1F;
TTHA	&#xC20;	&U0C20;
U	&#xC09;	&U0C09;
UU	&#xC0A;	&U0C0A;
VA	&#xC35;	&U0C35;
VOCALIC L	&#xC0C;	&U0C0C;
VOCALIC LL	&#xC61;	&U0C61;
VOCALIC R	&#xC0B;	&U0C0B;
VOCALIC RR	&#xC60;	&U0C60;
YA	&#xC2F;	&U0C2F;

TELUGU VOWEL SIGN

Character	XML	SPREAD
AA	&#xC3E;	&U0C3E;
AI	&#xC48;	&U0C48;
AU	&#xC4C;	&U0C4C;
E	&#xC46;	&U0C46;
EE	&#xC47;	&U0C47;
I	&#xC3F;	&U0C3F;

TELUGU VOWEL SIGN (Continued)

Character	XML	SPREAD
II	ీ	&U0C40;
O	ొ	&U0C4A;
OO	ో	&U0C4B;
U	ు	&U0C41;
UU	ూ	&U0C42;
VOCALIC R	ృ	&U0C43;
VOCALIC RR	ౄ	&U0C44;

Other Telugu

Character	XML	SPREAD
TELUGU AI LENGTH MARK	ౖ	&U0C56;
TELUGU LENGTH MARK	ౕ	&U0C55;
TELUGU SIGN ANUSVARA	ం	&U0C02;
TELUGU SIGN CANDRABINDU	ఁ	&U0C01;
TELUGU SIGN VIRAMA	్	&U0C4D;
TELUGU SIGN VISARGA	ః	&U0C03;

Telugu Numerals

Character	XML	SPREAD
telugu digit eight	౮	&U0C6E;
telugu digit five	౫	&U0C6B;
telugu digit four	౪	&U0C6A;
telugu digit nine	౯	&U0C6F;
telugu digit one	౧	&U0C67;
telugu digit seven	౭	&U0C6D;
telugu digit six	౬	&U0C6C;
telugu digit three	౩	&U0C69;
telugu digit two	౨	&U0C68;
telugu digit zero	౦	&U0C66;

THAI CHARACTER

Character	XML	SPREAD
ANGKHANKHU	&#xE5A;	&U0E5A;
BO BAIMAI	&#xE1A;	&U0E1A;
CHO CHAN	&#xE08;	&U0E08;
CHO CHANG	&#xE0A;	&U0E0A;
CHO CHING	&#xE09;	&U0E09;
CHO CHOE	&#xE0C;	&U0E0C;
DO CHADA	&#xE0E;	&U0E0E;
DO DEK	&#xE14;	&U0E14;
FO FA	&#xE1D;	&U0E1D;
FO FAN	&#xE1F;	&U0E1F;
FONGMAN	&#xE4F;	&U0E4F;
HO HIP	&#xE2B;	&U0E2B;
HO NOKHUK	&#xE2E;	&U0E2E;
KHO KHAI	&#xE02;	&U0E02;
KHO KHON	&#xE05;	&U0E05;
KHO KHUAT	&#xE03;	&U0E03;
KHO KHWAI	&#xE04;	&U0E04;
KHO RAKHANG	&#xE06;	&U0E06;
KHOMUT	&#xE5B;	&U0E5B;
KO KAI	&#xE01;	&U0E01;
LAKKHANGYAO	&#xE45;	&U0E45;
LO CHULA	&#xE2C;	&U0E2C;
LO LING	&#xE25;	&U0E25;
LU	&#xE26;	&U0E26;
MAI CHATTAWA	&#xE4B;	&U0E4B;
MAI EK	&#xE48;	&U0E48;
MAI HAN-AKAT	&#xE31;	&U0E31;
MAI THO	&#xE49;	&U0E49;
MAI TRI	&#xE4A;	&U0E4A;
MAITAIKHU	&#xE47;	&U0E47;
MAIYAMOK	&#xE46;	&U0E46;
MO MA	&#xE21;	&U0E21;
NGO NGU	&#xE07;	&U0E07;
NIKHAHIT	&#xE4D;	&U0E4D;
NO NEN	&#xE13;	&U0E13;
NO NU	&#xE19;	&U0E19;
O ANG	&#xE2D;	&U0E2D;
PAIYANNOI	&#xE2F;	&U0E2F;
PHINTHU	&#xE3A;	&U0E3A;
PHO PHAN	&#xE1E;	&U0E1E;
PHO PHUNG	&#xE1C;	&U0E1C;
PHO SAMPHAO	&#xE20;	&U0E20;
PO PLA	&#xE1B;	&U0E1B;
RO RUA	&#xE23;	&U0E23;
RU	&#xE24;	&U0E24;
SARA A	&#xE30;	&U0E30;
SARA AA	&#xE32;	&U0E32;
SARA AE	&#xE41;	&U0E41;
SARA AI MAIMALAI	&#xE44;	&U0E44;

The XML & SGML Cookbook

THAI CHARACTER (Continued)

Character	XML	SPREAD
SARA AI MAIMUAN	&#xE43;	&U0E43;
SARA AM	&#xE33;	&U0E33;
SARA E	&#xE40;	&U0E40;
SARA I	&#xE34;	&U0E34;
SARA II	&#xE35;	&U0E35;
SARA O	&#xE42;	&U0E42;
SARA U	&#xE38;	&U0E38;
SARA UE	&#xE36;	&U0E36;
SARA UEE	&#xE37;	&U0E37;
SARA UU	&#xE39;	&U0E39;
SO RUSI	&#xE29;	&U0E29;
SO SALA	&#xE28;	&U0E28;
SO SO	&#xE0B;	&U0E0B;
SO SUA	&#xE2A;	&U0E2A;
THANTHAKHAT	&#xE4C;	&U0E4C;
THO NANGMONTHO	&#xE11;	&U0E11;
THO PHUTHAO	&#xE12;	&U0E12;
THO THAHAN	&#xE17;	&U0E17;
THO THAN	&#xE10;	&U0E10;
THO THONG	&#xE18;	&U0E18;
THO THUNG	&#xE16;	&U0E16;
TO PATAK	&#xE0F;	&U0E0F;
TO TAO	&#xE15;	&U0E15;
WO WAEN	&#xE27;	&U0E27;
YAMAKKAN	&#xE4E;	&U0E4E;
YO YAK	&#xE22;	&U0E22;
YO YING	&#xE0D;	&U0E0D;

Thai Numerals

Character	XML	SPREAD
thai digit eight	&#xE58;	&U0E58;
thai digit five	&#xE55;	&U0E55;
thai digit four	&#xE54;	&U0E54;
thai digit nine	&#xE59;	&U0E59;
thai digit one	&#xE51;	&U0E51;
thai digit seven	&#xE57;	&U0E57;
thai digit six	&#xE56;	&U0E56;
thai digit three	&#xE53;	&U0E53;
thai digit two	&#xE52;	&U0E52;
thai digit zero	&#xE50;	&U0E50;

PUNCTUATION

Character	XML	ISO	SPREAD
apostrophe	&apos;		&U0027;
arabic comma	&#x60C;		&U060C;
arabic full stop	&#x6D4;		&U06D4;
arabic question mark	&#x61F;		&U061F;
arabic semicolon	&#x61B;		&U061B;
armenian abbreviation mark	&#x55F;		&U055F;
armenian apostrophe	&#x55A;		&U055A;
armenian comma	&#x55D;		&U055D;
armenian emphasis mark	&#x55B;		&U055B;
armenian exclamation mark	&#x55C;		&U055C;
armenian full stop	&#x589;		&U0589;
armenian question mark	&#x55E;		&U055E;
bullet	&#x2022;	&bull;	&U2022;
caret	&#x2038;		&U2038;
colon	&#x3A;		&U003A;
comma	&#x2C;		&U002C;
dagger	&#x2020;	&dagger;	&U2020;
ditto mark	&#x3003;		&U3003;
double dagger	&#x2021;	&Dagger;	&U2021;
double exclamation mark	&#x203C;		&U203C;
double high-reversed-9 quotation mark	&#x201F;		&U201F;
double low-9 quotation mark	&#x201E;	&ldquor;	&U201E;
double low line	&#x2017;		&U2017;
double prime	&#x2033;	&Prime;	&U2033;
double vertical line	&#x2016;	&Verbar;	&U2016;
em dash	&#x2014;	&mdash;	&U2014;
en dash	&#x2013;	&ndash;	&U2013;
exclamation mark	&#x21;		&U0021;
figure dash	&#x2012;		&U2012;
georgian paragraph separator	&#x10FB;		&U10FB;
greek ano teleia	&#x387;		&U0387;
greek question mark	&#x37E;		&U037E;
gujarati sign avagraha	&#xABD;		&U0ABD;
horizontal bar	&#x2015;	&horbar;	&U2015;
horizontal ellipsis	&#x2026;	&hellip;	&U2026;
hyphen-minus	&#x2D;		&U002D;
hyphen	&#x2010;	&hyphen;	&U2010;
hyphenation point	&#x2027;		&U2027;
ideographic closing mark	&#x3006;		&U3006;
ideographic comma	&#x3001;		&U3001;
ideographic full stop	&#x3002;		&U3002;
ideographic iteration mark	&#x3005;		&U3005;
inverted exclamation mark	&#xA1;	&iexcl;	&U00A1;
inverted question mark	&#xBF;	&iquest;	&U00BF;
lao ellipsis	&#xEAF;		&U0EAF;
left-pointing angle bracket	&#x2329;	&lang;	&U2329;
left-pointing double angle quotation mark	&#xAB;		&U00AB;
left angle bracket	&#x3008;		&U3008;
left black lenticular bracket	&#x3010;		&U3010;

Punctuation (Continued)

Character	XML	ISO	SPREAD
left corner bracket	「		&U300C;
left curly bracket	{		&U007B;
left double angle bracket	《		&U300A;
left double quotation mark	“	“	&U201C;
left parenthesis	(		&U0028;
left single quotation mark	‘	‘	&U2018;
left square bracket	[		&U005B;
left square bracket with quill	⁅		&U2045;
left tortoise shell bracket	〔		&U3014;
left white corner bracket	『		&U300E;
left white lenticular bracket	〖		&U3016;
left white square bracket	〚		&U301A;
left white tortoise shell bracket	〘		&U3018;
middle dot	·	·	&U00B7;
non-breaking hyphen	‑		&U2011;
one dot leader	․		&U2024;
oriya sign avagraha	ଽ		&U0B3D;
prime	′	′	&U2032;
question mark	?		&U003F;
quotation mark	"		&U0022;
reference mark	※		&U203B;
reverse solidus	\		&U005C;
reversed double prime	‶		&U2036;
reversed prime	‵		&U2035;
reversed triple prime	‷		&U2037;
right-pointing angle bracket	〉	⟩	&U232A;
right-pointing double angle quotation mark	»		&U00BB;
right angle bracket	〉		&U3009;
right black lenticular bracket	】		&U3011;
right corner bracket	」		&U300D;
right curly bracket	}		&U007D;
right double angle bracket	》		&U300B;
right double quotation mark	”	”, ”	&U201D;
right parenthesis	)		&U0029;
right single quotation mark	’	’, ’	&U2019;
right square bracket	]		&U005D;
right square bracket with quill	⁆		&U2046;
right tortoise shell bracket	〕		&U3015;
right white corner bracket	』		&U300F;
right white lenticular bracket	〗		&U3017;
right white square bracket	〛		&U301B;
right white tortoise shell bracket	〙		&U3019;
semicolon	;		&U003B;
single high-reversed-9 quotation mark	‛		&U201B;
single left-pointing angle quotation mark	‹	«	&U2039;
single low-9 quotation mark	‚	‚	&U201A;
single right-pointing angle quotation mark	›	»	&U203A;
soft hyphen	­	­	&U00AD;
solidus	/		&U002F;
triangular bullet	‣		&U2023;

Punctuation (Continued)

Character	XML	ISO	SPREAD
triple prime	&#x2034;	&tprime;	&U2034;
two dot leader	&#x2025;	…, ‥	&U2025;
wave dash	&#x301C;		&U301C;
wavy dash	&#x3030;		&U3030;

White-Space

Character	XML	ISO	SPREAD
em quad	&#x2001;		&U2001;
em space			&U2003;
en quad	&#x2000;		&U2000;
en space			&U2002;
figure space			&U2007;
four-per-em space	&#x2005;		&U2005;
hair space			&U200A;
ideographic space			&U3000;
line separator	&#x2028;		&U2028;
no-break space			&U00A0;
paragraph separator	&#x2029;		&U2029;
punctuation space			&U2008;
six-per-em space	&#x2006;		&U2006;
space	&#x20;		&U0020;
thin space			&U2009;
three-per-em space	&#x2004;		&U2004;
zero width space	&#x200B;		&U200B;

MARKS & SYMBOLS

Character	XML	ISO	SPREAD
ALEF SYMBOL	&#x2135;	&aleph;	&U2135;
ANGSTROM SIGN	&#x212B;	&angst;	&U212B;
BET SYMBOL	&#x2136;		&U2136;
DALET SYMBOL	&#x2138;		&U2138;
ESTIMATED SYMBOL	&#x212E;		&U212E;
EULER CONSTANT	&#x2107;	&epsiv;	&U2107;
FEMININE ORDINAL INDICATOR	&#xAA;	&ordf;	&U00AA;
GIMEL SYMBOL	&#x2137;		&U2137;
IDEOGRAPHIC DEPARTING TONE MARK	&#x302C;		&U302C;

Character	XML	ISO	SPREAD
IDEOGRAPHIC ENTERING TONE MARK	&#x302D;		&U302D;
IDEOGRAPHIC LEVEL TONE MARK	&#x302A;		&U302A;
IDEOGRAPHIC RISING TONE MARK	&#x302B;		&U302B;
KELVIN SIGN	&#x212A;		&U212A;
MASCULINE ORDINAL INDICATOR	&#xBA;	&ordm;	&U00BA;
MICRO SIGN	&#xB5;	&micro;	&U00B5;
NUMERO SIGN	&#x2116;		&U2116;
OHM SIGN	&#x2126;		&U2126;
PLANCK CONSTANT	&#x210E;		&U210E;
PLANCK CONSTANT OVER TWO PI	&#x210F;		&U210F;
RUPEE SIGN	&#x20A8;		&U20A8;
SERVICE MARK	&#x2120;		&U2120;
SOUND RECORDING COPYRIGHT	&#x2117;	&copysr;	&U2117;
TELEPHONE SIGN	&#x2121;		&U2121;
TRADE MARK SIGN	&#x2122;	&trade;	&U2122;
account of	&#x2100;		&U2100;
acute accent	&#xB4;	&acute;	&U00B4;
addressed to the subject	&#x2101;		&U2101;
adi shakti	&#x262C;		&U262C;
airplane	&#x2708;		&U2708;
all around-profile	&#x232E;		&U232E;
all equal to	&#x224C;		&U224C;
almost equal or equal to	&#x224A;		&U224A;
almost equal to	&#x2248;		&U2248;
ampersand	&amp;		&U0026;
angle	&#x2220;		&U2220;
ankh	&#x2625;		&U2625;
anticlockwise contour integral	&#x2233;		&U2233;
anticlockwise open circle arrow	&#x21BA;		&U21BA;
anticlockwise top semicircle arrow	&#x21B6;		&U21B6;
approaches the limit	&#x2250;		&U2250;
approximately but not actually equal to	&#x2246;		&U2246;
approximately equal to	&#x2245;	&cong;	&U2245;
approximately equal to or the image of	&#x2252;		&U2252;
aquarius	&#x2652;		&U2652;
arc	&#x2312;		&U2312;
aries	&#x2648;		&U2648;
ascending node	&#x260A;		&U260A;
assertion	&#x22A6;		&U22A6;
asterisk	&#x2A;		&U002A;
asterisk operator	&#x2217;	&lowast;	&U2217;
asterism	&#x2042;		&U2042;
asymptotically equal to	&#x2243;	&sime;	&U2243;
back-tilted shadowed white rightwards arrow	&#x27AB;		&U27AB;
balloon-spoked asterisk	&#x2749;		&U2749;
ballot box	&#x2610;		&U2610;
ballot box with check	&#x2611;		&U2611;
ballot box with x	&#x2612;		&U2612;
ballot x	&#x2717;	&cross;	&U2717;
beamed eighth notes	&#x266B;		&U266B;

Marks & Symbols (Continued)

Character	XML	ISO	SPREAD
beamed sixteenth notes	&#x266C;		&U266C;
because	&#x2235;	&becaus;	&U2235;
bengali isshar	&#x9FA;		&U09FA;
bengali rupee mark	&#x9F2;		&U09F2;
bengali rupee sign	&#x9F3;		&U09F3;
benzene ring	&#x232C;		&U232C;
between	&#x226C;		&U226C;
biohazard sign	&#x2623;		&U2623;
black-feathered north east arrow	&#x27B6;		&U27B6;
black-feathered rightwards arrow	&#x27B5;		&U27B5;
black-feathered south east arrow	&#x27B4;		&U27B4;
black centre white star	&#x272C;		&U272C;
black chess bishop	&#x265D;		&U265D;
black chess king	&#x265A;		&U265A;
black chess knight	&#x265E;		&U265E;
black chess pawn	&#x265F;		&U265F;
black chess queen	&#x265B;		&U265B;
black chess rook	&#x265C;		&U265C;
black circle	&#x25CF;		&U25CF;
black club suit	&#x2663;	&clubs;	&U2663;
black diamond	&#x25C6;		&U25C6;
black diamond minus white x	&#x2756;		&U2756;
black diamond suit	&#x2666;		&U2666;
black down-pointing small triangle	&#x25BE;	&dtrif;	&U25BE;
black down-pointing triangle	&#x25BC;		&U25BC;
black florette	&#x273F;		&U273F;
black four pointed star	&#x2726;	&lozf;	&U2726;
black heart suit	&#x2665;		&U2665;
black left-pointing pointer	&#x25C4;		&U25C4;
black left-pointing small triangle	&#x25C2;	&ltrif;	&U25C2;
black left-pointing triangle	&#x25C0;		&U25C0;
black left pointing index	&#x261A;		&U261A;
black lower left triangle	&#x25E3;		&U25E3;
black lower right triangle	&#x25E2;		&U25E2;
black nib	&#x2712;		&U2712;
black parallelogram	&#x25B0;		&U25B0;
black rectangle	&#x25AC;		&U25AC;
black right-pointing pointer	&#x25BA;		&U25BA;
black right-pointing small triangle	&#x25B8;	&rtrif;	&U25B8;
black right-pointing triangle	&#x25B6;		&U25B6;
black right pointing index	&#x261B;		&U261B;
black rightwards arrow	&#x27A1;		&U27A1;
black rightwards arrowhead	&#x27A4;		&U27A4;
black scissors	&#x2702;		&U2702;
black small square	&#x25AA;	&squf;	&U25AA;
black smiling face	&#x263B;		&U263B;
black spade suit	&#x2660;	&spades;	&U2660;
black square	&#x25A0;		&U25A0;
black star	&#x2605;	&starf;	&U2605;
black sun with rays	&#x2600;		&U2600;

Character	XML	ISO	SPREAD
black telephone	&#x260E;		&U260E;
black up-pointing small triangle	&#x25B4;	&utrif;	&U25B4;
black up-pointing triangle	&#x25B2;		&U25B2;
black upper left triangle	&#x25E4;		&U25E4;
black upper right triangle	&#x25E5;		&U25E5;
black vertical rectangle	&#x25AE;	&marker;	&U25AE;
blank symbol	&#x2422;		&U2422;
bottom half integral	&#x2321;		&U2321;
bottom left corner	&#x231E;		&U231E;
bottom left crop	&#x230D;	&dlcrop;	&U230D;
bottom right corner	&#x231F;		&U231F;
bottom right crop	&#x230C;	&drcrop;	&U230C;
bowtie	&#x22C8;		&U22C8;
breve	&#x2D8;	&breve;	&U02D8;
broken bar	&#xA6;	&brvbar;	&U00A6;
bullet operator	&#x2219;		&U2219;
bullseye	&#x25CE;		&U25CE;
cada una	&#x2106;		&U2106;
caduceus	&#x2624;		&U2624;
cancer	&#x264B;		&U264B;
capricorn	&#x2651;		&U2651;
care of	&#x2105;	&incare;	&U2105;
caret insertion point	&#x2041;	&caret;	&U2041;
caron	&#x2C7;	&caron;	&U02C7;
caution sign	&#x2621;		&U2621;
cedilla	&#xB8;	&cedil;	&U00B8;
cent sign	&#xA2;	&cent;	&U00A2;
centre line symbol	&#x2104;		&U2104;
character tie	&#x2040;		&U2040;
check mark	&#x2713;	&check;	&U2713;
chi rho	&#x2627;		&U2627;
circle with all but upper left quadrant black	&#x25D5;		&U25D5;
circle with left half black	&#x25D0;		&U25D0;
circle with lower half black	&#x25D2;		&U25D2;
circle with right half black	&#x25D1;		&U25D1;
circle with upper half black	&#x25D3;		&U25D3;
circle with upper right quadrant black	&#x25D4;		&U25D4;
circle with vertical fill	&#x25CD;		&U25CD;
circled asterisk operator	&#x229B;		&U229B;
circled dash	&#x229D;		&U229D;
circled division slash	&#x2298;		&U2298;
circled dot operator	&#x2299;		&U2299;
circled equals	&#x229C;		&U229C;
circled heavy white rightwards arrow	&#x27B2;		&U27B2;
circled minus	&#x2296;		&U2296;
circled open centre eight pointed star	&#x2742;		&U2742;
circled plus	&#x2295;		&U2295;
circled postal mark	&#x3036;		&U3036;
circled ring operator	&#x229A;		&U229A;
circled times	&#x2297;		&U2297;

Marks & Symbols (Continued)

Character	XML	ISO	SPREAD
circled white star	&#x272A;		&U272A;
circumflex accent	&#x5E;		&U005E;
clockwise contour integral	&#x2232;		&U2232;
clockwise integral	&#x2231;		&U2231;
clockwise open circle arrow	&#x21BB;		&U21BB;
clockwise top semicircle arrow	&#x21B7;		&U21B7;
cloud	&#x2601;		&U2601;
colon equals	&#x2254;		&U2254;
colon sign	&#x20A1;		&U20A1;
comet	&#x2604;		&U2604;
commercial at	&#x40;		&U0040;
complement	&#x2201;		&U2201;
conical taper	&#x2332;		&U2332;
conjunction	&#x260C;		&U260C;
contains as member	&#x220B;	&ni;	&U220B;
contains as normal subgroup	&#x22B3;		&U22B3;
contains as normal subgroup or equal to	&#x22B5;		&U22B5;
contour integral	&#x222E;	&conint;	&U222E;
copyright sign	&#xA9;	&copy;	&U00A9;
corresponds to	&#x2258;		&U2258;
counterbore	&#x2334;		&U2334;
countersink	&#x2335;		&U2335;
cross of jerusalem	&#x2629;		&U2629;
cross of lorraine	&#x2628;		&U2628;
cruzeiro sign	&#x20A2;		&U20A2;
cube root	&#x221B;		&U221B;
curly logical and	&#x22CF;		&U22CF;
curly logical or	&#x22CE;		&U22CE;
currency sign	&#xA4;	&curren;	&U00A4;
curved stem paragraph sign ornament	&#x2761;		&U2761;
cylindricity	&#x232D;		&U232D;
cyrillic thousands sign	&#x482;		&U0482;
dark shade	&#x2593;	&blk34;	&U2593;
dashed triangle-headed rightwards arrow	&#x279F;		&U279F;
degree celsius	&#x2103;		&U2103;
degree fahrenheit	&#x2109;		&U2109;
degree sign	&#xB0;	&deg;	&U00B0;
delta equal to	&#x225C;		&U225C;
descending node	&#x260B;		&U260B;
devanagari danda	&#x964;		&U0964;
devanagari double danda	&#x965;		&U0965;
devanagari om	&#x950;		&U0950;
diaeresis	&#xA8;	&die;	&U00A8;
diameter sign	&#x2300;		&U2300;
diamond operator	&#x22C4;		&U22C4;
difference between	&#x224F;		&U224F;
dimension origin	&#x2331;		&U2331;
divides	&#x2223;		&U2223;
division sign	&#xF7;	&divide;	&U00F7;
division slash	&#x2215;		&U2215;

Character	XML	ISO	SPREAD
division times	&#x22C7;		&U22C7;
does not contain as member	&#x220C;		&U220C;
does not contain as normal subgroup	&#x22EB;		&U22EB;
does not contain as normal subgroup or equal	&#x22ED;		&U22ED;
does not divide	&#x2224;		&U2224;
does not force	&#x22AE;		&U22AE;
does not precede	&#x2280;		&U2280;
does not precede or equal	&#x22E0;		&U22E0;
does not prove	&#x22AC;		&U22AC;
does not succeed	&#x2281;		&U2281;
does not succeed or equal	&#x22E1;		&U22E1;
dollar sign	&#x24;		&U0024;
dong sign	&#x20AB;		&U20AB;
dot above	&#x2D9;	&dot;	&U02D9;
dot minus	&#x2238;		&U2238;
dot operator	&#x22C5;		&U22C5;
dot plus	&#x2214;		&U2214;
dotted circle	&#x25CC;		&U25CC;
double acute accent	&#x2DD;	&dblac;	&U02DD;
double integral	&#x222C;		&U222C;
double intersection	&#x22D2;		&U22D2;
double prime quotation mark	&#x301E;		&U301E;
double subset	&#x22D0;		&U22D0;
double superset	&#x22D1;		&U22D1;
double union	&#x22D3;		&U22D3;
double vertical bar double right turnstile	&#x22AB;		&U22AB;
down arrowhead	&#x2304;		&U2304;
down right diagonal ellipsis	&#x22F1;		&U22F1;
down tack	&#x22A4;		&U22A4;
downwards arrow	&#x2193;	&darr;	&U2193;
downwards arrow from bar	&#x21A7;		&U21A7;
downwards arrow with corner leftwards	&#x21B5;		&U21B5;
downwards arrow with double stroke	&#x21DF;		&U21DF;
downwards arrow with tip leftwards	&#x21B2;		&U21B2;
downwards arrow with tip rightwards	&#x21B3;		&U21B3;
downwards dashed arrow	&#x21E3;		&U21E3;
downwards double arrow	&#x21D3;		&U21D3;
downwards harpoon with barb leftwards	&#x21C3;		&U21C3;
downwards harpoon with barb rightwards	&#x21C2;		&U21C2;
downwards paired arrows	&#x21CA;		&U21CA;
downwards two headed arrow	&#x21A1;		&U21A1;
downwards white arrow	&#x21E9;		&U21E9;
downwards zigzag arrow	&#x21AF;		&U21AF;
drafting point rightwards arrow	&#x279B;		&U279B;
earth	&#x2641;		&U2641;
eight petalled outlined black florette	&#x2741;		&U2741;
eight pointed black star	&#x2734;		&U2734;
eight pointed pinwheel star	&#x2735;		&U2735;
eight pointed rectilinear black star	&#x2737;		&U2737;
eight spoked asterisk	&#x2733;		&U2733;

Marks & Symbols (Continued)

Character	XML	ISO	SPREAD
eight teardrop-spoked propeller asterisk	&#x274A;		&U274A;
eighth note	&#x266A;	&sung;	&U266A;
element of	&#x2208;	&isin;	&U2208;
empty set	&#x2205;		&U2205;
end of proof	&#x220E;		&U220E;
envelope	&#x2709;		&U2709;
equal and parallel to	&#x22D5;		&U22D5;
equal to by definition	&#x225D;		&U225D;
equal to or greater-than	&#x22DD;		&U22DD;
equal to or less-than	&#x22DC;		&U22DC;
equal to or precedes	&#x22DE;		&U22DE;
equal to or succeeds	&#x22DF;		&U22DF;
equals colon	&#x2255;		&U2255;
equals sign	&#x3D;		&U003D;
equiangular to	&#x225A;		&U225A;
equivalent to	&#x224D;		&U224D;
erase to the left	&#x232B;		&U232B;
erase to the right	&#x2326;		&U2326;
estimates	&#x2259;	&wedgeq;	&U2259;
euro-currency sign	&#x20A0;		&U20A0;
excess	&#x2239;		&U2239;
farsi symbol	&#x262B;		&U262B;
female sign	&#x2640;	&female;	&U2640;
first quarter moon	&#x263D;		&U263D;
fisheye	&#x25C9;		&U25C9;
floral heart	&#x2766;		&U2766;
for all	&#x2200;	&forall;	&U2200;
forces	&#x22A9;		&U22A9;
four balloon-spoked asterisk	&#x2723;		&U2723;
four club-spoked asterisk	&#x2725;		&U2725;
four teardrop-spoked asterisk	&#x2722;		&U2722;
fourth root	&#x221C;		&U221C;
fraction slash	&#x2044;		&U2044;
french franc sign	&#x20A3;		&U20A3;
front-tilted shadowed white rightwards arrow	&#x27AC;		&U27AC;
frown	&#x2322;		&U2322;
full block	&#x2588;	&block;	&U2588;
gemini	&#x264A;		&U264A;
geometric proportion	&#x223A;		&U223A;
geometrically equal to	&#x2251;		&U2251;
geometrically equivalent to	&#x224E;		&U224E;
geta mark	&#x3013;		&U3013;
grave accent	&#x60;		&U0060;
greater-than but not equal to	&#x2269;		&U2269;
greater-than but not equivalent to	&#x22E7;		&U22E7;
greater-than equal to or less-than	&#x22DB;		&U22DB;
greater-than or equal to	&#x2265;	&ge;	&U2265;
greater-than or equivalent to	&#x2273;		&U2273;
greater-than or less-than	&#x2277;		&U2277;
greater-than over equal to	&#x2267;		&U2267;

Marks & Symbols (Continued)

Character	XML	ISO	SPREAD
greater-than sign	&gt;		&U003E;
greater-than with dot	&#x22D7;		&U22D7;
hammer and sickle	&#x262D;		&U262D;
heavy asterisk	&#x2731;		&U2731;
heavy ballot x	&#x2718;		&U2718;
heavy black-feathered north east arrow	&#x27B9;		&U27B9;
heavy black-feathered rightwards arrow	&#x27B8;		&U27B8;
heavy black-feathered south east arrow	&#x27B7;		&U27B7;
heavy black curved downwards and rightwards arrow	&#x27A5;		&U27A5;
heavy black curved upwards and rightwards arrow	&#x27A6;		&U27A6;
heavy black heart	&#x2764;		&U2764;
heavy check mark	&#x2714;		&U2714;
heavy chevron snowflake	&#x2746;		&U2746;
heavy concave-pointed black rightwards arrow	&#x27A8;		&U27A8;
heavy dashed triangle-headed rightwards arrow	&#x27A0;		&U27A0;
heavy double comma quotation mark ornament	&#x275E;		&U275E;
heavy double turned comma quotation mark ornament	&#x275D;		&U275D;
heavy eight pointed rectilinear black star	&#x2738;		&U2738;
heavy eight teardrop-spoked propeller asterisk	&#x274B;		&U274B;
heavy exclamation mark ornament	&#x2762;		&U2762;
heavy four balloon-spoked asterisk	&#x2724;		&U2724;
heavy greek cross	&#x271A;		&U271A;
heavy heart exclamation mark ornament	&#x2763;		&U2763;
heavy lower right-shadowed white rightwards arrow	&#x27AD;		&U27AD;
heavy multiplication x	&#x2716;		&U2716;
heavy north east arrow	&#x279A;		&U279A;
heavy open centre cross	&#x271C;		&U271C;
heavy outlined black star	&#x272E;		&U272E;
heavy rightwards arrow	&#x2799;		&U2799;
heavy round-tipped rightwards arrow	&#x279C;		&U279C;
heavy single comma quotation mark ornament	&#x275C;		&U275C;
heavy single turned comma quotation mark ornament	&#x275B;		&U275B;
heavy south east arrow	&#x2798;		&U2798;
heavy sparkle	&#x2748;		&U2748;
heavy teardrop-shanked rightwards arrow	&#x27BB;		&U27BB;
heavy teardrop-spoked asterisk	&#x273D;		&U273D;
heavy teardrop-spoked pinwheel asterisk	&#x2743;		&U2743;
heavy triangle-headed rightwards arrow	&#x279E;		&U279E;
heavy upper right-shadowed white rightwards arrow	&#x27AE;		&U27AE;
heavy vertical bar	&#x275A;		&U275A;
heavy wedge-tailed rightwards arrow	&#x27BD;		&U27BD;
heavy wide-headed rightwards arrow	&#x2794;		&U2794;
hermitian conjugate matrix	&#x22B9;		&U22B9;
hiragana iteration mark	&#x309D;		&U309D;
hiragana voiced iteration mark	&#x309E;		&U309E;
homothetic	&#x223B;		&U223B;
hot springs	&#x2668;		&U2668;
hourglass	&#x231B;		&U231B;
house	&#x2302;		&U2302;
hyphen bullet	&#x2043;	&hybull;	&U2043;

Character	XML	ISO	SPREAD
identical to	&#x2261;	&equiv;	&U2261;
image of	&#x22B7;		&U22B7;
image of or approximately equal to	&#x2253;		&U2253;
increment	&#x2206;		&U2206;
infinity	&#x221E;	&infin;	&U221E;
integral	&#x222B;	&int;	&U222B;
intercalate	&#x22BA;		&U22BA;
interrobang	&#x203D;		&U203D;
intersection	&#x2229;	&cap;	&U2229;
inverse bullet	&#x25D8;		&U25D8;
inverse white circle	&#x25D9;		&U25D9;
inverted lazy s	&#x223E;		&U223E;
inverted ohm sign	&#x2127;		&U2127;
japanese industrial standard symbol	&#x3004;		&U3004;
jupiter	&#x2643;		&U2643;
keyboard	&#x2328;		&U2328;
korean standard symbol	&#x327F;		&U327F;
l b bar symbol	&#x2114;		&U2114;
lao ko la	&#xEC6;		&U0EC6;
large circle	&#x25EF;		&U25EF;
last quarter moon	&#x263E;		&U263E;
latin cross	&#x271D;		&U271D;
left-shaded white rightwards arrow	&#x27AA;		&U27AA;
left ceiling	&#x2308;		&U2308;
left five eighths block	&#x258B;		&U258B;
left floor	&#x230A;		&U230A;
left half black circle	&#x25D6;		&U25D6;
left half block	&#x258C;		&U258C;
left normal factor semidirect product	&#x22C9;		&U22C9;
left one eighth block	&#x258F;		&U258F;
left one quarter block	&#x258E;		&U258E;
left right arrow	&#x2194;		&U2194;
left right arrow with stroke	&#x21AE;		&U21AE;
left right double arrow	&#x21D4;	&iff;	&U21D4;
left right double arrow with stroke	&#x21CE;		&U21CE;
left right wave arrow	&#x21AD;		&U21AD;
left semidirect product	&#x22CB;		&U22CB;
left seven eighths block	&#x2589;		&U2589;
left tack	&#x22A3;		&U22A3;
left three eighths block	&#x258D;		&U258D;
left three quarters block	&#x258A;		&U258A;
leftwards arrow	&#x2190;	&larr;	&U2190;
leftwards arrow from bar	&#x21A4;		&U21A4;
leftwards arrow over rightwards arrow	&#x21C6;		&U21C6;
leftwards arrow to bar	&#x21E4;		&U21E4;
leftwards arrow to bar over rightwards arrow to bar	&#x21B9;		&U21B9;
leftwards arrow with hook	&#x21A9;		&U21A9;
leftwards arrow with loop	&#x21AB;		&U21AB;
leftwards arrow with stroke	&#x219A;		&U219A;
leftwards arrow with tail	&#x21A2;		&U21A2;

Marks & Symbols (Continued)

Character	XML	ISO	SPREAD
leftwards dashed arrow	&#x21E0;		&U21E0;
leftwards double arrow	&#x21D0;	&lArr;	&U21D0;
leftwards double arrow with stroke	&#x21CD;		&U21CD;
leftwards harpoon over rightwards harpoon	&#x21CB;		&U21CB;
leftwards harpoon with barb downwards	&#x21BD;		&U21BD;
leftwards harpoon with barb upwards	&#x21BC;		&U21BC;
leftwards paired arrows	&#x21C7;		&U21C7;
leftwards squiggle arrow	&#x21DC;		&U21DC;
leftwards triple arrow	&#x21DA;		&U21DA;
leftwards two headed arrow	&#x219E;		&U219E;
leftwards wave arrow	&#x219C;		&U219C;
leftwards white arrow	&#x21E6;		&U21E6;
leo	&#x264C;		&U264C;
less-than but not equal to	&#x2268;		&U2268;
less-than but not equivalent to	&#x22E6;		&U22E6;
less-than equal to or greater-than	&#x22DA;		&U22DA;
less-than or equal to	&#x2264;	&le;	&U2264;
less-than or equivalent to	&#x2272;		&U2272;
less-than or greater-than	&#x2276;		&U2276;
less-than over equal to	&#x2266;		&U2266;
less-than sign	&lt;		&U003C;
less-than with dot	&#x22D6;		&U22D6;
libra	&#x264E;		&U264E;
light shade	&#x2591;	&blk14;	&U2591;
light vertical bar	&#x2758;		&U2758;
lightning	&#x2607;		&U2607;
lira sign	&#x20A4;		&U20A4;
logical and	&#x2227;	&and;	&U2227;
logical or	&#x2228;	&or;	&U2228;
low double prime quotation mark	&#x301F;		&U301F;
low line	&#x5F;		&U005F;
lower blade scissors	&#x2703;		&U2703;
lower five eighths block	&#x2585;		&U2585;
lower half block	&#x2584;	&lhblk;	&U2584;
lower half circle	&#x25E1;		&U25E1;
lower half inverse white circle	&#x25DB;		&U25DB;
lower left quadrant circular arc	&#x25DF;		&U25DF;
lower one eighth block	&#x2581;		&U2581;
lower one quarter block	&#x2582;		&U2582;
lower right drop-shadowed white square	&#x274F;		&U274F;
lower right pencil	&#x270E;		&U270E;
lower right quadrant circular arc	&#x25DE;		&U25DE;
lower right shadowed white square	&#x2751;		&U2751;
lower seven eighths block	&#x2587;		&U2587;
lower three eighths block	&#x2583;		&U2583;
lower three quarters block	&#x2586;		&U2586;
lozenge	&#x25CA;		&U25CA;
macron	&#xAF;	&macr;	&U00AF;
male sign	&#x2642;	&male;	&U2642;
maltese cross	&#x2720;	&malt;	&U2720;

Character	XML	ISO	SPREAD
measured angle	&#x2221;		&U2221;
measured by	&#x225E;		&U225E;
medium shade	&#x2592;	&blk12;	&U2592;
medium vertical bar	&#x2759;		&U2759;
mercury	&#x263F;		&U263F;
midline horizontal ellipsis	&#x22EF;		&U22EF;
mill sign	&#x20A5;		&U20A5;
minus-or-plus sign	&#x2213;	&mnplus;	&U2213;
minus sign	&#x2212;		&U2212;
minus tilde	&#x2242;		&U2242;
models	&#x22A7;		&U22A7;
much greater-than	&#x226B;		&U226B;
much less-than	&#x226A;		&U226A;
multimap	&#x22B8;		&U22B8;
multiplication sign	&#xD7;	&times;	&U00D7;
multiplication x	&#x2715;		&U2715;
multiset	&#x228C;		&U228C;
multiset multiplication	&#x228D;		&U228D;
multiset union	&#x228E;		&U228E;
music flat sign	&#x266D;	&flat;	&U266D;
music natural sign	&#x266E;	&natur;	&U266E;
music sharp sign	&#x266F;	&sharp;	&U266F;
n-ary coproduct	&#x2210;		&U2210;
n-ary intersection	&#x22C2;		&U22C2;
n-ary logical and	&#x22C0;		&U22C0;
n-ary logical or	&#x22C1;		&U22C1;
n-ary product	&#x220F;		&U220F;
n-ary summation	&#x2211;		&U2211;
n-ary union	&#x22C3;		&U22C3;
nabla	&#x2207;	&nabla;	&U2207;
naira sign	&#x20A6;		&U20A6;
nand	&#x22BC;		&U22BC;
negated double vertical bar double right turnstile	&#x22AF;		&U22AF;
neither a subset of nor equal to	&#x2288;		&U2288;
neither a superset of nor equal to	&#x2289;		&U2289;
neither approximately nor actually equal to	&#x2247;		&U2247;
neither greater-than nor equal to	&#x2271;		&U2271;
neither greater-than nor equivalent to	&#x2275;		&U2275;
neither greater-than nor less-than	&#x2279;		&U2279;
neither less-than nor equal to	&#x2270;		&U2270;
neither less-than nor equivalent to	&#x2274;		&U2274;
neither less-than nor greater-than	&#x2278;		&U2278;
neptune	&#x2646;		&U2646;
new sheqel sign	&#x20AA;		&U20AA;
nor	&#x22BD;		&U22BD;
normal subgroup of	&#x22B2;		&U22B2;
normal subgroup of or equal to	&#x22B4;		&U22B4;
north east arrow	&#x2197;		&U2197;
north east double arrow	&#x21D7;		&U21D7;
north west arrow	&#x2196;		&U2196;

Character	XML	ISO	SPREAD
north west arrow to long bar	`&#x21B8;`		`&U21B8;`
north west double arrow	`&#x21D6;`		`&U21D6;`
not a subset of	`&#x2284;`		`&U2284;`
not a superset of	`&#x2285;`		`&U2285;`
not almost equal to	`&#x2249;`	`&ap;`	`&U2249;`
not an element of	`&#x2209;`	`&notin;`	`&U2209;`
not asymptotically equal to	`&#x2244;`		`&U2244;`
not equal to	`&#x2260;`	`&ne;`	`&U2260;`
not equivalent to	`&#x226D;`		`&U226D;`
not greater-than	`&#x226F;`		`&U226F;`
not identical to	`&#x2262;`		`&U2262;`
not less-than	`&#x226E;`		`&U226E;`
not normal subgroup of	`&#x22EA;`		`&U22EA;`
not normal subgroup of or equal to	`&#x22EC;`		`&U22EC;`
not parallel to	`&#x2226;`		`&U2226;`
not sign	`&#xAC;`	`&not;`	`&U00AC;`
not square image of or equal to	`&#x22E2;`		`&U22E2;`
not square original of or equal to	`&#x22E3;`		`&U22E3;`
not tilde	`&#x2241;`		`&U2241;`
not true	`&#x22AD;`		`&U22AD;`
notched lower right-shadowed white rightwards arrow	`&#x27AF;`		`&U27AF;`
notched upper right-shadowed white rightwards arrow	`&#x27B1;`		`&U27B1;`
number sign	`&#x23;`		`&U0023;`
ocr amount of check	`&#x2447;`		`&U2447;`
ocr belt buckle	`&#x2444;`		`&U2444;`
ocr bow tie	`&#x2445;`		`&U2445;`
ocr branch bank identification	`&#x2446;`		`&U2446;`
ocr chair	`&#x2441;`		`&U2441;`
ocr customer account number	`&#x2449;`		`&U2449;`
ocr dash	`&#x2448;`		`&U2448;`
ocr double backslash	`&#x244A;`		`&U244A;`
ocr fork	`&#x2442;`		`&U2442;`
ocr hook	`&#x2440;`		`&U2440;`
ocr inverted fork	`&#x2443;`		`&U2443;`
ogonek	`&#x2DB;`	`&ogon;`	`&U02DB;`
open-outlined rightwards arrow	`&#x27BE;`		`&U27BE;`
open box	`&#x2423;`	`&blank;`	`&U2423;`
open centre asterisk	`&#x2732;`		`&U2732;`
open centre black star	`&#x272B;`		`&U272B;`
open centre cross	`&#x271B;`		`&U271B;`
open centre teardrop-spoked asterisk	`&#x273C;`		`&U273C;`
opposition	`&#x260D;`		`&U260D;`
option key	`&#x2325;`		`&U2325;`
original of	`&#x22B6;`		`&U22B6;`
oriya isshar	`&#xB70;`		`&U0B70;`
orthodox cross	`&#x2626;`		`&U2626;`
ounce sign	`&#x2125;`		`&U2125;`
outlined black star	`&#x272D;`		`&U272D;`
outlined greek cross	`&#x2719;`		`&U2719;`
outlined latin cross	`&#x271F;`		`&U271F;`

Character	XML	ISO	SPREAD
overline	&#x203E;		&U203E;
parallel to	&#x2225;	&par;	&U2225;
partial differential	&#x2202;	&part;	&U2202;
peace symbol	&#x262E;		&U262E;
pencil	&#x270F;		&U270F;
perspective	&#x2306;		&U2306;
peseta sign	&#x20A7;		&U20A7;
pilcrow sign	&#xB6;	&para;	&U00B6;
pinwheel star	&#x272F;		&U272F;
pisces	&#x2653;		&U2653;
pitchfork	&#x22D4;		&U22D4;
place of interest sign	&#x2318;		&U2318;
plus-minus sign	&#xB1;	&plusmn;	&U00B1;
plus sign	&#x2B;		&U002B;
pluto	&#x2647;		&U2647;
position indicator	&#x2316;	&target;	&U2316;
postal mark	&#x3012;		&U3012;
postal mark face	&#x3020;		&U3020;
pound sign	&#xA3;	&pound;	&U00A3;
precedes	&#x227A;		&U227A;
precedes but not equivalent to	&#x22E8;		&U22E8;
precedes or equal to	&#x227C;		&U227C;
precedes or equivalent to	&#x227E;		&U227E;
precedes under relation	&#x22B0;		&U22B0;
prescription take	&#x211E;	&rx;	&U211E;
projective	&#x2305;		&U2305;
proportion	&#x2237;		&U2237;
proportional to	&#x221D;	&prop;	&U221D;
quarter note	&#x2669;		&U2669;
questioned equal to	&#x225F;		&U225F;
radioactive sign	&#x2622;		&U2622;
ratio	&#x2236;		&U2236;
registered sign	&#xAE;	&reg;	&U00AE;
response	&#x211F;		&U211F;
reversed double prime quotation mark	&#x301D;		&U301D;
reversed not sign	&#x2310;		&U2310;
reversed tilde	&#x223D;		&U223D;
reversed tilde equals	&#x22CD;		&U22CD;
right-shaded white rightwards arrow	&#x27A9;		&U27A9;
right angle	&#x221F;	&ang90;	&U221F;
right angle with arc	&#x22BE;		&U22BE;
right ceiling	&#x2309;		&U2309;
right floor	&#x230B;		&U230B;
right half black circle	&#x25D7;		&U25D7;
right half block	&#x2590;		&U2590;
right normal factor semidirect product	&#x22CA;		&U22CA;
right one eighth block	&#x2595;		&U2595;
right semidirect product	&#x22CC;		&U22CC;
right tack	&#x22A2;		&U22A2;
right triangle	&#x22BF;		&U22BF;

The XML & SGML Cookbook

Character	XML	ISO	SPREAD
rightwards arrow	&#x2192;	&rarr;	&U2192;
rightwards arrow from bar	&#x21A6;		&U21A6;
rightwards arrow over leftwards arrow	&#x21C4;		&U21C4;
rightwards arrow to bar	&#x21E5;		&U21E5;
rightwards arrow with corner downwards	&#x21B4;		&U21B4;
rightwards arrow with hook	&#x21AA;		&U21AA;
rightwards arrow with loop	&#x21AC;		&U21AC;
rightwards arrow with stroke	&#x219B;		&U219B;
rightwards arrow with tail	&#x21A3;		&U21A3;
rightwards dashed arrow	&#x21E2;		&U21E2;
rightwards double arrow	&#x21D2;	&rArr;	&U21D2;
rightwards double arrow with stroke	&#x21CF;		&U21CF;
rightwards harpoon over leftwards harpoon	&#x21CC;		&U21CC;
rightwards harpoon with barb downwards	&#x21C1;		&U21C1;
rightwards harpoon with barb upwards	&#x21C0;		&U21C0;
rightwards paired arrows	&#x21C9;		&U21C9;
rightwards squiggle arrow	&#x21DD;		&U21DD;
rightwards triple arrow	&#x21DB;		&U21DB;
rightwards two headed arrow	&#x21A0;		&U21A0;
rightwards wave arrow	&#x219D;		&U219D;
rightwards white arrow	&#x21E8;		&U21E8;
ring above	&#x2DA;	&ring;	&U02DA;
ring equal to	&#x2257;		&U2257;
ring in equal to	&#x2256;		&U2256;
ring operator	&#x2218;	&compfn;	&U2218;
rotated floral heart bullet	&#x2767;		&U2767;
rotated heavy black heart bullet	&#x2765;		&U2765;
sagittarius	&#x2650;		&U2650;
saltire	&#x2613;		&U2613;
saturn	&#x2644;		&U2644;
scorpius	&#x264F;		&U264F;
scruple	&#x2108;		&U2108;
section sign	&#xA7;	&sect;	&U00A7;
sector	&#x2314;		&U2314;
segment	&#x2313;		&U2313;
set minus	&#x2216;		&U2216;
shadowed white circle	&#x274D;		&U274D;
shadowed white latin cross	&#x271E;		&U271E;
shadowed white star	&#x2730;		&U2730;
sine wave	&#x223F;		&U223F;
six petalled black and white florette	&#x273E;		&U273E;
six pointed black star	&#x2736;	&sext;	&U2736;
sixteen pointed asterisk	&#x273A;		&U273A;
skull and crossbones	&#x2620;		&U2620;
slope	&#x2333;		&U2333;
small contains as member	&#x220D;		&U220D;
small element of	&#x220A;		&U220A;
small tilde	&#x2DC;	&tilde;	&U02DC;
smile	&#x2323;		&U2323;
snowflake	&#x2744;		&U2744;

Character	XML	ISO	SPREAD
snowman	&#x2603;		&U2603;
south east arrow	&#x2198;		&U2198;
south east double arrow	&#x21D8;		&U21D8;
south west arrow	&#x2199;		&U2199;
south west double arrow	&#x21D9;		&U21D9;
sparkle	&#x2747;		&U2747;
spherical angle	&#x2222;	&angsph;	&U2222;
square am	&#x33C2;		&U33C2;
square c over kg	&#x33C6;		&U33C6;
square cap	&#x2293;		&U2293;
square cm cubed	&#x33A4;		&U33A4;
square cm squared	&#x33A0;		&U33A0;
square cup	&#x2294;		&U2294;
square dl	&#x3397;		&U3397;
square image of	&#x228F;		&U228F;
square image of or equal to	&#x2291;		&U2291;
square image of or not equal to	&#x22E4;		&U22E4;
square kl	&#x3398;		&U3398;
square km cubed	&#x33A6;		&U33A6;
square km squared	&#x33A2;		&U33A2;
square lozenge	&#x2311;		&U2311;
square m cubed	&#x33A5;		&U33A5;
square m over s	&#x33A7;		&U33A7;
square m over s squared	&#x33A8;		&U33A8;
square m squared	&#x33A1;		&U33A1;
square ml	&#x3396;		&U3396;
square mm cubed	&#x33A3;		&U33A3;
square mm squared	&#x339F;		&U339F;
square mu l	&#x3395;		&U3395;
square original of	&#x2290;		&U2290;
square original of or equal to	&#x2292;		&U2292;
square original of or not equal to	&#x22E5;		&U22E5;
square pm	&#x33D8;		&U33D8;
square rad over s	&#x33AE;		&U33AE;
square rad over s squared	&#x33AF;		&U33AF;
square root	&#x221A;	&radic;	&U221A;
square with diagonal crosshatch fill	&#x25A9;		&U25A9;
square with horizontal fill	&#x25A4;		&U25A4;
square with left half black	&#x25E7;		&U25E7;
square with lower right diagonal half black	&#x25EA;		&U25EA;
square with orthogonal crosshatch fill	&#x25A6;		&U25A6;
square with right half black	&#x25E8;		&U25E8;
square with upper left diagonal half black	&#x25E9;		&U25E9;
square with upper left to lower right fill	&#x25A7;		&U25A7;
square with upper right to lower left fill	&#x25A8;		&U25A8;
square with vertical fill	&#x25A5;		&U25A5;
squared dot operator	&#x22A1;		&U22A1;
squared minus	&#x229F;		&U229F;
squared plus	&#x229E;		&U229E;
squared times	&#x22A0;		&U22A0;

Character	XML	ISO	SPREAD
squat black rightwards arrow	`&#x27A7;`		`&U27A7;`
star and crescent	`&#x262A;`		`&U262A;`
star equals	`&#x225B;`		`&U225B;`
star of david	`&#x2721;`		`&U2721;`
star operator	`&#x22C6;`		`&U22C6;`
stress outlined white star	`&#x2729;`		`&U2729;`
strictly equivalent to	`&#x2263;`		`&U2263;`
subscript equals sign	`&#x208C;`		`&U208C;`
subscript minus	`&#x208B;`		`&U208B;`
subscript plus sign	`&#x208A;`		`&U208A;`
subset of	`&#x2282;`	`&sub;`	`&U2282;`
subset of or equal to	`&#x2286;`	`&sube;`	`&U2286;`
subset of with not equal to	`&#x228A;`		`&U228A;`
succeeds	`&#x227B;`		`&U227B;`
succeeds but not equivalent to	`&#x22E9;`		`&U22E9;`
succeeds or equal to	`&#x227D;`		`&U227D;`
succeeds or equivalent to	`&#x227F;`		`&U227F;`
succeeds under relation	`&#x22B1;`		`&U22B1;`
sun	`&#x2609;`		`&U2609;`
superscript equals sign	`&#x207C;`		`&U207C;`
superscript minus	`&#x207B;`		`&U207B;`
superscript plus sign	`&#x207A;`		`&U207A;`
superset of	`&#x2283;`	`&sup;`	`&U2283;`
superset of or equal to	`&#x2287;`	`&supe;`	`&U2287;`
superset of with not equal to	`&#x228B;`		`&U228B;`
surface integral	`&#x222F;`		`&U222F;`
symbol for acknowledge	`&#x2406;`		`&U2406;`
symbol for backspace	`&#x2408;`		`&U2408;`
symbol for bell	`&#x2407;`		`&U2407;`
symbol for cancel	`&#x2418;`		`&U2418;`
symbol for carriage return	`&#x240D;`		`&U240D;`
symbol for data link escape	`&#x2410;`		`&U2410;`
symbol for delete	`&#x2421;`		`&U2421;`
symbol for device control four	`&#x2414;`		`&U2414;`
symbol for device control one	`&#x2411;`		`&U2411;`
symbol for device control three	`&#x2413;`		`&U2413;`
symbol for device control two	`&#x2412;`		`&U2412;`
symbol for end of medium	`&#x2419;`		`&U2419;`
symbol for end of text	`&#x2403;`		`&U2403;`
symbol for end of transmission	`&#x2404;`		`&U2404;`
symbol for end of transmission block	`&#x2417;`		`&U2417;`
symbol for enquiry	`&#x2405;`		`&U2405;`
symbol for escape	`&#x241B;`		`&U241B;`
symbol for file separator	`&#x241C;`		`&U241C;`
symbol for form feed	`&#x240C;`		`&U240C;`
symbol for group separator	`&#x241D;`		`&U241D;`
symbol for horizontal tabulation	`&#x2409;`		`&U2409;`
symbol for line feed	`&#x240A;`		`&U240A;`
symbol for negative acknowledge	`&#x2415;`		`&U2415;`
symbol for newline	`&#x2424;`		`&U2424;`

Character	XML	ISO	SPREAD
symbol for null	&#x2400;		&U2400;
symbol for record separator	&#x241E;		&U241E;
symbol for shift in	&#x240F;		&U240F;
symbol for shift out	&#x240E;		&U240E;
symbol for space	&#x2420;		&U2420;
symbol for start of heading	&#x2401;		&U2401;
symbol for start of text	&#x2402;		&U2402;
symbol for substitute	&#x241A;		&U241A;
symbol for synchronous idle	&#x2416;		&U2416;
symbol for unit separator	&#x241F;		&U241F;
symbol for vertical tabulation	&#x240B;		&U240B;
symmetry	&#x232F;		&U232F;
tape drive	&#x2707;		&U2707;
taurus	&#x2649;		&U2649;
teardrop-barbed rightwards arrow	&#x27BA;		&U27BA;
teardrop-spoked asterisk	&#x273B;		&U273B;
telephone location sign	&#x2706;		&U2706;
telephone recorder	&#x2315;	&telrec;	&U2315;
thai currency symbol baht	&#xE3F;		&U0E3F;
there does not exist	&#x2204;		&U2204;
there exists	&#x2203;	&exist;	&U2203;
therefore	&#x2234;	&there4;	&U2234;
three-d bottom-lighted rightwards arrowhead	&#x27A3;		&U27A3;
three-d top-lighted rightwards arrowhead	&#x27A2;		&U27A2;
thunderstorm	&#x2608;		&U2608;
tight trifoliate snowflake	&#x2745;		&U2745;
tilde	&#x7E;		&U007E;
tilde operator	&#x223C;	&sim;	&U223C;
top half integral	&#x2320;		&U2320;
top left corner	&#x231C;		&U231C;
top left crop	&#x230F;	&ulcrop;	&U230F;
top right corner	&#x231D;		&U231D;
top right crop	&#x230E;	&urcrop;	&U230E;
total runout	&#x2330;		&U2330;
triangle-headed rightwards arrow	&#x279D;		&U279D;
trigram for earth	&#x2637;		&U2637;
trigram for fire	&#x2632;		&U2632;
trigram for heaven	&#x2630;		&U2630;
trigram for lake	&#x2631;		&U2631;
trigram for mountain	&#x2636;		&U2636;
trigram for thunder	&#x2633;		&U2633;
trigram for water	&#x2635;		&U2635;
trigram for wind	&#x2634;		&U2634;
triple integral	&#x222D;		&U222D;
triple tilde	&#x224B;		&U224B;
triple vertical bar right turnstile	&#x22AA;		&U22AA;
true	&#x22A8;		&U22A8;
turned capital f	&#x2132;		&U2132;
turned greek small letter iota	&#x2129;		&U2129;
turned not sign	&#x2319;		&U2319;

Character	XML	ISO	SPREAD
twelve pointed black star	&#x2739;		&U2739;
umbrella	&#x2602;		&U2602;
undertie	&#x203F;		&U203F;
union	&#x222A;	&cup;	&U222A;
up-pointing triangle with left half black	&#x25ED;		&U25ED;
up-pointing triangle with right half black	&#x25EE;		&U25EE;
up arrowhead	&#x2303;		&U2303;
up arrowhead between two horizontal bars	&#x2324;		&U2324;
up down arrow	&#x2195;		&U2195;
up down arrow with base	&#x21A8;		&U21A8;
up down double arrow	&#x21D5;		&U21D5;
up right diagonal ellipsis	&#x22F0;		&U22F0;
up tack	&#x22A5;	&bottom;	&U22A5;
upper blade scissors	&#x2701;		&U2701;
upper half block	&#x2580;	&uhblk;	&U2580;
upper half circle	&#x25E0;		&U25E0;
upper half inverse white circle	&#x25DA;		&U25DA;
upper left quadrant circular arc	&#x25DC;		&U25DC;
upper one eighth block	&#x2594;		&U2594;
upper right drop-shadowed white square	&#x2750;		&U2750;
upper right pencil	&#x2710;		&U2710;
upper right quadrant circular arc	&#x25DD;		&U25DD;
upper right shadowed white square	&#x2752;		&U2752;
upwards arrow	&#x2191;	&uarr;	&U2191;
upwards arrow from bar	&#x21A5;		&U21A5;
upwards arrow leftwards of downwards arrow	&#x21C5;		&U21C5;
upwards arrow with double stroke	&#x21DE;		&U21DE;
upwards arrow with tip leftwards	&#x21B0;		&U21B0;
upwards arrow with tip rightwards	&#x21B1;		&U21B1;
upwards dashed arrow	&#x21E1;		&U21E1;
upwards double arrow	&#x21D1;		&U21D1;
upwards harpoon with barb leftwards	&#x21BF;		&U21BF;
upwards harpoon with barb rightwards	&#x21BE;		&U21BE;
upwards paired arrows	&#x21C8;		&U21C8;
upwards two headed arrow	&#x219F;		&U219F;
upwards white arrow	&#x21E7;		&U21E7;
upwards white arrow from bar	&#x21EA;		&U21EA;
uranus	&#x2645;		&U2645;
versicle	&#x2123;		&U2123;
vertical line	&#x7C;		&U007C;
very much greater-than	&#x22D9;		&U22D9;
very much less-than	&#x22D8;		&U22D8;
victory hand	&#x270C;		&U270C;
viewdata square	&#x2317;		&U2317;
virgo	&#x264D;		&U264D;
volume integral	&#x2230;		&U2230;
watch	&#x231A;		&U231A;
wavy line	&#x2307;		&U2307;
wedge-tailed rightwards arrow	&#x27BC;		&U27BC;
wheel of dharma	&#x2638;		&U2638;

Character	XML	ISO	SPREAD
white-feathered rightwards arrow	&#x27B3;		&U27B3;
white bullet	&#x25E6;		&U25E6;
white chess bishop	&#x2657;		&U2657;
white chess king	&#x2654;		&U2654;
white chess knight	&#x2658;		&U2658;
white chess pawn	&#x2659;		&U2659;
white chess queen	&#x2655;		&U2655;
white chess rook	&#x2656;		&U2656;
white circle	&#x25CB;	&cir;	&U25CB;
white club suit	&#x2667;		&U2667;
white diamond	&#x25C7;		&U25C7;
white diamond containing black small diamond	&#x25C8;		&U25C8;
white diamond suit	&#x2662;	&diams;	&U2662;
white down-pointing small triangle	&#x25BF;	&dtri;	&U25BF;
white down-pointing triangle	&#x25BD;		&U25BD;
white down pointing index	&#x261F;		&U261F;
white florette	&#x2740;		&U2740;
white four pointed star	&#x2727;	&loz;	&U2727;
white frowning face	&#x2639;		&U2639;
white heart suit	&#x2661;	&hearts;	&U2661;
white left-pointing pointer	&#x25C5;		&U25C5;
white left-pointing small triangle	&#x25C3;	&ltri;	&U25C3;
white left-pointing triangle	&#x25C1;		&U25C1;
white left pointing index	&#x261C;		&U261C;
white nib	&#x2711;		&U2711;
white parallelogram	&#x25B1;		&U25B1;
white rectangle	&#x25AD;	&rect;	&U25AD;
white right-pointing pointer	&#x25BB;		&U25BB;
white right-pointing small triangle	&#x25B9;	&rtri;	&U25B9;
white right-pointing triangle	&#x25B7;		&U25B7;
white right pointing index	&#x261E;		&U261E;
white scissors	&#x2704;		&U2704;
white small square	&#x25AB;		&U25AB;
white smiling face	&#x263A;		&U263A;
white spade suit	&#x2664;		&U2664;
white square	&#x25A1;	□, □	&U25A1;
white square containing black small square	&#x25A3;		&U25A3;
white square with rounded corners	&#x25A2;		&U25A2;
white square with vertical bisecting line	&#x25EB;		&U25EB;
white star	&#x2606;	&star;	&U2606;
white sun with rays	&#x263C;		&U263C;
white telephone	&#x260F;		&U260F;
white up-pointing small triangle	&#x25B5;	&utri;	&U25B5;
white up-pointing triangle	&#x25B3;		&U25B3;
white up-pointing triangle with dot	&#x25EC;		&U25EC;
white up pointing index	&#x261D;		&U261D;
white vertical rectangle	&#x25AF;		&U25AF;
won sign	&#x20A9;		&U20A9;
wreath product	&#x2240;		&U2240;
writing hand	&#x270D;		&U270D;

Marks & Symbols (Continued)

Character	XML	ISO	SPREAD
x in a rectangle box	&#x2327;		&U2327;
xor	&#x22BB;		&U22BB;
yen sign	&#xA5;	&yen;	&U00A5;
yin yang	&#x262F;		&U262F;

Annotated Bibliography & References

[citation]	Title	Reference
Alschuler	*ABCD...SGML*	Liora Alschuler, International Thomson Computer Press, 1995. ISBN 1-850-32197.
App	*Computerized Collation of a Dunhuang Text*	Urs App, in *The Electronic Bodhidharma* (Journal), Urs App (ed.), International Research Institute for Zen Buddhism, Hanazono University, Kyoto. Number 4, June 1995. This paper is online at `http://www.iijnet.or.jp/iriz/irizhtml/maketext/xxly.htm`
Aquinas	*Summa Theologica*	St. Thomas Aquinas (1274). I recommend Thomas McDermott (translator and editor), Menthuen, London, 1991, ISBN 0-413-65300-5. Note that this translation removes the rigorous structure of medieval *disputation*: Each question was divided into articles. Each article has a conjecture, then objections, then replies to the objections.
ASCII	*American Standard Code for Information Interchange*	See [ISO 646].
ATA100	General name given to *Air Transport Association* DTDs	Part of the industry conventions *Spec 100* or *Spec 2100* DTD available from ATA, refer to `http://www.air-transport.org/pub/a100.htm`. Refer also to `http://tag.sgml.com/01201201.htm`
Bergström and Karlsson	*Fösverats Materielverk (FMV) Grund-DTD 1.0*	Peter Bergström and Leif Karlsson. This is the Swedish CALS DTD. The best source, and a good commentary on information units, can be found in the Web pages for the version 2.0 FMV *Grund-DTD* is `http://info.admin.kth.se/SGML/Bibliotek/DTDer/FMVGrund-DTD/introduction20.html`.
Bray	*XML: Report from the Front*	Tim Bray, Textuality, in *Proc. SGML/XML Asia Pacific '97*, GCA, 1997
Bringhurst	*The Elements of Typographic Style*	Robert Bringhurst, Hartley and Marks, Point Roberts, WA, 1992 ISBN 0-88179-110-5
Brown and Duguid	*Keeping It Simple*	John Seely Brown and Paul Duguid. Article in [Winograd].
CALS	*Continuous Acquisition and Life-Cycle Support*	`navycals.dt.navy.mil/`
CEN/TC304	*Information Technology – Character repertoire and coding for interworking with telex services*	Proposed European standard.
CGI	*Common Gateway Interface*	`http://hoohoo.ncsa.uiuc.edu/cgi/overview.html`

CJK.INF	China, Japan, Korea Information	Ken Lunde, `ftp://ftp.ora.com/pub/examples/nutshell/ujip/doc/cjk.inf` Also see [Ken Lunde].
Colby, Jackson, et al	*Special Edition Using SGML*	Martin Colby and David Jackson, et al. Que Corporation, Indianapolis, 1996. ISBN 0-7897-0414-5.
Cover		Robin Cover's SGML/XML web site is at `www.sil.org/sgml`
Crampton Smith, Tabor	*The Role of the Artist–Designer*	Gillian Crampton Smith and Philip Tabor. Article in [Winograd].
CSA Z243.4.1-1992	Collation Algorithm	CSA Z243.4.1-1992, Canadian Standards Association. (East Asian readers may also be interested in the Japanese standard JIS X 4061-1995.)
CSS	*Cascading Style Sheets*	Refer to `http://www.w3.org/Style/css/`
DaiKanwa Jiten		Taishuukan Shoten, 1986, Tokyo. This is a well-known and large Japanese book listing *kanji* and variants.
DeRose, Grosso	*Fragment Interchange*	TR9601:1996, SGML Open (now OASIS), `www.oasis-open.org`
Docbook	*DOCBOOK DTD*	Davenport Archive, the Davenport Group, refer to `www.ora.com/davenport/README.html`
DSSSL	*Document Style Semantics and Specification Language*	See [ISO 10179] and [XSL]
EBCDIC	*Extended Binary Coded Decimal Interchange Code*	A listing can be found at `http://www.ora.com/reference/dictionary/terms/E/Extended_Binary_Coded_Decimal_Interchange_Code.htm`
EBTI	*The Electronic Buddhist Text Initiative*	See [App] and [ZenBase]
ECMAScript	*ECMAScript*	Standard ECMA-262 ECMAScript: A general purpose, cross-platform programming language. Refer to `http://www.ecma.ch/stand/ecma-262.htm`
Ensign	*SGML: The Billion Dollar Secret*	Chet Ensign, Prentice Hall, 1997. ISBN 0-13-226705-5
ENV 1973:1995	*Minimum European Subset of ISO/IEC 10646-1*	A listing is at `http://www.indigo.ie/egt/standards/mes.html`
Eric Gill	*An Essay on Typography*	Eric Gill (1936), Lund Humphries Publishers, London, 1988. ISBN 0-85331-509-4
Gabriel	*Patterns of Software: Tales from the Software Community*	Richard P. Gabriel, Oxford University Press, 1996. ISBN 0-19-5100269-X. Gabriel is also the author of the important paper *Lisp: Good News, Bad News, Hpw to Win Big* (also known as *Worse is Better*) which influenced the development of XML: versions of this paper are on the World Wide Web, and in print in [UHH].

Gamma	*Design Patterns: Elements of Reusable Object-Oriented Software*	Erich Gamma, Richard Helm, Ralph Johnson, John Vlissides, Addison-Wesley Publishing Company, Massachusetts, 1995 ISBN 0-201-63361-2. However, readers of this are well advised to also refer to [Gabriel] for a more balanced view of patterns.
Gaur	*A History of Writing*	Albertine Gaur, The British Library, London, 1987 ISDN 0-7123-0145-3
GNU	*GNU's Not Unix*	Freesoft Foundation, `www.fsf.org/`
Goldfarb	*The SGML Handbook*	Charles F. Goldfarb, Oxford University Press, 1990. ISBN 0-19-853737-9
HTML	*Hypertext Markup Language*	`www.w3.org/REP` See also [ISO HTML].
HyTime	*HyTime*	See [ISO 10744]
HyTime '97	*HyTime 2d edition, 1997*	See [ISO 10744]
ICADD	*International Committee for Accessible Document Design*	Refer to the ICADD entry at `http://www.sil.org/sgml/gen-apps.html`, the Yuri Rubinsky Insight Foundation pages at `http://www.yuri.org/webable/` and the W3C pages at `http://www.w3.org/WAI/`
ISO/IEC 10036:1996	*ISO/IEC 10036:1996*	Information technology -- Font information interchange -- Procedures for registration of font-related identifiers
ISO 10179	*DSSSL*	ISO/IEC 10179:1996 Information technology -- Processing languages -- Document Style Semantics and Specification Language Refer to `ftp://ftp.ornl.gov/pub/sgml/WG8/DSSSL/dsssl96b.pdf`
ISO 10646	*Universal Character Set*	ISO/IEC 10646, Information Technology - Universal Multiple-Octet Coded Character Set (UCS) - Part 1: Architecture and Basic Multilingual Plane May 1993, with amendments. Refer to `http://osiris.dkuug.dk/JTC1/SC2/WG2/docs/projects` for recent developments.
ISO 10743	*Standard Music Description Language*	`ftp://ftp.ornl.gov/pub/sgml/WG8/smdl/10743.pdf`
ISO 10744	*HyTime*	Information processing -- Hypermedia/Time-based Structuring Language (HyTime) - 2d edition (ISO/IEC 10744:1997) `www.ornl.gov/sgml/wg8/document/1920.htm`
ISO/IEC DTR 11017:1996	*ISO/IEC DTR 11017*	Information technology -- Framework for internationalization
ISO 15445	*ISO HTML*	Refer to [JTC1\WG4].
ISO 2022	*ISO/IEC 2022:1994*	Information technology -- Character code structure and extension techniques
ISO 3166	*Country Codes*	ISO 3166-1:1997 Codes for the representation of names of countries and their subdivisions -- Part 1: Country codes ISO/DIS 3166-2 Codes for the representation of names of countries and their subdivisions -- Part 2: Country subdivision code ISO/DIS 3166-3 Codes for the representation of names of countries and their subdivisions -- Part 3: Code for formerly used names of countries

ISO 639-2	*Language Codes*	ISO 639:1988 Code for the representation of names of languages ISO/DIS 639-2 Codes for the representation of names of languages -- Part 2: Alpha-3 code
ISO 6429	*ISO/IEC 6429:1992*	Information technology -- Control functions for coded character sets
ISO 8859	ISO 8859	Refer to the ISO site www.iso.ch for up-to-date information. At the time of writing, the standards and draft standards were as follows: ISO 8859-1:1987 Information processing -- 8-bit single-byte coded graphic character sets -- Part 1: Latin alphabet No. 1 ISO/IEC DIS 8859-1 Information technology -- 8-bit single-byte coded graphic character sets -- Part 1: Latin alphabet No. 1 ISO 8859-2:1987 Information processing -- 8-bit single byte coded graphic character sets -- Part 2: Latin alphabet No. 2 ISO/IEC DIS 8859-2 Information technology -- 8-bit single-byte coded graphic character sets -- Part 2: Latin alphabet No. 2 (Revision of ISO 8859-2:1987) ISO 8859-3:1988 Information processing -- 8-bit single-byte coded graphic character sets -- Part 3: Latin alphabet No. 3 ISO/IEC DIS 8859-3 Information technology -- 8-bit single-byte coded graphic character sets -- Part 3: Latin alphabet No. 3 (Revisions of ISO 8859-3:1988) ISO 8859-4:1988 Information processing -- 8-bit single-byte coded graphic character sets -- Part 4: Latin alphabet No. 4 ISO/IEC DIS 8859-4 Information technology -- 8-bit single-byte coded graphic character sets -- Part 4: Latin alphabet No. 4 ISO/IEC 8859-5:1988 Information processing -- 8-bit single-byte coded graphic character sets -- Part 5: Latin/Cyrillic alphabet ISO/IEC DIS 8859-5 Information technology -- 8-bit single-byte coded graphic character sets -- Part 5: Latin/Cyrillic alphabet (Revision of ISO/IEC 8859-5:1988) ISO 8859-6:1987 Information processing -- 8-Bit single-byte coded graphic character sets -- Part 6: Latin/Arabic alphabet ISO/IEC DIS 8859-6 Information technology -- 8-bit single-byte coded graphic character sets -- Part 6: Latin/Arabic alphabet (Revision of ISO 8859-6:1987) ISO 8859-7:1987 Information processing -- 8-bit single-byte coded graphic character sets -- Part 7: Latin/Greek alphabet ISO 8859-8:1988 Information processing -- 8-bit single-byte coded graphic character sets -- Part 8: Latin/Hebrew alphabet ISO/IEC DIS 8859-8 Information technology -- 8-bit single-byte coded graphic character sets -- Part 8: Latin/Hebrew alphabet (Revision of ISO 8859-8:1988) ISO/IEC 8859-9:1989 Information processing -- 8-bit single-byte coded graphic character sets -- Part 9: Latin alphabet No. 5

		ISO/IEC DIS 8859-9 Information technology -- 8-bit single-byte coded graphic character sets -- Part 9: Latin alphabet No. 5 (Revision of ISO/IEC 8859-9:1989) ISO/IEC 8859-10:1992 Information technology -- 8-Bit single-byte coded graphic character sets -- Part 10: Latin alphabet No. 6 ISO/IEC DIS 8859-10 Information technology -- 8-bit single-byte coded graphic character sets -- Part 10: Latin alphabet No. 6 ISO/IEC DIS 8859-13 Information technology -- 8-bit single-byte coded graphic character sets -- Part 13: Latin alphabet No. 7 ISO/IEC DIS 8859-14 Information technology -- 8-bit single-byte coded graphic character sets -- Part 14: Latin alphabet No. 8 (Celtic) ISO/IEC DIS 8859-15 Information technology -- 8-bit single-byte coded graphic character sets -- Part 15: Latin alphabet No. 0
ISO 8879	*SGML*	Information technology -- Standard Generalized Markup Language. Full text available in [Goldfarb]. In 1997, several compatible enhancements were made to ISO 8879: normative annexes J and K, and informative annex L. These enhancements are collected together in `http://www.ornl.gov/sgml/wg8/document/1960.htm`
ISO 9070	*ISO/IEC 9070:1991*	Information technology -- SGML support facilities -- Registration procedures for public text owner identifiers
ISO 9541	*Font Information Interchange*	ISO/IEC 9541-1:1991, Information technology -- Font information interchange. Japanese readers should be aware of *Font Services User Guide: A Handbook on ISO/IEC 9541 (title tr.)* Dr Yushi Komachi, Tokyo, Japan, 1996 ISBN 4-542-30521-X (in Japanese)
ISO HTML	*ISO/IEC 15445*	(Standardization of HTML based on HTML 4.0, still in committee draft at the time of writing.)
Jan Tschibold	*Clay in the Potter's Hand*	Essay in Jan Tshibold, *The Form of the Book: Essays on the Morality of Good Design*, Hartley and Marks, Point Roberts, WA, 1991 ISBN 0-88179-116-4
Jelliffe	*Word Segmentation in Chinese*	Rick Jelliffe. `http://www.chilli.net.au/~ricko/chinaseg.htm` A reworked vesion of *Draft Proposal for Word Segmentation Standard* by (pron?) Wang Chu Yi and Zhang Li Li, paper circulated at China/Japan Korea Document Processing Group. (Translated from Chinese by Amy Shiu.)
Jorgensen		c. 1989, report by Eric Jorgensen, US Navy, David Taylor Model Basin - Carderock center, quoted by Len Bullard, *Re: IETM – interactive SGML browsers*, `comp.text.sgml`, 22-Feb-1996
JSML	*Java Speech Markup Language*	`http://java.sun.com:81/products/java-media/speech/forDevelopers/JSML/index.html/`
JTC1/WG4	*Working Group on Document Description and Processing Languages*	International Organization for Standardization, Joint Technical Committee 1, Working Group 4, `www.ornl.gov/sgml/wg8/document/wg8home.htm`
Kano	*Developing International Software*	Nadine Kano, Microsoft Press, Redmond, Washington, 1995 ISBN 1-55615-840-8

Ken Lunde	*Understanding Japanese Information Processing*	Ken Lunde, O'Reilly and Associates, Sebastapol, CA, 1993, ISBN 1-56592-043-0. Also see [CJK.INF].
Kennedy	*New Roles for SGML Consultants*	Dianne Kennedy, <TAG> vol 9, Aug 1996
Knuth	*Literate Programming*	Donald Knuth, CSLI, Stanford, 1992. ISBN 0-937073-80-6
Komachi, Hiyama, Furuse	*Open Markup Language for Publishing Japanese Documents by Electronic Distribution*	Yashi Komachi, Masayuki Hiyama, Yukihiro Furuse, *Proc. SGML Asia Pacific '95*, GCA, 1995
LTDR	*Lexical Type Definition Requirements*	http://www.ornl.gov/sgml/wg8/docs/ n1920/html/clause-A.2.html
Lunde	*Understanding Japanese Information Processing*	See [Ken Lunde]
Maler and el Andoloussi	*Developing SGML DTDs: From Text to Model to Markup*	Eve Maler and Jeanne El Andaloussi, Prentice Hall, New Jersey, 1996. ISBN 0-13-309881-1.
Malone, Yates and Benjamin	Except from *Electronic Markets and Electronic Hierarchies*	Thomas W. Malone, Joanne Yates, and Robert I. Benjamin. Article in [Stefik].
McGrath		
MID	*Metafile for Interactive Documents*	www.nawcsti.navy.mil/mid/mid.html
Mikes	*X window System Technical Reference*	Steven Mikes, Addison-Wesley, 1990. ISBN 0-201-52370-1
MIME	*Multipurpose Internet Mail Extensions*	See [RFC 2045] *et al.*.
MML	*Mathematics Markup Language*	Refer to http://www.w3.org/Math/
Nicholson Baker	*The History of Punctuation*	in Nicholson Baker, The Size of Thoughts, Vintage, London, 1997. ISBN 0-09-95791-5
Nihimura and Imago	*By Any Other Name: An SGML System Using Generic and Specific DTDs*	in *Proc. SGML Asia Pacific '95*, GCA, 1995

Okui	*General Japanese Style for Formatted Documents*	Yasuhiro Okui, Nihon Unitec, unpublished draft *General Japanese Style for Formatted Documents* , China/Korea/Japan Document Processing Group conference, Alaska, 1996. Japanese readers may also consult *Hajimete no SGML* by the same author, with others, ISBN 4-7741-0214-8, and *SGML no kakikata* ISBN 4-900710-01-6.
Okui, Matsuoka, Imago, Komachi	*Multilingual Document Interchange Using SDATA Entities, BUCS and Others*	Okui, Matsuoka, Imago, Komachi, in *Proc. SGML Asia Pacific '96*, GCA, 1996
OmniMark		`www.omnimark.com`
Palmer	*Re: SGML and multiple languages*	Greg Palmer, Active Systems, Ottawa. on `Comp.text.sgml`, Nov 16 1996
PDF	*Portable Document Format*	`www.adobe.com`
PICS	*Platform for Internet Content Selection*	Refer to the various reports and specifications at `www.w3.org/TR`
Pinnacles	*ECIX – Electronic Component Information Exchange*	`http://www.cfi.org/ecix/`
POSIX	*Portable Operating System Interface*	ISO/IEC 9945 Information technology - Portable Operating System Interface (POSIX)
Rainbow	*Rainbow DTD*	`ftp://ftp.ifi.uio.no/pub/SGML/Rainbow`
RFC 373	*Arbitrary Character Sets*	John McCarthy, 1972. `ds.internic.net/rfc/rfc373.txt`
RFC 1345	*Character Mnemonics & Character Sets*	Keld Simonsen, 1992. `ds.internic.net/rfc/rfc1345.txt`
RFC 1630	*Universal Resource Identifiers in WWW*	Tim Berners-Lee, 1994. `ds.internic.net/rfc/rfc1630.txt`
RFC 1700	*Assigned Numbers*	J. Reynolds and J. Postel `ds.internic.net/rfc/rfc1700.txt`
RFC 1738	*Uniform Resource Locators (URL)*	T. Berners-Lee, L. Masinter, M. McCahill (Eds). `ds.internic.net/rfc/rfc1738.txt`
RFC 1766	*Tags for the Identification of Languages*	H. Alvestrand `ds.internic.net/rfc/rfc1766.txt`, also note by the same author *IETF Policy on Character Sets and Languages, 1998* `ds.internic.net/rfc/rfc2277.txt.`
RFC 1808	*Relative Uniform Resource Locators*	R. Fielding `ds.internic.net/rfc/rfc1808.txt`
RFC 1922	*Chinese Character Encoding for Internet Messages*	HF. Zhu, *et al.* `ds.internic.net/rfc/rfc1922.txt`

RFC 2045	*Multipurpose Internet Mail Extensions (MIME) Part One: Format of Internet Message Bodies*	N. Freed, N. Borenstein ds.internic.net/rfc/rfc2045.txt
RFC 2046	*Multipurpose Internet Mail Extensions (MIME) Part Two: Media Types*	N. Freed, N. Borenstein ds.internic.net/rfc/rfc2046.txt
RFC 2047	*MIME (Multipurpose Internet Mail Extensions) Part Three: Message Header Extensions for Non–ASCII Text*	K. Moore ds.internic.net/rfc/rfc2047.txt
RFC 2049	*Multipurpose Internet Mail Extensions (MIME) Part Five: Conformance Criteria and Examples*	N. Freed, N. Borenstien ds.internic.net/rfc/rfc2049.txt
RFC 2070	*Internationalizatio n of the Hypertext Markup Language*	F. Yergeau, Gavin Nicol, G. Adams, M. Duerst ds.internic.net/rfc/rfc2070.txt
RFC 2141	*URN Syntax*	R. Moats ds.internic.net/rfc/rfc2141.txt
RFC 2152	*UTF–7: A Mail–Safe Transformation Format of Unicode*	D. Goldsmith, M. Davis ds.internic.net/rfc/rfc2152.txt
RFC 2231	*MIME Parameter Value and Encoded Word Extensions: Character Sets, Languages, and Continuations*	N. Freed, K. Moore ds.internic.net/rfc/rfc2231.txt
Robert Bringhurst	*The Elements of Typographic Style*	Robert Bringhurst, Hartley and Marks, Point Roberts, WA, 1992 ISBN 0-88179-110-5
Rogers	*Paragraphs on Printing,* illustration 54	Bruce Rogers, Dover Publications, New York, 1979. ISBN 0-486-32817-2.
Rubinsky	*SGML on the Web: Small Steps beyond HTML*	Yuri Rubinsky and Murray Maloney, Charles F. Goldfarb Series on Information Management, Prentice Hall, 1997. ISBN 0-13-519984-0. See also the Yuri Rubinsky Insight Foundation at www.yuri.org

Scheme	*Scheme*	IEEE P1178-1990, *IEEE Standard for the Scheme Programming Language*, ISBN 1-55937-125-0. Also, *The Revised ^ 4 Report on the Algorithmic Language Scheme*, W. Clinger *et al*, MIT (Nov 1991). The classic text using Scheme is *Structure and Interpretation of Computer Programs*, Harold Abelson and Gerald Jay Sussman with Julie Sussman, MIT Press, 1985, 0-07-000-422-6
SGML	*Standard Generalized Markup Language*	See [ISO 8879].
SGML '97	*Standard Generalized Markup Language*	As revised in 1997. See [ISO 8879]
SGML Open	OASIS	*Organization for the Advancement of Structured Information Standards*, www.oasis-open.org. Previously called SGML Open
SMDL	*Standard Music Description Language*	See [ISO 10743]
Smeijers	*Counterpunch*	Fred Smeijers, Hyphen Press, London, 1996. ISBN 0-907259-06-5
Smith	*A Study into the Wealth of Nations*	Adam Smith
Sommerville	*Software Engineering*	Ian Sommerville, Addison Wesley, Wokingham, England, 1989. ISBN 0-202-17568-1
SP	*SGML Processor*	James Clark (Software). www.jclark.com Available on the companion CD-ROM to this book.
SPREAD-2	*Public Entity Set for Universal Character Set, version 2*	Rick Jelliffe, Standardization Project Regarding East Asian Documents. Available on the companion CD-ROM to this book.
Stefik	*Internet Dreams: Archetypes, Myths, and Metaphors*	Mark Stefik, MIT Press, 1997. ISBN 0-262-69202-3
TEI	*Text Encoding Initiative*	For Writing System Declarations refer to http://etext.virginia.edu/bin/tei-tocs?div=DIV1&id=WD
TEIlite	Simpler version of the Text Encoding Intitiative DTD	Refer to [TEI]
TR 15285	ISO Font/Glyph Model	ISO/IEC Information Technology -- An operational model for characters and glyphs
TR 9573-13	*Public entity sets for mathematics and science*	ISO/IEC TR 9573-13:1991, Information processing - SGML support facilities - Techniques for using SGML
TR 9573-15	*Public entity sets for non-Latin based alphabets*	ISO/IEC TR 9573-13:1991, Information processing - SGML support facilities - Techniques for using SGML
Travis and Waldt	*The SGML Implementation Guide*	Dale Waldt and Brian Travis, springer-Verlag, 1995. ISBN 3-540-57730-0.
UHH	UNIX Haters' Handbook	Simson Garfinkel, Daniel Weise, and Steven Strassmann (eds), IDG Books. ISBN 1-56884-203-1

Unicode	*The Unicode Standard*	See next entry.
Unicode 2.0	*The Unicode Standard, Version 2*	The Unicode Consortium, Addison-Wesley, 1996. ISBN 0-201-48345-9. Unicode is an industry profile of [ISO 10646] with extra information.
URI	*Universal Resource Identifier*	See [RFC 1600], related RFCs and [W3C].
URL	*Uniform Resource Locator*	See [RFC 1738], related RFCs and [W3C].
Van Herwijnen	*Practical SGML*	Eric Van Herwijnen, Second Edition, Kluwer Academic Publishers, 1994. ISBN 0-7923-9434-8.
W3C	*World Wide Web Consortium*	`www.w3.org`
Web SGML	*Standard Generalized Markup Language*	As enhanced in 1997. See [ISO 8879]
WIDL	*Web Interface Definition Language*	P. Merrick and C. Allen, webMethods Inc. `www.w3.org/TR/NOTE-widl`
Winograd	*Bringing Design to Software*	Terry Winograd (ed.), ACM Press, Addison Wesley, 1996. ISBN 0-201-85491-0
Wirth	*Algorithms + Data Structures = Programs*	N. Wirth, Prentice Hall, 1976
XLL	*Extensible Linking Language*	At the time this book went to press, XLL was split into two parts: the linking elements making up XLink, and the Extended Pointer syntax, XPointer. Refer to `www.w3.org` for current details.
XML	*Extensible Markup Language*	Tim Bray, Jean Paoli, C. M. Sperberg (eds), `www.w3.org/REP` Refer also the excellent annotated version at `www.xml.com`.
XSL	*Extensible Style Language*	Refer to `www.w3.org` for current details.
Yergeau, Nicol, Adams, Duerst	*Internationalization of the Hypertext Markup Language*	See [RFC 2070].
ZenBase	*ZenBase*	Urs APP, ed., ZenBase CD 1. Kyoto: International Research Institute for Zen Buddhism, 1995. ISBN 4-938796-18-X

For information on SGML and XML, see the list of titles in *The Charles F. Goldfarb Series on Information Management* at the front of this book.

For further reading in print publishing, I have found the following very enjoyable:

Title	Reference
Better Type	Betty Binns, Roundtable Press, New York, NY, 1989 ISBN 0-8230-0484-8
The Book Before Printing: Ancient, Medieval and Oriental	David Diringer (1953), Dover Publications, New York, New York, 1982. ISBN 0-486-24243-9
A History of Reading	Alberto Manguel, Flamingo, London, 1997. ISBN 0-00-654681-1
Methods of Book Design: the Practise of an Industrial Craft	Hugh Williamson, Yale University Press, New Haven and London, 1983 ISBN 0-300-03035-5
The Design of Books	Adrian Wilson, Chronicle Books, San Francisco, CA, 1993 ISBN 0-8118-0304-X

Index

ISO Standard definitions of terms are indicated with **bold**.

The Public Entity Sets for Special Characters (Appendixes A to D) have their own indexes.

LICENSE AGREEMENT AND LIMITED WARRANTY

READ THE FOLLOWING TERMS AND CONDITIONS CAREFULLY BEFORE OPENING THIS CD PACKAGE. THIS LEGAL DOCUMENT IS AN AGREEMENT BETWEEN YOU AND PRENTICE-HALL, INC. (THE "COMPANY"). BY OPENING THIS SEALED CD PACKAGE, YOU ARE AGREEING TO BE BOUND BY THESE TERMS AND CONDITIONS. IF YOU DO NOT AGREE WITH THESE TERMS AND CONDITIONS, DO NOT OPEN THE CD PACKAGE. PROMPTLY RETURN THE UNOPENED CD PACKAGE AND ALL ACCOMPANYING ITEMS TO THE PLACE YOU OBTAINED THEM FOR A FULL REFUND OF ANY SUMS YOU HAVE PAID.

1.   **GRANT OF LICENSE:** In consideration of your purchase of this book, and your agreement to abide by the terms and conditions of this Agreement, the Company grants to you a nonexclusive right to use and display the copy of the enclosed software program (hereinafter the "SOFTWARE") on a single computer (i.e., with a single CPU) at a single location so long as you comply with the terms of this Agreement. The Company reserves all rights not expressly granted to you under this Agreement.

2.   **OWNERSHIP OF SOFTWARE:** You own only the magnetic or physical media (the enclosed CD) on which the SOFTWARE is recorded or fixed, but the Company and the software developers retain all the rights, title, and ownership to the SOFTWARE recorded on the original CD copy(ies) and all subsequent copies of the SOFTWARE, regardless of the form or media on which the original or other copies may exist. This license is not a sale of the original SOFTWARE or any copy to you.

3.   **COPY RESTRICTIONS:** This SOFTWARE and the accompanying printed materials and user manual (the "Documentation") are the subject of copyright. The individual programs on the CD are copyrighted by the authors of each program. You may <u>not</u> copy the Documentation or the SOFTWARE, except that you may make a single copy of the SOFTWARE for backup or archival purposes only. You may be held legally responsible for any copying or copyright infringement which is caused or encouraged by your failure to abide by the terms of this restriction.

4.   **USE RESTRICTIONS:** You may <u>not</u> network the SOFTWARE or otherwise use it on more than one computer or computer terminal at the same time. You may physically transfer the SOFTWARE from one computer to another provided that the SOFTWARE is used on only one computer at a time. You may <u>not</u> distribute copies of the SOFTWARE or Documentation to others. You may <u>not</u> reverse engineer, disassemble, decompile, modify, adapt, translate, or create derivative works based on the SOFTWARE or the Documentation without the prior written consent of the Company.

5.   **TRANSFER RESTRICTIONS:** The enclosed SOFTWARE is licensed only to you and may <u>not</u> be transferred to any one else without the prior written consent of the Company. Any unauthorized transfer of the SOFTWARE shall result in the immediate termination of this Agreement.

6.   **TERMINATION:** This license is effective until terminated. This license will terminate automatically without notice from the Company and become null and void if you fail to comply with any provisions or limitations of this license. Upon termination, you shall destroy the Documentation and all copies of the SOFTWARE. All provisions of this Agreement as to warranties, limitation of liability, remedies or damages, and our ownership rights shall survive termination.

7.   **MISCELLANEOUS:** This Agreement shall be construed in accordance with the laws of the United States of America and the State of New York and shall benefit the Company, its affiliates, and assignees.

8.   **LIMITED WARRANTY AND DISCLAIMER OF WARRANTY:** The Company warrants that the SOFTWARE, when properly used in accordance with the Documentation, will operate in substantial conformity with the description of the SOFTWARE set forth in the Documentation. The Company does not warrant that the SOFTWARE will meet your requirements or that the operation of the SOFTWARE will be uninterrupted or error-free. The Company warrants that the media on which the SOFTWARE is delivered shall be free from defects in materials and workmanship under

normal use for a period of thirty (30) days from the date of your purchase. Your only remedy and the Company's only obligation under these limited warranties is, at the Company's option, return of the warranted item for a refund of any amounts paid by you or replacement of the item. Any replacement of SOFTWARE or media under the warranties shall not extend the original warranty period. The limited warranty set forth above shall not apply to any SOFTWARE which the Company determines in good faith has been subject to misuse, neglect, improper installation, repair, alteration, or damage by you. EXCEPT FOR THE EXPRESSED WARRANTIES SET FORTH ABOVE, THE COMPANY DISCLAIMS ALL WARRANTIES, EXPRESS OR IMPLIED, INCLUDING WITHOUT LIMITATION, THE IMPLIED WARRANTIES OF MERCHANTABILITY AND FITNESS FOR A PARTICULAR PURPOSE. EXCEPT FOR THE EXPRESS WARRANTY SET FORTH ABOVE, THE COMPANY DOES NOT WARRANT, GUARANTEE, OR MAKE ANY REPRESENTATION REGARDING THE USE OR THE RESULTS OF THE USE OF THE SOFTWARE IN TERMS OF ITS CORRECTNESS, ACCURACY, RELIABILITY, CURRENTNESS, OR OTHERWISE.

IN NO EVENT, SHALL THE COMPANY OR ITS EMPLOYEES, AGENTS, SUPPLIERS, OR CONTRACTORS BE LIABLE FOR ANY INCIDENTAL, INDIRECT, SPECIAL, OR CONSEQUENTIAL DAMAGES ARISING OUT OF OR IN CONNECTION WITH THE LICENSE GRANTED UNDER THIS AGREEMENT, OR FOR LOSS OF USE, LOSS OF DATA, LOSS OF INCOME OR PROFIT, OR OTHER LOSSES, SUSTAINED AS A RESULT OF INJURY TO ANY PERSON, OR LOSS OF OR DAMAGE TO PROPERTY, OR CLAIMS OF THIRD PARTIES, EVEN IF THE COMPANY OR AN AUTHORIZED REPRESENTATIVE OF THE COMPANY HAS BEEN ADVISED OF THE POSSIBILITY OF SUCH DAMAGES. IN NO EVENT SHALL LIABILITY OF THE COMPANY FOR DAMAGES WITH RESPECT TO THE SOFTWARE EXCEED THE AMOUNTS ACTUALLY PAID BY YOU, IF ANY, FOR THE SOFTWARE.

SOME JURISDICTIONS DO NOT ALLOW THE LIMITATION OF IMPLIED WARRANTIES OR LIABILITY FOR INCIDENTAL, INDIRECT, SPECIAL, OR CONSEQUENTIAL DAMAGES, SO THE ABOVE LIMITATIONS MAY NOT ALWAYS APPLY. THE WARRANTIES IN THIS AGREEMENT GIVE YOU SPECIFIC LEGAL RIGHTS AND YOU MAY ALSO HAVE OTHER RIGHTS WHICH VARY IN ACCORDANCE WITH LOCAL LAW.

ACKNOWLEDGMENT

YOU ACKNOWLEDGE THAT YOU HAVE READ THIS AGREEMENT, UNDERSTAND IT, AND AGREE TO BE BOUND BY ITS TERMS AND CONDITIONS. YOU ALSO AGREE THAT THIS AGREEMENT IS THE COMPLETE AND EXCLUSIVE STATEMENT OF THE AGREEMENT BETWEEN YOU AND THE COMPANY AND SUPERSEDES ALL PROPOSALS OR PRIOR AGREEMENTS, ORAL, OR WRITTEN, AND ANY OTHER COMMUNICATIONS BETWEEN YOU AND THE COMPANY OR ANY REPRESENTATIVE OF THE COMPANY RELATING TO THE SUBJECT MATTER OF THIS AGREEMENT.

Should you have any questions concerning this Agreement or if you wish to contact the Company for any reason, please contact in writing at the address below.

Robin Short
Prentice Hall PTR
One Lake Street
Upper Saddle River, New Jersey 07458

ABOUT THE CD-ROM

This CD-ROM is a companion to *The XML & SGML Cookbook*, by Rick Jelliffe, part of the Charles F. Goldfarb Series on Open Information Management.

It contains the markup declarations from the book, entity declarations for working in many languages, and some of my favorite SGML applications. I hope you find it useful.

Installation Instructions:
Point your browser to /index.htm on the CD-ROM to start browsing.

Recipes

Markup Declarations from Part 1

Markup Declarations from Part 2

ISO Public Entity Set for Notations

Markup Declarations from Part 3

CADD DTD

Special Character Public Entity Sets from Appendixes

ISO

HTML

AAP/EJ

READ

Applications

I have included some of my favorite SGML applications, which I found valuable in writing the book.

T.I.M.E.L.U.X. EditTime

Thanks to Roger Schuetz for making this special demonstration version available. This version
write disabled. EditTime is an SGML/XML editor with the speed of a simple text editor. It sup
ports Unicode. For the most recent version and information, see www.timelux.lu. Binary for W
dows 95/NT.

OmniMark 3.0 Light Edition

Thanks to Andy Kowel for making this special version available. OmniMark is a text processi
language which can be used for many of the same jobs that Perl can be used for, but it is SGM
aware, and in my opinion has more maintainable code than Perl. OmniMark LE only allows
smaller programs, but is very useful. For the most recent version and information, see www.o
imark.com. Binary for PC.

James Clark's SP 1.3

Thanks to James Clark for making this version available. SP 1.3 is an SGML/XML processor w
several applications. It supports Unicode. For the most recent version and information, see
www.jclark.com/sp. C++ source code included, and binaries for Windows 95/NT. Also include
XML-tok, the source code for an XML parser.

Copyright and Disclaimers

See the various packages and files for particular copyright information and disclaimers.

Technical Support: Prentice Hall does not offer technical support for this software. Howeve
there is a problem with the media, you may obtain a replacement copy by e-mailing us with y
problem at: *ptr_techsupport@phptr.com*.

Platform/System Requirements
Software on this CD-ROM requires Windows 95, Windows NT or higher.